Three Volumes in One

THE DOCTRINE OF MERITS IN OLD RABBINICAL LITERATURE

and

THE OLD RABBINIC DOCTRINE OF GOD

Two Volumes in One

I. The Names and Attributes of God
II. Essays in Anthropomorphism

BY

A. MARMORSTEIN, Ph.D., *Rabbi*

KTAV PUBLISHING HOUSE, INC.

NEW YORK

THE DOCTRINE OF MERITS IN OLD RABBINICAL LITERATURE

BY

A. MARMORSTEIN, Ph.D., *Rabbi*

PROLEGOMENON BY

R. J. ZWI WERBLOWSKY

PROLEGOMENON

A wit, reviewing a scholarly work entitled "The Systematic Theology of the Ancient Synagogue" once wrote: there is no such thing as "the Synagogue"; and even if there were, it would have no theology; and even if it had a theology, it would not be systematic. Like all witticisms of this kind, this comment, true as it is, is at best a half-truth. For although the "Synagogue" or the "Ancient Synagogue" is largely a figment of the imagination of gentile scholars—after all, they needed some sort of theological abstraction which could be used as a foil to "the Church"—it is a fact that the ancient rabbinic sources do use the term *keneseth Yisra'el,* albeit in a sense very different from that of a teaching authority with a specific body of doctrine. In due course the "Synagogue" invented by the gentile theologians was replaced by "Judaism," and Judaism—with a capital J—was described as propounding certain ideas, doctrines and norms, and categorically rejecting others. I do not wish to disallow completely the word Judaism. It is, perhaps, a useful if somewhat vague term for indicating what Jews feel to be essential for the "Jewishness" of their existence and identity. But as a technical and doctrinal concept it is questionable on more than one score, and the reservations indicated here apply even to so excellent a work as G. F. Moore's monumental *Judaism* which, as Morton Smith has rightly pointed out,[1] should have been called more appropriately "Tannaitic Judaism of late second and third centuries."

Somewhat similar considerations apply to the term "theology." Here, of course, everything is a matter of definition, and it is not the historian's business to undo the semantic history of words which he wants to use. "Theology" is a word whose modern meaning—in all western languages—has been decisively influenced by its use and function in the history of Christianity. It would be foolish to pretend to ignore this fact. On the other hand it is true that Jews have always been thinking about God and about things pertaining to God: His actions, His will, and His relationship to His creation in general and to His people Israel in particular. In fact, they not only thought about these things but also expressed and articulated their thoughts in diverse literary forms. There may be more than one manner of thinking as well as of expressing thought, and some scholars (e.g. M. Kadushin and Isaac Heinemann) have attempted to analyze and describe the characteristic patterns of ancient rabbinic viz. aggadic thinking. The expression "Jewish Theology" is therefore not necessarily objectionable, although, to prevent misunderstandings, it should wherever possible be qualified with reference to the period, place and circle in which the theological notions under discussion were actually enunciated. Thus a posthumous collection of several of A. Marmorstein's articles has been published under the title *Studies in Jewish Theology* (1950), where "Jewish" clearly means Tannaitic and Amoraic (and not e.g., Hellenistic, or Karaite, or Kabbalistic) theology. But whilst greater precision of expression is always to be welcomed, the decisive and dominant influence of Tannaitic and Amoraic teaching on subsequent Jewish history may well justify a more generalizing manner of expression in this instance.

It is when considering the systematic character of doctrinal traditions that the student faces some of his most serious methodological and substantial problems. No doubt there were many systematic Jewish thinkers whose professed aim was to construct and elaborate a philosophical or theological system. Others were less systematic in their manner of thinking and presentation, yet a careful study of their thought clearly reveals an inner consistency and underlying pattern—in short, something like a system. The problem, in every specific case, is therefore to find out whether there is a system at all, and if there is, what kind of system it is (explicit, implicit, fully articulated, or merely exhibiting a certain coherence the criteria of which should first be established). It is only after answering these more, formal initial questions that there is any point in trying to present a collection of teachings as a system. As is well known, many of the earlier works on Jewish theology simply proceeded from types of systems current in Christian (and more especially Protestant) academic theology. By applying these to the rabbinic material, "systematic theologies" of Judaism were produced. And as the accounts of rabbinic theology by Christian scholars usually exhibited a great deal of anti-Jewish prejudice (as is amply evident even in the work of outstanding scholars like Bousset) [2], the theologies produced by Jewish authors inevitably bore the marks of their apologetic function. The apologetic and, indeed, polemical function even came to be projected into the method of analysis itself. It was assumed that every aggadic statement had a polemical address (e.g., gnostic, christian or philosophical heresies) and that only by discovering the latter could the actual *Sitz im Leben* of these statements be understood. It is undoubtedly true that outer and inner challenges, such as heresies and rival religions, often bring a religion to more articulate reflection and to a polemical definition of its doctrines. In fact, as Franz Rosenzweig pointedly observed, every *summa* is a *summa contra gentiles*. But this evident truth is still a far cry from the principle of smelling a polemical purpose behind every rabbinic utterance.

The presence or the lack of a systematic character in rabbinic teaching is a delicate problem. For it not only touches on the aforementioned general problem of "patterns of thought," the "rabbinic mind," "organic thinking," the "ways of the *aggadah*" and the like, but it also raises the narrower and more specific question regarding the alleged systems or doctrinal consistency of individual teachers and rabbis. Should we permit ourselves to regard aggadic statements as a chaotic jumble of *disjecta membra,* accounting for apparent contradictions by an appeal to the "homiletic" character of rabbinic teaching, or are we justified in attempting to look for a consistent doctrinal approach in the recorded sayings? Thus it has become customary to speak of a "school of R. Akiba" and a "school of R. Ishmael," and to explain all utterances of these two tannaitic teachers and their disciples in the light of what are held to be their respective systems. The tendency to view aggadic sayings as "doctrines" held in certain "schools of thought" can at times become a dangerous temptation which, it seems, Marmorstein himself has not always been able to avoid.

Yet the two—or rather three—major studies by A. Marmorstein, reprinted in this volume, are exemplary in their basic conception. Their avowed purpose is the modest, scholarly one of examining in precise detail the doctrines of a certain group of Jewish teachers, at a certain period, concerning certain well-defined subjects. Hence the studies on *The Doctrine of Merits in Old Rabbinic Literature* (1920) and *The Old Rabbinic Doctrine of God,* published in two parts: *The Names and Attributes of God* (1927) and *Essays in Anthropomorphism* (1937).

Little need be said here about Marmorstein the man and the scholar. The aforementioned posthumous volume *Studies in Jewish Theology* contains a full bibliography of his writings as well as a memoir by his son. A few remarks, however, may be in order on the subject-matter of the following three studies.

The rabbinic doctrine of merits has, perhaps more than any other, been discussed in the hothouse atmosphere of arrogant Christian prejudice and concomitant Jewish apologetics. As a matter of fact the rabbinic attitudes and views on the subject cannot be properly understood without taking into account their biblical antecedents and it is to be regretted therefore that Marmorstein, whose survey begins with Shemayah and Abtalyon, did not consider the biblical background. It is true, of course, that the Bible uses a very different vocabulary. There is little mention of "recompense" or "merits," but instead God does certain things and behaves in a certain (as a rule predictable) way in response to appropriate human behaviour—all this under the terms of his covenant with Israel. The terminology and the conceptual framework of the rabbis may differ from those of the Bible, but there is a certain continuity in the notion that man can qualify for one kind of treatment rather than another at the hands of God. As Marmorstein points out, the rabbis are unanimous in holding man capable of "acquiring merit before God." In spite of their humility and their profound awareness of human shortcomings and, indeed, sinfulness, they adhere to the basic position that men, in their actual lives, perform meritorious actions, even though a matter-of-course belief in one's own merits may be unpardonable pride and forgetfulness of the permanent possibility that one's sins may neutralize one's merits. In the words of G. F. Moore "Judaism has no hesitation about recognizing the merit of good works, or in exhorting men to acquire it and to accumulate a store of merit laid up for the hereafter."[3] The criticism of the notion of merit, noted also by Marmorstein, has been succinctly summarized by Moore. "The prejudice of many [Gentile] writers on Judaism against the very idea of good works and their reward, and of merit acquired with God through them, is a Protestant inheritance from Luther's controversy with Catholic doctrine, and further back from Paul's contention that there is no salvation in Judaism."[4]

This prejudice against the doctrine of merits has occasionally led to curious paradoxes—but then every stick was good enough to beat the ancient rabbis with. Thus, on the one hand, the rabbinic doctrine of *zekhuth* was said to lead to arrogance, "pharisaic" self-righteousness, and to a mercenary religion that lacked both a sense of the

tragic depth of the gulf separating man from God and an
awareness of the miracle of divine grace. On the other
hand the undeniable insufficiency of all human endeavour
and the awareness that one's merits almost necessarily fall
short of the required standard are said to plunge Judaism
into hopeless despair. On the one hand Judaism is accused
of a naive and self-righteous optimism; on the other hand,
as a *Leistungsreligion* with a quantitative calculus of
merits and demerits, it is supposed to be sunk in a hopeless pessimism. Prof. Rengstorf[5] consequently speaks of
the "curse of uncertainty" that haunts rabbinic religion.
All this is, of course, sheer and utter nonsense, and far
from demonstrating any *Fluch der Ungewissheit* in rabbinic religion, Prof. Rengstorf's highly revealing remarks
merely display some of the more dubious and unsavory
aspects of Lutheran *Heilsgewissheit*. But be that as it may,
the doctrine of merits is a major chapter of Jewish theology, expounded not only in aggadic statements but also
deeply embedded in the liturgy (e.g., on the one hand
the appeal to the merits of the patriarchs, martyrs and
pious men of old, and on the other hand such disclaimers
as "Not because of our righteous acts do we lay our supplications before thee but because of thine abundant
mercies" or the formula of thanksgiving "Who doest good
unto the undeserving, and who hast also rendered all good
unto me"). The history of this doctrine in medieval
thought would have to include philosophers, kabbalists
and moralists. But Marmorstein's purpose was to marshall
all the available rabbinic material from the early Tannaim to the last Amoraim. As it happens this is also the
most important and decisive period as far as the history of
this particular doctrine is concerned.

It is different with the subject of the names and attributes of God. The study of the names of God is essential
for an understanding of the development of biblical religion which looks forward to the day when "the Lord shall
be One and His name One." The names of God loom large
both in mysticism and in theurgic magic, and the doctrine

of attributes is the major theme of medieval Jewish philosophy. If God is essentially nameless, then every name is
an attribute and all names refer to divine manifestations
and qualities rather than to His ineffable essence. The
question "what is in a name" thus becomes the ultimate
question for the theologian. The names of a nameless God
(as, in other religious cultures, the images of a shapeless
God) thus have a paradoxical function. They represent
something which they are not, and hence they separate us
from the reality which they represent. At the same time
they also join us to that reality to which, otherwise, we
could have no contact at all. In fact, they not only "represent," but to the extent that their opaqueness can become
transparent they also "reveal." It was some such intuition
which made the German poet Rilke, thinking no doubt of
the "wall of images" (*ikonostasis*) in the Eastern Orthodox Churches, say

    Und deine Bilder stehn vor dir wie Namen.[6]

For the medieval kabbalists the whole of the Torah was a
mysterious combination of "Names of God"; in fact, the
Torah "is nothing but the one great and holy Name of
God."[7] In this long and variegated history of preoccupa-
tion with the name of God, the rabbinic period represents
but one, albeit important and influential stage. In keeping with the professed scope of his study, the author does
not go beyond the strictly rabbinic material and even his
chapter on "The Names of God in the Bible" deals with
the biblical names of God as understood and interpreted
by the rabbis; it is not meant as a contribution to the
theology of the Old Testament.

    Towards the end of the 19th century one of the greatest
classical scholars and historians of religion at the time
published a work entitled *Götternamen.* In this study of
mainly Greek and other Indo-European names of the
gods[8] Hermann Usener attempted to penetrate to the
"concept" behind the often opaque proper names. The
names used for God by the ancient rabbis are anything
but opaque, though occasionally (as in the case of

makom) the interpretation may pose some problems. But as a rule we are dealing not so much with names as with metaphors, epithets, by-names, circumlocutions, honorifics, homiletical formations (e.g. צדיקו של עולם) and referential phrases (e.g. מי שאמר והיה העולם). All these are subsumed by Marmorstein, perhaps in an unduly simplifying manner, under the heading "The rabbinic synonyms for God," but then there is a big difference between distinctions which *we* make and impose on our material, and those made in the sources themselves. Thus e.g. the Mishnah (*Shabuoth* iv.10) lists "merciful and compassionate" and "long suffering" together with *Elohim* as divine names—at least in matters of oaths. For other halakhic purposes several categories of names are distinguished, a particularly important distinction being that between the Tetragrammaton (the "Ineffable Name"), names of God, and epithets. But although the precise connotation of the rabbinic "synonyms" for God presents relatively few problems, the relative frequency of these synonyms, the time and circumstances of their emergence, and the reasons for their use or disuse are so many questions that require careful investigation.

Marmorstein, using all the sources available to him, insisted on dealing with these questions from a strictly historical point of view. Not all of his suggestions are equally convincing, e.g. his argument that the tradition associating the Tetragrammaton with God's attribute of mercy, and the name *Elohim* with his attribute of stern judgement, must be late because in an earlier tradition, represented by Philo, the association is reversed. There seems to be little proof of this thesis and Philo, whose interpretations are frequently the result of his peculiar exegetical constraints, is certainly no convincing witness—in the absence of other supporting evidence—of the existence of Jewish "traditions." On other occasions the author really seems to have hit the nail on the head. This seems to be the case with Marmorstein's important discovery that the well known rabbinic expression "the Holy One Blessed

Be He" came into use in the 3rd century C.E. only, oust-
ing other epithets that had been dominant until then,
especially the name *makom*. At a first glance Marmorstein's arguments do not appear very convincing and they
have, in fact, been harshly criticized.[9] Nevertheless it
appears that Marmorstein's thesis, in spite of the insufficiency of his arguments, is essentially correct. As E. E.
Urbach has shown,[10] a careful examination (including
statistical counts) of the names of God occurring in the
best available manuscripts suggests that *makom*, like
shamayim, is a predominantly Tannaitic expression, subsequently crowded out in the 3rd century by the Amoraic
ha-Kadosh Barukh Hu.

Shamayim—a metonymy for "He who dwelleth in
Heaven"—no doubt carries overtones of a transcendent,
omniscient, numinous God, though not necessarily of a
far-away God who is remote from all human concerns.
The latter idea, ascribed to the rabbis by e.g. Bousset, is
again one of the vain conceits fondly invented by gentile
scholars in order to persuade themselves that Judaism was
a religion without vitality and warmth, and devoid of any
sense of the nearness of God (and man's nearness to
Him). Even more fanciful is the more recent discovery
that the phrase "our father in heaven" —which, to an un-
prejudiced mind, would seem to evince a certain sense
of intimacy with God— still exhibits the remoteness of a
transcendent God. According to this view[11] the ordinary
Jew would at best say "my father" (*abi*), whilst only Jesus
could address God with the more intimate word *abba*. It
is hardly necessary to discuss these theories seriously in
view of the material assembled by Marmorstein under
אב שבשמים and שמים . But whilst *shamayim* does carry
overtones of numinous transcendence, *makom* is a metonymy meaning nearness, i.e. the One who dwelleth in
the place which He hath chosen. Marmorstein was not so
wide off the mark when he suggested, in the paragraph
on *Shekhinah*, that the two expressions *makom* and *shekhinah* were standing for one and the same idea. In fact,

as Urbach has shown, the Amoraic interpretation of *makom* as the space that contains the whole world (מקומו של עולם) is a secondary explanation which was offered precisely because the original meaning had been lost and the name had become "opaque." *Makom* is thus an *innerweltliche* place and not *ausserweltliche* space. Hence the notion of "He who dwelleth in the place He hath chosen" has evident affinities with the concept of *shekhinah* which, from the presence viz. the indwelling of God in his sanctuary, became the principle of divine immanence as such.[12] *Shekhinah* as God's actual presence or immanence consequently also designates the revelatory agent and as such is related to, though not identical with, the idea of the Holy Spirit.[13]

Of the *shekhinah* it is said the righteous are vouchsafed to behold it. The idea of the possibility of such a "beatific vision" leads us straight to the subject of anthropomorphism. Anthropomorphism i.e., the attribution of human, bodily as well as mental or psychological, qualities to the divine is a well-known phenomenon and problem in the history of religions. Anthropomorphism does not become less anthropomorphic by being reduced to mental or psychological expressions i.e., to anthropopathism (e.g. God loves, is wroth, has pity etc.) . God may have no ears, or his ears may be said to be purely metaphorical, yet he is still said to "hear" prayers. Even if these mental and feeling qualities are pruned away by suitable allegorical exegesis, we are still left with a basic, irreducible anthropomorphism: the conception of the Deity in "personalistic" terms, i.e. in analogy to the only type of "person" we really know—the human person. When every human discourse about God is only "symbolical," i.e. literally wrong and hence potentially misleading, and men nevertheless feel compelled to speak *about* God (e.g. in theology) and *to* God (e.g. in prayer) , then the question that demands an answer is what utterances are legitimate (though inadequate and possibly misleading) and which are entirely inadmissible. Thus the patriarchal monotheism of the Jews considers the epithet "father" as applied to God (Our Father, Our Father in Heaven) to be a legitimate anthropomorphism, although—to quote St. Jerome—*in divinitate nullus est sexus*. The expression "God our Mother," on the other hand, is utterly unthinkable. In fact, all anti-anthropomorphic qualifications have to be applied to the pronoun HE, which is the only one used of God, and not to the pronoun SHE. Isaiah, when he wanted to emphasize the utterly transcendent character of God asked "and what likeness will you compare unto him?" (Isaiah 40:18) and not "unto her."[14]

Indeed, it appears as if non-pagan, monotheistic religion is caught on the horns of an uncomfortable dilemma: either advocate a "negative theology" in which God easily becomes a bloodless abstraction, First Cause, or cosmic principle, or else risk to speak of God in human, all-too-human terms as Father, Shepherd, King and Lover. The rabbis boldly chose the latter risk, on the assumption that only by means of anthropomorphic imagery could the full, actual, vital relevance of God to our lives be brought out. The rabbis, it seems, could take this risk with equanamity since actual anthropomorphism was not considered a real danger by them. They could, therefore, permit themselves considerable latitude of expression. In this respect too the rabbis simply continued the biblical tradition. The days are passed when a naive evolutionism would arrange the biblical texts in a neat chronological order from the more "primitive" anthropological to the more highly developed spiritual passages. Biblical style and its choice of figures of speech are determined by many other factors. Anthropomorphic language is frequently contradicted by anti-anthropological expressions, and modern biblical scholarship is of the opinion that even the golden calves of the wicked Jerobeam were meant to serve as the pedestal for an invisible Deity and not as its actual representation.

Curiously enough the battle over anthropomorphism had to be fought over again in the late middle ages,

though for different reasons. As a matter of fact there are
several types of anthropomorphism,[15] and the genuine,
primitive and direct perception (or description) of the
divine in an anthropomorphic manner is very different
from the dogmatic affirmation that Scripture should be
believed literally. The former is original anthropomorphism, the latter is dogmatic literalism It is the latter
kind which we know so well from the history of both
Islamic theology and medieval Judaism. Nevertheless, the
Jewish fundamentalists against whom Maimonides ful-
minated and who, in their turn, accused him of modernistic heresy, must have had the authority of some kind of
tradition to appeal to. The orthodox diehards who accused both the philosophers of the school of Maimonides
and the mystics of the circle known as the German Hasidim of heretical innovations, certainly did not stage a
literalist revolution of their own. They had a tradition
behind them, and the persistence of this tradition is attested not only by Jewish polemicists but also by Christian
writers—from Justin Martyr to Agobard of Lyons. This
tradition, it had long been suspected, was that of the
Shiur Komah[16] on which so much new light has been
thrown by the recent researches of G. Scholem.[17] It seems
that the next major problem to which research ought to
address itself is that of the *Shiur Komah* type of gnosticism. The question is not only the exact date of its emergence, but whether we are dealing with a movement
within Jewry (which no doubt it is) or more specifically
within rabbinic Judaism. In the latter case we shall have
to accept that rabbinic Judaism was far more complex
than assumed hitherto. The weird macrocosmic anatomy
of the *Shiur Komah* would then have to be considered
not merely as part of the history of Jewish beliefs in the
Amoraic period but as an aspect of "The old rabbinic
doctrine of God."

Enough has been said to indicate the importance, rich-
ness and variety of the subjects treated, and of the issues
raised, in the three studies reprinted in the present vol-

ume. They also invite some reflections on the purpose and justification of offering this publication to the reader. For while it is not the business of a Preface to anticipate the kind of comments that ought to be made in a critical review, there are, nevertheless, some general considerations which it should not ignore. Marmorstein's historical approach is based—ideally—on as complete as possible a documentation and on a careful and critical analysis of the texts. But he himself immediately added a warning: "Our texts are unfortunately in such a condition that not much reliance can be put on them." Since these words were written considerable progress has been made on the textual front. Critical editions, based on known as well as on newly discovered manuscripts or fragments, have been published of many of the major Tannaitic texts, and some of Marmorstein's arguments must be revised (whilst others have been confirmed) in the light of the textual evidence. But also apart from purely philological matters, the conceptual apparatus required for dealing with the subject-matter of these studies should be capable of considerable refinement and improvement, both from the historical and the theological point of view. It is only by improved methods of "penetrating" a text that the utmost can be made of it. Marmorstein's writings are, moreover, often confusing because the way he organized his material —the architecture of his composition, as one might call it—involved unnecessary repetitions. Thus it happens that the material given in the form of chronological lists in one chapter is repeated in the next chapter under the guise of a systematic discussion. Theological and philosophical accounts which should conclude or sum up the historical presentation sometimes appear in the middle of an introductory chapter. The newly available texts and critical editions, as well as present-day standards of organizing and analyzing the material would make a renewed treatment of the subject by a competent scholar highly desirable. When there is genuine progress in scholarship, new studies are to be preferred above reprints of earlier classics. But alas, scholars capable of significantly improving on the work of their predecessors are few and far between. It is easier to criticize the shortcomings of earlier work than to supersede it by a more adequate, complete and definite modern synthesis of the same subject. Hence the growing tendency to reprint the classics of earlier research. It is a tribute to the scholarly labours of A. Marmorstein and to the abundance of the material which he has so indefatigably collected that his studies of *The Doctrine of Merits* and *The Old Rabbinic Doctrine of God* rank among these standard works.

R. J. Zwi Werblowsky

NOTES

1) Morton Smith, "The Work of George Foot Moore," *Harvard Library Bulletin,* XV.2 (April, 1967), p. 179.
2) G. F. Moore subjected the accounts of Judaism by Christian writers to a devastating review in an article in the *'Harvard Theological Review* XIV (1921), p. 197 ff.
3) G. F. Moore, *Judaism* vol. ii (1927), p. 90.
4) *Ibid.,* p. 93.
5) In Kittel's *Theologisches Wörterbuch* vol. ii, coll. 520-525.
6) R. M. Rilke, *Das Stunden-Buch.*
7) G. Scholem, *Major Trends in Jewish Mysticism*² (1946), p. 210.
8) H. Usener, Götternamen, 1896.
9) Particularly by S. Esch, *Der Heilige Er Sei Gepriesen* (1957), especially pp. 2-3, 14, 19.
10) In a forthcoming publication, the MS. of which Prof. Urbach has kindly allowed me to see.
11) Cf. T. W. Manson, *The Teaching of Jesus* (1931).
12) Cf. J. Abelson, *The Immanence of God in Rabbinical Literature* (1912).
13) As Marmorstein has shown in an article "The Holy Spirit in Rabbinic Legend," reprinted in the posthumous volume *Studies in Jewish Theology.*
14) No account is taken here of kabbalistic developments.
15) Cf. also Marmorstein's remarks in his Introduction, p.v.
16) As noted by Marmorstein himself.
17) In *Major Trends in Jewish Mysticism* and in *Jewish Gnosticism, Merkabah Mysticism and Talmudic Tradition* (1960)

INTRODUCTION

(1) THE doctrine, the history and meaning, the development and influence of the subject to be discussed and explained in the following pages, is based on two great ideas and ideals of Judaism, which dominate the sayings and thoughts of the sages of Israel in the first four centuries of the Common Era. These sages taught, with few exceptions, that one is able to acquire merits before God. There are two ways of accumulating merits: negative and positive. The Church Fathers speak of the former, the Rabbis of the latter. Since a man is justified by faith alone, without the works of the law (Rom. 3. 28), he can obtain merits only by avoiding the *indulgentia dei*, i. e. that which is not forbidden.[1] The Jews, however, were taught how one can obtain positive merits (Tert. *Apol.* 21, 4[1a]). Men and women can rise by positive deeds to such a height of moral beauty, virtue, and accomplishment, in spite of their natural shortcomings and innate faults, that they are regarded as meritorious before God. What else does this imply but the idea that each individual human life, every soul, is of immeasurable value? The inestimable value of every person imposes upon him high duties and responsibilities on the one hand, and allows him to participate in privileges and merits on the other. The former requires him to establish his life on the ethical sentiments laid down in the Torah, to walk on the 'path of life', and to contribute to the happiness and prosperity of the world.

[1] For instance, second marriage, to escape persecution, keeping away from wine and meat, from luxuries, *v.* Tertullian, *ad Uxorem*, I, 2 ; *de Uxore.* 18; C. Wirth, *Der Verdienst-Begriff in der christlichen Kirche nach seiner geschichtlichen Entwickelung*, Leipzig, 1892–1901.

[1a] v. H. Schrörs, *Zur Textgeschichte und Erklärung von Tertullians Apologetikum*, Leipzig, 1914, p. 43, 3.

The latter assures him of reward and saves him from punishment. Yet the theological speculations and philosophical teachings of the rabbis strove after something higher than reward, and sought for more than escape from punishment in the ordinary sense of the word. Our chief concern will be to describe how men or women can obtain merits, according to the teachings of the scribes, which shall benefit not merely themselves, but also their posterity, their fellow-creatures, their ancestry, their whole generation, not merely during their life, but even after their departure from the land of the living. Even in the hereafter their merits protect and heal others. Judaism further teaches, as a supplement to the doctrine of imputed merits, the law of imputed sin. The sin and evil-doing of the wicked react upon the life and fortunes of their children, their contemporaries, and others who ought to be spared and saved. This is nothing else but the law of the solidarity of mankind, of brotherhood of peoples and nations. Translated into the vernacular it means: One man, or one set of society, or even one people cannot do good or harm without influencing beneficently or adversely the fate of their nearest kith and kin as well as their whole environment, yea, even the whole world.

Our task will be to collect the Agadic material on this subject. The first chapter deals with the sayings and teachings of the Tannaim and the Amoraim as to the doctrine of imputed merits and sins. Since the 'anonymous' Agadah must necessarily be taken into consideration, they have to be connected with the problems arising out of this doctrine. The second chapter describes the views about the merits which were believed to have caused the creation of the world, which secure the existence of the Universe, and wrought the miracles as well as safeguarded the life of Israel as a religious community during its historical course. There must be a merit for everything. Without work nothing can be achieved. A reason has to be found, why the world was created. It was made for some purpose or aim. For whose sake? There are different theories trying to give a more or less plausible answer. The same is the case with the second question: Who or what are the moral pillars of this world? The scribes were even more deeply interested in the third problem. With profound feeling and truthful sentiment they endeavoured to give a philosophy of their ancient history by means of this doctrine. It was not an accident, it was not blind chance that God had chosen the fathers, had selected Israel among the nations, had redeemed the children of Abraham from Egypt, had divided the sea, given them manna and quails in the wilderness, made them cross the Jordan, inherit the Holy Land, and so on. They must have had merits; what were they? The third chapter deals with the various answers to these questions. They can be briefly grouped in two classes. The merits of the fathers, and those of the righteous. Hereto is added also a chapter on the merits of children which are available for the fathers, and the opposition which arose by some misrepresentations of the doctrine, to the idea of Zechuth Aboth. The last chapter speaks of the different means which acquire merits; they are based on: Faith, Work, and Love.

In the Introduction we have to treat first of all philologically the different terms which denote the ideas underlying this doctrine in their various forms. This leads to the description of the doctrine of God's grace as far as it is connected with our subject. Secondly, to the idea of treasuries upon heaven and the share in the future life. Thirdly, the theological, philosophical, ethical, and social aspects of this doctrine will be pointed out. A bibliography of works on and references to this doctrine in more recent literature will conclude this Introduction.

(2) All writers on ethics agree that the philological investigation of the words signifying the ethical conception is necessary for the understanding of the doctrine or idea. The word reflects as in a mirror the successive development or aberration of the way of thinking. Whilst,

however, the oral tradition does not appear always reliable,
that of literary documents offers a true description of the
feeling and notion. The words on which this doctrine
we are discussing is based, by which its meaning is
expressed, are many. The most familiar to all is the noun
זכות (Latin, *meritum*) and the verb זכה (*merere—mereri*).
These are. it is doubtful whether originally or not, legal
terms. However, in the conscience of the people, in
ordinary talk, זכי בי meant 'Do with me an act of charity
in order that thou mayest acquire a merit.' זכה meant
to most people, who happened not to be lawyers and
judges, 'He deserved, he got merits, he is worthy.' זכות
signified *a merit*, pl. זכיות *merits*. The noun is contrasted
by (*a*) חטא, (*b*) עבירה, and (*c*) חובה. It must be, therefore,
antithetic to sin, transgression, or guilt. For (*a*) we find
this contrast in the composition גרם חטא and גרם זכות.
A punishment *caused* by some sin, or a blessing caused by
some merit. A sin originates misfortune, a merit acquired
caused happiness. The same is the case in other constructions זכות תולה and חטא תולה.[2] The same contrast can be
discerned in המזכה and המחטיא.[3] The former causes others,
by his example, teaching, or conduct to acquire merits; the
latter as the originator of erroneous views or perverted
ambitions, to lead others astray. This merit to make
others imbibe high sentiments and to do good works,
guards a law-giver or teacher, a leader or worker, from
sin, and all the merits are ascribed to him who was the
spiritual father of those works (חטא הרבים v. זכות הרבים תלוי בו).
It is just the other way about with him who teaches sin
and shows the way to apostasy. Moses on one side,
Jeroboam ben Nebat on the other side, illustrate the case.
A later commentary gives a somewhat naïve explanation
for this fact,[4] yet we can understand the teaching very
well without it. Can there, namely, be a higher merit

[2] v. Mid. Cant. Z., p. 21.
[3] v. Aboth, 5. 18; Aboth R. Nathan, ed. Schechter, p. 120.
[4] v. Eccles. r. 4. 1.

than to teach others virtue? to strengthen those of little
faith in faith? and to show a higher outlook and aim of
life to those sunk in the depth of worldly pleasures,
ambitions, and desires? The sin of achieving the reverse
of this endeavour can have no pardon and atonement.
The historian will have to recognize that this is not an
arbitrary theory of what could and should have happened,
but a statement supported by the records reported in the
pages of history.

Just as 'merit and sin', so are contrasted 'merit and
transgression' (זכות v. עבירה). By performing the commandments, as well as by transgressing them, one gathers capital,
i. e. a treasure of good or bad deeds; yet the fruits are
different according to the character of the work.[5] Another
idea is conveyed by the antithesis of זכות and חובה 'merit
and guilt'. R. Hanina ben Gamaliel says: 'Merit and guilt
are never interchanged, except in the case of Reuben and
David'.[6] Great merits, acquired by one, cannot lessen his
burden of guilt, just as guilt does not diminish merits.
R. Simon ben Eleazar speaks also of both in his remarkable
saying, 'In the days of the Messiah there shall be neither
merit nor guilt.'[7] The same contrast as between מזכה and
מחטיא is repeated in מזכה and מחייב.[8] The righteous men get
merits, and cause advantages thereby to accrue to their
children and children's children (שמזכין לבניהם ולבני בניהם
עד סוף כל הדורות); the wicked, however, cause their own
guilt, and bring about punishment to late descendants.
Aaron and Canaan are given as examples. In the first
case the merit of the father helped the children (שעמד להם
זכות אביהם) so that they escaped the fate of their brethren;
in the second instance the guilt of Canaan prevented Tabi,
the slave of R. Gamaliel from being ordained (שחובת אביהם

---

[5] v. Isa. 3. 11; Prov. 1. 31; Tos. Pea., p. 18, l. 5, f., e. g. j. Pea. 16 B,
Aboth R. Nathan, p. 120.

[6] Sifrê Deut., § 347.

[7] b. Sabb. 151 B; Eccles. 12. 1, R. Hijja b. Nehemia, Lam. Z., p. 141.

[8] b. Joma 87 a.

גרמה להן). Instead of multiplying these illustrations, which have to be repeated in the course of this discussion, we may summarize our impression that זכות is something which is opposed to sin, transgression, and guilt. Both are influential in opposite directions on the life and justification of men. They revert not merely upon man's own works but upon contemporaries and posterity as well. The term זכות is used in the following compositions, put in alphabetical order : (1) בקש (v. also חפש), (2) גלגל, (3) גרם, (4) זכר, (5) כרע, (6) למד, (7) מצא, (8) נכה, (9) סייע, (10) עמד, and (11) תלה. Some were also found in connexion with חטא and חובה (e.g. 3 and 11). Very frequent is the contrast between זכה and לא זכה. This lexicographical apparatus is more instructive than it may appear at first sight. It enables us, namely, to get a closer acquaintance with the thoughts of the scribes. An anonymous teacher remarks to Gen. 12. 6, עד עכשיו נתבקש להם זכות בארץ[9]. Abraham passed through the land of promise, for he could not yet settle down, because a merit had still to be sought for the inhabitants of the land. God tries to find merits even for the Gentiles. God also seeks merits for Israel.[10] With reference to the sacrifice of Isaac, the phrase is used אם מבקשין שאחפוש להן זכות[11]. The composition גלגל זכות occurs in the saying מגלגלין זכות ליום זכאי וחובה ליום חייב[12]. One attributes and ascribes the reward of merits to a happy season (day), and the event arising out of guilt to an unhappy time. Merits cause reward (for instance, redemption, future salvation), guilt necessitates calamities (for instance, destruction of the Temple) ; they take place in seasons which are regarded as happy or unhappy. Both

---

[9] Gen. r. 39. 22, ed. Theodor, p. 379, 4 f.

[10] Exod. r. 30. 5 : וכשהוא רואה לישראל שעושין מצוותיו מתנחם על מה שעשה בציון ומבקש להם זכות.

[11] Tanh. f. 30 a, ed. Buber I, p. 115, reads : אם מבקשין הם שאהיה סולח להם. The proper reading might have been מבקשים להם זכות שאהיה סולח להם.

[12] b. Taanit 29 a, b. Erachin 11 b, R. Jose b. Sanh. 8 a.

זכות and חובה cause (גרם) either reward or punishment. R. Simon ben Jochai raises the question as to Deut. 6. 11: Certainly Israel could not fill the houses full of all good things, could not hew the cisterns, could not plant the vineyards, for they never entered the land? What is the meaning of מלאת, חצבת, and נטעת? It teaches that זכותך היא שגרמה, Israel's merit, brought it about that they were tilled, hewn, and planted at the time when they took possession of the land.[13] The merit causes something which does not happen in ordinary circumstances.[14] Hezekiah says to Isaiah: 'I will marry your daughter, maybe that both my and your merits will ensure it (אפשר דגרמא זכותא דידי ודידך), that my children shall be worthy, godfearing people.'[15] The merits of the fathers are supposed to annul the decree which Hezekiah saw by the Holy Spirit that his descendants would be unworthy.[16] The phrase זכר זכות is given Lev. r. 29. 6, Deut. z., p. 2, No. 6. Interesting is the conception which is implied in the composition הכריע זכות. Happy is he who performs a commandment, for he inclined (himself) towards the scale of merits, if he transgressed one thing, woe unto him, for he inclines towards the scale of guilt.[17] Or in another passage: 'Even if 999 angels accuse him (מלמדין עליו חובה), and one angel pleads for him (מלמד עליו זכות), God inclines him towards the scale of merits.'[18] The study of the Torah inclines God to judge man according to his meri-

---

[13] Sifrê Deut., § 38, p. 77 B.

[14] v. however, Friedmann's interpretation note ט"ו.

[15] b. Ber. 10 a.

[16] Tanh., f. 283 a remarks to Deut. 33. 1, ed. Buber, V, p. 54; Pes., p. 199 B מהו את בני ישראל שזכותו של ישראל גרמה לו. The meaning of this sentence is not as Buber (Pes., p. 199 B note, and Tanh. V, p. 54. note ט"ו) believes, Moses was called 'Man of God' for the merit of Israel, but, analogous to the view of R. Akiba, v. p. 44, for Israel's merit Moses was enabled to bless Israel. We have surely a fragment of a Tannaitic Midrash coming from R. Akiba's school before us which tried to explain the word את.

[17] Tos. Kid., p. 336, l. 24.

[18] j. Pea. 16 B; j. Kid. 61 D.

torious side.[19] The term למד זכות is used in Jewish Law
(v. M. Synh. IV. 1) as well. As to מצא זכות we refer to
Gen. r. 50. 1: the angels waited, perhaps they might find
merits for them.[20] He who trusts upon miracles מנכין לו
זכיותיו his merits are being diminished (b. Taan. 20 B). The
merits of the fathers support or help those who work
faithfully for the welfare of the congregation.[21] It is
identical with עמד.[22] Very frequent is the eleventh composition with תלה.[23]

Older than זכות may be the term מעשה.[23a] R. Eleazar
of Modiim speaks of the 'deeds of the fathers', meaning
nothing else but the idea of זכות אבות.[24] R. Akiba asked
a man: מה מעשים יש בידך? What works hast thou got,
i. e. what merits have you got to escape from sure death
in such a miraculous way?[25] R. Matja ben Heresh rules:
'There is no reward without corresponding deed',[26] yet
an anonymous teacher states: 'God does mercy with us,
even in case we have no works'.[27] The Agadists contrast
between the works of the just and those of the wicked.
The former bring forth fruits, the latter are fruitless.[28]
These righteous were called אנשי מעשה 'men of works'.[29]
They were neither Essenes nor any other kind of sectarians,[30]
but men like Hanina ben Dosa whose merits were shared
by other people. The whole world was created for the

---

[19] Aboth 6. 6; ומכריעו לכף זכות, v. also 1. 6.

[20] v. further Aboth R. Nathan, p. 107; M. Ct. z., p. 19; Exod. r., ch. 15. 4.

[21] שזכות אבותם מסייעתם Aboth, 2. 2; R. Gamaliel, III, son of
R. Judah, I.

[22] v. b. Joma 87 a; Gen. r. 56. 7; Lev. r. 36. 3; Pes. 156 a; M. Ps. 11 d;
Exod. r. 33. 3; Tanh., f. 28 B, ed. Buber, I, p. 11.

[23] v. M. Sotah 3. 4; Ber. 10 B; Joma 87 a; Aboth 5. 18; Gen. r. 49. 25;
Ct. r. 4. 3; Eccles. r. 1. 2; Eccles. Z., p. 83; Esther r., ch. 7.

[23a] v. II Baruch 14[7].   [24] Mech., p. 48 a.

[25] Eccles. r. 11. 1.   [26] Mech., p. 5 a.   [27] Mech. 42 B.

[28] Sifrê Deut., § 324, v. R. Judah ben Simon, Gen. r., l. 8.

[29] b. Sotah 49 a; b. Succah 51 a, 53 a; Taanith 24 a.

[30] v. however, Jost's *Annalen*, 1839, p. 145; Oppenheim in *MGWJ.*,
VII, p. 272; Frankel, *Zeitschrift*, III, p. 458; *MGWJ.*, II, p. 70;
Lightfoot J. B., *Dissertations on the Apostolic Age*, London, 1892, p. 330.

merit of such men as Ahab or R. Hanina ben Dosa.[31]
All creatures are supplied with food for his sake.[32] It is
therefore no wonder that his name is among the אנשי מעשה.
Among the Amoraim, R. Hanina ben Hama,[33] R. Joshua
ben Levi,[34] and others use מעשה for זכות. This can be
observed frequently in the anonymous Agadah. To Gen.
26. 28, ראו ראינו, we read: 'We have seen' thy works and
the works of thy fathers.[35] In the Midrash on Psalms
it is said: 'A man should not rely upon the works of his
fathers.'[36] David says: 'There are some who rely upon
their own good deeds, others who trust in the works of
their fathers. I, however, call unto Thee, O God.'[37] The
word מעשה occurs also in compositions with תלה [38] and זכר,[39]
just as זכות.

It seems that in the school of R. Ishmael the term בשכר
was used instead of בזכות.[40] In some sources the words
בשביל or בצדקה were put in exchange for בזכות. Many
examples occur in the following pages.

(3) The Doctrine of Zechuth, signified by various terms,
reveals to us one aspect of the relation between God and
man. Man has got the ability to acquire merits before his
Heavenly Father. However weak and frail man might
be physically or morally, he is in a position to gather
merits in the eyes of God. What kind of works must
he do to acquire merits? There are, of course, many ways
and means to give expression to this feeling and sentiment.
It is surely superficial to assume that God's relation to

[31] Rab., B. Ber. 61 a.   [32] B. Ber. 17 B.   [33] v. Gen. r. 50. 19.
[34] Exod. r. 44. 7.   [35] Gen. r. 64. 8.
[36] Ed. Prague, p. 68 c ; ed. B., p. 534.
[37] M. Psalms, p. 531.   [38] v. Eccles. r. 4. 5.
[39] M. Ct. z., p. 13.
[40] Thus Mech. 8 a: בשכר מצוה שאתם עושים ; Mech. 34 a, v. Tanch.
f. 81 B : בשכר אמונה ; Sifrê Deut. § 301 : בשכר שלשה ; b. Pes. 5 a :
בשכר ביאתינו ; b. B. M. 86 B : בשכר שלשה ; Gen. r. 55. 12, v. Mech. 27 a :
בשכר ב' בקיעות ; b. Hul. 88 B : בשכר שאמר אברהם. The author's
name is רבא, yet style and language suggest that we have, as often,
a quotation from an earlier Tannaitic source in the name of a Babylonian
teacher of the fourth century before us.

man has no other motive than the observance of the Law
on the part of man, and that there is no other form in
which God's relation to man appears except in the reward
for fulfilling and the punishment for transgressing the
Law.[41] It is superficial because the scribes had much higher
opinions of the Almighty than to think that He cannot
do kindness and show grace for His own sake, for His own
name (למען שמו).   And it is also misleading, for the Rabbis
knew that greater is the grace and salvation which man
can enjoy, when done for God's sake than a human
being, even the most perfect and just included, may deserve.
In the Amidah we read : ' And He brings the Redeemer
unto their children's children *for His name's sake* in love '
(ומביא גואל לבני בניהם למען שמו).   There was a view that God
created the world and man for the sake of His name, which
was, however, dropped on account of some misrepresentation
which it occasioned.

In spite of this we read in an anonymous Agadah: ' You
find that God created all things in the six days of creation,
He only created them for His glory, and to do His will
through them.'   There is a detailed support for this view
as to the work of each day.   I. Heaven and earth were
created for His glory according to Isa. 66. 1 and Ps. 19. 2.
Light, Ps. 104. 2.   II. רקיע (firmament) in order to make
a place for the angels, where they can sing His praise,
cf. Ps. 150. 1.   III. Herbs and trees.   Herbs praise God, cf.
Ps. 65. 14.   Trees, I Chron. 15. 33.   The trees are further
used in the Law for various purposes.   IV. The waters, Ps.
93. 4 ; sun and moon, Ps. 148. 3.   V. The birds.   VI. Animals
for sacrifices, v. Lev. 1. 14, and man for God's glory, Ps.
148. 8 f.   That is the meaning of the verse : ' All the works
has God made for His own glory (sake), Prov. 16. 4.[42]   In
the same sense was the passage interpreted by the scribes
who lived before the destruction of the Temple.[43]   Another
Agadist proved the same doctrine from Isa. 43. 7 combined

---

[41] Weber, *System der altsyn.-paläst. Theologie*, Leipzig, 1880, p. 47.
[42] Exod. r. 17. 1.   [43] v. B. Joma 38 a.

express this idea without giving us the name of the author. First of all the legend, quoted later on (p. 22), where we read that God gives from His unlimited treasures unto those who have gathered no treasures of their own.[52] Further to Ps. 23. 3 (He restoreth my soul) נפשי ישובב refers to the future world, He will cause me to return from the exile, not for my merits, but for His name's sake.[53] The teaching of the Mechilta[54] is enlarged and applied also to the future redemption of Israel, in the following words: It does not say 'for My own sake will I do it', but 'for my own sake, for my own sake'. God says: 'I do it only for the sake of My name, in order that My name shall not be profaned.' Why (is it said) twice? 'Just as I redeemed you from Egypt, so will I redeem you from Edom for My name's sake (v. Ps. 108. 8). Just as I redeemed you in this world, so will I redeem you in the world to come for the sake of My name.'[55] We conclude this list of proofs that the idea of God's grace for His name's sake was a reality, with a prayer by *R. Hoshaja* (R. Phinehas b. Hama in his name): 'Our fathers cried unto Thee in Egypt and Thou hast heard their cry, as it is written: "And the Lord went before them at daytime" (Exod. 13. 21); we, however, fasted, afflicted ourselves, we were entreating Thee and prayed day and night and Thou hast not done unto us miracles neither by day nor by night. If there are no good works among us, do it for the holiness of Thy name.'[56] We may surmise that this prayer, which might have been a peroration of some address, was said at a time of great distress, the exact details of which are unknown to us. The teachers of Judaism must have been aware, after all these sayings, that God can do kindness, show love, help and redeem even for His own name's sake.

(4) Yet man has power to acquire merits. The faithful observance of the Law and ceremonies is not unimportant,

---

[52] Exod. r. 45. 6.

[53] M. Ps. 22 c, ed. B., p. 202, Jellinek בה"מ, V. 163.

[54] p. 29 B.   [55] M. Ps., p. 461.   [56] M. Ps., p. 189.

but by no means the only way to acquire them. There are
many other methods of gathering merits. By performing the
commandments man is entitled to a reward, by neglecting
or transgressing them man is condemned to punishment.
The underlying principle of this conception is the old
doctrine of reward and punishment. In order to be able
to have merits, to get a reward, says *R. Hanania ben
Akasia*, God has given unto Israel many laws and commandments.[57] An unknown teacher applied this to Num.
8. 2. God says to Moses : ' Tell Israel, it is not for My
need of light that I command you to kindle a light before
Me, but in order that you may have merits.'[58] This
teaching is repeated by *R. Acha*.[59] The intention of the
teachers was to combat two views which were so often
pronounced against the Jewish Law. First of all the
opinion that the Law and the Ceremonies were a punishment for the stiff-necked people, who had worshipped the
golden calf. In consequence of this theory in the observance of these laws and keeping of these Ceremonies there
can be no virtue. Secondly, they argued, the observance
is senseless, for God does not need them, therefore they
are useless and superfluous. Or, as others put it, the Jews
have ceremonies and rites which cannot be for the Highest
God. The Agadists refuted these arguments by referring
to Scripture, which shows that the Laws and Observances

---

[57] M. Makkot, III, 16.

[58] Tanh. B., IV, p. 46 ; Num. r. 15. 2.

[59] Lev. r. 31, 7 ; Isa. 42. 21 : א״ר אחא יי חפץ למען צדקו יגדיל תורה
ויאדיר לא בראתי אלא לזכותך, and in another form in Tanh., II B,
p. 98 : שלא יטעה אותך יצרך לומר צריך הוא אורה, ראה מה כתיב
מחוץ לפרכת וגו' לא היתה המנורה צריכה להנתן אלא לפנים מן
הפרכת אצל הארון, והיא נתונה מחוץ לפרוכת, להודיעך שאינו צריך
אורה, למה אמר לך בשביל לזכותך למאור ; it seems that this was also
the meaning of *R. Judah ben Ilai*'s sentence : ואני צריך לאורה משלך אלא
למה אמרתי לך לעולם הבא, which can have no other sense than that by
performing the commandments you lay up treasures for the world to
come. בראתי in Lev. r. 31. 7 is to be read לא אמרתי.

were given to obtain merits. There is a reward for obedience to the Law.

The theoretical meaning of the Doctrine is expounded by *R. Jannai*. This teacher taught: A man who kindles light in daytime for his friend when it is light, what benefit has he derived? When does he obtain any advantage from light? In case he kindles it in the night-time, in darkness. The affection Israel has shown in the wilderness was kept for them from that time, from the days of Moses. And when was it repaid to them? In the days of Jeremiah, as it is said: 'I remember unto thee the affection of thy youth' (Jer. 2. 2). that is the meaning of the verse: 'O continue Thy lovingkindness (affection) unto them' (Ps. 36. 11).[60] The affection spoken of must be the willing reception of the Law at Sinai. By receiving, with joy and gladness God's Law, the Israelites stored up the merit which was remembered unto them in later times. The period of Israel's journey in the wilderness is remembered here as 'the affection of thy youth', for the sake of their willingness to take upon themselves the yoke of the Torah.

Yet a man who prays and mentions his own merits, or bases his supplication on the many good deeds he has performed, even in case he is heard, it is done not for his sake, but for the merits of others. If, however, he refers u his prayers to the merits of the fathers, and he has merits of his own, then he is heard for his own merits, and the deed is ascribed to him. *R. Jose ben Zimra* illustrates this theory with the case of Hezekiah and Moses. Hezekiah prayed: 'Remember now, O Lord, I beseech Thee, how I have walked before Thee in truth and with a whole heart, and have done that which is good in Thy sight.' The reply is: 'Thus saith the Lord, the God of David thy father, &c., for Mine own sake, and for

[60] M. Ps., p. 251 ed. Buber, Mech. 15 B cf. Dio Chrysostomus' saying (Zeller, *Die Philosophie der Griechen*, IV[3], p. 818): 'The great ones work for the benefit of others, not for themselves.' M. Ps. P., p. 38 c, אלו צדיקים שמניחים לבניהם פרי מעשיהם.

My servant David's sake' (2 Kings 20. 3–6). On the
other hand Moses cries: 'Remember Abraham, &c.' (Exod.
32. 12), and was heard for his own merits. 'Had not Moses
His chosen servant, stood before Him in the breach, to turn
back His wrath, lest He should destroy them?'[61] *R. Simon
ben Lakish* enlarges our knowledge on this subject a great
deal. He understood the meaning of this doctrine somewhat differently from Gfrörer or Weber, and preached
accordingly. 'All the blessings of the world, and all the
consolations come to the world for the sake of those who
pray for others, fast for the success of others, but for
themselves have no need whatever.' And *R. Simon ben
Lakish* knew such a man, whom he quotes as an instance,
i. e. Mar Zutra.[62] Such conduct and action cannot be

[61] Ps. 106. 23, b. Ber. 10 B; R. Jochanan in his name, Pes. B. 167 B.
R. Alexander adds a parable to this teaching : 'Two men gave myrtles to a
king. One gave it in his own name, and it "came out" for the name of
his grandfather, the other handed it over in his grandfather's name, and
it "came out" for his name.' We have here an allusion to an old rite.
It is known to all who have studied comparative religious history that
the myrtle has a chthonic character, it is holy unto the χθόνιοι, v. Erwin
Rohde, *Psyche*, 4 ed., p. 220, 2, therefore used at wedding and burial ceremonies, v. Eugen Fehrle, *Die kultische Reinheit im Altertume*, Giessen, 1910,
p. 240 f. The two men, whom R. Alexander had in mind, gave the
myrtles for some magic or religious purpose. In one case, where it was
given in the name of the grandfather, the man himself had some advantage,
and in the other case the benefit went to the grandfather. That is the
meaning of ויצאת. On the same idea or belief is *R. Levi's* parable based :
'A Matrona brought two myrtles to the king (i. e. when she married). She
lost one of them, and was very grieved. The king said : "Keep this one,
and I regard it as if you had still both of them "' (Pes. B. 117 B). The
myrtle is supposed to have a chthonic power, and the superstitious
matrona was afraid she might be lost (and go) to the evil spirits, when defended by one myrtle only. This explains further the curious habit of
R. Judah ben Ilai and *R. Samuel ben Isaac* who used to dance with three
myrtles before the bride. When the latter died, a storm of wind uprooted all the good trees of Palestine. Why ? Because he took myrtles
from them, and went before the bride. His colleagues, who were unaware
of the purpose of his doings, were annoyed, and said : 'Why does he do
this? He brings the Torah into contempt.' R. Zeira says : 'Leave him,
he knows what he does.' When he died a myrtle of fire appeared
(Gen. r. 59. 5 ; B. Ket. 17). We see that the belief existed in Palestine
that the myrtles have the power to avert the influence of evil spirits.

[62] v. j. Maaser Sheni 56 d ; Frankel, *Mebo Jer.*, p. 77 a. Other types of a

ascribed to the 'native business nature of the Jews'.
R. Judan preserved another version of R. *Alexander's*,
saying: 'an ox before its sinews are cut through can be
hanged on each of its sinews. After they are cut through,
however, how many strings and nails are necessary to
hang it on? The same happened with Solomon. Before
he sinned he could rely on his own merits, after his sin
he had to rely on the merits of his fathers.'[63] Before a
man sins, his merits are strong, being considered individually, keeping the character of man together; he
appears whole and undivided, in perfect harmony. As soon
as he sins these merits are cut through. They are broken
off, and unable, therefore, to support or hold together the
individuality of this man. Sin darkens all one's thoughts
and actions. To restore the broken individuality he has
to take refuge in the merits of his fathers.

We learn further that even wicked people are not
without merits. Esau obtained merits, according to
R. *Hama ben Hanina*, by honouring his father. A merit
to which the rabbis ascribed Rome's power and strength,[64]
for the scribes applied their philosophical theories to the
policy of the great world as well. Another heathen, Orphah,
was rewarded for the merit acquired by accompanying
her mother-in-law, by bringing forth four heroes, according
to R. *Levi's* view.[65] We see that even Gentiles can have
merits. *Simon ben Pazzi* warns people who accomplish
good deeds, and claim their reward at once. Had the
ancestors taken the reward of the smallest מצוה they did
in this world, whence could their merit have come for their
children, even for us? A man who does not do like the forefathers did is like a porter who says: 'There is the sack,
the money, and measure, go and take.'[66] The same view
was taught by R. *Phinehas b. Hama*. We gather that

similar character were R. Hanina b. Dosa, R. Simon ben Jochai, Hijja
and his sons, and R. Joshua ben Levi.

[63] Eccles. r. 1. 2.   [64] Gen. r. 66. 7.

[65] Tanh. B. I, p. 208 ; M. Ruth r. 2. 20 ; R. Judan in the name of R. *Isaac*.

[66] j. Sanh. 27 d ; Lev. r. 36. 3.

merits are to be obtained by not using the rewards we
are entitled to claim in this world. We learn, therefore,
(1) God has given the Law to enable man to obtain merits;
(2) by not using the reward which is due to him who
observes the Law, they are preserved for the later generations; (3) Jews and Gentiles are alike in acquiring merits
for goods deeds.

We have to mention finally two passages which throw
further light on the theory of the doctrine. The Rabbis
(colleagues of R. Levi) say: Abraham was afraid, and said:
' I escaped the fiery furnace, I escaped from battle, perhaps
I received my reward in this world, and there is nothing
left for me in the world to come.' God says: ' Do not be
afraid. What I have done to thee is all for nothing, thy
reward is kept for the next world.' [67] Another case is
that of Jacob. *R. Jannai* derived this theory from Gen.
32. 11 that a man should not stand on a dangerous place,
and trust in a miracle, because if he should escape he
diminishes his merits.[68] Both instances show the Rabbis'
view that we might use up the merits in this world which
ought to be stored up for the world to come. This leads
us to the conceptions of the heavenly treasures.

(5) ' He who works righteousness upon the earth has
a treasure in heaven ' [69] is an often-repeated teaching in
the Apocrypha and Pseud-epigrapha. II Baruch reports
that there are in heaven gathered the treasures of all
those who have been righteous in creation (24. 7); further,
that the pious have with God a store of works preserved
in treasuries (44. 12). And the Gospels preach: ' Lay not
up for yourselves *treasures upon earth* where moth and
rust doth corrupt and where thieves break through and
steal : but lay up for yourselves *treasures in heaven*, where
neither moth nor rust doth corrupt and where thieves do
not break through nor steal' (Matt. 6. 19–20) It was
assumed that the doctrine of the treasuries, where the good

[67] Gen. r. 44. 5.   [68] v. b. Sabb 32 B.
[69] Test. Lev. 13. 5 ; Test. Napht. 8. 5.

deeds of the pious were stored up, and used for the atonement for sins and for averting punishment of other people,
developed in Judaism through Persian influence and
example.[70] However that may be, we see the first part
of the Doctrine in the Apocrypha and Gospels. No trace
of the second part is to be seen. It is worth while investigating how far this doctrine penetrated into Rabbinical
Judaism. Charity is a treasure, as we find it in the story
of Monobazus. This king distributed among the poor his
property in years of famine. His brother reproached him,
saying: 'Your fathers gathered treasures, and increased
their fathers' treasures, and you distribute among the
poor your and your fathers' treasures.' He said: 'My
fathers stored up treasures on earth below, I store them
up in heaven above! They stored up treasures in a place,
whence they can be taken away, I do so where *they cannot
be taken away*.[71] They stored up treasures which can
bring no fruits, mine shall bear fruits ; they did it for this
world, I do it for the future world.'[72] This conception
differs from the view of R. Simon ben Jochai, according
to whom there is only one treasury, i. e. of those who fear
sin. It seems, however, that his colleague, R. Jose ben
Halafta, had a wider outlook, more in agreement with
that of Monobazus. Likewise did R. Nehemia teach that
all the souls of the righteous are gathered in the Heavenly
treasury. Bar Kappara also testifies that R. Simon ben
Jochai's doctrine has not enjoyed much popularity. Of
the Agadists of the Amoraic period only R. Abba b. Kahana
refers to this teaching.[73]

An anonymous teacher expresses the views held about
this doctrine by means of the following legend: Moses
ascends to heaven, and God shows him all the heavenly

[70] v. Spiegel, *Eranische Altertumskunde*, II, p. 64 f. ; *ZfWTh.*, 27. 356.

[71] v. my article, 'The Treasures in Heaven and upon Earth,' in the
London Quarterly Review, 1919, pp. 216–28.

[72] Tosefta Pea, p. 24, l. 11 ; pal. Pea, 15 в, b. B. B., 11 a ; Pes. r., p. 126 в.

[73] s., pp. 54 and 91.

treasures. Moses inquires: 'For whom is this?' God
replies: 'For those who observe the Law.' Moses: 'To
whom is this treasure due?' God: 'To him who brings
up orphans.' Moses passes from each treasury to the
other, and learns the merits for which they are kept.
Then Moses sees a big treasury, larger than all the others,
and asks: 'For whom, O Lord, is that?' God replies:
'He who has (merits) I give him his reward from his own;
to him, however, who has nothing, no merit at all, will be
given hence.'[74] From all these passages we learn that the
belief existed of the treasures of good deeds and performances gathered for the benefit of him who actually did
them. There is no reference to posterity or others.
Every one's merits are rewarded, he who has no merits
receives for God's sake.

On this conception is also based the teaching that each
Jew has a share in the future life, in the world to come.
The teachers of the Mishnah derived it from or supported
it with the words of Isa. 60. 21.[75] The exception enumerated
in the same Mishnah shows clearly that a good many Jews
were not found worthy of this share owing to dogmatic
reasons. Older and younger scribes enlarged this catalogue
of unworthies and supplemented the list by adding occasionally some transgressions which may deprive people of
this privilege. These negations have an historical ground,
which must be investigated individually and cannot be
dealt with summarily. The scribes are, however, reticent
as to the positive side of the doctrine. They never dared
to state plainly whether this or that person is a son of
the future world. Even men of great merits trembled
at the thought whether their share in the future life was
assured or not. Yet there are cases where people were
assigned as 'sons of the world' to come, of whom none
would have thought or imagined that such an honour was

---

[74] Exod. r. 45. 6, v. ארחות חיים, p. 51; Tanh. f. 127, a fuller description
in the Hebrew *Ascensio Mosis* (גדולת משה).
[75] M. Sanh. X. 1.

theirs, a fact which shows that not so much the open
merits counted in the eyes of those initiated, but just the
secret virtues and merits hidden to the sight of men, but
revealed to Him who sees everything. Not only Jews,
but pious heathens too, have a share in the future life.[76]
IV Ezra denies this share to heathens in general (13. 25),
yet Baruch (72. 2) grants it to pious heathens, just as
R. Joshua ben Hananiah did.[77] R. Meir's friend enlightens
us on this subject, when he says: 'This world belongs to
us (heathens), the world to come to you (Jews).'[78] We
know from Plato's *Republic* (II. 364) that already in his
days there were in Greece many begging charlatans, called
orpheo-telestae, whose business it was to knock at the doors
of the rich, with a heap of pamphlets under their arms,
supposed to have been written by Orpheus himself, out
of which they promised, in exchange for good money, to
perform some rites which, so they affirmed, or pretended—
and as a testimony of human cleverness found believers—
could purify and remove from those, who could afford to
pay, all traces of defilement and guilt, and assure them
a happy lot in the world to come.[79] The desire for a happy
lot in the future life existed in the heathen world later
on too, except in such circles to which R. Meir's friend
belonged, who may have been an adherent of Epicurus.
A pious Stoic was perhaps more anxious about his future
happiness. The teachers of Judaism, like R. Joshua ben
Hananiah, must have achieved many successes in these
circles, at least with wise men and wearied politicians or
soldiers who cared for their share in the future life. The
preachers of the Gospels had also not too difficult a task
with people who were anxious for their future life. This
broad view is mere theory. Actual life teaches differently.
Churches and denominations, ambitions and policies, are

[76] v. p. 40, n. 10.

[77] v. F. Rosenthal, *Vier apokryphische Bücher aus der Schule R. Akiba's*,
Leipzig, 1885, p. 83.

[78] v. p. 51, n. 48.

[79] v. Döllinger, *Heidenthum und Judenthum*, Regensburg, 1857, p. 138.

busy nullifying R. Joshua ben Hananiah's great teaching
that ultimately everything depends on piety and love o
God, in whatever form this appears.   Among Jews themselves there were *three* groups, often differentiated in the
sources: righteous, men of the middle way, and wicked.

(6) Of the four aspects on which the doctrine of merits
throws light, we deal firstly with the theological part.
God is, according to Rabbinical theology, all-mighty, all-
powerful.   None can prevent Him from, and none can help
Him in doing, anything.   That being so, what was the aim
of the Creation?   Why does this Universe exist?   Why
has He shown His great miracles and wonders in the
course of Jewish history?   Why was Israel chosen?   There
are two trends of theological speculation endeavouring to
satisfy people's curiosity.   One school inclined to the
opinion that 'everything is done for His Name's sake'.
Even the greatest personality does not come near the ideal,
or the best deeds are not sufficient recompense for God's
mercy shown in nature and history, in the past as well
as in the present time.   The second set has the general
tendency towards the opinion that nothing is caused but
for merits.   Approval and criticism can be equally divided
between both schools.   If God created the Universe for
His own glory, if He keeps the world going, does miracles,
&c., for His Name's sake, then He is in need of them, to
make known His name, and to be glorified.   God is,
however, without needs and requirements.   He who is
all-mighty needs nothing.   Yet the attempt of this school
was to show that the fundamental character of Deity is
mercy and goodness.   A human being or action cannot
be so great, so unselfish to deserve the revelations of God
in life and death by his own accomplishments.   The second
school had a better opinion of man's value.   We can acquire
merits, we can reach a height of perfection which makes
us worthy that a world shall be created for our sake, yet
could not God bestow upon us His mercy without our
work?   This school replied to the theorists : ' Without Faith,

Work, or Love nothing could come about, for it would not
be just, and God is just.' We see, therefore, the basis of
these various views is interwoven with the chief problems
of Jewish theology especially, and religious thought generally, namely, the nature (or attributes) of God (powerful,
good, just) and the Government of God. The later Agadists
must have come to a compromise, which enabled them to
combine both views. In this sense only are we justified
in speaking of merits in Rabbinical theology.

This appears even more strikingly in the differences
which can be discerned as to the merits themselves. Whilst
the great bulk of Agadists accept the doctrine of merits
unconditionally, they recognize only the value of self-
acquired merits, and would not admit the help or influence
of imputed merits. It is, according to their teachings,
quite in order that nothing should happen without merits,
yet we have to obtain our own merits. This does not
mean egotism or selfishness, but justice. Yet life contradicts this theory everywhere and in every way. This way
of thinking is too severe, and does not appeal to the masses.
Therefore, we observe that the second school which taught
and spread the doctrine of the merits of the fathers and
of the righteous enjoyed much greater popularity. To
trust in the merits of others is more convenient, especially
where and when moral qualities are considered. The
abuses and misinterpretations which the teaching might
lead to were obvious. A compromise was wanted, and was
actually found as early as in the time of Hillel, and carried
on by his school. In the later Agadah again the traces
of these differences were lost and the views assimilated
with each other. It is to be noted, however, that the
fathers or the righteous stand as representatives of ideals
in a good many cases. They personify the great moral
teachings for which Judaism lives.

There seems to be no dispute on the doctrine of imputed
sins. This was recognized generally. The ancient commentators of the Decalogue smoothed over the difficulty

arising out of this teaching by assuming that only those
children suffer for their fathers' sins who follow their
wicked fathers' footsteps.[80] The Agadists, however, take
this view for granted. Children suffer for the shortcomings
of their parents, and *vice versa*, just as in the case of merits.
Although one might be tempted to question the justice of
the children's suffering for the parents' sake, as one does
it in the analogous doctrine of merits, yet no dispute arose.
The reason may be found in the fact that the truth of the
fact is verified by daily experience, and secondly the
adoption of this view was less exposed to misconstruction
and harm than the other.

The merits are manifold. They are based on the principles of Faith, Works, and Love. The doctrine of merit
teaches, in common with the history of all ethical sentiments, that simple ethical notions develop into general
conceptions. They originally impersonate personalities and
events, who are the bearers of ethical ideas. The fathers,
the pious, the various biblical personages, whose merits
are spoken of, represent faithfulness, adherence to God's
word and obedience to His command, lovingkindness and
self-sacrifice, unselfishness and love. Speaking, therefore,
of the merits of these personalities means, if we divest
them of their names, idealizing the general notions of the
different merits. Rabbinical theology is generally reproached as preferring works to faith and love. One is
apt, however, to forget that these works, whether prayers
or charity, Sabbath or circumcision, sacrifices or tithes,
were never regarded as forms of words or forms of ceremony. They had, and have even now, a meaning which
is alive in them. They certainly were not looked upon
in themselves as possessing material or magical virtues.
Besides Judaism, firm on these ideals, stood the acid test
of history in very trying and dangerous moments. Any
form of religion which justifies man by faith and love
alone, without works, could not, as far as history teaches

[80] b. Ber 7 a, Mech. 49 a.

throughout the ages, withstand the enticing voice of selfishness and infidelity.

The development of this doctrine gives an illustration of the Agadic method. In more than one instance we can discern the influence of contemporary events, of actual life, of historical causes upon the teachings of the Agadists. It cannot be merely a chance when the rabbis of the third century changed suddenly their attitude by preaching: 'For Israel's sake was the world created, for Israel's sake does the world exist, for Israel's sake all blessing comes into the world', instead of the older view, ' For man's sake was the world created.' This was certainly neither chauvinism nor self-conceit on the part of the Rabbis. Its development is closely connected with the polemics of those days. The church and the porch, the cathedral and the temple revived the half-forgotten and totally ill-founded abuses against the Jews. The Jews are a useless nation, which had done nothing for the good of humanity.[81] The Jews, so the Agadists replied to the Church, are something more than witnesses of the veracity of the Church; they are the source of every blessing and happiness. How far this is true or false cannot be our task to investigate here, yet it is in any case nearer to the truth than the conception of the Church Fathers. The same apologetical tendency can be discovered in the teaching that for the sake of the pious women in Egypt Israel was redeemed. The accusations are well known, and it is worthless even to repeat them. The Agadists cannot be blamed when they availed themselves of this doctrine to repulse one of the most hideous and cruel misrepresentations of Jewish history. Other apologetical traces are shown in the doctrine of the merits of the fathers. From the writer of the Barnabas letter onwards, the story of the golden calf figures as a striking proof for Israel being forsaken by God. The Agadists retort that God has forgiven Israel for the merits of the

[81] Apolonios Molon, Josephus, c. Ap. 2. 14; Apion, ibid. 2. 12; Celsus, c. Cels. 4. 31; Julianus, p. 208 seq., 222 H.

fathers. That teaching gave rise to the problem as to how
long did the merits of the fathers influence the fate of
Israel ? Why did they not protect Israel in fateful hours
and crises ? Another, more internal, event occasioned the
argument : ' Why do the just men perish in time of plague ?
Why cannot their merits protect others as well as themselves ? ' On this basis they developed the doctrine of
imputed sins and imputed righteousness of the just.
Sometimes the latter dies for the sins of others, at other
times the death of the righteous prevents death or plague,
which threatens the whole community. In the homilies
of the scribes this aspect was forcefully emphasized to
warn against wickedness and to animate the hearers to
imitate the deeds of righteous men and women.

It is a general and a great mistake to criticize and pass
any opinion on the Agadah without considering the cultural
movements and philosophical streams in the environment
of the authors. The fundamental basis of our doctrine
finds its counterpart in Stoic thoughts. The contemporary
Stoics, whose philosophy bears a theological and ethical
aspect, were agitated by the same problems as the rabbis :
There must be some aim in the creation of the universe !
They taught further that the world will not exist for ever.
Any moment a great cataclysm may arise which will
shake the whole world to its foundations, and destroy it.
Only some merit keeps it together. Some deeper cause
prevents this threatening event being realized. It was
a teacher of the Stoa, who finally made the western world
acquainted with the doctrine that the descendants enjoy
the good works of their parents, just as the latter benefit
by the deeds of the children. Still the law of imputed
sin is one of the features of old Greek religion, as described
in the Homeric works and the Attic drama. Troy and her
inhabitants suffer for Paris' sin.[31a] It may be that the position of the ruler was so high that the punishment must be

---

[31a] v. also John 9. 2 : Master, who did sin, this man, or his parents, that
he was born blind ?

general, or that the conception is based on the idea of solidarity. The same occurs in the case of Niobe.[82] Yet the doctrine of imputed righteousness was never thought of before Judaism proclaimed it. The relation between the Stoa and Agadah appears not merely in this doctrine. There are besides this point many other problems which would tempt us to lay our material before the readers. Such an investigation is needed in spite of the attempts made by various students.[83] Space does not permit such an excursion. Yet it is more than probable according to our impression that the Stoics, especially those who hailed from the Orient or lived in Semitic environment,[84] adopted the greater part of their theological teachings from the Jews, and adapted them to their own system. However that may be, one fact is certain, that the speculations on the accumulation of merits were on the order of the day in the schools in the Orient as well as in the Occident in those days.

In other philosophical systems there are also some parallels to our doctrine. The Buddhist systems taught that people can acquire by asceticism such powers, and accumulate such great merits that the gods have to obey their wishes;[85] their merits are available for others.[86] One can transfer the accumulated merits from the living to the dead. This is also proclaimed by the Sayash la Sayash, which lays also great stress on the merit of repentance (VIII, 5–9). The wicked receive their reward for their good deeds.[87] Without great difficulty one can gather many parallels between the Jewish doctrine and various

[82] v. especially W. Wundt, *Ethik*, I, p. 93.

[83] v. esp. A. Bodek, *Marcus Aurelius Antoninus und Rabbi*, Leipzig, 1868, pp. 121–32, 141 ; Bergmann, *Iudaica, Festschrift zu Hermann Cohen's 70. Geburtstag*, Berlin, 1912, pp. 145–66 ; v. also Frankel, *MGWJ.*, 8. (1859), p. 399 f.

[84] v. Lightfoot J. B., *Apostolic Age*, p. 282 ff.

[85] Mahab., III, 122–5, *Visnu Purana*, I, 9.

[86] v. *JRAS.*, 1875, p. 7.

[87] v. M. N. Dhalla, *Zoroastrian Theology*, New York, 1914, pp. 56 f, 273–5.

religious systems; the material at our disposal shows,
however, that the importance of the doctrine does not
concentrate in its historical aspect, but in its ethical value.

The question of the origin of this doctrine leads to
negative results. Thinkers of many races and nations,
engaged in studying ethical problems, came to the result—
whether independently or not is a difficult, but irrelevant
question—that there is imputed righteousness as well as
imputed sin. The latter conception is older and wider, the
former reveals a higher development of ethical thought.
The objections to the ethical value of the merits are threefold: (a) they show a mercenary spirit; (b) they lead to
a craving after merits; and (c) they promote self-
righteousness. The history of our doctrine teaches us
that none of these dangers were overlooked, and none of
them darkened the brighter side of this conception. There
may or may not have been people who kept books of their
righteous works and good deeds. Yet the scribes warned
them and condemned their point of view! Besides, there
can be no mercenary spirit when the benefit or advantage
arising out of the merits and rewards cannot be enjoyed
in this world, but in a world to come—which itself is
a matter of faith and belief. Supposing some one reached
such a high standard of thought that he sees in his
devotion to study, in performing the observances, in giving
charity, an instrument to gather treasures for a future life,
is that a mercenary spirit? Is it not rather the strongest
faith one can imagine? It cannot be denied that Jews were
yearning to perform the commandments. Well, Moses desired,
according to the Agadic world-view, to enter the Holy Land,
because there were some observances which were meaningless
and valueless outside that country (b. Sotah 14 a R. Simlai).
They were craving not after rewards, but their desire was
to give worthy expression to that deep, immeasurable love
and unlimited faith in the Father in Heaven. They saw
in their works the means to bear witness to the existence
of God, to recognize His rule and providence, to acknow-

ledge gratefully His mercy in hours of success, and bow their head in sorrow with eyes turned to heaven in face of His chastisement. How far all this promoted self-righteousness it is impossible to see. The man who really obtained merits, or who was keen to accumulate them, did not do so for himself, but without his being aware of it, the merits benefited others. For the idea of merits in Judaism is something quite different from that in the Catholic Church. There a man gets merit who does something more or less than others do. He avoids things which God in His indulgence has not strictly forbidden. In Judaism, however, every one can get merits, not by negative, but by *positive* works. זכות is really neither Arete, Virtus, nor Tugend. These words signify some ideal which makes life appear good and desirable to the Greek, Roman, and Germanic races. They lay stress on external matters, like ability in society, military or forensic achievements, utility in art and craft. The Jews' ideal was to appear 'pure', 'undefiled' before the Creator. Thus he never approached the line of self-righteousness. Can one born of woman be pure before his Creator? The best example is that sage who spent his whole life in study and charitable work, and when he heard the news of his imminent martyr death, asked: ' Have I got a share in the future life?' Where is there self-righteousness here? We find further cases when the Rabbis were informed, by a way which it is not our duty to search here, of people whom every one regarded as wicked, unworthy, e. g. the Pentakaka, having supernatural powers. Do these examples leave any room for self-righteousness? Certainly not. It is also useless from the Rabbinical point of view to enter into discussion whether merits are rivals of duties,[88] or to distinguish between meritorious and autonomous works, for duty and merits are really the same. By doing our duty we acquire merits. We, of course, can object and say that discharging one's duty

---

[88] Kant, *Kritik der reinen Vernunft*, ed. Fehrnbach, pp. 103 ff., 186 ff.

cannot be a merit from the ethical point of view. Why,
then, did the scribes regard the observance of the Law,
which was the Jews' most sacred duty, as a merit? Yet
it seems that only the performance of those was considered
as meritorious in which the devotion to the faith in God
and lovingkindness found noble expression.

There are two other objections to Jewish ethics generally, and to our doctrine especially, which have to be
pointed out here. First of all the reproach that the ethics
of the Rabbis are materialistic, in so far that the terminology reminds us of legal aspects (for instance למד זכות)
or is caught in sensual phrases, like הכריע זכיותיו. Yet it
should not be forgotten that זכה is used in the Bible
originally in a more theological or ritualistic sense. We
observe further that in the whole discipline of ethics words
applied to worldly matters are used in speaking of moral
actions and ethical sentiments.[89] The second fault may be
found in the egotism, from which all eschatological conceptions suffer more or less. The latter are based on
future advantages. The rabbis, besides, exhausted the
pedagogical value which surrounds the agadic biographies
of biblical personages. Yet we cannot speak in this
connexion of having applied immoral motives for moral
aims,[90] because the motives themselves are by no means
immoral, indeed the reverse, because based on the highest
ideals of morality.

Finally, we have to point out the influence of the doctrine
on social life. In every form of social life merits and
demerits count; the former entitle us to esteem, praise, and
approbation ; the latter render us unworthy of these
qualities, and make us worthy of reproach and blame.
The merits are, however, dependent on the general moral
or ethical sentiments of the various social grades of different nations. Health of body, fortitude in war, skill in
the forum, beauty of appearance, were all merits which
may be beneficial to the individual. We speak, however,

[89] v. Wundt, *Ethik*, I, p. 29.   [90] v. Wundt, *l. c.* I, p. 100.

of merits by which the welfare of mankind, of a whole
community, of whole nations is promoted or secured, or of
demerits by which the fortune of future generations is
threatened. Such merits or demerits must be recognized
or blamed, revered or condemned. It is only natural that
those whose merits helped or were supposed to have helped
their contemporaries were in a somewhat exceptional
position in the community. Thus first of all the scribes
who were engaged in the study of Torah, who endeavoured
to raise the intellectual standard, to spread the word of
God by teaching and learning ; who comforted the mourning
and led the stumbling, by preaching and warning ; who
encouraged their brethren or compatriots in distress and
sorrow by unrolling before their eyes the glorious vision
of Israel's eternity. There was no field of human activity
or no branch of religious life where their benevolent and
unintrusive help was not wanted or their advice and
impartial judgement sought for in vain. Such men surely
deserved some signs of respect or reverence, recognition
or support for their merits. Even their children shared
the latter to a certain extent. Then we find that the rabbis
had to be lenient with people of great merits, as, e. g., in
the case of Honi ha Meagal, or Theodosius of Rome.[90a]
The strict law had to stand still in face of great merits.
These were, however, neither merits of birth, nor merits of
material wealth, but simply merits of works for the community. However great the esteem of people with merits
was, it was not of a material form. They had some social
privileges, but only on the fields they worked. No economic
advantages could be derived from them. Only in exceptional cases do we find that the lack of Zechut Aboth
influenced the career of a great man. If a suggestion
advanced by an Amora is correct and reliable, there was
on the one side the merit of wealth which was responsible
for R. Eleazar ben Azaria's election to the dignity of the

[90a] b. Ber. 19 a ; b. Pesaḥ. 53 a.

C

Patriarchate, and the lack of Zechut Aboth caused the defeat of R. Akiba in his nomination as R. Gamaliel II's temporary successor. This might also account for the legend that R. Meir, who was not liked by the intimates of the Patriarchal camarilla, was the descendant of the Emperor Nero. The problem of the merits of the proselytes has surely a social reason. It is to be noticed that in times of moral decline in Jewish history, antagonists, who by their spiritual value and moral light overwhelmed petty and selfish accusers, were abused or suspected as being of proselyte origin. Yet we find that the boasting of great ancestry, of noble birth, without one's own merits, was unpalatable to Jewish teachers.

The problem whether long life, children, and worldly wealth were an outcome of man's merits was discussed by the Alexandrinians and R. Joshua ben Hananiah.[91] The sage thought first that all these blessings depend on the merits of works. The sharp Alexandrians gave him, however, many instances which proved that even people with great merits died in their youth, or had no children and remained poor all their life. The scribe had to admit this, and gave them the advice to seek God's mercy. Some find this idea, that one's merits have no influence on his being rich or poor, in a saying of R. Meir.[92] The view is shared by R. Eleazar ben Pedath,[93] and expressed by the Babylonian Amora Raba (רבא): 'Life, children, and food do not depend on merits but on the influence of the planets.'[94] The fact that one dies early in life or in old age, childless or blessed with children, poor or rich, proves nothing as to one's merits, for the merits one accumulates are not rewarded in this world but in the world to come.

Quite different is the case of the demerits or sins. Their influence is felt in this world. One is disgraced and blamed for them in life. If one escaped them, then his

[91] b. Niddah 170 b.

[92] b. Kid. 82 a (v. p. 49), and Barzilais *Commentary to Sefer Yetzira*, p. 8.

[93] v. b. Ber. 5 b.   [94] b. M. K. 28 a.

descendants or family will have to suffer for it. Even strangers have to suffer for the sins of their wicked contemporaries. The righteous is taken away for the sin of his generation. This is the result, as will be shown, of the law of solidarity which was enunciated by the Jewish teachers. Thanks to Stoic philosophy a loftier conception of cosmopolitan teaching obtained among the intellectuals of the ancient world, and brought home to them the teaching that we are all members of one vast body. They made the soil, barren for so many ages, the heart, dried up by the tempest of selfishness, acceptable for an even higher teaching that all human beings, without difference of creed and nationality, race or position, are created in the image of God (R. Akiba, Aboth, IV. 15). There can be no other goal for life and history than the translation of this ideal of the solidarity of mankind into fact and reality.

The social aspect of this doctrine appears, finally, in the merits attributed to Jewish women. We will show later on that the view is primarily of apologetical provenance. This cannot prevent us deriving some truth and information as to the social position of women in those days. It must have been very high indeed, if the teachers and preachers could exclaim in their sermons and lectures: 'The merit of pious women delivered us from Egypt.' In this saying there is certainly more than a dry lifeless hypothesis of historical speculation. It teaches first of all that those scribes were perfectly aware and conscious of the self-sacrifice and motherly love with which noble womanhood watched their children's steps from their early youth, and, secondly, they knew and impressed their audience with that very same knowledge, which is verified by history and life, that the future, the existence of a religious community as well as of a nation, has its roots in family life, in the character of women. They have the privilege, but at the same time the higher duty, of working for the salvation of the world.

To these by no means exhaustive aspects of the doctrine

of merits—some aspects will occur naturally in the course
of the following pages—may be added a short bibliography
of this subject. The doctrine of merits has been often dealt
with and referred to in the last decades. Besides *Güdemann*[95] and *Kohler*,[96] we have essays treating on this
question by *S. Levy*[97] and *Schechter*[98] and *Wohlgemuth*.[99]
A new treatment of the doctrine seemed to us not out of
place, for these essays aimed mostly at one side, one aspect
of the question, the biblical origin or the liturgical value,
or at the merits of the fathers. We considered mainly the
historical development of the teaching. It is very convenient, in speaking of Jewish theology, to stigmatize any
attempt to show the historical development of its problems
as 'weaving ropes of sand' or 'building palaces out of sun-
beams'. The task has, however, to be undertaken.

[95] **Rahmer's** *Jüd. Literaturblatt*, XXI (1890), No. 18; *Jüd. Apologetik*,
Glogau, 1906, p. 171 f.

[96] *Grundriss einer systematischen Theologie des Judentums auf geschichtlicher
Grundlage*, Leipzig, 1910, p. 310.

[97] *Original Virtue and other short Studies*, London, 1907, p. 1–42.

[98] *Some Aspects of Rabbinic Theology*, 1909, pp. 170–98.

[99] In *Festschrift zum 40 jährigen Amtsjubiläum des Dr. S. Carlebach*, Berlin,
1910, pp. 98–145; v. also Ephraim Frisch, *Zechuth Aboth and the Akedah*,
in the Hebrew Union College Annual, Cincinnati, Ohio, 1904, pp. 253–
66; R. Travers Herford, B.A., *Pharisaism*, London, 1912, p. 213 f. and
p. 276 f.; and Gfrörer, F. A., *Das Jahrhundert des Heils*, Stuttgart, 1838,
pp. 134–94.

I.

(1) *Shemaiah and Abtaljon,* or Sameas and Pollion as
called by Josephus,[1] were the first to discuss a question
bearing on the subject of merits in Rabbinical literature.
The problem which agitated the mind of these two 'great
men of their generation'[2] was: 'What merit did the
Israelites possess that God divided the sea before them?'
Such a supernatural deed must have been caused or brought
about by some special merits. Shemaiah taught: 'Sufficient
is the *faith,* with which Abraham their father believed in
Me that I should divide the sea before them, as it is said:
And He believed in God, and He counted it unto him
(i. e. at the sea) for (doing) charity (with his children)'
(Gen. 15. 6). Abtaljon says: 'Worthy is the faith, they
(the Israelites themselves) believed in Me so that I shall
divide the sea before them, as it is said: "And the people
believed"' (Exod. 4. 31).[3] It is rather significant that at
the head of an historical review of one of the important
doctrines of the scribes, we do not find works and ceremonies emphasized, but the merit of faith, not an external
deed, but an innermost feeling, is demanded. Not 'opera
operata', but faith it was which produced an event which
seemed to the ancients one of the great miracles of Israel's

---

[1] Ant. XIV, 9. 4; XV, 1. 1; 10. 4. v. D. Hoffmann, *Der oberste Gerichtshof,*
pp. 43, 45; Büchler, *Das Synhedrion in Jerusalem,* p. 179 f.

[2] גדולי הדור b. Pes. 66 a; j. Pes. 33 a; גדולי עולם.

[3] Mech., p. 29 B: כדאי היא האמונה שהאמין בי אברהם אביהם שאקרע
להם את הים, אבטליון אומר כדאי היא האמונה שהאמינו בי שאקרע להם
את הים, v. Mech. of R. Simon ben Jochai, p. 48, where a fuller version of
the latter opinion is ascribed to the Rabbis generally. According to this
view the choice of Israel as God's chosen people is to be ascribed to
Israel's faith in God; v. also J. Oppenheim, האסיף, VI (1894), p. 95.

past. The dispute between the two scribes deals with a side issue, whether the faith of Abraham or their own faith made the Israelites worthy to experience and ask: 'What aileth thee, O thou sea, that thou fleest?' Their pupil and successor Hillel left us an epigrammatic saying which gave rise to various explanations; one at least calls for our attention. 'If I am not for myself, who is then for me? And if I am for myself, what am I?'[4] *Aboth of R. Nathan* explains this in the following words: 'If I do not acquire merits in this world, who will justify me in the world to come? There I have neither father nor brother. Our father Abraham could not ransom his son Ishmael. Our father Isaac could not redeem Esau. Even if they give all their Mammon they cannot ransom themselves. Whence do we know that brothers cannot redeem their brethren? Jacob could not redeem his brother Esau' (cf. Ps. 49. 8, 10).[5] Hillel's word may have been a warning, if he really meant it in this sense to those who misunderstood or misused the meaning of the teaching of merit. He turned perhaps against those who thought and said within themselves: ' *We have Abraham to our father* [6] in spite of whatever we may do or think.' Our forefathers cannot justify us in judgement, we ourselves have to abide by our deeds and consequences. Hillel would, in that case, have continued the teaching of his master Abtaljon, who pointed out against Shemaiah that individual merits helped Israel at the sea. In the second part of the saying we have a compromise. 'When I am for myself what am I?' i. e. what can man achieve? Even if we acquired merits, we still have no right to claim reward. All the good deeds a man does in this world are not sufficient to justify him. He has to rely on the works of the fathers. Thus or similarly sounded Hillel's teaching, if the pretty late interpretation understood it rightly. There is no cogent reason to doubt

---

[4] Aboth, I, 14.

[5] Ed. Schechter, p. 54, II version, I version much shorter.

[6] Matt. 3. 9; John 8. 39.

that, moreover, the views of Shemaiah and Abtaljon explain Hillel's saying in this sense and support such an interpretation. We find a striking parallel to this view of Shemaiah and Abtaljon in Luke 17. 5 f., where the apostles ask of Jesus : ' Increase our faith ! ' And Jesus said, if ye had *faith* as a grain of mustard seed, ye might say unto this sycamine tree (τῇ συκαμίνῳ) : Be thou plucked up by the root, *and be thou planted in the sea* ; and it should obey you.[7] If a faith as minute as a grain of mustard seed were sufficient to accomplish such miracles, the faith of Abraham or of Israel was surely sufficient to enable Israel to cross the sea.

It is doubtful whether the dialogue between the conqueror of Jerusalem, called Hadrian, and R. Jochanan ben Zakkai is genuine as related in Tanh. Buber, V, p. 6. Hadrian was proud, and boasted everywhere : ' I conquered Jerusalem with (my) power ! ' R. Jochanan ben Zakkai said to him : ' Do not boast, were it not from heaven (i. e. God's will) thou wouldst not have conquered it.' What did R. Jochanan ben Zakkai do ? He took Hadrian and led him to a cave and showed him the Amorites buried there, and one of them was eighteen cubits in length. I said to him : 'When we had merits, even these fell into our hands, and now that by reason of our sins, even thou can'st rule over us.'[8]

Of the contemporaries and pupils of R. Jochanan ben Zakkai we mention *R. Eleazar ben Zadok* first. He said to his father R. Zadok, who was healed by heathen physicians sent by the Roman Government at the request of R. Jochanan ben Zakkai : ' Father, give them their reward in this world, so that they have no reward through thee in the world to come.'[9] Even heathens,

[7] v. Matt. 17. 20 ; 21. 21 : Mark 11. 23.

[8] v. also the observations of Abba Saul on the fossil bones, b. Niddah 24 B. It is to be observed that the rhetors of the second and third century C. E. liked to refer to these fossil bones, so that the crowd should be attracted by the old hero worship, v. F. Kuhn, *Philostrat und Dyktys*, Hermes, 1917 (52), p. 614.

[9] Lam. r. I, 5, ed. Buber, p. 68 ; v. also Ps. Jon. Targ. Dt. 7. 10.

who do good deeds, have merits, which, however, are recompensed in this world. *R. Joshua ben Hananiah* held that Gentiles too, if they are worthy, have a share in the future life, in opposition to *R. Eliezer ben Hyrkanos*, who taught that no Gentile can have a share in the world to come, based on Ps. 9. 18.[10] The pious of the Gentiles have merits which entitle them to share the future life. Another dispute of these two scribes deals also with an aspect of our doctrine. R. Eliezer ben Hyrkanos refers, Eccles. 11. 2, 'seven' to the commandment of Sabbath, and 'eight' to that of circumcision, and reproduces Elijah's prayer (1 Kings 18. 14) in the following version: 'Lord of the World, if Israel has no other but these two merits alone, it is worthy that rain shall come down for these their merits.' R. Joshua ben Hananja refers both numbers (7 and 8) to the performance of the Pesach and Tabernacles festivals.[11] The merits of Sabbath and Circumcision, or of the festivals suffice to bring the blessing of rain to Israel. A third difference deals with the state of the children of the wicked, who died whilst they were minors. R. Eliezer ben Hyrkanos teaches they will neither live, nor be judged in the world to come (based on Mal. 3. 19). R. Joshua ben Hananiah, however, says they will come to the next world, and interprets the words: 'And he will not leave him root or branch' in the sense that there will be found no merit for them, upon which they can rely.[12] Both of these scribes knew the doctrine of merits. Not only Jews have merits, but Gentiles too. Among Jews, the wicked have no merits, yet the sin of the wicked

[10] v. M. Ps., ed. Buber, p. 90; b. Sanh. 105 a; according to Tosefta even R. Eliezer ben Hyrkanos does not refer to Gentiles generally, but merely to the wicked among them, ch. xiii, 434. 1 and ff. Cf. also Justin Martyr's dialogue with Tryphon, ch. viii, Graetz, *Geschichte*, IV, 4, p. 394; Gold-fahn, *MGWJ.*, 1873, p. 54.

[11] b. Erubin 40 B; Pesikta B. 192 a; Pes. r., 201 B; Eccles. r. 11. 2; v. Jerome's *Questiones* to Eccles. 11. 2; Brüll, *Jahrbücher*, I. 236.

[12] Aboth R. Nathan, I, ch. 36, p. 107; v., however, Tos. Synh., ch. 13, p. 434, 1. 1 ff., where *R. Gamaliel*, II, occurs instead of Eliezer, j. Seb. 35 c, b. Synh. 110 B.

parents cannot deprive the innocent children of their share in the future life. Of special merits they point out those of Sabbath and Circumcision on the one side, and on the other side that of observing the festivals. For these merits the blessing of rain is bestowed upon the people and the land. *Eleazar of Modiim* is the first among the Tannaites to lay stress upon the Doctrine of *Zechuth Aboth*, the merits of the fathers.[12a] This scribe had chosen his own path in many other teachings, so also in this doctrine. Standing under the continuous influence of the great political struggle of his days, his sayings reflect truly the feeling of a great mind and heart in the last fight of Judaea's independence, in the period between the destruction of the temple and the revolution of Bar-Kochba (70 C. E.–135 C. E.). Trembling for the fate of his beloved people, hoping for the glorious advent of freedom, fearing a crushing defeat, rejoicing at the wonderful reports of success of the few against the many, mourning at the news of death and terror, he found consolation in, and instilled encouragement in the hearts of his audience from, the narrative of the Bible. Perhaps at a moment, when the warriors of Judaea withstood and were about to repulse the sanguinary armies of Rome, he read to himself or to his fellow-citizens the fight of Israel with Amalek, and found there that Moses' reference to the merits of the fathers helped Israel to victory. He explains, namely, Exod. 17. 8 ('to-morrow I will stand on the top of the hill') in the sense: to-morrow we shall decree a fast, and pray, relying on the deeds of the fathers. R. Joshua ben Hananja takes the verse literally.[13] This doctrine is often repeated by the same teacher.[14] The remembrance of the

---

[12a] Hereto belongs perhaps a similar saying of Theodosius of Rome, M. Ps., ed. B., p. 229, ed. Ps., p. 25 a.

[13] v. Mech. 54 a, of *RSbJ.*, p. 82 ; Pes. B., p. 21 B, anonym. ; Ps. Jon. Targ. to Exod. 17. 8 : ראש = top = deeds of the father ; הגבעה = hill = deed of the mothers.

[14] v. L. A. Rosenthal in *Semitic Studies in memory of the Rev. Dr. Alex. Kohut*, Berlin, 1897, p. 465.

deeds of the Fathers and Mothers of Israel caused Moses' prayer to be heard and answered. The same explanation is given to v. 10, 'And they took a stone, and put it under him'; meaning the remembrance of the pious deeds of the Fathers.[15] He might have expressed his disapproval of military methods. Armies and arms will not help us, prayer and merits will lead us to victory. Historical circumstances help us to understand also R. Eleazar's explanation of the miracles connected with the Manna. In the time of starvation, in the besieged country, where they were cut off from all resources, he pointed out and explained the wonderful sustenance of the fathers in the wilderness. He finds in the word ויפנו, Exod. 16. 10, an allusion to the deeds of the fathers. 'They looked forward' to the works of the Fathers, for it is said 'the wilderness', just as there is nothing in the desert, so was neither sin nor iniquity with our first fathers.[16] Similarly he saw in הנני (v. 4) a reference to the merits of the Fathers.[17]

R. Joshua ben Hananiah disputes all these cases. He either takes the passages in their strict literal meaning, or he attributes the success of the fulfilment of the prayers to the merits of Moses, or of Israel. We cannot overlook in these different views and opinions the trains of thought we began with. We see Eleazar of Modiim following the way of Shemaiah; R. Joshua ben Hananiah, however, keeps strictly to the line marked out by Abtaljon. Hillel, who tried to establish a common ground for both views, has not succeeded in bringing the two different aspects of life together and harmonizing them. Under the blows of world-history and national catastrophes the old antagonism revived. Certainly, owing to the tragic events which followed the destruction of the Temple, and during the last great fight for freedom and independence, the view of Eleazar of Modiim became the general and dominant one. The conquered and down-trodden people lost with the

last shadows of its independence also its self-consciousness
and pride in itself, and from now on relied on the greatness
of the past, on the deeds and merits of the ancestors and
the pious of old. Few of the subsequent teachers emphasize
the self-acquired merits, or thought it sufficient to refer
to their own merits. A people under the heel of foreign
rulers dreams of the past or of the future, but does not
like to think too much of the present!

He, Eleazar of Modiim, expressed further the view that
the patriarchs prayed in their graves for their children,
when the latter were in distress and trouble, and their (the
fathers') prayers were heard, and their requests granted
by God. For the merit of these prayers was the Manna
given.[18] Finally we have to mention his view that people,
who transgress certain commandments, e.g. who profane
the sanctuaries (or the Sabbath, according to the reading
in AN), despise the festivals, who put their fellow-men
publicly to shame, destroy the covenant of our father
Abraham, and find in the Torah opinions contrary to the
Halachah, although they have knowledge of the Torah,
and good deeds, nevertheless they have no share in the
world to come.[19] The merits one has obtained must not
be damaged by faults, such as given in the catalogue
above, undoubtedly frequent among his contemporaries.
Eleazar ben Azarja searched and found that Israel was
delivered from Egypt for the merits of Abraham,[20] for the
merit of this patriarch was also the sea divided before Israel.[21]
In the school of *R. Ishmael* they discussed the question,
' for whose merit does the world exist?' And they taught,
' for the merits of the righteous'.[22] The dividing of the
sea he ascribes to the merit of Jerusalem,[23] and the revelation of God in Egypt and deliverance to the merit of the
performance and observance of the Law.[24] More frequent

---

[18] Mech. 49 a of *RSbJ.*, p. 77.   [19] Aboth., III, 112.
[20] Mech. 19 B.   [21] Mech. 29 B.
[22] Midr. haggadol, Genesis, 3 a, and above, p. 11, note 40.
[23] Mech. 29 a.   [24] Mech. 8 a and 12 a.

and varied is the information we get about our doctrine from the Agadah of *R. Akiba*. As to the theory of the doctrine we learn that the prayers of the children can save their parents from the punishment of hell.[25] According to him the delivery from Egypt was for the merit of the pious women,[26] and the division of the sea by the merit of Jacob.[27] Further, we hear that God spoke with Moses for the merit of Israel, and not for his own merit.[28] And finally we hear that Job was blessed by God for the merit of repentance and good deeds performed by him.[29]

Of R. Akiba's contemporaries we have to call attention first of all to *R. Tarphon*. We have a report of a meeting which took place in the shadow of the dovecot at *Jabne* on a Sabbath afternoon. After discussing a Halachic question, they were asked: 'Why does the text tell us all the details of the caravan of the Ishmaelites that came from Gilead, with their camels bearing spicery and balm and myrrh?' (Gen. 37. 25). The answer is: To teach you how far the merits of the righteous help them (להודיע זכותן של צדיקים כמה מסייעתן); for, had the Ishmaelites carried as usual hides, asphalt, and other evil-smelling things, he (Joseph) would have died.[30] A second question raised at that gathering was: 'For what merit was Judah worthy to be the king among his brethren?' (or the tribe of Judah to have the leading part in Jewish history). R. Tarphon said to the questioners: 'Answer yourselves!' They said: 'He was worthy to become king for the advice he gave

---

[25] v. p. 156 f.

[26] b. Sota, 11 B, R. Avira, Exod. r. 1. 16, read R. Akiba.

[27] Mech. 29 B, Exod. r. 21. 8.   [28] Mech. 2 a.

[29] Ruth r. 6. 6 and Parall.

[30] Mech. 31 B (Tos. Ber. 10. 15 has a different reading), reply: אלא שנתנו את הצדיק ההוא בין דברים החביבים והרי דברים קלוחומר ומה בשעת כעסן של צדיקים מרחמים עליהם בשעת הרחמים על אחת כמה וכמה. God shows mercy unto the righteous even in his wrath, how much more in 'the time of mercy'. The same teaching explains also Lev. 10. 6 and 1 Kings 13. 18. It amounts to the same as the phrase in the Mechilta, זכותן מסייעתן.

his brethren not to kill Joseph.' R. Tarphon objected to this suggestion on the ground that his advice, which saved Joseph's life, was good enough to atone for the selling of Joseph and the anxiety of his father, but never so praiseworthy as to get him the rulership. Then they suggested: 'For the merit of acknowledging his sin, and saving Tamar's life.' R. Tarphon rejected this view. The confession was sufficient to atone for his sin. A third suggestion was put forward. For he pledged himself for Benjamin. This hypothesis shared the fate of the previous one. R. Tarphon thought that there is no special merit in it, if a surety discharges his duties. Then they said: 'Now tell us!' R. Tarphon said: 'When the tribes stood before the sea, they debated who should enter first (v. Hos. 12. 1); the leader of Judah, Nahson ben Aminadab, put an end to this discussion, and jumped into the waves of the sea. Therefore was he chosen to the Kingdom.'[31]

There must have been a peculiar merit in Judah, thought these Rabbis, who discussed the question, which made Judah worthy to become the Ruler and King. Without merit, such a dignity seemed to them quite impossible. Judah's merit was his enthusiasm and self-sacrifice, of which he had shown signs. Further, we learn that this problem of merit was discussed in the school of R. Akiba, among his colleagues, as well as among his pupils. We have other proofs for this fact. Of *Simon ben Azzai* we know from other sources too that he thought of and taught of the merits for the sake of which the world was created. He saw the aim of the creation of the world in the obedience to God. 'For the one who fears God was the world created.'[32] According to some readings this view was held by another member of the company who

[31] Mech. 31 B; M. Ps., ed. Buber, b. 341; Tosefta 10. 1, 22 ff. gives a different report. According to the same the author is *R. Akiba*, and the problem discussed by four of his pupils: *Eleazar ben Matja, Hananja ben Hakinai, Simon ben Azzai*, and *Simon of Teman*.

[32] b. Ber. 6 B.

entered the Pardes, *Simon ben Zoma*. This sage is credited
with another saying, which looks like an enlargement of
R. Akiba's teaching. He teaches, namely, that not merely
with Moses but with all the other prophets did God speak
for Israel's merit, and not for their own individual merit.[33]

By another statement of *Ben Zoma* we are enabled to
establish the right authorship in the previous statement
(b. Ber. 6 B), which solved the great problem: 'For whose
sake was the world created?' For the sake of the pious.
Of Ben Zoma, we hear that he used to say, seeing the
crowds of people on the steps of the Temple Mount:
'Blessed be He who created all these to serve me.' Then
he compared the travail which Adam endured with the
great comfort he enjoys, and sums up: 'A good guest, what
does he say? May the owner be remembered for blessing,
how many kinds of wine, how many dishes did he set
before us. All he did was done for my sake. A bad
guest, what does he say? What have I eaten? A loaf,
one dish, I drank one glass of wine! All he did, he has
done for the sake of his wife and sons.'[34] Ben Zoma
teaches here that everything created by God was created
for man's sake, and he seems to disagree emphatically from
those scribes who taught that the world was created for
the sake of the pious alone. They are like the tactless
guests, who say: 'The master of the house (God) took the
trouble of preparing the meal merely for the sake of his
household (the pious and righteous).' 'No', Ben Zoma
preached, 'the table is laid for mankind, everybody has
a right to share it.'

Of the other scribes, mentioned among the four pupils
of R. Akiba, *Simon of Teman* also took part in another
discussion, which often and throughout Talmud and
Midrash engaged the attention of the teachers. What
was the merit of the Israelites that they were redeemed
from Egypt? that the sea was divided before them? We

[33] Mech. 2 a, v. p. 44.
[34] Cf. Job 36. 24; Tos., p. 14, l. 27–p. 15, l. 3; b. Ber. 58 a : j. Ber. 13 c.

can understand that the thoughts of the teachers after the destruction and before the defeat of Bar Kochba turned to that great period of biblical history which was through all ages a living well of inspiration for all those who longed for freedom and redemption from the chains of slavery! Simon of Teman says: ' For the merit of circumcision was the sea divided before them.' [35] *Eliezer ben Judah* of ברתותא ascribes this great event to the merits of the tribes, and *Simon of Katron* (קטרון) to Joseph, *R. Benaah* to Abraham.[36] From this brief list, to which we may add the opinion of R. Akiba and R. Eleazar ben Azarja, we see how far the view of Shemaiah over-ruled that of Abtaljon. With the exception of Simon of Teman, all the scribes found the merits in the past, in the life and deeds of Abraham or Joseph or the tribes, but not in the virtues of those who stood on the shores of the sea. Simon of Teman alone considered the deeds of those who were about to benefit by the miracle. Yet even R. Akiba could not shake off entirely the influence of Abtaljon's view, when he said that for the merit of the pious women in Israel were the Israelites redeemed from Egypt. This doctrine, as we prove later on, was advanced for apologetical reasons. Still an endeavour was made to find the virtues among the redeemed and those who shared the miracle, and not in those of their ancestors. Yet it must also be considered that one reading has instead of R. Akiba's name that of *R. Avira*, which is more plausible and likely. In spite of the general prevalence of Shemaiah's view, we find besides Simon of Teman other teachers before 135 c. e. as well as after that year, who still propagated and adhered to Abtaljon's conception. We have to mention especially *Matja ben Charesh*. In a homily based on Ezekiel 16. 6 this scribe says: ' The time came when God's promise to Abraham was to be fulfilled,' i. e. when He shall deliver the Israelites. Yet they had no commandments

---

[35] Mech. 29 B; cf. Jer. 33. 25.
[36] Mech. 29 B.

to keep, they had no observances to observe, for the merits
of which they deserved to be redeemed.   Therefore God
gave to them two commandments (i. e. the blood of circumcision and the blood of the Pascal offering), in order
that they shall be engaged with them, and shall have
merits to be redeemed.[37]   This scribe surely held all
vicarious merits insufficient to bring about the redemption.
He does not take into consideration the merits of the
fathers or the merits of the tribes, he points to actual
merits acquired by those who were about to obtain
freedom.   A story can give us illustration of the frame
of mind of the contemporary Rabbis, describing a meeting
which took place between *R. Jose ben Kisma* and *R.
Hanina ben Taradjon*.   The former was ill, and the latter
called on him according to prevailing custom and law.
R. Jose ben Kisma said to his visitor : 'Hanina ! My
brother ! dost thou not know that to this nation (Rome)
was given the rulership from heaven ?   A nation that has
destroyed His house, burnt His Temple, killed His pious
ones and His best ones and still exists !   Behold I heard
of thee that thou art sitting and art engaged in the study
of the law, and holdest the book in thy bosom.'   R. Hanina
said : ' May heaven have mercy.'   R. Jose replied : ' I told
thee words of common sense and thou sayest : May heaven
have mercy.   I wonder if they (the Romans) will not burn
thee with the scrolls of the Torah in fire.'   R. Hanina :
' Rabbi, *am I going to have a share in the world to come ?'*
(מה אני לחיי העולם הבא).   R. Jose : ' What hast thou done ? '
R. Hanina : ' Once I mistook my money put aside for
the Purim meal for money of charity, and distributed it
among the poor.'   R. Jose : ' I wish I had a share of
thine, would that thy lot were mine too.' [38]   This scribe,
who is also included in some writings among the ' self-
complacent ' Rabbis, ' idol-worshippers of the law ', the
' virtuosi of piety ', after hearing this terrible death sentence

[37] Mech. 5 a.   [38] b. A. Z. 18 a.

asked in all humility and modesty: 'Have I a share in future life?' He is not sure whether his life, devoted to the study of the Law and spent in deeds of charity, deserves future life. R. Jose ben Kisma has to tell him: 'I wish my share would be as thine, my lot as thine.' That means to say: you have plenty of merits, not merely for yourself, but also for others. This teacher, we see, thought that the merits of righteous men hold good and are available for others as well. As most significant in the whole story is the fact that R. Jose is not satisfied with the contempt with which Hanina ben Taradjon looked upon the prohibition of the Roman Government, which forbade the study of the Law, because according to R. Jose's party standpoint this attitude was exaggerated. Rome must have had merits, which enabled it to be a world-wide empire.

(2) We turn now to the teachers of a different period! The scribes, who lived after the catastrophe of Bethar, were faced by new problems on all aspects and turns of life. In the Halachah as well as in the Agadah the changed circumstances, the new environment, the varied activities left their sharp traces and signs. Just as the leaders of Israel could not rid themselves after the year of 68 C. E. of the memories and effects of the 9th of Ab, so the teachers after 135 could not wipe out from their hearts the impressions of the years of their greatest war for freedom and liberty. Under this influence we have to view the different aspects on our doctrine. The change is seen first of all in *R. Meir's* Agadah. For the general theory of our doctrine we learn that everything in life depends on the merits of man. There are rich and poor in all walks of life, in all professions and all occupations. One cannot say one art or business leads to wealth, the other to poverty. Worldly wealth or poverty are distributed according to merits.[39] Secondly he points out

[39] M. Kid. 4. 14; j. Kid. 66 d; b. Kid. 82 a; Tosefta, p. 343, l. 4, Rabbi.

the merit of charity, which has got the power to lengthen
life. He came namely to a place called ממלא, where he
could not detect an old man, for they all died very young.
R. Meir said to them: 'Are you, perhaps, descendants of
the High Priest Eli?' (v. 1 Sam. 2. 32). They said to
him: 'Rabbi pray for us!' He said to them: 'Go and
do charity (וטפלו בצרקה) and you will live long.'[40] Here
his saying ought to be mentioned: 'For the sin of Mezuzah
do young children die.'[41] In his Agadah we find special
attention paid to the merits of the study of the Law, of
circumcision, of hospitality, of the fathers, and last but
not least to that of the children. He who studies the Law
acquires many merits, it makes him worthy in such a
degree, *as if the whole world were created for his sake*
(ולא עוד אלא שכל העולם כדאי הוא לו). The study of the Law
brings a man to merits and removes him from sin.[42]
Accordingly R. Meir joins those who held that the world
was created for the merit of the students of the Torah.
Yet the world exists also for the merit of circumcision.[43]
In another passage R. Meir deals with this commandment
in a similar way.[44] Abraham did not become perfect until
he performed this law. Maybe that the reminiscences of
Hadrianic persecutions, which claimed so many good men
as sacrifices for the sake of these commandments, or the
agitation of the early Church induced R. Meir to emphasize
both of them. In his address to the people of Usha he
dwelt on the great merits of hospitality.[45] Significant is
his attitude towards his teacher Elisha ben Abuja, the
'Acher' of the scribes. People asked R. Meir, after the

[40] Gen. r. 59. 1; Midr. Sam., ed. Buber, p. 71, v. Prov. 16. 31.
[41] b. Sabb. 32 B.
[42] Aboth, VI, 1. I see in כדאי הוא לו an abbreviation: כדאי הוא
לו [שנברא בשבי], v. Hoffmann's translation: 'die ganze Welt ist es
werth, für ihn allein da zu sein'. *Bacher* renders it: 'ihm gebührt die
ganze Welt'.
[43] Pirke of R. El. in Jacob Hagoser's כללי המילה, p. 13.
[44] M. Ned. 31 a.
[45] Cant. r. 2. 5.

death of Elisha: 'In the world to come if they ask you whom do you want, your father or your teacher, what will you say?' R. Meir: 'First my father, then my teacher.' The questioners: 'And will they listen to you?' R. Meir: 'Certainly.' We learned it in the Mishnah: We rescue the cover with the book, the bag with the Phylacteries, 'we rescue Elisha for the merit of his Torah'.[46] Elisha, in spite of his heresies and apostasy, did not have to drink the cup of poison, as a greater philosopher and a smaller atheist in Athens, had not to flee, like the Stagirite, was not arrested like Anaxagoras, was not persecuted like Theodorus or Diogenes of Apollonia by the more enlightened Greeks,[47] although he lived among 'barbarous and fanatic' Jews. Why? For the merits of the Torah which he acquired. How could unlearned men bring a scholar to account for his opinions? This ordeal, it is true, Elisha has had to face, but much later, for in the last eighteen centuries the question of his opinions and thoughts was often handled in sermons and monographs. R. Meir had friendly relations, just as other scribes, with a Gentile, from whom we learn the doctrine that this world, with all its pleasures and good, belongs to the Gentiles, and the world to come is destined for the Jews.[48] For what merit? Certainly for the merits of the fathers. For R. Meir held that 'the dead of the Gentiles are dead, those of Israel are not dead, for by their merits the living exist' (חיים עומדין). An instance to support this view is given from history. When Israel did that deed (the golden calf), had Moses not mentioned and appealed to the merits of the fathers (Exod. 32. 13) Israel surely would have perished from the face of the earth.[49] On the other hand, R. Meir ascribes the revelation and the teaching of the Torah to

[46] Eccles. r. 7. 18; M. Sabb. 116 B; and Eccles. r., ed. Buber, p. 151; b. Hag. 15 B.

[47] v. Lange, *History of Materialism*, I, p. 5.

[48] Pes., p. 59 B; Pes. r., p. 82 B; Tanh. f. 245 B; Num. r., ch. 21. 18; M. Prov. 13. 25.

[49] Tanh. f. 57 a.

Israel as the merit of future generations and not of the
fathers. In the contrary way God would not accept,
according to the legend of R. Meir, the surety offered by
the patriarchs, they are themselves in need of sureties![50]
It may be that R. Meir's alleged alien origin—he was
supposed to have come of a proselyte family—induced him
to form this strange legend. He wanted to impress his
contemporaries that the triumph of the orah, or of the
ideals of the Torah, are to be sought in the future, and
not in the past.

Just as numerous, in comparison with the sayings in
the previous period, are the references in R. Meir's Agadah,
even richer is the Agadah of the second pupil of R. Akiba,
of *R. Simon ben Jochai* on the doctrine we deal with.
His Zechuth itself became proverbial through the ages. In
a saying of his we read: 'I am able to free the whole
world from judgement, from the hour of my birth up to
now. In case my son Eleazar be with me, I can do the
same for all creatures from the beginning of creation up
to now. In case Jotham ben Uzziah were with us, even
for those who will come into being from now up to the
end of the days.'[51] A somewhat different version is given
in a Palestinian source. 'If Abraham likes to justify (by
his merits) all people from his time up to my time, my
merits will justify them from now up to the time of the
Messiah, if not I join with Achiah השילוני, and we will
justify by our merits all creatures from Abraham up to
the time of the Messiah.'[52] The merits of Abraham, or
of Achiah, together with those of the speaker, can save all
the generations from judgement. Apart from the somewhat
difficult exaggeration of R. Simon ben Jochai's own merits,
it is clear that the merits of some persons can protect or
justify others. The same difficulty arises in another saying
of this teacher, where he says: 'I saw that those who have

[50] v. Cant. r. 1. 24 ; M. Ps., ed. Buber, p. 76 ; anonym.
[51] b. Sukkah, 45 B.
[52] j. Ber. 13 d ; Gen. r. 35. 2 ; Pesikta, 36 a.

a share in the world to come are very few, yet if there are three, I and my son (Eleazar) are two of them.'[53] Yet he teaches that the world cannot exist without the number of thirty righteous men, who are like Abraham; if they are less than thirty, even three, he and his son are always included.[54] There must have been something rather in the events of his life or his time, than in his nature and character, which induced this scribe to utter such sentences, which if understood literally sound like conceit, or taken allegorically mean nothing to us.

In other parts of our doctrine, we find that R.S.b.J. was not yet aware of the teaching that the world was created for the merit of Israel (v. p. 125). The world stands (or stood) firm for the sake of the Tabernacle. Before the Tabernacle was erected the earth was trembling, since the Tabernacle was established the world became firm.[55] He attributes the delivery from Egypt to the merit of circumcision,[56] the future redemption will come about through the merit of the observance of the Sabbath.[57] The surrounding and friends of the just man enjoy the merits, are prosperous for his sake, and share his blessing. R. Simon ben Jochai shows this in the case of Og,[58] of Lot,[59] and of Rahab.[60] Theoretically R. S. b. J. defines the idea of Zechut in the following words: ' If a man was just, a perfect righteous man all his life, and sinned at last, then he loses all his merits (Ezek. 33. 13 f.); if a man, however, be wicked all his life, and he repented at last, God receives him.[61] There is only one treasury in heaven with God, and it is that of ' fear of Heaven '.[62] He further

---

[53] j. Ber. 13 d; b. Sukkah, 45 B; Gen. r. 35. 2; Pes. 87 B, all given by Hezekiah in the name of R. Jeremiah.

[54] v. the same sources as in the previous note, and j. A. Z. 40 c; Hullin, 92 a.

[55] Pes. B., p. 6 a; Pes. r. 18 B.

[56] Mech. 19 B, 20 a.   [57] b. Sabb. 118 B.

[58] b. Niddah, 61 a.   [59] Tanh. f. 26 B.

[60] j. Ber. 8 B; j. Synh. 28 c; and Eccles. r. 5. 4.

[61] Tos. 337. 1 f.; b. Kid. 40 B; j. Pea. 16 B; Cant. r. 6. 1.

[62] יראת שמים R. Johanan in his name, b. Ber. 33 B.

emphasizes the merit of charity in his speech in Usha, which merit will bring about the resurrection of the dead.[63] Finally we have to enumerate his views on sin. Children die for the sins of their parents. Those of the generation of the flood, who perished before they reached the age of 100, therefore not liable to punishment, perished for the sins of their parents.[64] The family of the tax farmer or robber share the disgrace or punishment of the disgraced, for they protect them. The same applies to the family of the Moloch worshipper.[65] The persecution in the time of Haman came upon the Jews, because they ate the food of the Gentiles.[66] There is no punishment without sin, and the latter may be transferred from one person to another; just as the blessing or the merit of the righteous is available to the wicked, so the sin of the wicked is shared by his nearest, in case they support the wicked.

Of *R. Jose ben Halafta* we have only a few statements bearing on our subject. His questioner, a Matrona, wanted to know by what merit has Israel been chosen to be God's people? His reply was that God knows whom to choose,[67] which means Israel has merits which justify this choice. In another dialogue with the same Matrona, he taught that the souls of the righteous are put in the treasury.[68] This might be in opposition to R. Simon ben Jochai, according to whom only 'fear of Heaven' deserves a place in the treasury. The same reason may be given to his varied sayings which start, 'may my share be' (יהא חלקי), where he enumerates besides 'fear of Heaven' some positive duties.[69] R. Jose ben Halafta taught further that the good deeds of the children affect the fate of the wicked parents. Hannah, by her prayers, saved Korah and his company

[63] Cant. r. 2. 16.
[64] M. Ps., ed. Buber, p. 12; ed. Pr., p. 23, has *R. Simon ben Lakish*.
[65] Lev. 20. 5; Sifra, 81 b; Seb. 39 a.
[66] Cant. r. 7. 8; b. Meg. 12 a.
[67] M. Sam., ed. Buber, p. 70; Num. r. 3. 2.
[68] v. Eccl. r. 3. 27, and p. 21.   [69] b. Sabb. 118 B.

from Hell.[70]   Finally, we see R. Jose ben Halafta searching
for the reason, why proselytes suffer ?   They ought to
be happy and prosperous.   The theory advanced by this
teacher is, because they do not take care to learn the
details and particulars of the observances properly.[71]   As
the entire Agadah of R. Jose ben Halafta bears different
aspects and characteristics not to be found in that of his
contemporaries, which rightly suggests a certain independence of thought and aloofness of habit, so it is with his
problems, or his method of dealing with them, as far as
they are connected with our doctrine.

Another great teacher of this period was *R. Judah ben
Ilai.*   In his teachings we can more easily discover the
link between him and his contemporaries.   It is not certain
whether we have his view on the much disputed question
of the aim of the creation (v. p. 115).   In discussing the
merit of Judah he adopts the view of R. Akiba and
R. Tarphon.[72]   The redemption from Egypt was for the
merit of circumcision, as R. Matja ben Heresh and R. Simon
ben Jochai expounded.[72a]   The future redemption will arise
from the merit of charity.[73]   The patriarchs were blessed
for the merit of the tithe they gave,[74] just as the commandments were given to Israel to make them worthy to inherit
the world to come.[74a]   Wicked parents are saved in future
life by their innocent children (v. p. 158).   There is more
than one reference to the merits of the fathers.   For instance, in the case of Jethro's daughters (Exod. 2. 19),
where they said: 'He (i. e. Moses) drew water for us for
the sake of our father.'[75]   R. Judah ben Ilai adhered to

---

[70] j. Sanh. 29 a ;   M. Sam., p. 62, '*Rabbi*' ; Gen. r. 98. 2, '*Rabbanan*', in
R. Jose's name by *R. Joshua ben Levi.*

[71] b. Jeb. 48 B.

[72] v. pp. 45, b. Sotah, 37 a, against R. Meir, who held that Benjamin
was the first to set foot into the sea.

[72a] v. p. 144.   [73] b. BB. 10 a.

[74] Pes. r. 127 B ; Gen. r. 43. 10 ; Tanh. f. 32 a anonym. ; B. I., p. 119.

[74a] v. above, p. 16, n. 59.

[75] Cant. r. 2. 16 ; Exod. r. 1. 39

the view of Shemaiah, who did not emphasize those merits
which man acquires for himself, but those which have been
acquired by the fathers. Abtaljon's thought is pointed
out sharply in the teachings of R. Judah's opponent
R. Nehemia.[76] He informs us further that whatever merits
a man gathers, whatever good we do in this world, it
is merely a trifle in comparison with the mercy and grace
of God, which He bestows upon mankind. Our works can
never be good enough or sufficient to deserve God's lovingkindness.[76a] God shows us mercy for His name's sake.
R. Nehemia seems to be the first who revived and popu-
larized this old conception. Abtaljon's influence is felt in
his theory about the redemption from Egypt, although only
some sources ascribe to him the view that God delivered
Israel for the merit of the Elders and the pious men, who
lived in Egypt.[77] Yet in another source the Torah is
mentioned as the merit for redemption by him. Further,
we are told in his name that the merit of faith made the
Israelites worthy to sing the song on the sea, which betrays
the influence of Abtaljon's world view at once. Because
'to sing the song' is really a phrase signifying the seeing
of miracles,[78] whilst an anonymous teacher adopts entirely
in this case Shemaiah's theory, that the song was sung
for the merits of Abraham, Isaac, and Jacob.

R. Eleazar ben Shamua teaches us that the world exists
for the merit of one righteous.[79] Joshua and Elders after
the battle of Ai (Joshua 7. 6) referred in their prayers to
the merit of Abraham, for whose sake they expected
success.[80] They had no merits of their own, therefore they
relied upon that of Abraham. Parallel to this is his saying
that Aaron's surviving sons escaped the fate of their
brethren for the merit of Aaron, their father.[81] He points

---

[76] Exod. r. 15. 5.   [76a] Pes. 99 a ; Exod. r. 41. 1.
[77] v. Cant. r. 2. 19.
[78] Exod. r. 23. 6 ; v. M. Ps., p. 135.
[79] b. Hag. 12 B ; cf. Prov. 10. 29.   [80] Gen. r. 39. 24.
[81] Sifra to Lev. 10. 12, p. 44 B, v. p. 7.

out, finally, the merit of the study of the Law and good works, which protect men from the trouble and pain of the Messianic age,[82] and the great merit of dwelling in the Holy Land.[83] *Eliezer ben Jacob* might have attempted to contradict the poor opinion R. Simon ben Jochai had of his contemporaries, when he said: 'There is no generation which has not got a just man like Abraham, like Jacob, like Moses, and like Samuel.'[84] The world exists for the merit of the righteous, and there is no generation lacking such men. We ought to mention here also his saying: 'He who fulfils a commandment acquires for himself a (Parakleitos) defender. He who commits a sin, however, gets an accuser.'[85] A man who does a good deed acquires by it a defender and solicitor, which means nothing else but a merit. It is doubtful whether the saying of R. Eliezer ben Jacob, that Israel was redeemed from Egypt for the merit of Hananja, Mishael, and Azarja, is genuine.[86] If it is, then we learn first of all that he also took part in the discussions which attracted the attention of the sages of the second and third centuries as topics of their sermons and homilies, namely, for whose sake or for what merit was Israel released? And secondly, that he is one of the many teachers who taught that the merits of the children benefit the parents. And thirdly, we notice for the first time the act of martyrdom being applied to our doctrine. Maybe, he thought, the merits of those holy men who sanctified the name of God in the recent past, will accelerate our salvation, and our redemption too. It is significant that the merits of the martyrs were not exploited in the Judaism of the first centuries. *Eliezer the son of R. Jose the Galilean*, the third Eleazar of this period, expounds Ezek. 33. 24 on the basis of the doctrine of the merits. Abraham, who could not rely upon the merits of his fathers, inherited the Land of Promise; we who can rely

---

[82] b. Sanh. 98 B.
[84] Gen. r. 56. 9, and Gen. r. 74. 2.
[85] Aboth, IV, 11.
[83] Sifre Deut., § 80.
[86] M. Ps., p. 473.

upon the merits of the fathers, how much more hope have
we got to inherit the land of Israel.[87]   In agreement with
this view is another saying of the same Tannaite, when
he says: 'If thou seest a righteous undertaking a journey,
and thou also dost intend to take the same journey,
accelerate the journey by three days or delay it on his
account for three days, so that thou mayest go with him
together for ministering angels accompany him.'[88]   The
idea of the teaching is that the traveller will be prosperous
and successful on account of the merits of the righteous.
Yet if a wicked man plans a journey, one has to delay
or prearrange his proposed journey, for the angels of evil
accompany the wicked, and he might be caught by the sin
of his unlucky fellow-traveller.   He endeavoured further
to verify by Jer. 16. 5 the saying of R. Eliezer ben Jacob
that charity and good works acquire defenders.[89]   Further
he explained the merit of Noah's children.   Why were
they not punished, for only Noah found favour in the eyes
of God?   They were less than a hundred years of age,
and at that age, in the time of the flood, people became
responsible for their deeds after a hundred.[90]   In opposition

[87] Tos. Sotah, 305. 19, where the view of R. Eliezer is given in the name
of R. Nehemia, and that of R. Nehemia in the name of R. Jose the
Galilean.   However, as we have seen above, R. Nehemia never held this
view of Zechuth Aboth, therefore we have to accept the better reading of
Codex Erfurt, v. Zuckermandl's note.   *R. Nehemia's* saying corroborates
our observations made, p. 56.   Abraham, who had only one son whom
he was ready to sacrifice, and who inherited the land, how much more
we, who sacrifice many sons and daughters unto Moloch, *ibid.*, l. 17 f.
That is the doctrine of self-acquired merits.   That is the meaning of
Ezek. 33. 24.   Abraham was one (i. e. could not rely on the merits of his
fathers, R. El., or Abraham had sacrificed one son, R. Neh.), and he inherited the land ; but we are many (i.e. we have the merits of the fathers,
R. El., have sacrificed so many children, R. Neh., therefore have also our
own but greater merits), surely the land is given us for inheritance.

[88] Cf. Ps. 91. 11 and 109 b ; Tos. Sabb. 136. 20 ff. ; Jalk. Ps. 843 ; v. also
R. Ishmael ben Jochanan ben Beroka Aboth, R. Nathan and Tanh.
f. 42 a.

[89] v. Tosefta Peah, 24, l. 31 f. ; v. Tobit, 12. 8.

[90] Gen. r. 26. 2, ed. Theodor, p. 275 ; v. also above, p. 54.

to R. Simon ben Jochai, he taught that all the souls of the righteous are preserved in the treasury in heaven.[91]

R. Joshua ben Korha left the impression in a few of his sayings that he had thought a good deal about the question, which had engaged till his day a very few of the scribes, namely: 'For whose merit was the world created?' We have more than one remark on this subject by him. His view is, for the sake of man was everything created. The same opinion is expressed in his answer to a question: 'Why did the cattle and beast perish in the flood? There was a man who arranged a banquet for the wedding of his son. His son died meanwhile and the father destroyed everything. He said: "For whose sake have I done all this?" For my son. Since he died, there is no need for it at all. Likewise God said: "For whose sake have I created all these?" Not for man's sake? Twice he (man) sinned, for what purpose shall there be cattle and beast?'[92] Yet he seemed to have narrowed down this general view, and taught that merely for the sake of the righteous, among men, was the world created, and in a third passage we read even that the world was created for the sake of Abraham, who might have been thought of as the ideal just man. The latter point of view may be seen in the comparison drawn by the same teacher between Abraham and Moses, much in favour of the former,[93] and much to the detriment of the latter. As an eye-witness of the Hadrianic persecutions, it is only natural that he pointed out the great merit of circumcision. Great, he says, is the merit of circumcision, for even Moses' merit had not suspended the punishment or threat for a moment.[94] As to sins, he also was trying to find out

[91] Sifre Num., § 139; v. also Sifre Deut., § 344 anonym; v. above, p. 54, n. 68.

[92] b. Synh. 108 a.

[93] Gen. r., ch. 55. 16; Deut. r. 2. 4; Tanh., II, p. 9; Exod. r. 2. 6, anonym.; v. Hananja ben Akabja, Mech. 55 B.

[94] Mech. 58 a; M. Ned. 31 a, b. שלא נתלה זכות למשה.

the sins of people of whom chastisement and death is
reported in the Bible. One instance was given above,
another instance is the case of Elimelech (Ruth 1. 2) and
his children. They died because they ought to have
prayed to God for their contemporaries which they did not
do, and not, as *R. Simon ben Jochai* suggested, because
they left the Holy Land.[95] It is noteworthy that in the
Agadah of the school of R. Ishmael our doctrine was not
elaborated and is omitted in the teachings of the chief
exponents of that school, Jonathan and Josiah, although
we had to indicate some references as to our doctrine in
the name of the head of this school.[95a] There are very few
references to our doctrine in the Agadah of the sons of the
great teachers of the post-Hadrianic period. Their Agadah
is altogether poor compared with that of their teachers
and parents. The son of Simon ben Jochai, *Eleazar*, has
two statements on our subject. *R. Simon ben Jochai*
held that the merits of the righteous last even after
their death. His son Eleazar agreed with *R. Jose ben
Halafta*, who taught: 'As long as the just men are alive
blessing comes (for their merit) to the world, as soon as
they are removed, the blessing departs.' R. Eleazar held
further that the world was created for the merit of the
righteous.[96] He also took part in the discussion of the
question: for whose sin do little children die? His view
was for the sin of the parents, who do not keep their
vows.[97] Of R. Jose ben Halafta's sons, we have to mention
first of all *Ishmael*, who asked of, or was asked by *R. Judah*
the patriarch, for what merit do the Babylonians live?
'For the merit of the study of the Torah,' was the answer.
The Palestinians? 'For the merit of the tithes.' Israel in
the Diaspora? 'For the merit of honouring the Sabbath
and Festivals.' [98] The merits of the Torah, of tithe, and of

---

[95] b. B.B. 91 B.   [95a] v. p. 11, n. 40.   [96] Sifre Deut., § 38.
[97] b. Sabb. 32 B.

[98] Gen. r. 11. 3, ed. Theodor, p. 41; Pes. r. 119 B; b. Sabb. 119 a, Rabbi
is the questioner.

the Sabbath observance are here especially emphasized as
life-spending forces. His brother *Menachem* taught that
the merit of the Torah is greater than the merit of the
observances. The latter protects only in this life and
temporarily, the former for ever.[99] We see that Menachem
agreed with R. Simon ben Jochai who, in opposition to
R. Jose ben Halafta, the father of our author, held that
the merits are in force even after the death of him who
obtained them. A third son of R. Jose, *Eleazar*, repeats
and varies the saying of R. Eliezer ben Jacob. 'Charity
and lovingkindness bring peace and are Israel's defenders.'[100] The son of R. Judah ben Ilai, *R. Jose*, taught
that the well in the wilderness was given for the sake
of Miriam, the cloud for the merit of Aaron, and the
Manna for the merit of Moses. After their death these
three gifts ceased also.[101] R. Jose sided with R. Jose ben
Halafta and R. Eleazar ben Simon, and gave a special
instance for their doctrine that the merits of the righteous
are effective only in their lifetime and not after their
death. The problem which agitated the minds of these
teachers, and through them perhaps their contemporaries,
might have been whether the merits work in this world or
also in the world to come? Whether the good man spreads
blessing only in his lifetime, or even after his death? They
based their views on the teaching formulated by Simon ben
Jochai and Jose ben Halafta. Finally we have to mention
Hananja ben Akasja, whose date cannot be settled, who
taught certainly for apologetical reasons, that God gave
the observances to Israel to enable them to acquire merit.
R. Simon ben Eleazar taught: 'Hast thou ever seen
a beast or bird getting its food by any occupation? And
still they get their daily food without trouble. And behold
they were created to serve me, and I was created to serve
my creator, should I not get my daily bread without

[99] b. Sotah, 21 a.
[100] b. B.B. 10 a ; Tos. Pea. 24, l. 30 f, v. p. 571.
[101] Tos. Sotah, 315. 23 f. ; b. Taanit, 99 ; anonym. Seder Olam r., ch. 10.

trouble (or pain)? Yet I have spoilt my works and lost my sustenance.'[102] He held that the creation was for the sake of man. The same argument is used by *R. Simon ben Menassja* in order to prove that the heel of Adam was more brilliant than the sun. For God created him (Adam) for His service, and the sun for the service of man, how much more so that the Master shall be greater than the servant.[103] *R. Nathan* dealt with the question: 'For whose merit were the Israelites redeemed from Egypt?' His theory was, for the merits of the pious women.[104] Just as in. the case of imputed merits, he attributes the death of women to the vows of their husbands, which they have not fulfilled, to transmitted sins.[105] *R. Judah I* pointed out the merits of Torah, of tithes, and of the Sabbath in his dialogue with Ishmael ben R. Jose. He also taught that the nations are guarded by God for the sake of Israel.[106] As to the doctrine of subsidiary sin, we find first of all his view that little children perish for the unpaid vows of their parents,[107] and that calamities come into the world for the sins of the Amê Haarez.[108]

Before finishing with the Tannaitic Agadah, we must refer to the views of the teachers who may be regarded as colleagues and friends of the last-named Patriarch. First of all we have to mention *Bar Kappara*, who dealt with the same question which engaged the attention of his contemporary, R. Nathan, and that of older Tannaites. What were Israel's merits to be redeemed? He mentions four merits. They did not change their names and their language, they did not use evil language, and they were

[102] M. Kid. 82 a; Tos. Kid. 343. 13.

[103] R. Levi in his name, Pes., p. 36 B–37 A; Lev. r. 20. 2; Pes. r., p. 62 a; Eccles. r. to 8. 1; Tanh. III, p. 57.

[104] Mech. 5 a, 19 B; Lev. r. 32. 5; Cant. r. 4. 12; Jellinek, בית המדרש, 94; Pes. 83 a.

[105] b. Sabb. 32 B; Tos. 112. 18.

[106] Sifre Deut., § 40.

[107] b. Sabb. 32 B.

[108] b. B.B. 8 a.

chaste.[109]   He teaches further that parents enjoy the merits of their children (v. p. 161), that the wicked get their reward in this world so that they shall have no claim in the world to come.   He also informs us that he who mourns over the fate or death of a righteous man, his tears are preserved in the heavenly treasuries.[110]   Secondly we refer to *Hijja*, whose merits and those of his sons were embellished by many legends long after their death,[111] and were discussed by two of his prominent contemporaries, i. e. R. Ishmael ben Jose and R. Judah I.[112]   Of his own teaching referring to this doctrine mention has to be made, first of all of his view, shared also by *R. Simon ben Halafta*, that the world was not created for man's but for Heaven's sake.[113]   Maybe Simon ben Halafta was led to this view by his close observations of the state of piety in his time.   He informs us: 'Since hypocrisy increased, judgements became perverted, works spoilt, and no one can say: " My works are greater than thy works ".'[114] Man's merits are so little, so small, that creation for his sake cannot be imagined.   Yet he taught that the redemption from Egypt was for the merit of circumcision (v. p. 144, n. 101).   Another teacher of this circle was *R. Simai*, who speaks of Jethro's merits which were enjoyed by his descendants.   Jethro, together with Balaam and Job, were Pharaoh's counsellors at the time when the fate of the Israelites was discussed.[115]   Jethro fled so that he should have no share in the persecutions, for this merit his grandchildren were sitting among the members of the Synhedrion.[116]   The same thought is to be found in his teaching that God showed mercy to Israel in the wilderness, supplied and protected them as a reward for Abraham's

[109] Mech. 5 a ; Pes. B. 83 B ; Lev. r. 32. 5 ; Cant. r. 4. 12 ; Exod. r. 1. 33. *R. Huna* in his name, M. Ps., p. 472 ; Tanh. IV, p. 145 ; Num. r. ch. 20.
[110] b. Sabb. 105 B.   [111] b. Hullin, 86 a.
[112] b. Ket. 103 B ; b. B.M. 85 B.
[113] Pes. 98 B ; Tanh. B. IV, p. 24.   [114] b. Sota, 41 B.
[115] Exod. r. 1. 12.   [116] b. Sotah, 11 a ; b. Synh. 106 a.

hospitality.[117]   *R. Benaah* had taught that the merit
which caused the creation was the Torah (v. p. 129).   The
miracles at the sea happened for the merit of Abraham.[118]
R. Acha held that the latter was for the merit of Moses,[119]
and consequently might have directed his view against the
former view.   R. Benaah seems to have got impatient with
the doctrines of his contemporaries, who sought for the
reasons of every punishment.   He makes Saul (1 Sam. 15. 5)
say: 'If man sinned, what was the sin of the cattle?'
A heavenly voice answered, saying: 'Do not try to be
more just than thy creator!'[120]   This teaches that it is not
our duty to criticize God's ways and methods.   Finally we
have to mention *Eleazar b. Achwai*, who repeats R. Akiba's
saying that God spoke with Moses for Israel's sake,[121] and
to *R. Gamaliel III's* opinion that the merit of the fathers
help those who work faithfully for the welfare of the
community.[122]

(3) Before proceeding to review the teaching of the
Palestinian Amoraim about our doctrine, the following
facts must be emphasized.   We see first of all that the
difference of opinions between Shemaiah and Abtaljon
obtained up to the end of the period we reached in our
description.   More than half a dozen scribes can be put
on one side, and nearly a dozen on the other side.   Some
held that man's own deed and work and God's help are
needed for salvation, others believed in imputed merits, and
relied on the virtues of others.   Greater in number might
be the opinions of those who made a compromise between
these different schools of thought.   They saw the dangers
and shortcomings of both extreme views.   To those who
looked always and everywhere to the deeds of others, they

[117] Gen. r. 48. 10 ; Tanh. B. I, p. 86 f. ; Eccles. r. 11. 4 ; Pes. r. 57 a ;
Toa. Sota, 4. 1–6 ; Mech. 25 a ; Pirke, ch. 29 ; M. Ps. 104 ; Elia r., ch. 27.

[118] Mech. 29 b ; Exod. r. 24 ; Eccles. r. 10. 9.

[119] Mech. 29 b.

[120] Eccles. 7. 16 ; v. Eccles. r. 7. 31 and M. Eccles. z., p. 114.

[121] Sifra, p. 4 b.

[122] Aboth, II, 2–4.

said : 'If you are not doing good works for yourself what can man do for himself ? How can his own belief or work suffice without external support ?' It is therefore not at all so sure that Rabbinical theology adopted the doctrine of imputed merit. Shemaiah, who may be regarded as the first teacher of this doctrine, had many followers. We saw among them Eleazar of Modiim, Eleazar ben Azarjah, Eleazar ben Judah of Bartota, R. Benaah, Simon of קטרון, Jose ben Kisma, Judah ben Ilai, Eleazar ben Shamua, and finally Eliezer ben Jacob. Abtaljon's view was taken up by Joshua ben Hananja, the school of R. Ishmael (if our sources are reliable), Tarphon, Simon of Teman, Matja ben Heresh, Nehemia, Nathan, and Bar Kappara. Others, like Akiba, seemed to have accepted Hillel's compromise. A side issue of this third conception was, whether the merits of the righteous cease to work for others with one's death or not ? This question was especially dealt with by Simon ben Jochai and Jose ben Halafta on the one side, and by their sons and pupils on the other side. Whilst we see the teachers divided on the problem of imputed virtue, they seem to be unanimous, with the exception of R. Benaah, as to the doctrine of imputed sin.

The merits are personal and objective. To the first class we reckon those of the fathers generally, namely, Abraham, Jacob, Joseph, Moses, Aaron, and Miriam. Besides, there are the merits of individuals who were righteous and just. The wicked, who acquire merits, get their reward in this world. Some of them partake of the merits of their children. Further, great also was the merit of pious women. Stress is laid on the merits of faith, charity, hospitality, the circumcision, Sabbath and festivals, the study of the Torah, repentance, the Holy Land, the Tabernacle, Jerusalem, the tithe, and the observances in general. Some of these reflect immediately, at first sight, the special cares and troubles, needs and views of their time. Finally, we meet the merit of Israel. It is to be noticed that some

E

of these merits, e. g. of the merits of the fathers or of Israel, have not yet developed in this period to the height and importance which they will occupy in the age of the Amoraim. The historical reasons for this development must be left for later discussion, here it must suffice to establish the fact.

The second impression we gather from our review is that everything, fortune, misfortune, good or evil, is caused by a merit or by a sin. What merit was there for the creation and existence of the world? The answers can be divided into three groups. God created the world for His name's sake. The second view is, for the merit of the Torah. And the third for man's sake. The first teaching may be regarded as the oldest. God created this world for His own sake, in order that people shall serve and worship Him. Of course, the objection was raised, does God need the services even of the most pious or righteous? Equally may it be said that this view coincides with the next theory, which sees in man the purpose and meaning of the creation. Even this view was not admitted by many thinkers, as will be seen, and then as now they rejected the assumption that the universe and all that it contains was created for the sake of man. Of greater influence upon religious thought of the coming generations was the third opinion which saw in the Torah the aim and climax of creation. The first view is represented by Simon ben Azzai, Judah ben Ilai, Hijja, and Simon ben Halafta. The second opinion found its teachers in R. Meir and Benaah. And finally the last in Simon ben Zoma, Joshua ben Korha, Simon ben Eleazar, and Simon ben Menassja.

The third significant point in the teachings of the scribes of this period is their view about the share in future life, and their idea of the heavenly treasuries.

(4) The period of the Amoraim opens with the name of *R. Hanina ben Hama*, the great teacher of Sepphoris. There are two of his sayings which throw light upon his

views on the merit of the fathers. 'First of all ', he says, ' if a man is elevated to a dignity, then it is a merit for him as well as for all his descendants,' i. e. his children share his merits. ' Yet when this chain is interrupted or broken, it is on account of pride or haughtiness.' [123] He recognizes the value of the Zechuth Aboth in another of his sayings. Yet he gives the preference to the merit of the sacrifices. There may be a good reason for this. People surely asked, ' Why did Moses not try to achieve pardon for Israel, after the deed of the golden calf, by sacrifices ? ' The latter must be therefore valueless. R. Hanina says : ' Had Moses known then how the sacrifices are appreciated by God, he surely would have sacrificed all the cattle he could have secured, yet he appealed to the merits of the fathers.' [124] He points out with great emphasis the merit of Abraham. The ships which sailed on the Mediterranean and had a successful voyage, escaped for the merit of Abraham.[125] Further, he teaches imputed merits in a legend when he describes the objections of the angels to the creation of man. God shows them the deeds of the righteous, for whose sake Adam was created, concealing the works of the wicked.[126] Besides the merits of the fathers and of the children, there is preserved by him through *R. Eleazar ben Pedath* a remarkable saying on the merits of the just, who protect their contemporaries by their virtues. ' When a righteous man dies, he is lost to his fellow man. Like a pearl lost by the owner. The pearl remains a pearl, wherever it is, but the owner feels the loss. So the value of the just man remains even if he ceases to protect his surrounding.' [127] Noah had very little, just an ounce of merits, still he was saved by the grace of God.[128] Merits are accordingly neither weighed

---

[123] b. Zeb. 102 a ; b. Meg. 13 B. *R. Eleazar ben Pedath* is his name.
[124] Cant. r. 1. 9. [125] Gen. r. 39. 17, ed. Theodor, p. 376.
[126] Gen. r. 8. 4, ed. Theodor, p. 60 ; Pes. r., p. 166 B, has a different version, which was known to R. Berechjah.
[127] b. Meg. 15 a. [128] Gen. r. 29. 1 ; v. Tanh. I., p. 38.

nor measured, for the slightest merit can bring salvation
by the mercy of God. His older contemporary *R. Jannai*
provides us with some important information on the
theory of our doctrine (v. p. 17), with which is connected
his conception that a man can lose a good deal of his
merits by deriving too much therefrom in this world
(v. p. 20). Love of God in misfortune acquires merits.
Hezekiah ben Hijja expressed beautifully the idea of Israel's
solidarity with the doctrine of imputed sin. Israel is like
a sheep. Just as a lamb beaten on the head or on one of
its limbs feels it in all the parts of the body, likewise
is it with Israel. If one of them sins, all of them feel it,
i. e. are punished.[129] The leaders and teachers are taken
away on account of the sins of the generation, Israel is
one and undivided. If one sinned, the whole community
has to suffer. *R. Hanina ben Hama* dealt with the same
problem, when he said : ' The leaders of Israel die, because
they did not prevent the evil done by their fellow men.' [130]
They may have had in mind some especial event, of which
they were eye-witnesses, unknown to us. This assumption
finds confirmation in the Agadah of a third teacher, who
lived in the same days and dealt with the problem on
three different occasions. In a refutation of *R. Hanina
ben Hama,* who suggested that Adam ought to have lived
for ever, and the reason for whose death was because God
foresaw that Nebuchadnezzar and Hiram would declare
themselves gods—for this imputed sin Adam died—
R. Jonathan ben Eliezer says : ' Then the wicked shall
die, and the righteous live for ever ! Yet, the reason for
the death of the righteous is, lest the wicked will repent
in a hypocritical way and say : " Wherefore do the righteous
live ? " For they perform the commandments and good
deeds, we will do the same but it will not be for the sake
of God.' [131] In another passage he says : ' The righteous
do not die for their deeds,' i. e. because their deeds make

---

[129] Lev. r. 4. 6. [130] b. Sabb. 54 B.
[131] Gen. r. 9. 6, ed. Theodor, p. 70.

them liable to death, 'but for the words of My mouth', i. e. God's decrees.[132] And thirdly: 'Chastisement comes to the world on account of the wicked, but the righteous are taken away first.'[133] It is not improbable, and too adventurous to suggest, that we hear here echoes of the time of the great plague which claimed so many victims in Sepphoris in the days of these teachers.[134] R. Jonathan ben Eliezer raised also his voice against the misrepresentation of the doctrine of the merit of the fathers by unworthy children of worthy parents.[135] He was aware, as Hillel before his time, that the one-sided application of this doctrine is apt to be falsified and abused. Greater stress is laid by him upon the merits acquired by the good and righteous man himself. He who teaches the son of an Am ha-Arez Torah has got the merit and power to induce God to revoke His decrees.[136] If we paraphrase this somewhat hyperbolical phrase, we gather that there is nothing which such a good man cannot achieve for his fellow men with God. The chief merit pointed out by R. Jonathan ben Eliezer is: the merit of observances.[137] He emphasizes further the merits of chastity,[138] and pure family life,[139] which may be regarded as a benevolent warning against the corruption and immorality unfortunately prevailing in his time.[140] Only two sayings of the next Agadist of *R. Hoshaja* need be mentioned here. R. Hoshaja who lived in Caesarea, one of the important centres of Christianity in the East, the seat of Origen, said, certainly in refuting the argument of Christian Theology, that God had never

[132] b. Taan. 5 B, R. Samuel b. Nahman in his name.

[133] b. B. K. 60 a.

[134] v. pal. Taan., p. 66 c, also Graetz, *Geschichte*, IV, 4th ed., p. 233, and Büchler, *The Jewish Community of Sepphoris*, pp. 47, 53.

[135] b. Sabb. 89 B. [136] b. B. M. 85 a.

[137] b. Sotah, 3 B; b. A. Z. 5 a, in the same sense as taught above by R. Eliezer ben Jacob, v. p. 57, and by Eleazar ben Jose, v. p. 61.

[138] b. Meg. 10 b ; Sotah, 10 b.

[139] Erubin, 100 B; Pes. 72 B; Ned. 20 B.

[140] v. esp. Büchler, *The Jewish Community in Sepphoris*, p. 46, f. 53 and 57.

pardoned the sin of the golden calf, God had forgiven
Israel for the merit of receiving the Ten Commandments
upon themselves.[141]   None of the nations who were offered
the Torah—a general view in Jewish theology—accepted
it but Israel, and now the very same nations claim to be
the true Israel, on account of Israel's sin.   Israel's ready
acceptance of the Torah balances that sin.   In comparing
the two Kings Achaz and Menasseh, R. Hoshaja repeats
the doctrine of the merits of the children.   Menasseh has
no share in future life, although his father (Hezekiah) was
righteous, yet his son was wicked.   Ahaz, however, has
a share in future life, because his father as well as his son
(Hezekiah) were righteous.[142]   This teacher also inclined to
minimize the merit of the fathers and to give preference
to that of the children.   The next Agadist, *R. Jose ben
Zimra,* leads us back to Hillel's view of the relation
between man's own merits and those of his fathers.   He
who depends on his own merits and prays is heard for the
merits of his fathers.   He, however, who depends on the
merits of his fathers will be heard for his own merits.
As examples Moses and Solomon are given.[143]   From Jose
ben Zimra we hear also that God did not reveal Himself
unto Abraham so long as Lot stayed with him.[144]   The
sins of Lot made Abraham unfit for the revelation of
God.   It can be noticed again, as we saw in previous cases,
that teachers who accepted the doctrine of imputed sin
without reservation are not reconciled to a one-sided
interpretation of the ideas of imputed virtues.   *R. Simon
ben Jehozadak* leads us to an entirely different side of our
doctrine by emphasizing the sociological meaning of it.

[141] Based on אלה in Isa. 49. 15 and Exod. 32. 4.   Pes. 133 B, *R. Huna*
gives the same homily in the name of *R. Acha.*   R. Hoshaja's is given by
R. Eleazar b. Pedath ; b. Ber. 32 B.

[142] j. Synh. 27 d ; Lev. r. 36. 3.

[143] b. Ber. 10 B, v. Pes. 167 B in the name of R. Alexander, later p. 73
and above, p. 18, note 61.

[144] Tanh., I, p. 157 ; Pes. r. 10 a ; Gen. r. 41. 11, the same saying by
R. Nehemia.

God creates bands and societies of people. If one of the circle dies, let the whole circle feel the loss. If one of the society departs from life, the whole society trembles.[145] One member of the community is responsible for the other. There is a solidarity of mankind not only in the material, but also in the moral sense of the word.

One of the most fruitful Agadists of this period was *R. Joshua ben Levi*. His Agadah is rich in quality as well as in quantity as to information on our subject, and a different treatment from the previous teachers and their views seems necessary. He himself was supposed to have had especial merits, and we are told that in years of dearth his prayers for the community were most successful in bringing about rain. He was, however, only successful in his own place (Lydda), and even his prayer was not granted in another place (Sepphoris), where the merits of the community were very insignificant.[146] These rabbis, who were neither Cagliostros nor priests with 'keys' of heaven and earth, knew that their supplications were heard, when the merits of those for whom they entreated Heaven deserve it. They were merely the mouthpiece of the community. There must have been a special reason for Joshua ben Levi and his contemporaries to introduce a discussion on the question, 'whether the merits of the fathers ceased to operate, and to influence the fate of the Jewish people or not'. And if it ceased, when did it do so? We have three reports of this controversy, and in all of them R. Joshua ben Levi expresses the view that the merit of the fathers was effective till the time of Elijah, and not later.[147] It is not clear whether we have a purely academic dispute to deal with, or whether it originated in the apologetical tendency of the time, perhaps as a reply to curious inquirers. Why does the merit of the fathers not help you? Why could they not prevent the

[145] Ruth r. 2. 8; *R. Jochanan* in his name.
[146] v. j. Taan. 66 c; b. Taan. 25 a; Büchler, l. c., p. 37. 2.
[147] j. Synh. 27 d; Lev. r. 36. 5; b. Sabb. 55 a; Eccles. r. 12. 8.

destruction of your Temple? The devastation of your
land? Your exile and national catastrophe? Before the
time of Elijah, R. Joshua ben Levi sees in many events
of ancient history the work of Zechuth Aboth. He seems
to have been teaching very often and in various forms that
God pardoned Israel's sin in the wilderness for the merits
of the fathers.[148] This doctrine may account for his opinion
that Heman (1 Chron. 25. 5) was blessed with so many
children, for the merit of Hannah, who called God יי צבאות
' The Lord of Hosts '.[149] Yet the redemption from Egypt
he ascribes to the merit of erecting the Tabernacle. They
were released from Egypt on the condition that Israel
would erect the Tabernacle.[150] All the blessing which comes
to the world, whether to Jews or to Gentiles, is due to the
merit of the Tabernacle or Temple. After the destruction
of the Temple this merit was transferred to the people
of Israel.[150a] The same idea is to be found, perhaps,
in his statement that the world cannot exist without
Israel.[151] Original in his Agadah is the teaching that the
Gentiles are also punished for the sins of Israel. Not
merely for those which Israel commits through the violence
of the Gentiles, but even for those done independently.[152]
This sage proclaimed in modest words a teaching, the
understanding of which alone can bring blessing and
happiness to mankind, and the neglect of which was the
cause of woe and tragedies in the history of the world.
He applies the thoughts of solidarity in the community,
not to one race, but to the whole world. Just as a man
with a diseased limb, or a society of nations with an
organic disease cannot prosper, likewise a band of nations
suffers from the sins of individual nations or individual

---

[148] Eccles. r. to 4. 5 ; Exod. r. 44. 7, 8. *R. Zebida* in his name.
[149] M. Sam., p. 49.
[150] M. Ps., p. 473 ; Pes. r. 18 B ; Tanh. f. 204 B, Num. r., ch. 12.
[150a] Lev. r. 1. 11 ; Tanh. IV, p. 5 ; Num. r. 1. 3.
[151] b. Taan. 3 B ; cf. b. A. z. 10 B.
[152] Tanh. III, p. 109.

members. R. Joshua ben Levi repeats in a new form the
well-known and popular view that children die for the sins
of their parents. 'Tear your garments', he preached on
a solemn occasion, 'in repentance (Joel 2. 13), then you
need not tear them at the death of your sons and
daughters.'[153] We have a third passage where R. Joshua
ben Levi revealed his opinion on this problem. With
reference to Lev. 20. 16 he raises the question: Supposing
man sinned, what has the beast done? Because the sin
was committed through it (by means of it), therefore it
shall be stoned.[154] And lastly, his teaching that the pious
and righteous are judged according to the deeds, good or
evil, of the majority.[155]

R. Joshua ben Levi deals with other merits too: (1) of the
merit of the study and teaching the Torah,[156] and (2) of
the merit of the observances;[157] (3) of the merit of
Omer.[158]

Finally, we have to refer to R. Joshua ben Levi's endeavours to establish the number of the righteous.[159] His
contemporary, *R. Alexander*, derived the number of righteous
from the numerical value of יהיה (Gen. 18. 18).[159a] This same
teacher elaborated also the aspect of our doctrine we
quoted in the name of *R. Jose ben Zimra* (p. 70, above).
He exemplified by two different parables the meaning of

[153] j. Taan. 65 B; Pes., p. 161 B.

[154] Gen. r., 15. 8, ed. Theodor, p. 141; Pes., p. 142 B; *R. Berechja* and
R. Simon in his name.

[155] pal. Taan. 66 c; Jacob b. Idi in his name.

[156] Pes., p. 25 B; b. Mak. 10 a; M. Ps., p. 508. Ct. r. 6. 17, esp. the
support of the students of the Torah.

[157] b. A. Z. 4 B. All observances which Jews perform in this world will
testify for them in the world to come.

[158] Lev. r. 28. 6.; Pes. r. 92 B in the case of Gideon.

[159] He explained the word הנחילות, Ps. 5. 1, in the Notarikon fashion,
taking each work in its numerical value, ה = 5 = 5 books of Moses;
נ = 50 = 50 days of Omer; ח = 8 = 8 days of circumcision; י = 10 = 10
commandments; ל = 30 = 30 pious like Abraham, without whom the
world cannot exist. M. Ps., ed. B., p. 52 and j. A. Z. 40 c.

[159a] v. Gen. r. 49. 3, ed. Theodor, p. 500.

the teaching that he who refers to his own merits may
get his request or attain his desire by the help of his father's
merits, or vice versa (v. p. 18, note 61). Merits are not possessed by Jews only, they are international. With reference
to Zech. 12. 9: 'And it shall come to pass in that day that
I will seek to destroy all the nations that come against
Jerusalem', he asks: 'I will seek. From or by whom?'
i. e. how does such a word apply to God? God says:
'I will search in their books [בנניני]. If I find a merit
ascribed to them, then I will redeem them; if not, I will
destroy them.'[160]   The doctrine of merits is not confinèd
to race and religion, to members of one country or one
state, but everybody can accumulate merits.

We come now to one of the greatest teachers, and also
one of the greatest men Judaism has produced. Greatness,
of course, in the sense in which Judaism understands it.
He was great neither as a statesman nor as a warrior, nor
as an artist or linguist, but as a man of noble and great
ideals, as a thinker and servant of God. It may suffice
in order to prove this praise, to refer to one incident of
his biography. He sacrificed, like a Jewish Socrates, his
property, which was situated on the way between Sepphoris
and Tiberias, in order to devote himself to study and
work.[161]   And later on, when necessity and want drove
him to seek his daily bread, he returns to his school,
following the voice of his heart.[162]   That happened at a
time when philosophers and teachers in the civilized world
were still looked upon in a way that was so admirably
described by Lucian, the Epicurean of the second century.
The first problem which occupied this man's thoughts was:
'For whose sake does the world exist?' Many opinions
are related to *R. Jochanan b. Nappacha* on this question.
In one place we read: 'Even for *one* righteous person does

[160] b. A. Z. 4 a, v. Buber's *Pesikta*, p. 81 a, note כ"ט.
[161] Pes. 178 B; Lev. r. 30; Cant. r. 8. 7; Tanh. II, p. 119.
[162] b. Taan. 21 a.

the world exist.' [163] In another passage we hear: 'For the
merit [בצדקה used here in the sense of בזכות, v. p. 11] that
you received the Torah on Mount Sinai does the world
exist. Had you not received it, I had destroyed the whole
universe.' [164] He also took part in the discussion: When
did the merits of the fathers cease? We have no saying
of his referring to the merits of the fathers generally.
Yet he has a great deal to say about their merits individually. Of Abraham's merits he speaks in two instances.
First of all in a legend, given by *R. Keruspadai* in his
name, making Balaam advise Amalek to fight Israel.
'For', the false prophet says, 'if you fight them, or go
to war with them, you must certainly defeat them, because
they trust in the merit of Abraham. You are also descendants of Abraham, do the same, depend on the merit of
Abraham.' [165] The scribe ridiculed perhaps those extremists
who believed in the merits of the fathers as in charms or
magic, and meant: 'If one can be saved by the merits
of others, then Amalek had the same claims as Israel.'
That was, however, not R. Jochanan's intention. Moreover,
he held that some benefits derived from the great stock
of merits held by Abraham brought good to his surroundings too.[165a] This can be shown from another Agadah.
The daughters of Lot committed a great sin. How is it
that their unnatural deed took a natural course? R. Jochanan's answer is: 'It was for the sake of him who is the
father of the nations.' [166] Next to the merit of Abraham
he points out that of Isaac. It is remarkable that the

---

[163] b. Joma, 38 B. *R. Hijja b. Abba* in his name.

[164] M. Ps., p. 174 with *R. Eleazar ben Pedath* and *R. Phinehas*, perhaps
b. *Hama*, v. also Ruth r., Introd. 1, a similar saying to Ps. 76. 9 by
R. Jochanan, in his name, by *Hijja b. Abba*, 'The earth trembled in fear,
lest Israel would not receive the Torah, then it would return to water',
i. e. to nothing, Pes. r., p. 99 B.

[165] Esther r. 7, p. 22 a.   [165a] v. M. Cant. r., p. 18.

[166] מואב = מיאב Gen. r. 51. 14, *R. Judah ben Simon* and R. Hanin in his
name. To the interchange between ו and י in the Agadah, v. also Gen.
r. 23. 11; 42. 4; 56. 7.

merits of the second Patriarch do not figure in the same
degree in our doctrine as that of the other two. Individually
his (Isaac's) merits are seldom alluded to. The reason of this
will appear later on. R. Jochanan, however, puts the following prayer in the mouth of Abraham after the sacrifice—a
piece which may have been used in the Liturgy of the
New Year's service in the third century in Palestine.
Abraham said before God: 'Lord of the whole world,
when thou didst tell me to sacrifice my son Iaaac, I had
something to reply (to argue). Yet I did not do so, I subdued my inclination, and did Thy will. May it be Thy
will, O Lord my God, when the children of Isaac fall
into trouble, and they have no one to plead their case,
mayest Thou be their defender. Mayest Thou remember
the sacrifice of Isaac, their father, and be merciful to
them.' [167] When Israel passes through a time of distress
and visitation, on account of sins, or when Israel is being
judged, the sacrifice of Isaac appears as Israel's defender
and advocate. As to the merit of Jacob, we read that
Israel crossed the Jordan for his merits. This theory he
supports by passages taken from the three parts of the
Bible.[168] The existence of the world is ascribed to the
merit of Moses and Aaron, if we may trust certain readings
in the Talmudic text.[169] He repeats the teaching that
the well accompanied Israel for the merit of Miriam.[170]
Besides the merits of these biblical personages, he also

[167] j. Taan. 65 D, *R. Bibi b. R. Abba*, in his name Gen. r. 56. 15; Lev. r.
29. 8 with additions, anonym.; Tanh. I, p. 115; Pes., p. 145 where the
name of the teacher is given as R. Bibi b. R. Abba; somewhat different
Pes. r. 171 B. R. Jeremiah is a copyist's error for R. Jochanan. Jer. and
Tanh. read לידי צרה, Gen. r., Lev. r., Pes. לידי עבירות ומעשים רעום.

[168] Gen. 32. 11; Joshua 4. 22; and Ps. 114. 7, v. Gen. r. 76. 4,
R. Judah b. Simon in his name. In all the three instances the name
Jacob or Israel is used, Cant. r. 4. 6.

[169] b. Hulin, 89 a, there seems to have been copies in which the name
of the teacher was Raba the Babylonian school-head. Even if we keep the
first reading, there is no great difficulty in reconciling it with the view
cited at the beginning of our review of R. Jochanan's *Agadah*, v. p. 74 f.

[170] v. above under Jose ben Judah, p. 61; Cant. r. 4. 26.

speaks of God's grace. Wherever the word לולי is mentioned, help and salvation come for the merit of holiness
of the Name, i. e. for God's own sake.[171] In some cases
man is justified or a whole nation is saved by the grace
of God, without any outside help.

R. Jochanan also points out the merits of the Torah, of
the circumcision, of observances and the Omer. Together
with *R. Eleazar ben Pedath* he taught : ' The Torah
was given in forty days, the soul of every human being is
created in forty days. He who keeps the Torah has his soul
guarded. He who does not keep the Torah his soul is not
guarded.'[172] In another passage he regards a man who
studies the Torah for its own sake as one who protects
the whole world.[173] The merit of circumcision causes all
the joy which Israel derives in this world.[174] The merits
of the observances we find emphasized in the following
saying of R. Jochanan, given by R. Simon ben Pazzi on
Deut. 32. 35 : ' Mine is vengeance and recompense at the
time when their foot shall slide.' How is this to be reconciled with the might of God, that one should say : ' When
their foot shall slide, I will punish them ? '; but God said :
' When the observances which are customary (רגלם = הרגילות)
among them shall cease, and I can find no merit for them
before Me, at that time will vengeance and recompense
belong to Me.[175] The merit of the observances is great,
their neglect brings punishment.' Like *R. Joshua ben Levi*
he also puts stress on the observance of the Omer.[176] For

[171] Gen. r. 74. 10 ; M. Ps., p. 228, where a different interpretation is
given, כל לולי בזכות הקב"ה, based on Isa. 1. 9.

[172] b. Men. 99 b, v. above, p. 61, under *Menachem ben Jose.*

[173] b. Synh. 99 b. We have the opinions of most of the contemporary
teachers on this point, namely, of R. Alexander, Rab. (Babylonian) R.
Simon ben Lakish, R. Eleazar ben Pedath, R. Abahu, and Rabah רבה
(Babylonian).

[174] Cant. r. 7. 5 : כל חיטטין ופרנוקין שישראל מחטין ומתפרנקין בעולם
הזה בזכות מילה, v. Jalkut Machiri, Malachi, 20.

[175] Esther r. 1. 1, p. 6 a.

[176] Pes., p. 71 a ; Lev. r., ch. 28. 6.

the merit of the Omer Abraham inherited the land of
Canaan. There must be a good reason for emphasizing
this special commandment by R. Jochanan and R. Joshua
ben Levi, and later on by R. Samuel b. Nahman and
R. Levi.

His view on subsidiary sin must also be mentioned. He
who begins to perform a commandment, and does not
complete it, causes the death of his wife and children. As
an instance the case of Judah is given.[177] The righteous
die for the sins of the wicked. David (Ps. 26. 9) and
Daniel (2. 18) prayed to God that the pious should not be
taken from this world for the sake of or with the wicked.[178]
Finally we learn that the future redemption is to come
through the merit of repentance.[179]

The friend of R. Jochanan, *R. Simon ben Lakish*, to whose
Agadah we turn now, teaches the same view with regard to
the future redemption.[180] He agrees further with R. Jochanan in his view that the world stands for the merits of Israel
(v. p. 129), and that the world was originally created on the
condition that Israel in future would receive the Torah
(v. p. 72). R. Simon ben Lakish expressed this view also
in a third sentence, saying in the name of *R. Judah II,
the patriarch*: the world stands only through the breath
(הבל) of the school-children.[181] He is the first teacher who
taught expressly that the universe was created for Israel's
sake. In a beautiful legend based on Ps. 49. 14, he
composed a dialogue between God and the ecclesia of

---

[177] Tanh., I, p. 184; *R. Hijja b. Abba* in his name; Gen. r. 85. 3;
R. Judah ben Simon, and R. Hanin in his name. b. Sotah, 13 B gives
Samuel b. Nahman as author; v. also *PSEZ.*, ed. Friedmann, p. 45.

[178] M. Ps., p. 219.

[179] Exod. r., 25. 16. Here may be mentioned that R. Jochanan liked the
antithesis of זכה and לא זכה in his *Agadah* to Ps. 80. 14, v. Lev. 33. 5;
Cant. r. 3. 3; M. Ps. Pr. 182 a, v. my ed. of Midrash *Haseroth we Yeteroth*,
p. 44, note 185. The same method is applied by R. Joshua ben Levi (a) b;
Synh. 28 a; j. Taan. 63 d and (b); b. Sanh. 28 a, and by R. Hanina b.
Hama, Gen. r., ch. 8, v. p. 8, and by Nahman, son of R.S.b.N., Gen. r. 10. 5.

[180] Gen. r., 2. 5; Pes. r. 152 B.

[181] b. Sabb. 119 B.

Israel. The latter saying: 'A man who marries a second time does not forget and forsake his first wife; and Thou hast forgotten and forsaken me?' God says: 'Everything created was done for thy sake, and thou, sayest: Thou hast forgotten and forsaken me!' Israel: 'Since there is no forgetfulness before Thee, perhaps Thou wilt not forget the deed of the golden calf?' God replies: 'That will I forget!' Israel: 'Since there is forgetfulness before Thee, wilt Thou forget my deed on Sinai?' God says: 'I will never forget thee.'[182] This is a voice of the third century which reproduces the discussions which were held at that time all over the world where Christians and Jews met. Israel repeats the polemical views of the Church and God utters the replies of the Synagogue. Israel is forsaken by God and forgotten! A living body with a lifeless soul! Israel is remembered as an untrustworthy guardian of the highest ideals of Heaven. 'No', says R. Simon ben Lakish: 'God has not forgotten Israel. For Israel's sake was the world created. God has even forgotten Israel's sin.' We will see later on that R. Simon ben Lakish was the first teacher whom we know by name who spread this doctrine, and the context leaves not the shadow of a doubt for what purpose the teaching was propagated. Yet he acknowledges also the merits of the nations, for which they get their due reward.[183]

In his Agadah we hear further of the merit of Abraham; when Abraham obeyed the will of God, he was promised that the world shall never lack dew.[184] The Messiah is called (Dan. 2. 34) אבן (stone), for the sake of Jacob, i. e. he will destroy all the kingdoms of the world for Jacob's merit.[185] He thought a great deal of the merits of the righteous. Those unselfish righteous men who have no desire or wish for themselves, but pray and fast for the welfare of others,

---

[182] b. Ber. 32 B ; v. Jalkut Machiri, Isa., p. 179.
[183] Gen. r. 9. 15.
[184] j. Ber. 9 B ; j. Taan. 63 D ; R. Jacob of Kefar-Hanin in his name.
[185] Gen. 49. 24; Tanh. II, p. 92.

are the source of blessing for the world (v. p. 18). The righteous, however, die for the sins of their contemporaries, or are taken with the wicked together in times of plague or distress.[186] A typical instance for the merit of righteous fathers is given in the case of Saul. Saul deserved the Kingdom for the merit of his grandfather (ancestor) who spent money to light lamps for the community. It was said that there were dark alleys from his residence to the school-house, and he provided them with the necessary lights.[187]

R. Jose ben Hanina is represented in this survey with three sayings. The one refers to the merits of the righteous, for whose sake the world is created [v. p. 120]. The second illustrates the idea that the environment of the just derives some advantage from his merits. When Jacob came to Egypt the famine was only in its second year, still it ceased at once for the merit of Jacob.[188] And thirdly, by his endeavour to show that God always diminishes the balance of debt, and increases that of merit.[189] Another important Agadist, *R. Hama b. Hanina*, of this period, has left us only a few remarks on our subject. He emphasizes, first of all, the doctrine of Zechuth Aboth. 'Just as a son of a king, who had a case to defend before his father, is told: "If thou dost desire to be acquitted in my court (judgement), appoint for thy defence that solicitor (ניקולוגום), and thou shalt be acquitted." Likewise says God to Israel: "My children, do you desire that I shall justify you in My judgement, recall before Me the merits of your fathers and I shall pardon you."'[190] This merit of the fathers apparently did not cease in the time of the Kings, as most of R. Hama's friends held, but was still effective. Thus

---

[186] v. Gen. r. 9. 7; ed. Theodor, p. 71.

[187] j. Sebiit, 34 d; Lev. r., ch. 9. 2.

[188] v. Gen. r. 89. 10; Midrash, 32 Middoth par. 10; instead of Jose b. חייא read Hanina.

[189] j. Sanh. 27 c; j. Kid. 61 d; b. R. H. 17 a; b. Arachin 8 B; Pes. 167 a: M. Ps., p. 234.

[190] Or, justify you, Pes. 153 B; Lev. r. 29. 6.

he expresses his views in one of his six explanations of Gen. 29. 2. He sees therein a reference to the history of Zion. The well is Zion. The three flocks of sheep, the three first kingdoms, Babel, Media, and Greece. The big stone is the merit of the fathers. As the latter removed the yoke of the former kingdoms, so it will remove that of our present oppressors, Rome. For the influence of the merit of the fathers never ceased, and will never cease to be 'a well' of hope, and a source of consolation to Israel.[191] There must have been some cogent reasons which induced him to oppose his contemporaries, just as they were influenced by some important factors to spread and elaborate their view. The Manna came to Israel for the merit of Sarah or Abraham.[192] He also held that Rome's power is due to the merits of their ancestor Esau, who obtained it by honouring Isaac.[193] He finally points out the merits connected with the study of the Torah,[194] and with the sacrifices.[195] As to the doctrine of subsidiary sin there is his saying: 'Adam ought not to have died at all. Wherefore was death decreed against him? Because God foresaw that Nebuchadnezzar and Hiram will arise who will declare themselves as deities![196] Adam dies not for his own sin, but for the sin of some of his descendants.'

The next Agadist, of whose Agadah, as far as it concerns our doctrine, a brief account has to be given, is *R. Samuel ben Nahmani*. He revives the idea that the greatest things are done for God's grace. Thus the final salvation will come for His sake [v. p. 14 f.]. The forgiveness, when Israel made the golden calf, was for the merits of the fathers [v. p. 151 f.]. He also emphasizes the merit of Isaac. He saw, namely, in the ashes which were put on the heads of the worshippers on the fast day a remembrance of the

---

[191] Gen. r. 70. 8.
[192] Tanh. B., II, p. 67, v. Gen. r. 48. 13; Exod. r. 25. 5; b. B. M. 86 в.
[193] Gen. r. 66, 7.
[194] b. Ber. 16 a; Gen. r., ch. 92.
[195] Gen. r. 44. 17; R. Hijja b. Hanina, read Hama b. Hanina.
[196] Gen. r. 9. 6, v. already p. 68, n. 131.

merits of Isaac, in opposition to *Judah ben Menasseh*, who thinks of the merits of Abraham.[197] As to the merits of Jacob we have two references. First of all that Abraham was saved for the merit of Jacob (v. p. 136), which means that the view of the merits of children is implied. In another legend he points out that for the merits of Jacob and Joseph their masters (Laban and Potiphar) were prosperous.[198] Just as these were blessed for the sake of the two just men, who dwelt among them, so the world is blessed for the sake of Israel (v. p. 130). The Gentiles have also got merits for which they receive their reward in this world, as, for instance, the Canaanites.[199] He repeats the doctrine of merit of the Tabernacle (v. above, pp. 53 and 72), which established the world on a firm basis.[200] Although we learnt from him that the future redemption will be for God's own sake (v. p. 14), yet we hear that the merit of the purity of family life will also contribute to it a great deal.[201] As in the Agadah of some of his contemporaries, there is in R. Samuel ben Nahmani's, too, a reference to the merit of the Omer.[202] In another saying, we have a second instance of R. Samuel ben Nahmani varying a view commonly held in his time: ' When Israel does not do the will of the God, then He selects a pious, just, righteous, God-fearing man, who is among them, and removes him for the sin of the wicked.' [203] *R. Simlai* ascribes immorality as the source and reason of plague and pestilence (אנדרולומוסיא), which kill righteous and wicked people alike.[204] As a point of curiosity may be mentioned here also the defence of the nations of the world at the last judgement, in a visionary composition of this teacher, when the nations of the world

---

[197] j. Taan. 65 a ; b. Taan. 16 a ; Gen. r. 49. 23 ; cf. Lam. r., ed. B., p. 115.
[198] v. Gen. r. 84. 6 : זה נתברך בו חמיו וזה נתברך בו חמיו בשבילו.
[199] Gen. r. 100. 6.   [200] Tanh. II, 94.
[201] M. Ps., p. 175.   [202] Pes. 71 a ; Lev. r. 28. 6.
[203] Cant. r. 6. 6 ; j. Ber. 5 B. anonym.
[204] Gen. r. 26. 10, ed. Theodor, 278 f. ; Num. r. 9. 33 ; j. Sotah 17 a ; Tanh. I, 13 f.

pretend as if all the great things done in this world by them, all their achievement in culture and technique, were for Israel's sake, i. e. that Israel shall study the Torah in comfort.[205]

The following teachers are mostly the pupils of R. Jochanan ben Nappacha. Especially *R. Eleazar ben Pedath, R. Abahu, R. Ami, R. Hijja b. Abba, Simon bar Abba, R. Isaac, R. Levi, Simon ben Pazzi,* and *Abba b. Kahana,* whose views on the problems connected with our doctrine will be now described. *R. Eleazar ben Pedath's* Agadah may be introduced by his saying with reference to Ps. 62. 13, 'Unto Thee, O Lord, belongeth mercy; For Thou renderest to every man according to his work', and who has not got (any merits) Thou givest him from Thy own.[206] God in His mercy pardons him who has no merits. The world was created for him who fears God.[207] He expresses the same view in another saying: 'Even for the sake of *one* righteous man is a world created', based on Gen. 1. 4 and Isa. 3. 10.[208] It is doubtful, however, whether we have to attribute to him the opinion that the world stands for the sake of the one who keeps quiet at times of quarrel and strife.[209] Yet we have another statement of his to the effect that the world stands for the merit of the Torah.[210]

[205] b. AZ. 2 a–2 B.

[206] j. Peah.16 B: אמר' ר' אלעזר ולך ה' חסד כי אתה משלם לאיש כמעשהו ואי לית ליה את יהיב ליה מן דידך היא דעת יה דר"א, the same sentence j Kid. 61 d; j. Synh. 27 d, v. Ginzberg, שרידי הירושלמי, p. 228, l. 34; b. R. H. 17 B.

[207] B. Ber. 6 B to Eccles. 12. 13: 'Fear God and keep His commandments; for this is the whole man' אר אלעזר אמר מאי זה כל האדם? הקב"ה כל העולם כולו לא נברא אלא כשביל זה, v. b. Sabb. 30 B.

[208] b. Joma, 38 B: ואמר ר' אלעזר אפי' בשביל צדיק אחד עולם נברא שנ' וירא אלהים כי טוב ואין טוב אלא צדיק שנ' אמרו צדיק כי טוב. This identification of צדיק and טוב is older, v. R. Jannai, Gen. r. 3. 8; M. Ps., p. 323.

[209] b. Hul. 89 a. The text reads ר' אילעאי, Jalkut read Eleazar.

[210] b. Pes. 68 B; b. Ned. 32 a: דאמר ר' אלעזר גדולה תורה שאילמלא תורה לא נתקיימו שמים וארץ שנ' אם לא בריתי יומם ולילה, Jer. 33. 25.

For the merit of Abraham the Israelites were heard at Ai (Joshua 7. 6),[211] and the Manna was given to them in the wilderness for the same reason.[212]   When the destruction of Jerusalem in the time of Zedekiah was imminent the members of the Synhedrion prayed and mentioned the merits of Abraham and Jacob.[213]   Many references are to be found in R. Eleazar's Agadah to the merits of the righteous.   Rain comes for the merit of the just man.[214] The prayers of the righteous have the power to appease God.[215]   Blessing and happiness come to the world for the merit of Israel.[216]   Original is his view that Israel was redeemed from Egypt for the merit of future generations. The contemporaries had no merits.   Even the merits of the fathers could not hasten the hour of freedom.   The same was the case with the miracle at the sea.   They were redeemed for the merit of the children that they might proclaim the greatness and might of God.[217]   This statement does not contradict another saying of his which mentions the merits of the fathers as one of the five things which bring salvation, i. e. trouble (persecutions), prayer, the merit of the fathers, repentance, and the promised time of redemption (קץ).   R. Eleazar meant to say that these four requirements were wanting, therefore

[211] Gen. r. 39. 24, v. above under R. Eleazar ben Shamua, p. 56.

[212] Lev. r. 34. 8.

[213] מזכירין זכותו של אברהם מזכירין זכותו של יעקב, Lam. r. 2. 18, anonym, ed. B, p. 114; cf. b. Ned. 65 a in the name of R. Eleazar.

[214] j. Taan. 66 c: ר' ברכיה ור' חלבו פפא בשם ר' אלעזר פעמים שהנשמים יורדין בזכות אדם אחד בזכות עשב אחד בזכות שדה אחת ושלשתן בפסוק אחד ומטר נשם יתן לכם לאיש עשב בשדה, לאיש אבל לא לאנשים ולעשב אבל לא לעשבים ובשדה אבל לא בשדות; Zech. 10. 1; Lev. r. 35. 9 read ור' פפא ור' אלעזר.

[215] b. Sukkah, 14 a, v. b. Jeb. 64 a; R. Isaac, v. p. 69, n. 136.

[216] b. Jeb. 63 a: אפילו משפחות הדרות באדמה אין מתברכות אלא בשביל ישראל, אפילו ספינות הבאות מליא לאספמיא אין מתברכות אלא בשביל ישראל, v. above to R. Hanina b. Hama, p. 67.

[217] M. Ps., p. 268, ed. Buber; p. 28 d, ed. Prague; Jalkut has § 746 R. Eleazar.

the Zechuth of the fathers could not hasten the redemption, yet the merit of the children could do it.[218] We will mention a few sentences of his, which teach the doctrine of imputed sin. First of all his saying: 'He who forgets one thing of his learning causes exile to his children.'[219] Secondly, he says in a curious saying that the descendants of Abraham were caused to suffer slavery in Egypt for 210 years, because he forced the scholars to military service.[220] Thirdly, we have an instance of one righteous man being taken away owing to the sins of his generation.[221]

Another prominent pupil of R. Jochanan, a great teacher of this period, was *R. Abahu*, who has eight sayings on our doctrine. He discussed, like R. Eleazar, the question, 'for whose merit was the world created?' And expressed his opinion on the frequently debated problem, 'for whose merit does the world stand?' As to the second question he said that the world stands for the merit of Jacob (v. p. 123), as to the first, we hear that the world was created for the merit of the meek and modest people.[222] He revives the old doctrine of the merit of circumcision. For the sake of Abraham's circumcision God pardons Israel's sins,[223] and emphasizes that the Law of festivals and the Torah were given for the merits of the fathers, in order that Israel shall not come with empty hands before the Lord. Even in our time, says this great Agadist

---

[218] j. Taan. 63 d; Deut. r. 2. 21.

[219] Based on Hos. 4. 6; b. Joma, 38 B: כל המשכח דבר מתלמודו גורם גלות לבניו שנאמר ותשכח תורת אלהיך אשכח בניך גם אני. *R. Abahu* says that *he* is punished, but not his children.

[220] B. Ned. 32 a: מפני מה נענש אברהם אבינו ונשתעבדו בניו למצרים ר"י שנים ? מפני שעשה אנגריא בתלמידי חכמים שנאמר וירק את חניכיו; v. Büchler, *The political and social leaders*, p. 42[4].

[221] B. Ber. 62 B: א"ל הקבה למלאך המות טול לי רב שבהם שיש בו ליפרע מהם כמה חובות באותה שעה מת אבישי בן צרויה ששקול כרובה של סנהדרין.

[222] b. Hullin, 89 a: מי שמשים עצמו כמי שאינו שנ' מתחת זרועות עולם, he who is trodden down, he carries in his arms the world.

[223] Cant. r. 4. 14.

and Apologist, although we are persecuted, the Torah does
not depart from us. We are like a man whose case is
before the king, and his advocates defend him, likewise
if a man performs the commandments, studies the Law, or
does charity, even when Satan accuses him, his Torah and
charity defend him.[224] These words were said in Caesarea,
at a time when it was taught that the Torah and performances are punishments, and there is no good and value
in them. Do we wonder if R. Abahu pleaded the merits
of the observances? Another case of the merits of the
ancestors is shown in the biography of the prophet
Jeremiah; when he was rescued from the pit, he asked for
a ladder. God said to him: 'You want a ladder, is there
no merit in My hands belonging to thy ancestress (Rahab)?
Is it not written: Then she let them down by the cord
through the window (Joshua 2. 15)? Likewise did they
draw up Jeremiah with the cords' (Jer. 38. 13).[225] He taught
also about the merits of the children, for whose sake Noah
was rescued.[226] Just as the merits of the children benefit
the fathers, so the fathers die for the sins of the children.
Thus the wickedness of Esau shortened the days of
Abraham.[227] From *R. Hijja b. Abba's* Agadah we have
other proofs of the interest our problems roused in contemporary Judaism. We notice first of all his prayer:
'Unite, O God, our hearts to fear Thy name, remove us
from everything Thou dost hate, and bring us near to
everything Thou dost love, do unto us charity for Thy
name's sake.'[228] God does righteousness and charity for
His name's sake. He forgives Israel's sin for the merits
of the fathers (v. p. 151). He endorses his teacher's

---

[224] ומלמדין זכות, Exod. r. 31. 1.

[225] M. Sam., ed. Buber, p. 75.

[226] Tanh., f. 9 B. Gen. r. 29. 5 has the saying in the name of *R. Simon
ben Pazzi*, v. p. 90, and ed. Theodor, p. 270.

[227] Pes. r. 47 B, 49 B, v. Gen. r. 63. 16, anonym.

[228] Pal. Ber. 7 D : ר' חייאבר אבא מוסיף: ותייחד לבבינו ליראה את שמך
ותרחקנו מכל מה ששנאת, ותקרבנו לכל מה שאהבת ותעשה עמנו צדקה
למען שמך.

(R. Jochanan) view that the world exists, and stands for the merit of one righteous man.[229]   Lot became rich, whilst he accompanied Abraham for the merits of the latter.[230] Likewise Pharaoh's important dream is not to be ascribed to Pharaoh's, but to Joseph's merit.[231]   The sacrifices were given to Israel, so that they might acquire merits.[232]   God did not command sacrifices for his needs, but to enable Israel to obtain merits before Him.   Even greater is the merit of the Sabbath observance, for the merit of the Sabbath brings future redemption.[233]   Like most of his colleagues he endorses the view that the merits of the children atone for the parents' sins (v. p. 161), yet children die for the father's sins.[234]   More variety is to be discerned in the Agadah of *R. Isaac Nappacha.*   'Everybody,' he taught, 'is in need of God's grace, even Abraham, on whose account grace embraces the whole world.'[235]   There is no righteous or just man who can rely upon his own merit.   Everything in this world is for the merit of worship (הכל בזכות השתחויה), for instance, Abraham's safe return from the Mount Moriah, Israel's redemption, the Revelation of the Torah, the fulfilment of Hannah's prayer; likewise in future the gathering of the exiles, the rebuilding of the Temple, the resurrection of the dead will be for the merit of worship.[236]   In another saying we hear that the revelations, the re-establishment

[229] v. b. Joma. 38 B, my ed. of *Midrash Haserot we Yeteroth*, p. 36, note 150.

[230] Pes. r. 9 B, and Gen. r. 52. 5.

[231] Tanh. B., I, p. 190 : אלא ? חיא בר אבא חלום כלב המת חלום אלא "ר
לפי שעה על ידי הצדיק.

[232] Tanh. B., III, 96: למה, להודיע שאין לפניו לא אכילה ולא שתייה
אמר לי להקריב קרבן ? כדי לנכותך.

[233] Lev. r. 3. 1.   שאין ישראל נגאלין אלא בזכות שבת   Eccles. r. 4. 6.

[234] M. Ruth z., p. 47 : עד י"ג שנה הבן לוקה בעון האב.

[235] Gen. r. 60. 2: ר' חני בשם ר' יצחק הכל צריכין לחסד אפילו אברהם
שהחסד מתנלנל בעולם בשבילו נצרך לחסד   v. p. 13.

[236] Gen. r. 56. 3 ; M. Sam., ch. 3, p. 53 ; in a different order Pirke, R. Eliezer, ch. 31, shortened הכל לא נוצר אלא בזכות השתחויה שנ' רוממו
ה' אלהינו, based on Gen. 22. 3 ; Exod. 12. 17 ; Exod. 24. 1 ; 1 Sam. 1. 24 Isa. 27. 13 ; Ps. 95. 6.

of Israel in Palestine, the rebuilding of the Temple and
the appearance of the Messiah will come for the merit
of the festival plants.[237]   Among the different things
which depend on hope (בקיווי), R. Isaac enumerates in
a similar fashion the merits of the fathers.[238]   In an
explanation of Isa. 26. 10, R. Isaac makes Esau's father
say: 'Lord of the whole world! Let favour be shown to
Esau!' God replies: 'He is wicked.' Isaac: 'Yet will he
not learn righteousness?' God: 'In the land of uprightness will he deal wrongfully!' Isaac: 'Well then may he
not behold the pride of the Lord?'[239]   We have here an
instance of a father, just and righteous, entreating for his
wicked son. Yet he himself acknowledges God's judgement. R. Isaac repeats the opinion that for Jacob's merit
was Laban blessed. The same was the case with Joseph's
master.[240]   Aaron entered the Holy of Holies for the merit
of the twelve tribes.[241]   The merit of one just man saves
the city.[242]   As in all questions bearing on the Agadah
great attention must be paid here also to one of its greatest
teachers, *R. Levi*, who enlarges our knowledge on this
doctrine as on all other branches of Jewish theology.
Some of his views are quite original, others repetition, or
further development of earlier teachings. Thus when he
says the world was created for Abraham's merit.[243] A chief
feature in Levi's teachings is the great merit of Abraham.
With whomsoever Abraham entered into business transactions, the buyer or seller was blessed.[244] The events
in biblical history happened on the third day, likewise

---

[237] Lev. 23, 40, v. Gen. r. 63. 10 ; R. Haggai in his name ; Lev. r. 30,
15 ; by R. Berechja, in the name of R. Levi, Pesikta 185 a, the whole sentence
by R. Berechja in the name of *R. Abba b. Kahana.*

[238] Gen. r. 98. 20.   [239] b. Meg. 6 B.

[240] b. Sanh. 39 B.   [241] Exod. r. 38. 10.

[242] Gen. r. 49. 25 : א"ר יצחק עד כמה הוא מצוי חשבון לעיר אחת עד
אחד אם נמצא אחד בכל העיר תולין לה בזכותו.

[243] Gen. r. 12. 2, and Gen. r. 14. 6 ; v. however, Gen. r. 28. 2.

[244] Gen. r. 39. 17 : לא שם אדם פרה מאברהם עד שנתברך ולא שמה
לו עד שנתברך מאברהם.

such as are destined to take place in future on this day, for instance, the resurrection, the release of the twelve patriarchs, of the spies in Joshua's time, the revelation on Mount Sinai, the miracle of Jonah, of those who returned from exile to Palestine, the salvation in the days of Esther, all take place for Abraham's merit.[245] We have further a dispute between R. Levi and *R. Abba b. Kahana* on the question, for whose merit does the divine presence abide in Israel? One says and proves it from the Scripture that it was for the merit of Abraham, the other speaks of the merit of Jacob.[246] To judge from the previous statements we may say that R. Levi ascribed it to the merit of Abraham (v. p. 136). The tribe of Judah was worthy to sacrifice as the first for the meekness of their ancestor.[247] Besides Abraham's merits, R. Levi speaks at length of the merits of Moses. For his and Aaron's sake Israel was redeemed from Egypt (v. p. 143), the Manna came (p. 145), Moses was buried in the wilderness so that the dead of the generation of the desert, who died there, shall revive for his merit.[248]

An instance of the descendants benefiting by the good deeds of their parents is given in the case of Orpah. For the four miles Orpah accompanied her mother-in-law she was worthy that four heroes were among her children.[249] As to the doctrine of the merits of the fathers, we hear that its influence ceased before the destruction of the Temple.[250] There is another frequently repeated view of

---

[245] Gen. r. 56. 1 : באיזה זכות רבנן ור' לוי, רבנן אמרי בזכות יום השלישי
של מתן תורה ר' לוי אמר בזכות של יום השלישי של אברהם אבינו,
from R. Isaac's instances given above, compared with this it seems that such enumerations were in the latter part of the third century usual in public lectures.

[246] Cant. r. 7. 11.

[247] Gen. 44. 33 ; Pes. r., p. 27 B. *B. Berechja* in his name.

[248] Deut. r. 2. 5 : א״ל הקב״ה למשה אם אתה נקבר כאן אצלן בזכותך
הן באין עמך.

[249] Tanh. I, p. 208, against R. Isaac.

[250] v. Lam. r. Proem, 23, p. 18, ed. Buber.

R. Levi which was also taught by others who preceded
him, as well as by those who followed him. 'Blessing
comes', he says, 'to the world for Israel's merit.'[251] The
different means which prepare the way for merits are
numerous in R. Levi's Agadah. First of all there is the
merit of *faith*. Salvation comes for the merits of faith
and of the Torah.[252] Israel rejoices before the Lord for
the merits of the Sabbath and the tithes.[253] Like R. Jochanan
and R. Joshua ben Levi, he refers to the merit of the Omer,
which helped Israel in the days of Mordecai.[254] The merit
of circumcision is being especially emphasized. The redemption promised in Dan. 12. 1 will come for the merit
of circumcision, cf. Joshua 5. 2.[255] For at the circumcision,
in the time of Joshua, God promised to forgive Israel's sins
for the performance of that commandment.[256] Further, we
hear that God does charity with Israel for the merit of observing faithfully the civil laws.[257] Finally, R. Levi teaches
that for the sake of the soul, i. e. for man, the world was
created.[258] There are only a few items in the teachings
of *R. Ami*. Rain comes for the merit of those who have
faith.[259] *R. Simon bar Abba* emphasizes also the merit
of faith.[260] *R. Simon ben Pazzi* endorses the view of the
merits of the fathers and children.[261] As to the theory

---

[251] Gen. r. 66. 2 : אומה שכל טובה שהיא באה לעולם אינה באה אלא
בזכותה, הגשמים אינן יורדין אלא בזכותה, הטללים אינם יורדים אלא
בזכותה שנ' ויתן לך אלהים לך בזכותך ובך הדבר תלוי, Deut. r. 7. 8 :
רבנן אמרי בני כל טובות שבאות בעולם בזכותכם הן באות, and v. Cant.
r. 7. 1, like Gen. r. 66. 2.

[252] Gen. r. 74. 9.

[253] Pes., p. 96 B, מתחטאים; Aruch reads מתחטין, v. above, p. 77.
M. S. Carmoly adds זכות תורה.

[254] Pes. 71 B ; Pes. r. 93 a ; Lev., p. 28 ; Esther r. 10 ; b. Meg. 16 a.

[255] M. Ps. 19 B, ed. B., p. 175.

[256] Cant. r. 4. 14.

[257] Deut. r. 5. 6.   [258] Lev. r. 4. 2 ; Eccles. r. 7. 16.

[259] b. Taan. 8 a : ואין הגשמים באים אלא בזכות בעלי אמונה, and *ibid.*
for the sake of the righteous.

[260] Exod. r. 23. 5.

[261] Gen. r. 29. 5, v. above under R. Abahu, p. 86.

of the merits of the fathers, we learn that the reward not used by them during their lifetime is preserved for their children.[262] The nations have also merits.[263] *R. Hanina ben Papa* taught the merits of the children, when he says that Noah escaped from the catastrophe of the flood for the merit of Moses.[264] In *R. Abba b. Kahana's* Agadah most of the problems concerning our doctrine are discussed. Thus he tells us that for Israel's sake the world was created (v. p. 113), the world stands for the merit of the house of David.[265] Further he shows, in the example of Abraham, the view of the merits of the fathers and children in a combined form (v. p. 136 f.). The latter idea is also repeated by him in another instance. Noah and his children were saved for the merits of the pious and righteous men and women in future generations.[266] New is the teaching in his Agadah that Israel was redeemed from Egypt for the merits of Isaiah's generation,[267] which comes under the same category. R. Abba bar Kahana emphasizes especially the doctrine of the treasuries, which are kept for the righteous.[268]

----

[262] Lev. r. 36. 3 ; j. Synh. 27 d. [263] Tanh., p. 101 B.

[264] v. Gen. r. 26. 6 : אפילו נח שנשתייר מהם לא שהיה כדאי אלא בשצפה הקב״ה שמשה עתיד לעמוד ממנו שנאמר בשגם דחושבניה דין ויהיו ימיו, the Rabbis derived it from Gen. 6. 3 : הוא חושבניה דין מאה ועשרים שנה = the years of Moses.

[265] v. M. Sam., ch. 16, p. 94 (Buber) ; רבי ? באיזה זכות העולם עומד, 1 Kings 2. 24. אבא בר כהנא אמר בזכות מלכי בית דוד שנ' אשר הכינני. R. Simon ben Lakish says for the merit of Torah, and the Rabbis assume that for Israel's sake, cf. 2 Sam. 7. 22. Jalkut r. *R. Levi* instead of R. Simon ben Lakish, which reading appears more correct. There must be some reason for emphasizing the merits of the kings of the house of David! R. Hanina ben Papa also warned against any opposition to the house of David, v. b. Synh. 102 a. Maybe that the opposition to the Patriarch Judah II by the leaders of the schools induced these scribes to utter those words in defence of that institution? On this opposition v. *RÉJ.*, 67, pp. 59–66.

[266] Gen. r. 28. 5. [267] M. Ps., p. 473.

[268] v. p. 21, and also Cant. r. 7. 14 ; M. Ps. 31. 7 ; Deut. r. 7. 10 : אתם צפנתם לי תורה ומצות ואני צופן לכם מאותו הטוב שמתוקן לעתיד לבא.

To complete the thoughts and teachings on our subject the views of some scribes, of whom only occasional remarks on the doctrine of the merits are preserved in the old Rabbinical literature, must be added. *Zabdi ben Levi*, a contemporary of R. Joshua ben Levi, saw in the word לולי (except) an allusion to the merits of the fathers.[269] *Abba bar Zabda* expressed also his opinion in the debate on the question: 'When did the power of the merits of the fathers cease?' He found in 2 Kings 13. 23 a reference that it ceased in the days of Jehoash.[270] *Hilfa* or *Ilfa*, a friend of R. Jochanan remarks to Eccl. 1. 3, 'What profit hath man of all his labour under the sun', yet he has a treasure above the sun![271] *Jeremia ben Abba*, a pupil of the Babylonian Rab, gives us an instance how one can lose his merits. The book of Nehemia is not called by the author's name, for he wished to call it after his own name, whereby he lost his merits.[272] Of R. Jochanan's contemporaries and pupils we have to remember first of all *Tahlifa of Caesarea*. 'If Lot, who had no merits, was saved for showing honour to the angels, shall I not save you, for your merits and for the merits of your fathers?'[273] God saved Lot for Abraham's sake, how much more will the Lord lift up His countenance upon thee (Num. 6. 26). In *R. Judah ben Simon's* Agadah we find the doctrine that the world was created for the sake of the Torah, and for Israel's sake does the world stand.[274] The patriarchs acquired merits by the performance of the commandments of tithe.[275]

---

[269] Gen. r. 74. 9.

[270] j. Synh. 27 d ; Lev. r. 36. 5.

[271] Eccles. r. 1. 4.   R. Huna and R. Acha in his name.

[272] b. Sanh. 93 B, v. on the literature my ed. of *Midrash Haserot we Yeteroth*, p. 83, note 343.

[273] Gen. r. 50. 21: א״ר חלפתא קסרייא ומה אם לוט על ידי שכיבד את המלאך נשא לו פנים לך לא אשא פנים מפניך ומפני אבותיך ישא יי פניו אליך. Sifre Num. §. 42 reads (anonymous): ומה אם ללוט נשאתי פנים בשביל אברהם אוהבי לך לא אשא פנים מפניך ומפני אבותיך, v. also Num. r. 11. 7.

[274] Lev. r. 23. 3.   R. Azarja in his name, Cant. r. 2. 6; Exod. r. 24. 4.

[275] Gen. r. 43. 10: מכח אותה ברכה אכלו ג׳ יתידות גדולות בעולם

Judah ben Simon took also part in the discussion: 'For whose merit did Israel cross the Jordan?' He suggests, for Joseph's sake.[276] *R. Josiah* repeats the doctrine of the children's merits. God has patience with the wicked in this world, for they may repent or perform the observances, so that God will repay their reward in this world, or perhaps they will bring forth righteous children, as it was in the case of Ahaz and Hezekiah, Amon and Josiah, Shimei and Mordecai.[277] *Acha bar Hanina* was an outspoken opponent of those people who relied on the merits of the fathers. He applies Ezek. 18. 6 to a man who is just and does that which is lawful and right, who does not avail himself of the merits of his fathers (and hath not eaten upon the mountains, i. e. the merits of the fathers הרים = אבות מעשה), who is meek ('hath not lifted up his eyes to the idols', idolatry and pride are identical in the eyes of the Scribes), who does not trespass the craft of his fellow man ('hath not defiled his neighbour's wife'), and who claims nothing of the poor (i. e. 'hath not come near to a woman in her impurity').[278] This teacher looks with contempt, as it seems, upon a man whose only merit is to be an insignificant son of a great father, an unworthy descendant of a worthy and just ancestor. It may be that some of his contemporaries were referred to. *Zeira*, one of R. Jochanan's circle, a Babylonian by birth, teaches us that it was then proverbial in Palestine to promote charitable work with the words: בי זכי 'Acquire merits unto yourself by doing charity or good work'.[279] Another contemporary, *R. Samuel ben Isaac*, preserved also a Palestinian proverbial saying, which throws light upon an aspect of our doctrine: 'Shela sinned, and Jochana is punished.' The starvation which was in the days of David

אברהם יצחק ויעקב באברהם כתיב ויי ברך את אברהם בכל בזכות ויתן לו
מעשר מכל Gen. 24. 11 ; 27. 33 ; 33. 11.

[276] Gen. r. 84. 5, v. above to Simon of קטרון, p. 47.

[277] Eccles. r. 7. 32.   [278] b. Sanh. 87 a.

[279] Lev. r. 34. 7.

ought to have been in the days of Saul. Yet Saul was
but a branch of a Sycamore tree, i. e. too unimportant,
therefore did God bring it in the days of David.[280] This
Agadist speaks further of the merits of the children (v.
p. 161).

(5) The Agadah of the Amoraim of the third century,
from about 219 to 280, is the work of many great teachers.
This can be seen in the unusually large number of the
scribes on the one hand, and in the quality as well as in the
substance of their sayings on the other hand. Some of them
reached the highest possible standard of ethical teaching,
some of them merely reproduced or varied ideas and
teachings of previous generations. There is to be noticed
only a slight echo of the dispute on the question, whether
we owe our salvation and happiness and success to self-
acquired merits or to vicarious virtues, which was characteristic of the Tannaitic discussions. The teachers in
Sepphoris and Tiberias, at Lydda and Caesarea, recognized
and repeatedly emphasized in their teachings the doctrine
of the merits of the fathers, perhaps with the exception of
R. Eleazar of Modiim, more strongly than in the second
century. In the same manner the merits of Abraham, of
Isaac, of Jacob, of Joseph, of Moses and Aaron, are subjects
of various and frequent exegetical and theological aspects
to their mind.

Yet in this period we detect a stronger objection to the
abuses to which the doctrine of vicarious virtues might or
actually did lead. This accounts first of all for the greater
influence of the doctrine of God's grace in contemporary
theology. Secondly, this opposition appears in the outspoken censure or condemnation of those who have no
virtues of their own, wilfully neglecting their duties, men
who do not even try to get merits of their own, for they
rely upon the treasures gathered by their ancestors. It
is not difficult to see how far the old dispute between

---

[280] Gen. r. 25. 3, 40. 64; M. Sam., p. 131; Ruth r., ch. 1. 6; Pes. 113 в.
Macc. 11 a has the version טוביה חטא וזיגוד מינגד.

Shemaiah and Abtaljon was carried on with the old weapons and new arguments. Sometimes we find that the opponents are at the same time the defenders of the doctrine of vicarious merits. We see in the latter school the successors of that compromise ascribed previously to Hillel.

More developed in the Agadah of the third century is the doctrine of the merits of the children. By the piety and charity of the children, ancestors benefit in this world as well as in the world to come. There is really none so wretched who has no merits of his own. This applies, of course, first of all to Israel, as having more opportunities and means to acquire merits. But even the nations of the world have merits, either of their own or on account of their ancestors. Further, the nations derive great advantages from the merits of Israel. The origin of this conception lies in the aspect of the solidarity of mankind. There has to be solidarity in the individual himself, where merits and sins balance each other. Further, a solidarity between parents and children, members of one family, parts of a larger or smaller society, and finally between various societies, different nations and races. Just as one limb of the body when diseased causes pain to the whole body, so one sin in a man or family or nation imperils the whole body or bands of bodies, i.e. mankind. The same is the case with merits. The merits of the righteous protect even those who cannot boast of having virtues. Our merits as well as our sins are shared by our fellow men, posterity as well as by ancestors. Israel, as the bearer of God's word, has in this respect a special privilege and a higher responsibility. The latter is apparent in the great means of merits. The number of means acquiring merits is larger in this period than in the time of the Tannaim. Besides the merits of the study of the Law and of circumcision, in particular, the merits of the observances generally are more conspicuous. Other merits, like those of faith, of sacrifices, of chastity, of repentance, of tithes, are occasionally mentioned.

Vicarious sin is the counterpart of vicarious virtue. Just as the merits of the fathers influence most beneficently the life and fortunes of the children, so the sins of the fathers destroy the happiness of or bring evil to the children. The same relation is to be seen in the merits of the children and their sins respectively. Finally, we observe this relation in the advantages obtained by the environment of the righteous and just men, and in the death of the latter on account of their contemporaries' sins. Here in the effect of the sins, as there in merits, the ruling idea is: Human solidarity. One is responsible for the other for good or for evil.

We have seen that the Agadists were influenced by contemporary events in propagating or formulating their doctrines. Two outstanding events are to be pointed out here. One is of internal, the other of external character. The internal is signified by the peculiar social and economic conditions under which Jews lived in Galilee in the third century. In consequence of the abnormal political life, sacred earnestness and serious retrospect were lost, and the thirst for petty social advantages, and hunger for Mammon corrupted especially the so-called upper layers of society, who arrogated to themselves the leadership of the community. Sanctity of family life on one side, conscientious loyalty to Judaism on the other, were endangered by these changes; no wonder that most of the preachers—being good preachers—had the courage to tell their people their sins. Maybe the picture appears too dark, but there is no smoke without fire, and preachers like R. Hanina b. Hama or R. Jochanan b. Nappacha, must have well considered their reproaches, before they ascribed plague or pestilence to the sins of their communities, or held their contemporaries responsible for the death of the righteous men in their midst.

The second feature is the hostility of the outside world. The Church stood on the threshold of a world empire, on the eve of the great day when it was about to undo the ties which had bound it to Judaism. Jewish law and religion, history and life, past and present, were the target for centuries of cruel misrepresentations, and biased accusations. The Fathers of the Church learnt all the poisonous tricks of the old apostles of hate, the Alexandrinian Anti-Semites. The gospel of hate preached by the Fathers of the Church did more for the conquest of heathendom than the Gospel of Love taught by the founders of Christianity. The Greek mob was more delighted by the anti-Jewish denunciations of the teachers of the Church than by the Sermon on the Mount. This assertion sounds very strong, nevertheless it is true. In this period the old anti-Jewish polemic revived. One accusation frequently heard was—the uselessness and selfishness of the Jews. The Jews do and did nothing for humanity. Is it a matter of surprise if the Scribes tried to prove from the Scriptures that for Israel's sake the world was created, that the world exists, that blessing comes to mankind? Even stronger must have been the crusade against the observances and ceremonies. The latter were always a conscientious trouble to the Church. People were reminded of them, they take the same part of the Bible as chap. 53 of Isaiah. If the latter is to be taken literally, why not the other parts? The more or less fine theological theories and hypotheses were all very well for the academies and colleges; the plain man in the street was well aware that there was something wrong in the whole edifice. Then the leaders of the Synagogue might have been aware that the observances are the corner-stones of Judaism, despised by the builders of the new Temple. There is nothing more likely to imperil the future of Judaism than the neglect or extirpation of the observances. It is no wonder therefore that the Church Fathers do not get tired of teaching, preaching, and writing against them. They are idolatry! they are abhorred by God! they are everything else than good! Only a strong will and a firm conviction could withstand these attempts. The majority might have been

G

inclined to listen to the voice of the serpent. The Rabbis,
by preaching about the great merits of the observances,
did their share to avert the destruction which threatened
the House of Jacob.

(6) The list of the Amoraic Agadists in the fourth
century may be headed by *R. Helbo*, who derives from
Gen. 12. 16 that blessing in the home is to be attributed
to the merits of women, therefore man should be careful
to honour his wife.[281] A very remarkable saying on our
subject is preserved in the name of *R. Aibo.* He taught
that there are three groups of people. The first set holds
that it is quite sufficient reward for men having been
created to see the planets and stars. The second set does
not want any reward in this world. The reward may be
preserved for the world to come. The third set is that
of the lazy workmen who say : ' Give us now, for our deeds
as well as for the deeds of our fathers.'[282] There were
people who did not expect any reward at all for their good
deeds, for the charity and observances they performed.
The admiration of nature recompensed them for everything.
These philosophers may have been in a great minority.
Others would not forgo their reward, but did not claim
it in this world, and were satisfied to receive it in a future
world. Finally, the last group, which wanted to enjoy the
work of their hands in this world. Besides their own
reward, they tried to reap the rewards due to them on
account of the deeds of the fathers. These were the lazy
labourers. The world was created, we hear in another
saying, for man's sake. God prepared everything necessary
for man, and then man was created. Like a king who
had a palace full of the best things, if there were no people
to enjoy the good things, what pleasure would he derive

---

[281] b. B. M. 59 a : לעולם יהא אדם זהיר בכבוד אשתי שאין הברכה
מצויה בתוך ביתו של אדם אלא בשביל אשתו שנ' ולאברהם היטיב
בעבורה.

[282] M. Ps., p. 78, ed. Buber ; v. Cicero, *de nat. deorum*, II, 14 ; cf. Oppenheim, האסיף (IV), 5654, p. 88, note.

therefrom ? [283] God is the king; the palace, this world; the guests, humanity. What is the use of all good and enjoyable things without man? He repeats further the doctrine of the Gentiles' merits. Gentiles are able to acquire merits. To Isa. 63, 'I have trodden the winepress alone, and of the nations there was none with me.' Does God require the help or support of the nations that the prophet says: 'And of the nations there was none with me?' No, but God says: 'When I search the books (פנקסותיהן) of the nations, and there will be found no merit for them before Me, then I tread them in Mine anger, and trample them in My fury' (ibid.).[284] In Gen. 30. 22 R. Aibo sees a reference to the merits of Rachel (ויזכור אלהים תדרחל), of Leah (את רחל), of Jacob (וישמע אליה אלהים), and of the servants (ויפתח את רחמה).[285] The merit of circumcision brings atonement.[285a] R. Reuben also dealt with the question: 'For whose sake was the world created?' He thought, for Jacob's sake![286] R. Hanin repeats that the Manna was given to Israel for the merits of Abraham.[287] New is the idea that the Messiah will come for the merit of kindling the perpetual lamp,[288] and the thought that the cities of the coast, whose ill fame of immorality is often repeated in the literature, exist for the merit of one proselyte, of one God-fearing man, who arises in their midst yearly.[289] Here again we hear that the Gentiles too have merits, or in other words, even among the nations there are righteous, good men. We have no right to generalize by classifying between Israel and Gentiles, as if the former were absolutely good, the latter entirely bad. Another contemporary Agadist, R. Jeremia, found in the word 'Sulamith' (Cant. 7. 1) the thought that the world owes its existence and stability to Israel and to the Torah. Israel is called by God the peacemaker. A nation which solicits peace between God

---

[283] Gen. r. 8. 5.
[284] Esther r. to 1. 1.
[285] Gen. r. 71. 1.
[285a] Gen. r. 47. 9.
[286] Lev. r. 36. 4 ; Tanh. B., I, p. 132 based on Isa. 43. 1.
[287] Exod. r. 25. 5.
[288] Lev. r. 31. 9.
[289] Gen. r. 28. 5.

and the world. For, had Israel not received the Torah, God surely would have destroyed the world.[290] The same idea is taught by *R. Acha*.[291] This Agadist expresses it in different words, when he says: 'The world stands for the sake of those who walk in uprightness, for all the miracles and mighty deeds of God done in the world were performed for the merit of those that walk upright in the way.'[292] He took part in the great discussion which engaged the mind of the teachers in the third century, as to the period when the merits of the fathers ceased to work, and held that they never ceased and never will cease to operate.[293] As to the problem, for whose sake the world was created—a question dealt with by nearly all the important Agadists of this period—R. Acha derives from Deut. 33. 21 that it was for the merits of Moses.[294] God forgave Israel, after the deed of the golden calf, for the merits of Abraham.[295] Further, he derives from Ps. 123. 3–4 that Jerusalem will be rebuilt for the merits of the tribes;[296] and, finally, he repeats the view, often expressed by previous teachers, that the observances were given as an opportunity to acquire merits;[297] but not as it was taught by the Church as a punishment or degradation. *R. Judan* advances three theories on the problem for whose merits the world was created. The first teaches us that for Abraham's merits.[298] The second assumes that the world was created for the sake of the Torah.[299] In the third saying we are told: 'Great is the fear of God, for heaven and earth were only created for the merit of fear,' as it is said, Eccles. 3. 14, 'and God did it in

[290] Cant. r. 77. 1 ; Gen. r. 66 2 ; R. Idi.

[291] Gen. r. 66. 2.

[292] M. Ps., ed. Buber, p, 488.

[293] Lev. r. 36. 5 ; j. Synh. 27 d.

[294] Lev. r., ch. 36. 4, v. however, b. Synh. 98 B where the saying is attributed to Samuel ben Nahmani.

[295] Exod. r. 44. 4.

[296] Tanh. I, p. 174, M. Ps. Pr. 67 a.   [297] Lev. r. 31. 8.

[298] M. Ps., ed. Buber, p. 444 ; Gen. r. 12. 8 ; M. Samuel, 9. 2.

[299] Gen. r. 12. 2, v. however Pes. r., p. 14 a, *R. Judah b. Shalom.*

order that they shall have fear before Him.' [300]   There is, however, no contradiction in these three theories, for Abraham embodies the idea of Torah and the fear of God. The two latter ideas complete one another. Study or knowledge of the Torah is worthless without fear of God, just as the latter is incomplete without the former. The blessing in business and daily transactions in due to the merit of Jacob.[301]   For the merit of the song at the sea (Exod. 15. 2) Israel was clothed by God during the forty years' journey in the wilderness (Deut. 18. 4).[302]   Finally, we have to mention a catalogue of merits which are enumerated by R. Judan, for the purpose of explaining which merits enabled the High Priest to enter the Holy of Holies on the Day of Atonement. These merits are: (1) Torah (Deut. 4. 44); (2) Circumcision (Gen. 17. 10); (3) Sabbath (Isa. 56. 2); (4) Jerusalem (Ezek. 5. 5); (5) the Tribes (Gen. 49. 28); (6) Judah (Deut. 23. 7); (7) Israel (Cant. 7. 8); (8) the holy gifts (Exod. 25. 3); (9) tithes (Mal. 3. 10); and (10) sacrifices (Lev. 16. 3).[303]   *R. Joshua ben Nehemia* gives us also his opinion on a burning question of his time, when he says: 'For the merits of the tribes was the Universe created' (v. p. 124). In another passage he warned his audience not to rely too much on the merits of others. He makes God say in a legend: ' You think, O Israel! you may freely make Me angry, because the image of Jacob is engraved on My throne of glory. Lo! here it is, and He cast down from heaven the glory of Israel.' [304]   The image of Jacob engraven on the throne of glory in heaven— an old Agadic idea—misled many people, who erred, saying : ' We do not want our own merits, those of Jacob will protect us ! ' This teacher replied to them : ' You must get original merits, and do not rely on those of your

---

[300] Eccles. r. 3. 17.

[301] Cant. 3. 6, אבקת = ויאבק ; Gen. r. 32. 25 ; Cant. r. 3. 5.

[302] M. Ps., ed. B., p. 198.

[303] Pes. 176 a ; Lev. r. 21 ; Pes. r. 191 a, in all verses זאת is used just as in Lev. 16. 8 ; v. also Exod. r. 36. 8 ; Tanh. I, p. 102.

[304] Lam. 2. 1 ; Lam. 2. 1, v. also *R. Isaac* Lam r. 2. 7.

ancestors!' His contemporary *R. Phinehas ben Hama*
enters into the theoretical side of our doctrine, saying that
a man should not claim the reward for his good works
and deeds at once. Had the fathers claimed their due
reward at once, how could the seed of the pious have been
saved?[305] This teaching implies—especially as given in
Exod. r. 44. 3—that God pardoned Israel's sin for the
merits of the fathers; secondly, the surplus of merits which
the fathers or the righteous accumulate, holds good for
posterity or for their contemporaries respectively. We
can understand, therefore, why he thinks that the Israelites
were redeemed from Egypt for the merits of the pious
women (p. 142), or that the seventy rams Israel offered up
are done for the seventy nations. For these sacrifices rain
came down even for the Gentiles.[306]

One of the most prominent Agadists of the fourth
century was *R. Berechja*, who explains first of all the
theory of our doctrine, when he says: 'Even at a time
when Israel has no deeds, God helps them, so that His
might and name shall be known.'[307] Even without meritorious works God assists Israel. In agreement with this
saying is another teaching of the same scribe. In case
the merits of the fathers (the mountains) are shaken and
those of the mothers (the hills) tremble, i. e. cannot help,
God's grace never forsakes them.[308] The world was
created for Israel's sake,[309] it stands for the merits of the
righteous.[310] 'Although,' says God, 'I created and I bear
(carry) the world, still, when there are righteous men in
the world, it is as if they carry (keep up) it.' God does
not require the help of the righteous to keep the world
going. Yet as a sign of appreciation they are regarded

[305] j. Synh. 27 d ; Lev. r. 36. 3 ; Exod. r. 44. 3.
[306] Pes. 193 B ; Lam. r. 1. 23; Cant. r. 1. 15; 4. 1 ; M. Ps., p. 464 ; Tanh.
IV, p. 156; Num. r., ch. 21, 22, anonym.
[307] M. Ps., ed. B., p. 314 f.; Midrash in Jalkut, par. 792.
[308] j. Synh. 27 d, v. Lev. r. 36. 4, v. p. 13.
[309] Gen. r. 1. 1, based on Jer. 2. 3 ; Lev. r. 36. 4 ; Gen. r. 1. 4, R. *Acha.*
[310] *Agadath Bereshith,* ed. Buber, p. 115.

as co-bearers of this world. Of the righteous men and women he emphasizes particularly the merits of Moses, Aaron, and Miriam,[311] for whose sake the manna, the well, and the clouds of glory accompanied Israel in the wilderness (v. above, pp. 61 and 76, n. 170). Another doctrine, often discussed in the third century, was also developed by R. Berechja. Even in trouble and distress, he says, God remains Israel's friend. God chooses one just man who is able to uphold the course of judgement, and says : ' Enough ! This just man is a pledge for Israel.' His name is אשכל, i. e. who studied all branches of the Torah, he atones for all sins of Israel by means of the merits of the fathers of the world, who obeyed God like goats and received the blessing of the world.[312]

R. Abun repeats the doctrine that for Israel's sake was the world created (v. p. 109). The redemption from Egypt was not for the merits of the fathers, but for the sake of God's grace.[313] Yet when Moses prayed before God after the deed of the golden calf, he invoked the merits of the righteous, the patriarchs included.[314] The merit of the observances has power to change curses into blessing.[315] In R. Judah b. Shalom's Agadah we find likewise that the Universe was created for Israel's sake ;[316] and, secondly, the doctrine of God's grace. If we have merits of our own, if we have good deeds, then God gives us of our own ; if not, He does charity, and shows us grace of His own free will.[317] R. Azarja repeats and supports the view of R. Joshua ben Korha that the world was created for the sake of Abraham.[318] God's help in distress is also due to the merit of Abraham.[319] Like R. Judan, he ascribes Israel's success in this world in war or peace (study) to the

[311] Lev. r. 27. 6.   [312] Cant. r. 1. 60–61 ; Gen. r. 44. 6.

[313] Cf. Ps. 107. 1 ; Deut. 9. 4–6 ; M. Ps., p. 461, according to some MSS. for R. Huna Hakohen b. Abin.

[314] Exod. r. 44. 7.

[315] Lev. r. 35. 1 אם זכיתם.   [316] Tanh. I, p. 2.

[317] Isa. 3. 10 ; M. Ps., ed. B., p. 324.

[318] Gen. r. 12. 8.   [319] Gen. r. 44. 16.

merit of Jacob.[320] *R. Tanhuma*, the last of the great
Agadists, compares Israel with the vine. Just as the latter
is supported by dead wood, so living Israel relies on the
merit of the fathers.[321]

Of the other Agadists of this period, we have in general
very little material dealing with our doctrine. We have
to refer merely to six or seven scribes. *Ahaba ben Zeira*
is represented with a saying that even the sins of the
righteous bring blessing to the world. The children of
Jacob sold Joseph, and by doing so, brought blessing to
the world.[322] *R. Hanina ben Isaac*, older than R. Joshua
ben Nehemia, advances two theories on the problem of
the creation. In one saying he says: ' Heaven and earth
were created for the merit of Jacob.' [323] In another saying
of his, we have the doctrine that for Israel's merit the
Universe was created. He explains the name of שפרה
(Exod. 1. 15) who kept Israel alive,[324] for whose sake heaven
and earth were created.[325] In his theology the ' merits ' are
considered like charms. God says to the genius of Esau
when he fought Jacob (Gen. 32. 25): He comes against
you with five charms, with his own merit, with that of his
father, mother, grandfather, and grandmother. Consider
whether you are able to withstand even his own merit ? [326]
He sees further in Ezek. 9. 4 a proof for those who held
that the merits of the fathers ceased before the destruction
of the first temple.[327] Of *R. Hijja b. Nehemia* we have
the important saying that in the days of the Messiah there
will be neither merits nor sins.[328] According to *R. Hela*
just men are able to avert punishment which is about to

---

[320] Cant. r. 3 5; v. p. 101.   [321] Exod. r. 44. 1.

[322] Gen. r. 84. 16, עבירתן של שבטים זכות היא לעולם.

[323] Ps. 78. 5 and Deut. 4. 26; Lev. r. 36. 4.

[324] Read instead of שהעמידה ישראל לאלהים the words לעולם.

[325] שפרה, v. Job 26. 13; Exod. r. 1. 17.

[326] Gen. r. 77. 3; Cant. r. 3. 6.

[327] Lam. r. 1. 2, v. Samuel b. Sabb. 55 a.

[328] Eccles. r. 12. 1; Lev. r. 18. 1; v. above, p. 7, 7.

come to this world.[329]   R. *Idi* teaches that the world exists
for the merit of Israel.[330]   In a similar sense is his explanation of the word שולמות Chron. 2. 1 to be understood.[331]
R. *Nahman*, the son of R. *Samuel b. Nahmani*, ascribes the
redemption from Egypt to the merits of five righteous
men : Abraham, Isaac, Jacob, Moses, and Aaron. The
latter are like the five leaves which distinguish the thorn-
bush from all other trees.[332]   This scribe, who is one of
the last of the Palestinian Amoraim, expresses Hillel's
view. The merits of the fathers with the merits of the
contemporaries achieved the redemption.   He teaches
further, that for all the vanities and falsehood which
the sons of man, i. e. the children of Abraham, commit
in this world, the merit of Abraham is great enough to
atone.[333]   R. *Samuel b. Ami* taught the same idea,
finding a reference in Ps. 3. 3 to the merits of the
fathers.   David says: 'But Thou hast been a shield about
me, Thou hast protected me by the merits of the fathers.'[334]
Halafta ben Kahana repeats the often-mentioned view
that the world was created for the merit of Abraham, yet
not only this world, but even the world to come.[335]
Another Agadist, about whose age information is lacking,
Menachem b. Zeira was the only one who pointed out the
merits of the martyrs in the Hadrianic persecutions. God
rebuilt the world after the flood for the merits of these
martyrs.[336]   R. *Abba b. Hanina* taught that the merit of
the Synhedrion protects the whole world.[336 a]

(7) In the Agadah of the fourth century, we see that the
question for whose merit was the world created played
a most important part.   With very few exceptions, all the

[329] Lev. r. 2. 6, v. Bacher, *Agada der Pal. Amoräer*, III, p. 701, n. 6 ; read
perhaps R. Eleazar.

[330] M. Ps., ed. Buber, p. 32 ; Pes. r., p. 356 ; Cant. r. 7. 3 ; Tanh. II,
p. 105 ; v. p. 132

[331] Gen. r. 66. 2 ; *Agadath Cant.* to 2. 1, v. R. Acha, p. 100.

[332] Exod. r. 2. 5.   [333] Lev. r. 29. 7.

[334] Pes. 10 B ; Tanh. II, p. 106 ; M. Ps., ed. B., p. 38.

[335] Tanh. B. II, p. 6.

[336] Gen. 8. 21 ; Ps. 24. 2, 6 ; Gen. r. 34. 9.

[336 a] b. Synh. 37 a.

great teachers dealt with it, from one point of view or other. The majority held the view that for Israel's sake the Universe was created. This can and will be explained by the conditions prevailing in the communal and religious life on one side, and by the currents of intellectual growth or decline, the trend of philosophical as well as theological speculation, on the other. It must be more than a pure accident when R. Aibo, R. Reuben, R. Acha, R. Judah ben Shalom, R. Joshua ben Nehemia, R. Berechja, R. Abun, R. Azarja, R. Hanina b. Isaac, R. Idi, and Halafta ben Kahana, eleven Agadists, dealt with the same problem. These scribes, famous as teachers and successful as defenders of their religion and nation, fought for Israel's honour with the Scripture in their hands, and with immeasurable love in their heart. Israel despised by low and high, supposed to be forsaken by God—to suit the doctrine of the Church Fathers—a nation alleged to have done nothing for the human race, contributed no blessing for the advancement of mankind. Thus or similarly sounded the verdict of contemporary public opinion on Jews and Judaism. No wonder, when these Scribes of the House of Jacob raised their voice, and taught: 'For Israel's merit was the world created.' They settled in the same manner the problem: 'For whose merit does the world exist?' Certainly for Israel's sake, the bearer of the ideals embodied in the Torah.

Another important topic of the Agadah in this period is the frequent reference to the merits of the fathers generally, and to some of the biblical personages especially. The surplus merits of the fathers bring happiness and forgiveness in the hands of their children, and influence the wonderful course of Israel's history. Besides these merits, there are those of the righteous and pious women. It must be an eternal glory of those scribes, and reveals us their mentality, when they say: 'The blessing of the house is mainly in the honour and happiness of women!' What mothers and wives stood by the side of such teachers? They surely must have had in their own midst womanhood, worthy in piety and glorious self-sacrifice, of whom they could say: 'For their merits was Israel redeemed from Egypt.' Whilst they acknowledge vicarious merits they teach also the necessity of original virtue and the doctrine of God's grace. A slight opposition to the misuse of the doctrine is also to be observed in this period. This appears in a more or less clear condemnation of those who rely entirely upon the merits of others, as well as in the discussion, whether the merits of the fathers are still available or not. In this period we have for the first time a catalogue of merits.

(8) The Babylonian Agadah, much poorer than the Palestinian, preserved only a few sayings on our doctrine. R. Helbo quotes a prayer of Solomon, which was taught in the school of R. Sheila. Solomon says: 'If I have no works of my own, help for the grace of my father David.'[337] *Rab* says that the righteous man has the power to over-rule the decrees of heaven, and by doing so to protect his contemporaries (v. p. 69). He took part with *Samuel* in the discussion as to the period when the influence of the merits of the fathers ceased in Jewish history.[337a] Rab himself was regarded as a man of great merits,[338] likewise *R. Ada b. Ahava*. A saying by *R. Judah b. Ezekiel* on the aim of the creation (v. p. 115) is perhaps falsely ascribed to him. *Raba* (רבא) held that life, children, and riches do not depend on merits, but on the influence of the planets. He gives as an instance the lives of two great teachers, Rabbah and R. Hisda, who lived before him.[339] A man may have great merits, still he may have a short life, unworthy children, and poverty; on the other hand a man with no merits to speak of has often a long life, good children, and riches. Raba, typical Babylonian scholar as he was, believed in the rule of stars and planets.[340]

---

[337] Pes. r. 67 a: אם אין לי מעשים עשה בשביל חסדו של דוד אבי, v. *MGWJ.*, 1894, p. 176.

[337a] v. p. 104, note 327.

[338] v. b. Taan. 21 в.

[339] b M. K., p. 29 a.

[340] v. above, p. 34.

II

(1) *For whose sake was the world created?* This question attracted the attention of the scribes to the same extent as it occupied the thoughts of the philosophers and Church Fathers of the first four centuries. God, who created the world, must have had some purpose in view. What was that purpose? The answer of the *Stoics* was accepted by the early Church Fathers. This school of philosophers taught that the world was created for *the sake of man*.[1] In Hellenistic Jewry it was taught by Philo[2] and by the Sibylline Oracles.[3] The Apologist of the Church, *Marcus Aristides* of Athens, says in his letter to Titus Hadrianus Antoninus: 'I declare that God is the Lord of the Universe, and that He made everything for the sake of man' (I. 3). *Justin Martyr* says in the same way: 'And we were taught that He created of a formless matter everything *for the sake of man*' (*Apol.* I. 10. 2). The author of the letter *to Diognetus*, while opposing the teachings of the Jews, remarks: 'How is it possible to assume that some of the things, which God created for the use of mankind, should be good, and others bad?' (IV. 2), and more explicitly on another occasion: 'God loved all the creatures; for their sake has He created everything on earth, subdued everything beneath them, and given to them speech and understanding' (X. 2). We need not quote the similar

---

[1] v. Zeller, *Die Philosophie der Griechen*, 3rd ed., III, p. 172; Geffken, *Zwei griech. Apologeten*, p. 33. Seneca says: 'Gods are full of mercy and loving-kindness, everything they do is for our good, for our sake have they created all things,' v. Keim, *Rom und Christentum*, p. 32, and *Theophil. ad Autol.*, I, 6, II, 10.

[2] *De prov.*, II, 84; *De mundi opificis* (I, 12), and *De nominum mutatione* (IV, 340).

[3] IV, 16, cf. Geffken, *Komposition und Entstehungszeit der Oracula Sybillina*, pp. 18–21.

sayings in the kindred literature,[4] for our purpose it is sufficient to add the words of the *Clementine Recognitions* which include all the others: ' He made man, on whose account He had prepared all things, whose internal species is older, and for whose sake all things that were made, were given up to his service, and assigned to the uses of his habitation' (I. ch. 28).[4a] The Recognitions offer us the philosophical view in a clear and definite way. All things are made for man. Celsus, the heathen philosopher, throws light upon some points of controversy between Jews and Christians, teaching that both assume : 'All things are for their uses, earth, water, air, and planets; for their sake were all things created, for their services were all things appointed.'[5] According to this information the original idea went through a not unimportant altera- tion. Christians thought that all things were not created for man generally, but for the sake of Christians only. Likewise Jews. Origen himself adopts the Stoic view quoted above in its original form (v. IV. 74 and 99), yet Celsus must have had some evidence for his statement, which is confirmed by the Jewish writings. *R. Nehemia*, in the name of *R. Abun*, taught with reference to Isa. 40. 24 ('Yea, they shall not be planted, yea they shall not be sown ; yea, their stock shall not take root in the earth'), 'The Nations of the World have neither plant nor seed, nor root (Isa. 40. 24), and all the three are in one verse' ; but as to Israel, all three expressions are applied. They are planted, as it is said; 'I plant them in the earth' (Amos 9. 15), and it is written: 'To plant them in their land' (ibid.). They have seed (sowing), as it is written: 'I will sow them in the land' (Hos. 2. 25). They have a root, as it is said: ' He shall cause them that come of Jacob to take root' (Isa. 27. 6). This is to be compared to the dispute between the *straw, chaff,* and *stalk* in the

[4] v. Pred. Petri ; Clemens, *Strom.* IV, 5–40 ; Hermas, XII, 4. 2.

[4a] v. also Clem. Hom. III, 36 and XI, 23; cf. Schliemann, *Die Clementi- nen*, pp. 149 and 169.

[5] *Origen c. Cels.*, IV, 23.

parable. Each of them says : ' For my sake was the field
sown.' The wheat says to them : ' Wait until the time
comes, we shall be brought to the threshing floor, and we
will know for certain for whose sake the field was sown.'
When they are brought, then the owner starts to winnow,
the chaff is carried away by the wind ; he takes the straw
and throws it on the ground, then the stalk, and burns it, but
he takes the wheat and makes it into an heap. The same
is the case with the Nations of the World. Some of them
say : *We are Israel, and for our sake was the world
created !* Others say : *We are Israel, and for our sake
was the world created !* Israel says : ' Wait until the day
of the Lord comes, and we shall know for whose sake the
world was created ! ' [6]

The author of this parable is *R. Abun I* (about 300),
when Christians disputed among themselves as to which
sect has got the right to be called the true Israel.[7] Then
R. Abun proceeds to attack the Christians by saying that
they are fruitless—an argument often raised in the first
centuries by heathens against the Jews. Yet the idea of
the teaching that the world was created for Israel's sake
is older than R. Abun. Besides the testimony of Celsus,
we have a similar parable by an anonymous teacher.[8] We
also read the same parable in the Acts of the Martyrs
of Smyrna (about 250) in the speech delivered by Pionius
to the Jews of the same city. ' Imagine a floor filled with
wheat. Is the heap of chaff greater than that of wheat ?
When the farmer with the fork or with hand turns the
wheat, the chaff is blown away by the wind, the heavy
corn remains ' (IV. 14). This seems to be the answer to
the rabbis' contention that they are the wheat, and the
Christians the chaff. We may therefore rightly assume
that the idea and parable are older than R. Abun, just

---

[6] Cant. r. 7. 7, *vide* Wertheimer's בתי מדרשות, IV, 21 ; Pes. r. 36 a.

[7] On the subject see my *Religionsgeschichtliche Studien*, I, pp. 9–18.

[8] Gen. r. 83, 4 ; M. Ps., ed. Buber, p. 16 a. Israel is the wheat of the
world, v. Num. r. 1. 4 ; Tanh., ed. Frkft. 190 B.

as we have proofs that the teaching that the world was created for the sake of Christians is older than Origen, although he seems to pretend as if Celsus attacked the Christians for holding such views, without any justification. Hermas and the II Clemens letter (ch. 14) make it clear that the Church is older than the world, yea, for the sake of the Church was the world created.[9] It was, therefore, nothing else but pure defence, when the rabbis altered the original Stoic teaching that for the sake of Israel was the world created. Before we consider the sayings of the scribes, we have to refer to *IV Ezra* 6. 56 where the Apocalypsist says: 'I said all these before Thee, O Lord, because Thou didst speak that Thou createst this world for our sake, but all the nations are like nothing' (Isa. 40. 17).[10] We see that the author of this book preached that it was for His people's sake that the world was created. A similar teaching is preserved in the Syriac *Baruch*. The author is well aware of the Doctrine that the world was made for man generally. 'Thou didst say', he remarks, 14. 4 f., 'Thou wilt make man for Thy world, as a ruler of all Thy creatures, so that people may recognize that man was not made for the sake of the world, but just the reverse, the world was made for man's sake. And now, I see, the world made for man's sake continues to exist; we, however, for whose sake it came into being, perish!' God's reply is in the affirmative. 'Yes, it is so, but not for man generally. The world was made for the sake of the righteous' (15. 7). The world was created for such righteous men like Abraham, Isaac, and Jacob (21. 24). The *Assumptio Mosis* leaves no doubt whatever what its author believed. The world was created for the sake of Israel, or according to some emendation for the sake of the Torah [1. 12, if we read *legem* instead of *plebem*], which really, as will be seen later on, amounts to the same thing. For the Law, the Torah, was created from the very begin-

---

[9] v. Harnack, *Dogmengeschichte*, I, pp. 99 and 759.
[10] v. also 6. 59 and 7. 11.

ning of the world, as the first thing of the creation, yet
given to Israel and not to the children of Adam.

It is significant that the teaching as expressed by IV Ezra,
in the report of Celsus and in the Agadah of R. Abun is
unknown to the Tannaitic Agadah as well as to the earlier
Amoraim.   The first Agadist who taught so was *R. Simon
ben Lakish*, in the middle of the third century (v. p. 78 f.).
The whole context leaves no shadow of a doubt that
apologetical reasons induced the teachers to revive this
older view.   After R. Simon ben Lakish there is a whole
group of teachers who adopted or varied this teaching—
R. Levi, R. Abba b. Kahana, R. Berechja, R. Acha, R. Judah
ben Shalom, R. Hanina ben Isaac, and R. Acha ben Abba.
R. Levi avails himself of the simile of wheat.   Wherefore
is Israel compared with wheat?   Just as the landlord
when he comes to reckon with his tenant farmer (בֶּן בַּית),
what does he count?   What does he say to him?   Does
he perhaps say how many baskets (מַשְׁפֶּלֶת) of straw, or
how many baskets of stubble or thorns didst thou bring to
the storehouse?   Where does he put the straw?   Into
the fire!   Where does he throw the manure?   On the
dunghill!   Where the stubble?   To the wind!   What does
he actually say to the farmer?   'How much wheat hast
thou brought in?'   Why?   Because it is the vital element
of the world (חִיּוּתוֹ).   God is the landlord, for the whole
world belongs to Him (cf. Ps. 24. 1).   The farmer is Moses
(cf. Num. 12. 7).   God did not say to him: 'Make up your
mind to count the nations, who are compared with stubble
(cf. Exod. 15. 7; Obad. 1. 18), with thorns (Isa. 33. 12), with
straw (Job 21. 18)!   Moses was, however, commanded to
count Israel, who is compared with wheat.[11]   R. Levi must
have known the parable of wheat and straw; the underlying doctrine of which was that the field was sown for
the sake of wheat only.   For the sake of Israel only was
the world created.   Israel is compared with wheat in an

[11] Pes. r. 35 B–36 A.

anonymous saying, based on Cant. 7. 36: 'Thy womb is
like a heap of wheat', i. e. Israel, 'set about with lilies',
these are the righteous.[12] We may take it for granted
that R. Levi held the view of R. Simon ben Lakish, that
the universe was created for Israel's sake.

R. Abba b. Kahana derives this teaching from Jer. 2. 3.
Israel is holy unto the Lord, His first-fruit. How was
God's greatness recognized? By His work in creating the
heaven and earth. And for whose merit did He create it?
For the merit of Israel, as it is said: 'His first-fruit of its
produce.'[13] R. Berechja compares בראשית Gen. 1. 1, with
Jer. 2. 3, and derives the view that the Universe was
created for the merit of Israel.[14]

R. Judah ben Shalom found also a proof for this doctrine
in the word בראשית, which could have been replaced either
by מקדם or by בתחלה. The word was chosen deliberately
in order to allude to Jer. 2. 3, and teach that the Universe
was created for Israel's sake.[15] *R. Hanina ben Isaac*
refers to this doctrine in his explanation of the name שפרה
(v. p. 104), although he had another theory as well on this
question. *R. Acha bar Abba*[16] mentions this teaching in
a legend: God made up His mind to destroy the whole
world (באותה שעה בקש הקב״ה להחזיר את כל העולם כולו לתוהו ובהו),
and He said: 'The whole Universe which I created, I did
for the sake of these, as it is said: I will also smite My

[12] Aboth, *R. Nathan*, ed. Schechter, p. 12 f, 2nd version, and *Agadath
Shir Hashirim*, ed. Schechter, p. 91, v. also Cant. r. 7. 6. Cod. Parma, 626
has this teaching in the name of *R. Gamaliel*.

[13] Tanh., I, p. 6, v. my ed. of *Midrash Haserot we Yeteroth*, p. 29, note 121.

[14] Lev. r. 36. 4, v. however, Gen. r. 1. 5, where R. Berechja teaches that
the Universe was created for the merit of Moses. Yet this view is given
in Lev. r. 36. 4 in the name of *R. Acha*. There can be no doubt that the
correct reading ought to be : אמ׳ בניה העולם ומלואו לא נברא אלא בזכות
התורה, ר׳ ברכיה אומר שמים וארץ לא נבראו אלא בזכות ישראל, אמר׳
ר׳ אחא בזכות משה.

[15] Tanh. I, p. 4.

[16] v. on this name, *RÉJ*. 33, p. 44; *MGWJ*. 41, p. 607; Bacher,
Agada der Pal. Amoräer, III, 653, n. 8. Hyman, תולדות תנאים ואמוראים,
I, p. 122.

H

hands together, and will satisfy My fury (Ezek. 21. 22). The world I created, I have created only with My hands, as it is said: " And My hands have founded (established) the earth ", &c. (Isa. 48. 13). Now I will destroy it, and satisfy My fury!'[17]

We come across this view very often in the anonymous Agadah. A few instances may suffice. Moses said : מעונה אלהי קדם ' A dwelling-place is the God of Eternity' (Deut. 33. 27), that is Israel, for whose merits the world was created, and upon them (i. e. for their merits) the world exists.[18] Israel is the dwelling-place, for without Israel the world would never have been created, or without Israel's adherence to God's word the world could not exist. A second instance is taken from a homily based on Isa. 40. 25 : 'To whom will you liken me, or shall I be equal ? says the Holy One. Lift up your eyes on high, and behold, who has created these ? For whose merit were *these* created ?' (v. Gen. 2. 4 אלה תולדות). For the merit of Israel (Exod. 1. 1 אלה שמות), for whose merit the world exists, and for the merit of *these* statutes and command-ments (Deut. 4. 45).[19] A third instance occurs in Ps. Jonathan Targum to Num. 22. 30: And the ass said unto Balaam : 'Woe unto Balaam, the fool (חסיר דעתא)! Now I am but an unclean beast, destined to die in this world and to have no share in the world to come, and yet you cannot curse me, how much less can you do so to the children of Abraham, Isaac, and Jacob, for whose sake the world was created. And nevertheless you are going to try to curse them !'[20] Finally, a fourth instance may be cited, preserved in Massechet Gerim (1. 5), where we read the address to the Proselytes spoken by the authorities of the Court. They

[17] Pes. r., p. 135 a, b ; M. Ps. 66 a, ed. Buber, p. 523.

[18] Exod. r. 38. 5.

[19] Exod. r. 48. 2, v. Jalkut, *Machiri. Is.*, ed. Spira, p. 114.

[20] Jelamdenu, ed. Grünhut : הליקוטים 'ס, IV, p. 62 B, reads : ומה האתן שאין לה (לא) זכות ולא ברית אבות נצטויתי לתבוע עלבונה מירך, ישראל שיש להן זכות וברית אבית על אחת כמה וכמה שאתה מבקש לעקור.

said : ' Blessed art thou, who art going to join Him. Who spoke and the world was created. *The world was created for Israel's sake.* Israel is the child of Him. Who is Omnipresent. Israel alone is beloved by Him. What we spoke before (i. e. not to join us) we did in order to make thy merits greater !' These instances prove that the anonymous Agadah accepted the doctrine in the fourth century and onwards.[21] Nothing can prove more strikingly the difference between the address in Mas. Gerim on the one side, and that in the Baraita Jebamot 47 a, where this formulary is quite unknown. Moreover, we have positive proofs that the earlier Agadah differed widely from this conception. First of all we refer to the view that God created the Universe for His own glory. This view was supported by Isa. 43. 7. ' Everything called by My name, have I created for My honour. I formed them, and I made them.' [22] In the Tosefta this saying is attributed to the scribes of the time of the Second Temple, and is based on the text found in Prov. 16. 4: 'The Lord has made everything for His own purpose.' [23] We learn that the old sages held neither the Stoic view, that the world was created for the sake of man, nor was the later view, that the Universe was created for Israel's sake, known to them. A slight echo of this view is perhaps heard in the words of R. Judah.[24] ' God created everything in order that He might be feared.' R. Hijja Rabba and R. Simon ben Halafta seem to dispute the doctrine that the earth belongs to man. Each in a parable. The first speaks of a man who sells a garment in the market (באיטלים). Some one passes and contends: ' It belongs to me ?' The

---

[21] For the later Agadah, v. אותיות דר׳ עקיבה, ed. Wertheimer, p. ה, for Qalir, v. מחזור פסח, ed. Heidenheim, II, p. 100, ובשבילם גיא דוק יצרת.

[22] Aboth, VI, 11 ; Aboth of R. Nathan, 40. 16, ed. Schechter, p. 134.

[23] p. 184, l. 14, b. Jomah 38 a, pal. Jomah 3. 9.

[24] ben Ilai (?), the text refers to Judah b. Ezekiel, b. Sabb. 31 B, v. *Tanna debê Elijah*, p. 5 B.

merchant says: 'Very well, if it suits thee, then it is
thine, if not, it does not belong to thee.' Likewise spake
God with Job. God says: 'Is it not written about Me:
" Indeed, I fill heaven and earth " (Neh. 23. 24), and thou
sayest: "If My land cry against me"' (Job 32. 38).
R. S. b. H. has a similar parable. The merchant sells
a maid-servant. The test is whether she obeys the man
who claims to be the owner.[25] Both seem to teach that
the world belongs to God and for His own glory was it
created. The Church Father, *Irenaeus*, must have had these
Tannaitic doctrines in his mind when he wrote: 'It was
for man's sake, *not for God's glory*, that man was created
from the earth to which we belong' (Haer. V. 16. 1), or
'In the beginning God formed Adam, *not because he stood
in need of man*, but that he might have some one to
receive his benefits' (ibid. IV. 14. 1). It was pure benevolence which induced God to create us (ibid. 2).

Yet we have many traces in the Mishnah also of the
view that for man's sake was everything created. The
Mishnah has the following passage: 'A man who puts
a seal on different materials, they all look alike. How
different is it with God! He puts His seal on each creature,
still all of them are different. Therefore is each individual
obliged to say: 'For my sake was the world created!'[26]
No earth-born being has the right to claim privileges.
All of them are equal and alike, in spite of many differences. For our purpose it is sufficient to establish that
the Mishnah held the view that the Universe was made for
man's sake. *Simon ben Azzai* and *Simon ben Zoma* must
have had some lively discussions on this point. Whilst
Simon ben Azzai represents the view that the Universe
was created for the merit of the God-fearing man,[27] Simon

---

[25] Pes. 98 B; Tanh., *B. V.*, p. 24.   [26] b. Synh. 37 a.

[27] b. Ber. 6 B. The reading is not established beyond doubt, v. p. 45 f.
Saadya had in his text צוח לזה, v. Wertheimer, פי׳ רסע״ג על ברכות,
Jerusalem, 5668, p. 2 B, 'to obey'. Haj Gaon was also asked as to the
correct text of the passage, and reads: צות לזה, and comments: וביאורו

ben Zoma, however, teaches that the world was created for man's sake (v. p. 45 f.). God did not create the world merely for His household, the righteous or pious, but for all mankind.

In the following periods we find scribes who propagated the view of Ben Azzai, and others who sided with Ben Zoma. We turn to the latter first. In the second century R. Joshua ben Korha preached on this theme. On Eccles. 1. 4, ' One generation passeth away, and another generation cometh; but the earth abideth for ever', he remarks, ' Ecclesiastes ought to have said : " The earth passeth away and the earth comes again, but the generation (i. e. man) abideth for ever." Who was created for whom? Was man created for the sake of the earth, or the earth for the sake of man? Surely the earth for the sake of man. Why does Ecclesiastes give expression to the teaching in this way? To tell you: Man passeth away because he does not discharge his duties towards God (שאינו עומר בתפקידו של הקב"ה), but the earth which discharges faithfully God's commandments abideth for ever.' [28] The universe was created for man's sake. Not for a sect or a special nation, but for all mankind. There is no difference between Jews or Gentiles, Greeks or Barbarians, righteous or wicked. For all of them was the world created, yet the earth abideth for ever, whilst man passeth away. The same view was adopted by Simon ben Eleazar and Simon ben Menassja (v. p. 61 f.). They derive it from the life of nature. Beast and birds, sun and moon were created for the service of man. It is not impossible that we have here sayings before us directed against Celsus or other philosophers of the same mind and temperament, who denied that the

חברותא לזה והוא מפורסם בלשונינו שם החברותא צַוְתָא ואמר כי ה' קהלת Wertheimer, v. ,ברא העולם לחברותא לאנשי הדת מפני שהם החפץ שלמה, § 58. Nathan ben Jechiel read לצבות לזה, s. v. צבת 'to please him '. All readings seem to amount to the same thing. The Universe was created to please, or to obey, or to listen to the pious, v. also Rashi.

[28] Eccles. r. 1. 9, v. also above, p. 111 (Syriac Baruch).

world was made for man. The animals might even with
better reason regard themselves as the special objects of
God's care. Man seeks his food with pain and toil. 'The
animals neither sow nor plough, the earth supplies them
freely with all that they may need.' The Rabbis replied:
'If that is the case with the beasts, how much more is it
with man?' In the third and fourth centuries R. Levi [29]
and R. Aibo dwelt on this point. The former says, Eccles.
6. 2, 3, 7, 10; 7. 28; Lev. 4. 1, the word נפש is mentioned
six times, corresponding to the six days of creation. God
says to the soul: 'I created everything for the sake of the
soul, and the soul sinned!' [30]   R. Aibo speaks of people
who found satisfaction in the idea that the Universe was
created for their sake (v. p. 98).

We see that the view of Ben Zoma was represented by
a few scribes, that of Ben Azzai enjoyed much greater
popularity. The impression Ben Azzai's theory made upon
his contemporaries and the following generations can be
classified in two groups. The views of the first set can
be put briefly. The world was created for the sake of the
righteous. The wicked share the benefits and advantages
of the righteous. Righteousness is the aim of the creation.

Some tried to find this ideal of righteousness personi-
fied in the life and deeds of some biblical personages.
Others substitute the Torah, its ideals and teachings,
its duties and the way of life, for the individuals who
represent by their actions and works the ideals laid down
in the Torah. As a matter of fact both preach and teach
the same doctrine. The world was not created in vain. It
was called into existence for the development of that
righteousness, for which the Torah, and with it Judaism
stands. This will explain also the doctrine: For Israel's
sake was the world created.

[29] v. also above, p. 112 f., where R. Levi is represented as having taught
that for Israel's sake was the universe created. Israel as bearer of the
ideals laid down in the Torah may be regarded as the ideal 'man' for
whose sake everything was created.

[30] Lev. r. 4. 2 ; Eccles. r. 7. 16.

Now the question arises: What was the reason why this doctrine, namely, for Israel's sake was the world created, superseded the other view which taught that the Universe was created for man's sake? Secondly, we notice that some of the Apocalyptic writers proclaim the creation as having been made for Israel's sake; the more exclusive teachers of Judaism, the Agadists, adhere to the entirely universalistic view that for man's sake generally was the world created.[31] There must be some historical ground for these facts. Before we attempt to answer these questions, the development of Ben Azzai's doctrine must be stated.

The world was created for the merit of the righteous. Besides Ben Azzai we find this view expressed by 2 Baruch [15. 7–8, v. also 4 Ezra 6. 55]. 'On account of the righteous has this world come into existence, so shall be created the world to come on their account.' *R. Eleazar ben Simon ben Jochai* quotes this view as a generally acknowledged fact.[32] *R. Joshua ben Korha*, whom we saw representing the view that the world was made for man's sake (v. pp. 59 and 117), taught also, if we may trust our texts, that it was created for the sake of the righteous. He explains, namely, Isa. 65. 22 ('as the days of a tree shall be the days of My people'). Under 'Tree' we have to understand, according to Prov. 3. 18, the Torah. If the Torah, which was created for the glory (לכבודן) of Israel, endures for ever, how much more do the righteous, for whose merit the Universe was created.[33] There is also an anonymous statement, preceding that of R. Joshua ben Korha, which may be older than that of R. J. b. K., and expresses the same view somewhat differently, explaining the words 'like the days of heaven and earth' (Deut. 11. 21) as indicating that they will live for ever. Likewise it is said: 'Just as the new heavens and the new earth, which I shall make, will stand before me,

---

[31] v. Harnack, *Dogmengeschichte*, I, p. 99.

[32] Sifrê, Deut., p. 77 B: ק"ו לצדיקים שבעבורן נברא העולם.

[33] Ibid., 83 B. Jalkut reads *R. Simon ben Jochai*.

says the Lord' (Isa. 66. 22). If heaven and earth which
were created for the honour of Israel (לכבודן של ישראל)
stand and exist for ever, then as regards the righteous
for whose sake the world was created (לצדיקים שבעבורם נברא
העולם), how much more will they live for ever.[34] It is to
be noted that the world was not created for Israel's sake,
but for the sake of the righteous (שבעבורם—לכבודן). The
next Agadist who expressed this idea is *R. Jose ben
Hanina.* He gives the following parable. There was
once a king who prepared a banquet, and invited many
strangers. He expected them to come in the fourth, fifth,
or sixth hour of the day, yet they did not arrive. Towards
evening they came, and the king said to them : 'You have
done me a great deal of good (טובה גדולה אני צריך להחזיק לכם),
I have to thank you very much indeed, because if you had
not come, I should have thrown the whole of my banquet
to the dogs!' Thus says God to the righteous: 'I have
to thank you very much indeed! For your sake have
I created the world. Without you, to whom could I give
all the good things which I have prepared?'[35] The aim
of creation is therefore that good and righteous people
shall come, inhabit the earth, and enjoy the banquet which
is ready and prepared. *R. Eleazar ben Pedath* teaches also
in simple words that the world was created for the sake
of even one righteous and God-fearing man (v. p. 83). The
great work of creation is by no means wasted, by no means
futile, if at least one righteous, one God-fearing man is
to be found on it. *R. Abahu* puts meek and modest
people instead of righteous (v. p. 85). A beautiful anonymous Agadah carries this idea farther. 'There is one and
no second' (Eccles. 4. 8). There is one that is the Holy
one, blessed be He, as it is said: 'The Lord is our God.
the Lord is One' (Deut. 6. 4). There is no second one, for
He has no partner in this world (שותף). He has neither
a son, nor a brother. He has no brother, whence shall He

[34] Sifrê, Deut., p. 83 a.
[35] M. Ps., ed. Buber, p. 213, ed. Prague, p. 23 c, to Ps. 31. 20.

have a son? Yet because He loves Israel, therefore He calls them His children (cf. Deut. 14. 1), and calls them brethren and friends (Ps. 122. 8). And there is no end to all His trouble, for all He did in the six days of creation : For whom do I labour, for whom do I deprive My soul from good? Am I not doing it in order that (you shall) join His ways? If there were no righteous men who perform the commandments and do good deeds before Him, would it not be in vain that He created the world? [36] In other words, if there were no righteous people in the world, it would certainly be labour wasted to have created the world. The world was made in order that men shall become good, just, righteous beings, otherwise the creation of the world has no sense. It is childish to assume, according to this Agadist, that a world should have been created without some ultimate aim and ideal. The latter cannot be that men shall eat and drink, play and quarrel, live in travail and leisure, in joy and sorrow, but the purpose is to try to be righteous and good. The banquet is ready, the table is laid for everybody, although only few ought to share it on account of their righteousness. Some of the Agadists give examples of the ideal righteous man for whose sake the world was created. Whilst some have chosen Abraham for their ideal, others speak of Jacob, of the tribes, or of Moses in the same way. An anonymous statement contains the explanation of פתח האהל 'Thou hast opened a good opening (made a good beginning) for the travellers and for the Proselytes. Were it not for thee I had not created heaven and earth, sun and moon.' (The verses referred to are Isa. 40. 22 ; Ps. 19. 5 ; Job 25. 5 ; Gen. r. 48. 7 ; in all the verses אהל occurs.) The meaning of this passage can only be this, that heaven and earth, sun and moon were only created for Abraham's sake. How did the Agadist get this idea of these passages, and what did he mean by פתח טוב פתחת לעוברים ושבים, פתח טוב פתחת

---

[36] Eccles. r. 4. 13.

לגרים? The teaching was based on the two words פתח and האהל. The first word symbolizes Abraham's righteousness, whereby he was distinguished from his contemporaries. Abraham lives in the mind of the Agadists as a man who had shown in his time signs of lovingkindness unknown to the ancient world. He introduced, according to the Agadah, hospitality, a virtue unknown and despised by his selfish contemporaries. The ancient world was based on the principle of family ties. The members of a family have to care for each other, they are responsible for one another, they belong to each other. This praiseworthy virtue changed into narrow-minded selfishness, which limited love and care, human feeling and thought to members of the individual clans or tribes, excluding all others who were born or bred in different circumstances. Abraham was the first, according to the Agadah, who broke the chains of such narrow selfishness, and extended the rights of love and hospitality to all who were born 'in the image of God'. Secondly, he was the first who opened the door of the God-fearing people who, educated and brought up in idol worship, felt the ardent desire to recognize Him, who spoke and the world was created, and became a follower of the One and only God in heaven and on earth. That was the true type of a *Zaddik*, for whose sake the world was created. *R. Joshua ben Korha* finds for this idea a proof in the words בהבראם, which could be read by permutation באברהם, i. e. through the merit of Abraham.[37] The Tanhuma has this statement in the name of R. Tahlifa,[38] anonymously Pes., ed. Buber, p. 200 B. R. Azarja explains the view of R. J. b. K. in the following way: Why is all this trouble (ὄγκος)? For the merit of him, concerning whom it is said: 'Thou art the God who hast chosen Abraham' (Neh. 9. 6). *R. Judan* explains it by referring to Ps. 104. 18. It is not said 'the high mountains the wild goats היעלים', but

---

[37] Gen. r. 12. 8.   [38] Ed. Buber, I, p. 11.

ליעלים *for the wild goats*. Now the high mountains were
created only for the sake of the wild goats, how much
more was the whole world only created for the merit of
Abraham.[39] Independently of R. Joshua ben Korha we
find this view also in the Agada of *R. Samuel bar Nahmani*
and *R. Levi*. The former formulated an exegetical rule
that whenever the word ויהי occurs, it alludes to some
distress and trouble in those days. With regard to Gen.
14. 1 the question was raised: What was the trouble in
those days? There was war. A king had a friend in one
of his provinces, and for his sake he bestowed favour on
the province. Once the Barbarians came and made war
against this province. People said: 'Woe unto us! for the
king does not favour our province except for his friend's
sake.' Likewise was it in those days. The whole world
was not created except for the merit of Abraham. When
the kings came to fight against him the people said: 'Woe,
woe!'[40] R. Levi proved from Isa. 66. 2, ואת כל אלה ידי עשתה
'for all these things have My hands made, and so all
these things came to be, says the Lord. Even on him that
is poor, and of a contrite spirit, and trembleth at My
word.'[41] In another passage he (R. Levi) derives the
teaching from Joshua 14. 13, 'the great man among the
Anakim is Abraham'.[42]

Other Agadists held and proved that the world was
made for Jacob's sake. R. Abahu taught all things were
formed for the sake of *Jacob*,[43] based on Jer. 10. 16. The
portion of *Jacob* is not like them, for it was for his
(Jacob's) merit that all things were formed (בשביל יעקב נצר
הכל). The *Rabbis* go even a step farther, when they say
that even Abraham was not created but for the sake of
Jacob, because it is said: 'For I know him, that he will

[39] M. Ps., p. 444 ; Gen. r. 12. 8 ; fuller version, M. Ps. Prague 53 B.
[40] Ruth r., Introd. 7 ; v. also Tanh. I, p. 119, שבזכותו נבראו העולם
הזה והעולם הבא.
[41] Gen. r. 12. 2.   [42] Gen. r. 14. 6.
[43] s. Lev. r. 36. 4, v. *MGWJ.*, 1887, p. 124.

command his children, and his household after him, and
they shall keep the way of the Lord, to do justice and
judgement' (Gen. 18. 19). And justice and judgement
were to be found in Jacob only, as it is said: 'Because
there is justice and judgement in Jacob hast thou made
him' (i. e. Abraham).[44] *R. Hanina ben Isaac* has the
same teaching (v. p. 104). *R. Joshua ben Nehemia* attributes this merit to the twelve tribes.[45] Finally we have to
mention the opinion of R. Berechja according to whom
this merit belongs to Moses.[46] We may, perhaps, guess
the reason why Jacob or Moses were substituted for
Abraham, by assuming that all these Agadists had chosen
one typical example of a 'Zaddik' who typifies the teaching
that the world was created for the sake of the righteous.

There was another thought abroad in the schools and
synagogues of the second and third centuries which
declared that the world was created for the sake of the
Torah. First of all we refer to R. Meir who seems to have
taught that the world was created for him who studies
the Torah (v. p. 50). The merit of the Torah and the
merit of those who study it is the same in the conceptions
of the scribes.

R. Simon ben Jochai deals with this problem with
reference to Isa. 65. 22: 'Just as the days of the tree are
the days of My people.' Under tree (עץ) the Torah is to
be understood, as it is said: 'A tree of life is it' (Prov.

---

[44] Lev. r. 36. 4.

[45] שבטים based on Ezek. 48. 1 and Isa. 66. 2; Gen. r. 12. 2; Pes. r. 10 в,
v. also 14 a.

[46] Gen. r. 1. 6, s. however, p. 102, where R. Berechja teaches that the
world was created for Israel's merit, Lev. r. 36. 4, the name of the teacher
is *R. Acha*, based on Deut. 33. 21. It is to be noted that the source of
Lev. r. differed from Gen. r. and other Midrashim, in other respects too,
thus the view is attributed to R. Joshua ben Nehemia which was expressed
by R. Abahu, who quotes the same in the name of *R. Hanina b. Isaac*,
whilst this Agadist taught, as we saw, p. 104, בזכות ישראל נברא העולם.
The view of R. Abahu is uttered likewise by *R. Phinehas* in the name of
R. Reuben. It often occurs that Agadists quote views of earlier authorities
which they themselves do not hold.

3. 18). Who was created for whose sake? Was it the
Torah for Israel's sake, or Israel for the Torah's sake?
Undoubtedly the Torah for Israel's sake. Now if the
Torah, created for Israel's sake, endures for ever, how
much more so will Israel live for ever.[47] R. Simon ben
Jochai endeavours to demonstrate here, as on many other
occasions, the eternity of Israel in refuting the doctrine
of the Synagogue's bitter enemies, that Israel, forsaken by
God, has given over the historic part it had to play to the
Church. He does not seem to know the teaching that
the world was created either for Israel's sake or for the
Torah's sake. In his time the view was still held that
the world was created for man's sake. *R. Benaah* teaches
the world was created only for the sake of the Torah [48]
based on Prov. 3. 19, where חכמה is identified with
תורה. About seventy years later *R. Simon ben Lakish*
taught that God made all things conditionally. If Israel
would accept the Torah on Mount Sinai the world shall
exist; if not, He will destroy it.[49] *R. Judan* teaches the
same doctrine based on Lev. 26. 46.[50] The idea is referred
to in a legend of *R. Eleazar b.* אבונה in the name of
R. Acha. During twenty-six generations was the letter א
complaining (קורא תגר) before God, saying: 'Thou hast
placed me at the head of all the letters, and still Thou
didst create the world with the second letter (i. e. ב,
Gen. 1. 1).' God replies: '*My world was created only for
the sake of the Torah*, and in future when I come to reveal
Myself, and give the Torah unto Israel (cf. Prov. 3. 19),
I will place thee at the head of the commandments, and
commence with א!' [51] Another Agadist, whose name we
do not know, supports this teaching with the different terms

---

[47] Eccles. r., l. 9, v. p. 119.   [48] Gen. r. 1. 6.
[49] b. Sabb. 88 a; b. A. Z. 3 a, 5 a; also my edition of the *Midrash Haserot
we Yeteroth*, p. 39, note 163, *Menorat ha Maor*, par. 278, reads ר' תניא
שמעון אומר.
[50] Gen. r. 12. 2.
[51] Exod. 20. 1; Cant. r. 5. 8; Pes. r. 109 ʙ; Gen. r. 1. 14. An anonymous teacher derives this doctrine from Isa. 51. 16 (Tanh. B., I, p. 7).

used in the offerings of the princes.[52] *R. Tanhum bar Abba*
expounded the teaching of R. Simon ben Lakish as follows:
God saw in the future (צפה) that Israel will receive the
Law, otherwise He would not have created the world.[53]
These passages must suffice to show us the thoughts of
the teachers of Judaism. The idea expressed in these
various sayings is that the world was *created for the merit
of the Torah*. That means: the intention of the Creator
was to make the world a place where the Torah, with all
its beauties and blessings, could develop and spread. Or
in other words, the world is the body, the Torah its soul.
According to ancient thought the soul was created long
before the body comes into being. The body is the vessel
made to receive the soul, so the body is made for the soul's
sake and not *vice versa*. Likewise is it in the case of
world and Torah. Therefore the teaching of the Agadists
that the world was created for the sake of the Torah,
implies that it would be in vain to build a world which
has no chance to develop, spread abroad, and bring to
ultimate triumph the high ideals of the Torah. How can
this be done? How can we achieve this aim? How is
such a victory to be accomplished? The old teachers and
thinkers of Israel assumed rightly that the Torah is the
key which opens the door to the world's need of a peaceful
and glorious development in all the moral and social
struggles, in all the questions and thoughts concerning life
and death. This brings us nearer to the solution of the
question raised above, namely: How did they come to
teach that the world was created for Israel's sake? Yet,
before considering it, we have to mention three other
theories as well. *R. Meir* says: 'Great is the commandment
of מילה (circumcision) because all the commandments which
our father Abraham performed did not entitle him to be
called perfect (שלם), until he circumcised himself, as it is

[52] Num. r., ch. 14.
[53] Exod. r. 40. 1, based on Job 28. 27; v. also Simon ben Isaac's סליחה
in Heidenheim's ed. of *Selichoth*, 91 B.

said: "Walk before me, and be perfect"' (Gen. 17. 1).
Another explanation is: 'Great is the commandment of
מילה (circumcision), were it not for this commandment God
would have never created the world.' [54] It seems that this
Tannaitic Agadist at a time when the performance of this
duty was punished by death, saw in it the climax of piety,
the highest glory of self-sacrifice for whose sake the world
was created. He means to say: A man who has such
a love of, and a faith in, God that he is ready to die for
God, is surely a type for whose sake a world should be
created. There are two other views to be mentioned in
this connexion. *R. Huna* in the name of *R. Mathna*
taught that the world was created for the sake of חלה
מעשרות וביכורים,[55] and another view by an unknown teacher
that it was for Zion's sake the world was created.[56]

If we review the views dealt with up till now, we cannot
miss the answer to our question. We learn that the
earliest view was that *for God's glory* was everything
made. Secondly, we have the thought of the school which
held that all was created *for man's sake*. Thirdly, *for the
righteous*. The fourth view put forth is that of the
Torah's merit. And the last *for Israel's sake*. If we
understood rightly what the Agadists meant by the
teaching: For the sake of the righteous or for the merit
of the Torah was the world created, we shall have the key
to the meaning of the doctrine: for Israel's sake was
everything made. It does not mean that Israel, as such,
has the right to eat the fruits of this world, to enjoy life,
to partake of the good things of the earth. As a matter
of fact, Israel had the least share at the table of his
Heavenly Father, as history proves it, but Israel, as the
bearer of the ideal of the Torah, Israel as the assembly
which is able to bring forth the proper type of righteousness, has the opportunity to supply ideal personalities, for

[54] Mishnah Ned. 31 a.
[55] Gen. r. 16; v. Num. 15. 20; Deut. 18. 4; Exod. 23. 19.
[56] Tanh., I, 7 a.

whose merit it was fit to create this world. Yet the
Agadists did not proclaim this idea before the Church tried
to deprive the Synagogue of her spiritual rights and
privileges. Only when the Church put forth claims alleged
to be based on the Scripture, which led to a righteousness,
to a world conception, to an estimation of life far removed
from the true spirit of the Torah and Prophets, then did
the Agadists come forth with their dogma: *For Israel's
sake was the world created.* They had to imitate the
half-forgotten Apocalyptic writers who had the same
experience previously in a different circle, but under similar
circumstances. On the eve of Christianity becoming
a power entirely assimilated to heathendom such a
defence—and the apologetical tendency of the doctrine
is obvious—was not merely a necessity but a sacred duty.
The teaching, therefore, that the world was created for
Israel's sake is by no means a narrow-minded chauvinistic
view, which the leaders of Judaism proclaimed in their
pride and self-conceit as one who does not consider the
development of the idea might believe, but a well-considered
defence of their position in life and the world. The Temple
was destroyed, the people bereft of their national independence and rights, under the heels of a cruel conqueror,
were threatened by a dangerous attempt of misrepresentation and falsification on the part of the Church; how could
those thinkers and teachers, the Agadists, arm themselves
against despair and faintheartedness? In no other way
than by teaching that Judaism, by its adherence to God,
its faithfulness to the Bible and Prophets, by its institutions and doctrines, observances and laws, is the most
proper way whereby the ideal can be reached, for which
the creation of the world was not love's labour lost.

(2) Another teaching closely connected with our Doctrine
has to be dealt with in this place. It is just as the world
was created for Israel's sake, so the existence of the
world depends on the merit of Israel. In this point, too,
there is an agreement between Stoa and Agadah, both

of them holding that the end of the world will come sooner or later. Now there is nothing without cause, reason, or aim in the creation. For whose merit does the world exist? Aristides taught that the world exists merely for the sake of the Christians.[57] Turning to the Agadists, we have to mention first of all *R. Joshua ben Levi*, who says: 'Had the nations of the world known what a blessing the Tabernacle (or Temple) was to them, they would have surrounded it by fortresses (קסטריות) and trenches, in order to defend it. It was more useful to them than to the Israelites. As Solomon said in his prayer: 'And the stranger too who is not from Thy people Israel', and it is written: 'And do everything which the stranger prays for.' Yet when he (Solomon) comes to speak of Israel, what is written? 'And do and give to a man according to his way, as Thou knowest his heart' (1 Kings 8. 41). If he be worthy give him; if not, do not give him. And do not say (it was so at the time when) the Temple (stood), however, were it not for Israel, no rain would descend, the sun would not shine, because for their sake does God do good with the world (מריח).[58] And in the world to come the Nations of the World will see Israel, how God is with them, they (the Nations of the World) will endeavour to join them, as it is said: 'In those days ten men from all the tongues of the nations will get hold.'[59] This apology of R. J. b. L. teaches first of all that the sun shines, the rain descends for Israel's sake. At the time of the Temple this merit was attributed to the Sanctuary. The Nations of the World do not know this, but presumably deny Israel any virtue or merit. Then we find this teaching emphasized in the Agadah of *R. Simon ben Lakish*. This teacher makes the magicians of Ahasuerus say: 'If thou art going to extirpate Israel the world will

[57] Ch. XVI, v. Geffken, *Zwei griechische Apologeten*, p. 92.

[58] Tanh. f. 190 B.

[59] Zach. 1. 13; Num. r. 1. 3; Tanh. Num. IV, p. 5; Lev. r., ch. 1. 11; Cant. r. 2. 3; Tanh. II, p. 93.

I

not continue to exist.'[60]   *R. Eleazar* says that all the
inhabitants of the earth, even the ships which cross from
Gallia to Spain (Aspamia) are blessed for Israel's merit.[61]
R. Levi elaborates this teaching: 'Israel is a nation for
whose merit all the good things (blessings) come to the
world.   Rain and dew come only for Israel's sake to
the world.'[62]   An anonymous teacher explains why Israel
is compared with dust.   Just as the earth cannot exist
without dust, because if there were no dust, trees cannot
bring forth fruit, likewise the Nations of the World cannot
exist on the earth, if there be no Israelites.[63]   Further, the
view of *R. Samuel ben Nahmani* must be noticed.   The
Nations of the World who will pass away from the world
without leaving any trace do not say: 'The blessing of
God is upon you, Israel!'   Israel, however, says: 'We
blessed you in the name of the Lord!' meaning: 'Is it
not sufficient that you get so many blessings and consolations (נחמות) for our merit', and you say: 'Keep your
blessings for yourself!   You extort so many taxes from
us and lay so many burdens upon us.'[64]   These passages
reveal the apologetic tendency of the whole doctrine.
The Sages tried to reply to those of their enemies who
worried them with the question: 'What good has Israel
done?'   And what good does Israel do in the world?
Israel is a fruitless tree, which contributes nothing to the
welfare of the family of nations.   Has Israel really a right
to exist?   It is worth while to pay close attention to these
reproaches.   We know that the grammarian Apion with
his venomous pen poisoned the souls of his contemporaries
and posterity with his words: 'The Jews have never
brought forth a man who distinguished himself either
as an inventor or discoverer, as an artist or philosopher,
who left the slightest impression upon humanity or man-

---

[60] Esther r., ch. 7, p. 21 B, v. also pp. 20 a, 23 a, *Sifra de Agadta*, p. 47.
[61] s. b. Jebamot 63 a.   [62] v. p. 90, n. 251.
[63] Pes. r., p. 45 B.
[64] j. A. Z. 44 B ; j. Seb. 35 B, 30 A ; j. Gittin 47 B ; M. Ps., ed. B., p. 515.

kind.' [65]   What we have to think of this market journalist,
of this vain self-admirer, has already been said by Josephus.
Apion is a sad example of the stupidity of the masses
who are led by vainglorious, conscienceless leaders, and an
instance of how little brain is needed to influence even
great minds.   For even a serious historian like Tacitus
could not escape in this, as well as in other cases, the
bad influence of such a man as the *tympanum propriae
famae* or the *Cymbalum mundi*.   There is no wonder that
such a man as Celsus repeats these words.[66]   This question
is therefore older than the teachers of the third century.
As a matter of fact it was dealt with by the clever
Beruria, the wife of R. Meir.   A man, styled צדוקי, asked
her about the passage: ' Rejoice, O barren, that thou art
childless ' (Isa. 54. 1). What does that mean ? Who can rejoice
because one is barren ?   Beruria replied: ' You fool ! Why
do you not read the end of the sentence ?   " For more are
the children of the forsaken than of the wedded one, says
the Lord."   But what does it mean, Rejoice, O barren ?
Rejoice, O community of Israel, because thou art like the
barren woman who has not given birth to children, destined
for Hell, like this man is.' [67]   *R. Meir* himself expounded
the verse, saying: ' Israel was never fruitless, it is only
at present trodden down and destroyed by the nations '
[Pes. r. 141 a]. Hellenistic writers, apologists, and historians
had to take refuge in another theory.   Abraham or Moses
were, according to their historical constructions, the in-
ventors and teachers of all arts and wisdom.   The Jews
have their share, they wanted to prove, in the general
progress of civilization and culture.[68]   Christianity repeated
faithfully these reproaches as well as others.   The Jews are
a fruitless people, a people which proved unworthy, from
whom the Kingdom of Heaven was taken and given unto

[65] Josephus c., Ap. II, 13.

[66] *Orig. contra Cels.* IV, 31.   [67] b. Ber. 10 a.

[68] v. Freudenthal, *Hellenistische Studien*, I, p. 97 ; Bergmann, *Apologetik*,
p. 156.

a people that will bring forth good fruit.[69]   In the fourth
century *R. Judah ben Simon* taught that the world was
created for the sake of the Torah, but exists for Israel's
sake (v. above, p. 92).   He illustrates this doctrine with
the following parable.   A king had once an orchard, nicely
planted, one row of figs, one of grapes, one of pomegranates,
one of apples.   He gave it over to a tenant (אריס) and left
the place.   After many days the king returned and looked
into the orchard to see what the tenant had done.   He
found the whole orchard full of thistles and thorns.   He
brought cutters to cut them, and then he noticed one lily
among those thistles.   He took the lily, shielded it, and
was satisfied.   The king said: 'For the sake of the lily
shall the whole orchard be saved.'   Thus the whole world
was created for the sake of the Torah.   After twenty-six
generations God looked about in His world to see what
man had done, and found it full of sins.   He brought
cutters to cut it, v. Ps. 27. 10.   Then He noticed a lily,
i.e. Israel at the Mount of Sinai, and He was satisfied.
God said: 'For the sake of this lily shall the whole orchard
be saved, for the merit of Israel shall the world be saved.
For Israel's sake the world exists.'   *R. Idi* bases this
doctrine on Cant. 7. 3 : 'Thy womb is a heap of wheat.
Is a heap of pepper or of στροβυλος (nut pine) not better
than a heap of wheat?   Yet the world can live (exist)
without pepper or nut pine seeds, but it cannot exist without wheat, likewise is it with Israel, the world cannot
exist without it' (v. above, p. 105).

Older than this last conception is the view that the
world exists for the sake of the righteous.   It was taught
first in the school of R. Ishmael (v. p. 43).   R. Eleazar ben
Shamua found a proof for it in Prov. 10. 25 ('But the
righteous is an everlasting foundation').   Even one righteous
man is regarded as the pillar of the world (v. p. 56).
R. Jochanan b. Nappacha repeated the same saying (v.

---

[69] Ev. Matt. 21. 43.

p. 74). His friend *R. Eleazar ben Pedath* speaks of peaceful people as the keepers and supporters of the world (p. 83).[70]

A third theory held was that the world stands for the merit of the Torah or the Ten Commandments, i. e. for those who study and observe the Torah and its commandments.[71] Without the Torah the world could not exist. The world was established on a firm basis, since Israel uttered the never-to-be-forgotten words: 'We will do and obey.'[72] This view was taught by R. Hanina b. Hama,[73] by R. Jochanan ben Nappacha (p. 75), who speaks also in the same connexion of the merits of Moses and Aaron (v. p. 76), by R. Eleazar ben Pedath,[74] by R. Levi (p. 90), by R. Jeremia (p. 99), and R. Acha (p. 100). It amounts to the same when we read in the anonymous Agadah that the world stands for the merit of those who study the Torah.[75]

To a fourth group belong the views of those who ascribe the existence of the world to peculiar commandments. Thus R. Meir to that of circumcision (v. p. 50), R. Simon ben Jochai (v. p. 53). R. Joshua ben Levi (v. p. 72) and R. Samuel ben Nahmani (v. p. 82) saw, like R. S. b. J., in the merit of the Tabernacle the safeguard of the world, whilst R. Abba bar Kahana speaks of the merit of the Kingdom of David's house as of the basis of the world (v. p. 91). We distinguish four groups which dealt with our problem.[75a]

---

[70] The number of the righteous is given in various sources and by various authors differently. The usual number was thirty, v. Gen. r. 49. 7; Tanh. 27 B; ירא, 13; Pes. 88 a; j. A. Z. 40 c; M. Ps. 5. 5. In Babylonian sources we find the number thirty-six (Abajji b. Sukkah, 45 B; b. Synh. 96 B; Alphabeth of Ben Sira, 2 a, *Tanna debe Elijahu*, ch. 18, p. 57 B; *Aphraates Hom.* 22, p. 37 b, or 45, v. b. Hul. 92 a). Yet we have also the number three, M. Ps. 49 a; Midr. Tadshê, p. xli; Num. r. 3. 1; M. Sam. 44, v. also my ed. of the Midr. *Haserot we Yeteroth*, p. 30, n. 125, and p. 36, n. 150.

[71] v. Midrash Tadshê, p. xvi.

[72] v. Tanh. f., p. 280 B.   [73] Cant. r. 7; 1. 50.

[74] v. b. Pes. 68 B; Ned. 32 a.

[75] Tanh. f. 2 B and 10 a.

[75a] v. also Pirke of R. Hak, ed. Schönblum, p. 44 a, אין העולם מתקיים אלא על חסדו של מקום.

There are various theories and attempts to answer the question which must have seriously engaged the mind of people in the first four centuries. In the first theory we see undoubtedly apologetical tendencies. The latter alone, however, are not sufficient to account satisfactorily for the popularity of the theme. Jewish teachers held similar views as to the end of the world as the Stoics. The Synagogue as well as the Porch believed 'the world is going to perish through fire'.[76] This belief was widespread and feared. People asked, 'Since world destruction threatens us any moment, whose merit shall save us?' The teachers pointed out that the merits of Israel, the merits of the righteous, the merits of the Torah and Ten Commandments, of special observances and institutions could avert the disaster hanging over their heads. We, of course, do not believe in such ideas of world destruction, which the ancient sages and teachers thought possible or even imminent. Yet other dangers threaten our world against which we cannot arm ourselves by other means than by those which the ancients held the world was to be saved. That can be accomplished and achieved only by those ideals, by those teachings, by which Judaism in the interpretation of the scribes, stands or falls.

(3) The third problem which agitated the mind of the sages was much wider than the previous ones. Whilst the latter dealt with theoretical questions, for whose sake was the world created, and for whose merit does the world exist?—the third problem of our Doctrine was of a more practical issue. Thus when they asked: 'Why was Adam, who was by no means such a great success, made before Abraham, who was really the crown of the Creation?

[76] Paul Barth, *Die Stoa*, Stuttgart, 1903, pp. 33–41; L. Ginzberg, הגורן, VIII, pp. 35–51; Samaritans, v. Joshua, ch. VI; Herzfeld, *Geschichte*, II, p. 601. As to R. Abahu, v. *MGWJ.*, 1887, p. 72, as to Propertius, v. *Rheinishes Museum*, 55, p. 211, and 'Eine Zoroastrische Prophezeihung in christlichem Gewand', by Ernst Kuhn, in *Festschrift für R. v. Roth*, 1893, p. 217; Windischmann, *Zoroastrische Studien*, pp. 259 and 293; Rubin, מנחם הבבלי, p. 89 A.

Whose merit was it that Abraham's seed was chosen to be God's people? For whose merit were they delivered from Egypt after so many miracles? Why have they crossed the sea? Why have they received the Torah? Why did they receive manna, water, and protection in the wilderness? Why did they cross the Jordan? For whose merit did they inherit the land? Heaven's Providence? For whose sake do they exist? Is God present among them? Why did they experience God's mercy by having their sins forgiven so many times? Will they be redeemed in the future?' These and many more similar questions have to be considered in this section in order to see clearly the part the Doctrine of Merits plays in Rabbinical Theology. We will deal with some of the questions in the order given above:

(a) Adam's disobedience and punishment gave rise to many serious questions. Why was he formed by God's hand imperfect? Jews could not follow extravagant theories by striking out some passages which they did not like, or by declaring them forgeries (e. g. the Clementine Homilies). Every word of the Text is true and divine. Then, they argued, even the creature formed by the hands of Almighty God was imperfect! One of the answers which concerns us here, was that Adam is not the climax of creation, but Abraham, and he (Adam) was formed merely for the merit of Abraham. The case is compared with a king who prepared a banquet and invited a guest. Likewise did God create Adam for the merit of Abraham, as it is said: 'Thou knowest my sitting *in the Garden of Eden.* Mine uprising, i. e. *my exile therefrom.* Thou knowest for whose merit Thou hast taken counsel *to create me, for the merit of Him* who comes from afar (i. e. Abraham), as it is said: From a far country a man of his counsel.' [77] Adam was therefore not the crown of the creation, God knew that he was going to sin, and he was merely created for the

[77] Isa. 46. 11 ; Ps. 139. 2 ; Gen. r. 15. 5.

merit of Abraham.   In that case, people argued, Abraham ought to have been created before Adam.   To this we find a reply in the Agadah of *R. Levi* and *R. Abba b. Kahana.* R. Levi explains, Isa. 14. 15 : 'The man who was greatest among Anakim.'   'Man' refers to Abraham.   Why does the Text call him 'greatest'?   Because he was worthy to be created before Adam! (but why was he not created before Adam ?).   God said: 'Perchance he will sin, then there will be none to make amends.   Behold, I will create Adam first, and in case he sins, then let Abraham come, and do good instead of Adam.'   *R. Abba bar Kahana* compares the case with a man who has a pair of beams, where does he put them?   Surely only in the midst of the 'triclineum' (banquet-hall), in order to support those beams which are above and beneath.   In the same way God created Abraham in the midst of the generations in order to bear (the defective acts of) the generations before and after him.[78]   R. Abba b. Kahana might have seen the weak points in the theory of his colleague R. Levi, who based his arguments on the doctrine of *freewill.*   Yet if the will be free, well then it was just as uncertain that Abraham would reach the ideal, as it was in the case of Adam.   *R. Abba b. Kahana,* however, tries to show that there was some purpose in the creation of man.   'Adam was created for the merit of Abraham' means accordingly that the sinner Adam was created before Abraham, who is to be regarded as the climax of the creation.   There must be some cogent reason for such views, besides the question mentioned above, why did not the work of God appear faultless and without sin ?   This point was considered by Agadists scores of times.[79]   We have to discover some other reason too, because the views advanced by the

---

[78] Gen. r. 14. 6 ; Eccles. r. 2. 11 reads the parable in the name of *R. Judah ben Simon,* M. Ps. 22. 19 ; 49. 2 ; 34. 1 ; *R. Simon.*

[79] He was perfect when he was created ; by his own freewill, however, he spoilt his chances, v. my *Midrash Haserot we Yeteroth,* p. 18, n. 81 ; he was a great prophet, scholar, v. also *ZfWTh.* 28, p. 477.

anonymous sage, by R. Levi and R. A. b. K. answer this
question but partly or not at all.   Yet they entirely
weaken the often proclaimed dogma which identified Adam
with Christ either symbolically or historically.[80]   Now,
these scribes proved in their own way that Adam was
much inferior to Abraham, for whose sake Adam was
created.   Adam, the inferior, representing the Church can
in no possible way be superior to Abraham, representing
the Synagogue.   We must not overlook in this case, as in
so many others, some of which have been already mentioned, the apologetical origin of certain theological views
and doctrines.   Perhaps to emphasize this idea one of the
Agadists taught in an apologetical mood : ' Even Abraham
himself was not born but for the merit of Jacob, as it is
written : " Because I know," &c. in order to do righteousness
and justice (Gen. 18. 19), and there is no righteousness and
justice but in Jacob ' (v. Ps. 99. 4).[81]   Nowhere is צדקה ומשפט
to be found except in Jacob, therefore is it no good to argue
that Abraham had two sons, or that Isaac had two sons,
representing the Church and the Synagogue.   Which son
had the preference to the other ?   We, the descendants of
Jacob, say the Agadists are the bearers of Abraham's
inheritance of righteousness and justice.

There is another view that man was created for God's
glory.   We have already come across such an opinion
about the creation of the world (v. above, p. 115).   We saw
that the Church Father Irenaeus objected to it.   Yet we
find this teaching in the ancient part of the marriage
liturgy.   According to *R. Judah [ben Ezekiel]* the blessing
(ברכת חתנים) begins : ' Blessed art Thou, Lord our God, King
of the world, Who created everything for His own glory,
and Who created man.' [82]   This prayer must be older than

---

[80] v. Neander, *Kirchengesch.* I, p. 99; Dähne, *Jud. Alex. Religionsphilosophie*,
I, 66 ; *Christuspartei*, p. 255 ; Schliemann, *Die Clementinen*, p. 356.

[81] Lev. r. 36. 4.

[82] I. e. for his own glory, v. b. Ket. 8 a ; Tr. Kallah, 1. 1, ed. Jerusalem,
1912, p. 1 a, reads ושהכל ברא לכבודו בא"י יוצר האדם.

the third century, and is another testimony for the early age of the thought that all things were created for the glory of God. It seems that it was later on abandoned, although many traces of the idea remained in the Liturgy. II Baruch 21. 21 says: 'Because *on account of Thy name* (למען שמך) hast Thou called us a beloved people', answering the question: 'Why was Israel chosen as God's people?' II Baruch replies: 'You need not search for deeper reasons and hidden mysteries, He did it for His own name, just as He created the world or man, according to some opinions, for His own glory.' Yet the agitation of the Gnostics that the God of the Bible needed the world or man, rose to such heights that the view had to be dropped. This theme was discussed by the well-known Matrona and *R. Jose ben Chalafta*. The Matrona says: 'Whomsoever your God likes, He has chosen!' R. J. b. Ch. took a basket full of figs. The lady chose the best ones, and enjoyed them. R. J. b. Ch. said: 'You choose the best figs, and you assume that God is unable to have chosen the best ones. As a matter of fact, He too has chosen those (Israel) whom He regarded as the best ones.' [83] Here we see that Israel was chosen because it was the best of the nations. In another passage we read: 'If one tells you: "God makes rich and poor whom He likes, a king whom He likes, look at Abraham, He made him rich and a ruler when He wanted", you shall answer him and tell him: "Could you do what our father Abraham did?" "What has he done?"' the opponent will ask you. Tell him: 'Abraham was 100 years of age when a son was born unto him, and after all this anxiety he was willing to sacrifice his son for God's sake.' [84] That means to say it was not mere arbitrariness that God has chosen Abraham and his seed. They had real merits which made them fit to become God's people. God's rulership in the world and

[83] Num. r. 3. 2 ; Tobit 4. 19, 'The Lord gives all good things, He humiliates whom He likes, and at a time when He wants.'
[84] Gen. r. 55. 1.

history is by no means arbitrary, but just; therefore we have to show the merits, thought the ancient sages, explaining why God has shown mercy and miracles to His people.

(*b*) The first mercy shown by God to Israel was the chastisement meted out to the Egyptians, their oppressors. Besides R. Abun, who held that the redemption was not for the merits of the fathers, but for God's grace (v. p. 103), there are again four trains of thought endeavouring to satisfy the curiosity of the contemporaries on this subject. First we mention the general opinion that Israel was redeemed for the sake of the righteous men and women among them. The first group speaks of the merits of the dead patriarchs, namely, of Abraham, of Jacob. The second group of contemporary righteous men and women. To the latter belong the chaste and pious women who deserved by their conduct to bring freedom and salvation to their race. In spite of the apologetical tendency of this saying, there is a great truth in the words of those ancient teachers of Israel. It has to be emphasized again and again that Judaism recognized that, in a noble, unselfish, high-minded womanhood was the surety of the existence of the race on the one hand and the happiness and well-being of the coming generations on the other. A third group saw the reason of Israel's redemption in the merits of generations yet unborn. Thus R. Eleazar ben Pedath denies entirely the merits of the redeemed ones (p. 84), and speaks of the merits of future generations. R. Abba b. Kahana singled out those of Isaiah's generation (p. 91), whilst *R. Eliezer ben Jacob* speaks of the three young men who were ready to sacrifice themselves for God (v. p. 57).

Different from these conceptions were the teachings of those scribes who pointed to one or more merits, which the redeemed ones have had to acquire by their own work. Such are the merits of circumcision, of the Torah, the Paschal offering, the faithful adherence to ancient customs and the erection of the future Tabernacle.

We begin with the merits of the righteous, whose influence was felt beneficial even after their death. The merits of Abraham. Everything, says an anonymous Agadist, was done for the sake of Abraham, as it is said: 'He hath remembered His holy word unto Abraham His servant, and brought forth His people with joy, and He gave them the law of nations' (Ps. 105. 43). Why? In order that they shall keep His statutes and observe His laws (Ps. 105. 45).[85] *R. Eleazar ben Azarja* bases on these verses the theory that Israel was delivered from Egypt for Abraham's merit.[86] An anonymous writer puts the same view in different words when he says: 'God said to Moses, "Thou shalt redeem Israel for the merit of him with whom I spake between the pieces."'[87] In the Tanhuma we read that the Israelites were delivered from Egypt for the merit of Jacob, based on Ps. 105. 10, and Abraham himself was not delivered from Nimrod's fiery furnace but for Jacob's merit.[88] The idea which emphasizes the superiority of Jacob gives some interesting material for investigation. How did this thought arise? First we have to mention the saying of *R. Samuel ben Isaac.* Abraham did not escape from the fiery furnace but for the sake of Jacob. It is to be compared with a man who had a case before the ruler (judge), and he was condemned to death by fire. Then the ruler saw by astrology that this man would have a daughter, destined to be married to the king. Likewise Abraham was condemned to death by fire. God saw that in the future Jacob would come forth of Abraham, and He said: 'Abraham shall be saved for the merit of Jacob.'[89] The supreme contempt of logical thinking is apparent in this saying, yet just as clear is the fact that Jacob is esteemed higher than Abraham. We find the same statement by R. Berechja and R. Levi in the name of *R. Samuel*

---

[85] Exod. r. 15. 1.   [86] Mech. 19 B.
[87] Exod. r. 2. 5.
[88] Tanh. 62 B, v. דעת זקנים, 13 a; v. p. 137.   [89] Gen. r. 63. 2.

ben Nahmani.[90] It is possible that these teachers of the third century were not quite happy in their view that Abraham was the climax of creation, for the Church could always play and argue with the names of Ishmael and Isaac, Esau and Jacob (v. above, p. 137 f.). They felt it a necessity of the time to emphasize Jacob's superiority.

A third theory attributes the redemption of Israel from Egypt to the merit of the pious and chaste Hebrew women. *R. Akiba* says: 'The Israelites were delivered from Egypt as a reward for the pious women of those days.'[91] This view is often repeated in the Midrashic literature. A few instances will suffice. (*a*) R. Eleazar הקפר b. Rabbi says: Did they not have in their hand four commandments, for which enough reward there cannot be given [שאין העולם כדאי בהם], they were not suspected of having committed adultery, there was no evil speech (slander) among them, they changed neither their names nor their language.[92] (*b*) *R. Nathan* applies to them the verse Cant. 4. 12.[93] (*c*) Num. r. 3. 4 with reference to Ps. 68. 7: 'God makes the solitary to establish a house,' i. e. the Israelites who went to Egypt solitary in a group of seventy, and God formed them into houses. He brings out the prisoners into prosperity because they kept themselves aloof from adultery, therefore has He delivered them from Egypt. Likewise it is said by Solomon: 'A garden shut up is my sister,' &c. These were the maidens, 'A spring shut up.' These were the married women. God said: 'For their merit will I redeem My children,' that is what it is written: 'Thy shoots are an orchard of pomegranates,' for this merit will I send them out (שלחיך = ויהי בשלח), that teaches that the Israelites went out from Egypt for the merit

[90] Lev. r. 36. 4.

[91] Exod. r. 1. 16. 6. Sotah 11 B reads R. Avira.

[92] Mech. 5 a ; Pes. B. 83 c ; Lev. r. 32. 5 ; Hasit, s. v. גן נעול ; Exod. r. 1. 28 ; Nr. 20, end ; Tanh. בלק, 25 ; Pirke of R. El., ch. 48 ; *Tanna de be El.*, r. 10. 23, 24 ; M. Ps., ed. B. 472, ed. Prague, 57 a, v. p. 62.

[93] Mech. 5 a, n. ; Targum Cant. 4. 12 ; b. Joma 15 a ; Sifra, Emor, end.

of the pious women.[94] The investigator of the Agadah
cannot rest satisfied in this, as in all the other cases, in
spite of the passages from the Scriptures, and asks : Why
did the sages repeat this teaching so often and what led
them to enunciate such a doctrine ?   In this case the apologetical tendency of the saying is undoubtedly established.
It is well known that some ancient writers, who called themselves critics by nature, invented the cruel allegation that
the Jews were the illegitimate children of the Egyptians.
The latter ruled over the bodies as well as over the souls
of their wretched slaves.   This fruit of the perverse imagination of a mind like that of Apion or Lysimachus, the
name of the actual author is now unknown, is worthy of
its origin.   Even a less sensitive and proud people than
the Jews would see in such a libel an unheard-of humiliation ; how much more the Jews to whom immorality
appeared as the abomination of abominations?   The words
of the Agadists of the second and third centuries re-echo
the bitter feeling on the part of the Jews who had to
repudiate the 'historical theories' of the public-house
philosophers and degenerate politicians of the anti-Semitic
genius.   The greatest Agadists of those days combat this
harmful and shameless accusation of the apostles of
hatred.   R. Simon ben Halafta,[95] Joshua ben Levi,[96] Judah
ben Simon, Hoshaja,[97] R. Isaac,[98] Hijja b. Abba,[99] to
mention only a few, took up this subject and repelled
it publicly.   Our doctrine also tries to refute those libels.
The sages wished to say : 'You are entirely mistaken if
you dare to suspect and question the purity of our origin,
the chastity of our mothers and the virtue of Jewish
women ! The Scriptures show us that they were נשים

[94] v. also Cant r. 4. 24 ; *R. Phinehas*, R. P. in the name of R. Hijja ;
M. Ruth, Introd., p. 54 ; R. Acha ; cf. G. Friedländer, *Pirḳê de Rabbi Eliezer*,
p. 328, note 1.

[95] Tanh. 137 B.

[96] Cant. r. 4. 27 ; Pesikta, Buber, p. 82 a, b.

[97] Pes. 82 B ; Cant. r. 4. 42 reads R. Phinehas.

[98] Exod. r. 15. 17.   [99] Pes. B. 82 ; Lev. r. 32. 5.

צדקניות pious, God-fearing women for whose merit our fathers were delivered from Egyptian slavery.' In this, or in a similar manner, spoke these old teachers of the Agadah.

A fourth view was advanced by R. Nehemia (v. p. 56) and developed later by R. Levi. The redemption from Egypt was for the merit of Moses and Aaron. He compares the case with a king who wanted to marry a damsel. People came and said: ' Do not do so. She is very poor indeed, she has really nothing but two earrings. That is all.' The king said: ' Good, then I marry her for these two earrings. Likewise did God! It is sufficient that I redeem Israel for the sake of Moses and Aaron.' [100] It is quite superfluous, he means to say, to search for merits for Israel. For a people that had in its midst two men like Moses and Aaron it was undoubtedly worthy to lead a better life than to remain Pharaoh's slaves.

There is finally a fifth group of thought which does not ascribe the salvation of Israel from the Egyptian bondage to any particular individual, but to some self-acquired virtue or merit. Most significant for the whole doctrine of merits is the saying of *R. Matja ben Cheresh*. The time had come when God had to redeem the oath which He swore unto Abraham to deliver his children, but they had no observances (מצות) to observe in order that they might be redeemed. They were naked of all commandments. God therefore gave them two observances: the blood of the Paschal offering and the blood of the circumcision, in order that they might be redeemed. There is, namely, no reward without work (Mech. 5 a). ' Without work there can be no reward' is the basis of this teacher's ethics. The redemption must be the outcome of some merit, independent of eminent personages or ancestors. All who are to be redeemed must show themselves that they are worthy of the divine grace. Therefore they received the

[100] Exod. r. 15. 4.

commandments, which they had to observe and fulfil. In the *Pirke of R. Eliezer* this view is expressed by *R. Eleazar* (Eliezer?): 'God said, for the merit of the blood of circumcision and of the Paschal offering have I delivered you from Egypt, and for these merits am I going to deliver you at the end of the fourth kingdom.'[101] The apologetical tendency is more than obvious in this case too; Christian teaching aimed at the abolition of circumcision. The death of Jesus, the blood of the ideal Paschal lamb, made the old observance superfluous, so they argued. The scribes, how-ever, said: 'Just as in Egypt the blood of the Paschal lamb was mingled with the blood of the circumcision, do not therefore be persuaded and beguiled by the view that this ceremony is antiquated and obsolete, for the merit of this observance God will redeem us again. *R. Simon ben Jochai* put this view plainly when he teaches: 'For the merit of circumcision has God delivered them from Egypt.'[102] His contemporaries *R. Judah* (*ben Ilai*) and *R. Nehemia* dispute whether the redemption was for the merit of the law of circumcision or for the sake of the Torah which the Israelites were about to receive on Mount Sinai. R. Judah says it was for the merit of the circumcision (based as all the views above on Ezek. 16. 6). R. Nehemia says it was for the merit of the Torah.[103] The view of R. Nehemia occurs often.[104]

(c) The same five trains of thought can be recognized in the replies to the question: 'For whose merit was the sea divided before the Israelites?' For the merit of Abraham, according to *R. Benaah* בנאה,[105] but according

---

[101] Chap. 29, Friedländer, loc. cit., p. 210; v. also Exod. r. 19. 6; *R. Simon ben Halafta*; Cant. r. 1. 35; ibid. 1. 57; ibid. 3. 14; ibid. 5. 3; ibid. 7. 5.

[102] Mech., pp. 19 B, 20 a.

[103] וירא, Exod. 2. 25; ויראו, Exod. 20. 18; s. Pes. B. 63 B; Pes. r. 83 a; Exod. r. 17. 3; 19. 5; Tanh. וירא, 4; M. Ps. 474, and ed. Pr., p. 57 a; Agadath Ber., p. 35.

[104] s. Exod. r. 3. 5.

[105] Mech. 29 B; Mech. R. S. b. J., p. 48; ר' בניה, Exod. r. 21. 8; Gen. r. 55. 12, ר' בנאה ר' בי׃ם לה ותני מיאשא ר' בשם יוסי בר׳ חייא ר'.

to *R. Akiba* the merit was Jacob's,[106] or Joseph's, as *Simon of* קטרון held.[107] For the sake of the tribes the sea was divided before them, teaches *Eliezer ben Juda* of ברתותא.[108] The last opinion is chronologically the first; *Shemaja* says: 'Worthy is the faith with which their father Abraham believed in Me, therefore will I divide the sea before them.' *Abtaljon* says: 'Worthy is their own faith that which they believed in Me, so that I shall divide the sea before them.'[109] *Simon of Teman* speaks of the merit of circumcision.[110] This somewhat brief list shows that the principal features of the Doctrine of Merits are represented in this point as well as in the previous one. The significant features in both are: (*a*) the merits of the ancestors or prominent personalities, and (*b*) one's own merits.[111] The latter is to be divided in merits actually acquired (faith, circumcision), and to be accomplished in the future (the Torah). R. Eleazar ben Pedath (v. p. 84) cannot see in this miracle the influence of any merit, but attributes it to the merits of future generations.

(*d*) The same differences of opinion can be observed in the historical considerations paid to other outstanding facts of biblical events. Thus the Manna was, according to *Judah ha Levi ben Shalom* in the name of *R. Jonah*, given for the sake of Abraham;[112] according to an older authority, *R. Simai*, R. Eleazar in his name, all the supplies the Israelites had in the wilderness were a reward for the trouble which Abraham took in showing hospitality to the angels.[113] Yet we hear, according to R. Berechja in the name of *R. Levi*, that the Manna was given for the merit of Moses, the protection by the Cloud of Glory for the merit of Aaron, and the well of water for the sake of

---

[106] Mech. 29 B ; Exod. r. 21. 8.   [107] Gen. r. 87. 10 ; Mech. 29 B.

[108] Mech. 29 B.   [109] Ibid. 29 B.   [110] Ibid.

[111] There is also the merit of the Torah, v. Mech. 72 B ; Cant. r. 1. 48.

[112] s. Exod. r. 25. 5 ; Gen. r. 48. 13 ; R. Jonah in the name of *R. Hama b. Hanina.*

[113] v. also R. Hama ben Hanina, p. 81 and R. Hanin, p. 99 ; Gen. r. 48. 10 ; R. Isaac ; Exod. r. 24. 4.

Miriam.[114] No traces are known to us that the Manna
or any other benefit were for other merits other than those
of prominent personages.   The reason might be that
material advantages or benefits are given for material
works.   Older, however, than all these views is that of
R. Eleazar of Modiim that the Manna and the victory of
Amalek was due to the merits of the forefathers (v. p. 41).
The crossing of the Jordan was assigned by R. Jochanan
ben Nappacha to the merit of Jacob (v. p. 76), by Simon of
קטרין, and by R. Judah ben Simon to Joseph (v. pp. 47 and 92).

(e) Finally, we have to deal with the merits which will
bring about the future redemption of Israel, which explained to the Israelites of old the unique and marvellous
history of their people, its eternity and glory.   The opinions
are divided on this question as well as on all the previous
ones.   R. Samuel ben Nahmani (v. p. 81), and R. Eleazar
ben Pedath (v. p. 84) do not attribute it to any merit at all.
Such a great event cannot be brought about by merits,
it must be due to the Grace of God.   R. Jochanan and
R. Simon ben Lakish (v. p. 78) speak of the merit of
repentance, R. Hijja bar Abba (v. p. 87) of the great
merit of Sabbath observance.   R. Isaac mentions the merit
of festivals (v. p. 88), R. Levi ascribes it to the merit of
faith and Torah (v. p. 90),[115] and finally R. Hanin, who
speaks of the merit of the everlasting lamp (v. p. 99).
Only R. Simon ben Lakish (in a second saying, p. 78) and
R. Acha make use in this connexion of the merits of Jacob
or of his children.

---

[114] Num. 7. 1, 2; Tanh. 189 B; Telamd. Num. 26 a; Mech. Sifra, p. 129 a;
Seder Olam, ch. 10; Cant. r. 4. 13; Lev. r. 27. 6; Sifrè Deut., § 305, v.
also Ps. Philo, *JQR.*, X, 321.

[115] v. also Midr. Sam., ed. Buber, p. 135, ד"א בקר לא עבות שלא בא
בזכות אבות, בזכות מי בא? בזכותה שלתורה.

III

(1) THE history and biography, the virtues and deeds of the fathers, play a most prominent part in the teachings of the scribes. Under the name of 'fathers', the Rabbis understand not only Abraham, Isaac, and Jacob,[1] but all the biblical personages are included in this term. Sirach includes also in this praise of the fathers, besides the patriarchs κατ᾽ ἐξοχήν Abraham, Isaac and Jacob, Enoch, Noah, Moses, Aaron, Phinehas, Joshua, Kaleb, the Judges, David, Solomon, &c. (ch. 44. 50). In the Hebrew text of Sirach they are called אבות העולם, a term which frequently recurs in Rabbinic literature.[2] Besides this title, we meet frequently the term אבות הראשונים.[3] A third term was הרים (mountains).[4] Generally, however, all the terms

---

[1] Ber. 16 B : אין קורין אבות אלא לשלשה, to be emended according to Semahot, I, 14 : אין קורין לאבות אבינו אלא לשלשה האבות ולאמהות אמנו אלא לארבע, as a matter of fact Dereh'erez Zutta, ch. 1, speaks of seven fathers, ז' אבות כרותי ברית, with whom God made a covenant, Abraham, Isaac, Jacob, Moses, Aaron, Phinehas, and David; v. also Pirke, Rabbenu hakkadosh, ed. Grünhut, VII, 9.

[2] Gen. r. 58. 4 ; the burial-place is called קרית ארבע, because there were buried the four fathers of the world, namely, Adam, Abraham, Isaac, and Jacob, Tanh., ed. Buber, I, p. 119 ; cf. Gen. r. 65. 4 ; Pirke R. Hakkad, ed. Grünhut, III, 115. The fathers of the world include Abraham, Jacob, and Hezekiah, Deut. r., 2. 1 ; M. Ps. 13 d, 31 c ; Tanh., I, 196 ; Lam. r. 1. 24 ; Esther r., ch. 7 ; Mid. Lam. Zuta., p. 26 ; Jalkut, ibid., p. 148 ; Exod. r. 25. 10 ; Cant. r. 1. 60 ; Tanh. f. 57 B. 69 a ; M. Ps., ch. 16 (R. Phinehas, 13 d) ; Exod. r. 472 (R. Zebid in the name of R. Joshua ben Levi) ; Eccles. r. 75 refers by אבות העולם to Abraham, Isaac, and Jacob. Some of the scribes were also styled thus, like Shammai and Hillel, by R. Simon ben Jochhai (Gen. r. 1. 21 ; 12. 14'; Lev. r. 36. 1 ; Tanh. B., I, 15); M. Ps. 13 B ; Ishmael and Akiba (v. M. Edujoth, 1. 4 ; j. R. H. 56 d ; cf. MGWJ. 41. 22.

[3] Mech. 11 B : אבות הראשונים נהגו בדרך ארץ; Mech. R. S. b. J., p. 76 ; Gen. r. 68. 11 (R. Joshua ben Levi) ; Lev. r. 36. 3 ; Lev. r. 24. 4 (R. Levi) ; M. Ps. 3 B (R. Berechja) ; Aboth r. Nathan, ch. 9, p. 40 ; Tanh. f. 282 a.

[4] Sifre Deut., par. 353 ; Ps. Jonathan, Deut. 33. 15 ; R. Judah ben

primarily are applied to the three patriarchs. These fathers, the thought of whose creation preceded the creation of the world,[5] meet a different treatment in the theological teachings of the scribes. *R. Eliezer ben Hyrkanos* taught that for some reason or other the patriarchs could not stand in judgement before God (b. Arachin 17 a), they could not pledge before the revelation the success of the Torah, they themselves were in need of sureties.[6] With regard to the faults, says Irenaeus,[7] for which the Scriptures condemn the patriarchs and prophets, we should not censure them, nor act like Ham who ridiculed the shame of his father and so fell under a curse, but we should rather give thanks to God for them seeing that their sins were forgiven them. Even the *Pistis Sophia* [8] says : ' Abraham, Isaac, and Jacob, however, I forgave all their sins and shortcomings, and I revealed unto them the mysteries of light in the aeons, and have placed them on the place of Zabaoth and all the archontes who did repentance.' We may take it for granted therefore that when the scribes dwell on the faults of the fathers more vividly than pointed out in Scripture, it was done for some special purpose, sometimes hidden from us, sometimes for obvious reasons. Yet in the greater part of the literature there is no limit for the praise and the merit of the fathers.

(2) The merits of the fathers effects atonement and

Ilai and R. Nehemia dispute whether the word הרים 'mountains' signifies the ' patriarchs ' or the ' righteous men ' generally, Exod. r. 15. 5 ; Gen. r. 33. 1. Abraham is called הר, Gen. r. 50. 18 ; Agadath Ber. 50 ; Augustine *Sermones*, John 1. 1–5, calls the mountains the ' high ' souls, hills the ' small ' ones, cf. Ps. 71. 3 ; 120. 1. In later times the designation is most usual, cf. הרי עולם, Cant. r. 7. 3 ; (Eliezer ben Hyrkanos and Joshua b. Hananja) j. Jeb. 3 a ; Nazir. 54 d, v. שפת יתר, ed. Lippman, 2 a. In the Gaonic period, v. Harkavy, *Responsen*, p. 25, n. 132 ; Wertheimer, קהלת שלמה, pp. י״ח and נ״ז ; ibid., p. ס״א ; *Resp. of Solomon b. Adereth*, p. 110 c, d, no. 414, ed. Hanau, בית האוצר, p. 57 a ; אור זרוע, I, 15 в.

[5] Pirke, *R. E.*, ch. 3 ; Gen. r. 1. 5.

[6] v. Tanh. f. 52 в ; v. above, p. 51 f.

[7] *Adv. Haer.* I, 28. 1 ; III, 23. 8.

[8] Ibid., § 135 ; Schmidt, *Koptisch-Gnostische Schriften*, I, p. 230. 16.

forgiveness for their children's sins. This is especially emphasized by R. Hama ben Hanina (v. p. 80). The merits of these patriarchs appear as solicitors and advocates (ניקולוגוס) before God when He judges Israel. This is particularly the case on the Day of Judgement. This doctrine influenced a great deal the liturgy of the New Year and that of the Day of Atonement. They had a type of prayers and supplications, of hymns and poems called הזכרת זכות אבות, the remembrance of the merits of the fathers.[9] R. Abahu taught that the festivals and Torah were given to Israel for the merits of the fathers (v. p. 85). The three festivals were fixed by God, and the Torah was given for the merits of the fathers, means that the latter influenced indirectly the fate of the children. They were given so that Israel should not appear with empty hands before God. 'Even in our days', explains this teacher, 'although we are oppressed, the Torah does not depart from us. Just as a man who has his case before the king and his defenders (סניגורין), who plead for him, are able to appease the king, so the observances, charities a man does, who studied the Torah, when he is accused by Satan, his good deeds plead for him' (מלמדין זכות). It was a great mercy of God to give Israel these observances for the sake of the fathers.

Of all the fathers, Isaac has the greatest share in bringing about the atonement of Israel's sin. The sacrifice of Isaac is referred to in this connexion numerous times in the prayers and homilies in these centuries, although the merits of Isaac are very seldom alluded to in the Agadah.[10]

Besides the yearly atonement, there was in the past an

---

[9] v. Halachoth of Isaac ibn Gayyath, שערי שמחה, ed. Bamberger, p. 1 : ויורד שליח ציבור ואומר מה שירצה בדברי שבח והודאה והזכרת זכות אבות.

[10] v. Cant. r. 1. 59: אשכול הכופר זה יצחק שנכפת על גבי המזבח כאשכול הכופר שמכפר עונותיהם של ישראל; Gen. r. 1. 56. 15 ; Lev. r. 29. 8 (R. Jochanan) ; b. R. H. 16 a (R. Abahu) ; Pes. r. 73 в (R. Azarja) ; Lev. r. 36. 4 ; Tanh. f., p. 30 a.

event which called for atonement and forgiveness of sin,
and which was achieved for the merits of the fathers.
God did not destroy the people of Israel after the making
of the golden calf for the Zechut Aboth. This idea is
expressed at first by *R. Meir* who taught : The dead ones
of the gentiles are dead, those of the Israelites are not
dead, for through their merit the living exist (החיים עומדין) ;
an instance for this is, when Israel did that deed, had
Moses not mentioned the merits of the fathers [11] they
surely would have perished from the world.[12] In the
third century R. Meir's teaching was developed by R. Joshua
ben Levi, Hanina ben Hama, Hijja bar Abba and Samuel
b. Nahmani. The first of these scribes, *Joshua ben Levi*,
has two sayings in which he repeats and transcribes
R. Meir's thought. For the merits of the fathers *and* for
the merits of the *tribes* God forgave Israel.[13] In another
passage,[14] taught by R. Zebida, this teacher invented a
dialogue between Moses and God, in order to emphasize
the same teaching. Moses : 'Were the "fathers of the
world" just or wicked ?' God : 'Do make a difference
between these and those' (i.e. between the children of
Israel and between their fathers). Moses : 'If they were
wicked, then it is good to do unto them thus.' God :
'Why ?' Moses : 'Because their fathers have no deeds
(i.e. merits) with you. But if they were just, then give
them the deeds of their fathers.' The deeds of the just
are therefore kept with God for the benefit of their children.
R. Hanina bar Hama, in whose teachings this doctrine

---

[11] Exod. 32. 13.

[12] Tanh. f. 57 a. The teaching that the pious never die, or are called
'living' even after their death, is taught in the Wisdom of Solomon,
3. 1–4 ; 4. 16 ; V. 15 ; IV. Mac, v. Freudenthal, *Flavius Josephus*, p. 47 a,
69 ; Sifrè Deut., par. 357. Moses never died, but serves before God, Deut.
r. 9. 1 ; b, Sotah, 13 B ; j. Ber. 4 d. 6 ; Ber. 18 a ; Gen. r. 39. 7 (R. Isaac) ;
Zohar Trumah, 77 d ; Eccles. r. 9. 4 ; *Tanna debe Eliahu*, r., ch. 18. 61 B and
12 B ; Gen. r. 9. 6 ; *Alphabethum Sirac.* 20 a, v. also the *Sentences of Sextius*,
cf. Sänger, Geiger's *Jüd. Zeitschrift*, V, p. 31, and *Midrash Haserot we
Yeteroth*, p. 72, n. 176.

[13] Exod. r. 47. 8.   [14] Exod. r. 47. 7.

plays a great part, says : ' Had Moses known how appreciated the sacrifices are, he would have sacrificed all the
offerings mentioned in the Torah at the time when Israel
committed that deed, yet he ran and relied on the merits
of the fathers.'[15] This teacher seems to suggest that the
law of sacrifices was at the time yet unknown, otherwise
he might have tried to appease God by sacrifices. Anyhow
he taught that the prayer of Moses was successful, for he
referred to the Zechuth of the fathers. *R. Hijja b. Abba*
who pictures dramatically that scene, when Moses prayed
for his brethren and people (לא הניח משה זוית ברקיע שלא
נתחבט בה) says that Moses drove away three of the five
angels of destruction (מלאכי חבלה) by mentioning the merits
of the fathers.[16] The last of the Agadists enumerated
above, *R. Samuel ben Nahmani*, describes Moses standing
in prayer for forty days and forty nights that God might
forgive them the deed of the golden calf, yet without the
slightest result; but when he mentioned the merits of
the fathers, God at once forgave them.[17] The same conception is to be found in an Agadah of *Hezekiah bar Hijja*
and in many anonymous sayings.[18] It amounts to the
same, when Ps. Philo says: ' God has chosen the people
of Israel and has made this covenant with them for ever ;
if the children of Israel depart from God's ways and forget
His covenant, He delivers them for a time into the hands
of their enemies, but God is ever mindful of his covenant
with the patriarchs. He will always deliver the Israelites
and never abandon them ' (v. *JQR.*, X, 322). This leads
us to understand why, among other attempts to explain
and excuse the deed of the Israelites in the wilderness,
the teachers were eager to preach and proclaim that God
has forgiven that sin on account of the Zechuth Aboth.

[15] Cant. r. 1. 19.   [16] Deut. r. 3. 12.

[17] Exod. r. 44. 2. A fuller version but without name, Deut. r. 3. 15, the
words of R. S. b. N. were repeated by Tanhuma b. Abba, Exod. r. 44. 1,
v. also M. Ps. 8 a ; j. Ber. 8 B.

[18] v Tanh. I, 90 ; Agadath Ber., p. 14 ; Deut. Z., ed. Buber, no. 6.

The opponents of Judaism, from Barnabas to most recent times, found Israel unworthy of being God's chosen people, and added that the whole Law was given as a punishment for that deed.[19] The rabbis replied to all these more or less biased arguments and theories—which have a long and varied history—God forgave our forefathers for the merits of the patriarchs, and wiped out, not Israel, but Israel's sins.

In the following generation this view was taught and explained by R. Acha, R. Phinehas ben Hama, and R. Abun. R. Acha compares the case with a king who had a friend. The latter deposited with the king ten gems. After a short time the friend died and left a daughter. The king married her and gave her a chain of ten pearls. The queen lost the chain, and the king became so enraged for losing it that he wanted to divorce her. Then the queen's best man came in order to persuade the king that he should not carry out his intention. He was not successful at the first or the second attempt. When the best man saw that the king had made up his mind to divorce his wife, he said: 'You want to drive her away because she took your ten gems. Do you think I do not know that her father deposited with you ten gems? Let these be instead of the others.' When Israel committed that deed, God wanted to destroy Israel. Moses said: 'Why art Thou angry?' God: 'Because they nullified the Ten Commandments.' Moses: 'They have something to pay you with.' God: 'What?' Moses: 'Remember the Ten Trials of the fathers' (v. p. 100). R. Phinehas ben Hama says: 'If a man does a *Mitzwah* (i. e. performs a commandment), he should not ask for his reward at once (מיד ליד).' Why? That thou shalt not go out empty, for thou wilt not become free from thy sins and art called wicked, for thou didst not try to leave to thy children anything. Had

---

[19] v. Barnabas letter, cf. Harnack, *Texte und Untersuchungen*, 20, p. 132; Iren., *adv. haeres*, 15. 1; 10. 3; Tertullian, *adv. Marc.*, IV, 5; Diestel, *Die Ausleg. des A. T.*, pp. 55–60.

the fathers claimed the reward of their deeds, how could the seed of the righteous be saved ? The surplus righteousness of the fathers was preserved for the offspring. When they did that deed, God saved them (v. p. 102). R. Abun says: 'Moses referred to the righteous, who took no part in that deed, and included the merits of the fathers with them.' We see R. Abun combining the self-acquired merits with those of the fathers. Anonymous teachers found this doctrine expressed in Ps. 3. 3. Many people say to Israel: 'Such a nation, who committed such a thing, after having heard the Decalogue has no hope.' 'But', says Israel, 'God protects me for the merits of the fathers.' [20] Ps. Jonathan Targum frequently points out that Israel was saved in spite of its faults, for the merits of the fathers. To Deut. 1. 1 the Targumist adds, God wanted to destroy Israel when it asked for meat, yet it was saved for the merits of the fathers. To Deut. 9. 19 the fathers are represented as praying in their graves for their children. And finally to Deut. 28. 15 we read the following legend: 'When Moses, the prophet, began to say these words of reproof, earth and heaven quaked in terror, sun, moon, and stars were darkened, the fathers of the world cried bitterly from their graves, all creatures kept silence, the trees did not move. The fathers of the world said: "Have pity (mercy) upon our children when they are guilty. If these curses come upon them, how will they endure it? You might destroy them and our merits cannot protect them; besides us there is no one to intercede on their behalf." There came a "daughter voice" (Bath Kol) from heaven, saying: "Be not afraid, fathers of the world! Even if all the merits of all the generations cease to protect them, yours shall never cease to do so, just as My covenant with you will never be destroyed."' We see that the Targumist held the view that the merits of the fathers operate for the benefit of the children for ever.

[20] Pes., p. 10 a; Tanh. B., II, p. 106 : Pes. r., p. 39 a.

The Agadists were not unanimous on this point. R. Joshua ben Levi (p. 71), R. Jochanan (v. notes), R. Levi (v. p. 89), Abba b. Zabda (v. p. 92), R. Hanina b. Isaac (p. 104), and the Babylonian Amoraim Rab and Samuel (v. p. 107), give each of them different periods when the merits of the fathers ceased. R. Acha teaches that the merits of the fathers will never cease to influence the course of Jewish history (v. p. 100). The anonymous Agadah shows also traces of this antagonism in contemporary theological thought. Whilst one derives from Eccles. 8. 5, ותפר האביונה, the view that 'the merits of the fathers shall fail'.[21] another Agadist proclaims: ' Whensoever we are in trouble and distress, and we mention the deeds of the fathers before Thee, and their remembrance ascends before Thee, it is regarded as more than all the drink-offerings we offered on the altar.'[22]

(3) The merits of the fathers are emphasized in Agadah in all great events of biblical history. For the merits of the fathers was Israel redeemed from Egypt,[23] likewise was the Manna given and the victory over Amalek,[24] Israel inherited Palestine.[25] Zabdi ben Levi teaches that in all narratives where the word לילי occurs, there is an allusion to the merits of the fathers (p. 92).

The merits of the fathers appear especially in the numerous sayings which have reference to the merits of Abraham, Isaac, Jacob, Judah, Joseph and the tribes, Moses, Aaron and Miriam of the house of David, the contemporaries of Isaiah and of the martyrs.[26] The names of a few

[21] Eccles. r. 12. 8 ; Lam. r. 1. 23, ed. Buber, p. 22 ; M. Lam. Zutta, p. 130.

[22] Agadath Cant., ed. Schechter, 14. 1. 345.

[23] R. Judah ben Ilai, Exod. r. 15. 5.

[24] R. Eleazar of Modiim, p. 41 f.

[25] Eliezer the son of R. Jose the Galilaean, v. p. 57 f.

[26] Quite a number of teachers ascribe the creation of the world to the merit of *Abraham* (R. Joshua b. Korha, p. 59 ; R. Judan, p. 100 ; R. Azarja, p. 103, and Halafta b. Kahana, p. 105). The redemption from Egypt (R. Eleazar ben Azarja, p. 43), the miracle at the sea (Shemaja, p. 37; R. Benaah, p. 47), the supply in the wilderness, Manna (R. Simai, p. 65 ; Hama b. Hanina, p. 81 ; R. Hanin, p. 99), various deliverances through-

scribes who were regarded as men whose merits were beneficial to the world are: Hanina ben Dosa, Simon ben Jochai, Hijja and his sons, Joshua ben Levi, Adda b. Ahaba, and Rab. By mentioning these names we have turned from the merits of the fathers to the merits of the righteous, which shall be dealt with in one of the following chapters.

This enumeration of the merits of the fathers, collectively and individually, enables us to consider the ethical and philosophical ideas which the scribes thought of God and the world, of Creator and man, of Past and Present, of Israel and the Gentiles. The Patriarchs, as well as other personages of the Bible, accomplished or came near to

out history (Eleazar b. Shamua, p. 56 ; R. Eleazar, p. 84 ; R. Levi, p. 88 ; R. Azarja, p. 103), every blessing (Hanina b. Hama, p. 67 ; R. Levi, p. 88), even dew (Simon ben Lakish, p. 79) came or comes to Israel and to the world for the merit of Abraham. R. Levi says that the Shechinah was tabernacled in Israel for Abraham's sake. Few are the references to the merits of *Isaac* (v. above, pp. 75, 81, 149). More numerous are those to the merits of *Jacob*. For his merit was the creation of the universe (R. Reuben, p. 99 ; Hanina ben Isaac, p. 104), the rescue of Abraham from Nimrod's fiery furnace (R. Samuel ben Nahmani, p. 83), the miracle at the sea (R. Akiba, p. 44), and at the Jordan (R. Jochanan, p. 76), the Shechinah (R. Abba b. Kahana, p. 91) and success in life and business (Judan, p. 100 ; Azarja, p. 103). Similar methods were applied by the Agadists in pointing out the merits of *Judah*, his self-sacrifice at the crossing of the sea (R. Tarphon, p. 45), and his meekness (R. Levi, p. 88) made his tribe and descendants worthy of the leadership in Israel. Some attribute to the merit of *Joseph* the miracles of the crossing of the sea (Simon of Katron, p. 47) and that of the Jordan (Judah ben Simon, p. 92). Others speak of the *twelve tribes* generally for whose merit the world was created (R. Joshua ben Nehemia, p. 101), the sea was crossed (Eliezer ben Judah of Bartota, p. 97), and finally Jerusalem will be rebuilt (Acha, p. 100). Greater is, of course, the merit of *Moses* for whose merits the universe was created (R. Acha, p. 100), the world exists (together with the merits of *Aaron*) (R. Jochanan, p. 76), Israel was redeemed from Egypt (R. Levi, p. 89), crossed the sea (R. Acha, I, p. 100), had the Manna (Levi, p. 89 ; R. Berechja, p. 102), adds ' clouds of glory for Aaron's and the well for *Miriam's* merit, v. also R. Jochanan, p. 76, and finally those buried in the wilderness will be restored to life for Moses' merit (R. Levi, p. 88). Occasional references are to be found to the merits of the kings of the *house of David* (Abba b. Kahana, p. 91), the generation of *Isaiah* (p. 91), *the three martyrs* (Eliezer ben Jacob, p. 57), and to the *ten martyrs of the Hadrianic period* (p. 105).

perfection by their faith and love, unselfishness and charity, observances and performances, studies and works—of those ideals for which alone the world was worthy to be called into existence, and for which it deserves to exist. Thus they gathered treasures in heaven not for themselves but for others. By their works and charity their descendants experienced miracles and wonders in the course of their historical life. By their merits Israel escaped thousands of perils and dangers. For their sake Israel's immortality and eternity are assured.

(4) But not only do the merits of the fathers save or benefit the children, the merits of the children do a great deal of good to their parents. We have to mention first of all a story of *R. Akiba*. R. Akiba took a walk in a cemetery, and met a naked black man carrying on his shoulders wood, running like a horse. R. Akiba made him stand still, saying: 'If you are a slave, and your master is very cruel, I will redeem you. In case you are very poor, I will help you with money.' The man: 'I pray you let me go, because I am afraid that my superintendents in Hell will become very angry with me.' R. Akiba said: 'Who are you, and what is your work?' The man said: 'I am dead, and daily am I sent forth to gather wood, by which I am burnt.' R. Akiba inquired about his work before his death. The man confesses having been a publican (or tax-farmer), when he favoured the rich and tortured the poor. R. Akiba further inquires: 'Have you heard perhaps from your superintendents whether there is some hope for you?' The man replies: 'Yes, I heard something which is, however, impossible. They said: "If I had a son who would rise in the community to say Kaddish, and the members of the community would answer 'Amen', I could be saved." Well, I left my wife with child, and I do not know whether she gave birth to a boy or a girl, and supposing the first is the case, who will teach my son Torah, for he is friendless in this world.' R. Akiba took upon himself the duty to be this friend. R. Akiba asked him:

'What is your name?' He replied: 'Ukba.' R. Akiba: The
name of your wife? He: שישובא. R. A.: The name of
your place? לנקועה. R. Akiba immediately went to this
place where, after making the usual inquiries, the people
cursed the memory of the man, they told him that the
boy was not even circumcised. R. A. initiated him into
the covenant of Abraham and began to teach him Torah.
Love's labour was lost and R. A. spent forty days fasting.
Then he heard a voice from heaven: 'Akiba, why are you
fasting?' R. A. says: 'I pledged myself.' Then God
opened the boy's heart, and he learnt Torah, Kaddish, the
Amidah, Berachot, and grace after meals. He put him
before the community, where he said: 'Blessed be the
Lord to whom blessing is due.' The community replied:
'Blessed be the name of the glory of His kingdom.' And
he said Kaddish, and they replied: 'Amen'. By this
the boy saved his father from Hell. The man appeared
to R. Akiba in his dream, and thanked him especially.[27]
This story presupposes, as already well known in the
second century, the idea of the force and power of the
prayers uttered by the children for the well-being of
the parents after death. Some external, as well as internal, reasons show that the story cannot be very old,
the religious conceptions (like the walking of the deceased
spirits in the cemeteries, their being black and naked,
running like horses, the burning in fire, the superintendents, the fasting of forty days), as well as the historical
background (the position of the tax-farmer, the wealth
of R. Akiba, the names of man and wife, of Laodicea)
make the dating of the story quite uncertain, if not
impossible. Yet we find in the generation after R. Akiba

[27] Tanh. מנורת המאור, I, 1; Grünhut's הליקוטים ס', VI, p. 19 B, f.
and Introduction, to the references given there, v. also הגין נפש
by Abraham ben Hijja, p. lix, ראשית חכמה, p. 204 d. Read Laodicea
instead of לנקועה, v. also Gaster's המעשיות ס', p. 92; אנור, p. 29 a;
Gaonic Responsa, ed. Coronel, No. 94; Jellinek, בה"מ, I, 90; Mahzor Vitry,
§ 144; Friedmann, Ps. El. Zutta, p. 22.

teachings which closely resemble those contained in the
story of R. Akiba. We mention first the view of *R. Judah
ben Ilai*, 'And I returned and saw' (Eccles. 4. 1). R. Judah
says: 'These are the minors who die in the lifetime (of
their parents) *for the sin of their parents* in this world.
In the world to come they are standing in the company
of the righteous, and their parents will be among the
wicked. They (the children) shall say: "We died only
for the sins of our parents, *let them come to us for our
merits.*"' God says: 'Your parents sinned after your
death too, then let their sins accuse them.' Then Elijah
teaches them to defend the parents, saying: 'Lord of the
whole world! Which measure is greater, the measure of
mercy or the measure of punishment? Certainly the
former is greater, and the latter smaller. We died for
the sins of our fathers, if the measure of mercy be greater,
then naturally our parents ought to be with us.' Then
God says: 'You defended your parents rightly. Let your
parents come and be saved from Hell for the merits of their
children. Therefore let every one teach his children Torah
in order that they shall save him from Hell.'[28] We see
here that children, when very young, die for the sins of
their parents, and save them, through the study of the
Torah from the punishment of Hell. It must not be
forgotten that R. Judah ben Ilai was a contemporary of the
Hadrianic persecutions and endured the aftermath of the
Bar-Kochba war, when the study of the Law was prohibited
by the political authorities. How many were weak enough
to obey the threats and decrees of the tyrant? The idea
that children, whilst they are not responsible for their own
actions, die for the sins of their parents, is also expressed
in the Sifrê (§ 280): 'Each man shall die for his sin,
i. e. the parents die for their own sin, children die for the
sins of their parents.' Premature death of children comes,
according to the views of the Rabbis, for the parents' sins.

[28] Eccles. r. 4. 1.

R. Meir and *R. Judah ben Ilai* dispute on this point, whether death comes for the sin of neglecting the commandment of Mezuzah or Zizith.[29] *R. Nehemia* held for the sin of hatred, which is unjustified.[30] *R. Eleazar ben Simon* and *R. Judah I* dispute on the same question. According to one (R. E. b. S.) for the sin of vows, according to the other for the neglect of Torah.[31] The father of R. Eleazar, *R. Simon ben Jochai*, says that those of the generation of the flood, who did not reach the hundredth year, died for the sins of their parents.[32] A contemporary of these scribes, *R. Meir*, invented a dialogue between God and Israel before the revelation of the Law. God wanted sureties before He handed the Law to Israel. They referred first to the fathers and their merits. God found this unsatisfactory. Then they referred to the children, and their pledge was accepted.[33] Apart from the homiletical character of the whole passage, we see here clearly the idea that God gave the Law to Israel for the merit of future generations. *R. Josiah*, who was older than these Tannaites, and belongs to the pupils of R. Ishmael,[34] expressed our doctrine in clearer words, when he says: 'For three things shows God compassion to the wicked (האריך פנים) in this world: (*a*) perhaps they might repent, (*b*) they may accomplish good works for which they get their reward in this world, and (*c*) perhaps they will have righteous children. A biblical proof for the last category is Ahaz, who brought forth Hezekiah, Amon whose son was Josiah, and Simei whose protector was his son Mordecai.[35] The wicked fathers benefit by the piety of their children.

Some Rabbis differ from R. Judah ben Ilai and R. Nehemia in the explanation of Exod. 2. 13 as to the motive of Moses in killing the Egyptian, because he saw that no righteous man would descend from him, nor from

---

[29] b. Sabb. 32 B.   [30] Ibid. 32 B.   [31] Ibid.
[32] M. Ps. 12, ed. B., ed. Pr. has R. Simon ben Lakish.
[33] Cant. r. 1. 24, v. p. 55.   [34] v. however p. 93.
[35] Eccles. r. 7. 32.

his seed, to the end of all generations. When Moses recognized this fact, he consulted the angels and asked them: 'Is this man guilty of death?' They said, 'Yes.' That is the meaning of the text: And he saw that there was none who would plead the merits of this man.[36] 'And Moses saw by his wisdom and understood that no proselyte will come forth from this man.'[37] The action of Moses was objected to,[38] therefore the scribes endeavoured to explain away Moses' deed. For our purpose we see clearly that the merits of the unborn generations can save their ancestors from misfortune and trouble. The scribes held namely the Stoic doctrine that the souls of the yet unborn generations are created already, and are merely waiting for their turn to come into existence. R. Jose ben Halafta, a contemporary of these scribes, was influenced by the same doctrine, when he taught that Korah was released from hell for the prayer of his descendant, Hannah (v. p. 55). Again, R. Eliezer ben Jacob, who ascribes the redemption from Egypt to the martyrdom of Hananiah, Mishael, and Azaria (v. p. 57).

This conception influenced also to some extent the Halachah. There is a view that it is not permitted to announce publicly the losses which occurred to an Am Haarez.[39] There was, however, another opinion which allowed the advertisement of the losses of the Am Haarez. The reason is that sometimes the children of the Am Haarez will become Pharisees, and for the sake of the children the Am Haarez shares the rights of the Perushim. This rule was also emphasized in the case of the public informer. There is a view, namely, which does not permit the destruction of the property belonging to the public informer, because his children might choose a more decent

---

[36] שילמד עליו זכות, Exod. r. 1. 33 ; Ps. Jon. Targum, Exod. 2. 12.

[37] v. Illescas, אמרי נועם, p. 11 в.

[38] v. Clem. Hom. II, ch. 4.

[39] b. Pes. 49 в, ויש אומרין אף אין מכריין על אבידתו ; Pirke, *R. H.*, VI, 23, ed. Schonblum in the Text.

profession.[40] These opinions and views are expressed by
the Amoraim, yet it is not unlikely that they reflect the
thought of the Tannaites.

The Amoraic Agadah fully endorsed this view of their
predecessors. It will be sufficient to refer to some of
their statements. For instance, *R. Joshua ben Levi*, who
said that the community of Korah was sinking lower and
lower (שוקעת ויורדת) up to the time when Hannah prayed
for them.[41] The prayer of Hannah saved the Korahites
from further punishment. Similar is the teaching of
R. Hijja (bar Abba?): 'The bird (v. Deut. 22. 6) which
has got neither " the merits of the fathers " nor " covenants ",
and no oaths, still their young ones atone for them (i. e.
they save them from being sent away), how much more
should the merit of the children atone for one of Abraham's
or Isaac's or Jacob's descendants, in case they sinned.'[42]
R. Samuel ben Isaac derives from Isa. 29. 22 that Abraham
was saved from the fiery furnace for the sake of Jacob.[42a]

Older than *Samuel ben Isaac's* is a similar doctrine
of *Bar Kappara*, who explained to his audience why
Abraham was saved from Nimrod's fiery furnace. He
based his teaching on Cant. 8. 8 f. Abraham was like
a man who (מאחה) repairs with patches (קרע). He was
engaged performing commandments and charity whilst he
was little, and he had no ' breasts ' because he was not yet
obliged to perform commandments and charity. What
shall we do to him who repaired with patches (לאחותינו) on
the day we are speaking of (i. e. the day Nimrod the
wicked made him be thrown in the fiery furnace)? If she
be a wall, we will build upon her a turret of silver. 'If
she be a wall,' that is Abraham, God said : If he establishes
things like a wall, we will build upon it a turret of silver,
i. e. we will save him and establish him in the world.
And if it be a door, we will enclose it with boards of

[40] b. B. B. 119 a.   [41] 1 Sam. 2. 10 ; Synh. 4 a.
[42] Deut. r. 6. 3, I read שאם סרח אחד מהם שבנו מכפר עליהם.
[42a] v. Gen. r. 63. 2.

cedar. If he (Abraham) be poor, empty of good deeds
(דל), and his deeds are movable, i. e. not firm, like a door,
we will enclose upon it a board of cedar. Just as this
enclosure only holds for a short time, likewise he will not
be established for a long period. 'I am a wall,' Abraham
said before God. 'I am a wall, and I will establish good
deeds like a wall, and my breasts are like turrets, because
I shall bring forth many bands and companies, like me, in
Thy world. Then was I in His eyes as one that found
peace. God said to him : Just as thou descendest in the
furnace of fire, likewise will I bring thee out without
harm thence as it said : "I am the Lord who delivered
thee from the fire of the Chaldeans".'[43] The implication
of this long sermon must have been : For whose merit did
Abraham escape from Nimrod's fiery furnace ? Only for
the merit of the pious and righteous descendants who will
live after him. Bar Kappara taught, therefore, that the
escape of Abraham was not for Jacob's merit alone, but for
the merits of all the righteous in Israel. There are, of
course, in this sermon other Agadic types and problems,
for instance, the Doctrine of the observances by Abraham,
the figures of 'wall' and 'door' in the Agadah which
cannot be discussed here.

R. Eleazar ben Pedath taught that all the miracles
which God performed for Israel, e. g. the redemption from
Egypt and the crossing of the sea, were not for their
works, but for the sake of posterity that they should
relate God's praise among the nations.[44] *R. Simon* dealt
with our problem in connexion with the story of Noah.
'We find', he says, 'that God shows lovingkindness to
posterity for the sake of the fathers (הראשונים), whence do
we know that God does charity with the fathers for the
merits of posterity ? From Noah. And Noah found favour
with God for whose merit ? For the merit of his off-

[43] Gen. 15. 7 ; Cant. r. 8. 9.
[44] M. Ps. B., p. 268. According to Jalkut's rendering, Ps., par. 746 ;
Deut. r., ch. 3 ; j. Taanit 63 d ; Pes. r., p. 184 B.

spring.' [45]   *R. Juda ha-Levi ben Shalom* saw in 1 Chron.
22. 9 a proof that the birth of Solomon was a sign that
God has forgiven his father's sin.[46]

This teaching is, however, older than Simon ben Pazzi or
Abbahu.   For already the Book of Jubilees (5. 19) says:
'His person was accepted on behalf of his sons, whom God
saved from the waters of the flood on his account.'   Hanina
ben Papa proved in an agadic way that Noah was saved
for the merit of Moses (p. 91).

R. Jose ben Zimra (p. 70), and after him R. Alexander
(v. p. 73), prove that just as the merits of the fathers help
the children, we have instances in the Bible where the
merits of the children help the fathers.   We may regard it
as an established fact that the Rabbis of the second and
third centuries believed that the deeds and merits of the
children by their piety and faithfulness, by their study of
the law and prayers, can and do benefit their parents.   The
Kaddish prayer is based on this doctrine.   To whom the
meaning of the Kaddish is alive, the thought which the
words express present to his mind, it must always be
life-giving and comfort-bearing.   Unfortunately there are
people who think that the words of the Kaddish in themselves possess material and magical powers, and turn them
into charms, 'Then the purpose which they answer is to
hide God from us.'   The meaning of the doctrine is so
natural and clear that we find it everywhere where
common sense prevails in ethical thought and theological
speculation.

Here again we have to refer to Seneca, after having
enumerated the views of the Tannaim and Amoraim, who
says: 'The Gods help very often even those who are
unworthy of their help, for the sake of their descendants.
They know that some of the children or grandchildren
of this man are to become great and virtuous.   Some-

[45] Gen. r. 39. 5 ; Tanh. f. 9 B, v. *MGWJ.*, 1887, pp. 147, 120. This is
also taught in the name of *R. Abahu.*
[46] M. Ps., ed. Buber, p. 46.

times the wicked are saved, for they are descendants
of those who are God's beloved friends.[47] It is, therefore,
not 'Rabbinical craziness' which invents these theories,
but they show step by step the influence of Stoic thought.
The same view is to be found in the Shayas la Shayash,[48]
where we read: 'The duty and good works which a son
performs are as much the father's as though they had been
done by his own hand.' A mediaeval Jewish ethical writer,
Eliah de Vidas, concludes with a quotation: 'Greater is
the power of defence on the part of the children for their
parents, than *vice versa*.'[49]

(5) There is to be noticed a strong opposition to the
doctrine of the merits of the fathers! The idea had its
shadow as well as its light. From the educational point
of view the merits of the fathers have filled with zeal
numberless Jews to imitate the lofty examples shown by
the fathers. Yet knowing what human nature is, the
scribes became aware of or experienced the abuses to which
this doctrine led. We have seen that during centuries
a fight of opinions wavered between the two schools which
taught the doctrine of self-acquired and vicarious merits.
The latter remained victorious. The more was it opportune
to warn against the danger and onesidedness of the recognized school and opinion. There must have been people
who sinned and went astray, yet they relied on the virtues
of their fathers. They thought: 'We can walk after the
desire of our hearts, the "treasure" gathered by our fathers
will always hold good for us, will protect us, and grant
us forgiveness.' More than one earnest appeal is directed
against these in the anonymous Agadah. Fathers cannot
save their children. Abraham could not save Ishmael, nor
could Isaac protect Esau, as it is said: 'None can save
from my hands' (Deut. 32. 39). Whence is it derived that
a brother cannot save his brother? e.g. Isaac and Ishmael,

[47] v. Keim, *Rom und Christentum*, p. 33.
[48] X, 22; XII, 15.
[49] ראשית חכמה, p. 203 d.

Jacob and Esau? It is said: 'No man can redeem his brother' (Ps. 49. 8). Why? Because it is said: 'Too costly is the redemption of their soul.' Too costly is the soul of man, hence if a man sinned there is no ransom for his soul.[50] The righteousness and deeds, merits and virtues of the fathers cannot redeem the unworthy offspring from the punishment they fully deserve. This was the view of Abtaljon and his followers. This is implied in Hillel's words. This anonymous Agadah was used by the late compiler of the Aboth of R. Nathan in explaining Hillel's word. Very frequently is this disapproval expressed in the Midrash on Psalms. To Ps. 141. 1 an Agadist puts in David's prayer the words: 'There are some people who trust in their own good works, there are others who trust in their fathers' works, I trust in Thee!'[51] To Ps. 146. 3 we have a paraphrase of the passage in the Sifrê: 'A man should not trust in the works of his fathers. A man like Ishmael should not say: Abraham is my father! I will have of his share, and he will save me! Esau should not say: Jacob is my brother, and for his merits shall I be saved! No, as it is said: "No one can redeem his brother" (Ps. 49. 8). If a man does not perform good works by himself in this world, there is no use in trusting in the work of his fathers, therefore it says: "Put not your trust in princes" (Ps. 146. 3). Wherein shall you put your trust? In your own works (cf. Prov. 9. 12 and 16. 26). In the world to come none shall enjoy the works of his fathers, but each one shall eat of his own (Eccles. 6. 7; 3. 22). A man shall have no other merits but his own.'[52] There is a third passage to be mentioned of the same Midrash: 'On the day of judgement Israel will look forward to the fathers that they may plead on their behalf. Yet no father can save his son, and none his brother. Then Israel will look to God, the father in heaven, and will say: Thou art our father, for Abraham

[50] Sifrê, Deut., § 329; Midr. Tannaim, p. 202.
[51] Ed. Buber, p. 531.   [52] Ibid., p. 534.

does not know us' (Isa. 63. 16).[53] None can help Israel
but He who spake and heaven and earth were made.
These three anonymous passages convey to us a strong
opposition to those who relied upon their ancestors' merit,
and had no merits of their own. There is another passage
in the anonymous Agadah, perhaps much older than those
of the Midrash Psalms, which protests against the extreme
use of the merits of the fathers. The nations live for the
merits of Noah. Israel could be misled to believe: How
much more is due to us who rely on the merits of our
ancestors, Abraham, Isaac, and Jacob! Our eternity is
assured even without our own works or deeds. 'No',
says the Agadist, 'Israel lives for the merits of the observances, but not for the merits of the fathers.'[54]

In the sayings of the Amoraim we detect traces of this
opposition in the saying of R. Jose ben Zimra (v. p. 70).
People who rely entirely on their own merits, those who
get conceited as well as those who have no other merits
than those of their fathers are rebuked. There must be a
healthy proportion between one's own merits and those
of his fathers. R. Jonathan ben Eliezer paraphrases
Isa. 63. 16: 'For Thou art our father, for Abraham
knoweth us not, and Israel (Jacob) does not acknowledge
us,' by means of the following legend. At the day of
judgement God will say to Abraham and Jacob: Your

---

[53] Ed. Buber, p. 505, ed. Prague, 63 B.

[54] Midr. Tannaim, p. 62, v. note 9. There is no difference of opinion
between this passage and the view held in Sifrê, Deut., par. 94 or par. 184,
where we read הכל בזכות אבות because it refers to special promises and
predictions, namely, to Deut. 13. 18; ונתן and ישוב מחרון אפו, והרבך
לך רחמים, and Deut. 19. 8. אם ירחיב where the words כאשר נשבע
imply זכות אבות because such an oath is not explicitly mentioned in the
text. The same is to be observed with regard to Exod. 13. 5, where the
Mechilta of R. Simon, p. 32, reads: אשר נשבע לאבותיך הכל בזכות אבות.
Yet all these do not really contradict our passage, as the editors (Schechter
and Hoffmann) thought. The fact is that all the promises which conclude with the words כאשר נשבע לאבותיך, and are not given in Genesis,
contain an allusion to the merits of the fathers, הכל refers to the
promises.

children sinned. Yet they do not plead their children's case, but Isaac will do so. Then Israel praises Isaac for it, they say: Thou (Isaac) art our father! Isaac replies: Instead of praising me, come and praise God, for He is our father, our redeemer for everlasting is Thy name. He combines the merits of the fathers with God's grace, for which Israel obtains forgiveness of sin. R. Isaac (v. p. 88) has chosen the biography of Esau to illustrate that no father can help his son, procure for him forgiveness of sins. R. Acha b. Hanina (v. p. 93) found in Ezek. 18. 6 the praise of Him who does not rely upon the merits of the fathers. R. Aibo (v. p. 98) calls those people who do not work for their own salvation and justification before God, but trust in the deeds of the fathers, 'lazy labourers'.[55]

A second objection to this doctrine was raised from another quarter. If the 'merits of the fathers' were really of such importance as held by the Jews, so people asked: 'Why did those merits not prevent the destruction of the Temple? Could the fathers not avert the terrible misfortune and sufferings of the Jews? Why are the merits of the fathers not visible in our own days and life? Thus or similarly might the scribes have been interrogated by Jews and Gentiles alike who considered this doctrine critically. We saw that various teachers of the third and fourth centuries tried to show the time-limit when the influence of the fathers' merits ceased (v. p. 154).' There can be no doubt about it that these discussions originated by the question: Were the fathers indifferent as to the fate of Israel in moments of national catastrophe and tragedy? Some of the scribes give us even at length the prayers and intercessions of the fathers in times of distress.[56] In the fourth century the teaching prevailed, as we have shown, in spite of the previous objections,

[55] v. also R. Joshua ben Nehemia, p. 101.

[56] v. esp. Buber's ספרי דאגדתא, pp. 37, 47, and 49 ; R. Samuel b. Nahmani, Lam. r., Introd., par. 24 ; R. Hanina b. Isaac, Lam. r. 2. 4 and 2. 18; Pes. r., p. 133 ʀ.

which disappeared or lost their actuality, that the merits of the father will never cease. An anonymous saying which was the source of many liturgical productions in later centuries teaches that God listens to Israel's prayer in exile and brings redemption for the merits of the fathers. He explains, namely, Cant. 8. 14: 'Make haste, My beloved (deliver us) from the exile we are in, and stained by sins. And be thou like to a gazelle,' i. e. cleanse us like a gazelle. Or 'to a young hart', i. e. Thou mayest receive our prayers as substitute for sacrifices. Upon the mountains of spices may the good odour come before Thee for the merit of the fathers; the sweet savour of which ascends before Thee like spices (Cant. r. 8. 15). Even in exile, long after the destruction of the temple, the merit of the fathers protect Israel.

Of a quite different nature was the third objection raised against the doctrine. A very significant passage refers to Ps. 129. 2: 'When thou eatest the labour of thy hands', that is the Proselyte. He has got no Zechuth Aboth, yet we should not say: 'Woe unto me, in spite of all the good I do, since I have no Zechuth Aboth, I have my share merely in this world, but nothing in the world to come! No, he will eat the fruits of his works in both worlds.' [57] There must have been people who thought and taught that without Zechuth Aboth one can have no share in future life. This view was also contradicted by another anonymous writer. To Eccles. 7. 11, 'Good is wisdom with an inheritance', Good is wisdom which can be joined with the merits of the fathers. Happy is he who can trust upon Zechuth Aboth, and upon whose earthly path Zechuth Aboth throws light and blessing.[58] Our Agadist holds that even without Zechuth Aboth one can inherit future life.

The opposition to the doctrine of 'Zechuth Aboth' is to be found in the Gospels. 'And think not to say within yourselves: We have Abraham to our father: for I say

---

[57] Num. r. 8. 10.   [58] Eccles. r. 7. 22.

unto you that God is able of these stones to raise up
children unto Abraham.'[59] There might have been Jews
who boasted of Abraham and trusted that evil cannot
reach them. 'The Zechuth of Abraham cannot save you,
others will be called Abraham's seed', was the answer
to them. John 8. 38-40 has a similar saying: 'I speak
that which I have seen with my Father, and ye do that
what you have seen with your father.' They answered
and said unto him: 'Abraham is our Father.' Luke 16. 21
preserved further the Jewish doctrine that the dead are
carried by the angels into Abraham's bosom, but to
the rich man Abraham says: 'Son, remember that thou in
thy lifetime receivedst thy good things, and likewise
Lazarus evil things; but now he is comforted and thou
art tormented' (v. 25).[60] In the *Apost. Const.* 8. 41 we
find the prayer: Give him his lot in the land of the pious
that are sent unto the bosom of Abraham, Isaac, and Jacob
(v. also Pionius, ch. 14). The term of חיקו של אברהם, bosom
of Abraham, was, as we see, adopted by the Church. Did
the Synagogue know this idea? In the Tanhuma we
read: Whosoever is circumcised, does not descend to the
Gehinom (v. p. 180). In Gen. r. 48. 7 *R. Levi* says: In
the world to come Abraham will sit on the doormat of
Gehinom and will not allow a circumcised Jew to enter.
R. Levi, it seems, endeavours to contradict the teaching
of Luke, who draws a distinction between the beggar and
rich. There is no Israelite, he means to say, who will not
be carried into the bosom of Abraham. The same view
is held by the author of the Daniel Apocalypse: Abraham
will care for it that all of his seed, all Israelites, shall enter

[59] Matt. 3. 9.

[60] The same idea occurs in the Testament of Abraham (ed. James, p. 72),
in the Apocalypse of Zephania (*Zeitschrift für Aegypt. Sprache*, 1886, p. 121);
Apoc. Pauli (par. 27. 47); *Acta Andreae et Matthiae* (ed. Tischendorf, *Acta
Apoc.*, p. 145); Apocalypse of Daniel (Merx, *Archiv*, I, 425). In early compositions of Art illustrating the Last Judgement, e. g. on the West Portal
of S. Isophine of Arles, North Portal of Rheims Cathedral, West front of
Lincoln Cathedral, Bourges in the North Choir. In the mediaeval Vision
of S. Barontus, *c.* 700, of Pistoia (*Bollandist Acts*, March 25, p. 370).

into Paradise.[61] In b. Erubin 19 a the same view is expressed. Abraham saves all Jews from Gehinom except those who married heathen women. In the legend of Miriam bath Tanhum and her seven sons, the mother says to the youngest: 'What dost thou want that all of thy brothers shall be put into the bosom of Abraham, except thee?'[62] All these instances show that even the rich man is carried into the bosom of Abraham when he is worthy and of Abraham's seed.

Tertullian reproaches the Jews (*Apologeticum* 21. 5, v. Schrör's *Tertullian's Apologeticum*, p. 21): 'On account of their *great trust in the patriarchs* they are misled from the right path, they turned from their law in a manner which abrogates its holiness and forsook great things.' In the same manner preaches Chrysostom:[63] 'Him then let us also imitate and let us glorify God in all things by a heedful way of life, and *let us not feel confidence in the virtue of our ancestry, knowing the example that has been made of the Jews.*' In all these sayings, which can easily be multiplied, we see the antagonism of the Church to the doctrine of the virtues or merits of the ancestors. Yet, as we saw, there was no need for the scribes to wait for the warnings from outside. The Church itself adopted this teaching of the merits of good deeds before God as formulated by Tertullian and introduced by Cyprian.[64] It appears unjust to throw the burden of the evil consequences which a misunderstood aspect of this doctrine wrought upon the scribes. The Greeks praying before their gods remind us of their ancestors' works or their sacrifices.[65] When Gfrörer (*Jhdt. des Heils*, I², p. 187) says:

[61] Merx, *Archiv*, I, 425.

[62] Pes. r., p. 180 B, v. also Lam. r. 3. 65; Seder Elijah r., ch. 30; b. Gittin, 57 B; *RÉJ*. 54. 138, note 1.

[63] *Hom. Rom.*, p. 356.

[64] v. Wirth, H. Carl, *Der Verdienst-Begriff in der christl. Kirche nach seiner gesch. Entwickelung dargestellt*, 2 vol., Leipzig, 1892–1901; v. Smend, *Lit. Centralblatt*, 1901, no. 1674.

[65] v. Leop. Schmidt, *Die Ethik der Griechen*, I, p. 86; Ausfeld, *De Graecorum precationibus*, pp. 506 a, 526 f; *A. R. W.*, XI, 17 f. 18.

'It is just in the spirit of a business-like account, which was in the innermost nature of Judaism'[66] to teach such a doctrine, we would remind him of the prayers of Chryses in the introduction of the Iliad, where the allusion to the good works and merits acquired before God is nothing else but barter.[67]

[66] Gfrörer, A. Fr., *Das Jahrhundert des Heils*, II, p. 187.

[67] *A.R.W.*, XI, p. 18 ; v., however, Luthardt's *Kompendium der Dogmatik*, 1889, p. 290, for the biased Protestant conception. On the development of the doctrine in Islam, v. I. Goldziher, *Le Culte des Ancêtres et le Culte des Morts chez les Arabes* in *Revue de l'Histoire des Religions*, X, No. 2. In the Byzantine literature, v. *Life of St. Xenophon*, ch. 3, the prayer : 'Remember the works of our ancestors, and for their sake do not let us perish in the depth of the sea.' *Byz. Zeitschrift*, 19, p. 13.

IV

(1) THE merits of the righteous are equal to those of the fathers. זכות הצדיקים is, however, divided into those of men and women. Just as the Rabbis frequently refer to the merits of patriarchs (זכות אבות), and to the merits of the matriarchs (זכות אמהות), so do we find references to the merits of pious women (v. p. 141 ff.). It was often taught that the creation of the world was due to the merits of the righteous. Even one righteous man is sufficient for this purpose. The ideal righteous and just man is able to acquire such merits that the Universe should be created for his sake. A worthy appeal to mankind to be just and righteous! The others, the wicked and indifferent, enjoy the goods and fruits of this world for the merits of the righteous. This doctrine is a noble expression of the fundamental ethics of Jewish religion. The high esteem of each individual soul and of the solidarity of all human beings. Each individual hearer among the audience of those teachers can and should strive to become such a righteous, they meant to say, such a godfearing, good man, that his merits shall benefit the whole world. For his sake the world was created,[1] for his merits the world stands.[2]

The law of solidarity is also shown in another aspect of this teaching. The environment of the righteous benefit by and through the piety and charitable life of the pious. The small shopkeeper with whom Joseph stays becomes prosperous in his business. The prosperity of this man served as a pretext to the 'woman of Memphis' to persuade her husband to acquire Joseph as a slave.[3] In

---

[1] v. p. 116 f.   [2] v. p. 132 f.   [3] Test. of Joseph, § 3.

Rabbinical literature there are numerous instances of this conception. Lot, Laban, Pharaoh and Rahab are typical examples, illustrating this view. R. Simon ben Jochai in his Agadah (v. p. 53) dwells many times on this point. Moses was afraid the merit of Abraham might support Og. Lot became rich and honoured for Abraham's merit. The whole family of Rahab shared in her escape and good fortune. R. Eliezer, the son of R. Jose the Galilean, gives advice to travellers to start the journey when a just man is on the way, for his merit will benefit them (v. p. 58). R. Samuel ben Nahmani illustrates this on the prosperity which Laban and Joseph's master in Egypt enjoyed for the merits of Jacob and Joseph respectively (v. p. 82). R. Isaac teaches that the merits of one righteous person can protect a whole city (v. p. 88). They pray for others, not for themselves, and thereby achieve the salvation of their fellow citizens, they are able to nullify the decrees of heaven by their prayers and avert transient dangers.[4] The scribes disputed whether the merits of the righteous are effective only during their lifetime, or even after their death.[5] The merits of the righteous are applied also in explaining the history of Israel. The redemption was for the merits of the just.[6] Ps. Jonathan Targum, Exod. 40. 5 adds: 'And thou shalt set the golden altar for incense before the ark of testimony, for the sake of the wise men who study the Torah, and their smell is pleasant as incense. Put the screen of the door to the tabernacle for the merits of just men, who protect with their merits the people of Israel.' An illustration of this is found in Ps. Jonathan Targum to Num. 11. 31. The wind that went forth from the Lord to destroy the world was yet averted by the merit of the righteous, e. g. Moses and Aaron, averted it.[7]

---

[4] R. Hanina, b. Sabb. 63 a ; Jonathan ben Eliezer, p. 69 ; Rab, p. 107 ; Simon ben Lakish, p. 80 ; R. Abahu, b. M. K. 16 B ; R. Berechja, p. 103 ; R. Abun, p. 103.

[5] v. p. 60. [6] R. Nahmani, p. 105.

[7] Cf. Simon ben Lakish b. Joma, 75 B.

Just as one man enjoys the merits of a contemporary righteous man, so likewise a whole generation is protected by the works of a just man. *R. Simon ben Jochai* gives us two instances from the Scriptures, showing us the truth of this case as well as of the opposite one where the righteousness of contemporaries protects against the punishment due to the wickedness of one man. God wanted to destroy the world on account of the wickedness of Jehoiakim, yet He became appeased by considering his contemporaries. On the other hand He wanted to over-throw the world on account of the contemporaries of Zedekiah, yet he became appeased in considering Zedekiah.[8] The teaching is based on Jer. 26. 1 and Jer. 28. 1, where the word בראשית is used, and gave rise to this view. R. Simon ben Jochai surely contemplated it saying : 'Some-times one man saves many, sometimes, however, one man is apt to destroy many.' He shared of course the general view that there is a limit to this world which sooner or later is doomed to perish (v. above, p. 134). The same idea is repeated in another saying of *R. Simon ben Jochai*, to Ps. 36. 7 : 'Just as the mountains oppress the flood, to prevent the latter from going up and overflooding the world, so likewise the righteousness (of the just) keeps back a measure of punishment which is about to come to the world.'[9]

The merits of the fathers belong also to this category, for their virtues and merits are really based and estab-lished on the same principles and foundations as those of the righteous. They were all of them the bearers of lofty ideals to whom all generations looked up as examples of virtues and godfearing life ; their deeds and lives as put

[8] b. Synh. 103 a, by R. Jochanan.

[9] Tanh. Buber, I, 34; Agadath Bereschit, 4. 1, ed. Buber, p. 8 f. ; Pesikta Buber, p. 73 B ; *R. Jonathan in the name of R. Josiah*, Gen. r. 33, M. Ps., p. 250 ; likewise Lev. r. 27; Tanh. III, 86, anonymously. R. Josiah reads instead of צדקה 'charity, righteousness', כך מעשיהם של צדיקים 'the works of the just'. 'Mountains' הרים are here the just. The mountains are the fathers as well as the righteous.

down in the Scripture or pictured by the scribes are an everlasting inspiration to mankind.

(2) We come now to the means by which one acquires merits, by which the fathers of the world and the righteous were distinguished and enabled to become a source of continuous blessing to their contemporaries and posterity, by which children can save their fathers. These are some of the ideals of righteousness of the scribes. Some critics will deny altogether, or find it contradictory, to speak of ideals of the scribes. Those so-called 'whited sepulchres' could have had no ideals! Is not the basis of Rabbinic theology gross materialism, sometimes more or less balanced by a vague mysticism? Those scribes who live in imagination of old and modern theologians, filling the heaven with banking books, angels as clerks and with shop scales, balancing virtues and sins, surely had no ideals! we hear them saying. To describe those ideals would require a voluminous work on Rabbinical theology to which this modest description can offer only an unworthy contribution. We shall therefore confine ourselves to some observations on the merits of faith (אמונה), Torah and study of the Torah, Sabbath and festivals, circumcision and sacrifices, charity and repentance, observances and tithes, tabernacle and Palestine.

(a) *The merits of faith.* There is a general erroneous view abroad held by those who write or speak of Jewish religion, without either consulting or ignoring its sources, which make out that Jewish religion is based on works and not on belief or faith. Those who are wanting in faith are as severely reproached by the scribes as those of little faith in the Gospels.[10] He who says 'What shall I eat to-morrow?' is one of the מחוסרי אמונה according to R. Eleazar of Modiim, the chief champion of the doctrine of the merits of the fathers.[11] 'There is no need', this

---

[10] Matt. 6. 30.

[11] Mech. 47 B; Sotah, 48 a; Tanh. b. 88 B; Exod. r. 25. 14; cf. Ps. Jon. Targ. Num. 11. 32.

teacher preached, 'to provide for to-morrow, to gather wealth; have faith—and God won't forsake you.' Vividly are those of little faith described by an unknown teacher. When they saw and heard the Egyptians approaching, those of little faith began to pluck their hair, and tear their garments, till Moses soothed them down.[12] In another saying we hear: 'When God created the world He did it only with His word (במאמר), and not by oath. Who caused Him to give an oath? (Deut. 32. 40, 'For I lift up my hand to heaven.') Those who were of little faith.'[13] Hagar is called one of little faith,[14] and Noah by R. Jochanan b. Nappacha,[15] for he delayed to enter the ark till the water reached his knees. In a later source even he who prays loudly is regarded as of little faith.[16] Of Israel, R. Katina says: 'Even in the worst days of Jerusalem there never ceased men of faith.'[17] R. Ami says that rain comes down only for the merits of בעלי אמונה 'believers in God',[18] and illustrates their faith by the story of the weasel and well.[19] Israel believed in God and went after Moses.[20] For the merit of faith so many miracles happened.[21] Abraham inherited both worlds;[22] Israel sang the song at the sea;[23] the Schechinah was resting in Israel;[24] salvation will come to Israel.[25] The merit of faith, especially faithful work, is even more helpful than the merits of fathers.[26]

(b) *The merit of the Torah.* The word and term Torah meant to every Jew everything man holds dear and holy.

[12] Mech. 26 a.   [13] Sifrê, Deut., § 330.
[14] Gen. r. 53. 19.   [15] Gen. r. 32. 9.
[16] *Tanna debe Elijahu,* 71 B.
[17] בעלי אמונה, b. Hag. 14 a.
[18] b. Taan. 8 a.   [19] Ibid.   [20] Mech. 15 B.
[21] v. Shemaiah and Abtaljon, p. 37 ff., and Mech. 29 B, 30 a.
[22] Mech. 33 B.   [23] v. p. 56, R. Nehemia.
[24] Exod. r. 2. 22.
[25] v. p. 90, R. Levi, v. Mech. 33 B–34 a.
[26] Tanh. f. 39 B, מכאן אנו למידין שזכות מלאכה באמונה עומדת במקום שאין יכול זכות אבות לעמוד.

The estimation of and obedience to the Torah, the development and paraphrase of the contents of the Torah, the practical achievement and the theoretical interpretation of its tenets and ideals, show more clearly the history of the Jewish people than persecutions and liberties, worldly successes and temporary disappointments, material conditions and social upheavals. All the latter are merely the framework within which the Torah could develop. Dark dungeons and luxurious palaces, quiet schools and crowded synagogues, jails and places of banquet, testify to the progress as well as to the decline, the triumph as well as the defeat of the Torah. The development and intellectual growth of the Torah is *the* history of the Jewish people. By it one can measure and weigh with just measure and unbiased scales the worth and work of Israel in its own midst as well as in the world at large. There is no Torah without Israel! What is the world without Torah? Just as miserable as a Torahless world is, would be an Israel without Torah. This valuation of the Torah, established by the Agadists, is the keynote of the various doctrines taught about the merits of the Torah in Rabbinical literature. Surely if there is providence in the world, if there is an aim in life, if there is logical and natural purpose in history, the Universe must have been created for the merit of the Torah, and for those who study and spread, deepen and enlarge the ideals laid down therein! For the sake of the Torah and those who study and practise it was the Universe made.[27] The same idea underlies the views expressed by so many Agadists, that the existence and prosperity of the world is due to the merit of the Torah. This was pointed out especially by R. Jochanan, R. Simon ben Lakish, R. Jeremiah, and R. Acha. The world was created on one condition, i. e. if Israel accepts the Torah. If this should not come about, there is no reason for the world to exist. The Torah preceded the creation of the world so many centuries and generations; it was, so to say,

[27] v. p. 124 f.

M

the 'working vessel' (כלי אומנתו) by means of which the world was created.

The merit of the Torah causes not merely the welfare of Israel, the existence of His peculiar people, but the welfare and being of the whole world and of all the nations depends on the words of the Torah uttered by the school-children.[28] The head and leader of Palestinian Jewry of the third century was well aware that only the education of the coming generations based on the ideals of the Torah can safeguard the world. As a matter of fact there is no Agadist who had not in one form or another emphasized the great duty and high responsibility of teaching and studying, practising and spreading the words of the Torah. Bereft of or spared from all petty political machinations and ambitions, the sages of Israel knew only one aim of life, strove after one ideal: *the Torah.*

Apart from these functions [29] the Torah protects in this and future world.[30] R. Judah I sees in the study of the Torah a life-lengthening and spending merit.[31] Of historical events only R. Nehemia [32] ascribes the redemption from Egypt to the merit of the Torah. The world and life did not appear worth living for except for the merits of the Torah and those who study it.[33] All the worldly success is for the sake of Torah.[34]

Finally we hear that Israel will be redeemed in future for the merit of the study of the Torah, especially of the

[28] b. Synh. 99 B; R. Simon ben Lakish, in the name of R. Judah II.

[29] The merit of the Torah saves from punishments in Hell. R. Hanina b. Hama, Tanh. II, 130 B; Pes. 42 B; Gen. r. 44; M. Ps., ch. 52, end; M. Ps. 19 B; Pes. r., ch. 15; Mech. יתרו, ch. 9; Lev. r., ch. 13. Tanh. f. 137 adds the merit of sacrifices, Pes. r. 158 B; Jellinek, בה״מ, III, 68.

[30] R. Meir, p. 50; Eleazar b. Shamua, p. 56; Elisha ben Abuja; Aboth of R. Nathan, ch. 29; Sifrê, Deut., par. 48; b. Men. 99 B; Menachem ben Jose, p. 61; Jochanan, p. 77; R. Hama b. Hanina, p. 81.

[31] p. 60.   [32] v. p. 144, and also Exod. r. 3. 5.

[33] R. Judan, Cant. 3. 15, 3. 16, 3. 18, תוכו רצוף, אהבה זו זכות תורה ולומדיה.

[34] Exod. r. 2. 6: הר בשן שכל מה שאדם אוכל בשיניו בזכות תורה, and R. Eleazar ben Pedath, Gen. r. 69. 3, v. 71. 12.

Oral law. R. Huna says: 'The exiles will not be gathered but for the merit of those who teach the Mishnah.' [35]

(c) *The Observances* : A. *The merit of the Sabbath.* The observance and holiness of the Sabbath day was very early recognized as one of the pillars on which Judaism stands, and the neglect of which brings about its destruction. It is the 'precious gift' (מתנה טוה) which God kept in His storehouse, and gave to Israel.[36] In spite of the most cruel persecutions [37] and the derision the Jews were exposed to on account of the Sabbath, they adhered all the more to its observance. The teachers, as well as the common people saw in this institution one of the safeguards of the existence of Judaism and of its social-ethical foundations. The Jews in the Diaspora, having no other merits, live for the merit of the Sabbath observance.[38] The merit of Sabbath causes rain to come down,[39] brings joy,[40] and finally the future redemption.[41] An anonymous teacher sees in Zach. 4. 2 ('his seven lamps thereon') the merit of the Sabbath, which Israel observes once in seven days, 'seven pipes to the seven lamps', are the seven days of creation on one side and the seven patriarchs on the other.[42] He taught the view of R. Simon ben Jochai and R. Hijja b. Abba and saw in the words וגולה על ראשה, a reference to God,[43] who will redeem Israel for the merit of the Sabbath observance.

B. *Circumcision.* The merit of circumcision plays a much greater part in the Agadah than the merit of the Sabbath observance. It resembles the previous observance, however, in two respects. It was also the cause of cruel

---

[35] Lev. r. 7. 3 ; Pes. r. 83 B ; v. also *R. Simon b. Jochai*, Lam. r., p. 77.

[36] b. Beza 16 a ; b. Sabb. 10 B.

[37] Mechilta 104 B ; Sifrê Deut., par. 76.

[38] v. p. 60, and b. Sabb. 119 a.

[39] R. Eliezer ben Hyrkanos, p. 40 : v. also Pes. r. 201 B ; b. Erub. 40 B ; Eccles. r. 11. 2 ; Lev. r. 31 ; Cant. r. 7.

[40] R. Levi.   [41] R. Hijja b. Abba, p. 87.

[42] Pes. r. 29 B.

[43] Reading ונאולה instead of וגולה.

persecutions and subject to ridicule. On account of the latter the great merit of this observance was pointed out, just as that of the Sabbath.[44] Just as the Sabbath observer is immune from Gehinom, so is he who is circumcised.[45] Both observances are equal to all the other commandments of the Torah, and are signs and distinctions granted to Israel by God, not as a punishment, but as the greatest favour. If Israel, therefore, has no other merit, but the adhesion to this commandment, God complies with Israel's requests.[46] Both merits are instrumental in bringing rain,[47] future redemption,[48] forgiveness, atonement from sin,[49] and the possession of the Holy Land.[50] The greatness of this merit is especially emphasized by *R. Joshua ben Korha*.[51] For this merit does the world stand, and[52] Israel was redeemed from Egypt.[53]

C. *Sacrifice*. This merit is greater than that of the fathers.[54] Israel owes its existence to it,[55] and, like for the merits of Sabbath and circumcision, saves from the punishment of Hell.[56] The sacrifices were given so that Israel should be enabled to acquire merits, and not for punishment.[57] Whilst the two previous observances were still practised and performed, this one was merely a matter of memory and theory. The fact that Israel's existence was made

---

[44] v. Mech. 58 a.

[45] R. Meir, M. Ps. 7 b, כלמי שהוא מהול אינו יורד לגיהנם; R. Levi Gen. r. ch. 18. 6 b ; Erubin 19 a, v. Tanh. f. 32 a ; *PSEZ.*. ed. Friedmann, p. 46.

[46] Lev. r. 31. 4.   [47] v. p. 60.   [48] R. Levi, p. 90.

[49] v. p. 85 ; R. Abahu as to Sabbath observance, R. Jochanan b. Sabb. 119 b, R. Berechja, Eccles. r. 1. 3 ; Ps. Jon. Targ. Num. 23. 10.

[50] R. Judan, Gen. r. 46. 7.   [51] v. p. 59.

[52] R Meir, p. 50.

[53] Matja ben Cheres, p. 47 ; Simon ben Jochai, p. 53 ; Simon ben Halafta, p. 63, the great miracle on the Red Sea happened ; Simon of Teman, p. 47, v. also Pes. r. 63 b ; Tanh. וירא, 4 ; Pirke of R. Eliezer, ch. 29 ; Targ. Ezek. 15. 6.

[54] v. R. Hanina b. Hama, p. 67.

[55] v. p. 81, R. Hama b. Hanina and b. Taanith, 27 b.

[56] v. the passages, Index, s.v. Hell.

[57] v p. 87, Hijja bar Abba.

dependent on it is one of the many proofs of the doctrine
of merits having been available and emphasized by the
Apologists of the first four centuries. To the greater part
of the Stoic philosophers as well as to the Fathers of the
Church, sacrifices appeared as an unworthy form of
worship. The former fought against it and ridiculed it,
the latter used it for dogmatic reasons. They thought :
If sacrifices are abolished and antiquated, why should
people adhere to Sabbath observance and circumcision?
There are other means by which man can be justified.
The older legislation ordered sacrifices merely as a punishment for the people's sins. 'No,' replied the scribes, 'they
were never meant in this sense. Their purpose was to
enrich Israel with merits, for the sake of which Israel
exists.'

All this applies, of course, not only to these but to the
observances generally. 'All the commandments were
given,' says R. Judah ben Ilai, 'for no other reason and
with no other aim than to make Israel worthy to share the
future life.'[58] His contemporary, R. Jose ben Halafta,
singled out certain observers of a few commandments
whose portion in the world to come is assured.[59] Every
man who performs one of God's commandments acquires
a defender for himself in heaven.[60] According to Menachem
ben Jose the observances can protect merely in this world
and not in the world to come.[61] In opposition to this view
is that of R. Jonathan ben Eliezer, who speaks of the
future influence of the performed observances.[62] The
same teaching stands also in the name of R. Joshua ben
Levi.[63] This shows clearly that opinions differed whether
the observances can protect in the world to come just as in
this world, yet all agree in one point that they were given
to Israel, not for punishment, but to acquire merits through
them.[64]

[58] v. p. 16.   [59] v. p. 54.   [60] v. p. 57, Eliezer ben Jacob.
[61] v. p. 60 f.   [62] v. p. 68.   [63] v. p. 72 f.
[64] v. Tanh. III, p. 98; Lev. r. 30. 13.

For the merit of slaughtering the Paschal lamb, teaches R. Ishmael, revealed God himself unto Israel.[65] An anonymous teacher goes even further and proves from various passages that Israel does not exist in the world except for the merit of observing God's commandments, based on Num. 23. 10: 'Who is able to count the dust of Jacob?' i. e. the various observances Israel performs with dust, v. Deut. 22. 9–10.[66] R. Isaac assumes that for the merit of taking the fruit of goodly trees, &c. (Lev. 23. 40) God will redeem Israel, avenge it, build the temple, and send the Messiah.[67] Thus, either the observances generally or some of them especially were singled out to show the great results and the effects they can bring about by these works. R. Hanin, for instance, speaks of the observance of kindling the perpetual light as the merit which brings the days of the Messianic Age nearer to mankind.'[68] In the same sense is to be understood the homily of R. Meir,[69] when he assumes that the Holy Spirit is tabernacled with him who acquires the merit of hospitality, or, when R. Simon ben Jochai[70] states that the resurrection of the dead will come about by this merit.

The scribes emphasized another commandment, i. e. of the tithes, which throws light upon the methods and aims the Agadists pursued on the one side, and of the influence and effect of their teaching on the other side. It is an established historical fact that the Jews in Palestine, long after the destruction of the Temple, tithed their fruits and observed the laws concerning the tithe.[71] This was achieved by the continuous teaching that the patriarchs were blessed

---

[65] Mech. 8 a. 12 a.

[66] Pes. r. 41 в ; Num. r. 20. 16; Tanh. IV, p. 143, adds : Num. 19. 9 ; Lev. 19. 23 ; Num. 5. 17.

[67] Gen. r. 63. 10, v. p. 87 f.

[68] v. p. 99.   [69] v. p. 50.   [70] v. p. 54.

[71] v. Eccles. r. 11. 24 ; Lam. r. 1. 62 ; Zemach ben Paltoi, v. כפתור ופרח, ed. Lunz, I, p. 360; הלכות פסוקות, ed. Müller, n. ; v. on the subject Büchler, *Der gal. Am ha-Arez*, 1906, p. 27, note.

for the merit of the tithe.[72] The Jews in Palestine live for the merit of the tithe.[73] Joy comes to Israel for this merit.[74] Other Agadists like R. Joshua ben Levi, R. Jochánan, R. Samuel b. Nahmani, and R. Levi, refer to the merit of waving the sheaf of the Omer. For this merit did Abraham, and later Israel, inherit the Holy Land, Israel was saved in the time of Gideon (v. Judges 7. 13), of Hezekiah and of Mordecai.[75] The waving of the sheaf had certainly a deeper meaning. Allegorically it expressed nothing less than the acknowledgment of God's Omnipresence and Might.[76] In the same way the idea of tithes implied that we owe everything to God and act merely as God's appointed trustees in helping the needy.

D. *Charity and Lovingkindness.* It was proverbial in Palestine that doing charity acquires merits. The usual phrase was : ' Acquire merits through me ' (v. p. 6 and notes). R. Akiba points out the great merit of charity. He who gives charity to the poor gives a present to God, even if he sinned, and his judgement be given and sealed, the merit of charity will save him.[77] R. Meir teaches that charity lengthens life (v. p. 50); his colleague R. Judah b. Ilai regards this merit as a means of future redemption.[77a] The merit of charity makes even the sinner worthy to see the Shechina.[78] This merit of almsgiving is described in the same way by the author of the book of Tobit.[79] ' Almsgiving redeems from hell.'[79a]

If we mention only briefly the merits of repentance,[80]

---

[72] Gen. r. 43. 10 ; Pes. r. 127 B ; Tanh. f. 22 a, and Index, s.v. Tithe.
[73] v. p. 60.   [74] R. Levi, p. 90.
[75] v. Index, s.v. Omer, and Lev. r. 28. 6 ; Pes. 71 a, b ; Pes. r. 92 a, b ; b. Meg. 16 a ; Esther r. 10, ed. Buber, p. 40.
[76] v. Pesikta, p. 70 B ; R. Jose ben Hanina and R. Joshua ben Levi.
[77] Midrash Cant. r., ed. Buber, p. 19.
[77a] v. M. Cant. r., p. 70.
[78] M. Ps. 15 B, ed. Buber, p. 135, based on Isa. 40. 5.
[79] XII, 9, v. Hughes, *Ethics of the Apocrypha*, p. 44.
[79a] *Midrash* in המוסר ס', p. 4 a.
[80] By which Job was pardoned, v. R. Akiba, p. 44, or the future redemption will come, R. Jochanan and R. Simon ben Lakish, p. 78.

of the Tabernacle,[81] and of Palestine,[82] we have the catalogue of the most important merits nearly completed. These merits are based on three general principles which are the bases of Judaism. We mean *Faith, Work,* and *Love.* He who acquires merits is justified by faith. Faith alone, of course, was not sufficient, just as works without faith are valueless. Both must be united. They are inseparable. Faith in God, the Creator of Heaven and Earth, the *Omnipresent,* the *Omniscient,* the *Omnipotent,* is the basis of Judaism. Without these one cannot be a Jew, just as it is impossible to be a Christian without belief in Christ, or a Moslem without believing in Muhammed. Even faith must be taught and learnt, otherwise it is corrupted by superstition and idolatry on the one hand, and on the other hand it must be translated into works. The Torah teaches faith which a Jew has to believe, and leads us to works by which this belief can be kept fresh and alive. Faith must inspire man to action, and work must express this faith. The climax of both joined together is lovingkindness or charity. Rabbinical Judaism created and practised this virtue towards Jews and Gentiles. That charity is a virtue at all is one of the greatest glories and achievements *of the Jewish religion.* The genius of Judaism has endowed the world with institutions for the poor and needy, the sick and unhappy; has imposed upon humanity legislation and care for the suffering and unfortunate, and 'has assigned the highest place among human excellencies to charity'.[83] Is there in the world or nature an empty space in thought and work, in life and death, which *Judaism* has not filled with charity?

---

[81] By which the world stands, R. Simon ben Jochai, p. 53; R. Samuel b. Nahmani, p. 82, and blessing comes to the world, R. Joshua ben Levi, p. 72.

[82] v. b. Maccoth 7 a; Pes. r. 2 a.

[83] In spite of Wundt, *Ethik,* I, p. 251.

V

As a counterpart of the doctrine of subsidiary merits the scribes speak of and teach also imputed sins. Just as the merits of the fathers benefit their offspring, just as the merits of the children save their parents, just as the merits of the righteous protect and deliver their fellow men, so do the righteous suffer death and plague for the sins of their wicked contemporaries, likewise do fathers die for their children's evil deeds, and children are suffering for the iniquities of their parents. When *R. Jochanan* was visited by his pupils, they found him crying, they said: 'Our master, if thou art crying, what will happen to us?' R. Jochanan replied: 'My sons, should I not cry, being aware that I will soon be placed before my judges, and shown all my deeds.' Moreover, I shall be asked: 'Why did thy sons die during thy lifetime? and I was found unworthy to contribute my share to the establishment of the world! finally, those whose children die during their lifetime, will be brought to account.'[1]

An Agadist interpreting the words of Jacob, 'For I will go down into the grave unto my son mourning' (Gen. 37. 35) says: 'What is the meaning of "mourning into the Sheol?" I will die the *death of the wicked* in this world, and in the world to come. Why? Because God had promised me twelve tribes, and now one of them is dead, may be I was found unworthy to live in both worlds.'[2] This Agadist held that the death of children during the lifetime of parents comes about through the sins of the parents, and

[1] Friedmann's *PSEZ.*, p. 43.   [2] Tanh. B. I, 209.

they are responsible for it. *Ps. Jonathan Targum* renders
Gen. 46. 30 in the following way: 'And Israel said to
Joseph: In case I die now, I would be comforted, for I die
the death of the *righteous.*'   Another Agadist left us a
similar remark, when he explained Ps. 62. 13 (for Thou
renderest to every man according to his work) by the
following instance: There is a young man who has sown
his wild oats (בחור דלוק בעבירה), and becomes guilty of
death. What does God?   He waits till he marries and
begets children, and takes away one of his children for the
sin the father committed.[3] This is taught also by R. Eliezer
ben Hyrkanos and R. Joshua ben Hananja.   Other rabbis
enumerate different sins, on account of which young children
and women die or suffer.[4] R. Hama b. Hanina is represented
by the saying that Adam met with death for the sins of
future generations.[5] This view is also widespread in the
Agadah. We find, for instance, that Abraham died pre-
maturely because of Esau's sins. The aspect must have
been popular.[6] Finally we hear that plague and suffering
come for the just and unjust alike for the sins of the
Am ha-Arez.[7] Abraham was not visited by God as long
as Lot stayed with him.[8] The righteous are taken away

[3] M. Ps., ed. B., p. 308.

[4] R. Meir, p. 50; R. Eleazar ben Simon, p. 60; R. Nathan, p. 62;
F. Judah, I, p. 62; R. Jochanan, p. 78; Eleazar ben Pedath, p. 85; Hijja
bar Abba, p. 87; cf. Spiegel, Fr., *Eranische Altertumskunde*, III, p. 100, and
Büchler, A., *Der galiläische Am ha-Arez*, p. 199. 2.

[5] v. p. 81.

[6] The popularity of this aspect can be judged from the formulary
ברוך שפטרני מעונשו שלזה, the father says even nowadays, when his
son is called up to the Torah on the occasion of the בר מצוה. The
origin of the custom goes back to the saying of *R. Eleazar ben Pedath*
א"ר אלעזר צריך אדם להטפל בבנו עד י"ג שנה מכאן (Gen. r. 63. 14)
ואילך צריך שיאמר ברוך שפטרני מעונשו של זה. *R. Hijja b. Abba*
(v. p. 87, n. 234) teaches just the opposite view: עד י"ג שנה הבן לוקה
בעון האב. It is not impossible that R. Eleazar, a Babylonian by birth,
adopted the Persian view; v. Spiegel, l. c., p. 700, cf. b. Ket. 50 a.

[7] v. p. 62, R. Judah I.

[8] Jose ben Zimra, p. 70.

for the sins of their generation.[9] It became even proverbial Tobiah sinned, Zigud was punished.[10]

Both imputed sins and merits are based on the idea of human solidarity, as *R. Simai* explained it: 'Why has God created just *and* wicked people? In order that they shall atone for each other. Rich and poor, so that they may help one another.'[11] This solidarity is to be seen in man's and woman's every walk of life. A man or a woman cannot sin or do good without influencing either for good or bad one's fellow. It is further felt among members of one and the same family.[12] One cannot disgrace himself or be praised without bringing shame or causing pride to his family or tribe. One Israelite cannot sin without endangering the whole nation.[13] This is the reason why the innocent suffer for the wicked and *vice versa*, why the latter share the blessing caused by the former. But the idea of solidarity is not limited to one nation, it covers all members of the human family. This is shown admirably by R. Joshua ben Levi. If Israel sins, the Gentiles suffer with them, just as they partake of all the fruits of Israel's merits. The Gentiles themselves are not without merits. Apart from the righteous among them, who have a position in the future life, there reference is frequently made to the merits of the Gentiles.[14] God seeks for merits even among Gentiles,[15] some of them trust upon the merits of Abraham

---

[9] R. Simon ben Lakish, p. 80; Samuel b. Nahmani, p. 82; Simlai, p. 82; Eleazar ben Pedath, p. 85; Berechja, p. 103; v. however, Tanh. IV. B, p. 24, אלא בשעה שהדור מכעים לפניו הוא ממלט את הצדיקים ומאבד את הרשעים. According to Rab, R. Hanina b. Hama, R. Jonathan ben Eliezer, and R. Habiba, the righteous are taken away for neglecting to admonish or rebuke their contemporaries; v. b. Sabbath, p. 54 B; cf. Augustine, *De civ. dei*, I, 9, the very same idea.

[10] v. p. 93, n. 278.

[11] Pes. B., p. 191 a; *R. Tanhum b. Hijja*, p. 191 B; v. Eccles. r. 7. 30.

[12] v. R. Simon ben Jochai, p. 54; v. also M. Ps., p. 12.

[13] v. Hezekiah b. Hijja, p. 68.

[14] v. Index, Gentiles.

[15] v. Index, s.v. Gentiles.

their ancestor,[16] they get their reward for their merits in
this world,[17] Rome's might was due to Esau's merit.[18]

And, finally, if there are no merits among men, Israel
or Gentiles alike, then God does mercy for the sake of the
cattle.[19]   There is a kind of solidarity not only between
the members of one family, one race, one nation and
humanity, but even between the latter and the animal
world, between the different parts of God's creation, the
higher and lower.   Sometimes the latter are protected
for the merits of the former.   Yet there are cases when
humanity is barren of merits, and God takes pity on the
human race for the sake of the brute-creation.   That
happens, as in the case of the Alexander story, when
justice and right are trampled under the heels of violence
and might !

[16] R. Jochanan, p. 75.   [17] v. Samuel ben Nahmani, p. 82.
[18] v. Index, Esau and Rome.
[19] v. the Alexander story, Tamid. 32 a ; Gen. r. 33. 1 ; Lev. r. 27. 1 ;
j. B. M. 8 a ; *Midrash Ten Kings*, Pesikta 73 a ; v. R. Isaac, Jalk. Hos. 533,
בנוהג שבעולם אדם נכשל בעבירה הוא מתחייב עליה מיתת שמים מת שורו
אבדה תרנגלתו נשברה צלוחיתו נכשל באצבעו ומקצת הנפש ככל הנפש.

NOTES

Page 3. *R. Simon ben Rabbi* gives M. Macc. (III. 15) 23 B an instance of negative merits, saying: גזל ועריות שנפשו של אדם מתאוה להן ומחמדתן הפורש מהן על אחת כמה וכמה שיזכה לו ול דורותיו ולדורי דורותיו עד סוף כל הדורות, i.e. man is rewarded for not doing a thing, which appears to him abominable, how much more should he acquire merits by avoiding forbidden, but desirable things. The same idea recurs in a statement made by *Rabbi Eleazar ben Azarja*: Whence do we derive that one should not say, ' I do not like to wear a garment of two kinds of stuff mingled together! I do not like to eat pig-meat! I do not want to forbid intermarriage! ' but he should say, ' I would like to do it! yet, what I can I help, my Father in Heaven has decreed upon me not to do thus! ' therefore it is said, ' I have set you apart from the peoples ' (Lev. 20. 24). We find here that he, who says so, separates himself from transgression, and receives upon himself the Kingdom of Heaven (Sifra, p. 82 B). The same teacher gives two examples for accumulating merits unconsciously or unintentionally, for instance, the Egyptians (Deut. 23. 8, v. Sifrê Deut. § 225) and a man who dropped money found by poor people (Sifrê Deut. § 283, v. Sifra, 25 B, 26 A). *R. Akiba* relates a case of unconscious sin in Semaḥot 4. 34: אמר ר' עקיבא זו היתה תחלת זכותי לפני חכמים, השכמתי ומצאתי הרוג אחד והייתי מטפל בו ⸳בג' תחומי שבת עד שהבאתיו למקום קבורה וקברתיו, וכשבאתי והרצתי דברי לפני חכמים אמרו לי על כל פסיעה ופסיעה שהיית פוסע מעלין עליך כאילו שפכת דמים דנתי קלוחומר בעצמי ומה אם עכשיו שנתכוונתי לזכות חטאתי לרבות [לרבואות] מעוונתי אלו נתכוונתי על אחת כמה וכמה, וכשהיה אדם מדבר זה לפני ר' עקיבא היה אומר זה ומצאתי מת (2); תחלת תשמשי. j. Nazir 56 a reads (1) תחלת זכותי וכשבאתי אצל ר' אליעזר ור' יהושע (3); מצוה ונתפלתי בו כארבעת מיל; בשעה שלא נתכוונתי לזכות (5); ולזכות נתחייבתי (4). b. Kid. 82 B has a different version: ר' עקיבא כי מטא להאי פסוקא הוה בכי

אמר ומה מי שנתכוין לאכול בשר חזיר ועלה בידו בשר טלה אמרה
תורה צריכה כפרה וסליחה מי שנתכוין לאכול בשר חזיר ועלה בידו בשר
חזיר על אחת כמה וכמה (v. j. Nazir 53 a in the name of R. Jacob.)
כיוצא בדבר אתה אומר ולא ידע ואשם ונשא עונו כשהיה ר' עקיבא
מגיע לפסוק זה היה בוכה . ומה מי שנתכוין לאכול שומן ועלה בידו חלב
אמרה תורה ולא ידע ואשם ונשא עונו מי שנתכוין לאכול חלב ועלה
בידו חלב על אחת. כמה וכמה. From the Palestinian sources we
can gather R. Akiba's feeling at the reading of these passages.
His experience moved him to tears as often as he thought of that
event in his life.

Page 6. The saying זכי בי occurs in Lev. r. 34. 7, where
R. Zeira praises the style of the Palestinian Jews: אפי' שיחתן של
בני ארץ ישראל תורה הא כיצד אדם או מר לחבירו זכי בי או רכי בי,
זכי גרמך בי (v. p. 93); Lev. r. 34. 1. R. Jonah says: It is not
said, 'Happy is he that *giveth* unto the poor', but 'Happy is he
that *considereth* the poor'. Consider how you can acquire merits
through him. J. Sabb. 8 d: תרין תלמידין מן דר' חנינא הוין נפקין
מקטוע כיסין חמתין חדא איסטרולוגוס אמר אילין תרין מי נפקין ולא
חזרין, מן נפקין פגע בהון חד סב אמר לון: זבו עמי דאית לי תלתא יומין
חד בר נש אתא נבי חד מן קריבוי: דלא טעמית כלום j. Taanit 64 B:
דר' יניי א"ל ר' זכה עימי. These four instances may suffice to
show the spirit and meaning of Jewish charity. The well-to-do,
who shares his money or bread with the poor, is indebted to the
latter for the opportunity to acquire merits.

Modern expounders of the Agadah found in Jeroboam the proto-
type for the Gnostic *Marcion*, v. J. Oppenheim, המגיד, 1875, col. 436;
האסיף, 1893, p. 160, v. esp. j. A. Z. 1. 1, התחיל מפתה את ישראל, ibid.;
Lam. r. ed. Buber, p. 53 a; my ed. of *Midrash Haserot we Yeteroth*,
p. 53, note 232; further, M. Ps. 7 a, ed. Buber, p. 56. *R. Hanina b.*
Papa: שהוא (1 Kings 11. 29) ושניהם לבדם בשדה . פתר קריא בירבעם
שקול כאחיה השילוני, שישבו לברר מעשי מרכבה, ועמדו מלאכי השרת
לפני הקב"ה ואמרו לפניו שהוא עתיד להעמיד שני עגלים, את מגלה
לו מעשה מרכבה, אמר להן עכשיו מה הוא צדיק או רשע? אמרו לו
צדיק, אמר להן איני דן את האדם אלא לפי שעתו. Marcion really
dealt in his system with the subject of מעשה מרכבה, v. W. Bousset,
Hauptprobleme der Gnosis, Göttingen, 1907, p. 109 f. On Achiah
השילוני, v. p. 52, and Pes. B., p. 23 a; b. Taan. 20 a.

Page 7. R. Simon ben Eleazar's saying may appear clearer if
we compare it with the Persian conception, which taught that even
in the future world people will be treated according to their
merits or demerits (v. Spiegel, Fr., *Eranische Altertumskunde*, II,
p. 103). The scribe points out in opposition to that view, which
may have influenced large sections of Jewry in the East, that
Judaism does not share this doctrine. Weber, *System der alt-
synagogalen paläst. Theologie*, p. 362, reads into R. Simon ben
Eliezer's saying something the scribe surely never thought of.

Page 8. The conception of happy and unhappy days is to be
found with many nations. The Greeks call them δρύματα, v. *Rhein.
Mus.* 27. 635; *Byz. Zeitschrift*, 17. 552; Tylor, *Primitive Culture*,
I, 4th ed., p. 70 f.; Fr. Pradel, *Griechische Gebete*, p. 102; *Zeitschrift
des Vereines für Volkskunde*, I, pp. 200, 219; Güdemann, M.,
Geschichte des jüd. Erziehungswesens in Deutschland, p. 131. 2;
Magazin, XV, p. 146; v. also *R. Akiba*, b. Cant. 65 B; b. Ket.
107 B; *R. Bibi*, Esther r. 1. 2.

Page 11. Men who prayed successfully for others are enumerated by Kohler, *J.Q.R.*, 3 (1901), p. 567; v. additions in
Büchler's *Der galil. Am ha-Arez*, p. 336, n. 1. To אנשי מעשה,
cp. *PSEZ.*, ed. Friedmann, p. 6 : מעשה באדם אחד שירד מגליל העליון
לעשות מלאכה בדרום אמרו עליו על אותו האדם אעפ״ו שלא קרא ולא
שנה מאנשי מעשה הוה. v. b. Sabb. 127 B; v. Friedmann's note, 24.

Page 31. The story of Pentakaka is given j. Taan. 64 B איתחמי
לר׳ אבהו פנטקקה יצלי ואתי מיטרא נחית מיטרא שלח ר׳ אבהו ואייתיהי
שאל חמר עבין ההוא גברא עביד ההוא גברא בכל יום, מיגר זנייתא,
משפר תיטרון, מעיל מניהון לבני, מטפח ומרקד קדמיהון ומקיש בבוייא
קדמיהון, א״ל ומה טיבו עבדית, א״ל חד זמן הו׳ ההוא גברא משפר
תייטרון, אתה חדה איתא וקמת לה חורי עמודא בכייה, ואמרת לה מה
ליך ואמרה לי בעלה דההיא איתתא חביש ואנא בעיא מיחמי מה מעביד
ומפנינ׳ ובנית ערסא ופרים ערסי ויהבית ליה טימיתיה וא״ל הא לך פניי
בעליך ולא תיחטיי א״ל כדיי את מצלייא ומתענייא, v. Graetz, *Geschichte*,
IV, 4, p. 285. This event brings home to us the meaning of
a saying by R. Abahu in Agad. Bereshit, ed. Buber, p. 163:
א״ר אבהו לעתיד לבוא עתידין הכל להיות תמהין כנגד מי ששמעו להקב״ה
ואומר [ואומרין .r] : מה הוא כך פלוני שישב ולא שנה מימיו ולא קרא
מימיו והרי הוא יושב עם האבות ומסיח עמהן, והקבה אומר להן . מה

לכם תמיהין, לא זכי אלו אלא מפני ששמעו לי בחייהן, שנ' אזן שומעת
וגו' (Prov. 15. 31). The example of this Pentakaka may have
produced *R. Jochanan's* description of Esau, who committed on
one day *five* great sins (b. B. B. 16 B, v. p. 86, note 227). Of *Saul*
we hear in the Agadah (Pes. 74 a; Pes. r. 64 a; M. Sam., ed. B,
p. 97; Num. r. 11. 3; Tos. Ber., ch. 4) that he did five good
deeds: בזכות מי בזכות . שנמשך ומלך מיד באה זה שאול ועץ חיים תאוה
שהיה מעשים טובים שהיו בידו, שהיה עניו שהיה אוכל חולין בטהרה,
שהיה מבזבז את ממונו, כדי (שחם) לחום על ממונם של ישראל, ששקל כבוד
עבדו ככבוד עצמו.

Page 39. The number 18 is often applied in the Agadah; for
instance, the 18,000 worlds, v. b. Hag. 12 a; *R. Jose b. Hanina*,
אבני עשר ישמנה אמות היו, j. Sanh. 20 c; Pes. B. 169 a; Eccles. r. 2. 8;
Eccles. z., p. 90; Cant. r. 1. 10; *R. Levi*: ח שנה היתה בתקול יוצאת"י
ומכרזת בפלטין של נבוכדנצר ואומרת עבדא בישא זול ואחרב ביתה דמרך,
Eccles. z., p. 129.

Page 40. That pious gentiles have also a share in future life is
expressed in Sifre Deut. § 311: ד"א בהנחל עליון גוים כשהנחיל המקום
מן האומות יראי חטא וכשרים שבהם הפרידו בני אדם זה לוט.

Page 61. To Hananja ben Akasia v. above, p. 16, and Friedmann's *Ps. Seder Eliahu Zuta*, p. 21, ch. 2, note 46.

Page 69, note 136. The conception that the man of great
merits, a righteous, is able to annul the decrees of Heaven, is
expressed by R. Jonathan ben Eliezer in the words: כל המלמד
את בן חבירו תורה זוכה ויושב בישיבה, וכל המלמד את בן עם הארץ
תורה אפילו הקב"ה גוזר גזירה מבטלה בשבילו. A similar statement
is made by *R. Assi*, or according to some readings by *R. Hanina*,
b. Sabb. 63 a, with reference to a man who performs the commandments punctually: אפילו הקבה גוזר גזירה הוא מבטלה. *R.*
Abahu says (b. M. K. 16 B) as to 2 Sam. 23. 3 (the God of Israel
said, the Rock of Israel spake to me, He that ruleth over men
must be just, ruling in the fear of God). ה"ק אמר אלהי ישראל לי
דבר צור ישראל אני מושל באדם, מי מושל בי צדיק שאני גוזר גזירה
ומבטלה (והוא מבטלה r.). R. Ami teaches also that the prayer of
a חסיד (pious) causes rain to come down in times of dearth and
need (v. b. Tann. 8 a, ילך אצל חסיד שבדור וירבה עליו בתפלה), v. also
Cant. r. 1. 16; Pes. 102 b.

Page 75, line 5. It is doubtful whether R. Jochanan really

took part in the discussion of the problem: When did the merits of the father cease to help? b. Sabb. 55 a has ורבי יוחנן אמר מימי חזקיה, yet this view contradicts another saying of R. Jochanan, who explains the word תיו in Ezek. 9. 4 with תתן זכות אבות (v. Tossafoth, s.v. ושמואל אמר). We have to read *R. Jonathan* instead of R. Jochanan. Lev. r. 36. 5 gives this view (עד חזקיה) in the name of *R. Judan* (v. also j. Synh. 27 d).

Page 83. The names of ר' אלעזר and ר' אילעאי are often interchanged; for instance, Pes. B. 30 a, ר' ברכיה בשם ר' אלעאי, v. MS. Oxf. Lev. r. 26. 1; Gen. r. 32, בשם ר' אלעזר; Jalk. Ex. 370, א"ר אלעאי; and v. MS. Adler 2841; v. Praetorius *ZDMG.* 51 (1903), p. 528, and Büchler, *Der gal. Am ha-Arez*, p. 130. 2.

Page 85, 220. v. Büchler, *The Political and Social Leaders,* &c., p. 42. 2.

Page 93, note 278. v. b. Pes. 113 b and שערי תשובה, § 8, p. 2 B.

INDEX

THE OLD RABBINIC
DOCTRINE OF GOD

I. THE NAMES & ATTRIBUTES OF GOD

BY

A. MARMORSTEIN, Ph.D., RABBI

KTAV PUBLISHING HOUSE, INC.

NEW YORK

PREFACE

THE treatment of our subject requires no special apology or recommendation. There is as yet no comprehensive work dealing with our subject, which is somewhat surprising, considering its importance. The great masters of Jewish studies paved the path for grouping the works and classifying the teachers of the Haggadic literature. They left many branches of these studies untouched. Among these the theological conceptions and teachings have rightly the first claim. The first chapter of the Old-Rabbinic theology has to be devoted to the doctrine of God. The teachings of the Rabbis about God are like a mirror of the Jewish soul: without them the Jew, his history and glory, his suffering and joy, cannot be understood. These teachers exercised a greater influence on the world than some writers and scholars think, or would fain make others believe. We hope that this contribution to Rabbinic theology will help to prove the vitality of the old, dead teachers of Judaism. We regret that the work has to be printed in two parts. That this part, dealing with the names and attributes of God, can appear is due to Mr. S. Japhet, the esteemed Chairman of the Council of the Jews' College, whose kindness is hereby gratefully acknowledged. We have also to thank my friend, the Rev. R. Birch-Hoyle, A.T.S., Baptist minister, Belvedere (Kent), for his valuable assistance given me in reading the manuscript and proofs of my work.

A. MARMORSTEIN.

LONDON, 21st *April*, 1927.

CONTENTS

LIST OF ABBREVIATIONS

Aboth dRN, or AdRN	= Aboth di R. Nathan, ed. Schechter.
Ag. Ber.	= Agadath Bereshith, ed. Buber (= B).
A. Z.	= Aboda Zara.
B	= Buber.
B or Bab.	= Babylonian Talmud.
B. B.	= Baba Bathra.
B. K.	= Baba Kamma.
B. M.	= Baba Mezia.
Ber.	= Berakhoth.
Cant. r.	= Canticles rabba.
Deut. r.	= Deuteronomy rabba.
Eccl. r.	= Ecclesiastes rabba.
Exod. r.	= Exodus rabba.
Gen. r.	= Genesis rabba, ed. Theodor.
H. B.	= Hebräische Bibliographie.
J.	= Jerushalmi, v. also Pal.
Lam. r.	= Lamentations rabba.
Lev. r.	= Leviticus rabba.
M.	= Mishnah.
M. Sam.	= Midrash Samuel, ed. Buber.
M. Ps.	= Midrash Psalms, ed. Buber.
M. Tadshe	= Midrash Tadshe, ed. Epstein.
M. Tan.	= Midrash Tannaim, ed. Hoffmann.
Mekh.	= Mekhilta, ed. Friedmann. [Judentums.
MGWJ	= Monatsschrift für die Geschichte und Wissenschaft des
M.R.S.b.J.	= Mekhilta R. Simon ben Johai, ed. Hoffmann.
Num. r.	= Numbers r.
Pal.	= Palestinian Talmud.
Pes. B.	= Pesikta, ed. Buber.
Pes. r.	= Pesikta rabbati, ed. Friedmann.
Pirke R. E.	= Pirke di R. Eliezer.
B. Jon.	= Bends Jonathan Targum on the Pentateuch.
R. H.	= Rosh Ha Shanah.
R. É. J.	= Revue des Études Juives.
Ruth r.	= Ruth rabba.
S.E.R. or S.E.Z.	= Seder Elijahu rabba or zutta, ed. Friedmann.
Sifre	= ed. Friedmann.
T. K. or Tor. Koh.	= Torath Kohanim, ed. Warsaw.
Tanhuma	= ed. Buber, or F. ed. Frankfurt a. O.
Th.	= Theodor.
Tos.	= Tosefta, ed. Zuckermandel.
ZAW	= Zeitschrift für Alttestamentliche Wissenschaft
ZfNW	= Zeitschrift für Neutestamentliche Wissenschaft.

INTRODUCTION

'IF thou desirest to recognize Him who spake and the
world was created, learn Haggada, for through it thou wilt
recognize God, and cleave unto His ways.' These words are
quoted in the name of the old interpreters of signs called,
דורשי רשומות.[1] The old allegorists distinctly point out the
twofold aim of the Haggada: *the recognition of God*, and
the following in God's ways, or the *imitatio Dei*. Accordingly Haggada teaches the existence and unity, the essence
and attributes, the providence and love of God. It is true
that the very same Haggada knows of persons who, of themselves, recognized and arrived at the knowledge of God the
Creator, without teachers and books, preachers and study.[2]
The Haggada is still the best teacher to make the human
Divine and the Divine human. Modern thought concerning
the philosophy of religion draws nearer to this conception of
the real function of belief and religion. It seems, therefore,
worth while to consult these anticipators of present-day

---

[1] Sifre Deut., § 49, p. 85 A, דורשי רשומות אומרים רצונך שתכיר מי שאמר
והיה העולם למוד הגדה שמתוך כך אתה מכיר את הקב"ה ומדבק בדרכיו.
v. M. Tannaim, 44, שמתוך כך אתה מכיר את מי שאמר והיה העולם
ומדבק בדרכיו, and Sifre, p, 74 A. v. on the allegorists, I. Levy, *RÉJ.*,
lx, pp. 24–31, Jacob Lauterbach, *JQR.*, N. S., i, pp. 291–333, 503–531 and
D. Neumark, *Maybaum Festschrift*, Berlin., 1914, pp. 179 ff. Philo considers
the *recognitio dei* the ultimate aim of human life. Other passages pointing
out this function of the Haggada will be dealt with in the course of this
essay. Here we may refer to Midrash Psalms, ed. Buber, 230; R. Joshua ben
Levi says: כי לא יבינו אל פעלת ה' ואל מעשה ידיו יהרסם ולא יבנם אלו
האגדות. The neglect of haggadic studies leads to the disregard of the
works of God and to the destruction of the operation of His hands, Ps.
28. 6 (v. מנורת המאור, ed. Krotoschin, i, p. 19, Finn, האסיף, 1884, p. 94;
as to R. Joshua ben Levi's attitude towards the Haggada, v. Bacher,
Ag. Pal. Amoräer, i. 128). The popularity of the Haggada is often emphasized, v. Mekh. 46 A, 51 A, Yoma 75 A, Midr. Cant ed. Grünhut, p. 46 B.

[2] For instance, Abraham, Job, Hezekiah, and the Messiah, see Num. r. 14,
2, וזהו אחד מד' בני אדם שמעצמם הכירו להקב"ה איוב חזקיה ומלך המשיח,
as to Abraham, v. also Gen. r. 38. 8; 39. 1; 61. 1; 64. 4; b. Ned. 32 a;
Aboth R. N. ch. 33, M. Ps. 1. 13.

tendencies on the subject of religion generally. The phrase
'*Gotttrunkenheit*', rightly used or not of Spinoza, is appli-
cable to many of the Scribes. In the first four centuries
Palestine and Babylon produced many examples of that
type of men and women who were inebriated with the
glory and majesty of God. Their whole lives, from the
cradle to the grave, were devoted and dedicated to God. To
our thinking it is desirable to analyse and expound these
teachings in a work dealing with the Old-Rabbinic doctrine
of God.

Many attempts, scholarly and otherwise, serious and
superficial, unbiased and partial, have been made in the
last thirty or forty years to describe or distort the religion
of the Jews in the first century of the current era. One is
rightly surprised at the meagre result and the lack of
success achieved by the long rows of books which fill the
libraries. The causes of this great failure may be explained in various ways. It is due primarily to want of
thorough Rabbinic knowledge, and in the second place to
making use of that imperfect knowledge with utterly
wrong methods of application. Is it not amazing that we
possess no complete work describing and analysing, estimat-
ing or criticizing the sayings and teachings of the Jewish
teachers concerning the doctrine of God? No proper valuation of the religious life of an age or a community can be
attempted by scholars without seeing and examining the
teachings about God on such themes as His essence and
existence, His relation to the world and man, His providence, His universality and particular relation to Israel, His
creation and omnipresence, His Fatherhood and Rulership,
His omnipotence and omniscience, His justice and love. It is
no mean task to collect and explain all the sayings gathered
from the Rabbinic sources on these subjects, generally and
individually. There is scarcely a page in the many hundred
folios of Old Rabbinic literature without at least some lines
expressing one or more doctrines, or containing references
concerning God. Some of them appear to be uncouth,

others sublime; some are deposits from primitive ways of
thinking, some strike us as the climax of theological or
philosophical teachings. All Rabbinic teachings on the
most manifold aspects and subjects of this doctrine will
be treated in the following pages. There are different ways
of placing these doctrines before students and scholars.
We follow the historical method. We treat the themes
arising out of our material in chronological order. Neither
apologetical nor polemical motives influence our aims.
A good deal of true religious thought, advanced and proclaimed by those unassuming and quiet teachers of Judaea
and Galilee, became the common treasure of all civilized
religions. Every religion worth its name needs at least
some of them. Yet very often contemporary philosophy
and theology help us to find the real meaning of Rabbinic
teachings. Pagan, Gnostic, as well as Christian influence
can be traced in many words and sayings of our literature. History, with its good and bad effects, accompanies
Haggadic lore. The visible world throws its deep shadows
upon the invisible, and the latter inspires the former
with awe. Ages of peace and prosperity present different
problems of thought from those of war and suffering, and
these modify ancient beliefs. The advance and decline of
culture and civilization equally contribute their share to
shaking old-established dogmas and result in formulating
and altering ancient opinions concerning the Supreme
Being, and His relation to the children of men and the
world. How far our present-day belief and doctrine is
behind or ahead of the old Rabbinic doctrine of God is not
the present writer's wish or task to discuss. Having
weighed the words of hundreds of teachers of the first
four centuries, having examined their advanced position
in theology and their references to the doctrine of God in
the Bible, having listened at the fount of the ever fresh
waters to the life-giving force of their words, one is justly
entitled to pronounce the verdict of history that without
this contribution no religious enlightenment is to be thought

of. Thanks to these treasures of religious thoughts, theological speculations, and ever deepening piety, the ordinary Jew is equipped with a philosophy of religion which is not inferior to any other, however advanced and impressive. Neither Zoroaster nor Buddha, neither Jesus nor Paul, neither Origen nor Augustine can teach religion, can reveal God in a worthier way than that paved by these Scribes. We may point to Plato for parallels, we may cite the Stoics for some parables, we may refer to Cynics or Epicureans for criticism of heathendom and idolatry, yet they do not diminish the individuality of Rabbinic thought. The teachers of Judaism may have adopted foreign ideas, they may have assimilated pagan philosophical thoughts, they may have even adapted Babylonian or Egyptian, Greek or Barbarian myths and legends, but the teaching derived from them sounds quite new and original. For one thing is perfectly certain, there is no class of men in the world to whom the idea of God was so near, whose longing for God so ardent, whose zeal to do God's will so keen, whose ideal of piety, love, goodness, justice, purity, and holiness so supreme in all their actions and thoughts, deeds and meditations, as in the much-despised and unjustly judged Scribes. The majority of them are and will remain the living instances of religion in its most accomplished and perfect embodiment. There were, are, and will be times when the hearts of people will burn with desire to seek and see God. Likewise there are movements and periods when the masses turn shamefacedly away from their Father in Heaven. Both have deeper causes and are not without inner connexion with the doings of men and happenings of the world. Teachers of religion have the enviable and arduous task to stand firm in both cases, by spreading and preaching, affirming and enriching, deepening and amplifying the doctrine of God. We are not partial and biased in attributing the chief place in performing this duty on the part of the teachers of religion to the leading and moving spirits of the Jewish people—the immortal Tannaim and Amoraim!

Their contributions to the development of the teachings
concerning God and religion, ethics, and piety cannot be over-
rated, though they very often have been underrated. What
does that matter ? The law, the prophets, Jews and Judaism
have shared the same fate. Worldly success, earthly honour
is a very poor arbiter !

This work endeavours to present the doctrine of God
according to the sources of information as preserved in the
ancient writings of the Rabbinic teachers and sages,
homilists and thinkers. How far they touch our present
religious needs and troubles can be read between the lines
of their writings. On the whole one cannot but exclaim,
' How little mental conditions have changed in these last
eighteen hundred years or so!' The Rabbis had to face
almost the same problems and answer the same questions as arise nowadays. How far their answers and
points of view hold good to-day is another question altogether. The same is the case with some of their own
doctrines which on their part gave rise to new problems
and difficulties. Thanks to the studies and works of the
great masters of the last century, and to the scholarly
editions of old, lost and rediscovered, gems of Midrashic
lore, we are now able to arrange and classify with some
method the sources according to the times and countries of
their origin. Yet there are still many difficulties to be
tackled. There are, first of all, the many hundred folios
of this vast literature which have to be searched anew.
Their lines are full of teachings, sublime and primitive,
about God. The numerous teachers, Halakhists and
Haggadists, known and unknown, missed no opportunity
of airing and emphasizing their views about God. The
Divinity was felt by them, was present in their homes and
schools, glorified their life, sanctified their work—no space
or moment of existence, in the seen and unseen world, in
the shadow of life and beyond the grave could be imagined
without Him. Consequently, there is no aspect of primitive
or advanced religious thought which has ever agitated the

mind of man and has a bearing on Divinity and Godhead to which those sages remained indifferent, and to which they did not contribute their proper share in elucidating or developing them.

The vastness of our material is not the only trouble. Writers generally speak of Rabbinic belief, Rabbinic doctrines, as if they were held generally, paying not the slightest attention to the places and times of their origin. They do not see the differences between theological conceptions of the Tannaitic teachers and those of the Amoraic period, between South and North, between Palestine and Babylon, Alexandria and Jerusalem. Each saying must be judged in relation to the time and country of its teacher. We have to weigh and measure with the just *ephah* of the past and just *hin* of the future. The local and temporal conditions of the teachers, their cultural and religious standard, must never be lost sight of. Otherwise, one cannot arrive at a just estimate. These considerations account also for some striking facts we shall meet with in the course of our discussion, viz. treating one subject or side issue in one generation and neglecting it at other times. Life with its new and old problems and riddles cannot be divorced from the philosophy or theology of the surrounding world. Therefore, these external sources of knowledge have to be considered in the same way as human feelings and longings for the unseen or supernatural, in dealing with the highest and sublimest questions regarding God.

There are different ways of placing the wealth of Rabbinical material on this subject before the reader. The sages of the Middle Ages, from Sa'adya to Maimonides, who developed a philosophy of religion, are the best examples of the influence of their age on their theology. Whilst Sa'adya begins his work with the problems of the existence and unity of God, the great teacher of Cordova starts with the anthropomorphic conceptions in the Scriptures. Both methods can be easily justified. We limit our subject to the Rabbinic material and use the historical method. We

have to begin with the *Names of God*, dealing first with
the use of the old biblical names as far as they are
still used in our period and understood by the spokesmen of our time. Names were in antiquity of greater
importance than they are at present. To the primitive
mind a name is a mystery, powerful and of the greatest
importance for the well-being or ill-luck of a person. The
sacredness and awe of a name is the subject of many
investigations, which reveal a strange contrast between the
feelings of the present on one side and that of more remote
centuries on the other side. That being the case with the
name of an ordinary person, how much more with the Name
of God, the Name κατ' ἐξοχήν! The origin, development,
popularity, and abandonment of a divine name contain the
history of more than one religious movement. It is a step
in the evolution of religious thought and intellectual development. How did these Names originate? Were they born
under foreign influences, or did the religious genius of the
people invent them? Are they revealed by the Deity to the
chosen ones? Why are they, after a time, discarded altogether, supplanted by others, or relegated into dark
corners of magic or prayers? The history of the Divine
Names in our literature offers a good many observations on
and explanations of these questions. Some points are
shrouded in obscurity, others may become clearer by
investigation. We notice a very far-reaching difference
between Palestinian and Alexandrian theology concerning
the Tetragrammaton. A bitter struggle between Hellenists
and Hasidim centred around the pronunciation of the
Divine Name. A similar controversy arose afterwards
around the use of the name Elohim and even as to the
substitution of the Tetragrammaton. This led us to investigate the various Names applied by the Scribes to God.
Here a wealthy sanctuary of the most treasured religious
ideas and doctrines is opened to us, which invites entrance
to all who want to come nearer to God. Nowhere is the
creative genius of the pious scribes more at its best than in

this long list. Some of them occur in great variety. They teach us further, especially when reviewing our literary documents, that the Biblical names gave way to names designating God as the High, Heaven, &c. They were discarded in their turn by the term המקום (the omnipresent) till this Name became so holy that it was replaced by הקב״ה, 'the Holy One blessed be He'. We see here a development from the concrete to the abstract. Fortunately we are enabled to fix the dates of these changes. The names 'Heaven', or 'High', 'Highest' were in vogue till the Hasmonean period, המקום till the beginning of the third century C.E., when the great change, owing to external influences and internal movements, was made necessary. This is noticed in other domains of the Haggada generally and of our doctrine especially. Later on even this Name was altered to השם, or writers reverted to the oldest Name, Elohim. This history of the Divine Name or Names in our literary documents reveals many new aspects of Rabbinic theology. We are now enabled to fix the ages of older anonymous sayings interspersed in later Midrashic works, likewise to single out more recent material in the old Tannaitic sources. Our texts are unfortunately in such a condition that not much reliance can be placed on them. The burden of our proof had to be put on such works which are at our disposal either in critical editions or on the Talmudic text which support our contention in an unexpected manner.

The Names lead us to the second part of our doctrine, to the Attributes of God. The attributes of the divine being are in all advanced religions the points which differentiate between one religious form and the other, between monotheistic religions and polytheistic forms of worship. There is no contest of opinions on the generally recognized fact that the religion of the Pentateuch, Prophets, and Psalmists, in spite of all the crudities and blame attached to it by biased and short-sighted critics, reached a height which entitles it to head all the higher religious systems of antiquity. This would be even more generally recognized when speaking of the religion of the Rabbis. There, as in many other walks of life, the old truth of 'the wisdom of the poor', which is despised, finds its corroboration. Were it not Israel's heritage, the Jews' glory, the Rabbis' teaching, but some Mexican deity or Tibetan wise man, well, the adoration of the whole civilized world would be assured to it. But, it is the religion of the Jews!—moreover of the Rabbis, the Scribes, the Pharisees! That is enough to make it ignored or misjudged. These Attributes show the climax of the purest conception of the deity. God's Omnipresence, Omniscience, Omnipotence, Eternity, Truth, Justice, Benevolence, Purity, and Holiness are so many landmarks on the road leading to God. Some of them are to be met with in cruder forms of religious systems. Yet most of them are specially to be pointed out. The gods, even the highest of them, cannot be imagined as everywhere present or all-powerful. Even Zeus is the victim of some tricks which he cannot control or help. Then there is the ugly feature of the dying or reviving gods. We are firmly convinced that the teachings of the Scribes of the purity and holiness of God, if properly understood, will help all God-seeking people in their longing for a religious form of worship freed from all shackles of polytheism which still bind their religious outlook. The Attributes are of the utmost influence on human society and institutions. Our ideal life, life as it ought to be, and not as it is, is modelled upon attributes we ascribe to God. The fuller discussion of this point is part of the subject of the third chapter, dealing with the anthropomorphism and imitation of God.

Owing to technical reasons this work had to be divided into two parts. The second part will deal with the problem of anthropomorphism and anthropopathism, the relation of God to man and God to the world, the unity of God, and the existence of God. Some of the problems and attributes are so complex that the whole material can be judged only in connexion with the second part. The conclusion will give a survey of the contributions of the Scribes from

Simon the Just to the last of the Haggadists of the Amoraic period, to the doctrine of God. Whilst history aims at the description and study of the life and development of man, theology's subject is God. Historical theology has for its task to show the place of religion and its influence on society on one side, and man's drawing nearer to and developing clearer *the* most important problem of the mind— God—on the other. Our time is looking for God, searching after the Divine, longing for the unseen, hoping for redemption, dissatisfied with the past, and anxious for the future. May this modest contribution, based on the experience of seekers of God, help others to find Him, see Him, and imitate Him. God was through the ages, and remains up to this day, the beginning and end of Jewish thought, Jewish teaching, Jewish philosophy, Jewish poetry, Jewish mysticism, Jewish scholarship, and last but not least, Jewish life. The first step to recognize Him is to investigate the history of the Divine Names in Old-Rabbinic Theology.

A.

THE NAMES OF GOD

I.

The Pronunciation of the Tetragrammaton.

Greek philosophy, Jewish Alexandrinian theology, Christian apology and Gnostic lore concur in the idea of God's *namelessness*.[1] That God has no name, was taught by Aristotle,[2] Seneca,[3] Maxim of Tyre,[4] Celsus,[5] and Hermes Trismegistus.[6] The Seventy altered in several places the Hebrew text of the Scriptures in order to reconcile the philosophy of their adopted country with the doctrines of their ancestral faith.[7] Philo follows the footsteps of the Seventy.[8] Christian apologists emphasize this teaching again and again.[9] Apparently, Christians and Jews, who wrote for heathens, could not divert their attention from a teaching which was current in their days and countries. What was the attitude of the Palestinian teachers towards this apparently accepted philosophic dogma of their age?

The influence of Greek philosophy is felt in the LXX.

---

[1] Geffcken, J., *Zwei Griechische Apologeten*, Leipzig, 1907, p. 38.

[2] Περὶ Κόσμου, 7, Dio, *Or.* xii. 75.

[3] *Nat. qu.* 2. 45.   [4] 8. 10.   [5] Origen, i. 24.

[6] 5. 1. 10; v also Hennecke, *Judenchristentum*, p. 53

[7] v. Dähne, *Geschichtliche Darstellung der jüd.-alex. Religions-Philosophie*, Halle, 1834, ii. 27–32, v. also Gfrörer, *Jahrhundert des Heils*, i. 191, Or. Ltbl., 1849, 18.

[8] v. Dähne, loc. cit. i. 139 ff., 148 ff.; Zeller, *Die Philosophie der Griechen*, Leipzig, 1909, iv.⁴ 403.

[9] Aristides, Justin, *Apol.* ii. 6, 3; Tatian, 4; Clem. Strom. v. 12. 8, 3; Ps. Melito, 2; Cohort, 21; Min. Felix, 18. 10, Geffcken, loc. cit., p. 39.

They see in Lev. 24. 15 f. a prohibition of pronouncing the divine name (ὀνομάζων δε τὸ ὄνομα κυρίου θανάτῳ θανατούσθω). Philo, Josephus, and Aquila (et denominans nomen dei morte morietur) agree with their Greek Bible. Moses forbade, according to Philo,[10] to curse the name of false gods, in order that his pupils should not get used to treating lightly the name of God, because these designations require the highest respect and the deepest reverence. If, however, one dares to mention His name at an ordinary time he is guilty of death, not to speak of blaspheming the name of the Lord of all creatures and gods. Philo repeats himself very often, especially on subjects dear to him. He held with his teachers of philosophy that no name can adequately give an idea or expression of God.[11] New material is gained from the Magic Tablet of Adrumetum, where the important saying is inserted: ὁρκίζω σε τὸ ἅγιον ὄνομα ὅ οὐ λέγεται (lines 19, 20). 'I adjure thee by the sacred name which is not uttered in any place.' This is the old reading of Maspero: ἐν τῷ ἀδύτῳ, 'not even in the Temple'. Deissmann [12] considers it 'absolutely impossible that any one having any kind of sympathy with Judaism whatever could assert that the Holy Name was not pronounced in the Temple'. There is no doubt that the date of this exorcism was very old, and reflects the conditions on which the LXX is based. Yet there was a time when this prohibition was entirely unknown among the Jews in Egypt as well as in Babylon, not to mention Palestine. The Elephantine papyri taught many new things, dispelled many recent mistakes, and verified many old traditions. The writer of the Aristeas letter did not exaggerate in reporting that there were Jewish colonies in Egypt long before Alexander the Great. These Jews had a sanctuary dedicated to their God יהו. Many of the names found in that highly interesting collection

[10] De vita Mos. ii. 683.

[11] De Somn. i. 375 ; De vita Mos. i. 614, De nom. mutat. 1045 f.

[12] Biblical Studies, Edinburgh, 1901, p. 287.

begin or end with יהו or יה [13].   In the Babylonian documents of Nippur, dating from the time of Artaxerxes I
up to Darius Hystaspis we find many names ending with
יה, and Jama, which is equal with Jawa, יהו.[14]   Neither
in Egypt, nor in Babylonia, did the Jews know or keep
a law prohibiting the use of God's name, the Tetragrammaton, in ordinary conversation or greetings.   Yet, from
the third century B.C.E. till the third century A.C.E. such
a prohibition existed and was partly observed.   R. Levi, a
teacher of the third century, adopted literally this view in saying : ' He who pronounces God's name is guilty of death.' [15]
This Haggadist, R. Levi, who was not immune from foreign
influences, must have known the LXX.   The Aramaic
version of Ps. Jonathan adds ברם מאן דמפרש ומחרף שמא יקטול,
' He who pronounces the Name with *blasphemy* is guilty of
death '.   Onkelos agrees with R. Levi.   According to the
Mishna [16] only the blasphemer is guilty of death.   The view
must have been foreign to the teachers of the Mishna that
the Name of God must not be pronounced.   Yet there was
a time when the Hellenistic rule was well-known and
observed in Palestine.

We are told that the priests, after the death of Simon
the Just, either ceased altogether, or stopped for a short
period,[17] to use ' the Name' in pronouncing the blessing.
The Tosefta reads : ומת נמנעו חביריו מלברך בשם [18].   MS. W

[13] Cf. אביהו, יהוחן, יהושמע, יהותל, v. also מלכיה, מחסיה, ידניה, נמריה,
יהוישמע. v. Ungnad-Sachau, *Aramäische Papyrus aus Elephantine*, Leipzig,
1911, p. iii f. v. however, A. Cowley, JRAS., 1920, 170, *Aramaic Papyri*,
Oxf., 1923, p. xviii.

[14] Cf. Gedaljawa, *Son of Sabbatai* גדליהו בר שבתאי, v. Ungnad, loc. cit.,
p. iv, note ; cf. also S. Daiches, *The Jews in Babylonia in the time of Ezra and
Nehemia according to Babylonian Inscriptions*, London, Jews' Coll. Publ., No. 2,
1910.

[15] Pesikta R. K., ed. Buber, 148 A, כל מי שהוא מפרש שמו של הקב"ה
חייב מיתה, derived from נוקב שם ק', Lev. 24. 16.

[16] Sanh. 55 B, f.

[17] v. L. Blau, *Das Altjüd. Zauberwesen*, Budapest, 1898, p. 115, K. Kohler,
' The Tetragrammaton and its uses' in *Journal of Jewish Lore and Philosophy*,
i, pp. 19-32.

[18] ed. Zuckermandel, 329. 24.

and edd. read משמת שמעון הצדיק פסקו מלברך בשם. In the
Babylonian Talmud[19] the reading agrees with the Tosefta,
yet instead of חביריו we read אחיו הכהנים. The Boraita is
also quoted in the Pal. Talmud, yet the last sentence is
omitted. *Geiger*[20] connects this historical tradition with
the information derived from Hellenistic sources, according to which the pronunciation of the divine name was
strictly prohibited. *Weiss*[21] says: 'We do not know the
special reason for this reform, but it is quite clear that the
priests, seeing the decline of faith and fear of God, considered neither themselves nor their contemporaries worthy
of proclaiming or of hearing the name of God'. This
information contradicts many other traditions of the
Mishna. We read in the Mishna Sotah:[22] במקדש אומר את
השם ככתבו ובגבולין בכינוי. In the Sanctuary the priests said
the Tetragrammaton according to its writing, outside the
Temple by its substitute.[22a] In Sifre[23] the subject is discussed by two scholars belonging to the school of R. Ishmael,
e. g. R. Josiah and R. Jonathan. They agree with the rule
codified in the Mishna: 'Thus shall ye bless the children of
Israel' (Num. 6. 23) with the Name (בשם המפורש). There must
have been previously a law which objected to this custom.
Therefore the first-named Tannaite derives it from the word
שמי, 'my name', i. e. the שם המפורש. The second teacher is
inclined to base this law on Exod. 20. 24, expounding:
'Wherever *I reveal myself unto thee*, thou shalt pronounce
My Name', i. e. in the Sanctuary. There is a consensus of

---

[19] b. Yoma 49 B.   [20] *Urschrift*, 263, and Ozar Nehmad, iii. 117.
[21] דור דור ודרשיו i. 82–83.

[22] 38 b, v. Graetz, *MGWJ.* vi. 1857, p. 56, note, who thought that the prohibition of pronouncing the Tetragrammaton after the death of Simon
was limited to the synagogues outside the Temple (בגבולין). Graetz based
his theory on Tos. Sotah, ch. 13. The text משמת, however, does not
indicate or allow any difference between מקדש and גבולין. Besides the
MS. of the Midrash ha-Gadol preserved the reading מלברך בשם המפורש
במקדש, v. Königsberger, in Rahmer's *Jüd. Literaturblatt*, 1900, p. 85.

[22a] Mekh. 73 B, a law is quoted: מכאן אמרו שם המפורש אסור להאמר
בגבולין, derived from Exod. 20. 24, v. also M. R. S. b. J., p. 115.

[23] Num., § 39.

opinion as to the prohibition of using the Shem hamphorash
outside the Temple, yet in the service of the Temple the
Name was pronounced. The fuller version of this controversy is preserved in Num. r. 11. 10, which we put here
together with the text of the Sifre:

S.	*Num. R.*
כה תברכו את בני ישראל בשם	כה תברכו בשם המפורש, אתה
המפורש, אתה אומר בשם המפורש	אומר בשם המפריש או אינו אלא
או אינו אלא בכינוי ת"ל ושמו את	בכינוי, ת"ל ושמו את שמי על בני
שמי על בני ישראל בשם המפורש	ישראל ואני אברכם בשם המיוחד לי
ובנבולין בכינוי דברי ר' יאשיה.	יכול אף בנבולין נאמר כאן ושמו
	את שמי ונאמר להלן לשום את שמו
	מה להלן בשם המפורש מכאן אמרו
	במקדש בשם המפורש ובמדינה בכינוי
	דברי ר' יאשיה.

A third version is given in B. Sotah, 38 A, where the
view of R. Josiah is ascribed to R. Jonathan, and that of
R. Jonathan to R. Josiah. Anyhow, we learn that according to these Rabbis the Name was pronounced in the
Temple by the priests. This openly contradicts the first
report. One must not assume, however, that the Scribes
of the second century discussed a theoretic question or an
archaeological point which had no practical value. We can
cite R. Tarphon, who tells us as an eyewitness that the
priests used to pronounce the Name in the Temple. R.
Tarphon was of priestly descent, saw the Temple service, and
relates: 'Once I followed my uncle to say the priestly
blessing, and I inclined my ear near the High Priest, and
I have heard that he mixed (מבליע, lit. caused to be
swallowed) the Name with the tune of his brethren, the
priests.' [24] The Name was said, but not distinctly. We
must assume that after Simon the Just the name of God
was not pronounced. Later on, when the opposition to the
rule of the priests grew stronger, a compromise was

[24] B. Kid. 71 A.; v. also Pal. Yoma iii. 7, and Cant. r. 3. 11.

affected; the name of God should be pronounced in the priestly blessing, but בהבלעה, and not distinctly. In the service of the Day of Atonement, which is described in the ancient treatise of the Mishna called Joma, the confession of the High Priest is introduced by אנא השם (iii. 8, iv. 2, vi. 2) and אנא בשם (vi. 2). This is understood by most of our commentators as referring to the Name. The High Priest pronounced the Name according to its writing. The term היֹם obviates the idea that the High Priest had merely used a, or the substitute for the, divine name, which, of course, upsets the report about the usage after the death of Simon. There is a further passage which exhibits the same difficulty. M. Berakhoth, ix. 5, contains several institutions which are of the greatest importance for the knowledge of the intellectual movements of the first century. They instituted that people should greet their fellow men בשם 'by the Name'. The date of this arrangement must be very old. In the very Mishna it is put together with practices in the Temple. It must date back, therefore, before the destruction of the Second Temple. R. Joshua b. Levi enumerates it among the rules instituted by the Rabbis, which were sanctioned by Heaven. It ranges together with the arrangements for the reading of the Scroll of Esther on Purim, and with the discharging of the duties of the tithes during the time of the Second Temple. The passage occurs many times in the ancient Rabbinic writings. R. Simon relates in the name of R. Joshua b. Levi that three things were decreed by the earthly authorities and God agreed with them: the tithes, greeting by the name of God, and the reading of the Scroll of Esther.[25] The importance attached to the innovation is rather surprising. The date of this arrangement must coincide with that of

[25] v. Pal. Ber. 14 c; Ruth r. 4. 7; b. Meg. 7 A; b. Maccoth 23; M. Psalms, ed. Buber, p. 296; Tanhuma Buber, i. 109; Midrash Haseroth, ed. Marmorstein, p. 40, note 167, v. also Marmorstein, מאמר על איזה יהושע בן לוי תנועות רוחניות בדורו של ר' in Mélanges offerts à M. Israel Lévy, Paris, 1926, pp. i–xvi.

the other two reforms.   The weight of the proofs cited for
the support or the antiquity of the rule enhances its meaning.   The subject is of so much importance for the questions
here dealt with that the texts must be examined.   The Pal.
Talmud calls the author of our statement R. Joshua of
the South (דרומא), i.e. *Ben Levi*, Pal., has ג' דברים גזרו ב"ד
של מטן והסכים ב"ד של מעלה עמהן.   The three decrees are: (*a*) חרמה
של יריחו, (*b*) מגילת אסתר, and (*c*) שאילת שלום בשם.   R. Abun
adds in the name of R. J.b.L. (*d*) מעשרות.   Ruth r. mentions
as author R. Tanhuma in the name of the Rabbanan.   The
order of the decrees is *c*, *b*, and *d*.   It is noteworthy that
here the verse Jer. 23. 27 is first cited (who thought to
make my people forget *my Name*), upon which the references to Boaz and Gideon are given.   The Rabbis of the
third century see in the saying of Jeremiah a reference to
Athaliah, Mordecai, and Esther, or the three young men
respectively.   The chronological difficulties and impossi-
bilities do not worry the teachers of the Haggada.   In
Midr. Psalms the saying is by R. Simon in the name of
R. J. b. L.   The order is *d*, *c*, and *b*.   *a* is given in the name
of Rabbanan.   Tanh. reports the saying by R. J. b. L. in
the order of *d*, *b*, and *a*; here *c* is omitted altogether.   The
Bab. Talmud cites the sentence in the name of R. J. b. L.,
the order being *b*, *c*, *d*.   We have now to consider the
approximate dates of these innovations.

First of all, the arrangements about the tithes.   All reports agree that the duty of the tithes ceased to operate with
the destruction of the first Temple, and after the exile
of the Israelites into a strange land.   Yet the Israelites
voluntarily reserved the privilege of paying these duties.
The rearrangement of the tithes by Ezra, who bestowed
them on the priests that returned with him to the ancient
homestead, and punished the Levites who preferred Babylon
to the land of their ancestors, was often discussed and
pointed out, especially by Herzfeld and Graetz.[26]   We may

---

[26] v. the former's *Geschichte des Volkes Israel*, i. 138, and the latter in
MGWJ., 1886, p. 100 ff.

take for granted that we have before us a very ancient arrangement, dating probably from the time of Ezra, or, if later, from the time when Johanan, the High Priest, introduced his reforms. Yet, one may ask, why did R. J. b. L. in the third century call attention to the innovation of the tithes? It was surely not pure historical interest or archaeological zeal to bring these things to the notice of scholars and laymen alike? The cause is quite simple. We find a report that in the days of this great teacher a movement originated to abolish the existing practice of giving the tithes to the priests.[27] Thereon R. J. b. L. drew the attention of the people to the sacredness of this institution. It was arranged by Ezra, yet sanctioned by the heavenly court, by God Himself! The preachers of the third century exhort by various rhetorical methods at their disposal the merits of discharging this duty, and expatiate on the great sin of neglecting this singular observance. The frequency of both in the Haggadah of the period hints at the decline of the performance of this commandment.

We turn now to the second institution in the saying of of R. J. b. L. Whatever higher or lower critics may finally suggest about the date of the composition of the Book of Esther, the Jewish teachers saw in it an ancient work of the members of the *Synagoga magna*. The rules concerning the reading of the Scroll date back to the last two centuries preceding the destruction of the Temple. They are, apart from few minor points, anonymous and without controversies, such as occur, for instance, in connexion with the Feast of the Maccabees. In the third century again the book was subjected to many criticisms, and the teachers endeavoured, as in the case of the tithes, to establish its proper place. For our purpose it may be sufficient to say that this innovation must have been of very high antiquity. The same is the case with the pronunciation of the Name in greetings. We believe that this innovation was introduced in opposition to the priests, who after the death of Simon,

---

[27] Pal. Maaser Sheni 56 ʙ.

under Greek influence and Hellenistic teaching, held that
God has no name, or under the misuse of the Name for
magical practices prohibited the pronunciation of the
Tetragrammaton.   After a long struggle, the teachers
re-established the old usage of pronouncing the Divine
Name in the Temple.   Moreover, even in common greetings,
they succeeded with their reform.   The Mishna emphasizes, having always in view an opposition to this usage,
that the Name was pronounced in the Sanctuary according
to its writing.[28]   The בשם in the greetings must have a
similar meaning, otherwise the whole institution appears
superfluous and meaningless.   Yet one difficult and weighty
argument cannot and must not be overlooked!   We think
of the fact that in the Tannaitic sources, we referred to
above, we find clearly stated that the Name was pronounced
according to the writing in the Sanctuary only, but never
in the provinces.   Well, if this usage was not permitted in
the divine service in the synagogues, where substitutes
were used, how can we assume that the use of the Tetragrammaton was unscrupulously permitted in ordinary
greetings?   Secondly, even in the lessons from the Scriptures, they were commanded to change the Tetragrammaton
into the substitute of it—אדני.[29]   Thirdly, we are informed
by a reliable eye-witness—R. Tarphon, a priest—who
minutely watched and carefully observed the Blessing
pronounced by the High Priest in the Temple, and he tells
us, as we learnt above, that he once followed his uncle to
the platform (דוכן), stood listening near the High Priest,
and heard that he mingled (הבלעה) the Name with the tune
of his brethren, the priests!   According to the Jerushalmi

---

[28] v. Tamid vii. 2.

[29] v. Pes. 50 A; R. Nahman b. Isaac, העוהז לא כעולם הזה העולם הבא
נכתב ביו"ד ה"י ונקרא באלף דלת אבל לעולם הבא כולו אחד נקרא
יה, b. Kid. 71 A, it is the answer of ההוא סבא to ביו"ד ה"י ונכתב ביו"ד יה
R. Abina's question; the Pal. Talmud, Sanh. 28 B, ascribes a similar
saying to R. Jacob b. Aha, who explains Abba Shaul's sentence, which
will be discussed later on, by נכתב ביה ונקרא בא"ד.

we have to put it that R. Tarphon stood among the priests his brethren in the same row, and directed his attention towards the High Priest, &c. As to the manner of pronouncing the Name, however, there is a consensus of all reports. It seems that even in the Temple the pronunciation was not distinct. The High Priest tried to utter the Name in such a way that the people listening to the blessing should not hear the same distinctly. How shall we imagine that ordinary people in the street were permitted to pronounce the Name in their greetings? Finally, Abba Shaul registers those who utter the Name by its letters, i. e. as it is written, among those who have no share in future life.[30] What was his attitude toward the injunction in the Mishna of Berakhot?

All these questions and arguments can be settled if we examine the relation of the Tosefta to our Mishna. The Tosefta reads: בראישונה שהיתה תורה משתכחת מישראל היו זקנים מבליעין אותה ביניהן שנ' והנה בועז וכו' ואומר יי עמך גבור חחיל.[31] Two eminent Rabbis, who were also great scholars, Dr. Perls and Dr. Szidon, dealt with this Boraita in the Hungarian Jewish Review.[32] Dr. Perls saw that our Boraita is defective and unusual. This we certainly accept. We can, however, consent neither to his suggestion, nor do we find satisfactory the solution advanced by his critic. We agree that the style of the Boraita is not what we are used to in Tannaitic sayings of a similar type. These begin with בראישונה, depicting the conditions of the good old times, and put the state of the present circumstances, adding to it the changed law or rule. That is the general experience and observation. Here the antithesis is missing. From Hillel's sentence, which is a commentary to the previous saying, we learn that the antithesis was:

---

[30] M. Sanh. x. 1, Aboth R N., ed. Schechter, i. 35, p. 54, this saying is mentioned in the name of R. Johanan ben Nuri. Some readings limit this prohibition to countries outside Palestine, cf. Ber. Sanh. 101 B.

[31] vii. 23, ed. Zuckermandel, p. 17, ll. 14, 16.

[32] *Magyar Zsidó Szemle*, xii, 1895, 348–56, and xiii, 1896, 207 ff.

(a) בשעה שהתורה חביבה על ישראל

(b) בשעה שהתורה משתכחת

Therefore we assume, following Dr. Perls, that between
בראשונה and שהיתה תורה there must be a good deal missing.
Further, it seems obscure what the verses referring to
Boaz and Gideon are to prove in their present context.
Examining the Mishna, we find there that the quotations from Prov. 23. 22, and Ps. 119, 126 do not fit in
the context, in the Tosefta again Ruth 2. 4, and Judges
6. 12 are entirely out of place. This difficulty was
raised by the earliest interpreters of the Mishna. The
original text read most probably like this, gathered
from the Mishna and Tosefta, the words from T. are in
square brackets: התקינו [בראשונה שהיתה תורה חביבה על ישראל]
שיהא אדם שואל את שלום חבירו בשם שנ' והנה בועז בא וגו' ואומר ה'
עמך גבור החיל [משהיתה תורה משתכחת מישראל היו זקנים מבליעין
It is .אותה ביניהן שנ'] אל תבוז כי זקנה אמך, ואומר עת לעשות וגו'
especially noteworthy that the second part does not refer
to the priests, but to Zekenim, scholars and spiritual
leaders. Accordingly we can discern the following stages:
(1) After the death of Simon the use of the Name was
discontinued; (2) in the time of the early Hasidim the old
custom was re-established in the Temple and extended to
ordinary greetings in order to counteract Hellenistic influence; (3) with the establishment of the synagogues a line
was drawn between the service in the Temple and outside;
and (4) the greetings and the pronunciation in the Temple
by the Name were done בהבלעה, and not distinctly. This
reconstruction of the Boraita is preferable to that of
Dr. Perls, who suggests the following reading: בראשונה
שהיתה תורה חביבה על ישראל היו זקנים מבליעין את השם משקלקלו
המינים והיה תורה משתכחת מישראל התקינו שיהא אדם שואל את
We cannot agree to this .שלום חבירו בשם שנ' והנה בועז וגו'
for various reasons. The reform was not directed against
the early Christians, whom P. sees in the Minim of the
text, but against the Hellenists whose praxis is well

established. The whole Mishna and Boraita is doubtless to be dated from the time of the Temple, and not later. Yet the הבלעה was a later development, as is seen from R. Tarphon's report, than the greeting by the Name. The quotations from Proverbs and Psalms still remain obscure according to Dr. Perls's reconstruction of the Boraita. Hillel's parallel application of the terms תורה חביבה and תורה משתכחת seems to confirm our reading. Another corroboration of this order of things can be derived from a similarly composed Boraita, which reads : ת״ר בראשונה שם בן י״ב אותיות היו מוסרין אותו לכל אדם משרבו הפרוצים היו מוסרים אותו לצנועים שבכהונה וצנועים שבכהונה מבליעים אותו בנעימות אחיהם הכהנים.[33] This Boraita is parallel to our re-established Tosefta and Mishna. For both the more general custom prevailed at first, and was altered later. There can be no shadow of a doubt that the שאל בשם is the primary, and מבליעין the secondary degree of piety. Similar Tannaitic reports are preserved in the Palestinian Talmud. The first reads : בראשונה היה אומרו בקול גבוה משרבו הפרוצין היה אומרו בקול נמוך. The second sounds similarly : בראשונה הוא נמסר לכל אדם משרבו הפרוצין לא היה נמסר אלא לכשרים.[34] The first refers to the High Priest. In earlier periods the High Priest pronounced the Name in a loud voice, since the Peruzim increased it was uttered in a low voice. We may here suggest that קול נמוך is identical with בהבלעת נעימת הכהנים. The second is the same as the Borajta in the Babli, when we see in the כשרים the צנועים שבכהונה. Graetz is inclined to see in the Simon the Just of the report Simon b. Boethos Kantheras, who was raised to the High Priesthood by Agrippa I after the dismissal of Anan b. Anan.[35] There are weighty objections

---

[33] v. B. Kiddushin 71 A, as to the term צנוע; v. Simon, הצנוע, Tos. Kelim i. 1, 6, and other passages; Büchler, *Priester und Cultus*, Wien, 1895, 22; v. also b. Nidda 12 A : כל המקיים דברי חכמים נקרא צנוע, v. also Cant. r. 3. 11 : בראשונה היו מוסרין אותו לכל אדם משרבו הפושעים התקינו שלא יהו מוסרין אותו אלא לצנועים שבכהנה והצנועין שבכהונה היו מבליעין אותו בתוך נעימת הכהנים.

[34] Yoma 40 D (iii. 7).   [35] *MGWJ.*, 30, 1881, 108.

to an otherwise very ingenious hypothesis, the difficulties
and improbabilities of which were not hidden from our
great historian.   The treatises Yoma and Tamid, which are
of the period before the Destruction do not know of the
fact that the Name was not pronounced according to its
writing. It is also impossible to see in the term שנמנע מלברך
בשם the equivalent of מבליעים אותו.   Then, if the pronunciation was stopped, what was the good of handing on the Name
to the pious priests?   Finally, if the pronunciation was
not heard at all, how could the people respond with בשכמל״ו?
Apart from all these difficulties, Graetz cannot present the
slightest corroborating facts for the 'piety' of the High
Priest Kantheras, and a reason for his surname 'the Just'.
Moreover, is it not more likely that the compilers or copyists, who attribute to him the proclamation about Caius
Caligula, confused him with Simon the Just I, whom they
credited with such prophetic powers?   The piety of
Agrippa I surely could not make Simon Kantheras enjoy,
or attain to, the title of הצדיק.

Whilst Graetz was inclined to establish that the prohibition was the final stage in the history of the Name, his
pupil, B. Jacob, who contributed a very important and
erudite work on our subject [36] comes to the conclusion that
the latest tendency gave the use of the Name quite free to
every one in order to counteract Gnostic and Christian
tendencies. The action of the priests after the death of
Simon the Just is limited to a day's duration, or to the
time of the surviving contemporaries.   This is so done
because, otherwise, the difficulties would be insurmount-
able.[36a]   We tried to find a key to open the gate of these
difficulties. Dr. Jacob's theory would not be acceptable,
even if the riddle could not be solved, for a good many
reasons. How does Dr. Jacob account for all the sources,
which are older than Gnostic and Christian influences, and
which permit and encourage the use of the Tetragram-

[36] *Im Namen Gottes*, Berlin, 1903.
[36a] v. Tosefta Yadaim, p. 684, l. 6. שאתם מזכירים את השם.

maton ? How does he explain the undoubted antipathy of
the Palestinian as well as Alexandrian Jews in the earliest
period against the use of the Tetragrammaton, before magicians could have availed themselves of it ? It has often been
pointed out, and found very strange that the author of the
Scroll of Esther never mentions the Name of God.   Yet
the matter seems so simple. . The author lived in an age and
in a country where and when the pronunciation of the Name
was strictly forbidden.   It is exactly the time after the death
of Simon the Just.   The Bible translators in Egypt must
have lived at the same period and brought this Halakhah
with them from their native country.   The Samaritans
accepted also the law that the Tetragrammaton must not
be pronounced, but substituted the same by אלהים or שמא.[37]
One cannot get over the difficulty that there was a time
when the pronunciation of the Tetragrammaton was strictly
forbidden. The Hellenistic writer Artapan relates a Midrash :
' Moses released by supernatural power from prison went to
the royal palace, found the gates open, the guards fast
asleep, awoke the king, who was at first terrified at the
sight of Moses, then told him mockingly *to name the God
who sent him*.   Moses *whispered* the name in the king's ear,.
whereupon the king dropped down ; *caught* by Moses he
revived.   Later on Moses wrote the Name on a tablet and
sealed it.   A priest who blasphemed the writing died in
great agony.' [38]   Whatever *Jacob Freudenthal* thought of
this writer and his work,[39] we may cite him for a witness
that the Jews in his time and environment would not be
inclined to pronounce the Tetragrammaton.   The king
asked for *God's Name*.   Moses whispers, but does not pronounce the same.   All these materials show clearly that
the report of the Rabbinic writings about the contemporaries of Simon the Just is reliable and has to be

[37] Cf. כרמי שומרון, ed. Kirchheim, p. 94 ff. ; Gaster, M., *The Samaritans*,
p. 67.   Pal. Sanh. xi. 1 ; Geiger, *Urschrift*, p. 262; Herzfeld, *Geschichte,*
ii. 601.

[38] Euseb., *Praep. Ev.* 18. 23. 27.

[39] *Hellenistische Studien*, p. 143 f.

seriously and earnestly considered by students of that
period and on the Name of God. The difficulties presented
can, however, be removed when we assume that at some
later period the innovation of the priests became antiquated
and was removed by a reform, which made it a duty to
pronounce the Name in greetings. We saw that the custom of הבלעה followed this reform. The text of the Mishna
and Tosefta, as re-established above, confirms this.

Yet we have other proofs at our disposal to show that
the custom of הבלעת השם was the usual one in the last
decades of the Temple. R. Judah b. Ilai, who is a very
reliable historical witness, tells us that at the processions
around the altar the words אני והו הושיעה נא, and not אנא יי,
were uttered.[40] The Rabbanan do not know of it. They
know of אנא ה'. It is clear that there can be no contradiction or a controversy about facts. R. Judah as well as the
teachers of that Mishna, could have consulted eye-witnesses
by asking them: What did the people say at such
and such an occasion? There must have been among
scholars and unlearned, priests and laymen alike, in the
earlier part of R. Judah's life, men of standing who could
have satisfied R. Judah's or his opponents' curiosity on this
point. Yet the matter is quite in agreement with the
facts. The first part of the Mishna describes the earlier
custom which prevailed before they introduced the הבלעה;
R. Judah refers to the later usage in the last decade or
perhaps decades of the existence of the Temple. The
second part of the Mishna, where we read that they
surrounded the altar seven times on the day of the *Arubah*,
teaches that in taking leave from the altar was said:
יופי לך מזבח, lit. 'Beauty unto thee, altar', which sounds
rather strange. Scholars recognized that יופי is really a substitute for God's Name.[41] This Mishna was already altered
according to R. Judah, or taught according to his views.
An older Tannaite, R. Eliezer b. Hyrkanos said that ליה ולך
מזבח was uttered, and preserved the original words.

[40] M. Sukka, iv. 5.   [41] v. esp. Blau, *Das Altjüd. Zauberwesen*, p. 115.

A second instance leads away from the precincts of the Temple to the Courts of Law, where life and death was decreed. The Mishna teaches that a man who blasphemed God is not guilty of death unless he uttered the Tetragrammaton according to its writing.[42] The Mishna must have been taught when people knew the proper pronunciation of the Tetragrammaton, before the restrictions of publishing the same abroad were issued, before the institution of the הבלעה, and after the period which followed the death of Simon the Just I. Similarly to the יופי = God (Tetragrammaton), R. Joshua b. Korha relates that יוסי was applied instead of God (Tetragrammaton). It is to be noticed that both יופי as well as יוסי contain four letters like the Tetragrammaton.[42a]

Before we enter into an inquiry as to the nature of the greetings referred to in our source, and the reason for pointing it out in the third century, we have to settle another historical report. We are told that a day was especially marked, e. g. the 3rd of Tishri, in the Jewish calendar, on which the אדכרתא was removed from the public documents.[43] Let us consider the original text first: בשלשה בתשרי אתנטילת (בטילה) אדכרתא מן שטריא. On the 3rd of Tishri the אדכרתא was taken away or annulled from the documents. In the Scholion, and in the Babylonian Talmud we read: שגזרה מלכות יון גזרה שלא להזכיר שם שמים על פיהם וכשגנברה מלכות חשמונאי ונצחום התקינו שיהו מזכירין שם שמים אפילו בשטרות וכך היו כותבים בשנת כך וכך ליוחנן כהן גדול לאל עליון וכששמעו חכמים בדבר אמרו למחר זה פורע את חובו ונמצא שטר מוטל באשפה וביטלום ואותו היום עשאוהו וגו'. In the Scholion there are a few variants. First: שהוא משמש לאל

[42] M. Sanh. 55 B.

[42a] D. Oppenheim, *Kobak's Jeschurun*, iv. 1864, German part 90-98 identifies יוסי with Jovis, I. Levy, ibid., Hebr., pp. 4-6 with Jesus, the son of Josef. Needless to say that neither explanation can be considered satisfactory.

[43] Meg. Taanith, ch. 7; B. R. H. 18 B; Geiger, *Urschrift*, 33; Graetz, *Geschichte*, iii. 2, 572; Bornstein in *Hatekufah*, viii. 289; and S. Zeitlin, *Megillat Taanith*, Philadelphia, 1922, p. 97 f.

וכששמעו חכמים בדבר אמרו וכי מזכירין שם שמים בשטרות and ,עליון
למחר, a sentence which was omitted by the copyists of the
Talmud.[44] This text deserves a careful analysis.

First of all we have to investigate the term אדכרתא.   In
all our sources on this subject we find the word שם for the
Tetragrammaton. R. Jose ha Gelili and R. Tarphon use
this term denoting the Tetragrammaton with reference to
the Books of the Minim.[45] Yet one may reasonably doubt
whether this is the original term for the Tetragrammaton.
This term never occurs in old Tannaitic sources. We
can trace it only from the time of the Boraita collector
and compiler, R. Hijja, who was a half-Tannaite, and
onwards.   R. Hijja says : השומע אזכרה בזמן הזה אינו חייב לקרוע,
' He who hears the Azkarah in this time need not rend his
garments '.[46] The discussion of the Talmud qualifies this
statement to the use of the substitutes of the Name by
a non-Jew. Samuel taught : השומע אזכרה מפי העובד כוכבים
אינו חייב לקרוע.[47] A Jew who hears the Azkarah from a Gentile need not comply with the duty of קריעה, i.e. rending his
garments. R. Jonathan b. Eliezer says that the books of the
last three prophets contain 93 Azkaroth.[48]   R. Hona
examined the books and found only 83. Both sayings are
rather surprising. We find the Name in Haggai 30 times,
in Zechariah 126 times, and in Malachi 46 times. How do
the facts agree with the teacher's assertion that they are
mentioned 93 or 83 times respectively ? Yet, omitting the
Names, where the Tetragrammaton is connected with צבאות,
&c., we find the Name in Haggai 15 times, in Zech. 72, and
in Malachi 19, which amounts to 106. Eliminating now
13 passages where the Name occurs twice we get the total
pointed out by R. Jonathan. Yet what does this artificial
calculation teach us ? Nothing less than the very important fact that the Tetragrammaton alone was called
Azkarah or Adkartha. Such appellations as יי צבאות, or

---

[44] v. *Meg. Taan.*, ed. Amsterdam, 1711, Prague, 1795.

[45] Tos. Sabb. 13. 5. and parall.   [46] v. b. Sanh. 60 A.

[47] b. Sanh. 60 A.   [48] pal. Hag. 79 D ; R. S. b. N. in his name.

יי אלהים, or יי אלהי ישראל are not included. R. Nathan b.
Abishalom, who took part in a discussion, or whose view is
mentioned together with that of R. Jose b. Halafta and
R. Jonathan b. Joseph, says of the בעל קרי that he may study
the Talmud אם מציע את הגמרא ובלבד שלא יאמר אזכרות שבהן.[49]
He must have belonged to the Amoraic period, otherwise the
term גמרא would be out of place. Here the אזכרות again refer
to the Tetragrammaton Rabba b. R. Huna speaks of the
one אזכרה that was on the ציץ, and the many אזכרות, which
are to be found in the phylacteries.[50] *R. Hillel, the son of
R. Samuel b. Nahmani,* sees in the Eighteen Benedictions
a parallel to the 18 אזכרות in Ps. 29; *R. Joseph,* in the 18
אזכרות of the שמע.[51] The Babylonian Amora counts
אלהים as Azkaroth. The teaching of R. S. b. N. is
reported in the Pal. Talmud by R Levi, כנגד י"ח הזכרות
שכתוב בהבו ליי בני אלים[52] and R. Abba of קרטגינא, as
to the Nine Benedictions for the New Year's Day,
כנגד תשע אזכרות שכתוב בפרשת חנה.[53] R. Hoshaja, R. Judah
b. Simon in his name, counted from Gen. 1. 1 to Gen. 3. 17
71 Azkaroth. Since the Tetragrammaton occurs only 16
times, and אלהים 39 times, we must assume that R. Hoshaja
reckoned 39 (אלהים) + 16 (יי) + 16 (יי אלהים), together 71.[54]
R. Hoshaja, who lived in Caesarea, kept to the Babylonian
tradition in seeing in Elohim also an Azkarah, which did
not agree with the Palestinian praxis. We may derive

[49] b. Ber. 22 A.

[50] b. Men. 36 B; b. Sabb. 12 B; Yoma 7 B.

[51] Deut. 6. 4–9 (three times), 11. 13–21 (four times), Num. 15. 37–41
(four times); one must therefore add : אלהים and אלהיכם (seven times in
Num.), אלהיך, אלהינו (twice in Deut. ch. 6), and אלהיכם (once in ch. 11),
together 7 and 11 = 18 ; v. also Lev. 5. 1–8.

[52] pal. Ber. 8 A; pal. Taanith 65 c; Tanh. B., i. 71 B. Similar explanations are being advanced by R. Judan ענתוריא as to the Seven Benedictions for Sabbath, כנגד ז' אזכרות שכתוב במזמור שיר ליום השבת
Ps. ch. 92. Here again אלהינו in v. 14 is not counted.

[53] v. 1 Sam. 2. 1–10, where כאלהינו ver. 2, and אל דעות ver. 3, are
not counted ; vide also pal. Taanith 65 c, where we read ענתו דריא and
קרתיגנא respectively.

[54] Gen. r. 20. 6; Num. r. 14. 12; M. Tadshe, ch. 10.

from our material the conclusion, that אזכרה was used
since the latest Tannaim and first Amoraim to denote the
Mishnaic שם. It is now most surprising that we find in
the M. T. אדכרתא, and not השם. It seems that איתנטלית השם
or בטילת השם would sound too drastic, therefore the rather
unusual אדכרתא was put in its place. Let us turn to the
Scholion! Here it is distinctly stated that the Greeks
prohibited the mentioning of the name of Heaven.
R. Simon b. Lakish, in the third century, had a similar
historical tradition. The Jews were commanded to write
on the horn of the ox: 'We have no share in the God of
Israel ',[55] which perfectly agrees with the word of the
Scholion, ואמרו להם אין לכם חלק באלהי ישראל. Here we have
the real explanation for the action of the priests after the
death of Simon the Just. Hellenistic opposition to the
religion of the Jews, the apostasy of the priests and
nobles, introduced and established the rule not to pronounce
the Tetragrammaton in the Sanctuary. The reaction came
before, or in the time of the Hasmoneans. One counter-
action we saw already in the rule to use the Name of God in
greetings. The second was in the formulary of documents.
According to the Boraita, they wrote, 'in the ·year so and
so of X, High Priest to the Highest God'. Yet what did
they write in the time of a king, who did not adorn the
dignity of the High Priests? .Or was the custom in use
only as long as the High Priests were the highest digni-
taries? When was this usage abolished? Geiger, who is
followed by Zeitlin, dates it to the Roman period, to the
time of the great wars against the Romans, i.e. 65 C. E.
It was the work of Menahem, son of the scribe Judas, the
Galilean.[56] Is it likely that the M. T. would celebrate
a victory of the enemies of the Pharisees? Further, why
did they eliminate the Name of God, and not that of the
High Priest, since the Jews 'were subject to God alone'?

[55] Mekhilta 71 B; Gen. r. 2. 4; v. Marmorstein, *Jahrbuch für Jüd. Volkskunde*, i. 307 f.
[56] Zeitlin, pp. 98 f.

We would expect that they removed the ruler's name, and not the Name of God. One cannot grasp the objection of the Greeks to the term אל עליון, that was well known, and frequently to be found with them as well. Finally, the question of the Galilean proves the praxis that the Name, the שם, was still in use in documents in the time before the destruction of the Temple. We are therefore obliged to accept the view that we have here a victory of the Pharisees over the Sadducees.[57] It is the same development which we find established in the history of the pronunciation of the Name. Ed. Baneth[58] came to a similar result as to the date and origin of the passage in M. T. and the M. Ber. without basing his theory on the report as to the conduct of the priests after the death of Simon. Baneth thinks that the institution of greeting with the divine Name is connected with the movement ascribed by him to Jewish sects, who endeavoured to remove the divine Names מקום and שמים, and substitute in their place טובים. Why should the Rabbis object to טובים, and prefer מקום or שמים? The name טובים, or טוב, is actually used in Rabbinic sources for God. The real reason for this institution must be sought somewhere else.

A reminiscence of this struggle for the pronunciation, and against the use, of the Tetragrammaton can be seen in some of the Psalms. Notably in Ps. 129. Israel may rightly say: 'Many a time have the nations afflicted me from my youth' (verse 1). Egypt, Assur, Babylon, the Medes, and now the Greeks. Yet they have not prevailed against Israel (ver. 2). Some of these, at one time mighty enemies, are in the dust; Israel is still alive. They plowed like plowers on Israel's back. God in his righteousness has cut asunder the cords of the wicked (verses 3–4). All the haters, enemies of Zion, are confounded and turned back (ver. 5). They may become as the grass on the housetops,

---

[57] v. Graetz, *Geschichte*, iii A. 572.

[58] *Ursprung der Sadokäer und Boethosäer*, Berlin, 1882, p. 53 f.

which withereth afore it groweth up (ver. 6).   The next
sentence seems artificial at the first sight.   The mower
filleth not his hands, nor he that bindeth sheaves his bosom
(ver. 7).   And the passers-by did not say : ' The Blessing of
'' be upon you : we bless you in the name of '''' ' (ver. 8).
Who are the enemies of Zion ?   Why did they not greet
with the old greeting of Boaz any more ? (Ruth 2. 4).   The
enemies are the Jews who joined the Greeks in removing
the Name, and even when the Scribes re-established the old
greetings, they, the Hellenists, still refrained from applying
it.   The same background must be ascribed to Psalms 128
and 134.   The man who feareth God must be blessed with
the words : יברכך יי מציון (128. 4 f), and not, as it was done
before, without employing the Tetragrammaton.   Ps. 134
concludes, after having appealed to bless the Lord, with the
blessing : יברכך יי מציון עושה שמים וארץ (ver. 3).   The same is
the case in Ps. 135 (ver. 21).   The house of Israel, the house
of Aaron, and those who fear the Lord are invited to bless
the Lord (verses 19–20).   Even those who fear God need not
refrain from uttering the Tetragrammaton in their benedictions and greetings.   This psalmist, or these psalmists,
may have been contemporaries of Ben Sira, who alludes in an
unmistakable manner to this movement among his people.
In ch. 41. verses 17–22 he enumerates things of which man
should and must be ashamed, which are followed by a catalogue of virtues of which one need not be ashamed.   Graetz
rightly saw in these portions a very valuable historical
source, which throws light on the religious and social conditions of the author's period and enabled him to establish
Sirah's approximate date.   We draw attention especially to
ch. 41, ver. 20 A : ' Be ashamed of keeping silent when you
are greeted '.   The Hebrew has two versions : (a) מישאל שלום
מהחריש, and (b) משאול שלום מחריש.   The second reading means :
' to greet silently ', and the first : ' not to return a greeting,
keeping silent, when greeted '.   It is true that the Rabbis
rebuke the proud who do not return their fellow men's

greeting.[59] Yet it is hardly to be believed that Sirah meant the same. He, surely, wanted to say more than that the rich are too haughty in their dealings with the poor; that they are ashamed to accept the greetings of their less fortunate brethren. It does not fit in the context, rebuking impudence, falsehood, treachery, larceny, breaking covenant and oath, inhospitality, cruelty, adultery, and sexual immorality. Surely he meant that people refrained from using the 'Name' in their greetings, or, at least, have been ashamed of doing so.[59a]

We arrived at the question, What was the meaning of these greetings? Why did the scribes emphasize their importance and attach to it the Tetragrammaton? We are told that R. Johanan b. Zakkai greeted Jews as well as heathens, even before they saluted him.[59b] Did R. Joh. b. Z. use the Tetragrammaton? Did he pronounce the name in greeting Jews and Gentiles alike? R. Meir and R. Judah speak of two kinds of greetings. Greetings out of honour, and those out of fear.[60] A Boraita teaches: הנכנס לבית המרחץ מקום שב"א עומדין לבושין יש שם מקרא ותפלה וא"צ לומר שאילת שלום ומניח תפילין ואצ"ל שאינו חולץ. In a bath, where people stood dressed, one can read the Bible, deliver the prayer; needless to say that they may greet each other, &c. Where people stood dressed and naked, there greetings were exchanged, but there was no room for reading and prayer. Where people stood naked there was no place for greetings.[61] The distinction made between reading and prayer on one side and between greetings on the other side suggests that the latter were not on the same high level as the former. From the discussion of the Amoraim it appears

---

[59] b. Ber. 6 B. R. Helbo in the name of R. Huna. כל שיודע בחבירו שרגיל ליתן לו שלום יקדים לו שלום.

[59a] v. now Marmorstein, Zur Erklärung von Jes. 53, in ZAW., N. S., iii (1926), p. 263.

[59b] b. Ber. 17 A, אמרו עליו על רבן יוחנן בן זכאי שלא הקדימו אדם שלום מעולם ואפלו נכרי בשוק.

[60] Mishna, Ber. ii. 1.

[61] Tosefta Berakoth 2. 23; pal. Ber. 4 c; b. Shabb. 10 A.

that in their time the Tetragrammaton was not used any
more.   Had they still used it, one would never allow it to
be pronounced in a place where people were naked.   In the
third century we hear of scholars who went to greet
(סלק למשאל בשלמי הדר) their teachers or friends, as
R. Jochanan b. Nappaha went to R. Haninah b. Hama,[62]
and R. Levi [63] to the Patriarch of his time.[64]   R. Johanan b.
Nappaha was very angry with R. Eleazar b. Pedath, who
did not greet his master and colleague.   The Babylonians
were rather backward in this respect.   Another Babylonian contemporary, Zeiri, neglected also this sign of
respect towards his teacher.[65]   R. Johanan teaches us
further that the greeting was expressed by the words
שלום עליך רבי ומורי.[66]   The same phrases of greetings were
exchanged between R. Jose b. Halafta and Elijah.[67]   R. Jose
b. Qisma met a stranger, and we read that they exchanged
greetings.[68]   Babylonian scholars sent greetings to their
Palestinian friends.[69]   Certain rules as to greetings were laid
down by various teachers.[70]   The preachers liked to refer in
their sermons to this custom of greetings.[71]   Certain families
had the privilege of greeting the Patriarch every day.[72]   In
all these instances we may safely gather that the old custom
was already abolished.   It is true that the Scribes saw in
the word שלום a name of God, but the old greeting with the
Tetragrammaton ceased.   Yet there was actuality in this
point of R. J. b. L.'s saying, just as the references to the

[62] Gen. r. 5, 6 ; Lev. r. 10. 9 ; 21. 7; Pes., ed. Buber, 177 A.
[63] Or R. Simon b. Lakish.   [64] Gen. r. 78. 15 ; 80. 1.
[65] pal. Ber. 4 B; v. also pal. MK. 83 c, pal. Shek. 16 c.
[66] pal. Ber. 4 B, v. B. B. K. 73 B.   [67] v. b. Ber. 3 A.
[68] נתן לו שלום והחזיר ושלום; v. Kinjan Tora, M. 9, Tractate Derek Erets
r. ch. vi.
[69] b. Ber. 9 B.
[70] v. Rab b. Ber. 14 A, before prayers; Ulla, b. Sabb. 10 B, in the bath ;
R. Huna, b. Ber. 6 B, &c.
[71] v. R. Akiba; Cant. 2. 19 ; Gen. r. 45. 5 ; R. Meir, ושאל בשלמה של ;
עלובה ; Deut. r. 4. 8 ; Cant. r. 7. 4 ; Tanh. B. ii. 80, and other instances.
[72] pal. Sabb. 13 c ; Hor. 48 c ; Jeb. 12. 3 B ; Sachs, *Beiträge*, i. 17 ; *MGWJ*.,
1885, 481.

reading of the Scroll and the tithes were not arbitrary or theoretical. For in this time, in the first half of the third century, a great change in the use of the name of God is to be noticed, which brought about many changes in Jewish theological and philosophical lore, the influences of which are felt up to this very day. This will be the subject of the next chapter. Yet, before concluding this chapter, we have to point out that the knowledge of the 'Name' was not yet extinct. Samuel heard a Persian woman cursing her son with one letter of the Name.[73] A doctor of medicine in Sepphoris wanted to teach R. Phinehas b. Hama the use of the Name.[74] Similar stories are related about R. Haninah b. Hama and Aninai b. Nahson. According to Pirke R. Eliezer[75] the President of the Academy in declaring the New-Moon pronounced the Tetragrammaton in the same way as the High Priest on the Day of Atonement.

[73] pal. Yoma 3. 7.   [74] Ibid. Eccl. r. 3. 11.
[75] Ch. 8, v. *JQR.*, xiv, 1902, 469.

II

The Names of God in the Bible.

THE Mishna gives an official list of the divine Names of
the Bible for several purposes. Mishna Shebuot, iv. 10,
teaches : ' If a man said " I put an oath on you, I command
you (by oath), I bind you (by oath) ", he is guilty ; " By
heaven and earth ", he is free ; By the names (a) א"ד, (b) י"ה,
(c) שדי, (d) צבאות, (e) חנון ורחום, (f) ארך אפים, (g) רב חסד, and
(h) by all the substitutes, then he is guilty.' [1] This list contains two difficulties. First of all that the name אלהים, or
אל, is altogether omitted. Secondly, that א"ד is mentioned
before י"ה, and is called a real name, whilst it ought to be
treated as one of the substitutes. A second catalogue of
names, which may be deleted in writing, or may not be
treated so, gives under the latter category : (a) אל with all
its composites, (b) אהיה אשר אהיה, (c) א"ד, (d) י"ה, (e) שדי, and
(f) צבאות, and in the first category are added to (c), (d), and
(e) of the Mishna also : הגדול, הגבור הנורא האדיר והחזק והאמיץ
והעזוז.[2] The omission of אלהים in the M. is to be ascribed to
the fact that all sayings with that name belong to a group
of curses (אלה). The order of א"ד and י"ה is kept in the
Boraita as well. The treatise of Soferim adds [3] : אבל רחום
וחנון וארך אפים ורב חסד מלך מלכים גדול עליון צדיק וישר חסיד תמים
גבור הרי אלו נמחקין. The chief divine names are also given
in the introductory words of the Book of Yezira : יה ה'
צבאות אלהי ישראל אלהים חיים אל שדי רם ונשא שוכן עד וקדוש.[4]

Reviewing these names we notice that some of them
occur even in the Bible only once, some are repeated only
a few times, others occur more or less frequently. They

---

[1] M. Shebuoth, *Yer. and Babli* חנון ורחום as God's names occur also
Sifre, Deut., § 49, Midr. Tannaim, p. 43.

[2] b. Sheb. 35 A ; Soferim, iv. 1 ; A. R. N. 34. 2, v. also a Tanhuma fragment in Yalkut Makhiri Psalms, 92, 26.   [3] iv. 9.

[4] v. about the readings פירוש ס' יצירה, by Judah b. Barzili of Barcelona,
ed. S. Halberstamm, Berlin, 1885, p. 116.

are landmarks in the religious development and education
of the old Hebrews and Israelites. The most ardent intellectual endeavours and religious zeal are attached to these
names, which left their indestructible marks and irremov-
able imprints on the mind and soul of the whole world.
Whatever moderns may think of those prophets and
priests who uttered them for the first time, and grew not
weary in repeating them, these Names prepared for the religious enlightenment of the world. His Name became great
among the nations all over the earth from sunrise to sunset
(cf. Mal. 1. 11). A psalmist calls upon all the nations to
sing and praise Him, whose Name became the guide and
comfort of the whole world (Ps. 117. 1). Yet some of these
names have never been repeated, at least not in their
original form. The divine Name אהיה אשר אהיה is mentioned
only once (Exod. 3. 14). The name שדי is more frequent.
The teachers of the third century endeavour to explain the
meaning of this term. All of them see in it a kind of
notarikon : אני הוא שאמרתי לעולם די, ' I am He, who said to
the World, Enough ! ' meaning that otherwise the creation
of heaven and earth would never have been completed.[5]
There was an older interpretation by R. Eliezer b. Jacob,
who sees in שדי the idea that the whole universe and all the
fullness thereof is not worthy (כדיי) of the Godhead. The
Haggadist quotes the Greek words of Aquilas' translation :
ἄξιος and ἱκανός. The first word means ' everlasting ' and
the second ' all powerful '.[6]

The name צבאות gave rise to several explanations. What

---

[5] Rab (R. Judah b. Ezekiel in his name); R. Simon b. Lakish, Hag. 12 A;
R. Alexander Tanh. i. 202; R. Abbahu; Tanhuma, בראשית, 12 ; i. 80,
i. 197 ; R. Aha (trans. by R. Nathan), and R. Isaac (trans. by R. Berekhja;
Gen. r. 5, ed. Theodor. pp. 37 and 460) ; R. Hoshaja (trans. by R. Phinehas
b. Hanna, Gen. r. 92. 1), and Pirke R. E., ch. 3.

[6] Gen. r. ch. 17. 1, ed. Theodor, 401 ; v. also Tanh. i 80 ; Levy, H. W. B.,
s. vv. אקסיום and איקנום; Z. Frankel, Über den Einfluss der paläst.
Exegese, Leipzig, 1851, 28 ; Lerner, Quellen und Anlage, 57 ; Krauss, in
Steinschneider Festschrift, 152 ; Lehnwörter, s.v. and Preuschen-Bauer, Griech-
Deutsches Wörterbuch ; Giessen, 1926, col. 122 and col. 583, v. also Marmor-
stein, Miscellen, in ZfNW, 25, 1926, p. 253 f.

is צבאות ?   A sign (אות) in his hosts.[7]   A notarikon which
shows that the original meaning of the name was lost to
the later generations.   A teacher of the fourth century,
R. Abba b. Kahana, R. Berekhja in his name, remarks that
the name of God is Zabaoth.   R. Judah b. Simon adds, ' even
one letter of His name is capable of creating hosts as the
the whole of His name '.[8]   In Hebrew-Aramaic and Greek
magic צבאות is put together with ια ια αδωναι σαβαωθ.[9]
R. Eleazar b. Pedath emphasizes that Hannah was the first
to use this name.[10]   The teachers add : Hannah saw the
multitudes of Israel in the precincts of the Temple, and
she said in her prayer : 'Thou hast brought forth all
these multitudes (צבאות) and unto me dost Thou withhold
a son ?'[11]

The other names, like אד, יה and אל were also relegated
to the language of prayers and magic, as will be shown in
the next chapter.   But before attempting to describe the
history of these names in Rabbinic theology, their meaning
must be dealt with at some length.

Rabbinic lore preserved the teaching that the Tetragrammaton implies or expresses the measure of love and mercy ;
the name Elohim, that of judgement.   Philo taught just
the reverse ; the term θεός = אלהים means εὐεργέτης, the
good, the God of love and benevolence ; κύριος = אדני
expresses God's Lordship, Rulership, Judgement.   Dähne,
the old, but not antiquated, historian of Jewish-Hellenistic
philosophy of religion, wrote about ninety years ago :
'Philo names the benevolent world-creating power (δύναμις)
God (θεός), and the mighty world-ruling power Lord
(κύριος).   Philo himself asserts that in doing so he relies
on the usual phraseology.'[12]   Many passages in Philo's
works confirm this statement.   The first modern Jewish

---

[7] צבא, Mekh. 35 A.   [8] Pes. r. 104 A.

[9] v. Blau, *Zauberwesen*, p. 91 ; b. Yoma, 84 A, and b. B. B. 73 A.

[10] b. Ber. 31 B.

[11] v. ib. ; M. Samuel, ed. Buber, p. 48 f., R. Levi and R. Joshua b. Levi.

[12] *Geschichtliche Darstellung der jüd. alex. Religions-Philosophie*, Halle, 1834,
p. 231 f.

investigator of the Septuagint, *Zacharias Frankel,* was
puzzled by this view of Philo, and ascribes this great
difference between the Palestinian way of thinking and
between Philo's hermeneutics to the latter's ignorance of
Hebrew.[13]   Philo's assumed ignorance alone does not explain the great discrepancy between Alexandrinian and
Palestinian teachings.   Besides, Philo clearly points out
that his conception goes back to reliable authorities.   Who
were they ?

We have to examine the midrashic material at our
disposal in order to see the real state of our doctrine.   The
first teachers in whose sayings the terms מדת הרחמים and
מדת הדין occur are R. Meir and R. Simon b. Johai.   R. Meir's
name is attached to the saying based on Isa. 26. 21 : כי הנה
ה' יוצא ממקומו יוצא ממדה למדה ממדת הדין למדת הרחמים.   'God
goes out from His place ?   God is omnipresent !   How could
it be that He goes from one place to another ?   It was
taught in the name of R. Meir that He changes the
measure of judgement with that of mercy.'   Apparently
the meaning is : ה' (the measure of mercy) steps in the place
of אלהים (the measure of judgement).[14]   R. Simon b. Johai
sees in אל, Ps. 36. 7, an allusion to God's judgement.[15]   The
doctrine that the term אלהים means judge is several times
ascribed to R. S. b. J.   Yet the old Tannaitic Haggada does
not seem to know the terms מדת הרחמים and מדת הדין.[15a]
Instead we read the terms מדה טובה and מדה פורענות, 'the

***

[13] v. *Vorstudien in der LXX,* Leipzig, 1851, p. 178 f., esp. his note, and
Über den Einfluss der palästinensischen Exegese auf die alex. Hermeneutik, Leipzig,
1851, p. 26.

[14] v. pal. Taanith 65 B ; Pesikta, ed. Buber, 162 A and 164 A, where the
text can be completed with the help of Yalkut Makhiri on Hosea, ed.
Greenup, 2.

[15] v. Tanh., ed. Buber, i. 34 ; Ag. Ber. 4. 1.   See, however, Pes., ed.
Buber, 73 A ; Lev. r. 27 ; Gen. r. 33 ; M. Ps. ch. 36, cf. Lev. r, 27. 1, Tanh.
B. iii. 71.

[15a] The dispute between R. Ishmael and R. Akiba, whether אלהים in
Ex. 22. 27 means "God", or "Judge", could not have arisen if the later
meaning of Elohim had been known in their days, v. Mekh. 79 A, b. Sanh.
66 A, pal. Sanh. 7. 8, Soferim 4, 5.

measure of goodness and the measure of punishment'.
A saying of R. Meir contains the latter, and not the former
terms. 'Whence do we derive that one must bless God for
the good as well as for the evil?' because it says, 'Which the
Lord thy God has given thee'. He is thy judge in all
judgements He passes on thee, whether with the measure of
goodness or with that of punishment.[16] The Tannaitic
Midrash usually adopts these earlier terms.[17] None of
these, however, enables us to glance at the inner meaning
of the use made of the divine name. One can see in 'ה the
מדת פורענות, and in אלהים the measure of goodness, or *vice
versa*. Yet a few passages show clearly that not only
Philo but even the older Rabbis did not know of the
exegetical norm we are dealing with, in spite of being well
acquainted with the Hebrew Bible, a knowledge of which
Philo could not boast, according to Frankel. In Mekhilta 8 A
we read: אני יי בשבועה אני נפרע מהם קו"ח ומה אם מדת פורענות
כו"כ ע"א מרובה טובה מדה ועשה לעשות הקב'ה אמר מעוטה. Here the
name יי occurs, and it is understood to convey the meaning
of a threat, a future punishment in case of disobedience.
Although the Midrash of the Tannaim contains the rule of
ה = מדת הרחמים, and אלהים = מדת הדין,[18] yet the text never uses
these terms, but always the older terms מדת טובה and מדת
פורענות. In one place the new term, מדת הרחמים, is actually
used, but not with reference to 'ה. Mekh. 37 A contains a
text, reading: אל אלהי אבי עמי נהג במדת רחמים ועם אבותי נהג
במדת רחמים ומנין שאין אלי אלא מדת רחמים שנ' אלי אלי למה עזבתני,
ואומר אל נא רפא נא לה, ואומר אל יי ויאר לנו. 'God, the God of
my father. He treated me with the measure of mercy, just
as He treated my father with the same measure.' Whence

---

[16] b. Ber. 48 B; also Hijja b. Nahmani; Mekh. 19 B; Tosefta, 14, p. 181;
v. also R. Akiba, Mekh. 72 B.

[17] v. M. 7 B, 26 A: ומה אם מדה פורענות מעוטה מי שהתחיל בעבירה
קו ומה אם מדת פורענות 14A, לוקה תחלה קו"ח למדת טובה שמרובה
מועטת העושה בסתר הקב'ה מפרסמו בגלוי מדה טובה מרובה ע"א כו"כ;
49 A; 68 B. R. Eleazar of Modiim, 95 B, 100 A; Sifre Num., § 115; Sifre
Deut., § 286, and several more.

[18] Sifre Deut., § 27.

do we know that אל denotes *the measure of mercy*? From
Ps. 22. 2, Num. 12. 13, and Ps. 118. 27. Friedmann corrects the texts according to Nahmanides, and earlier commentators, and changes the second מדת הרחמים in the term
of מדת הדין. The correction is based on the assumption that
the old Haggadah knew the norm of אלהים being the
measure of judgement. That is not so. The fact is that the
ancient Haggada, just like Philo, saw in ה' the מדת פורענות
= the judgeship or rulership of God, and in אלהים the love
and mercy of God. The first traces of a change of views and
attitude do not lead farther than the age of R. Simon and
R. Meir.[18b]

The rule is repeatedly quoted in the Midrash. The oldest
mention of it is to be found in the Sifre, § 27. Here it
reads: כל מקום שנ' ה' זו מדת הרחמים כל מקום שנ' אלהים זו מדת
הדין. For the first half of the rule we are referred to
Exod. 34. 6, and for the second to Exod. 22. 8 and 27.
Secondly, the first half of this rule is quoted in Gen. r. ch. 33,
ed. Theodor, p. 308, in a sermon of R. Samuel b. Nahmani.
The second half is cited by an anonymous preacher in
Eccles. r. 7. 17: באותה שעה בקשה מדת הדין לפגוע בו, דכתי' וידבר
אלהים ואין אלהים אלא מדת הדין ונא' ויאמר אליו אני ה' א'ל את ב'ו
לא יכולת לסבול אותם אני ה' רחמן בעל הרחמים במדתי ארחם.
Tanh. iii. 39 reads: שנ' ויקרא ה' אלהים אל האדם, אין ה' אלא
מדת הרחמים שנ' ה' ה' אל רחום והנון, הקדים לו מדת רחמים למדת
הדין, הוי כי לא אל חפץ רשע, שאינו חפץ לחייב בריה. Num. r. 9. 16:
יתן ה' אותך אוי להם לרשעים שעושים מדת רחמים אכזריות בכ"מ שנ' ביוד
ה"א מדת רחמים שנ' ה' ה' אל רחום. This Midrash uses also in
another place the term מדת אכזריות instead of מדת הדין, as
seen in 10. 17: כך תפלתן של צדיקים מהפכין מדת אכזריות למדת
רחמניות. M. Ps., ch. 56, ed. Buber, p. 294, ascribes this rule
to R. Nehorai (most of the MSS. omit this name) teaching:
מקום שנ' אלהים הוא מדת הדין ה' זו מדת הרחמים. According to
this information the authorship of the saying is to be

[18b] A Boraita of R. Hijja in Lev. r. 23. 9, preserved traces of the older
Agada, which says: למה אני ה' ב' פעמים אני שפרעתי מדור המבול וג'
אני עתיד ליפרע ממי שהוא עושה.

attributed to R. Nehorai. Nehorai and Meir are identical
names.[19] This also bears out our suggestion that the rule
was formulated by, or originated in the time of, R. Meir.
The teachers of the previous generations use, as we saw,
different terms. In genuine Tannaitic sources the new
terms are rare; very frequent, however, the older terms
מדת פורענות and מדת טובה. Some instances from the
Tannaitic Midrashim have been given already above. Here
other sources shall be consulted. Exod. r. 3. 18 has a
sentence, written in a style which can be ascribed to an older
Tannaitic Midrash, containing these terms. The passage
reads: ד״א מכאן שהפורענות (r. ש מדת) שהוא על הצדיקים לבא
ומדת הטוב ממהרת לבא. In the Bab. Talmud, Sabb. 97 A,
the saying is quoted by Raba, according to other readings
by R. Jose b. Haninah in the old Tannaitic form: מדה טובה
ממהרת לבא ממדת פורענות. The Amoraim preserved, as the
language shows, the original form of the sayings by earlier
teachers. The Midrash השכם [20] contains a question of
R. Joshua (b. Hananja): ' Which measure is greater? That
of goodness, or that of punishment? Certainly the former.'
Here again the Bab. Talmud preserved a fuller form of this
statement.[21] Here R. Joshua proves that the measure of
goodness surpasses that of punishment. If in punishment
the sins of the parents are visited on their children, how
much more that in the measure of goodness, i.e. reward,
their children will enjoy the fruits of their deeds in the
hereafter. There, by the same method, God's goodness is
demonstrated as enabling the righteous as well as the
wicked to bear the bounty of goodness and the severity of
punishment respectively. R. Ishmael deals with the same
question with reference to the faithless woman.[22] We are
therefore entitled to see in passages, where these older

[19] v. B. Erubin, 13 B.

[20] ed. Grünhut, הליקוטים ס׳, I. Jerusalem, 1892, 4 B.

[21] b. Sanh. 100 A–B; v. also b. Yoma 76 A.

[22] Sifre Num., § 9; cf. b. Sotah, 20 B; Tosefta, ch. 1; Num. r. 9. 39;
similarly R. Jose, the Galilean (Sifre Num., § 15; Sotah, 28 A; Num. r. 9.
45, fuller than in the other sources).

terms occur, Tannaitic Haggada. Thus Tanh. v. 49, where we learn that all Israelites are surety for each other. If there is one righteous, the whole world stands (exists) for his sake. If one man sins, the whole generation suffers on account of him. This is the law of solidarity in Israel and the world.[23] For this the example Achan is quoted. The homily concludes: מדת פורענות מועטת והדור נתפש מדה טובה מרובה על אחת כמה וכמה. The phrase occurs in a discussion between R. Gamaliel II and R. Akiba.[24] Once we find the terms in the name of R. Simon b. Abba;[25] it is, however, doubtful whether it is not a repetition of an older saying. For in the Amoraic Haggada these terms are not used. Even in some of the sayings of R. Meir[26] and R. S. b. J.[27] the old forms are still alive. It was surely a period of transition. Their contemporaries, R. Jose b. Halafta and R. Judah b. Ilai,[28] use still the old names.[29] Yet the latter Scribe is reputed to have used the new terms. He says: כך אמר משה בשעה שאמרת לי ועתה לך ואשלחך אל פרעה במדת רחמים אמרת לי שאתה עתיד לגואלן שמא עד שבאתי נהפכה למדת הדין, א'ל הקב'ה אני ה' במדת רחמים אני עומד הוי ויאמר אליו ה'.[30] We deduce from our material that this rule, just as the terms of מדת הדין and מדת הרחמים, are not older than the middle of the second century. We traced back the earlier view, which agrees with Philo's interpretation, that ה' signifies the מדת הדין, and אלהים the מדת הרחמים to the Palestinian Haggadah.

A further proof for this observation can be advanced from the translation of the name Elohim in the literature

[23] v. Marmorstein, *The Doctrine of Merits*, pp. 185 ff.

[24] Midr. Psalms, 119; cf. Sanh. 81 A; Maccoth, 24 A.

[25] Gen. r. ch. 9, ed. Th., p. 73.

[26] A. b. R. N. ch. 30, ed. Sch., p. 89.

[27] Tanh. i. 34: כך צדקה כובשת על מדת הדין ועל הפורענות כדי שלא יבוא לעולם, where either מדת הדין or מדת הפורענות is superfluous.

[28] Eccl. r. 4. 1, where we have to read instead of בשם ריב"ל, according to Midrash hashkem בשם ר' יהושע בן חנניה; cf. also b. Sanh. 100 A.

[29] v. Tanh. ii. 116; Exod. r. 45. 6: כל טובי מדת הטוב ומדת הפורענות.

[30] Exod. r. 6. 3.

of the Targumim. The late Chief Rabbi, Dr. Nathan
M. Adler, ז״ל, one of the most successful and competent
commentators of the Targum Onkelos, makes the following
important remark in his general introduction to the
Targum Onkelos (iv. 2): 'Behold, in the whole of the
Torah the Targumist translates the name of God " Elohim "
as the Tetragrammaton.' Similarly in his comments on
Gen. 1. 1 (ed. Wilna, 1874, p. 3 a): 'Elohim is translated in the whole of the Pentateuch as the Tetragrammaton'. The same observation can be made in
studying the Targum of the Prophets. The so-called
Ps. Jonathan has some exceptions from this rule. The
same can be observed in some of the Targumim of the
Hagiographa. The latter are surely post-Tannaitic just as
the Ps. Jonathan, which shows Amoraic influence in
Halakah as well as in the Haggada. We are inclined
to ask: If Onkelos really knew this most pronounced and
far-reaching theological distinction of the meanings attached
to the two names, Elohim the measure of judgement,
Adonaj the measure of mercy, how could he ignore this rule
and see in Elohim the Tetragrammaton? Surely, Onkelos
is *older* than the *later* distinction of the Rabbis and agrees
with Philo, who held the view that Elohim = Measure of
love, and Adonaj = Measure of judgement.

The next step to be taken in the course of our investigation must be to answer the question what motives or
circumstances moved the scribes to alter the established
rule that ה' is the Lordship, Judgement of God, and אלהים
the Love of God? Philo, surely, never invented these terms,
but took them from Palestinian sources. There never
was a discrepancy between Philo and the Rabbis in this
respect. Therefore we must find a cogent reason for such
a far-reaching change. What was it? R. Simon b. Johai
took a conspicuous part in opposing the views and doctrines
of the Dualists. These, as we are informed by Irenaeus, saw
in the two Names an affirmation of their theories of two
Gods. Let us quote the very words of this Church Father,

D

who was a contemporary of R. Simon b. Johai, and the
other scribes, in whose Haggada we found the two new
terms. The Bishop of Lugdunum, who is considered the
father of Christian dogmatics, writes: 'If, however, any
object that, in the Hebrew language, diverse expressions
occur in the Scriptures, such as Sabaoth, Eloë, Adonai, and
all other such terms, striving to prove from these that there
are different powers and gods, let them learn that all expressions of this kind are but announcements and appellations
of one and the same Being. For the term "Eloë" in the
Jewish language denotes God, while Eloeim and Eloeuth in
the Hebrew language signify "*that which contains all*". As
to the appellation Adonai, sometimes it denotes what is
nameable and admirable; but at other times, when the letter
Daleth in it is doubled, and the word receives an initial gut-
tural sound—thus, Addonai—it signifies, "One who bounds
and separates the land from the water, so that the water
should not subsequently submerge the land." All the other
expressions likewise bring out the title of one and the same
Being; as, for example, the Lord of Powers, the Father of
all, Gòd Almighty, the Most High, the Creator, the Maker,
and such like.'[31] This passage leaves no doubt that the
two names stood in the centre of Gnostic speculations. It
seemed natural that κύριος should be interpreted as the God
of the Jews, the God of rigid judgement, and Elohim, the
general name of God, as the Highest God, the most perfect
God, the God of love and mercy. Consequently the teachers
of the middle of the second century changed the order.

Even this new interpretation did not remove all the
difficulties. First of all there are very numerous passages
which contradict this rule. For instance, in Gen. 8. 1, we
read ויזכור אלהים את נח; here, plainly, a measure of love
and mercy is spoken of, yet the text uses אלהים, v. also
Exod. 2. 24, וישמע אלהים את נאקתם ויזכור אלהים, and Gen. 30. 22,
ויזכור אלהים את רחל. There are many instances of יי being
connected with punishments, chastisement, and threats,

---

[31] *Ag. Heresies*, ii. xxxv. 3, cf. *ZfNW.*, loc. cit., p. 257.

cf. Gen. 6. 5–7, and others. R. Samuel b. Nahmani deals
with these verses in a homily, which says : 'Woe unto the
wicked, for they change the measure of love into a measure
of punishment. Blessed are the pious, who change the
measure of judgement into that of love!'[32] Moses is mentioned as one typically pious, who changed the measure of
judgement into that of mercy by his prayer.[33] Secondly,
the אלהים in the story of creation must have given rise to
many objections The creation is a sign of God's mercy and
goodness. For God's glory and man's merit was the world
created. Why, then, in the first chapter of the Book of Genesis
is the term אלהים, and not ", to be found? The reply to
this is that the Bible does not mention the full name of
God, the Tetragrammaton, before the creation was fully
accomplished. A third point was, Why does the first
chapter of Genesis mention the term אלהים, the measure
of judgement in connexion with the creation of man ? Again
the preachers of the third and fourth centuries dwell on
this. R. Joshua b. Levi says : 'When God created man, He
created him with the two measures, and in driving him out
from the garden, He applied also both measures.'[34] He
means to say that neither the work of creation, nor the
punishment after the sin, could have been the measure of
the Demiurgos, for in both cases the two measures were
jointly applied. R. Berechja preached on the same subject.
When God created man, He foresaw that righteous and
wicked people would come forth, and said : 'If I create
man there will arise wicked people, if I do not create him,
there is no chance for pious men to be born!' What did
God do? He put aside the thought of the wicked, and
joined the measure of mercy with that of judgement.[35]

[32] Gen. r. ch. 33, ed. Th. 308, ib. 73. 2.

[33] v. Eccles. r. 8. 1 ; Tanh. iv. 113 ; Pes. B. 36 A ; Pes. r. 166 B ; M. Ps.
388 r. שהכריע מדה״ד למדה״ר ; the previous sources read שמשנה מדה״ד,
Tanh. B. iv. 70 ינצח מדה״ד למדה״ר.

[34] Gen. r. ch. 21, ed. Th. 202, כשבראו בראו במדת הדין מדת הרחמים,
וכשטרדו טרדו במדת הרחמים.

[35] Gen. r. ch. 8, ed. Th. 59 ; M. Ps. 1. 22 ; R. Eljakim, Pes. r. 166 B ;
R. Haninah.

An anonymous preacher varies this idea by saying : ' God said, " If I create the world with the measure of love, then sins will be too many; with that of judgement, the world cannot exist; but I will join both measures, and I wish that the world should stand." ' [36] This teaching of the two measures connected with the divine name is responsible for the doctrine developed in the third century, that God does nothing without the counsel of His heavenly court, and that the term וי implies His Court of High ; a doctrine which contradicts the views of the foregoing centuries. God is the only judge. He judges without assistants and coun- sellors. Very cogent reasons must have prevailed to change the older doctrine, which was more in accordance with the purer monotheistic belief of the Jews.[37] We conclude this investigation of the Biblical names of God with a saying of K. Abba b. Mamal : ' God says to Moses, " Thou wilt know my Name ? I am called according to my deeds. When I judge the creatures, I am אלהים; when I fight the wicked, I am צבאות; when I leave the sins of man in suspense, I am שדי; and when I am compassionate, I am וי !" ' [38] This teacher lived in the third century, and was a contemporary of R. Joshua b. Levi. What was the reason for these explanations of God's Names ? R. Abba b. Kahana, also a teacher of the same age, informs us that two generations used the Tetragrammaton in their prayers : the generation of the Great Assembly and that of the שמד.[39] Some scholars[40] thought that this referred to the Hadrianic perse- cutions. Yet, דורו של שמד, the generation of the persecutions

[36] Gen. r. ch. 12, ed. Th., p. 112 f. ; Pes. r. 167 A ; M. Cant., ed. Grünhut, 39 A.

[37] For a fuller treatment of this point v. Marmorstein, ' Some Greek and Rabbinic ideas of God ', in the *Jewish Chronicle Supplement*, January, 1925, pp. v–vii, where the material is given, and further on.

[38] Exod. r. 3. 6 ; for similar explanations of the divine names, v. also a fragment quoted in Yalkut Makhiri Psalms, 92, 26.

[39] M. Ps. 36. 3, ed. Buber, 251.

[40] v. Graetz, *Geschichte*, iv. 2. 452 ; Bacher, *APa.*, ii. 478 ; v., however, Marmorstein, ' Eine messianische Bewegung im 3ten Jahrhundert ', in Dr. Wohlgemut's *Jeschurun*, xiii (1926), pp. 16–28, 171–86, and 369–83.

is distinguished from the generation of the Hadrianic persecutions in our texts.[41] R. Joshua b. Levi, who stood
under the influence of the Hasidic teacher, R. Phinehas
b. Jair, who taught that if Israel used the Tetragrammaton,
they soon would be redeemed.[42] R. Joshua b. Levi, who
lived in a time of great religious persecutions, tried to avail
himself of this advice, and introduced such a ' reform '. To
justify his action, he reminded his contemporaries of the
ancient rule about the greetings with the Name. Other [43]
liturgical innovations of a similar kind were also introduced. R. Joshua b. Levi had to face great opposition on
account of his ' reforms ', although he supported them with
ancient precedents. R. Levi, belonging to the school of
Tiberias, opposed, as we saw in the beginning of our
investigation, this praxis.[44] We shall understand now why
the scholars of Lydda were stigmatized by their colleagues
of the North as ' haughty ' people.[45] For no other reason
but because they taught and thought of making use of the
Tetragrammaton. This weighty and extraordinary controversy between North and South, Tiberias and Lydda,
R. Joshua b. Levi and R. Johanan, led to new developments
in the history of the divine name. Before attempting to
describe this new departure, we have to survey the complete list of the names of God in our Rabbinic sources.

[41] v. *Jeschurun*, loc. cit., p. 183.

[42] Pes. r. ch. 22, ed. Friedmann, 114 B, מתפללים ואינן נאנים ריב"ל בשם
רפב"י מפני שאינם יודעים סוד שם המפורש.

[43] v. Midr. Ps. 14. 6, B. 114 : ר' יודן בשם ר' יהושע בן לוי אמר לפי
שהתינוקות של בית רבן אומרים שני פעמים ביום שחרית וערבית שובנו אלהי
ישענו והפר כעסך מעמנו ; Ps. 85. 5 ; Pes. r. ch. 41, ed. Friedmann, 174 A,
לפי ששני פעמים התינוקות אומרין בבית הכנסת אחת בבקר ואחת R. Huna,
בערב הושיענו אלהינו לפיכך הקב'ה אומר שני פעמים מי יתן מציון . This
prayer for redemption is closely connected with the Messianic expecta-
tion of the third century.

[44] v. above, p. 19.

[45] jer. Pes. 32 A ; b. Pes. 63 A ; *Jeschurun*, loc. cit., 184. On the sin and evil
of a haughty spirit v. b. Sota, 5 A, the sayings of Mar R. Joseph, R. Eleazar,
and R. Alexander; further b. Sanh. 101 B, R. Nahman ; v. also R. Joshua
b. Levi, b. Sanh. 43 B, and Sotah 5 B.

III

The Rabbinic Synonyms for God.

WHILST the names of God in the Bible have often been investigated during the last two thousand years, those in the Rabbinic writings have never been completely gathered and explained. The scribes speak of God's seventy names, and register them. A Midrash on Canticles enumerates them; so the later Midrash on the Alphabet, attributed to R. Akiba, but surely later than the second century.[1] The collection is by no means free from artificiality and owes its origin to the popularity of this number. Numbers, as we now know, were of great importance in popular science and mystic speculations. The number 'seventy' shared this ancient partiality. No such predilection is known in the number of God's Names in the Rabbinic writings. An attempt has been made by *E. Landau*[2] to form such a collection. This scholar enumerates fifty-seven names, some of the names are doubled, but a good many omitted altogether. We have left aside some (like נצחונו של עולם, ' the Victory of the World') which occur only in mystic writings, like the Bahir. This book is outside the sources used for our investigation. Yet our collection comprises more than

---

[1] v. Agadath Shir ha Shirim, ed. Schechter, p. 79, and Midrash Cant. Zutta, ed. Buber, 11, Zunz, G. V. 262; v. also Pes., p. 22 החלוץ, iv. 71, ס' חשק, Lemberg, 1865; H. B., xiv. 6; *JQR.*, vii. 731 (שערי אורה), בדי ארון, p. 35; *MGWJ.*, viii. 145; *ZDMG.*, xxxv. 167; *Jüd. Literaturblatt*, xiii, no. 7–8.

[2] *Die dem Raume entnommenen Synonyma für Gott in der neu-hebräischen Littera-tur*, Zürich, 1888, 6–10; v. earlier attempts by Leop. Löw, *Die talmudische Lehre vom göttlichen Wesen, Ben Chananja*, 1866, no. 35, coll. 85–92, = Ges. *Schriften*, i. 177 ff.; and Bartolocci, *Bibliotheca magna rabbinica*, 552–642, *Diss, de Deo, sc. id quod sentiunt Rabbini Talmudistae*, full of errors and prejudice, some of them corrected by Löw.

ninety designations of God. It is needless to emphasize
the wealth of religious fervour and enthusiasm, deep
thought and high intelligence which lie behind these
words. Many strenuous mental struggles, often lasting for
centuries, phases of the conflicts between ignorance and
culture, the growth of religious advancement from lower
to higher stages, and the increasing war between light and
darkness are concealed within these words. They bear
eloquent witness to Israel's victory over gods and their
temples. Products of Israel's gestation, these names fertil-
ized in turn nations and peoples, doomed without them to
decay and death.

Internally and externally they purified the air of religion, cleansed the hearts, freed them from superstition and
idolatry, and brought salvation to the perishing world under
the dying culture of Hellas and Rome, of Byzantium and
Persia. Many spiritual forces and material tempests, many
wars and revolutions of the history of the world originated
these names, caused their changes, and influenced their history. The religious genius of the Rabbis in the first four
centuries manifests itself as a living and imperishable source
of real piety and true knowledge of God, which is unsur-
passed in the history of religions. Surely teachers and
preachers, who could express God's relation to men and the
world's relation to God, His attributes and nature in such
manifold ways and names, are entitled to be heard in all
questions which bear on the problem of religion. No
student of the history of religion, no searcher in the fields
of religious thoughts and the philosophy of religion can
pass unnoticed these works of the greatest teachers of this
subject.

Our list gives ninety-one Names. This catalogue of Names
may appear to some more technical. Unfortunately our
branch of research is not yet furnished with the apparatus
which would enable us to dispense with such investigations. Our material is arranged in alphabetical order. The
chronology of the names and their frequency in different

periods of Jewish history will be dealt with in the following chapter.

The Names of God in the Rabbinic Writings.

(1) אב הרחמים

'Father of Mercy.' SER. 69. ' God, the Father of Mercy, finds it hard to destroy men who studied the Torah and Mishna and are stained by ugly conduct and unworthy deeds.' Ed. Venice reads בעל הרחמים, v. sub voce.[3]

(2) אב שבשמים

'Father in Heaven', also אבינו שבשמים 'Our Father in Heaven', אביכם שבשמים ' Your Father in Heaven', and אבי, אביהם, אביו, אביך. There is no basis for Kohler's assumption that this appellation is of Essene origin.[4] It is so often used by all the teachers of Judaism in the first four centuries that there is not the slightest ground for ascribing it to one sect or section of Jews. Similarly must we regard Dalman's assertion or information that this name of God does not appear in Rabbinic literature before the end of the first century.[5] Simon b. Shetach, who lived in the first century B.C.E., says to Honi, the circle drawer : ' Thou art like a son, who endears himself to his father, and his father complies with all his requests'.[6] The great pacifist,

---

[3] The term is very usual in liturgical pieces, v. Elbogen, Gottesdienst, p. 203, and second edition, p. 549; further J. Davidson, Thesaurus of Mediaeval Hebrew Poetry, i, New York, 1904, nos. 37, 39 †, 40, 44 †.

[4] v. Kohler, Grundriss einer systematischen Theologie, Leipzig, 1910, p. 78, and Hebrew Union College Annual, i, 1924, p. 398.

[5] v. Die Worte Jesu, Leipzig, 1898, p. 152.

[6] v. pal. Taanith 67 A; b. Taan. 23 A: כבן שהוא מתחטא אל אביו. Pseudo-Rashi explains לשון חטא, an expression of sin, we take it, according to Aruch, s.v. חט 1, to mean ענין ענות. The real meaning of the expression is corroborated by several Haggadic sayings. First of all by the sentence of R. Levi, who says : בזכות ב' דברים שישראל מתחטין לפני המקום בזכות שבת ובזכות מעשרות בזכות שבת דכתיב אם תשוב משבת רגלך, מה כתיב בתריה אז תתענג על ה, ובזכות מעשרות דכת' ושמחת בכל הטוב, cf. Isa. 58. 13 f., Deut. 26. 11, Pes. B. 96 B, Tanh. v. 22. There are different read-

R. Johanan b. Zakkai, taught in the time of the war between Rome and Judea the greatness of spreading peace between husband and wife, cities and nations, basing his homily on the law, Exod. 20. 25, ' For the stones of the altar are peacemakers between Israel and their Father in Heaven '.[7] The same teacher uses the words : ' Blessed be the God of Israel, who gave a son to our father Abraham, who is able (knows) to expound and to grasp the glory of our Father that is in Heaven ! ' in blessing his pupil, R. Eleazar b. Arakh.[8] *R. Gamaliel II* sees the cause of persecutions in the days of Haman in the sad fact that the ' beloved sons of God ' provoked the displeasure of their ' Father in Heaven '.[9] This saying deserves more than passing attention. First of all for the phrase ' *beloved sons of God* ' (בניא חביביא). Nicodemus, son of Gorion, went to the Temple and prayed : ' Lord of the world, show that there are in Thy world men loved by Thee ' (אהובים).[10] Josephus speaks of a certain Onias, a righteous and God-beloved man.[11] The patriarch surely thought here of Israel in general, who are called God's (ידידים) friends, beloved.[12] The same passage furnishes us with some materials as to the inner life of the age in Judaea. It was a period of unjust judges and corrupt witnesses, of informers

ings in the texts, מתחטטין, מתחננין, and מתעננין. The verb occurs similarly in a saying of R. Eleazar b. Pedath : כל חיטטין ופרנוקין ישראל מחטין ומתפרנקין, v. Cant. r. 7. 5, cf. Marmorstein, *The Doctrine of Merits*, 77, note 174. A clear exposition of the term מתחטא is given in the Boraita : ' The child says, Father, take me to the bath, give me nuts ', &c. This sentence was inserted in order to avoid any mistake of the verb מתחטא in the sense of Pseudo-Rashi. R. Abbahu in the name of R. Jose b. Hanina uses the verb in the sense of privileges, rights, when he says : כמה מתחטאין ויש להם פתחון פה לעושה מצוה, v. Tanh. v. 45. The underlined words are here again put as a commentary to the otherwise difficult מתחטאין; v. also Büchler, *Some Types*, p. 252 f.

[7] v. Mekh. 74 A ; M.R.S. b. J., 67. 116 ; Torath Kohanim 84 A ; Tosefta B. K. 358 ; M. R. S. b. J. r. שמטילות כפרה בין ישראל.

[8] Tosefta 234 ; Pal. Hag. 77 A.   [9] Esther r. 1. 9.

[10] b. Taanith 19 B.

[11] *Antt.* 14. 2, 1 ; v. Büchler, *Some Types*, p. 199.

[12] v. Mekh. 33 B ; Men. 53 A.

and confiscations, of increasing arrogance and decreasing honour. *R. Eliezer, the Great*, reflecting on the sad changes in the inner life of the scholars and people, concludes with the words: על מי יש לנו להשען על אבינו שבשמים 'In whom can we trust? In our Father in Heaven'.[13] *R. Joshua b. Hananja* depicts Amalek endeavouring to hurt Israel 'from under the wing of their Father in Heaven'.[14] *R. Eleazar b. Azarja* teaches: 'A man must not say, "I will not do this or that prohibited by the law, because I have no desire to do so," but he should say, "I would like to do so, eat this, but what can I do? *My Father in Heaven* decreed upon me not to do it or eat it!"'[15] *R. Ishmael*, speaking of the writings and scrolls of the heretics, says: ומה לעשות שלום בין איש לאשתו אמרה תורה שמי שנכתב בקדושה ימחה על המים הללו שמטילים קנאה ואיבה ותחתרות בין ישראל לאביהם שבשמים ע'א כו"כ. 'And if in order to make peace between husband and wife the Torah did allow the Name written in holiness to be blotted out by water, how much more these books which stir up enmity, envy, and strife between Israel and their Father in Heaven'.[16] R. Ishmael follows here the teaching on peace expressed by R. Johanan b. Zakkai (v. above, p. 57). The same sentence is reported in a Haggadic legend taught by R. Hisda in the name of Ahitophel ומה לעשות שלום בין איש לאשתו אמרה תורה שמי שנכתב בקדושה ימחה על המים לעשות שלום לכל העולם כולו על אחת כמה וכמה.[17] Attention may be drawn to the differences between the two sayings. Ahitophel speaks of peace between the

---

[13] M. Sotah, 49 B. R. Eliezer concludes his prayer on behalf of R. Jose b. Durmaskis with יהי רצון מלפני אבינו שבשמים שיחזרו עיני יוסף למקומן, v. M. Ps. 25. 13, ed. B. p. 214, cf. Yadaim 4. 3; Tosefta Yadaim, ch. 2, Hag. 3 B. M. Ps. 94. 2, ed. B., p. 418 preserved a saying of R. Eliezer b. Jacob, which is omitted in the original sources of Mekhilta and Sifre, reading: ומי גרם לכם לרצות לאביכם שבשמים? הוי אומר יסורין. Suffering brings peace between man and his heavenly Father.

[14] Mech. 56 A; v. the reading in M. R. S. b. J. 84: מחחת כנפי השמים.

[15] Torath Kohanim, 82 B.

[16] Boraita Shabbath, 116 A; Tosefta, 129

[17] b. Sukka, 53 B; b. Maccoth, 11 A.

Father in Heaven and the whole world, whilst R. Ishmael refers to the same between God and Israel. In the legend the whole world is threatened with the flood of waters, whilst R. Ishmael refers to a ceremony limited to Israelites.[18] *R. Akiba's* prayer, ' Our Father, our King, we have no other king besides Thee ! Our Father, our King, have mercy upon us for Thine own sake, and let rain come down ', is well known.[19] He combines here the two ideas of God's Fatherhood and Kingship. In a second homily, presumably delivered on the Day of Atonement, he says : ' Happy are ye Israelites ! Before whom are ye purifying yourselves ? Who purifies you ? Your Father in Heaven !'[20] He is comforting the old generation that saw the Temple with its sacrificial ceremonies and despaired of atonement. He is also admonishing the new generation that is seeking for means of atonement in new doctrines and conceptions. God, and not sacrifices ; God, and not priests or magicians, is purifying and atoning Israel. Speaking of Moses, R. Akiba says : ' He was worthy to become an intermediary between Israel and their Father in Heaven.'[21]

The teachers of the period after Bar-Kokhba discussed, from some cogent reason, the relations between God and Israel, the children to their father, as will be seen from a further chapter devoted to this aspect of the Old Rabbinic doctrine of God. The name ' Father in Heaven ' is also very frequent in this age. We refer first of all to *R. Simon b. Johai*, who asks : ' Why did the Manna not descend once a year (sc. and supply them with food) ? In order that Israel should turn their heart to their Father in Heaven.'[22] R. Simon b. Menasja expounding Prov. 23. 15, says : ' My son, if thine heart be wise, mine heart shall rejoice, even mine.' This means to say that not only the earthly, but also the heavenly Father rejoices at the student's or scholar's

---

[18] v. variants of Ishmael's saying, Sifre Num., § 16 ; b. Ned. 61 B, and Hullin 141 A.

[19] b. Taan. 25 B.   [20] M. Yoma 85 B.   [21] Tor. Koh. 110 B.

[22] Sifre Num., § 89 ; cf. Yoma 46 B ; cf. also Sifre, Deut. 84 B.

success in wisdom and learning.[23] *R. Phinehas b. Jair* concludes his lament at, or over, the conditions prevailing after
the destruction of the Temple, with the same words used
by R. Eliezer b. Hyrkanos.[24] *R. Eliezer b. Jose* varies the
older saying of R. Johanan b. Zakkai, who saw in the altar
the peacemaker between Israel and their Father in Heaven.
Our teacher puts charity and loving-kindness in the place
of sacrifices.[25] *R. Simon b. Eleazar* sees in the word שעטנז
(Lev. 19. 19, Deut. 22. 11) the idea that he who wears a
cloth or a garment of mixed kinds turns away from God,
and causes his Father in Heaven to turn away from him.[26]
R. Nathan reflects upon the persecutions of the Jews in his
days. Jews are crucified, killed, put to death in the most
cruel ways. Why? Because of their observances of Sabbath, circumcision, &c. All these punishments, says Israel,
cause to make me beloved to my Father in Heaven.[27]
Judah ben Temah says: ' Be bold as a leopard and light
as an eagle and swift as a gazelle and strong as a lion to do
the will of thy Father which is in Heaven.' [28] Owing to
the religious persecutions in the second half of the second
century, depicted by R. Nathan, all one's boldness, strength,
and swiftness were required in order to do the will of God.

The sayings of the Amoraic Haggadists offer abundant
instances of the familiar use of this name in the third and
fourth centuries. Here again a few instances shall suffice.
R. Johanan b. Nappaha concludes one of his homilies with

---

[23] Sifre Deut., § 48, reads R. Simon b. Johai; the correct reading is
preserved in Yalkut, Midr. Tannaim, 43; Yalkut Makhiri; Prov. 23. 13;
and Gen. r. ch. 63, ed. Th., p. 678, where, as usual, הקב'ה is read instead of
אביו שבשמים.

[24] v. above, p. 58.

[25] v. the references, Marmorstein, *The Doctrine of Merits*, p. 61, note 100.
We have, perhaps, to read פרקליט גדול [ועושה] שלום גדול instead of
ושלום גדול ?

[26] Sifre Deut., § 232; Torath Kohanim 78 B; M. Kel. 9. 8; Tos. Kelaim;
9. 8.

[27] Mekh. 68 B; M. Ps. 110.

[28] Aboth v. 23; v. Num. r. 20. 24; Tanh. iv. 148 לעשות רצון קונו; v. ib.,
4. 21; A. b. R. N. i. 41, ii. 48; b. Pes. 112 A.

a peroration explaining Jer. 3. 19 : ' What is the business
of a father ? He loves his son. What is the son's business?
He is longing for the delights of his father, who feeds him.
Likewise ye Israelites shall be longing after your Father in
Heaven.' [29] *R. Jose b. Hanina* explains the name Simon,
שומע בקול אביו שבשמים, ' he who hearkens to the voice of his
Father in Heaven '.[30] *R. Jose b. Jeremiah* raises the question : ' Wherefore are the prophets of Israel compared to
women ?' (e. g. היפה בנשים, Cant. 1. 8). ' To tell thee that just
as a woman is not ashamed to ask for the needs of the
house (לתבוע צרכי ביתה), similarly are the prophets proud
to ask for Israel's need from their Father in Heaven.' [31]
R. Menahem b. Abin explains the names in 1 Chron. 4. 22.
אשר בעלו למואב is interpreted by ' his pleasant deeds came
and ascended before his Father in Heaven '.[32] *R. Huna*
interprets Cant. 2. 2 : ' Israel is like the lily, for even if they
are tortured by taxes and duties (ארנוניות and בורסגניות) their
heart is turned to their Father in Heaven.' [33] *R Levi* uses
the name פטרון בשמים instead of אב שבשמים.[34] There can be
cited also a goodly number of passages from the anonymous
Haggada, which show what we think by now to have
demonstrated, viz., the great popularity of this divine name
For our present purpose this may suffice.

אב לכל העולם (3)

' Father of the whole world.' In Midrash Prov. 10. 1 we
read : אין אב אלא הקב'ה שהוא אב לכל העולם שנ' אבי יתומים.[35]
' Father is the Holy One, blessed be He, for He is the Father
of the whole world ', cf. Ps. 68. 6. The sentence אין אב אלא
הקב'ה occurs in a saying of R. Hanina b. Papa.[36] Further,

---

[29] Tanh. iv. 82.   [30] Gen. r. 71. 4.
[31] Pes. B. 101 A ; M. Prov., ch. 31 ; Cant. r. to 1. 7.
[32] Ruth r. 2. 4 ; v. also ib., 2. 1. ושבאתה ונדבקה בישראל ועלו מעשיה
לאביה שבשמים
[33] Cant. r. 2. 2.   [34] Tanh. iii. 95 ; Pes. B. 79 A ; M. Ps. 26.
[35] M. Prov., ed. Stettin, 13 A.
[36] b. Ber. 35 B : כל הנהנה מן העוהז בלא ברכה כאילו גוזל להקב'ה וכנסת
ישראל, based on Prov. 28. 24, where Father = God, mother = the com-

in an anonymous homily based on a Boraita,[37] which describes the five duties of a father to his son. The preacher extends these to God also, by saying האב זה הקב״ה.[38]

אדון (4)

'Lord': v. also מרי and רבון in Aramaic. We find this name combined with אדון העולם 'Lord of the world', אדון העולמים 'Lord of the worlds', or כל העולמים 'of all the worlds', אדון לכל המעשים 'Lord of all the works' [38a], אדון כל הבריות [39] 'Lord of all the creatures', אדון לכל באי העולם 'Lord of all who come into the world'. R. Simon b. Johai observed that Abraham was the first to call God אדון 'Lord' (cf. Gen. 15. 2).[40] R. Aha contradicts or ignores this earlier teaching. He taught that Adam was the first to call God אדן 'Lord'.[41] This teacher makes Adam say: 'Thou art worthy to be called "Lord" for Thou really art Lord of all Thy creatures, and Lord of all the worlds.' [42] The Tannaitic Midrash uses the term אדון לכל באי עולם,[43] which is identical with אדון כל הבריות. The old Tannaitic Haggada altogether prefers the term כל באי עולם to כל בריות. R. Hijja the Great [44] follows R. Simon b. Johai

munity of Israel, and חבר לאיש משחית =Jeroboam b. Nebath, who led astray Israel from their Father in Heaven.

[37] Quoted j. Kid. 61 A; b. Kid. 29 A; Tosefta Kid., ch. 2; Mekhilta, Eccles. r. 9. 9; and Num. r. 17. 1.

[38] Tanh. iv. 71.   [38a] Ben Azzai, Tr. Derek Erets, ch. 4.

[39] In a homily on Deut. 3. 23 we read: ואתחנן במיני תחנונים בעת ההיא לאמר, שאין תל לאמר אלא א״ל הודיעני אם אני נכנם לארץ ואם לאו אדון ,אדון לכל באי העולם, אלהים בדין בראת את העולם, v. Sifre Num., § 134.

[40] b. Ber. 7 B. R. Johanan in his name, and the remark of Rab about Daniel; v. also Agadath Bereshit, B. 112: שהוא עשה הקב״ה אדון כל בריותיו; v. also אדון כל הבריות; Sifre, Deut. 31; Mak. 102 A; Exod. r. 29; Ruth r. beg.

[41] Gen. r. 17. 4; M. Ps. 8. 2 B, p. 74; Pes. B. 34 A; Pes. r. 34 A; Eccles. r. 7. 23; Marmorstein, Midrash Abkhir, Dwir i. 131 and 136; and Tanh. iv. 111.

[42] אדון לכל בריותיך ואדון כל העולמים, v. Midr. Abkhir, p. 131; cf. Midrash Temurah, ed. Wertheimer, 9. הקב״ה אדון לכל דבר.

[43] § 134, ed. Horowitz, 180.   [44] רבה, or הגדול.

when he lets Moses ask before God: 'Through me dost
Thou want to redeem the children of Abraham, who caused
Thee to become Lord of all creatures?'[45] *R. Isaac* speaks
of God as אדון כל העולם [46] 'the leader, the Lord of the whole
world'. Some explain Ps. 9. 21 (שיתה ה' מורה להם): 'There
are some who arrogate to themselves the character of
divinity; make known unto them, teach them that Thou
art the Lord over all of them.' (אדון על כולם) [47]. Pharaoh
called himself 'Lord of the world'.[48] It may be that the
preacher refers to the emperor-cult in his days. R. Samuel
b. Nahmani explains the name אדון (Isa. 1. 24): 'The Lord
who uproots the dwellers of the land and settles others in
their place'[49] (cf. Isa. 3. 11). 'God is the Lord of the
heavenly (i. e. angels) and the earthly hosts (i. e. Israel).'[50]
R. Abbahu explains the names of places in Neh. 7. 61:
כרוב אדון ואמר, 'God said: The Lord said, "I thought that
Israel will be before me like a cherub, and they became
leopards."'[51] An anonymous Haggadist[52] makes Mordecai
say to Haman: 'There is a Lord, who is more exalted than
all the high ones; how can I leave Him and worship the
idols?' Finally we mention a homily combining Exod. 22. 24
('If thou lend money to any of my people') with Ps. 112.5
('A good man sheweth favour and lendeth'). The preacher
chose as the subject of his sermon the theme: 'There is no
creature who does not owe something to God. Yet God is
gracious and merciful, and forgives the earlier debts'
(i. e. sins). Then the preacher illustrates the teaching by

---

[45] Exod. r. 3. 21; v. also 3. 20: אמר משה להקב׳ה אתה אדון העולם וכי
אתה רוצה שאהיה שלוח הכי לא איש וכו'.

[46] Gen. r. 39. 1; Th. 365, אני הוא המנהיג אדון כל העולם.

[47] Tanh. ii. 31.   [48] Exod. r. 5. 19.

[49] Pes. B. 123 A: אוקר דיורין ומכנים דיורין.   [50] Exod. r. 15. 7.

[51] b. Kid. 70 A: אמר אדון אני אמרתי יהיו ישראל לפני חשובים ככרוב
והם שמו עצמם כנמר. Another version reads ששמו אע״פ אמר אדון
עצמם כנמר הן חשובים לפני ככרוב.

[52] Esther r. ch. 6: יש אדון המתגאה על כל הגאים ואיך אני מניחו
ואשתחוה לע״ז.

a parable. Once a man borrowed money from a דיוסטוסו[53]
and forgot to pay. After a time the borrower comes to
the lender and says: 'I know that I owe you money
The lender says: ' Why didst thou remind me of thine old
debt ? I have lost sight of it already !' Thus, *the Lord of
the world !* The creatures commit sins. He looks with
patience, and they do not repent. Yet, when they return
to Him and remind Him of their earlier transgressions,
God does not remember them.[54] Owing to the unsatisfactory state of our texts [55] we are unable to establish
whether אדון העולמים was not the original, instead of אדון
העולם. It is quite impossible to assume that the Gnostic
doctrine of the Jewish God as the Lord of this world, the
Satan, the Demiurgos,[56] the source of Evil, should not have
influenced the theological speculations and the apologetical
tendencies of the Rabbis. We will show later on that many
homilies and teachings are due to this cause.

(5) אדיר

'Mighty.' Four are called 'mighty': e.g. God (Ps. 93. 4,
אדיר במרום י"), Israel, Egypt, and the waters. 'The Mighty
(God) will come and punish the mighty ones (Egypt) on
behalf of the mighty ones (Israel) by means of the waters,
which are called mighty.'[57] This saying is ascribed to
R. Ezra, the grandson of R. Euptolemaeus, a descendant of
R. Eleazar b. Azarja. It is also to be found in the Mekhilta.[58]

(6) אדם

'Man.' R. Judah b. Simon sees in Eccles. 2. 21 (אדם) one of
God's names, based on Ezek. 1. 26.[59] This anthropomorphic
designation of God is rather striking. We shall have to

---

[53] A moneylender, read דניסטוס, Danista, or δανειστής, v. Levy,
H. W. B., s. v. and Preuschen-Bauer, loc. cit., col. 266.

[54] Exod. r. 31. 1.   [55] v. further, p. 98.

[56] Marcion, Irenaeus i. 24.

[57] Men. 53 A ; v. also Midr. Prov., ed. Stettin, 12 A.   [58] 41 A.

[59] v. Tanh. i. 24 ; Gen. r. 27. 1 ; Eccles. r. 2. 21 ; Gen. r. also refers to
Dan. 8. 16.

consider whether the Haggadist was not influenced by the christological development of the term 'Son of Man'.

אֶחָד (7)

'One.' This name occurs even in the Tannaitic Haggada. R. Ishmael b. Jose says: 'Judge not alone, for there is none save One (God), who judgeth alone.'[60] Some[61] see this name in Dan. 8. 13 (וָאֶשְׁמְעָה אֶחָד), which means: 'I heard אֶחָד, i.e. God, קרוש, who is called the Holy One by all, מדבר, He decrees hard decrees on his creatures.' R. Abbahu uses the name in his exposition of Deut. 1. 2: אחד עשר יום מחורב במיוחד שבעשרה חטאתם, בשמי שהוא אחד שהוא ראש לכל הדברות שנ' אנכי ה'[62] 'Ye have sinned against the chief commandment of the Decalogue, against my name, that is אחד, the first of the Words' (i.e. Commandments). The Scribes may have found this name alluded to in Zech. 14. 9.[63]

אִישׁ (8)

'Man.'[64] R. Simon b. Johai saw in Prov. 15. 23 שמחה לאיש (joy to a man), an allusion to God, cf. Exod. 15. 3.[65] R. Joshua b. Levi sees in Gen. 43. 14 לפני האיש the name of God.[66] 'The brethren stood before their heavenly Judge.' Interesting is R. Aha's sermon, who says: 'When Israel went into exile the nations of the world greatly rejoiced[67] that Israelites were driven from their places. It does not say נודי (thou shalt move), but נודו (ye shall move). They (the nations of the world) spoke against God (כלפי מעלה)

---

[60] Aboth iv. 8; v. Mekh. 33 A; Pappus דן יחידי לכל באי עולם; Pal. Sanh. 11 A, and Marmorstein, 'Some Greek and Rabbinic Ideas of God', loc. cit., p. vi.

[61] Gen. r. 21. 1, ed. Th. 198.   [62] Exod. r. 42. 6.

[63] v. Tr. Derekh Erez r. ch. 2: יחיד ושמו אחד ושוכן בשבעה הרקיעים, v. also Sifra 74 B as to Mal. 2. 15.

[64] v. Marmorstein, 'Some Remarks on the Slavonic Josephus' in the Quest., 17 (1926), 3.

[65] Gen. r. 19, ed. Theodor; v. also Gen. r. 3. 3.   [66] Gen. r. 92. 3.

[67] M. Ps. B. 97 reads: היו או'ה אומרים להגלותן ממקומם; v., however, Yalkut Makhiri, 66: היו או'ה שמחים להגלותם ממקומם.

E

and Israel (כלפי מטה). Like as a bird is moving from its
nest, so a man (God) wanders from his place' (Prov. 27. 8).[68]
Nahum, the son of Simai,[69] preached in Tarsus on Exod. 12. 3
ויקחו להם איש : 'Take *God* unto you. By performing the
duty of sacrificing the Paschal lamb the Israelite draws
near to God.'[70] This extraordinary homiletical contribution seems to be directed against Christological conceptions
of the Paschal lamb, and it is rather a curious coincidence
that it should have been delivered in Paul's native place!
We find similar expositions of Biblical verses, which are
most instructive instances of the allegorical methods and
sermons of the Palestinian preachers. We mention here
some of them. On Num. 5. 12 a preacher remarks: 'The
faithless woman commits a sin against God (איש של מעלה),
and against her husband (איש של מטה).[71] Others apply
Num. 15. 24 to explain Israel and God's mutual relation.
A third preacher combines Num. 11. 16 with Prov. 22. 11.
'Why does the text say שבעים איש and not שבעים אישם?
They shall be similar to God and Moses, both of whom are
called איש' (v. Exod. 15. 3 and Num. 12. 3).[72] A fourth teacher
dwells on Num. 19. 9. ואסף 'God, who gathered the exiles of
Israel' (cf. Isa. 11. 12), איש 'God' (cf. Exod. 15. 3), טהור 'God'
(cf. Hab. 1. 13), shall gather 'the ashes of the heifer, i.e. the
exiles of Israel, and lay them without the camp in a clean
place, i.e. Jerusalem.'[73] A fifth preacher saw in ברו לכם איש
(1 Sam. 17. 8) 'choose unto you a man', i.e. God.[74] Further,
we find that Isa. 2. 9; וישפל איש, was expounded as the

[68] '*A man*' means God, 'from His place' = his sanctuary. They
meant to say that God ceased to rule and exist.

[69] Pes. B. 55 B. R. Berekhja in the name of R. Abbahu, whose relations
to Christians in Caesarea are well proved, דרש נחום בשם ר׳ סימאי,
ר׳ ברכיה בש׳ר אבהו דריש .MS. Oxf. and Pes. r. ביש׳ר אבין איש נחום Yalk.
נחום ב׳ר סימאי בטריסים.

[70] Tanh. iv. 30 ; Num. r. 9. 1.

[71] Num. r. 9. 54: והביא האיש זה הקב׳ה, את אשתו זו כנסת ישראל.

[72] Tanh. iv. 60: איש שהם דומין לי ולך.

[73] Tanh. iv. 120 ; Pes. B. 44 B.

[74] Tanh. iii. 49, anonym. ; b. Sotah, 42 B ; R. Johanan.

humiliation of God by the sins of His creatures.[75] As a
characteristic instance shall be quoted a homily on Exod.
21. 7, where איש 'the man is God', בתו 'his daughter', the
Torah, לאמה ' to Israel '.[76] All these and other [77] homilies are
based on Exod. 15. 3. The old Tannaites asked already: ' Is
it possible to speak thus of God ? Behold, the Heavens and
the earth do I fill, saith the Lord ' (Jer. 23. 24, cf. Isa. 6. 3,
2 Chron. 6. 18, and Ezek. 43. 2). Owing to His love of
Israel, Israel's holiness, does God sanctify His name through
Israel, as it is said: ' For I am God, and not man ' (Hos.
11. 9).[73] We have plenty of evidence at our disposal to prove
that this Midrash belongs to the school of R. Ishmael, who
were averse to anthropomorphic explanations of R. Akiba's
method, and consequently objected to and opposed the
identification of איש with God.

(9) אלהים

' God.' It is a well-established fact that the name
Elohim was not used in the schools and synagogues of the
first four centuries in Palestine except in quotations from
the Bible, in prayers, and magic. This innovation has to
be regarded as one of the most important intellectual movements in old Israel. We do not know by whom or when
this reform was introduced. The history of this alteration
is shrouded in antiquity and carries with it important
consequences, for such a change must be regarded as
highly momentous in the development of religious thought
in antiquity. One of the most remarkable days in the
history of Israel was that moment in the life of the Jews
when it dawned even on the minds of the broad masses,
that the God who spoke to them through Moses and the

[75] b. Sotah 48A : וישפל איש שגורמין שפלות לשונאו של הקב׳ה ואין איש
אלא הקב׳ה. R. Johanan sees in איש, Zech. 1. 8, the divine name, and
Ulla, in Prov. 7. 19, ' the man is not in his house ' = God, after the
destruction of the Temple.

[76] Midrash quoted in כד הקמח, 3A ; cf. Exod. r. 30.

[77] v. further Cant. r. 1. 14, s. v. אשכול הכופר.   [78] Mekhilta 38A.

E 2

Prophets, who admonished them through the Scribes and teachers, who appealed to them through the word of the Torah and the symbols of the observances, was different from the deities of Egypt and Babylonia, Greece and Rome, of the philosophers and astrologers. Therefore the term אלהים was no longer sufficient to express their religious needs and requirements. No longer did it convey the higher, purer, and clearer idea of God, which became more and more the religious view of the whole people. We have already seen that the Scribes fought for the retention of the Tetragrammaton in spite of the opposition of the Hellenists and the conservative instincts of the Sadducees. Whether the alteration of the name אלהים gave rise to a spiritual struggle in an opposite direction, where the combatants changed places, is not known to us. Examining closely our literary documents, it may be that we must come to the conclusion that the Scribes and preachers did not use the name אל, אלהים unless they quoted a passage from the Scriptures, or spoke Aramaic. They used it in reference to the idols, or in speeches of heathens, and in dialogues with sectarians and strangers. Even some of the usages of אלהים in the Bible were considered profane when applied to idols, to judges, and to mortals. No wonder that the attempts of scholars and the feeling of the common people, owing to the ambiguity of the term, showed necessary caution in their mode of expression and favoured the elimination of the term 'Elohim'. Yet it was retained together with the Tetragrammaton in prayers, or in oaths without, and with Israel אלהי ישראל (v. no. 11) in exorcism.

The rich material at our disposal requires us to treat these different aspects individually and point out their various significances.

(a) אלהים or אלוהות for Idols.

R. *Akiba* explains the את in Gen. 1. 1 by saying to R. Ishmael: 'If it read בראשית ברא שמים, one would assume

that heaven and earth are gods !' [79]   R. Hoshaja : 'Where
is there a nation whose Godhead agrees with her ?' [80]
R. Hama b. Hanina speaks of God's foreknowledge that
the heathen would worship the sun and moon and planets,
and make them gods.[81]   R. Samuel b. Nahmani depicts
the future judgement, when God will call the nations with
their gods (ואלהיה עמה) to be judged.[82]   R. Levi makes
Pharaoh produce דיפתרא של אלוהות, the scrolls of parch-
ment on which the lists of gods were written.[83]   An old
Midrash knows of four applications of the term אלהים.
First for God, secondly for the idols, thirdly for Israel, and
fourthly for angels.[84]   In the time of the Scribe, just as in
the period of the Holy Writings, the name Elohim was still in
vogue among the heathen.   Some indication as to the movement aroused by our problem may be gathered from the old
discussions on the name אלהים attached to the strange deities
(Exod. 20. 3).   These discussions, as will be shown later on,
began in the first century C. E., if not earlier, and were continued till the third century.   The questions and objections
on this ground may have led to the avoidance of the name
altogether.

(b) The Name in the Dialogues.

In the numerous dialogues between heathens and scribes
the former speak of God as אלהיכם.   In some sources, from
custom or set purpose, as will be proved in the next
chapter, הקב׳ה is put for אלהים.   We mention here R.
Gamaliel II, R. Joshua b. Hananja, R. Akiba, and R. Jose
b. Halafta, with various men and women, where our texts

<hr/>

[79] Gen. r., ed. Th., 12 ; v. also Tanh. i. 6 and parall.

[80] איזה אומה שמסבים אלהיה עמה, v. M. Ps. B. 43.   God consents to
Israel's arrangements ; not so the idols.

[81] שאו׳ה העולם עתירין לעשותן אלוהות, Gen. r. Th. 40 ; v. also Th. 70,
Tanh. ii. 23-4, a similar saying about the assumed divinity of Nebuchadnezzar, Hiram, &c.

[82] M. Ps. B. 229 ; v. also B 21 and parall.

[83] Tanh. ii. 19, and parall.

[84] Marmorstein : מדרש חסירות ויתירות, London, 1917, p. 59, note 263,
where parallels are to be found.

generally read, 'Your God', &c. (אלהיכם). When heathen,
like Ahasuerus, Alexander, Titus, &c., speak of Jews and
their God, they use the term אלהיהון דיהודיא. Even Jews
speaking in Aramaic use אלוה or אלהיא. Very interesting
are R. Levi's proverbs in which this word occurs.

(c) *The Name* אלהים *referred to Mortals.*

We saw that angels are designated by this term. It is
applied to Israel generally, further to the judges and some
prominent individuals, like Adam, Abraham, Jacob, Moses,
&c. No wonder that owing to the manifold meaning of the
word some doubts arose in exegesis and Massorah as to
the sanctity of the word in many places of the Scriptures.

(d) *The Use of the Name in Oaths and Prayers.*

Many instances can be shown where האלהים is used in
exclamations of oath.[85] In prayers it was connected with
the Tetragrammaton, e. g. יי אלהינו. A recent writer,
Dr. Finkelstein, on the '*Development of the Amidah*',[86]
states: 'It will be found that the contemporaries of
R. Gamaliel II *never* used the term ה' אלהינו in their prayers,
while the Rabbis of the following generation always used
it.' A careful investigation of our material does by no
means justify such an assertion, and refutes the far-reaching theories based on it. We refer first of all to R. Dosa
b. Hyrkanos, who says: העובר לפני התיבה ביום טוב הראשון של
ר'ה אומר החליצנו יי אלהינו את יום ר'ח הזה וכו'.[87] R. Johanan
b. Zakkai arose and kissed R. Eleazar b. Arakh, saying:
ברוך יי אלהי ישראל שנתן בן לא"א.[88] In the Temple they said:
ברוך יי אלהי ישראל מן העולם ועד העולם.[89] The Tetragrammaton
was used in the Temple, even in greetings. The High-
Priest, Ishmael b. Elisha, who ministered in the Temple,
says: פעם אחת נכנסתי להקטיר קטרת לפני ולפנים וראיתי אכתריאל

[85] v. Marmorstein, *Religionsgeschichtliche Studien*, ii. 69, note 2.
[86] *JQR.*, N. S., xvi., 1925, 1 ff.   [87] M. Erubin iii. 9.
[88] Tos. Hag. ii. 1, p. 234. 2 and parall.   [89] Ib., i. 11.

יה ה' צבאות (b. Ber. 7 A). R. Eleazar b. Zadok reports
that his father used to pray on the eve of Sabbath :
נתת לנו יי and מאהבתך יי אלהינו שאהבת את ישראל עמך וכו'
אלהינו.[90] Nehunja b. ha Kana used the words, both when
he entered and when he left the house of study : יהי רצון
מודה אני לפניך ה' אלהי and מלפניך ה' אלהי respectively.[91]
The High Priest also used the introductory words יהי רצון
מלפניך ה' אלהינו in his prayer on the Day of Atonement
(v. Tanh. iii. 59, and paralls.). All these authorities
are either older than, or contemporaneous with, R.
Gamaliel II. The whole assumption is based on the omission by the copyists of ה' before אלהינו in the story of
R. Gamaliel.[92] R. Eleazar b. Zadok quotes a prayer of his
father's, and not as we read, *JQR.*, loc. cit., p. 8, note 22,
' The prayer cited by R. Eleazar b. Zadok by his son ',
which is inaccurate. Ed. Zuckermandel reads : א'ר אלעזר בר
צדוק אבא היה וכו'. R. Eleazar b. Zadok says : ' My father
used to pray ; ' i. e. R. Zadok, since the father used the
words ה' אלהינו, the son surely followed his example, albeit
that the words are omitted. The same is the case with the
prayer of R. Eliezer b. Hyrkanos. There is no real basis
for the theory that before R. Akiba, or in the time of
R. Gamaliel II the formulary יי אלהינו in prayers may have
been unknown. Is it feasible to believe that R. Gamaliel
would have used אלהינו without יי, having experienced that
אלהים alone gave rise to many misunderstandings and misinterpretations ? Comparing this formulary in the ancient
documents, *some* of which must be older than R. Akiba, we
always, without any exception, meet the formulary : יהי רצון
מלפניך יי אלהינו.[93]

[90] Tos. Ber. 3. 7.
[91] b. Ber. 28 B. To the reading of this Mishna, v. H. B. vi. 72, החלוץ
ii. 119, קבוצת חכמים, 119.
[92] v. Midr. Tannaim 172.
[93] v. M. Ber. x. 6 ; Tos. Ber. 7. 2 ; b. Ber. 14 B, 16 B ; b. Shabb. 30 B ;
Gen. r. 60. 7, 68. 11, 85. 5 ; b. Taan. 5 B ; Tanh. iv. 9–10 ; S. E. R. 18 ; v. also
Boraita b. Ber. 19 A.

אלהים חיים (10)

'Living God.'[94] In the story of Hillel,[95] we read 'in order to hear the words of the living God out of the mouth of Shemaja and Abtaljon'. R. Abba says in the name of Samuel: 'Three years lasted the dispute between the houses of Shammai and Hillel. Each of them insisting on their opinion, till a בת קול was heard, saying: "Both are the words of the living God."'[96] R. Matja b. Heresh says to R. Josiah: מה לך לעזוב דברי אלהים חיים, 'Wherefore dost thou forsake the words of the living God?'[97] A Boraita mentions God (cf. Jer. 10. 10) among the ten things that are called חיים.[98]

אלהי ישראל (11)

'The God of Israel.' This name appears mostly in exorcism and magic. A few instances must suffice. The Greeks compelled the Jews to write on the horn of the ox that they have no share in the God of Israel.[99] Vows are given to the God of Israel.[100] R. Johanan b. Nappaha promises by oath אשתבע לאלהא דישראל that he will not reveal a secret.[1] In the confession we say: 'I sinned against the God of Israel.'[2] In excommunication R. Hisda says: ליהוי בשמתא דאלהי ישראל.[3] Finally we find the term in introductions to sermons by the preachers.[4]

אלופו של עולם (12)

'The friend of the world.' The teachers of the Midrash saw in Prov. 16. 28 an allegory of the story of Eve and the serpent. The froward man (איש תהפוכות), i. e. the serpent. 'Why?' 'Because he turned his words against his Creator'

[94] v. Dan. 6. 27, אלהא חיה.   [95] b. Yoma 35.
[96] b. Erubin, 13 B; cf. b. Gittin, 6 B; Sotah 3. 4, ר"ת, a Boraita.
[97] Aboth R. N. i, ch. 1, p. 1.   [98] Ib. i. 34; Sch. 103.
[99] v. above, p. 35, note 55.
[100] Ned. 8 A, 22 B; R. Asi.
[1] Yoma, 84 A; A. Z. 28 A.   [2] Yoma, 86 A.
[3] b. Hullin, 133 B; v. also Hekhalot in Jellinek's בית המדרש, iii. 84;
Testament of Naphtali in Hebrew, ed. Wertheimer, בתי מדרשות, 2. 14; Sota, 8. 3.
[4] v. A. b. R. N. i. 3, p. 17; Jeb. 121 A.

(בוראו). ' He is the whisperer, because he whispered words against his Creator. Thus did he divide them from the chief Friend of the world.'[5]   R. Judah, the Meturgeman of R. Simon b. Lakish, explained Micah 7. 5: ' If the evil inclination told thee, " Go, sin, God is forgiving !" do not trust him, for it is said, " Do ye not trust the Evil One ", and the יצר הרע is the evil [cf. Gen. r. 8. 21], nor do ye trust a Friend (אלוף)! (i.e. God [cf. Jer. 3. 4], scil. God will not forgive him).'[6]

(13) אמת

' Truth.' [v.אותיות דר'ע, ed.Wertheimer, p. 1 ; Or Zarua i. 5 A; Maimonides, מאמר הייחוד, ed. Steinschneider, p. 32, note 17].

(14) אני

' I.'   Some see this name in Hillel's saying : אם אני כאן [Aboth i. 14] and in the exclamation at the festival of water drawing (b. Sukka 45 A, 53 A).

(15) בודק לבבות

' Searcher of Hearts.'   R. Berekhja uses this term in reply of God to Esau (Gen. r. 67. 8): לית את ידע די אנא בודקיהון דלבביא, ' Dost thou not know that I am the searcher of Hearts ?'

We have also חוקר לבבות (cf. Jer. 17.10) and בוחן כליות ולבבות. The first occurs in a speech of Abraham before God: ' A man tests his friend, for he does not know what is in the heart of his friend. Thou, however, who art *the Searcher of hearts and reins*, dost Thou need this ? Was it not revealed before Thee, when Thou saidst that I shall sacrifice my son then I will surely be eager to slaughter him with a willing heart?'[7]   The second is frequently used in the Seder Elijahu[8] and in the later Haggada.[9]

---

[5] Gen. r. 182.   [6] b. Hag. 16 A and parall.
[7] Tanh. i. 114.
[8] v. pp. 30, 44, 48, 126.   [9] v., for instance, Exod. r. 11. 2.

(16) בורא

'Creator.' One of the most usual names of God. The Tannaitic Haggada knows this term in the sayings of R. Judah b. Ilai,[10] R. Simon b. Jochai,[11] and R. Judah I.[12] More frequent is the term in the sentences of the Amoraim. We begin with R. Joshua b. Levi. Jacob said: מה אנא מובד סברי סברי מן ברײ ח׳ו לית אנא מובד סברי מן ברײ יי אלא עזרי מעם 'Why do I lose my hope in my Creator? Far be it from me to do so; my help is from God!'[13] R. Johanan bar Nappaha, R. Hanina b. Hama, and R. Simon b. Lakish dispute at what age Abraham recognized God, his Creator.[14] R. Isaac b. Merjon adds to Gen. 2. 4, 'Their *Creator* praises them; who can reprove them? Their Creator glorifies them; who can find fault with them?'[15] The saying is surely directed against Gnostics,

[10] M. Ps. 399: ולכך היה מכוין לבוראו, derived from Gen. 28. 11: ויקח מאבני המקום; v. Gen. r. 68. 11, where this sentence is omitted; Pirke, R. El., ch. 35.

[11] M. Ps. 172; Lev. r. 5. 8: תני רשב׳י כמה גבורים הם הם הצדיקים שהם יודעים לפתות את בוראם, ויודעין היאך לקלם. A similar saying by R. Josiah; M. Ps. 366 f., Gen. r. 29. 4, Pes. B. 152 A: שיודעים לפתות את בוראם; some MSS. read הקב׳ה instead of בוראם. בוראם בתרועה ובקול שופר.

[12] Tanh. i. 215: קברו אותי בכלים לבנים, שלא אבוש במעשי להקביל פני בוראי, v. Gen. r. 97, Gen. r. 100. 2, jer. Kel. 32 B, Ket. 35 A. R. Josiah, instead of R. Judah; v. also the saying of Jose משיתא, Gen. r. 65. 18 לא הוה לך להרגיז ווי אוי אוי שהכעסתי לבוראי, Tanh. iii. 82; R. Nathan להכעיס את בוראי, ib., 167 בוראך, Tanh. iv. 165; M. Sam. לעשות רצון בוראי להרגיז על בוראי 120.

[13] Gen. r. 68. 2; v. also p. 556. Anonymous, Sarah says: מה אנא מובדה סברי מן ברײ חס ושלום לית אנא מובדה סברי מן ברײ אלא אני ביי אעלוזה, v. also R. Abba b. Kahana, M. Sam. איה דסברינין פסיק, R. Jonathan b. Eliezer, Gen. r. 61 למד מבוראך שברא, Tanh. i. 190 צדיקים בטוחים על בוראם 'The righteous trust in their Creator' (R. Hijja b. Abba), Tanh. i. 163, R. Hanina b. Isaac אשה שכך אשריו לילוד אשה שכך שמע מבוראו, ראו כל מה שתבע מבוראו הבטיחו.

[14] Gen. r. 30. 8. 64. 64: ר׳ יוחנן ור׳ חנינא תרוייהון אמרין בן מ״ח שנה מ׳ח שנה ג׳ שנים הכיר אברהם את בוראו; R. J. b. L. says: הכיר אברהם את בוראו, Tanh. i. 119, and Gen. r. 95. 2.

[15] Gen. r. 138; v. also, p. 99: בוראן משבחן ומי מגנן בוראן מקלסן ומי יתן בהם דופי.

who found fault with and criticized the creation of God.   R.
Eleazar explains Gen. 4. 16 : ויצא קין מלפני ה' 'and Cain went
from before God', כמפרים ומרמא בבוראו 'as one who cheated
and deceived God'.[16]   R. Levi accuses the serpent of having
slandered God.[17]   He found further Akabja b. Mehalalel's
famous saying [18] indicated in Eccles. 12. 1 : 'Remember thy
Creator, i.e. God.'   R. Phinehas b. Hama says of Eve:
'She added to God's commandment, and was ready to
fulfil her Creator's will.' [19]   Further, to Gen. 49. 2, ושמעו
אל ישראל, he says: 'Your father Israel is (like) God! As God
is a Creator of worlds, so Israel created worlds.' [20]   R. Berekhja
makes all the trees of the garden talk to Adam, saying: 'Lo,
the thief, he has stolen the mind of his Creator; he has stolen
the mind of his Lord!' [21]   Very often in anonymous homilies.[22]
In a sermon based on Job 4. 17 : 'Can a human being be
more just than his Creator?   Can he be purer than his
Creator.' [23]   'The just are like their Creator.' [24]   Abraham
preaches to his contemporaries: 'What do ye want of God,
who sits high above?   Did He say to you, "Go, trouble, and
supply Me with food?"   Behold, He is the Creator; He is
supplying you!' [25]   David says: 'God, too, gives evidence on

[16] Gen. r. 202, Pes. 160 A, Lev. r. 10. 4 read Eleazar bar Simon. The
chronology does not fit in M. Ps. 100. 2, Tanh. i. (בראשית) 25.

[17] Gen. r. 172 : התחיל אומר דילטוריה לבוראו ; M. Ps. 10 : הנחש אמר
לשון הרע על בוראו ; Tanh. iii. 47 ; Exod. r. 3. 14.

[18] Aboth iii. 1 ; j. Sota, 18 A ; Lev. r. 18 ; Eccles. 12. 1 ; Lam. r. 17.

[19] Gen. r. 38 f.

[20] Gen. r. 98. 4 to בורא עולמות ; v. also R. Abbahu, Gen. r. 9. 2, and
R. Tanhuma, Eccles. r. 3. 11, M. Ps. 244, Gen. r. 3. 7.

[21] Gen. r. 140 ; v. Ps. 36. 12 : רגל גאוה = רגל שנתגאה על בוראה 177,
only הא גנבא דגנב דעתיה דבריה , Pes. B. 142 B.

[22] v. above, sub אלופו של עולם , sub no. 12.

[23] Gen. r. 555, Pes. B. 123 B, M. Sam. 98 : שאול אל תהי צדיק יותר
מבוראך.

[24] Gen. r. 67. 7 ; R. Eleazar b. Jose ; v. also Tanh. i. 31, 'Noah was
called just because he supplied food to God's creatures ; therefore he
became like his Creator' (נעשה כבוראו). Ib., i. 132, 'Jacob was a partner
with his Creator in everything' (שותף עם בוראו). The wicked, however, לא היה לבם שוה לבוראם , M. Ps. 427.

[25] Tanh. i. 99.

my behalf, and says, " The Lord has chosen for Him a man
according to His heart (1 Sam. 13. 14) "; he (David) put his
name together with that of his Creator' (וכינה שמו לבוראו).‎[26]
David says: 'Stir up my honour before the honour of my
Creator; my honour is nothing before the honour of my
Creator.'[27] 'Our duty is to praise and magnify our
Creator.'[28] There is a dialogue between God and Jeremiah.
God: 'If thou descendest with (Israel) to Babylon, I remain
here; or if thou remainest here, I go with them to Babylon.'
Jeremiah: 'If I went with them, what good can I be to
them? Let their Creator (ברייהו) go with them, and He will
help them!'[29] Three times did the nations of the world
rejoice, and said: 'Now can Israel dispute with their
Creator?'[30] Finally, we notice that even heathens used
this term in speaking of God.[31] R. Johanan sat before the
Babylonian synagogue of Sepphoris and preached there.
An official (ארכונא) passed and the scribe did not rise before
him. The slaves of the Archon wanted to punish R.
Johanan, but their master commanded them: 'Leave him
alone, he is engaged with the Law of his Creator!'[32]

בחור (17)

'The Chosen One.'[33]

[26] M. Ps. 4.

[27] M. Ps. 184, 298; Pal. Ber. (8. 1) 2 D; Lam. r. 2. 22 (p. 120); Ruth r.
6. 1; Pes. B. 63 A: אין כבודי כלום לפני כבוד בוראי; v. also Bloch in
H, Cohen, *Judaica*, 165.

[28] M. Ps. 381. The relation between God and world.

[29] Pes. B. 113 A; Lam. r., Intr., p. 34.

[30] Pes. B. 76 B; R. Samuel b. Nahmani, Cant. חכו ממתקלם; Num. r.
10. 1; Lev. r. 27.

[31] Pal. Ber. 5. 1 (νόμος) דבריה הוא עסיק ארפוניה בנימוסיא.

[32] v. further for the use of this term S. E. R. 97. Until that time
(Abraham) did not yet recognize his Creator, v. to הביר בוראהו above note 14,
and p. 130 חמה ולבנה וכו' כולם משבימים ומעריבים לעשית רצון בוראם,
and Pirke R E. 51 והקשה הירח את ערפו לעשות רצון בוראו. In this work
we find the term about six times, cf. chaps. 11 (three times), 13, 21, 27,
48 (twice) לשם בוראו.

[33] Tanh. iii. 74; v. Gen. r. ch. 8: 'An earthly king does not allow others
to wear his titles, e. g. Augustus, God calls Israel אלהים', Ps. 82. 6; חכם

בעל הבית (18)

'The Master of the House.' Simon b. Zoma, when beholding the crowds in Jerusalem, used to say : ' Blessed be He who created all these in order to serve me !' Likewise he used to point out the difference between a good and a bad guest. The latter does not thank the Lord of the House, the former is grateful for every gift, every trouble, and every service offered him. There can be no doubt that Ben Zoma meant under the good guests the faithful, and under the bad guests the Gnostics, who found faults and blasphemed the Lord of the House, i.e. God.'[34] R. Tarphon in his famous saying of the shortness of the day, the greatness of the task, the sluggish workmen and the urging master of the house,[35] saw in the master of the house none else but God. The master of the house, like the king, is a most popular figure in the Haggada, just as in the parables of the Stoics,[36] and in that of the Gospels.[37] Some of these contribute a good deal to our knowledge of the Rabbinic conception of the divinity, and, therefore, must be dealt with here. ' The master of the house has two cows; one is strong, the other is weak. Upon which does he put the yoke ? On the former. God, the בעל הבית, tests the righteous, the strong ones.' [38] R. Aha [39] illustrates the idol worshippers by the simile of התושב מפנה לבעל הבית ' the stranger (the idols) remove the master of the house ' (God). R. Helbo depicts the relation of God to Israel in the parable of the orphan and the בעל הבית. The orphan was brought up and supplied with

Deut. 4. 7, and God is also called by the same name, Job 9. 4 ; דודים or דוד, cf. Cant. 5. 10, 5. 1 : בחור = ib. 15 and Deut. 7. 6, 7 and חסיד, Jer. 3. 12, Ps. 50. 5, קדוש Is. 6. 3, Lev. 19. 2.

[34] Pal. Ber. ix. 1 ; Tosefta Ber. vii. 2, pp. 14–15 ; B. Ber. 58 A.

[35] Aboth ii. 15.

[36] Epictet iii. 22. 4, 27. 19, the οἰκοδεσπότης.

[37] Luke 12. 39, Matt. 13. 27 ; v. also Theophilus ii. 17 ; Tert., *De cultu fem.*, ii. 10.

[38] R. Eleazar b. Pedath, Gen. r. 32. 3 ; Gen. r. 55. 2.

[39] Deut. r. 2. 13, v. also Jelamdenu, Genesis ed. Grünhut 26 B : שנר ותושב אומר לבעל הבית פנה את כליך.

everything by the latter. The same orphan boasted of
having deserved all by his work and in lieu of his wages.
The master of the house says : 'Truly, all that you enjoyed
is for the pail of water you have drawn, for the piece of
wood you have hewn, but your real wages are kept by me.'
God is the master of the house, Israel the orphan, the goods
of this world for the sufferings, but the real reward is kept
for the world to come.[40]   Another teacher speaks of a master
of the house and thieves who were caught drinking wine.[41]
The master of the house says : 'May ye enjoy yourselves,
but please put the bottles in their right place.'   God is the
בעל הבית, the brethren of Joseph the thieves; they are commanded to return Joseph to Palestine.   R. Levi explains the
reason for Israel being compared with wheat, and says :
'God is the master of the house, Moses his steward, Israel
is the wheat, which is carefully counted.'[42]

(19) בעל ברית

'Confederate.'[43]

(20) בעל דין

'Accuser.' R. Eleazar ha Kappar enumerates this too
among his seven names of God.[44]   We find this name earlier
in a saying of R. Eleazar b. Azarja : 'Woe unto us because
of the day of judgement ! Woe unto us because of the day
of rebuke ! When Joseph the Just, who was a mere human
being, rebuked his brethren, they could not stand his rebuke:
God, who is a judge, an accuser, and sits on the Throne of
Judgement, and judges each person, how much more shall
we not be able to stand before Him ?'[45]

---

[40] Deut. r. 3. 7.   [41] Deut. r. 8. 5.
[42] Pes. r. 32 B and parall. Cant. r. 7. 3 ; v. also Pes. B. 199 A ; M. Ps.,
pp. 481, 482, 514, and others.
[43] Aboth R. N. i. 17, 66. R. Eliezer : דע לפני מי אתה עמל ומי הוא
בעל בריתך.
[44] Aboth iv. 22.
[45] Gen. r. 93. 11 : הקב׳ה שהוא דיין ובעל דין ויושב על כסא דין ודן כל אחד
ואחד ע׳א כ׳ו שאין כל בשר ודם יכולים לעמוד לפניו ; v. Tanh. i. 207. R. Eleazar
b. Simon in the name of R. E. b. A. somewhat differently : כשיבא הקב׳ה
להתווכח עם כל אחד ואחד מן הבריות ולומר לו מעשיו כמו שכתוב כי הוא

בעל חוב (21)

Creditor.[46]

בעל מחשבות (22)

'Lord of thoughts, Who knows the thoughts of all.'
Judah b. Tabbai, or Simon b. Shetah uses this name when
saying אבל היודע ובעל מחשבות הוא יפרע מאותו האיש.[47]

בעל מלאכה (23)

'Employer.'   R. Eleazar and R. Tarphon, both use the
same term in emphasizing the certainty of the payment of
reward.[48]

בעל המשפט (24)

'Lord of Judgement.'[49] God loveth judgement (Ps. 37. 28)
because He is called בעל המשפט, cf. Isa. 30. 18. God says :
'I am called בעל המשפט, I try to send my hand forward
against Esau, but I cannot do so unless I have rewarded
him the small commandment he performed in this world.'[50]

Tanh. v. ; יוצר הרים וכו' . על אחת כמה וכמה שאין בריה יכולה לעמוד
10 on Deut. 3. 26 : רב לך בעל דין שלך כבר הוציא עליך גזירה שתמות
וכל הבריות כמותך. The בעל דין is not Adam, as Buber thought,
note 32, but God !

[46] The Babylonian Amora, Rabbah uses the legal axiom, אין אדם מעיז
פניו בפני בעל חובו, v. b Ket. 18 A; B. K. 107 A; B. M. 3 A, 5 A; Gittin
51 B ; Shebuot 42 B ; which can be and is applied to describe man's relation
to God, v. already Seneca, *De benefic.*, v. 21, and Marc. Aurel. 10. He is the
worst debtor, who reproaches his creditor.

[47] Mekh. 100 A ; v. b. Sanh. 37 B read היודע מחשבות ; v. Tosefta Sanh.
ch. 8, p. 426, l. 24 ; Pal. Sanh. iv. 9 also היודע מחשבות ; v. J. Derenbourg,
Essai sur l'histoire, p. 149.

[48] Aboth ii. 14 and 16 : ונאמן הוא ; v. also vi. 5 : שישלם לך שכר פעולתך
בעל מלאבתך שישלם לך שכר פעולתך.

[49] Tanh. i. 185.   [50] Tanh. ii. 83.

בעל הנחמות (25)

'Lord of Consolations.' This name is used in the old blessing said in the house of the mourners: ' Our brethren, who
are suffering and pained by this sad event, make up your
mind concerning this! This is standing (sc. the common lot
of man) for ever. It is a path designed since the six days
of creation. Many have drunk (sc. of this cup), and many
shall drink it. The lot of the latter ones is as that of the
former. Our brethren, may the Lord of Consolations comfort
you. Blessed be He, who comforts the mourners.' [51]

בעל העולם (26)

'Lord of the World',[52] used by Philo [53], and in the Mekhilta,[54] שלא יהיו בזויי העולם אומרין מפני שהוא אלוה ובעל עולם עושה
דבריו שלא כדת ' in order that the lowly people should not say,
" Because He is the God, the Lord of the world, therefore
he acts in all things against law and right ".' Surely the
Haggadist reproduces here the actual words of contemporary Gnostic teachings.

פקדונות, or בעל הפקדון (27)

'Lord of Pledge, or Pledges.' R. Aha says : ' God is the
owner of pledges (with reference to Gen. 21. 1). Amalek
deposited bundles of thorns, and He returned him the same.
Sarah deposited pious and good deeds, and God returned
her the same.' [55]

בעל הרחמים (28)

'Lord of Mercy.' [56] R. Nehemja, the father-in-law of
R. Levi, said : לעולם אין בעל הרחמים לוקח נפשות תחלה עד שנפרע מן

---

[51] v. Ket. 8 B ; Judah b. Nahmani, the Meturgeman of R. Simon b.
Lakish.

[52] v. also above, sub אדון העולם. or העולמים.

[53] De decal. ii. 189 ; Geffcken, loc. cit., p. xxvii.

[54] Mekh. R. S. b. J., p. 2.

[55] Gen. r. 53. 5 ; ed. Theod. 560 ; M. Sam., ch. 18 ; Pes. r. 181 A.

[56] v. also above אב הרחמים.

הממון 'The Lord of Mercy does not punish the soul before he punishes man's wealth'.[57]

בעל השבועה (29)

'Lord of Oath.' In a legend[58] we read: 'God says to Moses, "In case Jethro says a word about your oath, tell him the Lord of Oath has already released me from it".'

גבוה (30)

'High.' This term is one of the oldest in Rabbinic theology. In our sources it occurs almost exclusively in the Halakha, and here also in very ancient parts. It seems that in the period of the Tannaim and Amoraim this name or designation was already antiquated. In old texts גבוה is opposed to הדיוט, e. g. M. Kid. i. 6, אמירתו לגבוה כנתינתו להדיוט, or put together like Pal. Peah, i. 3, אחד לגבוה אחד להדיוט. We find it in the language of both schools of Shammai and Hillel.[59] R. Eleazar b. Azarja also uses this term.[60] There are also some instances of the use of this term in the Haggada.[61]

גבהות העולם (31)

'The Height of the World.' Eccles. 12. 5, גם מגבוה יראו (also of the high they shall be afraid) is explained, גם מגבהו

---

[57] Pes. B. 65 B ; Pes. r. ch. 17 מעין גנים, ed. Buber, p. 6 ; Lev. r. ch. 17 ; Ruth r., v. Buber's note in Pes. B. 5 B, 71.

[58] Exod. r. 4. 4 : אם יאמר לך יתרו כלום מן השבועה אמור לו בעל השבועה התיר אותי מן נדרי לכך וילך משה וכו'.

[59] B. AZ. 52 B, 63 A ; b. Pes., Peah 1. 3 ; Nazir 6. 1.

[60] Sifre, § 104 : ומה אם גבוה אין אדם רשאי להחרים את כל נכסיו ע"א כו"כ שיהיה אדם חייב להיות חס על נכסיו, 114. The service of God in the Temple is called עבודת גבוה, pal. Sanh. 25 B ; R. Zeira. Pal. Nazir 51 A שהחמיר בהדיוט Num. r. 8. 4 ; (חרם) לשון גבוה הוא האומר לחרם לא וכו' יותר מבגבוה.

[61] v. R. Avira, or R. Eleazar b. Sota, 5 A : הוא גבוה ורואה את השפל ; באותה שעה הקב"ה נעשה גבוה בעולמו and M. Lam. 19 Tanh. iii. 72 ; ומגבוהו של עולם נתירא to Eccles. 12. 5 ; נבוה של עולם.

F

של עולם ממ'ה מתירא ' he was afraid of the highest of the
world, the King of all kings.'[62]

נבורה (32)

' Might.' This term is also older than the Tannaitic period,
and occurs mostly in sayings of that period. It is generally
used to emphasize the doctrine that Moses did not enjoin
the commandments of his own authority, but מפי הגבורה
' from the mouth of the all-powerful, Almighty'.[63] The
repeated reference to this phrase alludes to grave doubts and
scepticism on the part of powerful heretic movements as
to the reception of the Law from Sinai. The name is also
used in other connexions.[64] In the later Midrashim the term
occurs mostly in passages copied from older works.[65]

גדול העולמים (33)

' The Great One of the Worlds.' Gen. 21. 8, משתה גדול,
is explained with reference to Deut. 30. 9,[66] by R. Judah b.
Simon and R. Jose b. Hananiah as meaning that God was
also present. It is difficult to reconcile this Haggada with
the doctrine of God's omnipresence. God is everywhere
present. It is no wonder that some corrected the text
in גדולי עולם ' the great of the world were present at the

---

[62] v. Eccles. r. 12. 8 : גם מגבהו של עולם ממ'ה הק'ב'ה ; v. also Midrash,
Yalk. Daniel, § 1064, באותה שעה הקב'ה הוא גבוה בעולמו, cf. Tanh. B.
iii. 72.

[63] Mekh. 26 A : עדשאמר להם משה מפי הגבורה ; ib. 71 A, R. Akiba ואין
לא נסעו על פי משה אלא ע'פ הנבורה ; 77 B, 54 B דבר שלא יצא מפי הגבורה
S. N. 112, R. Ishmael אלא הכל מפי ; ib. 46 שנאמר למשה מפי חגבורה ;
ולא מעצמי אני אומר לכם אלא ; T. K. 3 B, S Deut. 9 משה ומשה מפי הנבורה
מפי הגבורה .

[64] Mech. 59 B : צא והמלך בנבורה ; v. also 60 A ; ib. 66 A משה משיב
בעיני הנבורה ; A. R. N. 37 דברים לפני הנבורה ; B. Sota, 37 A R. Meir
אושפזיכין לגבורה .

[65] Tanh. i. 196, ii. 63, iv. 35, 41, 42, 91, 163, v 31 ; M. Lam. 38 ; Pes. B.
20 A, 36 B, 61 B, 126 A, 166 A ; M. Ps. 317, 395, 415 ; Exod. r. 50. 2 ; S. E. R.
91, 198 ; P. R. E. chaps. 5, 16, 41.

[66] Gen. r. ch. 50 ; ed. Th. 565.

banquet.' Yet the more difficult reading is corroborated by another Haggada. R. Isaac teaches that ' the Great of the Worlds ' was present at the funeral of Jacob. Here, in order to obviate a mistake, another old reading (ואית דאמרן) has : כבוד חי עולמים ('the Glory of the Everlasting').[67]

גלגל עינו של עולם (34)

'The Eye of the World.' This term occurs twice in a Midrash[68] of R. Aha, whom we know as very clever in forming names of God ; he speaks of the five Kings who fought the Eye of the World, God.

דוד (35)

'Beloved.' When R. Hijja b. Ada died, the nephew of Bar Kappara and R. Simon b. Lakish, delivered funeral addresses based on Cant. 6. 2 : 'My Beloved is gone down into his garden, to the beds of spices, to feed in the gardens and to gather lilies '. דודי (my beloved), i.e. God ; לגנו, i. e. the world ; לערוגת הבשם, i.e. Israel ; לרעות בגנים, i.e. the nations of the world, to gather the lilies ; i.e. the pious, whom he removes from their midst.[69]

דיין (36)

'Judge.' The term אלהים was identified by R. Simon b. Johai with דיין (judge). Thus he substituted for בני אלהים Gen. 6. 2, בני דיינים, and cursed all those who translated בני אלהיא.[70] This is in agreement with R. Simon b. Johai's rule אין אלהים אלא דיין.[71] His teacher, R. Akiba, denies the saying of some of his generation : 'There is neither judgement nor judge ', by emphasizing, ' Yes, there is judgement,

---

[67] Gen. r. ch. 100. 6.

[68] Gen. r. ch. 41 ; ed. Th. 401 : לא באו ליזדווג אלא לתוך גלגל עינו של עולם, and 412.

[69] v. Pal. Ber. 2. 8 ; Cant. r. on 6. 2 ; v. also Tanh. iii 74.

[70] Gen. r. ch. 36 ; Th. 247.   [71] Mekhilta 1 a, *MRSJ.*, p. 6.

and there is a Judge ', i.e. God.[72]   This conception of God's
judgeship is one of the most important aspects of our
doctrine, and will be dealt with at length in a following
chapter.   Here may be repeated the saying of R. Eleazar b.
Azarja : 'He is a Judge, and Accuser, who is seated on the
Throne of Judgement and judges each person individually '.[73]
R. Simon b. Johai says : 'Blessed be the true Judge, before
whom is no injustice or respect of person '.[74]   The attribute
of God's justice, and the doctrine of reward and punishment
are closely allied with this name.   God as Judge is also the
source of moral law, justice, and righteousness.

(37) הוא

' He.'   In several sayings God is called הוא ' He ', without
any other designation or explanation.   Hillel has a saying :
ולקילוסן הוא צריך, does He require their praise ? [74a]   R. Meir
says : 'He will perform miracles and mighty deeds, and ye
shall stand, keeping silence.' [75]   R. Eleazar b. Pedath, in his
often-repeated saying : כל מקום שנ׳ ויי הוא ובית דינו.[76]   R. Aha
also adopted this name.[77]   Pythagoras likewise used the
name ' Ipse ' for the Godhead, v. Cicero, De natura deorum,
i, 5, L. Dukes, Or. Ltblatt, 1849, 396.

(38) הימנותא

' Faith.'   This term is mentioned very rarely, and it is
doubtful whether it was known to Palestinian Jews as well
as to Babylonian Jews.[78]

---

[72] Gen. r. ch. 26 ; Th. 252, and parall.
[73] Gen. r. 93, end : שהוא דיין ובעל דין ויושב על כסא דין ודן כל אחד
ואחד ; v. above בעל דין.
[74] Sifre Deut., § 304 : ברוך דיין אמת שאין עולה ומשוא פנים לפנין.
[74a] pal. Sukka, 5. 4 ; b. Sukka, 53 A.
[75] Mekh. 29 A : הוא יעשה לכם נסים וגבורות ואתם תהיו עומדין
ושותקין ; v. also Tanh. iii. 71 הוא נגאל.   Mishna, M. K. iii. 5 כע״ל הוא
אומר, Gen. r. 37. 4 ; Esther r. ch. 1.
[76] Gen. r. 51, p. 533, and parall.   [77] Gen. r. 63, p. 678.
[78] b. Shabbath, 10 B.

(39) חי העולמים [79]

'Life of the Worlds'. This term, expressing the attribute of God's eternity, is bound to take a spacious place in Rabbinic theology. It is, with the doctrines of omnipresence and omnipotence, the unbridgeable contrast between the Jewish doctrine of God, on one side, and all the other religions, primitive and higher as well, on the other side; the proper place of its treatment will be in one of the next chapters.

(40) חהם

'The Wise'. God is called wise, cf. Job 9. 4.[80] Some see this name indicated in Eccles. 8. 1; cf. Prov. 3. 19.[81]

(41) חסיד

'The Pious.' The Haggada which attempts to demonstrate the idea of the *imitatio dei* by pointing out that Israel is called by the same names as his Maker, puts together אלהים (v. no. 9), דוד (v. above, no. 35), חכם (v. above, no. 40), בחור (v. above, no. 17), and חסיד. God is called חסיד, cf. Jer. 3. 12; Israel Ps. 50. 5.[82] Sifre Dt. § 49, מה הקב׳ה נקרא חסיד.

(42) טהור

'The Pure.' In the allegorical homily on the red heifer we read טהור, i. e. 'God', based on Hab. 1. 13.[83]

(43) טובו שלעולם or טוב

'Good', or 'the Goodness of the World.' The eulogy, ברוך הטוב והמטיב, expresses this attribute of God to be met with in all higher religions.[84] The identification טוב = הקב׳ה is taught by R. Meir standing at the grave side of

---

[79] As to the pronunciation of חֵי or חַי there were many disputes among the codifiers and liturgical scholars of the Middle Ages, v. Marmorstein, שבלים וזאת ליהודה in, Budapest, 1926, p. 212.

[80] Tanh. iii. 74.

[81] Pes. B. 36 A; Eccles. r. 8. 1; Num. r. 19. 4.

[82] Tanh. iii. 74; v. M. Ps. B. 123; cf. Ps. 86. 2, and ib., p. 372.

[83] Tanh. iv. 120 and parall. [84] Gen. r. 57, ed. Th. 613.

his teacher Elisha b. Abuja.[85]   Again, in a statement which
groups the things which are called טוב, e.g. God, Torah,
Moses, and Israel.[86]   The name of God is based on
Ps. 145. 9.   The name טובו or טיבותו ' of the world', occurs
in a saying of R. Simon b. Halafta, saying : ' The arrogant
prevailed over the pious, and more so over the Goodness of
the World.[87]

(44) ידיד

' Friend.'   Six are called friends, among them God ;
cf. Is. 5. 1.[88]

(45) יודע מחשבות

' He who knows the thoughts' of men; v. above, *sub*
בעל מחשבות.   R. Jose b. Halafta has a saying [pal. Sanh.
1. 1] אין אני יודע דין תורה אלא היודע מחשבות יפרע מאותן האנשים
מקבלין עליכון מה דנא אמר לכון.

(46) יוצר עולמים

' Creator of the World ', or shortened יוצר, used very
frequently, especially to denote man's relation to God, and
occurs in Tannaitic as well as in Amoraic sources.   The
Hebrew Testament of Naphtali has the passage [89] : רק אני
מזהיר אתכם על אהבת היוצר ולעבדו ולדבקה בו.   The Alfabetha of
Sira says [90] : יגלה את לבו ומעשיו ליוצרו ' Let him reveal his
heart and deeds to his Creator'.   Stoics and Philo often
use the parable of the potter (also יוצר) in their teleological
proofs of God's existence.[91]   This parable is very often
repeated in the Haggada.[92]   Great is, says R. Judan, the
power of the seers, for they can compare the figure with
the artist.[93]   Generally some homilists found fault with

---

[85] j. Hag. 77 c ; Ruth r. 6. 13.   [86] B. Men. 53 B ; M. Ps. B. 510.

[87] j. Taan. 2. 1 ; Pes. B. 161 A.

[88] Sifre Deut., § 352, p. 115 ; b. Men. 53 B ; Pirke R. Hakadosh, vi. 38,
ed. Schönblum, 17 B.

[89] ed. Wertheimer, בתי מדרשות, ii. 9.   [90] Or. Brit. Mus. 5399, 81 B.

[91] De decal. ii, 189 ff. ; Geffcken, loc. cit., xxvii.

[92] v. Gen. r. 34. 1, ibid. 14. 7 ; Pes. r. ch. 24. 125 A.

[93] Gen. r. 27. 1 ; v. also M. Ps. 2 B ; Eccles. r. 2. 24, 8. 1.

people who dare to put the created thing higher than the Creator, or artist.[94] The teachers speak of יוצר בראשית ויוצר עולם,[95] and יוצר המאורות, or אור.[96] The name is connected with the idea of doing the Creator's will, or annoying Him.[97]

יחודו של עולם (47)

'The Unique of the World'. This name we meet in a saying of Ben Azzai, who preaches that Israel was not sent or driven into exile until he denied ביחודו שלעולם.[98] R. Judan preserved a homily of Aquilas, which teaches that God is worthy to be called God (אלוה). A king is being eulogized before he built public buildings for the city (δημόσια), or before he presented honours (προκοπή). The יחודו של עולם is different. First he does, then he is praised.[99] R. Judah b. Simon explains Gen. 3. 22 באחד by יחודו של עולם.[100] Similarly כאחד, Gen. 49. 16; Dan[1] is like יחודו של עולם, 'who needs no help in battle'; finally, Job 14. 4 : מי יתן טהור מטמא לא אחד 'who gives the pure out of the impure?' like Abraham of Terah, Hezekiah of Ahaz, Mordecai of Shimei, Israel of the nations? The יחודו של עולם = אחד.[2] R. Phinehas b. Hama ascribes God's justice, R. Juda Halevi b. Shalom, God's omniscience to His uniqueness, i.e. His being יחודו של עולם.[3] We find further in answer to questions like מי עשה זאת ?, or מי צוה כן ?, not הקב'ה, but יחודו של עולם.[4]

94 R. Hoshaja, Gen. r. 24. 1 ; R. Samuel b. Nahman 1. 3 ; M. Ps. 12 D, and Buber, p. 111, Wisdom of Solomon, 15. 16.

95 v. בתי מדרשות, ed Wertheimer, i. 9 ; pal. Ber. 1. 5.

96 b. Ber. 11 A, B.

97 v. Ruth r. 3. 1 ; b. Ber. 17 A ; R. Johanan b. Nappaha.

98 Lam. r. 1. 1.

99 Gen. r. ch. 1 ; Th., p. 10. The same idea is expressed by Ben Azzai and R. Simon b. Johai ; v. also Pes. B. 30 B ; Pes. r. 21 B ; Num. r. 12. 5 ; Tanh. תשא 17.

100 Gen. r. 21. 5, Th. 200.

1 Gen. r. 98. 18, 99. 11 ; R. Joshua b. Nehemiah, Midrash ha-Gadol, Gen. 742 ; Num. r. 10. 5.

2 Pes. B. 29 B and parall ; v. also מעין גנים, ed. Buber, p. 45.

3 Tanh. B. i. 97, ii. 9.

4 Tanh. B. iv. 103, 104 ; v. also iii. 30.

<u>ישב בסתרו של עולם</u> (48)

'He who dwells in the hidden places of the world.'
R. Simon b. Lakish explains Job 24. 15 : ' " The eye also of
the adulterer waiteth for the twilight, saying, ' No eye shall
see me ', and disguiseth the face." Thou shalt not say :
" He who sins with his body is an adulterer ; " even he who
sins with his eyes is also an adulterer, as it is said, " The
eye is an adulterer. He sits and waits for the twilight, for
the evening " (Prov. 7. 9). He does not know that He who
sitteth in the Secret (בסתר) appoints (ישים) watchmen to make
known his intentions (בלקטירים = פנים).' [5]

(49) יי

v. above, *sub* אלהים, and chapter 1.

<u>ישרו של עולם</u> (50)

'The righteous of the world.' The righteous will see
God and God the righteous.[6]

<u>כבודו של עולם</u> (51)

'The Glory of the World.' This name is very frequent
in the Targumim (יקרא), but rare in Rabbinic writings.
We met the name in connexion with חי העולמים.[7] In
Tannaitic sources we have כבודו של עולם for אלהים.[8] R. Anja
b. Susi says : פעמים שאין העולם ומלואו מחזיקים כבודו.[9] Very
often speaking of God, כבודי or כבודך or כבודו is substituted.[10]

[5] Pes. r. ch. 24. 124 B ; Lev. r. 23. 12.
[6] M. Ps. ch. 11. 101 B, : אלא הם יראו פני ישרו של עולם וישרו של
עולם יחזה פניהם של ישרים.
[7] v. above, *sub* no. 39, p. 85.
[8] Mekh. 58 A ; v. esp. 60 A. R. Joshua b. Hananja : ישלחו בכבודו של
עולם.
[9] Gen. r. Th. 28.
[10] Tanh. B. i. 69 : אמר הקב׳ה אני ; ii. 101 : אילולי שיתפתה בכודך עמי
והבסא דומה : Midr. Ps., Buber, 209 ; v. also iv. 17 and 18 ; ארד בכבודי
לכבודו ; Pirke R. Eliezer, chaps. 10, 26, and 53 ; Seder Elijahu r., p. 53.

(52) כבשונו שלעולם

'The Secret of the World.' It is doubtful whether this can be regarded as a name. The name occurs only once,[11] and means the secrets of the world, i.e. of creation and theosophy, which must not be revealed.

(53) לבו של ישראל

'The Heart of Israel.' R. Hijja b. Abba proves that God is called the heart of Israel from Ps. 73. 26.[12]

(54) מבין

'Who understands.' Occurs in the Mishna[13] in the list of names enumerated by R. Eleazar ha-Kappar.

(55) מזנא דעלמא

'The Supplier of the World.' In Cant. 7. 4 אל יחסר המזג we read the remark : לא נחסר מזנא דעלמא ; cf. Ps. 23.[14]

(56) מי שאמר והיה העולם

'He, who spake and the world was.' This is one of the characteristic Tannaitic terms for God. Almost in all cases where this Name occurs one can assume that the saying is of Tannaitic origin. Some of the oldest Scribes known to us by name used it. Yet it has been discovered in an old Sumerian Psalm, therefore must be very old. 'Overpowering, exalted, at Thy word which created the world, Lord of Lords, Lord of the Word of Life, Father, Shepherd, &c.'[15] Owing to the discovery of this ancient name in Sumero-Babylonian literature, we can trace the origin of this term to the oldest stage of religious thought.

---

[11] b. Hag. 13 A.

[12] Cant. r. 5. 2 ; Tanh. B. i. 137 ; Pes. B. 46 B ; Lam. r., ed. Buber, 13.

[13] Aboth iv. 22.   [14] Cant. r. 7. 6.

[15] Langdon, *Sumerian and Babylonian Psalms*, 127.

מי שענה ... (57)

'He who heard', scil. the prayers of Abraham, Isaac, &c.
The name was invoked in great public distress or serious
calamities. and is to be found in the ancient order of service
for Public Fast days as described in the Mishna (Taanith ii.
3 ff.), v. Zunz, *Synagogale Poesie*, p. 83, *Ritus*, p. 122 f.,
Kaufmann, *Ges. Schriften*, iii. 517.

מי ששיכן את שמו בבית הזה (58)

'He who caused His Name to dwell in this House.'
According to R. Helbo, the priestly division, that left on
Saturday the service of the Temple greeted the entering
division with the words: may He, who caused his Name
to dwell in this place, grant you love and affection, peace
and friendship.[16]

מלך מלכי המלכים (59)

'King of all kings.' The Apocrypha and Pseudepigrapha offer many parallels to this name.[17] In all cases
without הקב'ה. Our sources add in the majority of cases
this latter term, which, as will be seen afterwards, belongs
to a later period. The name occurs in the earliest sources,
and we are entitled to assume that הקב'ה is a later addition,
to distinguish between God and the Roman or another
emperor, who aspired to this honoured, ancient title.
The original name was מלך מלכי המלכים ברוך הוא, the latter
words have been frequently added to המקום, שמים and other
names. The Apocrypha offer also instances of עליון ברוך הוא[18]
or חי עולמים ברוך הוא.[19] 'King of all kings' is used by the
oldest authorities in our sources.

---

[16] b. Ber. 12 A, מי ששיכן את שמו בבית הזה הוא ישכון ביניכם אהבה
ואחוה ושלום וריעות. Other Names beginning with מי are: מי שברך
אבותינו, v. Zunz, *Ritus*, p. 9; and מי שעשה נסים לאבותינו.

[17] Bousset, loc. cit., 360.　　　[18] Jub. 22, 27.

[19] Enoch i. 77. 1. The Hebrew text of the Test. Naph., ch. ix, has
הקב'ה, most probably a later addition.

מעון (60)

'Abode.' The name מעון is used especially in oaths,[20] and was derived from Deut. 33. 27 and Ps. 90. 1. R. Isaac explains similarly to R. Jose b. Halafta's interpretation of the name המקום : We do not know whether מעון is the abode of the world, or the world is His abode ; from Ps. 90.1, one can learn that God is the abode of the universe.[21] This exegesis, surely, is far from pantheistic conceptions. It endeavours to emphasize the doctrine of God's omni-presence, as will be shown in the attributes of God.

מעלה (61)

'Above', or 'High.' This name is generally used to signify that nothing happens on earth unless it is provided or ordered by God. R. Hannina b. Hama says : אין אדם נוקף אצבעו מלמטה אא'כ מכריזין עליו מלמעלה [22] 'A man does not hurt his finger below, unless it is decreed from Above.' R. Samuel b. Nahmani makes the serpent say : אפשר דאנא עביד כלום דלא מתאמר לי מן עליותא [23] 'Is it possible for me to do some-thing which I was not commanded to do from Above ? ' This was repeated and enlarged by R. Abba b. Kahana : לעולם אין הנחש נושך אלא אם כן נלחש לו מלעיל, ואין הארי טורף אא'כ נלחש לו מלמעלה, ואין המלכות מתגרה בבני אדם אא'כ נלחש לו מלעיל [24] The three names מעלה, שמים, and עליון occur in the same sense. The saying of these teachers coincides with R. Simon b. Johai's sentence : אפילו צפור מבלעדי שמיא לא אצדיא ' No bird is caught by the fowler without the consent of Heaven '.[25] Another version of the saying reads : מה צפרין חוץ מדעת עליון אינן נתפסין אנו חוץ מדעת עליון נתפסין [26] The change between these terms appears noteworthy.

[20] v. my *Religionsgeschichtliche Studien*, ii. 69.

[21] Gen. r. 68 and further under המקום.

[22] Cf. Ps. 37. 23 and Prov. 20. 24 ; b. Hullin, 7 B.

[23] Lev. r. 26. 1 ; Num. r. 19. 2.   [24] Eccles. r. 10. 14

[25] Pes. B. 89 A ; MS. Oxford. r. לא יבדא, Pal. Shebiith, 9. 1 ; לא יבדה v. Arukh, s. v. בדה, Tos. A. Z. 16 B, s. v. דימוס, Eccles. r ; חופר גומץ Esther r. ch. 3.

[26] M. Ps. 17.

Secondly, מעלה is used when the Scribes express or report man's feelings for or speech against God, כלפי מעלה[27], or to avoid and weaken anthropomophism, e.g. עין של מעלה אינה רואה[28]. Thirdly, it stands for מרום, e.g. מיד תלה עשו את עיניו,[29] or עליון[30] and in connexion with כבוד של מעלה[31].

מקום (62)

'Place.' This name is often discussed. Some scholars see in it Hellenistic-Alexandrian influence,[32] others derived it from the Bible,[33] a third view looks to a Persian origin.[34] Bousset thought that this Name seems to have had its origin very late, although it occurs frequently in the Mishna. There is no trace, according to Bousset, of it in the literature of the first century.[35] Our investigation shows that Simon the Just,[36] c. 300 B.C.E., was the first of whom we know with certainty that he used this term. It is very significant for the date of the Targumim, as well as of the Gospels that neither המקום, nor its Greek (τόπος), or Aramaic (אתרא) equivalents are used or known.[37] Our material shows that the oldest strata of the Tannaitic sources used המקום. A small Midrash called מדרש תמורה[38] preserved the report that מקום was the Name used by the

---

[27] Gen. r. 119, 572; Tanh. iii. 66; R. Simon b. Lakish ibid. v. 39; R. Joh. b. Nap.; Ms. Ps. 97, R. Aha.

[28] Num. r. 94.   [29] Tanh. i. 4, v. 25.

[30] Tanh. i. 19 : בקש לגנוב דעת של מעלה.

[31] M. Ps. 177, R. Aha.

[32] Gfrörer, *Jahrhundert des Heils*, Stuttgart, 1838, p. 290 f.; Dähne, *Gesch. Darstellung*, pp. 72, 282; Siegfried, *Philo*, pp. 202, 204; Freudenthal, *Hell. Studien*, p. 66; Geiger's *Jüd. Zeitschrift*, xi, p. 222; A. Berliner, *Targum Onkelos*, Berlin, 1884, 102, note; Heinemann, *MGWJ.*, 66, 1922, p. 310, note, who denies the use of המקום in Hellenistic writings altogether.

[33] Geiger, *Nachgelassene Schriften*, iv. 424; Schürer, *Jahrbücher für prot. Theologie*, ii. 1876, 168.

[34] E. Landau, *Synonyma für Gott*, Zurich, 1888, 41 ff.

[35] *Die Religion des Judenthums*,[2] 363.

[36] And not Simon b. Shetach, as Landau, loc. cit., 43, on which his theory of Persian origin is based, thought.

[37] Already noticed by Dalman, *Worte Jesu*, Leipzig, 1898, p. 189.

[38] ed. Wertheimer, Jerusalem, 1914.

אנשי לשכת הגזית,[39] i.e. the Synhedrion. The antiquity of some parts of this Midrash is corroborated by the use of המקום, and old material preserved in it,[40] although the final redaction of the Midrash may be put in the Amoraic period.[41] In the third century, when המקום was already displaced by the Amoraic term הקב'ה, the Haggadist R. Ami pondered on the meaning of this name. This also corroborates our contention that the change must have taken place in this century. The movements in favour of a change started earlier. It can be traced back to the last decades of the second century, when the sages were moved to give explanations or defend its use, as it was done by R. Jose b. Halafta, or according to others, by R. Meir.[42] For our purpose here it is sufficient to point out the antiquity of this Name, and its disappearance in the time of the earlier Amoraim.

מרום (63)

'High', 'Heaven.' Identical with עליון and שמים, and especially used in connexion with prayers, like תלה עינו במרום.[43]

מרותיה של עולם (64)

'The Lordship of the world.' R. Phinehas b. Hama interprets the word מוריה by עולם של מרותיה למקום.[44]

מרי (65)

'My Lord.' R. Jose b. Halafta speaks of מרי שמיא 'Lord of Heaven', in replying to a heathen: 'We trust in the

---

[39] With reference to Middoth, v. 6: ברוך המקום; cf. also Mekh. 52 B.

[40] Marmorstein, 'Die Nachrichten über Nekyomanteia in der altrabbinischen Literatur, in ZfNW. 22, 1923, p. 303.

[41] v., however, Zunz, Gottesd. Vortr. 118; Rab Pealim, 123; Jellinek, Bet ha Midrash i, p. xx, certainly older than 1250.

[42] Gen. r. 68; M. Ps. 90, 10; Pes. r. 107 B; Exod. r. 45. 6; Pirke R. E., Tanh. B. ii., and according to Simon b. Zemach Duran, in his commentary on Aboth ii. 9, in the third chapter of Pal. Maccoth, which is, however, not to be found in the editions: v. now ed. Theodor, p. 777.

[43] Gen. r. 65. 5.

[44] Gen. r. 55. 9; Tanh. i. 113; v. also Tanh. ii. 38, R. Aha: שלא קיבלו מרותו שלעו'.

Lord of Heaven, who will show us His countenance in the future world.[45]　Corresponding to אדון העולם and רבון העולם we find also מריה דעלמא.[46]

עד (66)

'Witness.'　Eleazar ha-Kappar, in his list of God's names, gives also this designation.[47]　In the Tanhuma the question is raised : 'Whence do we know that God is called עד?'　The reply refers to Jer. 29. 23 : ואנכי היודע ועד נאם ה'.[48]

עליון (67)

'High.'　This name, as one of the oldest, heads the list of God's names enumerated in an old Midrash.[49]　It is frequently used in Psalms and Pseudepigraphic writings. In our period it had already an archaic sound, but it was still used in a few instances.　R. Aibo speaks of כגונב דעת העליונה,[50] or אלא שנשתנית ימין של עליון.[51]

עשירו של עולם (68)

'The Wealthy of the World.'　R. Tanhuma combines Deut. 3. 23 with Prov. 18. 23.　The poor, who speaketh entreaties is Moses, who comes before his Creator with supplications.　The rich, who answereth roughly is the Rich of the World, whose reply was, 'Do not continue to speak to me any further.'[52]

עתיקו של עולם (69)

'The Ancient of the World.'　This name occurs once. Its proper meaning is also a matter of conjecture owing to

---

[45] Gen. r. 131 ; M. Ps. 30 ; M. Lam. r. 28 ; b. Ber. 6 A תפילין דמארי עלמא.
[46] Gen. r. 272, 99. 3 ; M. Ps. 236 ; M. Lam. r. 84.
[47] Aboth iv. 22.　　　　　　　　[48] Tanh. iii. 9.
[49] Agadath Shir ha-Shirim, ed. Schechter, Camb., 1896, 9 ; Yalkut Makhiri, Ps. 97 A ; Midrash Zutta, ed. Buber.
[50] Gen. r. 220 ; v. R. Berechja, 140 : דגנב דעתיה דמריה ; v. also Tanh. i. 19 : דעת של מעלה ; Pes. B. 160 A.
[51] M. Ps 267 ; v. also p. 344.
[52] Deut. r. 2. 3 ; v. Sifre Deut., § 26.

the bad texts. Ruth r. reads: ר' איבו אמר אפילו דברים
שנתעסקו בהם החזירם שנ' פסל לך וג' הדברים הללו נאמרו במעתיקו
וחדברים עתיקים ר' איבו ורבי סימן: reads [54] Yalkut .של עולם[53]
אומר הדברים האלו אומרים מעתיקו של עולם. The words speak
of the ancient of the world. The term is identical with
the well-known עתיק יומין, or עתיק יומיא, v. also b. Ber. 17 A
ופעמיך ירוצו לשמוע דברי עתיק יומין.

פועל (70)

'Maker.' R. Eleazar, the son of R. Jose, the Galilean,
says: מהו אמרו לאלהים, אמרו לפועליך הטוב והישר.[55]

פנים (71)

'Countenance.' In sayings, as כאילו כנף מכסה את הפנים,[56]
in order to avoid anthropomorphic ideas, or כל הפנים שוות,
'All the deities are alike.' [57]

צור עולמים (72)

'The Rock of the Worlds.' R. Simai in his prayers
invokes God, as אדון כל הבריות, אלוה התושבחות צור העולמים
חי העולם יוצר בראשית 'The Lord of all the creatures, God of
praises, Rock of the Worlds, Everlasting Creator.' [58] 'The
Rock' is a favourite simile in Biblical as well as Baby-
lonian-Assyrian hymnology.[59] We find further the saying
אין צור אלא הקב"ה, v. b. Berak. 6 A.

צדיקו של עולם (73)

'The Righteous of the World.' Also צדיק חי העולמים.
We begin with a sermon of Bar-Kappara, reported by
R. Huna, based on Ps. 31. 19, 'Let the lying lips be put to
silence, which speak grievous things proudly and contemp-
tuously against the righteous.' תאלמנה ('let them be put
to silence') means (a) אתפרכן 'they shall become tied',
cf. Targum to Gen. 37. 7 ; (b) איתחרשן 'deaf and dumb',

---

[53] Ruth r. ii. 1.   [54] Chronicles, § 1074.
[55] Tanh. ii. 54.   [56] Tanh. v. 45.
[57] M. Ps. 47, and Parall ; Pes. B. 29 A, 162 B.
[58] Pal. Ber. 1. 5.
[59] *Keilinschriftliche Bibliothek*, ii. 79, 83.

cf. Exod. 4. 11 ; and (c) 'silenced, for they speak against the Zaddik, the Everlasting, things which He removed from His creatures.' [60]   Another teacher explains, Is. 3. 10: אמרו צדיק כי טוב ' say unto the Righteous of the World that He is good', combining the attribute of righteousness with that of goodness.[61]   Prov. 21. 15 : שמחה לצדיק עשות משפט ' It is a joy to the righteous of the world when He performs judgement ', for he then is exalted in the world.[62] A fourth teacher combines Gen. 9. 18 and Ps. 37. 16 : טוב מעט לצדיק ' Better are Israel in the eyes of the righteous of the world although they are only a few (cf. Deut. 7. 7) than the hosts of the wicked.' [63]   Abraham says to God, according to R. Judah [b. Simon] : לא את צדיקו של עולם צרף עצמך עמהן ויעלו מנין חמשים.[64] ' The Righteous of the world knows even the soul of his cattle; (cf. Prov. 12. 10) even in His anger He shows His love to His creatures.' [65] Eccles. 3. 16 is explained : מקום הצדק שמה הרשע, מקום אחד היה לצדיקו שלעולם בהמ'ק המיוחד לשכינה והרשיעו מנשה.[66] ' God is the Righteous of the world because he is omniscient ; He knows and sees our hearts and sinews.' This saying connects the two attributes of God's knowledge and justice.[67]   R. Judah b. Shalom identifies צדיק, Is. 3. 10, with God ; cf. Ps. 11. 7.[68] Prov. 13. 25, צדיק אוכל לשובע נפשו, is referred to God and

---

[60] Gen. r. ch. 1, Th., p. 2, ; j. Hag. 77 c

[61] M. Ps. B. 481 ; Pes. B. 73 B ; v. also M. Ps 324.

[62] M. Ps. B. 33, another reading for שמחה לצדיקו ש׳ עולם שנעשה מדת הדין בביתו והחריבו ; v. on this idea, Marmorstein, *Einige messianologische Vorstellungen des dritten Jahrhunderts neu beleuchtet*, in *Jeschurun*, xi, 1924, pp. 323–42.

[63] Ag. Ber. B. 23 f. ; v. also the term צדיק עולמים above, sub no. 73, חי העולמים, sub no. 39.

[64] Gen. r. ch. 48, Th., p. 510.

[65] Tanh. B. i. 35 ; Ag. Ber. r. יודע צדיקו של עולם אפי בחמתו instead of בהמתי ; v. Tanh. B. iii. 95 : צדיק זה הקב׳ה ; Pes. B. 78 B.

[66] Tanh. B. iii. 6.

[67] M. Ps. B. 67 ; v. further, p. 98 : צדיק העולם הוא הקב׳ה מה פעולה ; מה הנייה יש לך בעולמך ובפעולתך secondly ; הניחו לך בעולמך and finally צדיק העולם מה פעולה פעלת.

[68] M. Ps., p. 323 ; v. also above, note 61 ; v. also ib., p. 465 on Isa. 41. 2.

the sacrifices accepted by Him.[69] R. Hanina sees in Job
17. 9 references to God. צדיק is God ; cf. Ps. 15. 7. טהר ידים ;
v. Hab. 1. 13 ; יוסיף אומץ ' for He strengthens the power of
the pious to do his will.[70]

הקדוש ברוך הוא (74)

'The Holy One, blessed be He.' It will be shown later
on that this name was introduced in the third century, and
took the place of the earlier המקום. We have shown that
it is a late addition in the name מלך מלכי המלכים הקב'ה.
Here we point to the fact that neither the Apocrypha and
Pseudepigrapha, nor the N. T. know this name. Targum
Onkelos must have been compiled before this name was
introduced in the schools and synagogues. The later
Targum, ascribed to Jonathan b. Uzziel,[70a] which borrowed
liberally from the Midrashim, use it very often. The great
step by which the religion of Judaism advanced in adopting this name, will be fully dealt with in speaking of God's
holiness. It suffices to hint at the fact that all-important
and vital external and internal problems, which threatened
the whole fabric of Jewish religion, brought about such
a change. All the forces, Paganism and Gnosticism, Christianity and Atheism, arrayed against Jewish teaching and
belief, combined to threaten the very existence of Israel.
The idea of holiness hallowed Israel, just as Israel sanctified God !

קדמונו של עולם (75)

'The first of the World.' R. Eleazar b. Simon sees in
Gen. 11. 2 (ויהי בנסעם מקדם) an allusion to the thoughts of
the generation of the separation. They removed from the

[69] Pes. B. 60 A.

[70] Pes. B. 166 A ; v. further Midrash Othijoth of R. Akiba, ed.
Wertheimer, 48 B, and Sifre, § 49 : מה הקב'ה נקרא צדיק.

[70a] We have this name also in Aramaic : קודשא בריך הוא, v. b. Ber.
5 B, 6 A, 7 A, 10 A, מי חשיד קודשא בריך הוא דעביד דינא בלא דינא, or
ומי איכא רותחא קמיה דקודב'ה, or ומי משבח קודב'ה בשבחין דישראל,
and ומה דניחא קמיה דקודב'ה הוא לעביד.

first of the world, saying : 'We do not want either Him, or His Godhead.'[71] A similar explanation is given to Gen. 13. 11 with reference to Lot.[72]

כונה (76)

'Creator', 'Possessor.' In the Mishna we read : כל שלא חס על כבוד קונו ראוי לו שלא בא לעולם.[73] Further, in a saying of R. Johanan b. Zakkai : זה השוה כבוד עבד לכבוד קונו.[74] A Boraita teaches that Sandalphon קושר כתר לקונו.[75] R. Levi quotes in the name of R. Jose b. Nahorai : כל זמן שהיו ידי קוניהם ממשמשים בהם היו מותחים והולכים כיון שנחו ידי קוניהם נותן להם ניחה וינח לעולמו.[76] In anonymous sayings we come across sentences like דיו לעבד להיות שוה לקונו,[77] which reminds us of R. Johanan b. Zakkai's homily, or השוו עבד שהלך בתמימות,[78] further, 'לעשות רצון קונו שבשמ'[79] and עם קונו.[80] The wife of R. Simon b. Halafta says to her husband : שמא הטרחת את קונך?[81] These instances show the double meaning of the name : Creator and Master.

רבון כל המעשים (77)

'Lord of all works.' R. Joshua b. Hananja repeats the question of the generation of Amalek : אם רבון כל המעשים 'If He is the Lord of כשם שהוא רבון עלינו נעבדנו ואם לאו לא all works just as He is our Lord, then we will worship

---

[71] Gen. r. ch. 38, Th. 356.

[72] Gen. r. ch. 40, Th. 394 ; v. Tobia b. Eliezer in his לקח טוב, i. 62, who saw in נסע מקדמונו של a reference to Abraham : קדמונו שלעולם עולם זה אברהם שהיה ראש אמנה. M. Aggada 28, reads : מקדמותו שלעולם ; Rashi, ed. Berliner, p. 24 : הסיע עצמו מקדמונו של עולם אמר אי אפשי באברהם ולא באלהיו.

[73] M. Hagiga, ii. 1, 11 A ; v. also R. Joshua b. Korha, Pirke R. E. ch. 25.

[74] Mekh. 91 B 6 ; B. K. 79 B ; v. also Mekh. 37 A : וכי אפשר להנוות לקונו.

[75] B. Hag. 13 A ; Pirke R. E. ch. 4.

[76] Gen. r. Th. 86.

[77] Tanh. i. 79 ; v. also M. Ps. B. 532 : שעבד נכנם לדין עם קונו ; v. also Agad. Bereshith B. 34.

[78] Ib. iv. 125.   [79] Ib. iv. 178, usually לעשות רצון המקום.

[80] Ib. v. 2.   [81] M. Ps. B. 408.

Him, otherwise not.' [82]   In another source [83] the very same question is quoted in a Haggada of R. Judah b. Ilai.

רבון כל העולמים (78)

'Lord of all Worlds.' This name is one of the most frequently used in addressing God. Our texts have רבון העולמים and רבונו של עולם. The former is the more correct. It is most unlikely that the rabbis should have paid no attention to the contentions of the Gnostic sects, who saw in the God of the Jews 'the Lord of this world.'

רואה ואינו נראה (79)

'He who sees and is invisible.' A blind man says to R. Hoshaja: את פייסת דין דמתחמי ולא חמי 'Thou didst appease one who is seen and cannot see'. דין דחמי ולא מתחמי יקבל פיוסך 'May He, who sees everything, but cannot be seen, accept thy apology.' [84]   In Hebrew very frequently הרואה ואינו נראה is applied, for instance, in the comparison of God to the soul: 'God is invisible and sees everything, so the soul sees everything and is invisible.' [85]

רוח הקודש (80)

'The Holy Spirit.' This term has been discussed more recently by various scholars, and deserves a new and full treatment from more than one aspect. From a survey of the whole material in our sources we gather that generally the rabbis understood by it the spirit of prophecy or divination. Many a time it bears the same meaning as the term שכינה. It occurs in the following connexions: (1) רוח הק' אומרת, (2) השיבה, (3) צווחת, (4) שראה, (5) הופיע, (6) להקביל, (7) צפה, (8) ברוח הק', (9) ראה ב', (10) חזא ב', (11) כינס ב', ביטלה ממנו, (12) נסתלקה, (13) נצנצה בהם, (14) שואב רוח הק', (15) סוכים ברוח הק', (16) משיח רוח הק', (17) סמך ברוח הק', (18) השתמש ברוח הק', (19) נזקק לרוח הקדש, (20) זכה לרוח הק', (21) קפצה עליו רוח הק',

[82] Mekh. 52 B.   [83] Pes. B. 28 A.

[84] Peah 8. 8 ; v. also the story of the blind man and R. Eliezer b. Jacob.

[85] B. Ber. 10 A and parall.

(22) מכרחת, and (23) נתקררה. In some instances רוח הקודש
means God, and acts as a substitute for the Divine Name.
Two examples will suffice to show this. A homily on
Eccles. 8. 2 has : אמר להם רוח הקודש משביע אני עליכם שאם
תגזור עליכם מלכות גזרות אל תמרדו עליה 'The Holy Spirit
says to Israel, " I put an oath on you ; if the Government
put hard decrees on you, do not revolt." ' Some editions
actually have הקב׳ה instead of רוח הקודש.[86]   In another
passage : ורוח הקודש צווחת ואומרת להם אתם סבורים שאתם עושין
בסתר ואינו גלוי לפני 'The Holy Spirit cried, " Ye think that
ye are doing your work in hidden places, and it is not
revealed before me ! " ' [87]   Many other instances are available which cannot be enumerated in this place.[88]   They all
belong to the Amoraic period, when the change from המקום
to הקב׳ה was really accomplished. Do we find traces of this
use also in the Tannaitic age ? There is no old saying of
that period known in which רוח הק׳ is used as a Divine
Name. A somewhat lengthy dialogue, which will engage
our special attention later, between Israel and the Holy
Spirit,[89] shows clearly that the Tannaim understood under
רוח הקודש, prophets and prophecy.

רומו של עולם (81)

'The Height of the World.' A Haggadist reports a
dialogue between the Egyptian and his horse. The former
says to his horse : ' Yesterday I led thee in order to give
thee water, and now thou desirest to drown me in the sea '.
The latter replies : ' רמה בים. i.e. see (ראה) what is (מה) in
the sea ? I see the Highest of the world whom I see in the
sea ' (רומו של עולם אני רואה בים).[90]

רועה (82)

'Shepherd.' God as shepherd of all men is an old name
for God in the Prophets and Psalms. The same was not

---

[86] Tanh. B. i. 38 ; Ag. Ber. ch. 7, ed. Tanh. הקב׳ה.
[87] Tanh. ii. 68.   [88] v., for instance, M. Ps. B. 137, 138.
[89] Sifre Deut., § 355.   [90] Exod. r. 23. 14.

unknown to polytheistic speculations on the Godhead.[91]
In the Haggada God is generally the owner of the flock,
and Moses the shepherd.[92]   Yet there are instances of the
older conception.   R. Abba b. Kahana says that 'God
delivered Israel from Egypt, as a shepherd delivers the
young from the mother's womb'.[93]   R. Hanina, the son of
R. Aha compares Job's case to a shepherd who is taking
a look over his flock: suddenly comes a wolf and threatens
it; the shepherd puts a goat at his disposal.[94]   God is the
shepherd, Satan the wolf, Job the goat.

(83) רחמנא

'Merciful.'   Although this term is more frequent in the
sayings of the Babylonian teachers in the period of the
Amoraim, we find the same also with Tannaim and Palestinian Amoraim.   R. Huna says in the name of Rab, who
said it in the name of R. Meir, and it was likewise taught
in the name of R. Akiba : 'One should accustom oneself to
say : כל מה דעביד רחמנא לטב עביד "Whatever God does is
done for the best." '[95]   It is to be noted that the saying is
Aramaic, and R. Akiba must have used it as a well known
and accepted maxim.   It is not impossible to assume that
Hillel brought the same with him from his Babylonian
native country and his pupils spread it abroad.   R. Simon
b. Johai [96] uses it in his saying, also preserved in Aramaic :
אלו הוינא קאים על טורא דסיני בשעתא דאתיהיבת תורה לישראל הוינ' מתבעי
קומו רחמנא.   The antiquity of this name is proved by its use
in prayers and blessings.   It is used interchangeably with
המקום.[97]   Prayers or homilies are introduced by בריך רחמנא.[98]
R. Phinehas b. Hama notes to Eccles. 6. 2: 'God does not give

---

[91] v. Farnell, *Greece and Babylon*, 105.
[92] v., for instance, Ruth. r. ch. 5 ; M. Ps. 22 A, 34 B; Mekh. 33 B.
[93] M. Ps. 462.   [94] Gen. r. 57. 3.
[95] b. Ber. 60 B.   [96] b. Ber. 1. 2.
[97] b. Sabb. 12: המקום יפקדך לשלום ; in Aramaic : רחמנא ידכרוך
לשלם.
[98] v. the Galilean before R. Hisda Sabb. 88; R. Shela b. Ber. 62; b.
Ber. 53 B, 54 B ; Pes. 57.

wealth, property, and honour only to those whom He likes '.
‏אלא במי שירצה בו הקב׳ה‏.[100] [99]; in Hebrew: (‏מאן דרחמנא רעי ביה‏)
We mention finally R. Jeremiah's saying: ‏לא ליהוי לימא איניש‏
‏רחמנא ירחיק חטאה אלא ירחיק חטאה מינן‏,[1] and R. Judan who
says: ‏מאן דאמר רחמנא וותרן יתוותרון בני מועהי‏.[2]

‏רם ונשא‏ (84)

'The High and Lofty One.' In an old mystical Midrash
dealing with cosmogony we read: ‏ומנין שנקרא הב׳ה רם ונשא‏
‏שנ׳ כי כה אמר רם ונשא שוכן עד וקדוש שמו‏.[3] The Midrash
Haggada[4] contains the passage: ‏מי עשה זה הקב׳ה שהוא רם‏
‏ונשא‏. The name is derived from Isa. 57. 15. This verse
suggested to some teachers of the third century the idea of
God's humility. God is high and lofty, yet He is with him
that is contrite and humble in spirit. We mention here
only R. Johanan[5] and R. Eleazar b. Pedath.[6] The latter
preached very strongly and frequently against the vice of
pride and haughtiness, as will be shown later.[7]

‏שוכן עדי עד‏ (85)

'He who dwells for ever.' This name occurs only once,
and is formed by scholars of Babylon. It is given here for
completeness' sake. R. Huna b. Nathan asked R. Ashi
about the names ‏קינה דימונה ועדעדה‏ in Josh. 15. 22. R. Ashi
said: 'The text enumerates the boundaries of the land of
Israel.' R. Huna: 'Do you mean to suggest that I am not
aware of this fact?' but R. Gebiha of Arqiza gave the

---

[99] M. Sam. B. 44.   [100] Eccles. r. on 6. 2.

[1] M. Ps. 436.

[2] ib. 93 Pal. ; Shekalim, 48 D ; Taanit, 68 D ; Beza, 62 B ; Gen. r. 67. 4 ;
Esther r. ch. 7 ; Tanh. ‏כי תשא‏, 26 ; B. K. 50 A.

[3] v. ‏מעשה בראשית‏ in Wertheimer ; ‏בתי מדרשות‏, ii. 15.

[4] ed. Buber, Ex. 145.

[5] b. Meg. 5 A : ‏כל מקום שאתה מוצא גדולתו של הקב׳ה שם אתה מוצא‏
‏עניתנותו‏ ; he proves this from all the three parts of the Bible.

[6] Jelamdenu, v. Tanh. B. i. 84 : ‏בשבע מקומות השוה הקב׳ה את עצמו‏
‏בחבורת הנמוכים‏.

[7] v. Sota 5 a.

following explanation : ' He who is jealous of his fellow
man and keeps silent, He who dwells for ever will judge on
his behalf'.   R. Ashi replied : ' How will you explain the
names צקלג ומדמנה וסנסנה ?'   ib. 15. 31.   R. Huna said : ' If
R. Gebiha could be present he surely would expound it'.
R. Aha of Be Huzaah explained it thus : ' He who has a
complaint against his fellow men of ruining his trade
(צעקת לגימא), and he keeps silent, He who dwelleth in the
thorn bush will do his judgement ' (מי ששוכן בסנה).[8]   The
teachers delighted in deriving ethical and moral teachings
from geographical or personal names.

שומר עולמים (86)

' The Guardian of the Worlds.'   In a homiletical exposition
of Isaiah 21. 11 we read : ' Israel said to the prophet. " Our
teacher Isaiah ! tell us what will deliver us of this night ?" '
Isaiah says : ' Wait till I have asked !'   After he had asked,
he returns to them.   They ask : ' What did the Guardian of
the Worlds say (שומר מה מילל) ?'[9]   In the Hebrew Sirah[10]
we find the term שומר ישראל, which occurs also in the old
prayer beginning השכיבנו.[11]

שכינה (87)

' The Divine Presence.'   Landau[12] asserts that Shekhina
is the latest of God's names used in the last period before the
redaction of the Mishna.   Then he points out that R. Akiba,
who shows many variants in using God's names,[13] was
probably the first to apply it.   If our texts are reliable we
could trace it back to R. Gamaliel II, who said : אלא ללמדך
שאין בארץ מקום פנוי מן השכינה.[14]   R. Zadok, a contemporary

---

[8] b. Gittin, 7 A.   [9] j. Taan. 67 A.   [10] ch. 51. 12.

[11] v. Marmorstein, Jesus Sirach, 51. 12 ff. in ZAW. 29 (1909), p. 291.

[12] Synonyma für Gott, 48.

[13] Like המקום, אבינו שבשמים, גבוה, רחמנא, אבינו מלכנו, שמים and
מי שאמר והיה העולם.   The same can be proved in the cases of others,
e. g. R. Johanan b. Zakkai, or the Amoraic Haggadist, R. Aha, and many
more.

[14] Pes. B. 2 B, also Num. r. 14. 4 ; v. however, Midr. Ct. r. 3. 9 ; Exod. r.

of R. Gamaliel says: מצינו גדול מרבן גמליאל ומאברהם ששימש
את הבריות א'ל אי זה זה אמר להם שכינה שכל שעה מספיק מזון לכל
באי עולם כדי צרכן.[15]   R. Eleazar, of Modiim, speaks of proselytes: ואקרבם תחת כנפי השבינה.[16]   R. Ishmael, the opponent
of R. Akiba, uses the same term in the Halakha, which
would support the idea that Shekhina is a much older
term, if we can rely on the experience made with other
terms, e.g. שמים, or גבוה.[17]   The name is frequently put
together with נהנה מזיו, סלק, השרה, and זנו עיניהם.   It may be
that the people, after the destruction of the Temple, popu-
larized this name in order to indicate that in spite of the
loss of Temple and land, the divine presence was still in
Israel.   Its frequent occurrence in the Targumim is most
noticeable.   It is by no means impossible that the שבינה
stands in the Aramaic versions for מקום, both of which
point to the dwelling·place of God.   This would help to
throw light on the still unsettled, very important literary
problem as to the date of the various versions.   Here
again it is most noteworthy that the N. T. does not contain any reference to this name.[18]

שלום העולמים (88)

'The Peace of the Worlds.'   R. Berekhja interprets the
word שולמית (Cant. 7. 1) by ' אומה ששלום העולמים דר בתוכה a
nation in whose midst the peace of the worlds dwells.'[19]
In the Midrash, ed. Grünhut, p. 43 B, we read: ואומה מי
ששמו שלום דר בתוכה.   Ulla and other Babylonian scholars
also saw in שלום one of God's names.[20]   The name is based
on the peace-bringing and peace-making efforts of God.[21]

2. 9; R. Joshua b. Korha.   The former reading (R. Gamaliel) is given in
Mekh. R. S. b. J. 2.

[15] Mekh. 59 A; Siphre Deut. 38; b. Kid. 32 B.   [16] ib. 60 A.

[17] Sifra 1 B: קל וחומר לשבינה.

[18] v. Dalman, loc. cit., p. 187.

[19] Gen. r. 66. 3; Cant. r. 71; some read: אומה ששלום חי העולמים וכו.

[20] b. Shabb. 10 B.

[21] Pes. B. 2 B–3 A: המלך שהשלים מעשיו עם הבריות, and המלך שהוא
עושה שלום בבריותיו.

He reconciles the conflicts between and within His creatures.
The Tannaitic Midrash derives this name of God from
Judges 6. 24.[22]

(89) השם

'The Name.' R. Joshua b. Hananja says: הושע השם את
עמך ישראל.[23] R. Ishmael and R. Akiba speak of קידוש השם
without שם שמים[24]; R. Phinehas b. Jair of חלול השם.[25] In
some sources השם substitutes the older המקום or רחמנא.[26]

(90) שמים

'Heaven.'[27] Bousset is inclined to see in this name of God
another influence of Persian religion on Jewish theology,[28]
whilst Jewish scholars[29] thought of Greek prototypes.
The truth is with neither party. Most origins are dark
and obscure. Very seldom can one lift the veil of antiquity.
One thing is certain that the use of this name is earlier
than both Persian and Greek periods. 'The God of
Heavens and Earth' is known to all readers of the Bible.
In our period the name was used exclusively in a ritual
and legal sense. The Nazirite, who relates his story to
Simon the Just, offers a good example. He defeated his evil
inclination by sanctifying his beautiful hair to heaven.[30]
This lad was an ordinary shepherd from the South. He
did not believe in a transcendental God, who is far away
removed in Heaven. He felt His presence near in the
meadow, near the well, where his senses tempted him to
commit a sin. We find therefore in vows,[31] offerings to the

---

[22] Sifre Num., § 42 : ששמו של הקב׳ה נקרא, ed. Horowitz, p. 47 ; some
read המקום instead of הקב׳ה.

[23] M. Ber. 29 B.   [24] b. B. K. 113 A.   [25] ib.

[26] Midrash Agada, Ex. 177 : השם יעמידך למקומך לשלום, instead of
רחמנא ידבריגך לשלם, or המקום יפקדך לשלום.

[27] v. also רקיע, cf. b. Ber. 3 B : מי איכא ספיקא קמי רקיע.

[28] Die Religion des Judentums², Berlin, 1906, 359, n. 3.

[29] v. Jacob Brüll, מבוא המשנה, i. 14 ; v. also Pseudo-Hekataios, cf
Geffcken, loc. cit., p. xi and p. 19.

[30] Sifre Num., § 22, and Parall.

[31] b. Pes. 56 A ; Sifre Deut., § 306.

sanctuary,[32] oath,[33] and prayers [34] the name of Heaven mentioned. The examples, which were taken from daily life,
show that the name was really antiquated and belonged to
the language of cult or law.　Just as אלהים, or אלהי ישראל
after they were eliminated from daily conversation, were
retained on such occasions, so the name השמים. In legal
portions of the Halakha the terms מיתה בידי שמים or נקי בידי
שמים corroborate the same conception.[35] R. Akiba, who
uses one of these terms, knew that 'Heaven and Earth'
were regarded by some, especially by the Greeks, as deities,[36]
surely would have objected to the use of such a name. As
a matter of fact the more expressive 'Father in Heaven'
took the place of the older and shorter שמים. It is true
that Antigonos of Soko[37] still speaks of fear of Heaven
(מורא שמים), which phrase is repeated by others and changed
later in יראת שמים, yet he most probably meant, 'the fear of
the Father in Heaven'. In connexion with sanctifying or
profaning God's name, we find always מקדש שם שמים or חלול שם שמים
שם שמים. Thus in the sayings of Shimon b. Shetach,[38]
Abtaljon,[39] and many others.[40] The pious are spoken of as
devoting and performing all their actions, directing all their
thoughts and deeds לשם שמים.[41] The use of שם יהוה in the
Bible offers the best parallel to our case. In times when
the Tetragrammaton *alone*, for some reason or other, did
not satisfy all the longing, could not express all the

[32] Lam. r., p. 61 A.

[33] b. Ber. 53 B ; Sifre Deut., § 301, 354 ; Sotah, i. 31 ; *AbRN*. i. 38, 114.

[34] b. A. Z. 52 B ; Men. 59 A ; b. R. H. 55 A ; Pes. Buber, 6 B, and *DEZ.*,
ed. Tawrogi, p. 16.

[35] Sifre Deut., § 96 ; Torath Kohanim, 83 B ; A. R. N. 44 ; pal. Sotah,
i. 7 ; Meg. i. 6 ; v. also Chwolson, *Ssabier*, ii. 724.

[36] Gen. r. 1, ed. Theod., p. 12.

[37] Mekh. 53 B ; Aboth i. 3 ; iv. 12.

[38] B. Taanith, 23 A.　　　　　[39] Aboth i. 11.

[40] v. Pes. 57 A, Ker. 28 A : יששכר איש כפר ברקאי שמכבד את עצמו ומחלל
קדשי שמים ; v. J. Derenbourg, *Essai*, p. 233 ; B. M. K. 17 A ; R. Ilai : אם
רואה אדם שיצרו מתגבר עליו ילך וכו' ואל יתחלל שם שמים R. Simon
b. Johai, Gen. r. 1. 17 and Paralls., Mekh. 37 B.

[41] Tos. B. K. ch. 8 ; b. Taan. 23 A ; Sifre Deut., § 42 ; pal. Sotah, 9. 10.

religious thoughts, of men, because it might lead to mis-
understanding, then the Tetragrammaton had to be combined with שם. The same process took place when שמים
alone became too familiar among Jews and Gentiles alike,
and could not express without a prefixed שם the meaning
attached to it. Many instances show that שמים was used in
the sense of the other names, e. g. רומו של עולם, מעלה, גבוה,
e.g. in sayings מן השמים, or שמים 'coming from above',
'from High', and afterwards 'the Highest', as in the
saying of R. Simon b. Johai and others.[42]

תוקפיהון דישראל (91)

'The Strength of Israel.' R. Tanhum b. Hanilai translates אביר ישראל, Isa. 1. 24, by תוקפיהון דישראל. Targum has
תקיפא דישראל.[43] According to a legend the angels call God:
הא תקיף הא תקיף, הא אלהא.[44] A Boraita of Bar Kappara
translates: וכעצם השמים לטהר (Exod. 24. 10) by כתקיף שמיא.[45]

---

[42] v. b. A. Z., 18 A; Eccles. r. 1. 8, 9. 7; Sifre Num., § 78; b. Sabb.
157 B; b. Ber. 58 A; B. B. 91 B; Eccles. r. 11. 8.

[43] Pes. B. 123 A.   [44] Pes. B. 152 A; Lev. r. 29. 3.

[45] pal. Sukka, iv. 3; cf. Lev. r. 23. 8.

IV.

The Sources.

(1) The *Mishna* is the oldest post-biblical literary work
which we can consult for our investigation. As a halachic
compilation it does not offer as much material for the
treatment of our subject as we would desire, yet the little
we can glean from its pages is of decisive value and an
eloquent witness for the history of God's name in Judaism.
Here we find confirmed and proved, the first time, the
great and important development through which Judaism
passed during the first three centuries. The fact that the
name הקדוש ב'ה is so very rare in the original portions of
the Mishna, must give rise to serious reflection. We will
prove that in the original Tannaitic sayings the word הקב'ה
either does not occur at all, or, if it occurs it is a late
addition or alteration. We put our material chronologically to enable students to judge for themselves. The
importance of this theory for the distinction between
the earlier parts and the later Amoraic additions need not
be specially emphasized. The views about the oldest and
more recent parts of the Mishna are still fluctuating.
Certain portions can, with some certainty, be ascribed to
the periods prior to the destruction of the second Temple.
Our investigation will show how far these results can be
relied upon. Further, we gain by this method a standard
by which to test the genuineness of the oldest material
in the Mishna.

We start with *Antigonos, the man of Sokho.* He added
to his famous saying, which deals with man's relation to
his Maker, the very significant admonition, ' Let there be

the fear of Heaven upon you.'[1] Man should see in God
a master, who has to be served for His own sake, without
expecting a reward. Yet this lack of reward must not lead
to the abrogation of duties. The fear of Heaven (God)
should urge man to discharge his duties towards his Master.
Abtaljon enjoined his contemporaries to avoid the profanation of the name of Heaven.[2] The predecessor of Abtaljon,
Simon b. Shetach, uses the term המקום, and his contemporary,
Honi, the circle drawer, expresses the relation of God to
man in the form of a father to his son, which is shared
fully by Simon b. Shetach. The fatherhood of God seems to
both of them a well-established and known conception of
their theology.[3] *R. Johanan b. Zakkai* preached that Job
did not serve God from love, but fear. This teacher used
the term המקום.[4] *R. Joshua b. Hyrkanos* proved that Job
served המקום in love.[5] Another pupil of R. Johanan,
R. Joshua b. Hananya[6] concludes, after reviewing the sad
events which passed since the destruction of the Temple,
like *R. Eliezer b. Hyrkanos*, with the saying: 'We have
none to rely on besides our *Father in Heaven*' (אבינו
שבשמים).[7] In another prayer of R. Joshua we find: 'Help,
O God (השם).[8] *R. Gamaliel II* speaks of the Kingdom of
Heaven (מלכות שמים),[9] of המקום,[10] and אלוה,[11] when referring
to the character of the gods generally. *Akabja b. Mehalalel*,
who lived before the destruction of the second Temple,[12]
uses המקום and מלך מלכי המלכים הקב'ה. Yet the text is not
firmly established.[13] *R. Dosa b. Hyrkanos* speaks in a

---

[1] Aboth i. 3 : ויהי מורא שמים עליכם; A.R.N. i. 5 adds : כדי שיהיה
שכרכם כפול לעתיד לבא.

[2] Aboth i. 11 ; the passage is omitted in A. R. N.   [3] Taanith ii. 8.

[4] Sotah v. 5.   [5] Ib. v. 4.   [6] v. also ib. v. 5.

[7] Sotah ix. 20, 21.

[8] Originally the Tetragrammaton, Berakhoth iv. 4.

[9] Ber. ii. 5.   [10] Pes. x. 5 : שפסח המקום.

[11] Ab. Zar. iii. 4.   [12] Ed. v. 6.

[13] So Aboth iii. 1; Tanh. Gen. Buber, p. 120, shows clearly that the
original reading was בוראך זה הקב'ה; Tanh. reads : המקום ב'ה בוראך;
למקום שאתה עתיד ליתן דין וחשבון. The word למקום gives no sense.

prayer for the New Year's Day of אלהינו ה',[14] likewise
R. Akiba in a prayer, יי אלהינו [15]; otherwise this teacher uses
the term, 'Your Father in Heaven' אביכם שבשמים [16] and המקום.[17]
R. Eleazar b. Azarja has המקום [18] and שמים.[19]   R. Tarphon
likes to describe God as a בעל הבית and בעל מלאכה.[20]   God
is a landlord who urges the lazy workmen to finish their
work, for which they are paid very well.   Or, God is like
a trustworthy employer, who rewards those who work for
their master.   The same term and aspect is in R. Eleazar's
teaching.   He admonishes the diligent study of the Torah
in order to be able to reply to the Epicureans, and to be
perfectly aware, before whom one toils and who the
employer is, who will faithfully pay his reward.[21]   Hanina
b. Dosa [22] speaks of מקום.   The saying attributed to
R. Hananja b. Taradjon has הקב'ה.[23]   The first part of the
sentence ascribed to R. Hananja uses the term שכינה for God.
The later part of the Mishna is altogether suspicious.
A Geniza fragment has the reading: מנין אפילו אחד, שיושב
ושונה מעלה עליו הכתוב כאלו קים כל התורה כולה שנ' ישב בדד וידם
כי נטל עליו.[24]   We have here the third instance showing that
the term הקב'ה is a later insertion or addition.

The Mishna further furnishes us with some scanty
material as to the terms used by the great teachers after
the Bar-Kokhba period.   We have mentioned already once
R. Judah b. Ilai's version of the saying in the Temple on

Originally it was בוראך המקום, later on הקב'ה was put ; v. also pal.
Sotah, 18 A, where the sentence is quoted with the interpretation of
R. Levi : בוראך לפני מי שאתה עתיד ליתן דין וחשבון ; v. also Lev. r.
18. 1 ; Eccles. r. 12. 1 : בוראך זה מלך מלכי מלכים הקב'ה.   It is obvious
that the sentence was altered in the third century.

[14] Erubin iii. 9.   [15] Pes. x. 6.
[16] Yoma x. 9.   The continuation אף הקב'ה מטהר את ישראל is a later
gloss provided by some Amora of the third century for a purpose, namely
that the treatise should not conclude with the word את הטמאים.
[17] Aboth iii. 15.   [18] Yoma x. 9.
[19] Yadaim iv. 3.   [20] Aboth ii. 15, 16.
[21] Ib. ii. 14 ; v. also ch. vi. 4.   [22] Ib. iii. 11.   [23] Ib. iii. 2.
[24] A similar text was known to R. Joseph Ashkenazy ; v. מלאכת שלמה
in בית הבחירה, Wien, 1854, 15 A.

the Feast of the Water-drawing.[25] *R. Meir* has the terms
שכינה [26] and מקום.[27] In the first instance it is asserted
that God is grieved on account of the violent death
caused to the wicked: how much more when inflicted
upon the righteous. *R Simon b. Johai* speaks of מקום,[28]
but also of הקב'ה.[29] Similarly in the well-known saying
of *R. Hananja b. Akasja,* רצה הקב'ה לזכות את ישראל, the
term cannot be original, since edd. and MSS. preserved
the older form המקום. No doubt, owing to the liturgical use of the saying the newer form displaced the
older one.[30] R. Gamaliel, the son of R. Judah I, admonishes
those who are engaged in communal work, to work for the
name of Heaven (לשם שמים).[31] R. Jose, the priest said before
this teacher: 'All thy works shall be for the name of
Heaven' (לשם שמים).[32] This was a high degree of piety.
R. Johanan b. Baroka says: 'He who profanes (כל המחלל
שם שמים the name of Heaven privately will be punished
publicly.' As to the profanation of the Name there is no
difference between a presumptuous and an unconscious
action.[33] R. Johanan, the סנדלר, distinguishes between
gatherings לשם שמים and שלא לשם שמים,[34] and R. Eleazar b.
Shamua enjoins: 'Fear thy master, as thou fearest Heaven.[35]
Judah b. Tema speaks of God as 'thy Father in Heaven',
whose will has to be done with the strength of a leopard,
the lightness of an eagle, swiftness of a deer, and the force
of a lion.[36]

Finally we have to refer to the sayings of R. Joshua
b. Levi and R. Simon b. Halafta, who belong to the post-
Tannaitic period, which contain already the name of הקב'ה.[37]

[25] v. above, p. 31.   [26] Sanh. vi. 5.
[27] Ib., and Aboth vi. 6.   [28] Aboth ii. 13.
[29] Sanh. x. 6 ; v. however Sifre Deut., § 95, where אמר הקב'ה is *not to
be found.*
[30] Maccoth iii. 16.
[31] Aboth ii. 2.   [32] Aboth ii. 12.
[33] Aboth iv. 4.   [34] Aboth iv. 11.
[35] Aboth iv. 12.   [36] Aboth v. 20.
[37] Ukazin iii. 12.

This list, which may appear technical and not in the
least attractive, is very instructive indeed.   For we learn
that in the time of the Mishna the name הקדוש ברוך הוא was
not commonly used by the Tannaim.   It must have been
introduced for some reason or other in the generation
immediately after the redaction of the Mishna.   This can
be especially proved from the saying of R. Eleazar
ha-Kappar, who enumerates God's names and attributes.
In his words the names of God are: אל (God), יוצר (the
Former), בורא (the Creator), המבין (the Omniscient, cf. Ps.
33. 15), דיין (the Judge), עד (Witness), בעל דין (Accuser).[38]
The term הקב'ה is not given, although the sentence concludes with: לפני מלך מלכי המלכים הקב'ה.   It is quite likely that
הקב'ה stands here also for המקום.[39]   Our theory is corroborated by the sayings in the Mishna, which are cited
without the special names of their authors.   Ber. vi, reports
that the 'Early Hasidim' waited a short while before
starting their prayers in order 'to prepare their heart to
God' (כדי שיכוונו לבם למקום).[40]   Shek. iii. 2 we read: לפי שאדם
צריך לצאת ידי הבריות כדרך שצריך לצאת ידי המקום ;   Sotah. i. 6:
אתם באים בנצחוני and המקום גילה ;   Sanh. viii. 1: המקום נוולה
של מקום.   In one Mishna we have הקב'ה and המקום in one
and the same sentence: מי לנו גדול ממשה שלא נתעסק בו אלא
הקב'ה — אלא שכל הצדיקים שהמקום מאספן, yet Edd. and MSS.
read in both cases המקום.   We further notice very frequently
that when the name המקום occurs twice in a saying, the first
or the second was altered by the copyists in הקב'ה.   We
find further the term הקב'ה twice in Sanh. iv. 5.   The whole
passage contains a refutation of the Minim, who say that
there are two powers in Heaven: ולהגיד גדולתו של הקב'ה שאדם
טובע כמה מטבעות בחותם אחד, וכולן דומין זה לזה: ומלך מלכי
המלכים הקב'ה.   The passage is quoted in Seder Elijahu r.,

[38] Aboth iv. 22.

[39] According to A. R. N., 2 rec., ch. 34, the saying belongs to Eliezer, the
son of Eleazar ha-Kappar, who flourished in the days of Rabbi, when the
term became already known.

[40] v. Men. xiii. 11 : ובלבד שיכוון אדם את דעתו לשמים.

ch. i, ed. Friedmann, p. 10, with שנו חכמים במשנה, and reading in both cases ממ'ה הקב'ה. One is permitted to doubt
whether the whole of דבר אחר seems an integral part of the
Mishna. It is a later addition.[41] Similar is the case with
M. Ned. iii. 6. The last Mishna of this chapter is introduced
by דבר אחר and contains a sentence: שאילמלא היא לא ברא
הקב'ה. Here, again, we have a later addition to the Mishna.
Yet, while in the first case we are forced to work with
a hypothesis, here we have something to rely on. The
Palestinian Mishna [42] marks this Mishna as a later interpola-
tion by the word תוספה 'addition'. Most of the passages with
הקב'ה were met with in the Aboth, the text of which was
specially apt to be altered. We have here to refer to
passages in the sixth chapter, which are external Mishna-
joth, and, therefore, cannot upset our theory; rather do they
confirm it.[43]

Next to מקום the most usual term is שמים. It is used in
the term: עול מלכות שמים 'the yoke of the heavenly kingdom', or 'the yoke of Heaven', (עול שמים) [44] 'the Father in
Heaven',[45] especially with reference to vows and sanctification,[46] or punishment by Heaven.[47] In prayers,[48] in oaths,[49]
the Biblical names were used, אלהים and אלוה to signify

---

[41] Other instances of דבר אחר in the Mishna are Ber. ix. 5; v. Sifre
Deut., § 32, R. Jacob, Yalkut reads R. Akiba; v. Tosefta Sanh. viii. 5.

[42] מתניתא רבי מערבא, ed. W. H. Lowe, Cambridge, 1883, p. 85 B, l. 25.

[43] Aboth vi. 10: ג' קנינים קנה לו הקב'ה; v., further on, Mekh., p.
43 A, and vi. 11: כל מה שברא הקב'ה לכבודו בראו.

[44] Ber. ii. 2; v. R. Joshua b. Korha.

[45] Kel. iv. 8; v. R. Simon b. Eleazar; cf. Sifra, p. 78 B; M. R. H. iii. 9.
כל זמן שישראל מתכלין כלפי מעלה ומשעבדין את לבן לאביהן שבשמים,
twice, Sotah iv. 24; Sanh. vii. 10 read אבינו שבשמים instead of אלהינו
שבשמים?

[46] Ned. i. 4, once, שמים; v. ע'ז, then v. כהנים, iv. 3; v. ix. 3; Sheb.
iv. 13.

[47] Zeb. iv. 13; Judah ha Temani: כרת בידי שמים; Sanh. xi. 5: מיתתו
בידי שמים; v. בידי אדם.

[48] Ber. vii. 7.   [49] Sheb. iv. 13.

idols or gods.[50]   In many cases the noun השם substituted
the divine name.   Finally we find the old term קונה.[51]   We
are entitled to draw the deduction that המקום was the most
usual term in the period of the Tannaim.   The term
אב שבשמים 'Father in Heaven', enjoyed the same popularity. 'Heaven', שמים and 'High' גבוה, were already somewhat antiquated; הקב'ה not yet used.   We have, fortunately,
other Tannaitic sources which may prove or disprove our
contention. We turn, therefore, to the Tosefta, then to the
Tannaitic Midrashim, and finally to the fragments of
Tannaitic works preserved in the Babylonian and Palestinian Talmud.[51a]

(2) The second source at our disposal is the *Tosefta*.
This work contains more Haggadic material than our
Mishna, therefore, it offers more material for our investigation.   Yet, owing to the fact that the redaction of the
Tosefta must be put in the Amoraic period, the change of
the name המקום into הקב'ה is more clearly discerned than in
the Mishna. We will treat first the passages in which
הקב'ה occurs. They are:

(*a*) ii. 15 : שבשברא הקב'ה את האדם לא בראו ערום.   The
whole sentence introduced by the words אף על פי שאמרו is
an Amoraic tradition based on an older Tannaitic exposition
of Job 38. 9 by R. Eliezer b. Hyrkanos, R. Joshua b.
Hananja, and R. Akiba.   Nakedness was condemned by
the Rabbis.   Sifre Deut., § 320, might have been the
source of the Tosefta.   There we read : בלא עם אלו הבאים
מברבריייא ומטונס וממורטניא שמהלכין ערומים בשוק אין לך אדם בזוי
בשוק ערום המהלך אלא בעולם ופגום.[52]   Just as the Sifre singles
out those of Barbary, Tunis, and Mauretania as walking
naked on the market squares, so Philostratus of Tyre, in

---

[50] Ber. ix. 4, v. above, pp. 68–9; Yoma iii. 8, iv. 2, vi. 2 ; Sanh. vi. 4,
vii. 5.

[51] Hag. ii. 1 ; Kid. iv. 13 ; R. Simon b. Eleazar.

[51a] v. also A. Spanier, 'Die Gottesbezeichnungen המקום und הקדוש
ברוך הוא in der frühtalmudischen Literatur, in *MGWJ*. 66, 1922, pp. 309–
314.

[52] T. r. : אין שבחו של אדם להיות יושב ערום.

the Life of Apollonius of Tyana points to the wise men of
Ethiopia (Photius, Library, i. 37) and Hippolytus (Ref.
i. 21), to the Brahmans, who pass their life naked. The
Book of Jub. (i. 31) also enjoins that people should not
uncover themselves as the Gentiles do.[53] This passage of
the Sifre is quoted in the Babylonian Talmud, where we
read : במתניתא תנא אלו אלו אנשי ברבריא ואנשי מרטנאי שמהלכין ערומים
.בשוק שאין לך משוקץ ומתועב לפני המקום יותר ממי[54] We are entitled
to assume that המקום was the original rendering in our text
as well.

(b) Peah i. 4, we read : מחשבה טובה המקום מצרפה למעשה,
מחשבה רעה אין המקום מצרפה למעשה ' A good thought is considered by God as an accomplished action—good deed. A
bad thought, plan, is not regarded as an action'. The
teaching is based on Ps. 66. 18, ' If I regard iniquity in my
heart, the Lord will not hear me.' The teaching was,
however, objected to on account of Jer. 6. 19, ' Behold, I will
bring evil, the fruit of their *thoughts*', and amended thus :
' A good thought, which does good, God (המקום) considers as
a deed, but a thought which does no good, God (הקב'ה) does
not regard it as a deed '. Here we may assume that all the
four names were originally המקום, or that the alteration of
the doctrine is of Amoraic origin. The Tannaitic origin of
the teaching is confirmed by the Mekhilta[55] : ויעשו, וכי כבר
עשו אלא משקיבלו עליהם לעשות מעלה עליהם כאילו עשו. Old

---

[53] About nakedness in Jewish literature ; v. also M. Abba Gorion, 13 ;
Pirke R. El. ch. 49 ; Td. E. 93 B ; M. Ps. B. 523. In the rites of
various people, Weinhold, *Abhandlung. der Berl. Ak.*, 1896, 30, ZdVsfVK. 21,
1911, 305 ; Samter, *Geburt, Hochzeit und Tod.*, 109 f, ; W. A. Müller, *Nackt-
heit und Entblössung in altorient. u. altgr. Kunst. Diss.*, Leipzig, 1906 ; Fehrle,
E., *Kultische Keuschheit*, p. 11, and 62. 6 in the Lupercalia ARW. 1910,
491 ; Wensinck, *Some Semitic Rites*, p. 98.

[54] b. Jeb. 63 B ; Yalkut 945, v. מברברי ומבריטניא ; Pes. z. only, מברבריאה.
About the Barbarians in the Haggada, v. Gen. r. 75. 9 ; R. Hama b. Hanina ;
Gen. r. 23. 11 ; R. Hanina ; M. Zutta, p. 90 ; R. Judah ; Gen. r. 42. 4 ;
R. Samuel b. Nahmani, Esther r. 39 ; R. Levi ; Exod. r. 18. 6 ; Jel. Num.
7 A ; Midr. Abba Gorion, p. 20 ; M. Ps. 215 ; Pes. B. 48 A. Nearly all of
these references date back to the third century, when the Roman Empire
was trembling for fear of the Barbarians.

[55] p. 13 A.

H 2

witnesses read : והעלה עליהם המקום כאלו עשו.[56] The doctrine
is very often repeated,[57] and not without reason. Stoics
taught that sin consists in intention, and not in act.[58] The
Testaments teach that God takes account of intentions and
motives even for evil. Sins of the flesh can be committed
in thoughts.[59] The Pastor Hermas threatens also those
who sin in thought.[60] The earlier Tannaitic Haggada
opposed this view, yet the alteration agreed with the
teaching of the external literature. This dogmatic change
bears out our theory, that המקום represents the older, הקב׳ה
the younger stratum of the saying.

(c) Demai v. 18 : לפיכך הקב׳ה מביא עליהם שלש פורענות כנגד
שלש עבירות. Here the Palestinian Talmud, Demai vi. 2,
supplies us with the reading : המקום מביא עליהן ג׳ פורענות.

(d) Shabb. vii. 25. *R. Simon b. Gamaliel* praises the
Emorites : אין לך בבל העממין מתון יותר מן האמורי שכן האמינו
בהקב׳ה. ונלו לאפריקא ונתן להם המקום ארץ יפה כארצם. Here
again the Palestinian Talmud enables us to establish the
right text. Jer. Shebiit vi. 1, quotes a saying by
R. Samuel b. Nahmani, v. Tosafoth Gittin 46 A, *s. v.* ויביון,
where the sentence occurs : נירגשי פינה והאמין לו להקב׳ה והלך
לאפריקי. Therefore the original sentence of R. Simon b.

---

[56] Rashi, Yalkut.

[57] v. b. Ber. 6 A ; *R. Ashi* (v. R. Assi) : חשב אדם לעשות מצוה ונאנם
ולא עשאה מעלה עליו הכתוב כאילו עשאה ; b. Shabb. 63 A, the same, in
the name of R. Ami : מעלה עליו הכתוב ; b. Kid. 40 A ; R. Assi ; after
this our Boraita is quoted ; v. also p. 39 B : מחשבה רעה אין הקב׳ה מצרפה
מחשבה שעושה,with the alteration,which reads : למעשה שנ׳ און אם ראיתי
פרי הקב׳ה מצרפה למעשה מחשבה שאין בה פרי אין הקב׳ה מצרפה.
Jer. Peah., i. 1, the Boraita is quoted : מחשבה טובה המקום מצרפה למעשה
מחשבה רעה אין המקום מצרפה למ׳. It seems that our Tosefta is based
on the Pal. Talmud, using the commentary given thereon. R. Levi
expresses this view with reference to the sacrifice of Isaac, Gen. r. 55. 5 :
ביצחק אעפ׳י שלא נעשה מעשה קבלו בגומר מעשה ; v. Theodor, p. 588 ;
Ag. Ber., p. 51 : אין הק׳ דן אלא לפי המחשבות. On further developments of this thought v. *Midrash Haseroth*, London, 1917, p. 19, note 86.

[58] Seneca, *de Benef.* 5, 14, and 19 ; Ep. Mor. 95.

[59] Test. Iudah vii. 2 ; Joseph ix. 2 ; v. also Naph. ii. 9 ; Gad v. 3.

[60] i. 8 ; v. also Wisdom Sol. iii. 15.

Gamaliel read: אין לך בכל העממין מתון יותר מן האמורי ונתן להם
המקום ארץ יפה כארצם. Later copyists or teachers inserted
the words of R. Samuel b. Nahmani as a comment.

(e) Shek. i. 6: אף כך אמר הקב׳ה יתמשכנו ישראל על שקליהם
T. W. and T. A. read המקום. Similar evidence can be
brought forward from Edd. and MSS. for מקום instead of
הקב׳ה, being the original reading in Yoma ii. 5: אמרו לא
שלא יהו עושין כן לע׳ז; [61] further: ברא הקב׳ה את עולמו אלא לכבודו
כדרך שעושין להקב׳ה, Sotah iii. 7,[62] iii. 9, iii. 19, vii. 4, viii. 6,
x. 5.

(f) Yoma ii. 7, says Simon b. Loga to R. Akiba: אף
אמר לו על הכבוד. Pal. iii. 9 reads: שהקב׳ה עתיד לשמח את בניו
המתוקן לצדיקים לע׳ל, where the name is altogether omitted and
the whole sentence is put in a less anthropomorphic form.
Sotah vii. 4, we find in W. and T. A. the reading שבשהשביע
וכן מצינו שבשהשביע הקב׳ה את ישראל בערבות מואב instead of משה.
Sanh. viii. 9: זה מלך מלכי המלכים הקב׳ה שברא עולמו בשבועה,
yet Sanh. viii. 5 we find the form: למה נברא יחידי להגיד גדולתו
של מלך מלכי המלכים ברוך הוא, v. Mishna Sanh. iv. 5. The
original form was מלך מלכי המלכים 'the King of kings',
which was later on supplemented by הקב׳ה.

(g) Erakhin i. 10: אמר להן הקב׳ה לענני כבוד רצו טל לפני בני
והקב׳ה מרביץ לפניהם טללים .... Comparing the sentence in
the Tosefta with R. Joshua b. Levi's saying in the T. and
M. we are justified in seeing in the same a teaching of this
Amora, or an older sentence reshaped by the teacher of the
third century.[63]

We must bear in mind a few facts resulting out of this
material. That most of these instances belong to the
anonymous Haggadah, and even here we were able to show
the original reading מקום. Where this proof could not be
established, we have furnished proofs for the later date, the
post-Tannaitic origin of the doctrines. The well-known
Tannaim use the older names for God, e.g. מקום or שמים.

---

[61] v. above, M. Aboth vi. 11, and Marmorstein, *The Doctrine of Merits*,
p. 115 f.
[62] v. Mekh. 35 B. [63] v. Shabb. 88 B; Mekh. 71 B.

The former is to be met with in the majority of sayings
and sentences : R. Johanan b. Zakkai,[64] his pupils,
R. Eliezer ben Hyrkanos,[65] and R. Joshua b. Hananja.[66]
R. Akiba considers every one favoured by God (המקום),
who is popular with man.[67] R. Ishmael derives the law
that the books of the heretics may not be saved from fire
on Sabbath by a comparison with the law of the suspected
woman. In the latter God (המקום) commands the blotting
out of His name, in order to make peace between husband
and wife; how much more in this case! These books throw
enmity, jealousy, and strife between Israel and their
Father in Heaven.[68] Ben Azzai says : אין שכחה לפני המקום.[69]
'There is no forgetfulness before God.' R. Meir,[70] R. Jose
b. Halafta,[71] R. Simon b. Johai,[72] R. Menahem b. Jose,[73]
and R. Simon b. Eleazar[74] use the same term.[75] The
anonymous Haggada in the Tosefta uses throughout המקום.[76]

[64] B. K. vii. 10 : בוא וראה כמה חם המקום על כבוד הבריות.
[65] Yoma iv. 17 : כך יהיו איבי המקום ; Sanh. xiv. 3 : אלא כך אמר
המקום הריני נותן אותם לרחמים ומטיל אהבתי בלבם.
[66] Sanh. xiii. 6 : שאין המקום מניח להן מצוה.
[67] Ber. iii. 4 : כל שרוח הבריות נוחה הימנו רוח המקום נוחה הימנו אבל כל
שאין וכו' ; v. Aboth iii. 10, attributed to R. Haninah b. Dosa, missing
A. N., ch. 29 ; v. above, p. 110 ; Ed. i. 14 : אע'פ שהימים והלילות כחוט
השערה לפני המקום.
[68] Shabb. 13. 5.   [69] Yoma ii. 7.
[70] Sanh. viii. 6 : שינה המקום מראה פנים דעת וקול : Men. vii. 9 :
בזמן שישראל ברצון לפני המקום כבנים שמתפרנסים מאביהם.
[71] Sotah vii. 1.
[72] Sanh. xiv. 4.   [73] Sanh. xiii. 6.
[74] Sanh. xiv. 10 : כשם ששמחה לפני המקום בקיומן של צדיקים כך
שמחה לפני המקום באבדן של רשעים ; Sotah vi. 7.
[75] Other instances : Hasid, Peah iii. 8 : כל מצוה שבתורה נתן לנו המקום
אונדם ; לדעתינו זו שלא לדעתינו שאילו עשינו ברצון לפני המקום
ben Levi, Yoma ii. 8 ; Hasid, Taan. iii : אבל בטוחין אנו שאין המקום מביא
מבול לעולם ; R. Eleazar, the son of R. Jose, the Galilean ; Sanh. i. 2 ;
R. Eleazar, Sotah ii. 3.
[76] Ber. iii. 77 : וקידש שמו של מקום ; iv. 16 : שאין נבהות לפני המקום ;
iii. 16 : סומא ומי שאין יכול לכוין את הרוחות מכונין לבם לפני המקום ;
T. W. reads instead of המקום = שבשמים אביהן ; T. B. : אביו שבשמים ;

We have to enumerate here, also, the terms which contain
the ideas of God's kingship, as expressed by Rabbi
(Ber. ii. 1), corresponding to R. Joshua b. Korha's 'Kingdom of Heaven'. The 'Fatherhood of God' is to be found
several times in the sayings of R. Johanan b. Zakkai [77]
and R. Eleazar b. Jose.[78] The use of שמים is in the Tosefta
similar to that in the Mishna.[79] In prayers the Biblical
names of God, יי אלהינו, are repeated.[80] Speaking of strange
deities אלוה is used.[81]

We observe that some of the Psalms and the majority

Pal. למעלן. We saw above, p. 112, that כיון לבו occurs with מקום as well
as with שמים. Yoma ii. 7 : כדרך שעושין לפני המקום ; R. H. ii. 3 :
ללמדך שבית דינו של ירובעל גדול לפני המקום כב'ד של משה ; Sotah,
iii. 9, 12, 13, 14, 18 ; v. 12 ; x. 3, 4, 5 ; Kid. v. 17, 21 ; B. K. vii. 7 ; A. Z.
iv. 5 ; Men. xiii. 22.

[77] Hag. ii. 10 : בכבוד אבינו שבשמים (twice) ; B. K. vii. 6 ; v. also vii. 7 ;
v. also R. Ishmael, above, to Shabb. xiii. 5 ; R. Eliezer b. Hyrkanos,
Hullin, ii. 24.

[78] Peah iv. 20 : מנין שהצדקה וגמילות חסדים פרקליט גדול ושלום בין
ישר' לאביהם שבשמים.

[79] R. Akiba, Shek. ii. 1 : הטוב בעיני שמים והישר בעיני האדם ; Yoma
ii. 8 : שנתחלל שם ; v. 8 : הם ביקשו להרבות כבודם ולמעט כבוד שמים ;
שמים ; Sotah v. 12 : שם שמים נתחלל and השמים ביני לביניך ; v. also
vi. 7, xiv. 4 : עול מלכות שמים, v. ופרקו מהם עול שמים ; B. K. vi. 16,
ix. 31 : דינו מסור לשמים ; B. K. vii. 5 ; R. Johanan b. Zakkai, like
Sotah xiv. 4 ; B. K. viii. 13 : אמרו עליו על ר' יהודה בן בבא שהיו כל
אין מן השמים מוחלין, v. above, p. 111 ; Sheb. iii. 1–3 : מעשיו לשם שמים ;
כך כל המכנים בריה בריה אחת תחת כנפי השמים ; Kor. ii. 7 ; לו עד שישלמו ;
Nid. v. 16 : הקדיש קרדום אחד לשמים.

[80] For instance Ber. iii. 5 : אחרים אומרים צורכי עמך מרובים ודעתן
קצרה יהי רצון מלפניך יי אלהינו שתתן לכל אחד ואחד וכו' ; ib., R. Eleazar
b. Zadok, in the name of his father : מאהבתך יי אלהינו שאהבת את ישראל
עמך . . . . . נתת לנו יי אלהינו את יום השביעי הגדול וכו' ; ib. vii. 2 :
יהי רצון מלפניך יי אלהינו שתיעקר עבודה זרה ; ib. vii. 16 f., Ben Azzai :
מודה אני לפניך יי אלהי and יהי רצון מלפניך יי אלהינו.

[81] Ab. Zara v. 6 : את שנוהג לשום אלוה אסור ואת שאינו נוהג בו לשום
כל זמן שאתם בארץ כנען הריני לכם לאלוה, באין אתם ; iv. 4 : אלוה מותר
בארץ כנען כביכול איני לכם לאלוה.

of the Apocryphal writings give some preference to the name עליון 'the Highest', 'Most High'. The Tosefta preserves the same as גבוה, in opposition to הדיוט, or uses the word עליון itself. The first is to be found[82] in a dispute between the Schools of Shammai and Hillel. The latter in a saying of R. Johanan b. Zakkai,[83] where the name קונה, again a very old term, is also mentioned.[84] Other names, either familiar to us from the Mishna or new ones, are: מי שאמר והיה העולם (4), דיין (3), בעל הבית (2), בורא (1), שכינה (9), הקודש (8), רוח הקודש (7), רחמן (6), יודע מחשבות (5) and (10) השם. The first one, בורא, 'the Creator', is referred to in the dialogue between the philosopher and R. Reuben, in Tiberias, where the latter says: זה הכופר במי שבראו,[85] and Sotah vii. 12: אל אחד בראן 'one God created them all'. The second, בעל הבית, is known from the Mishna; here it is derived from a saying of Ben Zoma.[86] The third is used by R. Eliezer b. Hyrkanos and R. Meir.[87] The fourth by Simeon b. Shetach.[88] The fifth by R. Meir[89] and R. Jose b. Halafta.[90] קודש, Taan. ii. 10, occurs only once in the saying: מפי הקודש אני עולה. This term is unique in the Tosefta, and will be discussed in connexion with the parallels in the Tannaitic Midrash. רוח הקודש stands sometimes for God, likewise שכינה and השם. The name רחמן 'All-Merciful', is mentioned by R. Judah b. Ilai in the name of R. Gamaliel II: 'When thou art merciful, the All-Merciful will be merciful to thee' (B. K. viii. 13). B. Shabb. 151 B, quotes this saying by R. Gamaliel b. Rabbi כל המרחם על הבריות מרחמין עליו מן השמים, שאינו מרחם על הבריות אין מרחמין עליו מן השמים. The same saying is mentioned in Sifre Deut., § 96: כל זמן שאתה מרחם על הבריות מרחמים עליך מן השמים. Midr. Tannaim, 69, does not supply the teacher's name, and reads: אם ריחמת מרחמין עליך ואם לאו אין מרחמין עליך.[91]

[82] Hag. ii. 10 ; Erakhin iv. 32 ; R. Judah b. Batyra.
[83] B. K. vii. 2.
[84] v. also Ber. vi. 1 : אלא בכבוד קונהו.
[85] Sheb. iii. 6.   [86] Ber. vii. 2.
[87] Hullin ii. 24, and Ber. vii. 1.   [88] Sanh. viii. 3.
[89] B. K. vii. 10.   [90] B. M. vi. 17.
[91] v. also Fragment, ed. Schechter, JQR., 1904, p. 699 ; M. T., p. 41.

The Tosefta is a faithful witness that המקום was the name used by the Tannaim ; הקב׳ה is a later substitute for המקום, or of Amoraic origin altogether. Half-a-dozen or so passages with הקב׳ה have been dealt with above, and it was shown that parallels offer instead of this name המקום, or that some can be classified with the Haggada of the Amoraim. If the latter found a place in the Mishna, no wonder that the same happened in the Tosefta. On the whole, however, the old tradition that these works, Mishna and Tosefta, were (apart from minor glosses) editorially finished in the period of the Tannaim, is well established. The final redaction might have taken place in the School of R. Joshua b. Levi, who, as we saw, was closely connected with the problem of pronouncing the name of God and the alteration of המקום into הקב׳ה.

(3) Our third source is the Mekhilta on Exodus. Two books with the title of Mekhilta are now in our hands. One belongs to the School of R. Ishmael, the other to that of R. Akiba. Although we are able to establish many theological differences between the two schools, we have no traces of different treatment accorded to the divine names in these schools. To a large extent both Mekhiltas cover the same ground, therefore enable us to verify the proper readings. We find that in most of the passages of our text of the Mekhilta, where הקב׳ה occurs, parallel passages, or Mekhilta of Rabbi Simon b. Johai, preserve the reading מי שאמר והיה העולם or המקום. It confirms the result we gained from the previous sources, Mishna and Tosefta, that הקב׳ה was not known as a name of God to the teachers of the Tannaitic period. The Mekhilta offers, owing to its wealth of Haggada, more material for our observations. We propose to give an account of it by grouping first of all the passages containing the name אב שבשמים, expressing ' the Fatherhood of God '. Secondly, the terms שמים ' Heaven ', מי שאמר והיה העולם ' the Creator ', גבורה ' All-Powerful ', מקום and הקב׳ה.

In the Mekhilta the term אב שבשמים is found five times.

P. 3 A : ‏אחת לל' יום מגביהים עיניהם לאביהם שבשמים‎. The Talmud
quotes a similar passage as ‏תנא דבי ר' ישמעאל‎,[92] saying : ‏אלמלא‎
‏זכו ישראל אלא להקביל פני אביהן שבשמים כל חדש וחדש דיים‎.
P. 45 B : ‏אחרים אומרים היו ישראל מתחננים ומתפללין לפני אביהם‎
‏שבשמים כבן שהוא מתחנן לפני אביו וכתלמיד שמתגדר לפני רבו כך‎
‏היו ישראל מתחננין ומתגדרים לפני אביהן שבשמים ואומרים לפניו רבש'ע‎
‏חטאנו לפניך‎. In the Mekh. of R. S. b. J.[93] the passage reads :
‏באותה שעה היו ישראל מתחננים ומתגרים לפני אביהם שבשמים כבן‎
‏שמתחטא לפני אביו כתלמיד שמתחגרה לפני רבו אמרו לפניו רבש'ע‎
‏חטאנו שנתרעמנו אל המים‎. A Geniza fragment[94] preserved
also the reading ‏מתחטים‎ instead of ‏מתחנגים‎.[95] The phrase is
similar to that used in the story of Honi.[96] P. 56 A,
R. Joshua b. Hananja says : ‏כשבא עמלק להזיק את ישראל מתחת‎
‏כנפי אביהם שבשמים אמר משה לפני הקב'ה רבש'ע רשע זה בא לאבד‎
‏בניך מתחת כנפיך‎. In the M. R. S. b. J.[97] this saying is in the
name of R. Eleazar of Modiim in a more original form :
‏לפי שבא לאבד את ישראל מתחת כנפי השמים אמר משה לפני המקום‎
‏רבש'ע רשע זה בא לאבד את בניך מתחת השמים ס'ת שנתת להן מי‎
‏יקרא בו‎. This text proves, for which we have many other
witnesses, that ‏שמים‎ is an abbreviated form for ‏אביהם‎
‏שבשמים‎. The older term ‏המקום‎ was changed into the newer
form ‏הקב'ה‎. P. 68 B, R. Nathan depicts the persecutions
the Jews suffered in his age. Jews were burnt for reading
in the Torah, crucified for eating the Passover bread,
punished with one hundred strokes for taking the Lulab,
and concludes : ‏מכות אלו גרמו לי ליאהב לאבי שבשמים‎. Another
source[98] has besides : ‏שעשיתי רצון אבי שבשמים‎. The same
version is preserved in the Midrash on Psalms : ‏על שעשיתי‎

<hr />

[92] b. Sanh. 42 A.   [93] p. 72.
[94] MS. Adler.   [95] v. p. 56 for the explanation.
[96] v. b. Taanith, iii. 8, and above, p. 56, note 6. Fr. reads ‏מתגדר‎ ;
Yalk. ‏מתגרר‎ ; H. ‏מתנרה‎.
[97] p. 84. About the terms ‏לוקה באפרגל‎, ‏ליצלב‎, and ‏לישרף‎ v. S. Krauss.
in ‏הדביר‎, i. 5683. pp. 112, 107.
[98] Lev. r. 32. 1. Here the saying is by R. Nehemia, a contemporary of
R. Nathan. Here the sins of the martyrs are the observance of Sabbath,
eating the Mazzah, taking the Lulab, observing the laws of Tephillin and
Zizith.

‏רצון אבי שבשמים‎.⁹⁹ P. 74 A, *R. Johanan b. Zakkai* says:
‏ומה אם אבני מזבח שאינם לא רואות ולא שומעות ולא מדברות‎
‏על שמטילות שלום בין ישראל לאביהם שבשמים אמר הקב'ה אל תניף‎
‏עליהם ברזל וכו'‎. M. R. S. b. J.¹⁰⁰ reads ‏שמטילות כפרה‎ instead of
‏שמטילות שלום‎. Here we have another proof for the fact
that the original ‏המקום‎ was removed for the later ‏הקב'ה‎.
The Tosefta¹ reads: ‏אבנים שמטילות שלום בין ישראל לאביהם שבש'‎
‏על אכו'כ שיהיו שלמים לפני המקום‎, and ends ‏אמר המקום וכו'‎. The
same sentence which occurs in the Mekhilta is repeated in
the Sifra,² where we also read ‏אמר הכתוב‎ instead of ‏אמר‎
‏הקב'ה‎.

More frequent is the use of ‏שמים‎ for God. P. 7 B: ‏פסח‎
‏לשם המיוחד‎.³ ‏הוא ליי שיהו כל מעשיהם לשם שמים‎. Sifre reads
P. 53 B we read ‏מורא רבך כמורא שמים‎; here surely ‏אביך שבש'‎
has to be added. The teaching is given in another place⁴
in the name of R. Eleazar b. Shamua, and quoted in the
Palestinian Talmud as a Mishna.⁵ The Didachê⁶ borrowed
this teaching from the Rabbis, substituting Lord for ‏שמים‎.
It says: τιμήσεις δὲ αὐτὸν ὡς κύριον. P. 57 A: One of
Jethro's names was ‏קנ‎ because ‏שקנא לשמים וקנה לו תורה‎.
Mekh. of R. S. b. J., reads ‏שקנה העולם הבא‎.⁷ Our explanation
attributed in Sifre to R. Jose b. Halafta. The reading is
is somewhat different. P. 58 B: ‏אינו בא אלא לשום שמים‎, 'for the
name of Heaven.'⁸ R. Eleazar of Modiim uses the phrase

---

⁹⁹ M. Ps. 12. 5, ed. Buber, p. 108. The reading differs from that oᵣ
Lev. r. ‏שבש'‎. ‏מה לך לוקה בפרוגין על שעשיתי רצון אבי שבש'‎. There is missing a whole sentence. Read ‏מה לך לוקה בפרגל על שעשיתי סוכה וכו' על‎
‏שעשיתי רצון אבא שבשמים‎. All sources conclude with the words of
R. Nathan in the Mekhilta.

¹⁰⁰ p. 116. The conclusion reads ‏בני תורה שהן כפרה לעולם על אכו'כ‎.
The term ‏בן תורה‎ is younger than ‏תלמיד חכם‎.

¹ B. K. vii. 7, ed. Zuckermandl, p. 358, l. 16, v. above, p. 118.
² 84 A; v. also Semahoth, ch. viii, r.: ‏יהיו שלמים לפני הקב'ה‎.
³ Deut., § 128; v. above, p. 111, note 31; Aboth ii. 12; Tos. Bk. xiv. 4.
⁴ Aboth iv. 12, v. above, p. 111.
⁵ Ned. 41 B; v. also Exod. r. 3. 22.
⁶ ch. iv, ed. Lietzmann, Bonn, 1907, p. 6.   ⁷ p. 86.
⁸ Num., § 78. The text reads: ‏שקנה שמים וארץ‎, v. MS. ‏שקנה את‎
‏השמים‎. On the names of Jethro, v. Exod. r. 27. 7 (seven names); Pirke

in his saying: 'God says: [9] אני הוא שאמרתי אני המקרב ולא
המרחק שנ' האלי מקרוב אני נאם ה' ולא אלי מרחק אני שקרבתי את
יתרו ולא רחקתיו אף אתה כשבא אדם אצלך להתגייר אינו בא אלא
להכנים תחת = לשם שמים. Mekh. R. S. 67 reads for לשם שמים
כנפי השכינה.[10] P. 61 B, R. Johanan b. Zakkai said, when
he went to Meon Jehuda and saw a girl gathering barley
under the hoofs of a horse: לא רציתם להשתעבד לשמים הרי אתם
משתעבדים לפני גוים, לא רציתם לשקול בקע לגולגולת הראיתם שוקלים
ט'ו שקלים במלכות אויביכם. Here לשמים has to be supplemented
with מלכות, i.e. 'the Kingdom of Heaven'. P. 92 B,
R. Akiba speaks of מיתה בידי שמים and בידי־אדם. The same
terms occur 101 B: מה שמחה אמורה באדם בדבר הראויה לבא בידי
אדם אף שמחה אמורה בשלמים דבר הראוי לבא בידי שמים.

The *third* term very frequently used in the Mekhilta is:
מי שאמר והיה העולם 'He who spake, and the world was
created'. We find the same about eighteen times, P. 12 A:
והלא אבות ונביאים שהלכו לעשות רצונו של מי שאמר והיה העולם נהגו
בדרך ארץ. P. 33 A, R. Akiba says to Pappajus: אין להשיב
על דברי מי שאמר והיה העולם אלא־דן הכל באמת והכל בדין. Mekh.
R. S. b. J.[11] reads the sentence: שלא להשיב על דברי מי שאמר
והיה העולם שהכל בדין והכל באומר. P. 33 B: 'Great is the faith
which Israel believed in' מי שאמר והיה העולם. M. R. S. b. J.
reads: גדולה אמנה לפני מי שאמר והיה העולם.[12] Ib., 'He who
believes in the faithful shepherd is as if he believed in
מי שאמר והיה העולם. He who speaks against the faithful
shepherd is as if he spoke against מי שאמר והיה העולם.[13]
P. 35 A: אבל מי שאמר והיה העולם אינו כן אלא כל מה שמקלסין

R. ha Kadosh, ed. Grünhut, 7. 7; v. also B. Königsberger, in Rahmer's
Jüd. Literaturblatt, xxiii, 1892, pp. 201 ff., 204 ff.

[9] This is a variation of the name מי שעשה את העולם, v. further on
p. 135.

[10] p. 87; v. also Sifre Deut., § 305, where the name of the girl's father
is given as Nakdimon b. Gorion. The teaching is different. It contains
the well-known antithesis . . . . כל זמן שישראל עושין רצונו של מקום
וכשאין ישראל עושין רצונו של מקום. The story is also related Midr.
Lam., ed. Buber, p. 86, differently; v. also Tos. Ket. chaps. 5, 6; Ket.
66 B; Pal. Ket. 5, 11; Ab. R. N. ch. 17.

[11] p. 54; v. also the parallel, Cant. r. 1. 9.

[12] p. 54; v. Marmorstein, *The Doctrine of Merits*, p. 175 f.

[13] M. R. S. b. J., p. 54; Num. r. 19.

אותו הוא יותר מקילוסו[14] ' An earthly king is praised. They flatter him with his strength, wisdom, wealth, goodness, justice, and faithfulness; in fact, he is weak, foolish, poor, cruel, unjust, and untrustworthy'. God (מי שאמר וה' הע') cannot be duly praised. No praise comes anywhere near to His real attributes. His wisdom (Prov. 3. 19 and Job 12, 13), wealth (Deut. 10. 14, Hag. 2. 8), lovingkindness (Exod. 34. 6, Deut. 4. 31), justice (Isa. 30. 18, Ps. 82. 1), trustworthiness (Deut. 7. 9, cp. 32. 4), beauty (Ps. 89. 6, 89. 9, 86. 8, Cant. 1. 10), and power (1 Chron. 29. 11). The Mekh. enumerates God's attributes differently: power (Deut. 10. 17, Ps. 24. 8, Isa. 42. 13, and Jer. 10. 6), wealth (Deut. 10. 14, Ps. 24. 1, 95. 8, Hag. 2. 8, Ezek. 18. 4), wisdom (Prov. 2. 6, Dan. 2. 21, Jer. 10. 7), loving-kindness (Exod. 34. 6, Deut. 4. 31, Ps. 25. 6, 145. 9, Dan. 9.9), justice (Deut. 1. 17 and 32. 4, Ps. 82. 1), trust (Deut. 7. 9). P. 37 B : שהרי מי שאמר והיה העולם עתיד להלחם בהם. P. 38 A : אבל מי שאמר והיה העולם אינו כן אלא אני יי לא שניתי[15]. Here again we have a long list of God's attributes compared to the character of an earthly king. God's power,[16]

---

[14] M. R. S. b. J., p. 57. Tanh., f. 82, alters מי שאמר והיה העולם into הקב'ה. The attributes are given there in the following order : might, wealth, wisdom, mercy, justice, and trust, like Mekh.

[15] Also M. R. S. b. J. 61.

[16]

Mekh.	M. R. S. b. J.
יש גבור במדינה ועליו כל כלי זיין אבל אין לו כח ולא גבורה ולא תכסים ולא מלחמה אבל הק' אינו כן יש לו כח וגבורה ותכסים ומלחמה.	Missing.

The second sentence, dealing with the same attribute in a different aspect, is preserved in both sources.

Mekh.	M. R. S. b. J.
יש גבור במדינה וכחו עליו בן מ' שנה אינו דומה לבן ס', ולא בן ס' לבן ע' אלא כל שהוא הולך כחו מתמעט אבל מי ש' וה' הע' אינו כן אלא אני יי לא שניתי.	יש גבור עומד במלחמה וכחו עליו כבן מ' שנה אבל אין דומה לבן ס' או לבן ע'.

God's strength is unchangeable.

love,[17] lovingkindness,[18] omnipresence,[19] is described, and he
is the sustainer of the whole world.[20] The edition of the
Mekh. reads הקב׳ה in two instances where the M. R. S. b. J.
has מי שאמר והיה העולם. We may assume that the original
had in all the five instances the name מי שאמר, and not הקב׳ה.
P. 70 A, Rabbi says : חביב כבוד אב ואם לפני מי שאמר והיה העולם
ששקל כבודן ומוראן לכבודו ולמוראו. M. R. S. b. J. (p. 110) has a
similar saying in the name of R. Simon b. Johai : גדול כבוד
אב ואם שהשוה הקב׳ה כבודן לכבודו ומוראן למוראו. Ib., R. Eliezer
ben Hyrkanos says : גלוי וידוע לפני מי שאמר והיה העולם שאדם
מכבד אמו יותר מאביו וכו׳ וגלוי וידוע לפני מי שאמר והיה העולם שאדם

[17] Mekh.	M. R. S. b. J. 62.
יש גבור במדינה שמשקנאה וגבורה	יש גבור עומד ומשקנאה וגבורה
לובשתו אפי׳ אביו ואפילו אמו ואפילו	לובשתו אפילו אביו ואפילו אחיו
קרובו הכל מכה בחימה והולך לו,	ואפי׳ קרוביו אינו מבחין אלא מכה
אבל הקב׳ה אינו כן יי איש מלחמה	והוליד בחמה, אבל מי שאמר והיה
שהוא נלחם במצרים שהוא מרחם על	העולם אינו כן הוא עושה מלחמה
בריותיו.	וא׳ע׳פי כן ה׳ שמו רחמן הוא על כל
	בריותיו.

God's love is shown even in battle and punishment.

[18] Mekh.	M. R. S. b. J.
יש גבור במדינה בשעה שהחצי	יש גבור וכו׳ ומשחין יוצא מידו אין
יוצא מידו לא יכול להתגרה אליו	יכול להתגרו אבל מי שאמר והיה
אבל הקב׳ה כשאין ישראל עושין	העולם אינו כן אלא כשאין ישראל
רצונו כביכול גזרה יוצאה מלפניו	עושין רצונו של מקום גזרה יוצאה
עשו תשובה מיד הוא מחזירה.	מלפניו, עשו תשובה הרי הוא
	מחזירה.

[19] This point is not in the M. R. S. b. J. in the present edition. Mekh.
reads : מלך בשו׳ד יוצא למלחמה ומחנות קרובות באות ושואלות צרכיהן
מלפניו אומר להן זעוף הוא למלחמה הוא יוצא לכשינצח וישוב באין אתם
ושואלין צרכיכם מלפניו אבל הקב׳ה אינו כן שהוא נלחם במצרים שהוא
שומע צעקת כל באי העולם.
[20] Mekh. : מלך בו׳ד עומד במלחמה אינו יכול לזון ולא לספק אבסניות
לכל חיילותיו והקב׳ה אינו כן אלא שהוא ילחם במצרים שהוא זן ומפרנס
לכל באי העולם ;P. 43 B : חביב בית המקדש לפני מי שאמר והיה העולם
likewise M. R. S. b. J. 70 ; v. however M., p. 44 A : חביב בהמ׳ק לפני הקב׳ה
מי שאמר והיה העולם M. R. S. b. J. has again שכשברא הקב׳ה.

מגיד הכתוב שבל מי שמחלל את P. 70 B: .מתיירא מאביו יותר מאמו
השבת מעיד לפני מי שאמר והיה העולם שלא ברא עולמו לששה ימים ולא
נח בשביעי וכל מי שמשמר את השבת מעיד לפני מי שאמר והיה העולם
בשביעי; v. also p. 104 A. P. 72 B, שברא עולמו לששה ימים ונח
Rabbi: 'קל וחומר לכבודו של מי ש' ו' ה. P. 87 A, R. Ishmael:
בא וראה רחמיו של מי שאמר והיה העולם על בשר ודם שאדם קונה
את עצמו בממון מידי שמים. P. 95 B, R. Akiba said, when
R. Ishmael and R. Simon were put to death by the Romans:
גלוי וידוע לפני מי שאמר והיה העולם שפורענות גדולה עתידה לבא
בדורינו וסילק אלו מבינותינו. The same term is given in other
reports of the same event as well.[21]

The fourth name we find in the Mekhilta is גבורה, P. 26 A:
לא נסעו אלא על P. 44 B: .מפי הגבורה נאמר לי שאתם בני חורין
פי משה ושאר כל המסעות כולן נסעו על פי הגבורה. R. Eliezer says:
לא נפנו על פי הגבורה נסעו. P. 48 A, R. Joshua b. Hananja:
למדנו שהמלחמה הזאת. P. 54 B, R. Eliezer: עד שנתגלתה גבורה
צא והמלך בגבורה. P. 59 B: לא היתה אלא על פי הגבורה P. 60 A,
the same. P. 66 A: מנין שהיה משיב דברים לפני הגבורה. P. 71 A,
R. Akiba: ואין דבר שלא יצא מפי הגבורה ונחצב על הלוחות.

Special attention has to be paid to the fifth and sixth
name of God in this Midrash. We mean the terms מקום and
הקב׳ה. The first is to be found about one hundred times.
Yet by comparing some of the passages which have הקב׳ה
with other texts, we observe that מקום was displaced by the
more usual הקב׳ה. Or, in some instances, the sentences with
הקב׳ה are of a later period, as we saw similar cases in the
previous Tannaitic sources. The Mekhilta offers a special
object lesson in this respect.

We give first the list of those passages where Mekh. has
וכן אתה מוצא בברוך בן נריה שהיה מתרעם לפני (1) P. 2 B: המקום
המקום; (2) ib.: בא וראה מה המקום משיבו; (3) ib., R. Akiba:
מצינו שמותיהן של צדיקים P. 19 A: (4) והראה המקום את כולן באצבע
על כן נתן להם P. 23 B: (5); ומעשיהם גלויים למקום עד שלא נוצרו
המקום קבורה P. 24 B: (6); והמקום עכב לה במדבר P. 25 A: (7):
באותה P. 28 B: (8); כשהמקום פורע מן האומות שמו מתגדל בעולם
אמר P. 30 A: (9); שעה הראה להם המקום תורמיות תורמיות של מה׳ש

21 v. Semahoth, ch. viii.

(10) P. 30 B (five times): ; המקום למשה, משה בני נתונים בצרה

מיד אמר המקום למשה ידידי טובעים בים והים סוגר :P. 31 B (11) ; וכן אתה מוצא שלא נפרע המקום מאנשי דור המבול ומאנשי סדום וכו'

אף עוברין שבמעי אמן פתחו פיהן ואמרו שירה :R. Meir (13) ; וכו' :ib. (12) אמר המקום מי שהמלכני על הים אעשהו מלך על ; ישראל

מה עשה המקום ? מרכיב את האדם על הסום ;P. 37 B, R. Simon (15) : לפני המקום וכו' ולא ישראל בלבד אמרו שירה לפני המקום :P. 36 B (14)

כשישראל עושין רצונו של מקום אז מתגדל שמו בעולם :b. Eleazar ; כשישראל עושין רצונו של מקום הן עושין שמאל לימין :P. 39 A (16)

ראה כמה חביבים ישראל לפני המקום ולפי שהן חביבין :b. Gamaliel ; וכשאין ישר' עושין רצונו וכו' :P. 27 A (17) ; ולא היו לו (לאברהם : כמה עבדים אלא לכבוד המקום ;P. 46 A, R. Eleazar of (18) : ושם ניסה המקום את ישראל ;P. 47 A, R. Simon (19) : Modiim

כאן המקום ממיך ומשה מגביה ובמקום :P. 52 A (21) ; אמר להם המקום אם תשמרו שבת זו עתיד אני ליתן לכם :Modiim ; לפניו שינה עליהם מעשה בראשית ;P. 51 A, R. Eleazar of (20)

ויהא המקום יחידי בעולם ותהי מלכותו לעולם ולעולמי עולמים :ib. (24) ; המקום קראו מסה ומריבה :P. 56 A, the same (23) : Modiim ; אחר המקום מגביה ומשה ממיך ;P. 52 B, R. Eleazar of (22) ; שש מדות טובות

רעואל שהיה כריע למקום, חבר שנעשה כחבר למקום ;P. 58 A (27) ; המקום בכסא־הכבוד שלו :P. 57 A (26) ; חובב שהיה חביב למקום, ;P. 56 B, R. Eliezer (25) ; הנס הזה שעשה משה בגיני עשאו :נשבע

עשאן המקום כתים כתים ;P. 60 A (30) : R. Joshua b. Hananja ; לכן בקש המקום להרגו :ib., R. Jose b. Halafta (28) ; כשאמר לו המקום הוצא את עמי בני' :R. Joshua b. Korha ; (29) ib.,

הבאר שנתן לנו המקום :R. Eleazar of Modiim (33) ; המן הזה שנתן לנו המקום :P. 58 B (32) ; מכעיסין למקום ;P. 61 B (31) : והמקום הודה לדבריך ;P. 58 B, R. Joshua b. Hananja (34) P. 58 B,

מנין א'א שאמר הקב"ה למשה וכו' גדול משה שהודה לו המקום :b. Ilai ; ולא עמד א' מהם לברך למקום עד שבא יתרו :P. 63 B, R. Jehuda (36) ; עתיד המקום ליתן לנו שש מידות :P. 58 B, Papajos (35) : R. Eliezer

מלמד שאמר המקום :P. 65 B (39) ; אלא שאמר המקום למשה לפרוש מן ה' :ib. (38) : P. 67 B (37) ; כך אמר המקום לישראל אנכי :P. 66 A (40) ; למשה הריני קורא לך מראש ההר ואתה עולה :מנין ; מלמד שהסכים המקום על ידו

הקיש מוראת ;ib. (44) ; היקש כבוד אב ואם לכבוד המקום :Rabbi ; אמר להם המקום :P. 67 B, R. Jose b. Halafta (43) ; P. 70 A, ; שהודה המקום לדבריהם :P. 67 A (41) : המקום (42)

הקיש קללת או׳א לקללת המקום (45) ib.: ;או׳א למוראת המקום

שכל מי שעובד ע״ז מעלה עליו הכתוב כאילו מנאף מנאף אחר B 70 .P (46)

מנין אתה אומר שהראה המקום R. Nathan: ,B 71 .P (47) ;המקום

׳לאברהם אבינו גיהנם וכו R. Eliezer (Yalkut r. ,B 100 .P (48)

כשישראל עושין רצונו של מקום הם עושין שמיטה :R. Ishmael)

׳אבל המקום קרוי לשון שבח אל B: 101 .P (49) ;אחת בשבוע וכו

׳אלהים שדי צבאות אהיה אשר אהיה חנון ורחום ארך אפים וכו

בזמן שישראל עושין רצונו של מקום מלאכתן נעשית A: 104 .P (50)

על ידי אחרים ;also p. 104 B, and M. R. S. b. J. in the name of
R. Ishmael.

We have seen a few instances of interchanges between
מי שאמר והיה העו׳,[22] and הקב׳ה, likewise between המקום and
הקב׳ה.[23] We are enabled to show that many times, where our
texts have הקב׳ה, the original form must have been המקום. In
other cases, where such evidence cannot be brought forward,
we assert that the alteration was effected in the Amoraic
or later period, or the passage is of a post-Tannaitic origin.
We register first of all the passages which have been altered
by a later hand. These are: (1) P. 11 A : שמשה חלק כבוד
לא במקום אחד. Sifre iv, § 92, reads: ׳לזקנים וכן הקב׳ה אמר לי
ולא בשנים המקום חולק כבוד לזקנים ובכל מקום שאתה מוצא זקנים
המקום חולק כבוד לזקנים. The compiler of Exodus rabba[24]
quotes this saying as a תני ר׳ שמעון בן יוחאי, (2) P. 14 A : הן עשו
בסתר, והקב׳ה פרסם אותם בגלוי; in the Tannaitic source preserved
in b. Sotah 9 A we read a similar sentence: ד׳א היא עשתה בסתר
שהיו קוברים מיתיהם והודו ושבחו ;(3) P. 24 A : המקום פירסמה בגלוי
ושבחו לשם; M. R. S. b. J. reads להקב׳ה שלא ראו אויביהם (4)
P. 28 B: באותה שעה הראה להם הקב׳ה תורמיות תורמיות של,
מה׳ש, v. above under מקום, No. 8, where the text reads
המקום in the very same sentence; (5) P. 31 A : וכן אתה
מוצא שאין הקב׳ה עתיד ליפרע מן הרשעים בגיהנם אלא ברוח קדים

<hr>

[22] v. p. 126.   [23] v. pp. 121.

[24] 5. 15 : תני ר׳ שמעון בן יוחאי בכמה מקומות שנינו שחלק הקב׳ה
דתני ר׳ שמעון בן יוחאי לא במקום ;v. also Lev. r. 11. 5 : כבוד לזקנים
;אחד ולא בשני מקומות מצינו שחלק הקב׳ה כבוד לזקנים אלא בכמה מקומות
Tanh., Exodus, ed. Buber, p. 17, r. : אמר הקב׳ה בעוה׳ז חלקתי כבוד
.לזקנים

I

v. p. 30 A : ‏שלא נפרע המקום מהם אלא ברוח קדים‏ ; (6) ‏.‏P. 31 B :

Tos. 12, l. 8 : ‏א׳ל הקב׳ה מי שקידש שמי על הים יבא וימשול על ישראל‏

‏גדולה אמונה לפני הקב׳ה‏ : (7) P. 34 A : ‏א׳ל מפניו שקידש שמו של מקום‏ ;

M. R. S. b. J. 57 reads ‏שבשכר אמונה שרתה עליהם רוח הקודש‏

‏וכן אתה מוצא שאין הקב׳ה‏ : (8) P. 36 B : ‏לפני מי שאמר והיה העולם‏ ;

M. R. S. b. J. ‏עתיד להפרע מן המלכיות לע׳ל עד שיפרע משריהן תחלה‏

58 : ‏שאין המקום נפרע מן המלכיות עד שמפיל את שריהן‏ ; (9) P. 36 B :

M. R. S. b. J. 59 : ‏והרי כל אומות שבעולם אומרים שבחו של הקב׳ה‏ ;

‏שהרי אומות העולם אומרין ניאותו ושבחו של מי שאמר והיה העולם‏ ;

(10) P. 37 A : R. Jose, the Galilean : ‏לפני‏ ‏ניינו ושבחו של הקב׳ה‏

‏או׳ה‏, M. R. S. b. J. 60 : ‏אדבר בשבחו בניאותו ובשבחו של מי שאמר‏

‏והיה העולם‏ ; (11) ib., R. Akiba : ‏אדבר בנאותיו ובשבחיו של הקב׳ה‏,

M. R. S. b. J. 60 : ‏אומר ניאותו ושבחו של מי שאמר והיה העולם לפני‏

‏או׳ה‏; (12) P. 38 A, v. already above, p. 125 ; (13) P. 39 A :

Sifre Num., ‏מגיד שכל מי שקם נגד ישראל כאלו קם נגד הקב׳ה‏ ;

(14) P. 39 B : ‏שבל מי שקם נגד ישראל כאלו קם נגד המקום‏ : 84 §

‏וכל‏ : 84 § ., Sifre Num ‏וכל מי שעוזר לישראל כאלו עוזר להקב׳ה‏

(15) P. 41 B : ‏מי שעוזר לישראל כאלו עוזר למקום‏ ; ‏אבל הקב׳ה אומר‏

‏אבל הקב׳ה אומר עיצרת הדברים באחת‏ : .ib, ‏שני דברים בדיבור אחד‏,

M. R. S. b. J. 6 B : ‏אבל מי שאמר והיה העולם אינו כן אלא אמר עשר‏

(16) P. 41 B : ‏אבל הקב׳ה אינו כן אלא מוראו‏ ; ‏הדברות בדיבור אחד‏

M. R. S. b. J. 67 : ‏אבל מי שאמר והיה העולם‏, ‏על קרוביו יותר מרחוקיו‏

‏שלא‏ introduced by, ‏אינו כן מוראו על הקרובים יותר מן הרחוקים‏

ib. : ‏אבל הקב׳ה אינו כן אדם תאב‏; (17) ‏כמדת בשר ודם מדת המקום‏

M. R. S. b. J. ‏לבנים נותן לו תאב לחכמה נותן לו, תאב לנכסים נתן לו‏,

67 : ‏אבל הקב׳ה בונה‏ ; (18) ib. : ‏אבל מי שאמר והיה העולם אינו כן‏

‏שלא כמדת בו׳ד מדת‏, M. R. S. b. J. 67 : ‏העליון ואח׳כ בונה התחתון‏

(19) ‏המקום — אבל מי שאמר והיה העולם אינו כן אלא בונה עליון‏;

P. 42 B : ‏אבל הקב׳ה צר צורה במים‏, Mekh. R. S. b. J. 67 :

introduced, ‏אבל מי שאמר והיה העולם אינו כן אלא צר צורה במים‏

by ‏והקב׳ה צר צורה‏ : .ib (20) ; ‏שלא כמדת בשר ודם מדת המקום‏

‏בעפר‏ ; M. R. S. b. J. 67 reads instead : ‏אבל מי שאמר והיה העולם‏

‏צר צורה באפילה‏ ; (21) ib. : ‏אבל הקב׳ה צר כולה כאחת‏, M. R. S. b. J.

67 : ‏אבל מי שאמר והיה העולם אינו כן אלא כשהוא צר צורה צר הכל‏

‏כאחד‏; (22) P. 41 B : ‏אבל הקב׳ה אפילו כל באי עולם באין וצועקין‏

‏אבל מי שאמר והיה העולם‏, M. R. S. b. J. 67 : ‏לפניו הוא שומע צעקתם‏

‏אינו כן אלא כל באי עולם עומדין בתפלה לפניו ושומיע תפלתם‏;

(23) P. 42 A : מגיד שבל הנפשות בכף של הקב'ה, M. R. S. b. J. 67 :

כשהקב'ה : (24) P. 72A ; מגיד שבל הנפשות ביד מי שאמר והיה העולם

מניד הבתוב בשהמקום : M. R. S. b. J. 67, נוטה ידו רשעים כלים מן העולם

אמר הקב'ה אתם : (25) P. 42 A ; מטה את ידו הרשעים פונין מן העולם

; אמר להם המקום אתם : M. R. S. b. J. 67, צדקתם עליכם את הדין

אלא הצדיקים היו מובטחים ויודעים שהקב'ה עושה להם : (26) P. 44 A

: נסים וגבורות עת שיוצאין ממצרים התקינו להם וכו' ,M. R.S. b. J. 71

מובטחין עם יציאתן ממצרים שהמקום עושה להם נסים וגבורות ולפיכך

בא וראה כמה : (27) P. 45 B, R. Simon b. Gamaliel ; נטלו

מפורשין דרכי הקב'ה מדרכי בו'ר, בו'ד במתוק מרפא את המר,

M. R. S. b. J. 73 reads R. Ishmael b. R. Johanan b. Berakha :

א'ל עד : P. 47 B ; (28) כמה מפורשין דרכי בשר ודם מדרכי המקום

שאתם ישינים במטותיכם הקב'ה מפרנס אתכם ,M. R. S. b. J. 76 :

מ'א למד ששקולה יציאת מצרים כיצד .(29) ib, ; המקום מפרנס אתכם

: כל הנסים וגבורות שעשה הקב'ה לישראל ,M. R. S. b. J. 76 שעשה

: שבשם שגזר הקב'ה בן היה : (30) P. 48 A ; המקום לישראל ,Yalkut

וכל כן למה אמר הקב'ה מוטב שילקה : (31) P. 48 A ; שבשם שגזר המקום

המקום נגלה : M. R. S. b. J. 76, עמוד הענן ואל יסקל משה ואהרן

; בעמוד ענן אמר המקום מוטיב ילקה עמוד הענן ואל יסקל משה וא'

,אם כן זמן הקב'ה למבעיסיו ק'ו שישלם שכר טוב לצדיקים : (32) P. 48 B

Jalkut : זמן המקום ; (33) P. 49 A, R. Tarphon : כביכול פשט

הקב'ה ידו ונטל תפלתן של אבות ,M. R. S b. J. 77, R. Eleazar of

Modiim : כביכול פשט המקום את ידו וקבל תפלתן של אבות ;

(34) P. 50 B, 51 A, R. Joshua b. Hananja : אם תשמרו שבת זו

M. R. S. b. J. 78, עתיד הקב'ה ליתן לכם שש מדות טובות

R. Eleazar of Modiim : אם תזכו לשמור שבת עתיד המקום ליתן

י' : אמר לו הקב'ה כל מקום שאתה מוצא רגלי : (35) P. 52 B ; לכם א'

אמר לו [המקום] כל מקום : M. R. S. b. J. 81, אדם שם אני לפניך

וכי ידיו של משה מגברות ישראל : (36) P. 53 B ; שאתה מוצא וכו'

או ידיו שוברות עמלק אלא כל זמן שמגביה ידיו כלפי מעלה היו ישראל

מסתכלין בו ומאמינין במי שפקד משה לעשות כן והקב'ה עשה להם נסים

וגבורות ,M. R. S. b. J. 82, R. Eliezer b. Hyrkanos : אלא בזמן

שישראל עושין רצונו של מקום ומאמינים במה (במי read) שפקד המקום

: למשה המקום עושה להם נסים וגבורות ,v. above, M. R. H. iii. 29 A

אלא כ'ו : M. R. S. b. J. 83, והקב'ה עשה להם רפואות : (37) P. 54 A

שישראל עושין רצונו של מקום ומאמינין במה שפקדן הן מתרפאין ;

: המקום חס עליהן ; (38) ib. : M. R. S. b. J. 83, הקב'ה חס עליהם

אמר משה לפני הקב'ה רבש'ע על ידי הוצאת את ישראל : (39) P. 54 B

(40) P. 56 A, ‏אמר משה לפני המקום‎ : 83 .M. R. S. b. J, ‏וכו'‎;
R. Joshua b. Hananja : ‏כשבא עמלק להזיק את ישראל מתחת כנפי‎
M. R. S. b. J. 84, ‏אביהם שבשמים אמר משה לפני הקב'ה רבש'ע‎
R. Eleazar of Modiim : ‏לפי כשבא לאבד את ישראל תחת כנפי‎
(41) P. 57 B, R. Eleazar of ‏השמים אמר משה לפני המקום רבש'ע‎;
Modiim : ‏בשעה שאמר הקב'ה למשה לך הוצא את עמי‎, M. R. S. b. J.
86 : ‏אימתי שלחה בשעה שאמר לו המקום‎; (42) P. 65 B, R. Eliezer :
‏מניין אתה אומר שאין הקב'ה מדבר עד שמשה אמר דבר שכבר קבלו‎
‏כן הוא הדבר וכו' אלא מלמד שנתן הקב'ה‎ : and R. Akiba, ‏עליהם בניך‎
‏כבוד גדול חלק‎, v. M. R. S. b. J. 101 : ‏כח וגבורה במשה והיה הקב'ה‎
(43) P. 65 B : ‏לו המקום למשה שלא היה המקום מדבר עד שאמר וכו'‎;
‏מלמד שהרכין הקב'ה‎, v. also p. 72 B, R. Akiba, cf. M. R. S. b. J.
114; (44) P. 88 B, in the well-known ‏מלמד שהרכין המקום ב'ה‎;
saying of R. Johanan b. Zakkai : ‏חס הקב'ה על כבודן של בריות‎,
v. above, p. 117, to Tos. B. K. vii. 10 : ‏חס המקום‎, v. also B. K.
79 B; (45) P. 94 B, R. Simon b. Johai : ‏כל המשתתף שמו של‎
‏כל המשתתף שם שמים וד'א‎, v. b. Sanh. 63 A : ‏הקב'ה בע'ז חייב כלייה‎,
the same reading must have been the original in the previous sentence beg. ‏אלולי ששתפו‎, and M. R. S. b. J., p. 50;
(46) p. 102 A, R. Simon b. Johai, Yalkut r. R. Ishmael,
v. also Sifre Deut., § 104: ‏כנגד ג' בריתות שכרת הקב'ה‎, v.
M. Tann. 75 : ‏שכרת המקום‎, v. also, p. 57, R. Simon b. Johai :
‏שלא כרת ע' המקום מ'ח בריתות‎.

In these forty-six passages we have been able to show that
there are other readings besides ‏הקב'ה‎. We propose, now,
to deal with the passages, with reference to which we have
no literary evidence enabling us to substitute the original
term. In some of these cases the fact must be ascribed to
an accident, or we have to deal with an Amoraic supplement or gloss. Most of the sayings to be dealt with belong
to the anonymous Haggada, but there are some ascribed to
older authorities, who, according to our experience, could
not have used the term ‏הקב'ה‎. We will deal with a few
passages: (1) 2 A : ‏שלוחי הקב'ה לא כשלוחי בו'ד‎, b. B. B. 25 A,
our saying is quoted in the name of R. Hoshaja: ‏שלוחיך לא‎
‏כשהקב'ה גוזר גזירות טובות ורעותעל‎ : ib. (2); ‏כבשר ודם שלוחי בו'ד וכו'‎
‏ישראל על הטובה מחזירים לפניו וכו'‎. The saying is quoted Yalk.

Ezra 349, and Job 924, in the name of R. Josiah; perhaps it belongs also to R. Hoshaja? In the Babyl. Talmud the saying is quoted in the name of *R. Aha b. Haninah* with slight alterations. (3) 57 B, from שבשעה שאמר הקב'ה למשה לך הוצא את עמי בנ'י, does not belong to the saying of R. Eleazar of Modiim, but is an addition from the Amoraic Haggadah, P. 59 A: שכל מי שמוציא דין אמת לאמיתו מעלה עליו הכתוב כאלו כאלו שותף במעשה, M. R. S. b. J. 89 reads היה שותף עם הקב'ה במ'ב בראשית. Here we have reliable literary evidence that the original saying was altered by the Mishna teachers of the Amoraic period. B. Shabb. 10A, R. Hijja b. Rab, of דפתי, quotes this saying with some other additional words: כל דיין שדן דין אמת לאמיתו אפילו שעה אחת מעלה עליו הכתוב כאילו נעשה שותף להקב'ה במעשה בראשית. Other variants of this saying also suggest that this sentence is of Amoraic origin. R. Samuel b. Nahmani says in the name of R. Jonathan b. Eliezer: כל דיין שדן דין אמת לאמיתו משרה שכינה בישראל, based on Ps. 82. 1 (v. also Exod. r. 30. 20, and b. Zeb. 109 B). P. 63 B: In the sayings of R. Judah and Rabbi הקב'ה and המקום are alternately used. We saw already above, p. 128, that the copyists or teachers availed themselves of this method, in order not to repeat the same term twice. Mekh., R. S. b. J. 96 reads in R. Judah's saying also הקב'ה, v. also 66 A. P. 66 B, ולא על הנגלות בלבד נגלה הקב'ה עליהם לכרות ברית, is probably a gloss from the Tanhuma, v. ed Frankfurt a. M., 96 B. P. 66 B, R. Nathan says: מכאן תשובה למינים שאומרים שתי רשויותהן שכשעמד הקב'ה. All texts read so, v. Yalkut Lekach Tob. ii. 133. Neither שמים nor מקום nor שכינה would do in such a case. There must have been quite a different phrase, which was altered for some reason. P. 71 B, באותה שעה אמר הקב'ה, and in the saying of R. Judah b. Ilai, אמר הקב'ה, v. above to Tos. Erakhin, i. 10, p. 116, esp. note 63. M. R. S. b. J. 113–4 these additions are not given. P. 98 A, שאין הקב'ה מקפח שכר כל בריה, is quoted in the Talmud and Midrash in the name of Amoraim. B. K. 38 B, by R. Hijja bar Abba in the name of R. Johanan, with the additional clause, אפילו שכר שיחה נאה; v. also Pes. 114 A, Nazir 20 B, Hora-

joth 10 B, Exod. r. 31. Similarly is the phrase, מיום שברא
הקב׳ה עולמו, p. 104 B, an Amoraic phrase.

It is true that there are still a few sayings left which
contain הקב׳ה. Especially Haggadic portions which are
ascribed to such authorities as R. Eliezer b. Hyrkanos and
R. Joshua b. Hananja, or R. Matjâ b. Heresh, &c. The
previous list has convinced us that the Tannaim did not
use the term הקב׳ה. R. Joshua b. Hananja and R. Eliezer
b. Hyrkanos figure in that list conspicuously as having
used המקום. The same observation can be made in the
Mishna and Tosefta. Considering the fact that the *final*
redaction of the Mekhilta must be placed in the Amoraic
period and can be classed as one of the latest of the
Tannaitic Midrashim, there can be no surprise that the
name הקב׳ה occurs more frequently than in the other old
sources.

Besides these principal names, e.g. השמים, המקום, מי שאמר
והיה הע׳, and הקב׳ה, there are numerous others, most of
which are dealt with in the previous chapter.[25]

In the Mekhilta of R. Simon b. Johai the term הקב׳ה was
also substituted for המקום. The final compilation of the
Midrash is. with good reason, ascribed to Hezekia, the son of
R. Hijja. Thus we find pp. 1 f in the sayings of R. Simon
b. Johai, R. Jose, and R. Joshua, מפני מה נגלה הקב׳ה, although
the first saying contains in the latter part המקום, and the
second, מי שאמר והיה העולם. Both terms belong to the Tannaitic
Haggada. In the second sentence of R. Joshua we read
בוא וראה כמה רחמיו וחביותיו של הק׳בה על ישראל, varying the teaching of Akiba, that 'God shares Israel's troubles and exiles,
but also rejoices in his people's joy'. The dialogue between
a heathen and R. Gamaliel shows clearly that the term
הקב׳ה is due to editorial alterations. The questioning
heathen or philosopher generally refers to God as אלוה or

---

[25] v. אדיר, אלהים and אלוה. דיין, הוא, יודע מחשבות, חי העולמים, יוצר,
רבון, קונה, עליון, מעלה, מרום, מלך, כבודו של עולם, יחודו של עולם,
שם and שכינה, רוח הקודש.

אלהים; here הקב׳ה was put instead of the heathen's term.[26]
The saying of R. Eleazar b. Arakh has both terms, חקב׳ה
and המקום (p. 2) : מפני מה נגלה חקב׳ה משמי מרום — לפי שיכול
המקום שידבר.[27] The same teacher quotes in his diatribe the
words of the heretics against God's justice and righteousness, calling them בזויי העולם ' the despised of the world ', in
which the terms אלוה and בעל העולם occur. ' Lord of the
World ' is a special gnostic term for the Demiurgos. The
objection of the latter was to the expression ויחר אף ד׳ במשה
(Exod. 4. 14), which ascribes anger and feelings of wrath
to God. The explanation of R. Eleazar b. Arakh לא דבר
דברה תורה הקב׳ה אלא בדרך ארץ (p. 2) means nothing else but
בלשון בני אדם. Yet, even in this overworked text there are
traces of המקום (p. 3). Similarly attention may be called to
the name בעל הרחמים ' Lord of Mercy ' (p. 3).

The Mekhilta to section וארא contains the exposition of
ten Tannaites on Exod. 6. 2. The ten sayings are not in
chronological order, and show the signs of a more recent
arrangement. It is no wonder, therefore, that the later
term הקב׳ה stands for המקום. The term deserves attention
(אני־הוא שאמרתי והיה העולם) in R. Eliezer b. Hyrkanos's saying,
and אדון העולם in that of R. Judah b. Ilai. The reading,
רבון העולמים instead of רבון העולם in R. Eleazar of Modiim's
sentence is also remarkable.

To a greater extent this Mekhilta reads המקום, even where
our Mekh. has הקב׳ה, as we have shown already. Here
some passages will be quoted in which the older terms
occur. P. 13 : ד׳א אני ה׳ מלכות וכל מקום שמזכיר גיאה של ע׳ז שם
מזכיר שבחו של המקום. The idols are referred to as אלהים. P. 17:
the old term גבוה is used, and in Abba Saul's sentence, בידי
שמים occurs in opposition to בידי הדיוט. P. 18 (v. also p. 27) :
מלמד שצבאות מקום נקראו צבאות ישראל וצבאות ישראל נקראו צבאות
מקום, v. to Mekh. 10 A, where צבאות מה׳ש stands for צבאות מקום.

---

[26] v. Exod. r. 2. 9, where R. Joshua b. Korha disputes with the heathen,
and Num. r. 14, R. Gamaliel.
[27] Likewise were the other sayings of the same scribe altered, like היה
לא דבר הקב׳ה עם משה and מכחיש הקב׳ה.

P. 21 : גלוי וידוע לפני מי שאמר והיה העולם שבשישראל   P. 22 :

28. לפי שמצינו שפרשה ראשונה אמ׳ל המקום למשה — שמע מפי הקודש

P. 24 : ואין המקום מוחל לו לאדם עד שיפיים את חבירו ; this saying
agrees with that of R. Eleazar b. Azarja, b. Joma, 85 B ;
v. above, p. 110. P. 25 : The Egyptians feared the Israelites
as people fear their God (כבני אדם שיראים מן קוניהם). P. 47,
R. Simon b. Johai : לעשות רצון אביו שבשמים. P. 50 : אדון
אדון כל המעשים and המעשים ברוך הוא.

(4) Our fourth source, the *Siphra*, offers less material
for our purpose than the Mekhilta. R. Akiba, R. Eleazar
b. Azarja, and R. Simon b. Eleazar speak of God as ' the
Father in Heaven.'[29] R. Eleazar b. Azarja uses the term
גבוה.[30] גבורה is applied in the usual way when speaking in
the name of God.[31] God as creator is called either מי שעשה
את העולם[32] or more frequently מי שאמר והיה העולם.[33] Similar
to גבוה is the term מעלה.[34] More frequent are the names
signifying God's kingship, by Abba Saul (p. 75 B : פמליא
למלך ומה עליה להיות מחקה למלך), R. Eleazar b. Azarja
(82 B : נמצא פורש מן העבירה ומקבל עליו מלכות שמים), R. Simon
b. Johai (p. 74 B), Rabbi (p. 95 B), and in several anonymous
sentences.[35] Secondly שמים, especially in sanctifications or
in connexion with God's name. Pappus and Lulianus, the
martyrs, say אנו חייבין מיתה עד לשמים (93 B), R. Simon b.

---

28. v. also p. 41 : מפי הקודש.

29. 110 B, R. Akiba : משה שליח בין ישר׳ לאביהם שבשמים ; 82 B, R. 96 A :
אבל אפשי ואבי שבשמים נזר עלי ; 78 B, R. S. b. J., v. M. Kelaim, above,
p. 113, and 87 A (anonymous) : אדם שעושה את התורה ועושה רצון אביו
שבשמים.

30. pp. 96 B, 104 B, 114 B.

31. p. 3 B : את הדברים לפני הגבורה.

32. p. 11 A : לשם מי שעשה.

33. Rabbi 74 B : מי . . א׳ל ולא אחד עשה . . גלוי וידוע לפני מ׳ ש׳ ו׳ ה׳,
אני ה׳ שאמרתי ; v. also 74 A : שברא את ישראל הוא ברא את האומות
והיה העולם.

34. p. 76 A.

35. מניין שאין אהרן לובש בגדים לגדולתו אלא כמקיים גזירת המלך : 71 B ;
על כורחכם שלא בטובתכם אני ה׳ : 110 B ; הפי זו גזירת המלך : 113 A
שקבלתם מלכותי עליכם במצרים א׳ל הין והין קבלתם מלכותי קבלו גזירותי.

Johai (7 A: לבטלה—לא יזכיר שם שמים), and Rabbi (83 B), who
speaks of death imposed by Heaven (מיתה האמורה בידי שמים).
Further, several times in sayings like בידי שמים,[36] מן השמים,[37]
and others.[38] In the majority of cases we read מקום. Thus
R. Eliezer b. Hyrkanos,[39] who says, 'God does not bring
a punishment on Israel unless he warned them first'.
R. Eleazar b. Azarja speaks of דברים שבינך ובין המקום.[40]
Pappus and Lulianus say to their tyrant: הרבה מזיקים למקום,[41]
and R. Simon b. Johai.[42] Many anonymous sayings: 6 A,
שהמקום רוצה לו; 71 A, עבירות שבין אדם למקום, v. above, p. 110;
75 B, הקיש מורא או'א למורא המקום, and similar sentences as to
honour and curse; 83 B, על אחת כמה נכמה שיעבירנו המקום מן העולם;
84 A, אם לפני בו'ד עושים כן ק'ו; 68 A, חס עליהם המקום מלהעבירם
מלמד 108 A, מבקשים שכרם מלפני המקום; 108 B, לפני המקום
כבר הבטיח המקום 110 B, שהמקום מתאוה שיהו עמלים בתורה
לישראל שאין דן אבות ע'י בנים.[43] The term הקב'ה, however, is
to be found only twice; some of them are surely Amoraic
insertions, others perhaps not original. In any case this
Tannaitic work also confirms our observations that הקב'ה
was not known to and used in the Tannaitic Haggada.

Besides these names there are occasionally the terms כבוד,
by R. Akiba (3 B), R. Simon b. Johai, especially when the
seeing of God by human beings is spoken of; v. also 76,
חייבים בכבודי. The rule that אלהים denotes the judgeship of
God is four times quoted (74 A, 74 B, 75 A, 82 B). Finally

---

[36] 6 A.   [37] 8 A.

[38] 110 A; דינר לשמים; 106 B, לשמים; מעשיהם לשם שמים, p. 108 B;
על מלכות שמים, 106 B; and 11 A, יכוון את דעתו לשמים

[39] 109 B: אין המקום מביא פורענות בישראל עד שמעיד בהם תחלה.

[40] 71 A, v. also 44 A: שריחם המקום על אהרן.

[41] 93 B.

[42] 108 B: אימתו הוא שבחו של מקום.

[43] T. K. 2 B: מלמד שהרבין הקב'ה, v. already above, p. 132, 3 A, 9 A,
v. מפי הקודש or מפי חנבורה, the usual term for this is שומע מפי הקב'ה
חם הקב'ה על הרשעים ק'ו על כבודן של צדיקים, parallels 3 A, 71 A, p. 84:
have המקום; 109 A: הקב'ה אמר להם לצדיקים, further עתיד הקב'ה מטייל
אין אומר הקב'ה לאו'ה seem to be of Amoraic עם הצדיקים, and finally
origin.

שכינה (1 A, 98 B, 78 A, 81 A, 81 B, 110 A) is often repeated, and
שם (15 A, 75 A, 93 B, 99 B, 100 A, 110 A) is also frequent.

(5) For the Tannaitic Midrashim on the fourth Book of
the Pentateuch we can avail ourselves of the critical edition
published by H. S. Horowitz.[44] It is highly interesting to
see that in this work the use of the term הקב'ה is almost
unknown, while those of מקום and שמים, but especially the
former, are the rule. The study of this text kindles the
desire to see a critical edition of the whole Tannaitic Midrash
of both schools. We enumerate first the passages which
have to be corrected in מקום: (1) § 42, גדול השלום ששמו של
הקב'ה שלום; R.[45] and R. b.[46] read מקום. About God's name being
שלום, v. further, on p. 104; (2) § 42 has further a sentence,
כשהקב'ה קורא הכל עונים, which the editor, rightly, considers as
belonging to a later gloss;[47] (3) § 61, R. Akiba, והראה לו
הקב'ה באצבע, R. Mekh. מקום, v. also Men. 29 A, Pes. B. M. 5,
Pes. r. 15, Exod. r. 15, Num. r. 15. 4, Tanh., Num., and שמיני;
(4) § 61, R. Nathan, להודיע שבחו של משה שבשם שא'ל הקב'ה כן
כאן הקב'ה ממיך ומשה מגביה, R. reads מקום; (5) § 90, עשה,
המקום מקום R. , Yalkut, MS. London, Midrash Hakhamim r. המקום;
(6) § 91, שהראה הקב'ה, all MS. and Yalk. read שהראהו; (7) § 92,
מפי הגבורה, M. H. reads more correctly לשמוע דיבור מפי הקב'ה;
(8) § 100, והלא אף עם האבות דבר הקב'ה, no variant, perhaps
the editor's gloss (?);[48] (9) § 102, שלא כמדת בו'ר מדת הקב'ה,
בקש מלפני and עד שהשיבו הקב'ה; (10) § 105, מדת המקום ב'ה R.;
כשפדה הקב'ה את זרע אברהם, M. r. המקום; (11) § 115, הקב'ה,
אין הקב'ה מואס תפלתן של R. r. המקום; (12) § 135, R. Nathan,
בא וראה, R. r. המקום; (13) § 137, R. Eleazar of Modiim, רבים
לפני מי שאמר, Yalk., M. and R. כמה צדיקים חביבים לפני הקב'ה;
עד שהשיבו הקב'ה, Yalk., London, M. and והיה העולם; (14) § 138,

---

[44] Leipzig, 1917.   [45] = MS. Vatican.   [46] = Num. r.
[47] The passage in § 58, כשהקב'ה מדבר הכל שותקים and כשהקב'ה
מדבר בקול גדול may also be later additions, or originally כשהמקום stood,
which was altered, because one cannot speak of מקום as speaking or
calling.
[48] v. also § 106, § 111, הקב'ה הסגירה, הקב'ה טימאה וכו'; ומהיכן התחיל
§ 119, R Eleazar ha-Kappar, הראה הקב'ה ליעקב בהמ'ק; § 141, הקב'ה;
§ 142, כן אמר לו הקב'ה; מה צוה הקב'ה את משה בשמחה.

R. המקום ; (15) § 143, Simon b. Azzai, שאחד מרבה ואחד מ' לפני

המקום .L. M, מקום .R ,הקב'ה. We see that the term הקב'ה is,
on the whole, very rarely used, and, with the exception of
very few cases, the literary evidence goes very far to prove
that the use of it is not primary. If we are comparing now
with this the use of המקום, it is almost mathematically proved
that הקב'ה was not known to the teachers of the Tannaitic
period.

Let us now investigate the occurrence of the name הקב'ה
in the Sifre zutta. P. 249: ד'א אתה אומר חביב הוא השלום
שאלו ברא הקב'ה מדה יפה יותר מן וכו'. P. 249, R. Simon b. Johai:
וכן אתה מוצא שלא נתן הקב'ה שכר : P. 250. מדתו של ממ'ה הקב'ה
שאין הקב'ה עתיד לנחם את ירושלם and תלמוד תורה אלא שלום
זה קידש שמו של הקב'ה על הים והוא ראוי: P. 252. [49] אלא בשלום.
משה לא היה יודע אימתי הקב'ה מדבר עמו : P. 254. להוריד השכינה.
אלו אדם שלא : P. 265. ובלעם היה יודע מה הקב'ה עתיד לדבר עמו and
בך אמר הקב'ה איני מהלך שתאמר לי לך : P. 267. הכיר נסין של הקב'ה.
P. 268, R.Gamaliel: לפי שהלשינו ישראל על הקב'ה ואמרו היוכל וכו'
שמיום : P. 274. כך אמר הקב'ה לישראל : P. 272. וראה הקב'ה
והלא הקב'ה ואמר לו כתוב : P. 279. שדבר הקב'ה עם משה. The
difference between the Sifre and Sifre Zutta is noteworthy. It is due either to a later redaction, or, more
likely, to the fact that we have no old literary witnesses to
establish the right reading in these cases. Yet, even here, the
passages with המקום outnumber those with הקב'ה.

Besides המקום our source contains all the old terms of the
Tannaitic period, like מי שאמר, גבורה, קונה, שמים, שם, שכינה,
והיה העולם (not as frequently as in the other Tannaitic
works!) and מעלה.

(6) In the Sifre on Deuteronomy, our sixth source, again
we have plenty of proofs that the הקב'ה in the text is not
original. P. 64 B, § 1, ed. reads כך אמר הקב'ה לישראל זו ותירה
כך אמר המקום ברוך הוא לישראל הא ,M. T. 2; לכל מה שעשיתם
יתירא כל מה שעשיתם. P. 65 A, in the saying of R. Judah
b. Ilai (v. M. T., p. 3), אלו הנסיונות שנסו אבותינו הקב'ה; M. T.
reads שניסו אבותינו את המקום, M. Aboth, v. 4, has הקב'ה, yet

49 v. also שלא כונן הקב'ה את מלכות בית דוד אלא בשלום.

MS. Adler, 2585 r. את המקום (v. Mishna). P. 67 B, § 10,
המקום אמר לאבינו M. T. 6 reads ; הקב'ה הבטיח את אברהם אבינו
אברהם—המקום לא נתן קצבה לברכתינו. Here a whole sentence
is missing from the edition. We compare the two texts
with each other:

Sifre.

אמרו לו רבינו משה אי איפשי
לנו שתברכנו הקב'ה הבטיח את
אברהם אבינו אמר והרבתי את
זרעך וכו' ושמתי את זרעך וכו'
ואתה נותן קצבה לברכותינו משל
למלך שהיו לו נכסים הרבה וכו'.

M. T.

אמרו ישראל למשה רבינו אי
אפשינו שתברכינו אנו מובטחים
על ברכות הרבה המקום אמר
לאבינו אברהם כי ברך אברכך
וכו' ואתה נתתה קצבה לברכותינו,
א'ל אני בו'ד אני ישלי קצבה
לברכותי ה' אל' הר' את' ה' אלהי
וכו' . אמרו לו המקום לא נתן
קצבה לברכותינו אמר להן זו משלי
וכו' משל למלך.

Through a copyist's error the whole passage between
קצבה לברכותינו and קצבה לברכותינו was omitted. Sifre, p. 69,
§ 21, .M. T., p. 11, וייטב בעיני הדבר ולא בעיני הקב'ה ; בעיני היה
; כך אמר משה לפני הקב'ה Sifre, p. 10 B, § 26, טוב ולא בעיני המקום
in M. T., ib., לפני המקום, א'ל המקום ; דוד המלך אמר לפני הקב'ה
M. T., לפני המקום ; Sifre 70 B, § 26, כך משה מבקש מלפני הקב'ה
M. T. 15, כך משה היה מבקש מלפני המקום ; Sifre, p. 71 A, § 27,
יש שקראו עצמם עבדים והקב'ה קוראם עבדים ; M. T., p. 16, והמקום
; אלא במדת הקב'ה Sifre, p. 73 A, § 31, קרא אותם עבדים ; M. T.
25, אלא במדת המקום ; Sifre 74 A, § 33, באי זה צד אוהבים את הקב'ה
M. T. 26, המקום ; Sifre 75 B, § 37, אמר להם הקב'ה ; M. T. 29,
הזהרו שלא תמרדו בהקב'ה שאין אדם מורד ; Sifre 80 B, § 43, המקום
; בהקב'ה אלא מתוך שרעה M. T. 36, הזהרו שלא תמרדו במקום שאין
; אמר להן המקום ; ib., אמר להן הקב'ה ; M. T., אדם מורד במקום אלא
ib., אף הקב'ה פתח להן ; M. T., המקום ; ib., אמר לו הקב'ה הרי לי
שנים עדים ; M. T., המקום. Sifre 81 B, אלולא שתפו ישראל שמו
Sifre ; של הקב'ה בע'ז היו כלים מן העולם ; M. T. 38, שמו של מקום
85 A, § 49, אלו דרכי הקב'ה ; M. T. 43, אלו דרכי המקום ; Sifre 86 A,

;ונתן לפנינו המקום ,M. T. 45; ונתן הקב׳ה לפנינו ב׳ דרכים § 53,
לא נתכוונו להקריב אלא דבר שהקב׳ה שונא ,Sifre 91 B, § 81,
א׳ר עקיבא חס ושלום אלא מה שהמקום שונא; Sifre 92 A, M. T. 55,
שהמקום מעמיד; M. T. 63, שהקב׳ה מעמיד חמה ולבנה. These
instances can easily be increased to show that מקום is the
primary reading, and was displaced by the term of the
Amoraic period, namely הקב׳ה. There are many passages
where the original המקום stands in our texts as well.

This survey of the Tannaitic writings teaches clearly
that the oldest sources comprise sayings without the name
הקב׳ה. The later they are the greater appears the influence
of the Amoraic Haggada. Wherever and whenever critical
resources, even in a limited way, are at our disposal, we
cannot help feeling that הקב׳ה must be the secondary, and
המקום the primary term used by the ancient sages. Yet we
have still other proofs to corroborate our contention.

(7) The Haggada in the two works of the Talmud, the
Babylonian and the Palestinian, can be used as a test to
prove or disprove our theory. It is impossible to give here
the whole of our material. It will be consulted and quoted
eventually in the course of this treatise. In order to avoid
unnecessary repetition we will draw from various parts of
the Talmudic Haggada.

The stories, which aim at teaching that a man should
give credit to his fellow men for good and not for evil, refer
to events in the life of people who lived in the first century,
and in all of them the concluding phrase sounds : כשם שדנתי
לכף זכות המקום ידין אתכם לכף זכות (b. Shabb. 127 B). The
whole passage is taken from a Tannaitic source, when the
name הקב׳ה was not yet in use. In the story of R. Joshua
b. Korha with a certain eunuch, the former says : ברוך המקום
שמנעו לאותו האיש מכולם (b. Shabb. 152 A). A Boraita is
quoted : תלמיד אחד היה לו לר׳ אליעזר בן יעקב שנתחייב בשריפה למקום
(b. Erubin 54 A). Abba Hanan, in the name of R. Eliezer,
mentions the old saying of בזמן שישראל עושין רצונו של מקום
(b. Joma 3 B). In another Boraita we read יש בהם חובת מצוה
למקום (ib., 11 A). An old Boraita has : הרואה אותם צריך שית

שבה לפני המקום (b. Ber. 54 B). In the story of Hillel with
the proselyte, the latter says : ומה ישראל שנקראו בנים למקום
(b. Shabb. 30 B). R. Judah b. Ilai and R. Jose b. Halafta
used to say when visiting the sick : המקום ירחם עליך (ib., 12 B).
These instances, which can easily be multiplied, may suffice
to show that the redactors or editors of the Babylonian
Talmud preserved faithfully their sources. If that would
not be the case one could hardly explain the fact why
Simon b. Shetach, Abba Helkijahu, Hillel's proselyte, and
others should speak of המקום and not הקב'ה ? There must
be a cogent reason for this remarkable fact. We see in
this fact the most eloquent evidence for the genuineness
and veracity of our Rabbinic sources.

Many other similar observations can be made in reviewing our material derived from the Palestinian Talmud.
R. Eliezer b. Hyrkanos says that ' one should comfort a
friend at a loss of a slave or cattle with the words המקום
ימלא לך חסרונך (pal. Ber. ii. 8) '. At the end of a Boraita :
והיו שמחין שהסכימה דעתן לדעת המקום (pal. Sotah ix. 16) ; also
ib., 11 : וכי יש שינה לפני המקום, and כעם הוא לפני המקום ; j. Sotah
v. 6, vii. 7, R. Eleazar b. R. Simon, j. Sotah v. 6, R. Eleazar
b. Azarja to R. Akiba, and many more passages.

In many cases the Talmudic texts enable us to reconstruct
the original readings in the Tosefta or Tannaitic Midrash.
It is true that both Talmudic texts embody sayings by
Amoraic Haggadists in which המקום figures. Yet we can
account for them in one of two ways. First of all the
saying may be of Tannaitic origin altogether. Secondly,
some of the later preachers reveal an antiquarian practice
of using old phrases. The two texts of the Talmud really
belong to the third period of the Rabbinic writings. The
latter have to be divided into three groups. First the
sources, in which המקום is the general term, הקב'ה the exception or a later gloss ; the second, in which המקום was
displaced by הקב'ה ; and the third where הקב'ה is the rule
and המקום the exception. This latter group will be briefly
characterized in the next division.

(8) Our observation is even more fully confirmed by the
Midrashim, which undoubtedly belong to the period of the
Amoraim. We consider first the *Genesis rabba*. There we
learn the terms: (1) אדון לכל בריותיך (156), or אדון כל העולם
(365, R. Isaac), 'Lord of all Thy creatures', or 'Lord of the
whole world;' (2) איש, Man. (19, R. Simon b. Johai, and
92, 3, R. Josiah, r. Joshua b. Levi); (3) אלה, אלוהות when
idols are spoken of, or heathen in dispute with the Rabbis
referring to God ; (4) אלוף (182, אלופו של עולם); (5) בודק לבבות
(67. 8, R. Berechja, א׳ל הקב׳ה לית את ידע דאנא הוא בודקיהן
דלבבא); (6) בורא, Creator, very frequently; (7) בעל דין
(93. 11); (8) בעל פקדונות (560, R. Aha); (9) גדול העולמים (565,
R. Judah, R. Joshua b. Hananja, 100 8, R. Isaac); (10) גלגל
עינו של עולם (R. Aha, 401, v. also 412); (11) דיין (85, 246,
R. Simon b. Johai, 252, R. Akiba, 334, R. Meir, 519, R. Levi,
93, 11, R. Eleazar b. Azarja); (12) הוא (678, R. Aha);
(13) חי העולמים (418, 654, 661, 66. 2, 100. 6); (14) יוצר, several
times; (15) יחידו של עולם (24, 198, 200, 354, 511, 98, 18);
(16) כבוד, v. 28; (17) מי שאמר והיה העולם (28, 54, 230, 291,
593, 73. 4; (18) מלך מלכי המלכים, seven times; (19) מעלה
(119, 572); (20) מרום (65, 5); (21) מרי (114, 131, 140, 272,
99. 3); (22) עליון (220, R. Aibo); (23) צדיק חי העולמים (3) or
צדיקו של עולם (570); (24) קדמונו של עולם (356, R. Eleazar b.
Simon); (25) קונה (86); (26) רוח הקודש, several times;
(27) שכינה, very often; (28) שלום עולמים (66. 2); and
(29) שמים. Yet, whilst הקב׳ה occurs many hundred times,
the term מקום is mentioned altogether three times. First,
67. 2, in a saying of R. Hama b. Haninah, מי הוא זה שעושה
סרסור ביני לבין המקום, and 84. 13, in a saying of R. Jannai,
נסעו מזה ממדותיו של מקום. Both teachers belong to the first
generation of Amoraim, when probably the reform of the
name was not yet definitely carried through. The third
passage (68. 10) is by R. Huna in the name of R. Ami, when
the name מקום was entirely discarded and out of use. The
teachers and preachers at that time inquired as to the
meaning of the term, and advanced their theories.

(9) The same result can be gathered from a thorough

examination of the Tanhuma (I. Buber). Here we meet
the same names, with some additions as in the Genesis
rabba. Throughout the name הקב'ה is dominant, which
occurs several hundred times. The term מקום is mentioned
altogether five times (v. ii. 116, R. Jose b. Halafta : הנה אני
במקום הזה אין אין כתיב כאן אלא הנה מקום אתי מקומי טפל לי ואני טפל
למקומי, iii. 64 ; v. however ib., R. Simon, iv. 55, iv. 88, 120,
144, and v. 22, R. Levi). R. Samuel b. Nahman, who speaks
of מקום של רחמים and מקום של פורענות, does not seem to assume
that the term מקום is still connected in the popular mind
and speech with the name of God (i. 99).

(10) Pesikta of R. Kahana has also הקב'ה as a most significant feature ; מקום, however, in six places. These are
(1) 15 A, R. Huna, in the name of R. Idi, חם המקום על כבודו
של צדיק ; (2) 96 B, R. Levi, מתחטאים לפני המקום ; (3) 147 A,
R. Simon b. Johai, וישראל מצפים לישועתו של מקום ; (4) 182 B,
עושים רצונו של מקום ; (5) 165 A, הוא צוה לפני המקום ; and (6)
165 A, R. Levi, אנו באים לפני המקום. We may assume that
here, as well as in the Tanhuma, these Tannaitic sentences
remained unchanged.

(11) The Midrash on Psalms contains fourteen passages
with מקום, whilst the majority have הקב'ה. Some of these
passages are surely of Tannaitic origin or belong to teachers
of the early Amoraic period, others are borrowed from
Tannaitic sources.

(12) Midrash Samuel (ed. Buber, Cracow, 1893). This
Midrash has אלהים (pp. 70, 79, 109, 133), either in dialogues
by heathen, like the Matrona, or with reference to heathen
deities, but never as substitute for המקום or הקב'ה, we observed
in some books (e. g. Exodus rabba and Numbers rabba).
Further בורא (pp. 98, 120), בעל פקדונות (p. 98, R. Aha), the
old Tannaitic מי שאמר והיה העולם (p. 77, היה העכבר אומר לספסל
אני שלוחו של מי שאמר והיה העולם, originally from Sifre
Num. 88, cf. Yalkut Samuel, 91, in a saying of Abba b.
Zutra in the name of R. Samuel b. (Nahmani), אבל מי שאו'ה
ר'בא, Cant. r. 4. 5, v. ב"ה אינו כן אלא מתקן את הרטיה ואח'כ מכה
בשם ר' שמעון ; here the source of the idea can be traced back

להודיע שבחו של משו'ה שהוא מקרב את 134, to Tannaitic sources,
הרחוקים ושמח וכו', further מלך and מלכות שמים (pp. 63, 84, R.
Simon b. Johai, Simon b. Menasse, 64 and 141, ממ'ה הקב'ה),
and מקום once in a saying of R. Isaac, p. 52, v. however Gen.
r., ch. 48, ed. Th., 480. Tanh. B, i. 84, ed. F., and Ag. Ber.,
ch. 19, may be that the alteration is due to the quotation in
Tanh., בכל מקום ; the latter name occurs only once, and even
there it is doubtful. The name הקב'ה is quoted very frequently. Most of these sayings belong to the teachers of
the third century. There are one or two exceptions. In a
dialogue of the Matrona and R. Jose b. Halafta, p. 62, the
question is לכמה ימים ברא הקב'ה את עולמו ? It is rather
unusual that the interlocutor should use this term instead
of the usual אלהיכם. Gen. r. 68. 4, Lev. r. 8. 1, Pes. B. 11B
have the same reading. All are dependent on Gen. r., where
the tendency is proved to have prevailed to substitute הקב'ה
for other terms. The same may be the case in Bar Kappara's sentence, p. 74, עשה הקב'ה את שאינו נראה. There are
further the terms רבון כל חעול מים (pp. 47, 48, 64, 83), רחמנא
(p. 44, R. Phinehas b. Hama, אלא במאן דרחמנא רעי ביה), שכינה (in
the sayings of R. Hijja, 71, אלא כל זמן שהוא ? וכי שכינה היה עומד
כל המעיז, and R. Judan, 141, עומד לפני כאלו עומד לפני השכינה
שפרקו עול שמים (p. 64, פניו במלך כאילו מעיז פניו בשכינה), and שמים
p. 84, R. Simon b. Johai ; v. above מלך, sc. מלכות שמים, and
כבוד שמים 124, in antithesis to כבוד עצמו).

(13) Other Midrashim, like Lam. rabba, Eccles. rabba,
Cant. rabba, Leviticus rabba show the same characteristics.
The term המקום is found very rarely in them, and in such
form that we are enabled to recognize their origin at once.[50]
The later Midrashim, however, which have many excerpts
from older works, and in which the term הקב'ה was antiquated and supplanted by the older אלהים, have המקום more
frequently. Such are the younger Jelamdenu, Exodus
rabba, Numbers rabba, Seder Elijahu,[51] and Pirke R. Eliezer.

[50] Lam. r. has המקום twice, 27 and 42 ; M. Samuel once, 52 ; Agadath
Bereshith, twice, 11 and 32.
[51] We give here the names of God in the Seder Elijahu or Tanna debe

The Palestinian and Babylonian Talmud report the Tannaitic sayings mostly with the old terms. There is no better proof for the authenticity of a saying than the term for God's name. In a genuine old saying the term שמים or מקום ; in an overworked or later report הקב'ה occurs. Now it is very interesting to observe that in the eleventh and twelfth centuries הקב'ה of the third group and the האלהים of the later Midrashim have been supplanted by המקום, even in Amoraic sayings. This is a specially characteristic feature

Elijahu rabba (ed. Friedmann, Wien, 1900). This work offers fifteen names. Some of them occur only once or twice, e. g. אב הרחמים (pp. 19, 67). אלוה in speeches or questions of heathen, like p. 5. מפני מה ברא אלוה שקצים וכו', p. 31. 'Happy this people, whose portion is the Lord, their God', p. 27. Terah is told, 'make me a God' (אלוה), likewise אלהות for deities, pp. 52, 151,? וכי יש אלוה לעולם, but האלהים is also used in the fashion of Exod. r. and Num. r., v. p. 145. Once אלהי ישראל, p. 51, and יראת אלהים, p. 83, and אלהים שבשמים, p. 8, instead of אב שבשמים and יראת שמים respectively. The author likes the name בוחן לבות וכליות for God, pp. 30, 44, 48, 126. בורא occurs twice, pp. 27, 139. Like Midrash Samuel, S. E. R. calls God בעל הפקדון, p. 8. The term גבורה is used in a somewhat different sense from that in the older Midrashim, pp. 91, 108; all are drawn and go out from before the Geburah, or, 'thus the angels of destruction descend on the command of the Geburah, and take them. God is the judge' דיין (pp. 5, 56, &c.). Very frequent the old Tannaitic מי שאמר והיה העולם (pp. 4, 5, 9, 15, 17, 22, 31, 69, 96, 97, 103, 104, 105, 124 (twice), 132, 133 (twice), 139 (nineteen times), some of which may well have been excerpted from Tannaitic sources. Especially interesting is p. 69 : שמו של הקב'ה מי שאמר והיה העולם ברוך הוא. 'God's kingdom', 'the kingdom of Heaven'. God as King of all kings is very much emphasized in this work. The term מעלה occurs in connexion with כלפי מעלה, פנים של מ', כבוד של מעלה, and מעלה של מעלה. כנגד ב"ד של מעלה. Exceptional is the very frequent use of the term המקום in the S. Elijahu R. The sermons and meditations generally begin with ברוך המקום ברוך הוא, giving expression to the doctrine of God's omniscience, goodness, justice, wisdom, omnipresence, and creatorship. Yet the passages with הקב'ה are even more numerous. It seems that the S. E. R. adapted the old introductory form of ברוך המקום, which is to be found in the Mishna and Tosefta. This work is also rich in passages with רבון העולם, or rather רבון כל העולמים, שכינה and שמים. There is no other Midrash which offers such a rich source for the understanding and explanation of the term 'Father in Heaven', as will be seen in the chapter treating on the relation of God to man.

of the Midrash collections and excerpts coming from the school of Rashi. There must be some deeper reason for these alterations, the finding of which is, however, outside our task. It can be solved only on the other hand with the help of all the manuscripts available. For our present purpose we must be content to have shown the development of the post-Biblical names of God, which are really Prolegomena to the Old Rabbinic doctrine of God.

B.

THE ATTRIBUTES OF GOD

(1) *Omnipresence.*

God is everywhere present, in heaven and on earth, in
the upper and lower worlds ; He fills this and all the other
worlds, which are numerous ; there is no space, whether on
the ground or in the hollow of the air, which is not filled
by the divine majesty, or thought of as free from the
Shekhina.   In this attribute, as in many other outstanding
and significant problems of our doctrine, we can feel the
influence of external polemics, and the impulse of internal
creative power in dogmatic developments.   We have, to
begin with, *R. Gamaliel II.*   His dialogues on this subject
are to be analysed in the chapter of God's existence and
unity.   He is invisible, His place is not known, but there
is no place void of the Shekhina.   The teaching was repeated
and elaborated in the School of R. Ishmael.[1]   The Shekhina
is everywhere.   This view is opposed to that taught in the
Mekhilta[2] that the Shekhina does not dwell in the countries
outside Palestine.   We may see in this point also a difference
between the two Schools.   Many passages in the Bible are
quoted to show the doctrine of God's omnipresence, like
Ps. 139. 6–10, Zech. 4. 10, Prov. 15. 3, Amos 9. 3, Job 34. 21.
Yet this School seems to have made a distinction between
Shekhina and God.   R. Jose b. Halafta was surely moved
by heretic theories when he preached, ' Never descended the

---

[1] v. b. B. B. 25 a : ‏ואף ר׳ ישמעאל סבר שכינה בכל מקום‎ .
[2] 1 b.

Shekhina to the earth, and never did Moses or Elijah ascend to Heaven.[3] One cannot fail to express amazement at such a sentence, which ignores many words in the Bible, like Exod. 19. 20. A Boraita enumerates ten of God's descents, and details them by enumerating some passages from the Bible. They played a great part in Haggadic lore.[4] The same scribe revealed his opinion on our problem in another saying of his addressed to his son, R. Ishmael: 'If thou wilt behold the countenance of the Shekhina in this world, study the Torah in Palestine.'[5] God is everywhere present, but can be seen only through study of the law in Palestine. Thirdly, R. Jose b. Halafta deals with our problem in an often-quoted sentence, 'We do not know whether God is the place of His world, or the world is His place'. From Exod. 33. 21 we derive that God is the place of His world, and not *vice versa*.[6] Although the tradition as to the authorship of this saying is not perfectly established, inner reasons entitle us to ascribe it to this Tannaitic teacher of the second century. The deep thought expressed by this teacher anticipated metaphysical teachings of many a great thinker in the last centuries. A contemporary of our teacher, R. Meir, convinces us that the Scribes were interrogated about our teaching. According to our texts R. Meir was asked by a Samaritan to explain Jer. 23. 24: 'Behold I fill heaven and earth'. How could God speak to Moses

---

[3] b. Sukka, 8 A ; b. Shabb. 89 A.

[4] v. Pirke R. Eliezer, chaps. 14, 25, 39, 40, 41, 48 ; Aboth R. N. ch. 34 ; Gen. r. 38. 12, 49. 10, תני רשב״י ; Tanh. f. 13 A. The Hellenist, Aristobul, tried to explain these descents in a spiritual sense and to do away with the anthropomorphic conception, which contradicts the doctrine of God's omnipresence.

[5] M. Ps. 105. 1, ed. Buber, 448 : אמר ר' יוסי בן חלפתא לר' ישמעאל בריה מבקש אתה לראות פני שכינה בעולם הזה עסוק בתורה בארץ ישראל.

[6] So Gen. r. ch. 68, ed. Theodor, 777 ; Exod. r. 45. 6 ; R. Jose b. Hanina, Midr. ha Gadol, 446 r. ; R. Jose b. Abun ; Tanh. Ex., ed. Buber, תשא, 16, has also R. Jose b. Halafta ; it was also in the lost parts of pal. Makkoth and Sifre, v. S. b. Z. Duran, מגן אבות, ii. 9 ; v. now also M. Tannaim, 222, and above as to the history of מקום as God's name, p. 92.

from between the two divisions of the ark? R. Meir demonstrates by bringing large and small mirrors—that the figure of man changes according to the size of the looking-glass. If that is possible in the case of a human being, how much more likely is this with God.[7] Both teachers, as we know from other sources also, were well aquainted and in frequent communication with intellectuals and philosophers of their respective places of residence, Sepphoris and Tiberias. No wonder that the doctrine and its relation to the Bible cropped up in their discussions. The difficulty gave rise to the theory developed on the lines of R. Meir's reply to his interlocutor, of God concentrating His Shekhina in a certain place.[8]

Turning now to the teachings of the Amoraim, we notice that R. Hoshaja took trouble to repeat the teaching of R. Ishmael's school that God is omnipresent. He bases his homily on Neh. 9.6: 'Thou, O Lord, art alone, Thou hast made the heaven, &c. Thy messengers are unlike the messengers of earthly kings. The latter return to the place whence they are sent forth, but God's return at the place whither they were sent to'; cf. Job 38.35, 'Where-ever they are they are in God's presence'.[9] R. Joshua b. Levi remarks to Neh. 9.6 ('and the hosts of heaven bow down before Thee'): 'Come, let us be grateful to our ancestors, who taught us the place of prayers'.[10] The same teacher forbids to walk proudly on account of Isa. 6.3 ('full is the whole earth of His glory'): 'It looks

---

[7] Gen. r. 4, ed. Th. 27 f. : אמר לו אם שאתה בשר ודם משנה עצמך בכל מה שתרצה מי שאמר והיה העולם ע׳א כו׳כ.

[8] Called צמצום.

[9] b. B. B. 25 A : שלוחיך לא כשלוחי בו׳ד, שלוחי בו׳ד ממקום שמשתלחים לשם מחזירין שליחותן אבל שלוחיך למקום שמשתלחין שם מחזירין שליחותן. v. Mekh. 2 A has the same saying anonymously : שלוחי הקב׳ה לא כשלוחי בו׳ד ששלוחי בו׳ד צריכין לחזור אצל שולחיהם אבל לפניך אינו כן וכו׳ בכל מקום שהן מהלכין נמצאו לפניך. We have here one of the many Amoraic interpolations of the Mekhilta.

[10] b. B. B. 25 A, meaning to say that every place is fit for prayer.

as if the creature would boast himself before his maker '
(b. Kid. 31 A). He developed further R. Jose b. Halafta's
idea of God's omnipresence in a sermon based on Jer. 23. 24.
One might infer from this passage that God fills merely
heaven and earth, the upper and lower worlds. This is a
mistake! The whole universe together is not greater
than God's smallest finger can contain or touch (M. Ps. 8. 6,
ed. B. 78: לפי שהקב'ה אומר להן והלא את השמים ואת הארץ דעו,
כי העליונים והתחתונים אין בהן אלא מעשה אצבעותיך, fuller ib., 19. 6,
p. 165: אין בה אלא כדי מישוש אצבעו של הקב'ה). The parable
leaves no room for doubt that the whole sermon is directed
against the critics of God's creation, the Gnostics, who
alleged the inferiority of the 'Jewish' God (v. also Tanh.
iv. 29: כביכול הקב'ה מלא עליונים ותחתונים שנ' הלא את השמים,
ובמקום שבא הנואף לנאוף הלא הקב'ה בכבודו שם שנ' מלא כל הארץ
כבודו, and M. Ps. 62. 3, p. 307, R. Hijja b. Abba of Jophe:
מניין שהקב'ה מלא חללו של עולם שנא' הלא את השמים; further
Num. r. 9. 9, Tanh. נשא 8 to Prov. 15. 3, Zech. 4. 10, אמר הקב'ה
אפילו בחללו, אני ממלא העליונים והתחתונים, Mekh. Deut. r. 2. 28,
של עולם). R. Simon b. Lakish follows R. Jose b. Halafta in
explaining the saying of God's descent on Mount Sinai.
Although it appeared as if God descended on Sinai
(Exod. 19. 20), yet the Sinai was dependent on Him ; cf.
Ps. 68. 18).[11] R. Levi expounds Exod. 40. 35 by the parable of
a cave, which was situated near the sea. It once filled with
water, but the waters of the sea were not diminished. The
Tabernacle was full of God's glory, yet the world did not
lack anything of the glory.[12] R. Isaac, R. Ammi, and
others repeat R. Jose b. Halafta's saying as to God being
the habitation of the world, and not the world the
habitation of God.[13] R. Phinehas b. Hama expresses the
thought in this way: 'A worldly king can be either in
his bed-chamber or in his reception room, but he cannot
be in both of them at one and the same time. God ﹀

[11] M. Ps. 68. 10, ed. Buber, p. 319.
[12] Pes. 2 B ; ib. r. 19 B ; Cant. r. 3. 10 ; Num. r. 12. 4 ; Tanh. ii. (ויקהל).
[13] Gen. r. 68. 9 ; M. Ps. 90. 10, p. 390.

fills both in the same moment'. Cf. Ps. 148. 13 and Jer. 23. 24.[14]

The often-quoted parallel between God and the human soul dwells on the fact that the soul fills the whole body, likewise God the whole universe. This idea is derived from R. Gamaliel II's reply to his questioner.[15] The doctrine is further illustrated in a legend. R. Tanhuma relates that once a whole company of pagans boarded a ship, and a Jewish child was among them. A great storm threatened the boat, and all the lives on it were in the greatest danger of being lost. Each of the passengers took his idol in his hands, prayed to it, but to no good purpose. Then, seeing that their gods could not help, they turned to the Jew, and said to him: 'Boy, rise and entreat your God, for we have heard that He hears your supplication whenever you cry unto Him!' He poured out his heart in prayer. God heard his request, and the sea became silent. When they reached a port, all of them went to provide themselves with the supplies for their journey. The Jew remained on the boat. His fellow travellers asked: 'Do you not buy any provisions?' The Jew replies: 'What do you want of such a poor stranger as I am?' They said: 'You a poor humble stranger? We are strangers. Some of us are here, and our gods in Babylon or Rome ; others carry their gods with them and derive no benefit from them whatever. You, however, wherever you go, your God is with you.'[16] 'God', says R. Isaac, 'is with his creatures on the scaffold, in fire, water, in the den of lions, and saves them, which cannot be said of a human friend, even of the mightiest of kings, because they are confined to one place, and cannot

---

[14] Num. r. 12. 4. He emphasizes also that God is near to all His creatures, although He seems to be far removed, whilst the idols seem to be very near, yet they are indeed very far away, unable to hear the prayers of those who entreat them ; pal. Ber. 13 A ; M. Ps. 4. 3.

[15] b. Sanh. 39 A ; Exod. r. 29 ; Pirke R. El. ch. 7 ; M. Ps. 103. 5 ; b. Ber. 10 A ; Lev. r. iv. 8 ; Deut. r. 2. 37.

[16] pal. Ber. 13 B.

appear everywhere.' [17] It is natural that this doctrine
was developed in no other religious system as in Judaism.
The whole doctrine is alien to the spirit of polytheism.
The teachers of Jewish religion advanced religious thought
immensely by putting this idea in the forefront of their
speculations. A correlative of this doctrine is the universalistic aspect of the Rabbinic doctrine of God, which will
engage our attention in the chapter dealing with God's
relation to man. This is a subject which has not met
with much appreciation on the part of modern theologians.[18]

(2) *Omniscience.*

With the conception of omnipresence is closely connected the doctrine of the omniscience of God. Since God
is everywhere present, He knows man and the world,
history and life, wherever they happen to be and whenever
they originate and pass away. He knows the thoughts of
men before they are conceived, and foresees actions prior
to their existence. Since the omnipresence is not only in
space but also in time, as a consequence God's knowledge
has no limit either in space or in time. There must be
a cogent reason for repeating and emphasizing this idea so
often. We notice even in the apocryphal and pseudepi-
graphical writings that great stress is being laid on this
doctrine. The writers of those books, with very few exceptions, do not get weary of repeating God's omniscience.
This was surely due to some mighty opposition to this
theological conception. God knew the world before it was
created. He knows the secrets of the heart before they
rose in men. No sinner can hide his misdeeds before Him.
The teaching found its way into one of the most solemn

[17] pal. Ber. 13 A ; v. also R. Eleazar, ib., 13 B.

[18] v. however, now, Moore, *History of Religions*, ii, 1920, p. 69, and
G. Kittel, *Probleme des pal. Spätjudentums und Urchristentums.* Stuttgart
1926, p. 133 f.

prayers in Jewish liturgy. 'Thou knowest the secrets of
the world, and the hidden thoughts of every life ; Thou
searchest the chambers of the womb, and testest the sinews
and heart !' is the Jew's prayer on the Day of Atonement.
' Nothing is hidden from Thee, nor is anything covered from
before Thy eyes !'[1] The preachers introduced their homilies
by announcing emphatically this attribute of God: ברוך המקום
ברוך הוא שמכיר בראש ובסוף, ומגיד מראשית אחרית מקדם עד שלא נעשה
ויודע מה שנעשה ומה שעתיד להיעשות וצופה לטובה ואין צופה לרעה.[2]
R. Johanan b. Zakkai explained to his pupils why the Law
dealt more severely with the thief than with the robber.
The latter treated master and slave in the same way. The
former thought of God's eye, as if it could not see, and His
ear, as if it could not hear (cf. Isa. 29.15, Ps. 94.7, Ezek. 9.9).
They had to contend against those who thought that God
cannot see and discern human actions.[3] R. Joshua b.
Hananja is reported to have been asked by the Romans
(רומיים): ' Whence do we know that God will revive the
dead and knows the future ?' The scribe replied by quoting
Deut. 31.16: ' And the Lord said unto Moses, "behold thou
shalt sleep with thy fathers, and rise up, and the people will
go whoring after the gods "', &c. The questioners were not
satisfied, for they read : ' And the people will rise up', &c.
R. Joshua said: 'Do admit at least that God knows the
future !'[4]   R. Johanan repeats the same doctrine in the
name of R. Simon b. Johai,[5] who dwells on this teaching
in another homily, also saying: 'A human being does not
know his minutes, times, and hours, but God knows them'.[6]
R. Ishmael asks as to Exod. 12.12 (' when I see the blood ').
' Is not everything revealed before Him ? He knoweth
what is in the darkness, and light dwelleth in Him ' (Dan.

[1] Mahzor Vitry, 390–91.

[2] S. E. R. ch. 1, p. 3 ; M. Tadshe, p. ix ; E. D. Z. in Yalkut Deut., § 827 ;
Tanh., f. 74 A.

[3] B. K. 79 B, and paralls. : השוה כבוד עבד לכבוד קונו כביכול עשה עין
שלמעלה כאילו אינה רואה ואזן של מעלה כאילו אינה שומעת.

[4] b. Sanh. 90 B ; v. also Oppenheim, האסיף, vi. 1894, 97.

[5] Ib.   [6] Gen. r. 10.10, ed. Theodor, 85.

2. 22). ' Yea, the darkness hideth not from Thee' (Ps. 139.
12).[7] The verb does not mean to say that God saw, but
that God revealed Himself as a reward for performing the
duties connected with the Passover. According to a second
interpretation God remembered the sacrifice of Isaac.[8] The
Siphre Zutta explains the term אלהי הרוחות ' God of Spirits'
(Num. 27. 16) : ' God, who knows the mind and spirit of each
individual, whether high or low, whether humble or quarrel-
some', implying the teaching of God's omniscience.[9] There
were other passages in the Scriptures which gave rise to
many objections to this teaching and called for doubts.
Sayings like Gen. 13. 17, 32. 12, Jer. 18. 8, Jon. 3. 10,
1 Sam. 15. 35 caused trouble to the ancient translators,[10]
Philo [11] and the writers of the Clementines.[12] The latter
saw in all these instances later insertions of the Jews.
One of these objectors asked R. Joshua b. Korha about
Gen. 6. 6: ' Do you not say that God knows the future?'
R. J. b. K.: ' Yes.' Heathen : ' How do you account, then, for
God's repentance and grief ?'   R. J. b. K.: ' Well, have you
got a son ?' H. : ' Yes.' R. J. b. K.: ' What did you do when
he was born ?' H. : ' I rejoiced and caused others to rejoice
with me !' R. J. b. K.: ' Did you not consider that the boy
would die ?'   H. : ' Yes, but one should rejoice at the time of
joy, and mourn in time of death.' R. J. b. K.: ' The same
is the case with God !' [13]

Great stress was laid by the Amoraic preachers on the

---

[7] Mekh. 8 A, 12 A.

[8] Ps. Jonathan translates in this sense : ואחמי ית זכות אדמה, i. e. of
the Passover-sacrifice and of the circumcision (12, 13), yet v. 23 he translates literally. ויחמי ית אדמא; v. Onkelos, וחזי ית דמא.

[9] v. ed. Horowitz, p. 320.

[10] v. Dähne, Gesch. Darstell. ii. 38.

[11] Quod deus sit nesciunt, 296.

[12] Schliemann, *die Clementinen*, 198.

[13] Gen. r. 27. 7 ; 1 K. H. 57 A : אין הקב'ה רואה את הנולד. The heathen
questioner speaks of הקב'ה, v. above, p. 69. On the opposition of the
Gnostics to this doctrine, v. Harnack, *Origines*, i. 32 ; about similar
inquiries in the Middle Ages between Jews and Christians, v. Beth
Talmud, iii. 12.

idea that sinners cannot hide their evil deeds or wicked thoughts before their Maker. R. Hoshaja[14] expounds Isa. 29. 15, a passage which R. Johanan b. Zakkai used already for the same purpose,[15] rebuking those 'that seek deep to hide their counsel from the Lord, and their works are in the dark, and they say : ' Who seeth us and who knoweth us ? ' Like an architect, who built a palace with all its rooms, channels, and underground places, and became their tax-collector, and said : ' I built all these secret places ; from whom do ye hide yourselves ? God formed man and he wants to hide himself from Him, and thinks that God does not know and see ! R. Jannai [16] treats this doctrine at some length with reference to Ps. 11. 4, ' The Lord is in his holy temple, the Lord's throne is in heaven ; his eyes behold, his eyelids try the children of men '. Like a king who owned an orchard, he gathered workmen into it. At the gate of the orchard there was a treasury full of precious things. The king said : ' Whoever will discharge his work whole-heartedly shall get his wages ; hence the others will be judged in my palace '. God is the King of all kings. The world the orchard. Children of men the workmen. Those that observe faithfully the Torah will receive their reward in the Garden of Eden, the others will be punished in Hell. God says : ' Although I seemingly removed my Shekhina from the sanctuary, yet my eyes behold !' R. Johanan bar Nappacha must have had special reasons to recur so often to our doctrine. We saw above that he preserved a saying of R. S. b. J. on our subject [17] : ' God can behold the upper

---

[14] So in edd. Gen. r. 24. 1 ; v., however, Th. 229 ; R. Levi ; M. Ps. 14. 1 ; Tanh. B. iv., נשא, 8 ; Num. r. 9. 1.

[15] v. above, p. 154.

[16] Tanh. ii. 6 ; Exod. r. 2. 2 ; M. Ps. 11. 3, ed. B. 99, quotes another parable similar to that given above, p. 152, in the name of R. Phinehas b. Hama, to illustrate God's omnipresence : מלך בו'ד כשהן נכנסין לטרקלין אינו רואה מה בקיטון אבל הקב'ה אינו כן. If a king enters the triclinium, he cannot see what happens in the κοιτών ; not so God. His throne is in Heaven, yet He צופה ומביט בכל העולם ואין עין שולטת בו, sees everything, though he is invisible.

[17] v. above, p. 154.

and lower world with one glance ; not so a human king'.[18]
'God beholds the deeds of all creatures [19] at one glance.'
R. Simon b. Lakish taught that God foresaw both worlds
with one glance.[20] The same teaching is further developed
by R. Abbahu and R. Hijja bar Abba.[21] The former teaches
that God foresaw the deeds of the wicked and righteous,
the latter speaks of the building, destruction, and rebuilding of the Temple. The 'foresight' of God is one of the
most favoured motifs of the Haggada.[22] God knew that in
future righteous and wicked would arise, that Israel would
receive the Torah and sin ; Moses and Thorah passed before
His eyes long before their birth, the knowledge of the nations,

[18] Gen. r. 9. 3, ed. Th. 68 : מלך בו׳ד בונה פלטין מביט בעליונים ראיה
אחת ובתחתונים ראייה אחת אבל הקב׳ה מביט בעליונים ובתחחונים ראייה
אחת ; v. also 12. 12 : אבל הקב׳ה ברא העליונים ואת התחתונים ברייה אחת
'All the worlds were created at the same time'.
[19] b. R. H. 18 B, Rabba b. Hama, in his name : וכולן נסקרין בסקירה אחת
v. also Num. r. 11. 6.
[20] Gen. r. 9. 3 : העולם הזה והעולם הבא הבים בהם הקב׳ה ראיה אחת.
[21] Gen. r. 2. 5, ed. Th. 18, according to Gen. r. ch. 3. 10, ed. Th. 23,
one would be inclined to suggest R. Jannai instead of R. Abahu, and
R. Hijja 'the great', instead of R. Hijja b. Abba. In that case R. S. b. L.
developed the teachings of the earlier Haggadists.
[22] A few instances will suffice. Gen. r. 1. 5, ed. Th. 6 f. ; R. Samuel b.
Isaac, צפה הקב׳ה שאחר כ׳ו דורות ישראל וכו׳ ; Gen. r. 4. 8 ; R. Tanhum
b. Hanilai, ed. Th. 30, מתחלת בריית העולם צפה הקב׳ה משה כי קרוי טוב ;
Gen. r. 6. 1, R. Hanina b. Hama, ed. Th. 40, אלא צפה הקב׳ה שאו׳ה עתידין ;
Gen. r. 8. 4, R. Berekhja, ראה צדיקים ורשעים יוצאים ממנו ; Gen.
r. 9. 6, R. Hanina b. Hama, צפה הקב׳ה שנ׳נ וחירום מלך צור עתידיו
מתחלת בריתו של עולם ; Gen. r. 9. 13, R. Joseph, לעשות עצמן אלוהות
צפה הקב׳ה שהוא עתיד לקרוא ; Gen. r. 17. 5. R. Aha, צפה הק׳ במדה
וצפה הקב׳ה שיעקב ; Gen. r. 63. 2, R. Samuel b. Isaac, עליה תנר לפיכך
עתיד לעמוד ממנו, v. above, Gen. r. 1. 5 ; Gen. r. 74. 2, R. Abbahu, צפה
; Gen. r. 98. 4, R. Judah b. הקב׳ה שלא היתה כוונתה אלא לשם שמים
Simon ; Exod. r. 41. 3, R. Phinehas b. Hama, צפוי וגלוי לפני הקב׳ה
צפה הקב׳ה וראה שישראל, v. also Exod. r. 3. 3 and 40. 1, שעתידין ישראל
מקבלין התורה ; Tanh. iv. 23, צפה הקב׳ה שקרח עתיד לעמוד ; Tanh.
iv. 24, צפה הקב׳ה שעתידין ישראל להכעים לפניו. We find the verb צפה
in connexion with the knowledge of the future of many biblical persons,
v. Gen. r. 11. 2 (Adam), Ag. Ber. 12 (Jacob), Gen. r. 3. 2 (the earth), &c.

idol-worship as well as the deifying of the individual, dates
back to the creation of the world. The Haggadists and
Liturgists further furnish the phrase, רבהע' גלוי וידוע לפניך
' Lord of the whole world, it is revealed and known before
Thee!' by which the prayers of biblical personages in the
Haggada are introduced. The fact that God knows past
and future, the thoughts of human souls, and sees all movements of the body, is one of the most firm religious con-
victions of the Scribes. A few instances of these Haggadic
prayers will bear out the truth of this observation, which
was of great influence on the earliest liturgical compositions.[23] The omniscience of God is due, according to some,
to His creatorship; according to others, to His uniqueness
or unity. The first thought is expressed by R. Hoshaja [24]
or R. Levi, and also in anonymous sayings.[25] R. Levi,
R. Eleazar b. Pedath and R. Berekhja see it proclaimed in
Ps. 33. 15, ' He who formed together their heart, understands all their deeds '.[26] Others, like R. Phinehas b. Hama,
R. Judah b. Shalom, and R. Abun base it on Job 23. 13,
' He is One '. Owing to His Oneness He knows the judgement and mind of His creatures.[27]

Many other Bible verses teaching the omniscience of God
were amplified and elaborated in the homilies and teachings
of the Scribes (1 Chron. 28), ' The Lord searcheth all hearts,
and understandeth all the imagination of the thoughts '.
God understands man's thoughts before they have been
formed.[28] Even before man is born his thoughts and

---

[23] For the phrase גלוי וידוע v. R. Simon, Pes. 43 B : וכבר גלוי וידוע
גלוי וידוע ; ib., 200 A, R. Abbahu : לפניך שאין או׳ה מקבלים את תורתך
לפני מי שאמר והיה העולם שאין או׳ה מקבלין את התורה.
[24] v. above, note 14 ; M. Ps. 14. 1.
[25] Tanh. נשא, 6–8.　　　　　[26] pal. Ber. 13 A.
[27] Tanh. וירא, 21 ; Exod. r. 14.
[28] M. Ps. 45. 4, ed. B., p. 270 : עד שאין אדם צר את המחשבה בלבו
הקב׳ה עד ש/א ידבר אדם הוא יודע מה בלבו : Exod. r. 21. 3 ; הקב׳ה מבין,
where the saying is ascribed to R. Eleazar ben Pedath ; v. also Gen. r. 9. 3,
where the teaching is repeated by R. Haggai and R. Judan in the name
of R. Isaac. The first reads : קודם עד שלא נוצרה מחשבה בלבו של אדם

actions are known to God. Secondly, Jer. 23. 24, 'Can
anyone hide himself in secret places that I shall not see
him?' R. Levi makes the Holy Spirit say to those
Israelites who left the manna, so that insects issued from
their tents: 'You think that you are acting in secret
places, and I do not see? Can a man hide in secret', &c.[29]
R. Benjamin b. Levi interprets the sentence: 'If anyone
hides himself in secret, shall I not show him and put him
to shame before the world?'[30] Thirdly, Isa. 46. 10, 'Declaring the end from the beginning, and from ancient times
that are not yet done. Everything is foreseen by God',[31]
which is merely a repetition of, or a support for, R. Akiba's
saying, הכל צפוי 'Everything is foreseen'.[32] The doctrine
of divine foreknowledge is older than R. Akiba. R. Johanan
b. Zakkai and his pupil, R. Joshua b. Hananja, taught the
same. Both were preceded by Simon b. Shetach, who used
בעל מחשבות 'Lord of Thoughts', or יודע מחשבות, as one of
God's names.[33] Fourthly, Ps. 139. 4, 'Thou, O Lord, knowest
all'. David says before God: 'Thou knowest my resting
and rising, all my steps I am going to walk in future
(Job 14. 16), even before I was born (Jer. 1. 5), there is no
word on my tongue Thou dost not know!'[34]

Owing to God's omniscience he is also called הרואה ואינו נראה
'The Invisible, Who beholds all'.[35] He is not seen even
by the creatures who carry His throne, according to

קודם עד שלא נוצר יצור כבר מחשבתו .the latter r כבר היא גלויה לפניך
גלויה לפני.

[29] Tanh. B. ii. 68.

[30] Tanh. B. iv. 29; Num. r. 9. 9, reading אֲראֵנוּ instead of אֶרְאֵנוּ, combining it with Zech. 4. 10 and 2 Chron. 16. 9, 'the eyes of the Lord,
which run to and fro through the whole world'; v. also Tanh. i. 24;
v. also Prov. 15. 3.

[31] Tanh. iv. 68; Num. r. 16.   [32] Aboth iii. 17.

[33] v. above, p. 79.

[34] M. Ps. 528.

[35] v. R. Hoshaja, j. Peah 8. 8: דין דחמי ולא מתחמי אל קבל פיוסך ; b. Hag.
5 B: תזכו להקביל פנים הרואים ואינן נראין ; Deut. r. l. 9, R. Berekhja:
ומי הוא אלוה האלהים הרואה ואינו נראה ; M. Ps. 91. 1, R. Judah b. Simon:
b. נחשא פרוזדוק .R, כל המעשים רואה ואינו נראה in his name; Ps. Jon.
Gen. 24. 12 and 25. 11.

R. Akiba.   Simon b. Azzai adds that even the everlasting ministering angels cannot behold His glory.[36]

(3) *Omnipotence.*

This attribute is another characteristic doctrine which places the religious thought of the Israelites higher than the climax of all the religions of Egypt, Mesopotamia, Persia, Greece, and Rome.   Christianity, owing to the influences of Hellas and Rome on one side, the Mystery Religions on the other, could not adapt itself completely to this higher conception.   The nature-of polytheism and magical conceptions contradicts or denies this attribute of the Godhead.   If magic could influence God, if God Himself was addicted to magical performances, then His strength is not worth much.   If a god, even the highest, is not free in his actions and deliberations, and even the Greek Zeus is dependent on the members of his household, the Zara-thustrian god hindered by his counterpart, then there is no room for the idea of omnipotence.   A great drawback of the polytheistic religions is the idea of the sexes among Gods. Here again the Christian religion could not rid itself entirely of pagan teachings.   The goddess curtails by her sympathies and antipathies, likings and dislikings, weakness of judge-ment and strength of feelings, the plans of the highest God. The religion of the Rabbis was free from all these shackles of superstition and misconception.   Israel knows no god-dess, and is free from magic and witchcraft, which perished in the long fight during centuries, and disappeared from the soil of Palestine.   Whatever remained in dark corners of life and love, habits and beliefs, law and religion, adapted themselves to a purer monotheism.   There can be no doubt that people and scribes, educated and uneducated, priests and laymen, consented to the belief and thought that ' God's strength and might fill the earth '.[1]   When the teachers

---

[36] Siphra 4 B ; Num. r. 14. 22.

[1] Cf. Ps. 106. 2 ; Pirke R. E. ch. 3 ; v. also b. Megilla, 16 B, R. Eleazar.

and preachers in the schools and houses of worship spoke of גבורה ' Might ', all the hearers knew without any need of further information that the all-powerful God, the Almighty Father in heaven was meant. Curiously enough this most expressive word was not used when describing or depicting the miracles of life, the wonders of nature, the riddles of the universe, and the almost incomprehensible work of creation, but to the great revelation of God's being and teaching to His people Israel on Sinai.[2] By this testimony these men testified their own greatness and worth. For man's greatness lies not in his contribution to material progress of mankind, but by making visible by moral and spiritual light, by piety and wisdom the light of the unseen worlds. The ' Gebhurah ' was ' the Power of God ', manifested in the light of the Torah. The Gospels (Matt. 26. 64, Mark 14. 62) quote this word ($\delta\acute{v}\nu\alpha\mu\iota\varsigma$), and knew that God = גבורה = $\delta\acute{v}\nu\alpha\mu\iota\varsigma$ have the same meaning. Luke did not understand it, therefore he added ' the might of God ' ($\tau o\hat{v}\ \theta\epsilon o\hat{v}$), which is superfluous (Luke 22. 69). We have seen that many Scribes of the first and following centuries knew this name.

The Scribes contribute a good many new points to the elucidation of this attribute. We do not meet at this stage of doctrine the idea of the incomprehensibility of God's power. We do find, however, many traces of the teaching that man is unable duly to express God's greatness and power. They must have had their own theories, some of which are recorded, some unknown, about nature and history, life and death. God was the centre of all that is great and powerful, of wisdom and might. The rebukes and warnings against those who tried to give utterance to God's greatness and might, presuppose that there existed conceited people who pretended to do so. They were put in their right place. ' Who can express by words the mighty acts of God, and who can show forth all his praise ? Is there a being in existence who is able to utter the mighty deeds of God, or who can praise Him according to His

[2] v. p. 82.

L

greatness ? No, not even the ministering angels are able to do so !' The angels, we learnt above,[3] cannot see God's glory, nor can they utter all His praise, power, and greatness. Such an attempt was earnestly rebuked and severely criticized by the teachers. There is a good historical reason for the fact that the teachers of the third century devote much attention to this problem. Strong words were used to condemn the heaping up of epithets in prayers or sermons. R. Johanan b. Nappacha, one of the authoritative spokesmen of the age, says : ' He who speaks or relates too much of God's praise will be uprooted from this world (life).'[3a] Since those expressions, נעקר מן העולם, or נטרד מן העולם, and מתבלע מן העולם are always used to express disfavour of heretic, especially Gnostic, ideas and thoughts, we can guess whom the teacher of Tiberias had in his mind when he pronounced his statement. Gnostics thought that by their intuition and magic one could penetrate into the chambers of heaven ; they dared and pretended to reveal in their theosophical studies God's power. We are told that R. Johanan and R. Jonathan, when visiting a place in the South, heard a reader, who may or may not have been an adherent of some Gnostic sect, say in the Eighteen Benedictions, האל הגדול הגבור והנורא האדיר והאמין, and these scribes ordered him to be silent ![4] All the names and attributes, synonyms, and expressions, can never convey the idea of God's power and might. R. Huna, another teacher of this age, seems to imply the thought of the incomprehensibility of God's might. Basing his words on Job 26. 14, he says : ' All that thou seest is merely an infinitesimally small part

---

[3] v. p. 159 f.

[3a] b. Meg. 18 A, based on Job 37. 20 ; pal. Ber. 12 D ; M. Ps. 19. 2, ed. B. 163. In the first place R. Abba b. Hana, in the second and third R. Abbahu teaches this in the name of R. Johanan. The first preserved the saying : המספר שבחו של הקב׳ה יותר מדאי נעקר מן העולם, the second : אם בא אדם לספר גבורותיו של הקב׳ה מתבלע מן העולם.

[4] pal. Ber., 12 D ; v. however M. Ps. 163, where, more correctly, R. Haninah b. Hama went with R. Jonathan, and not R. Johanan ; v. also b. Ber. 33 B.

of God's ways. Man cannot conceive the meaning of the
thunder, hurricane, storm, the order of the universe, his
own nature ; how can he boast of being able to understand
the ways of the King of all kings ? ' [5] In this age the
opinion was repeated that even the greatest men of antiquity, like Moses, &c., could not reach a proper view of God's
greatness. It is too much for the human mind. Moses
prays for such a revelation, according to R. Johanan, but
his request is not complied with.[6] The words of Zophar,
the Naamathite (Job 11. 7) were understood to teach the
incomprehensibility of God's creation on the part of man.
Moses admitted the futility of man's endeavours to penetrate into the riddles of God's might, and David confesses,
after many disappointments of research and seeking to
reach it, that man cannot come near to the knowledge of
God's greatness and power.[7] It has been pointed out
already [8] that the omniscience of God, his wisdom, fostered
the value of knowledge, encouraged research, and put
learning and wisdom on a very high level, but there are
barriers before the human mind, which cannot be broken
down, which prevent access to the gnosis of God's power,
origins of world and man. The answers to Whence and
Whither are withheld. The scribes, with all their love of
and longing for, the gnosis, admitted modestly their
inability to satisfy their desire of expressing God's
omnipotence. If all the seas were ink, all the forests
supplied pens, all the heavens folded into parchments,
all the hands and tongues of men could not approxi-
mately describe or depict God's power and greatness.
Mortal man is too weak or insignificant, small and power-
less to utter immortal God's power and might ! This

---

[5] Gen. r. 12. 1 ; Eccles. r. 2. 12.

[6] M. Ps. 25. 6, ed. Buber, 211, R. Berekhja, in his name ; v. also the
parable of the medical practitioner. God's answer is אין אתה יכול לעמוד
על מדותי 'man cannot fully grasp God's attributes'.

[7] M. Ps. 139. 1, ed. B. 527 ; v. also Tanh. iii. 80 : אין בריה יכולה לעמוד
על מעשיו, or אין אדם יכול להגיע לגבורותיו של הקב׳ה.

[8] v. above, p. 157, note 22.

thought was repeated in homilies and parables. A very
remarkable homily furnishes us with material on our
problem particularly, and on the attributes of God
especially. To Exod. 15. 1, ' I will sing unto the Lord ', an
ancient preacher remarked: ' Unto God it is meet to
attribute greatness, power, glory, victory, and majesty ;
cf. 1 Chron. 29. 11. When a king enters a city, he is
praised as a hero, whilst he actually is weak ; as a wise man,
whilst he is a fool ; as a rich man, whilst he is poor ; as a
kindhearted man, whilst he is cruel ; as a just judge, and
he has none of these virtues. Quite different is the case
with God (מי שאמר והיה העולם) ! His power, wealth, wisdom,
love, justice are much higher than the praise which can
be expressed by man. In this sense sang the Israelites on
the sea : "I will sing unto Him "!' [9] In another homily a
preacher explains Ps. 19. 2, ' A king ruled over many cities.
The people of these places said : "The king has so much
gold, silver, &c., so and so many slaves, jewels, &c."' A
clever old man, who listened to them, said : ' Whence do you
know all this ? You are living so far from your king ?
Have you seen his wealth ? The people of the city, where
he dwells, are entitled to speak of the king's wealth and
praise him.' Thus says David : ' The whole earth and its
fulness is unable to relate God's praise. Who is able to do
so ? The heavens relate the glory of God.' [10]

[9] v. Mekh. 35 A, M. R. S. b. J. 57 proves the attributes of *wisdom*, from
Prov. 3. 19, Job 12. 3 ; *wealth*, Deut. 10. 14, Hag. 2. 8 ; *love*, Exod. 34. 6,
Deut. 4. 31 ; *justice*, Isa. 30. 18, Ps. 82. 1 ; *faithfulness*, Deut. 7. 9 and 32. 4 ;
beauty, Ps. 89. 7 and 9, 86. 8 ; Cant. 1. 10–16. We see here that not the
Greeks alone attach importance to the attribute of beauty, as Farnell,
(*Attributes of God*, Oxford, 1926, p. 211, although he refers to the Psalmist's
' Out of Zion hath God appeared in perfect beauty '), assumes, but the
rabbis did so likewise. The Mekh. R. S. b. J. omitted here the passages for
the attribute of power. Mekh. supplies Deut. 10, Ps. 24. 8, Isa. 42. 3,
Jer. 10. 6. Altogether the quotations and biblical proofs for the attributes
are more complete in the Mekh. than in the M. R. S. b. J. For *wisdom*
Mekh. cites also Prov. 2. 6, Dan. 2. 21, Jer. 10. 6 ; for *wealth* Ps. 24. 1,
Ezek. 18. 4 ; for *love* Ps. 25. 6, 145. 9, Dan. 9. 9 ; for *justice* Deut. 1. 17,
and 32. 4. The M. is quoted Tanh. B. ii. 1 in a shortened form and
M. Ps. B. 454.

[10] M. Ps. B. 112.

A teacher [11] extends this deficiency of human knowledge even to the understanding of God's providence and care for His creatures. 'Wherefore does the text say, it is asked, לעושה נפלאות לבדו He, who performs wonderful things by Himself?' Does anyone help Him? or does He require help? No, but man is unable to relate God's greatness and wonders, which he (man) enjoys. 'Therefore', says R. Aha,[12] 'man cannot express the multitude of God's kindnesses experienced by, and shown to him.' R. Berekhja formulates this thought: 'Praise Him as much as you can, and you will not find it sufficient!' Other contemporary teachers point out: 'David praised God with all the limbs of his body, and yet all his efforts proved unsatisfactory.'[13]

In spite of this conscious weakness of the human mind, the Haggadists did not neglect preaching on and dealing with this doctrine. They applied similes and parables to bring home this conception to their hearers. One tannaitic Haggadist develops the following aspects of our teaching:[14] (a) God has power and strength, soldiers, and leads in war;[15] (b) His power and strength are unchanged through the ages; (c) God does not change His love and mercy even in chastising His creatures; (d) God *changes* His decrees issued against His creatures, in case they repent; (e) God hears all who pray and cry unto Him in their distress; and (f) God's providence extends, even during His fight against the Egyptians. None of these deeds can be imitated by a human being, however mighty he may be. Every reader who has followed with any attention the history and problem of the philosophy of religions, must credit this teacher of the first or second century with

[11] M. Ps. B. 271; Yalkut Ps., § 751 r. R., פרוזדוריא בר נחשא; v. also M. Ps. 106. 1 B, 453, 136. 2, B. 518; pal. Ber. 9. 1.

[12] M. Ps. 88. 1, ed. B. 380.

[13] v. M. Ps. 18. 2, B. 135 f.; Tanh. ii. 1; R. Judah ha Levy b. Shalom; Huna, the priest, b. Abin; R. Simon and R. Abin ha Levy.

[14] Mekh. 38 A; M. R. S. b. J. 61 has only nos. 2, 4, 3; nos. 1, 5, 6 are not given there.

[15] תכסים, i. e. battle-order.

deep insight in religious philosophy. He touched, and in
the original probably dealt at length, with the attributes of
omnipotence, the problem of God's immutability and infinity
and the doctrines of God's love and mercy. He can be
excused for cramming so many vital questions of religion
in such a brief space. In the hand of Philo such a series
of subjects would require books or a volume. Yet the
state of our literary documents is responsible for the
brevity of the tradition. The chief idea is, however, quite
apparent. God's power is unparalleled in this world, bears
no comparison to our conception of power. What God can
do no human might can perform, or come near to His work.
So far the tendency is clear. Why has he filled it also
with the other doctrines? One can understand his references to God's love and mercy even when sitting in judgement over people. The attributes of love and mercy do not
contradict His omnipotence. All of them are infinite. His
omnipotence is manifested further in the efficacy of prayers.
The latter again touches very closely on the mutability
of God. By the way, there seems a hopeless contradiction
between b. (God's power is unchangeable), and d. (God
changes his decrees). To see clearly, we must first of all
discuss the question of prayer, and secondly, that of repentance in relation to God's immutability.

The efficacy of prayers was often, seriously and lightly,
argued about. Here the question may have been : ' How
can God hear all the prayers uttered at different places at
the same time? How can God fulfil the contradictory
requests of the various worshippers in the same place?'
One wants rain, the other drought? Thirdly, if God's
decrees are settled, how can prayer upset them? Consequently, if God decreed death, poverty, or barrenness, how
could human prayer affect life, wealth, and children? It is
a well-established doctrine of Rabbinic theology that prayer
can bring about changes and is effective. Prayer is a means
by which death, famine, plague, drought, flood, earthquake,
war, and storm can be averted from the individual as well

as from the community. Instances for this generally-held
view can be brought from history as well as legends,
homilies, and teachings. It is interesting to compare here
the views on this subject of the Church Father, Tertullian,
with those of the rabbis. The former writes in chap. xxix
of his treatise on prayer, which is styled *Of the Power and
Effect of Prayer*: 'For what has God, who exacts it, ever
denied to prayer coming from spirit and truth? What
mighty specimens of its efficacy do we read, and hear, and
believe! Old-world prayer, indeed, used to free from fires,
and from beasts, and from famine; and yet it had not then
received its form from Christ?'[16] Similar sayings are
reported in the names of various scribes. R. Jose b. Halafta,
who is an older authority than Tertullian, says: 'There are
appointed times for prayer' (cf. Ps. 69. 14). Which time is
the most favourable? When the community deliver their
prayers.[17] Therefore must man rise early for prayers, for
there is nothing greater than prayer. Do know, it was
decreed concerning Moses that he should not enter the land,
and not see it, Thanks to his prayers, God has shown him
the land (cf. Deut. 34. 1). Hezekiah prayed, and the decree
was annulled. So Jacob, in sending his sons to Egypt,
prayed on their behalf.[18] R. Eleazar b. Pedath, who may
be the author of the latter part of the saying, teaches:
'Great is prayer before God.' R. Eleazar says: 'Dost thou
want to know the strength of prayer? If it does not
accomplish the whole of it (*sc.* request), it does half of
it.' The instance of Cain is illustrated, who owed it to his
prayer that the עֹנ of his punishment was forgiven, though

---

[16] v. also the Apology of Aristides, ch. xvi, Sirach uses the phrase,
'The prayer of the humble pierceth the clouds', 35. 17; v. Hebrew,
32. 14.

[17] As to the importance of communal prayers, v. Tr. Kallah, ch. R. Meir,
ed. Coronel 16 A, b. Ber. 6 A, b. Ber. 8 A, R. Nathan מנין שאין הקב'ה
מואס בתפלותן של רבים, b. Ber. 5 A, R. Joshua b. Levi to his son, ib.,
M. Prov. 10 B, ed. Stettin, R. Simon b. Johai, R. Johanan in his name.

[18] pal. Maccoth, ii. 9; Pes. B. 127 B; M. Ps. 65; M. Lam. s. v. סכותה;
Tanh. B. i. 197. Some texts have b. Tahlifa, and without these instances.

the נוד (=נד) remained. As a second illustration there
also the case of Hezekiah, who recovered from his illness
and fifteen years were added to his life, is mentioned.[19] It
was an accepted belief that prayers are useful and necessary, especially the prayers of the community. We read in
another homily :[20] 'God hears all the prayers which are
delivered in the same time. God's ears hear all the supplications and entreaties addressed to him!' It is one side of
God's omnipotence. This is only possible with God, who is
all-powerful. There may have beén a more popular solution of this difficulty which answered it by applying an
angelological doctrine. 'An angel is appointed over prayers.
He collects them and gathers them. Making a crown of
them he puts them on God's head.'[21] We note here in
passing that *to crown* in Hellenistic phraseology is identical
with to pray.[22] The angel to whom this function is allotted
is called Sandalfon.[23] This extraordinary power of God is
also the subject of another homily in the Tannaitic
Midrash.[24] We have nineteen parallels drawn between
the might of God (מי שאמר והיה העולם, or המקום) on one side,
and the weakness of idols and men respectively ρn the
other side. 'Idols have eyes, ears, nostrils, hands, legs,

---

[19] Deut. r. 8. 1 ; Pes. r. ch. 47, 188 в f., gives similar teachings and
instances in the name of R. Juda b. Hijja, R. Joshua b. Levi, and R. Levi ;
v. also Gen. r. 22, Tanh. Sanhedrin 37 A, Lev. r. 10, Jeb. 64, jer. Ber. 9. 1,
M. Ps. B. 475. Daniel's prayers, b. Ber. 31 A.

[20] M. P. 65. 2 ; B. 312 ; Exod. r. 21. 4.

[21] M. Ps. 19. 7 ; B. 167 ; R. Phinehas in the name of R. Abba ; ib.,
88. 2 ; B. 380 ; R. Phinehas ; Exod. 21. 4 ; R. Phinehas in the name of
R. Meir ; R. Jeremiah in the name of R. Hijja b. Abba. Obviously in the
first place the names of R. Meir, R. Jeremiah, and R. Hijja have been
omitted.

[22] v. Gfrörer, *Urchristentum*, ii. 376 ; Dukes, *Zur Kenntnis der neuhebr. rel.
Poesie*, Frankfort, 1842, 108.

[23] b. Hag. 13 в, הקושר כתרים לקונו ; Deut. r. 2. 26. R. Berekhja says
that Israel is called ten times כלה, corresponding to the ten garments of
glory with which Israel crowns God ; v. Cant. r. s. v. מה יפו דודיך, Jellinek,
בה"מ, iii. 70 ; Qalir, Mahzor ר"ה i, ed. Heidenheim, מלך אזור ; Yalk.
Is. 506, Ps. 847.

[24] Mekh. 41 в ; M. R. S. b. J. 66 f., fuller than the Mekh. ; v. also 66 A,
69 A ; Sifre Deut., § 233 ; the text is based on the M. R. S. b. J.

and cannot use them, men have thoughts and cannot
control them. God, however, has none of these things;
yet He sees everything at the same time (Zech. 4. 10,
Prov. 15. 3), *He hears the prayers of all* (Ps. 65. 3, 10, 11),
He accepts the sweet savour of the sacrifices, His hands
created the Universe, He goes to war, and His thought is
full of sweetness. God can utter two words at the same
time, hear all the creatures praying at the same moment,
fulfil the desires of all of them, their wishes for offspring,
wisdom, and wealth, and grant them. His fear is greater
on those who are near to Him than those who are far off.
His creative power in forming the Universe and children
of men is also unparalleled.' Here again in this remarkable homily great stress is laid on God's power. This is
really the chief theme of this homiletical gem. The conception is laid down that with God it is possible to hear so
many prayers and requests at the same time. The old
Haggadist ignores or does not know that any intervention on
the part of the angels is wanted. This wonderful thing is
possible with God. God's power equals his immutability.
But, does He not change His decrees at the prayers or signs
of repentance on the part of the condemned or the wicked?
Is there no contradiction between these two attributes?
How shall we reconcile with this doctrine the often repeated
idea that the prayers of the just remove or upset God's
decrees? Is there no change in God's relation to his creatures caused by man's repentance and prayer? Are there
not manifold instances in primitive and higher belief that
owing to prayers, good deeds, and repentance God's judgement is altered? Our preacher treated these vexed questions rather lightly. When pointing out the third great
attribute of the doctrine of God, His love and mercy, he
apparently lost himself in contradictions. Love and mercy
induce God, in spite of His general immutability, to change
His plans and actions. There, he moved in a circle. Or,
did he think of God's power as finite?

The general trend of rabbinic theology inclines to the

doctrine that God's decrees are subject to change. R. Johanan taught in the name of R. Jose b. Halafta: ' No word which went out from the mouth of God for good, even conditionally, was withdrawn.'[25] Only those which are for the good of the world, not so the decrees for evil and punishment, which are subject to alteration. An anonymous Haggadist[26] sees in God a father who condemned His son to death ; then the son repented, and the father cleanses him of his sins. An older[27] source puts it that all the decrees for evil are put only conditionally, and are not fixed. God's decrees are, therefore, not changed, but originally made on condition. The saying of R. Eleazar that prayer, charity, and repentance remove all evil decrees, may also be understood in this sense.[28] Likewise the popular belief that the Zaddik annuls the decrees of God.[29] The Haggadists also like to contrast the power of a human king with God's. The former promises and decrees, and does not or cannot keep his words; God, however, גוזר ומקיים, decrees and keeps them.[30]

The Jewish doctrine of the all-powerful God met with severe criticism in the pagan world. Such a view was alien to the heathens, who were used to threaten and punish their gods in times of misfortune and disappointment. Romans, who saw the failures of the Jews in politics and war, could not suppress their contempt for the weakness of the God whose temple they destroyed, whose nation they crucified, whose land they devastated, whose state was low and miserable. They came to the conclusion: ' The God of the Jews is weak, and not omnipotent.' This state of mind is well reflected in the Titus legend, often repeated in our sources. Titus is supposed to enter the most sacred parts of the Temple accompanied by two harlots, tearing

---

[25] b. Ber. 7 A ; v. also Tanh. B. תצוה 8 ; Pes. r. ch. 40 ; Yalk. Ps. 877, and Midr. Agada, B. 176, based on Ps. 119. 89.

[26] M. Ps. 82.   [27] Sifre Zutta, Yalk. Deut., 813.

[28] Eccles. r. 7. 29 ; Pes. r. 200 B.

[29] v. Marmorstein, *Beiträge zur Religionsgeschichte u. Volkeskunde*, ii, pp. 51–3 62.   [30] Pes. B. 30 and parall.

asunder the veil of the Holy of Holies, and asking : 'Where is the God who has slain Sisera and Sennacherib? I am in His dwelling-place, under his authority; well, let Him come and defeat me if He is really all-powerful ?' On his homeward journey he met a terrific storm, and provokes the 'God of the Jews'. It seems to him that the God of the Jews has power over the water and storm. The generation of the flood, Pharaoh, perished by water. On the dry land, however, his power vanished; he is weak. God replies; 'Shall I fight with thee? No, I will send the smallest of my creatures, a despicable flea, and it will conquer thee!' *Abba Hanan* sees God's greatness and power in His long-suffering and patience with sinners like Titus.[31] This explanation is dependent on Ben Zoma's conception and idea of power and strength generally.[32]

It would, however, be a mistake to assume that only pagans held such views about God's power as ascribed to Titus. There must have been many Jews after 68 c.e., and after the catastrophe in the year 135, who doubted God's might. R. Eleazar b. Hyrkanos and R. Joshua b. Hananja actually repeat the words of their fellow Jews, who said : 'If God is the Lord of all works, just as He is our God, then we will acknowledge Him! If God is able to supply us with all our needs, we will obey Him!'[33] These words are quoted by these two Tannaim with reference to Exod. 17. 7 and attributed to the Israelites trembling before Amalek. Amalek is the Imperial Rome of the first century. The very words are repeated in the next generation by the contemporaries of R. Judah b. Ilai and R. Nehemia.[34] According to the latter source the Jews doubted the three cardinal attributes of God: the universalism, the omnipo-

[31] The Titus legend is preserved in Aboth R. N. i. 6, ii. 7 ; Gittin 56 B ; Lev. r. 20. 5, 22.3 ; Gen. r. 10. 8 ; M. Eccles. Zutta, 104 ; R. Aha, Eccles. r. 5. 9 ; M. Ps. 63 c ; Lam. r. i. 32 ; Pirke ch. 49 ; Tanh. B. iv. 99 ; Num. r. 18. 22 ; Pugio 258 ; v. also I. Barukh 21. 20.

[32] Mishna Aboth iv. 4.   [33] Mekh. 52 B.

[34] Pes. B. 28 A ; Tanh. B. v. 42 f.   M. R. S. b. J. 81 reads instead of R. Eliezer b. Hyrkanos, R. Eleazar of Modiim.

tence, and the omniscience of God. In another legend [35]
again, a Roman, Tineius Rufus, says to the martyrs of
Lydda, Julianus and Pappus, before they were about to be
executed: 'He', i.e. God, 'cannot save you, as He saved the
three young men, because He grew old since then, as it is
said: "The Lord does not see, and the God of Jacob does
not understand"' (Ps. 94. 7). The martyrs replied: 'They',
i.e. the three young men, 'were pious, and the king also
worthy that a miracle should be performed through them.
Thou, however, art unworthy, and we also are not without
guilt. There are many wild beasts that could or should
put us to death at God's command. Thou art one of them!'
The Roman dignitary, just like Titus in the legend, knew
the history of the Jews in the last decades of the Temple
and after the destruction, must have been convinced that
the 'Jewish' God became weak, old, and helpless. Another
martyr, though not of the Synagogue, but of the Church,
Justin, corroborates these words of the Midrashim.[36] He
says: 'Should some think, in case we acknowledge a God,
who is able to help, well, we should not suffer by people,
who are not just, we should not be tortured by them!'
These doubts, felt and expressed by sceptics, must have
been re-echoed by some contemporaries of the last Tannaim,
otherwise we could not account for the fact that nearly all
the teachers dealt with this subject. R. Simon b. Eleazar
dwells at length on Num. 11. 23, 'Is it possible that Moses
should say: "God (המקום) is unable to supply us and our
cattle. The Nile in Egypt supplied us with fish, and
there was also enough for the Egyptians and their cattle!"?
No, that was not Moses' question. What he said was this:
"Lord of all the worlds, is it right to do so, that Thou
shouldst give them food, and afterwards slay them? Does
one say to his friend: 'Take a loaf of bread, and go to
Sheol'? Does one say to an ass: 'Take a khor of barley

[35] Sifra Emor 9; Eccles. r. 3. 6; Taanith, 18 B; Semahoth, ch. 8;
Midrash Zutta, 98.
[36] *Apology*, ii. 5; v. Zöckler. *Apologetik*, 42.

and we will cut off thy head ' ? " God replied : " Is it better
that they should say, ' God is unable to supply us with
food ' ?   Let them and hundreds like them perish, but My
hand is never short to give even for a short while." ' [37]
This curious dialogue between God and Moses and the
treatment of the doctrine of God's power surely reproduced
the scepticism of the age.   This accounts for the remarkable fact that nearly all the teachers of this age, the last
three decades of the second century, deal with and elaborate
this attribute of God.   R. Nathan teaches : ' God said, " Even
if all the magicians of the world gathered together and
united their forces, they could not change day into night,
and night into day.   Just as I separated between light and
darkness (sc. which no human power can alter any more),
so did I sanctify Aaron." ' [38]   R. Simai uses the parable of
the sun, asking : ' Have you ever heard that the sun is sick,
and is unable to discharge his duties ? that the moon is sick
and unable to do her work ?   God's servants are free from
weakness ; can God Himself be sick ? ' [39]   Bar Kappara
teaches that God can make the impossible possible, the
invisible visible.[40]   Finally, Rabbi, i.e. R. Judah I, if our
reading of the name is correct, repeats the parable of the
sun, like R. Simon b. Johai and R. Simai, in order to demonstrate the doctrine of God's omnipotence.[41]   Christians
must have been taunted by the same arguments as Jews :
' If God is powerful, why does He not help ? '   R. Simon b.
Johai, a contemporary of Justin Martyr and Tineius Rufus,
repeats the parable of the sun to refute the attack on our
doctrine.[42]   ' Have you ever heard ', asks the Haggadist,

[37] Tos. Sotah vi. 7, ed. Z. 305. 1 ff.

[38] Tanh. B. iv. 87.

[39] Pes. B. 130 A. ; v. also further on, where it is quoted in the name of
Simon b. Johai.

[40] M. Sam. ch. 9, ed. B. 74.

[41] v. Mekh. 72 B.   The text reads : ומה [שמש] אחד משמשי שמשין הרי
הוא בא במקומו ושלא במקומו ק״ו לכבודו של מי שאמר והיה העולם   ' In
spite of the omnipresence of God, we can speak of God's descent and
Moses's ascent ; everything is possible with God '.

[42] Lam. r. 2. 23, ed. B. 5. 9 ; r. R. Isaac, and the moon is substituted
for the sun ; v. also above, in the name of R. Simai.

' of the sun being ill ? or being too weak in discharging its
duties ?   God's servant cannot become ill, or weak, or old ;
how can such a thing be thought of God Himself ? ' These
instances, which are taken from the Apologies of Rabbis,
and can easily be multiplied, prove plainly that some Jews
and Gentiles alike must have raised serious doubts as to
the omnipotence of God. Our purpose in treating this
point at some length is to throw light on an otherwise
surprising idea in connexion with our subject. We read
in many Midrashim the teaching that as long as Edom, or
Amalek, rules in this world the Kingdom of Heaven, the
Name of God, or His Throne is not complete, firm, or absolute.[43]   Here, again, the tendency of the finite power, which
God seems to have, ruled in the theology of the third
century. We observe similar ways of thinking of the
doctrine of God's Unity, which can be here merely alluded
to.   God's Unity will be perfect only in the future, when
all nations will live as citizens of the heavenly kingdom.
The Unity of God is, therefore, at present limited to Israel
and the pious believers in God among the nations.   God's
power is also limited by His heavenly Court, as we have
mentioned above. These points are reserved left for discussion in the chapter treating the Unity of God.

   The attribute of God's power is closely connected with
God's Unity, with the problem of Dualism and consequently also with that of God's character as Creator of man
and the Universe.   The latter point must be treated in the
chapter of God's relation to both man and the world.
Here, before closing this discussion of the doctrine of God's
omnipotence, one problem must be touched : God's power
to produce miracles. How are the supernatural miracles,
like the dividing of the Red Sea, and Jordan, &c. to be
explained ?   If changes of the laws of nature are possible,
the doctrine of God's immutability is also threatened.

---

[43] The teaching is ascribed to R. Hama b. Hanina and R. Abba b.
Kahana; Pes. B. 29 B; Pes. r. ch. 12; M. Ps. 10 B; Tanhuma; v.
Marmorstein, *Midrash Haseroth witheroth*, p. 27, note 106.

The belief in miracles and wonders, whether natural or supernatural, was general in the ages of the Tannaitic and Amoraic teacher.[44] The miracles served the purpose of sanctifying God's name and of making His name great and recognized among the nations.[45] Doubts and negations were expressed as to the truth of the Biblical wonders.[46] Some of the teachers repelled scepticism by the favourite theory that the just in this world perform similar deeds; they revive the dead, heal the sick, bless the barren, &c. If human beings are able to do so, how much more God Himself.[47] R. Judah b. Simon taught with reference to the great changes in the world to come, to the eschatological wonders, that such great things were already performed by the pious in this world.[48] The greatest of the wonders to be performed is the resurrection from death.[49] There is a consensus of opinion that Almighty God in His power can and will accomplish such a miracle. This belief, joined with the dogma of God giving or withholding rain in due season, is regarded as the גבורות especially. Both dogmas comprise together the second number of the Eighteen Benedictions.

There were teachers who displayed a more rationalistic tendency regarding this problem. R. Johanan and R. Jeremiah b. Eliezer,[50] inclining to a conception of a finite power of God, teach that the rending of the sea, the bowing of the heavens before Moses (Deut. 32. 1), the standing still of sun and moon in the time of Joshua, the feeding of Elijah by the ravens, the escape of the three young men

[44] v. Lev. r. 10. 8; R. Judah b. Ilai, Exod. r. 18. 8, Eccl. r. 3. 17; R. Simon b. Lakish, Gen. r. 5. 4, M. Ps. 18. 6; R. Simon b. Judah, Cant. r. 3. 4; R. Eleazar b. Pedath, Tanh. i. לך לך, 9; R. Simon b. Lakish, Cant. r. 1. 5; R. Berekhja, Gen. r. 43. 4; R. Judah and R. Nehemjah, Taan. 25 A: R. Hanina b. Dosa, Taan. 21 A; Nahum of Gimso.

[45] Sifre Deut., § 306, 132 B.

[46] R. Simon b. Lakish; v. Num. r. chap. 17.

[47] Deut. 10. 3; v. Jellinek בהמ', iii. 69. 77.

[48] Gen. r. 77. 1.

[49] v. the material collected, Marmorstein, *The Doctrine of the Resurrection*, in 'Journal of American Theology', 1915, pp. 577–591.

[50] Gen. r. 5. 4; Exod. r. 21. 6; Midr. Konen; Marmorstein, *Midr. Has. witheroth*, p. 39.

from the fire, of Daniel in the lion's den, the opening of the
Heavens to Ezekiel, and the saving of Jonah in the whale,
were all laid down as conditions at the creation of the
world. God stipulated with fire and water, lions and
whales, that they should change their nature on these
occasions. Nature does not change, but they were ordered
from the beginning so as to provide for these miracles.
The whole world was created only conditionally, if Israel
accepts the Torah or not.[51]

(4) *The Eternity of God.*

R. Simai, a teacher of the latter period of the Tannaim,
prayed: 'Lord of all creatures, God of all praises, Rock of
the worlds, the everlasting Creator of the Universe, who
quickenest again the death.'[1] It seems natural to assume
that the attribute of God's Eternity is a consequence of His
power, or that the latter is an outcome of the fact that
God is eternal, or the life of the world. It is an
everlasting merit of the Rabbinic theologians that they
reopened the older prophetic conception and, without any
reservation, taught the Eternity of God. Whatever may
have been believed in Old Israel in the pagan period of the
Jewish people about growing and perishing, reviving and
decaying gods, Judaism left and kept no traces of such
religious aspects. This is another deep contrast between
monotheism and polytheism, in which the former excels
the latter, in spite of the fact that Christianity could not
entirely free itself from the influence of the latter. The
names of God mentioned in the prayer of R. Simai contain
also חי העולם, which may mean 'the Life of the World' or
'the Everlasting'. More frequent than this is the term
חי העולמים. R. Johanan b. Zakkai wept when his pupils
surrounded the master's death-bed in the last hour of his
life. They were surprised, and asked: 'Light of Israel,
right pillar, strong hammer, wherefore dost thou weep?'

---

[51] *Midrash Haseroth*, p. 39, note 162.
[1] pal. Ber. 1. 5.

R. J. b. Z. said : ' If I were carried before an earthly king, who is here to-day and to-morrow in his grave, if he were angry it would not last for ever, if he would bind me and kill me, it could not be for ever ; moreover, I could appease him with words, or bribe him with money, yet I would surely cry. Now that I am about to appear before the King of all kings, who lives and exists for all generations, whose anger, punishment, and sentence of death are eternal, who cannot be bribed by words or money, should I not tremble and fear ? '[2] The belief in an everlasting God could not be expressed in a more impressive way than in these words of the departing scribe. Another scribe ordered, when mentioning God, the righteous, the everlasting righteous, to bless Him.[3] The ark of God, the Everlasting (חי העולמים) was carried during the journey in the wilderness next to the ark of Joseph, and people asked : מה טיבו של מת להלוך עם ארון חי העולמים.[4] The blessing at drinking water is, to Him who created many souls and supplied their needs, ' for all that Thou hast created', and who is 'Everlasting'.[5] R. Eleazar of Modiim praises a scholar who had heard the word of the law from his teacher, and regards him as if he had served, ministered before Him, who lives and exists for ever.[6] The prohibition of idolatry is extended to all generations from the word על פני (Exod. 20. 3). Just as God lives and exists for ever, similarly the prohibition of idolatry holds good for everlasting generations.[7] Moses[8] rebukes his people for being rebellious against or before חי וקיים לעולמים. We see that the Tannaitic Haggada frequently emphasizes this doctrine.

---

[2] b. Ber. 28 B.

[3] Mekh. 19 B. 7 : ר' אומר זכר צדיק לברכה כשהוא מזכיר את הצדיק; v. b. Yoma צדיק חי העולמים שנ' צדיק ה' בכל דרכיו תן ברכה אמן 37 A, Hananjahu, the nephew of R. Joshua b. Hananja : אמר להם נביא לישראל כשאני מזכיר צדיק עולמים אתם תנו ברכה צדיק חי עולמים. Yalkut Exod. 219, agrees with ed. Mekh.

[4] Mekh. 24 B ; Sotah 13 A and Parall.

[5] Mekh. 31 B ; b. Ber. 44 A ; Tosefta and Parall.

[6] Mekh. 46 A ; v. also Sifre Deut., § 41 : כשומע מפי הקב'ה.

[7] Mekh. 67 B.   [8] Mekh. 48 A.

M

R. Judah b. Ilai uses the name of God חי העולמים in explaining
the geographical name באר לחי ראי (Gen. 16. 14).[9] Bar
Kappara joins it with צדיק, speaking of צדיק חי העולמים, about
whom sectarians talk blasphemies.[10] We find also the term
כבוד חי עולמים, the Glory of the Everlasting just as the
Everlasting Righteous.[11]

R. Tanhum b. Hanilai developed R. Johanan b. Zakkai's
teaching, and adapted it in his homily on Ps. 12. 7 : 'A king,
flattered by the eulogies of the city, promises them town
halls, public buildings and baths, and water supply. He
goes to rest in the evening, and does not awake any more.
Where is he, and where his promises ? Not so God. He is
a truthful God' (Jer. 10. 10). Why is He truthful ?
R. Levi says : ' Because He is a *living* and *everlasting* God.[12]
The teacher combines here, as in other cases also, two
different attributes, e.g. Truth and Eternity. R. Levi
illustrates a similar antithesis between God and the idols.[13]
R. Joshua b. Levi depicts Pharaoh first searching the scrolls
containing the divine names of tribal and national deities, of
Moab, Amon, Edom, and Zidon &c., and afterwards unable
to discover the names of the God of the Hebrews. R. Levi
illustrates this with a parable. ' There was once a priest who
owned a slave. The priest had to leave for another place
without the knowledge of the slave. The latter went about
looking for his master, and sought also in the cemetery.
People asked him : ' Who is your master ? ' The slave replied: 'So and so, the priest!' People said: 'You fool! you
are looking for a priest in the cemetery?' Thus Pharaoh. He
sought God in his dead scrolls. 'The gods in your hand
are dead ones ; our God is alive, and exists for ever' (v. Jer.
10. 10). In another source [14] R. Levi depicts a father, who
lost his son, and was looking for him in the cemetery. A
clever man meets him, and asks : ' Was your lost son alive or
dead ? ' The Father replies: ' Alive ! ' The stranger says :

[9] Gen. r., pp. 654, 661, ed. Theodor.
[10] Gen. r. 1. 7.   [11] Gen. r. 100. 6 ; R. Isaac.
[12] Pes. B. 30 b ; Tanh. iv. 104, R. Abin instead of R. Levi ; Lev. r. 26. 1.
[13] Tanh. ii. 18.   [14] Lev. r. 6. 6.

'You fool! is it customary to look for the dead among the living, or the living among the dead? The living provide for the necessities of the dead; do the dead care and toil for the living?' Likewise, continues the preacher, our God is living, and exists to all eternities. The gods of the nations of the world are dead (cf. Ps. 115. 3 ff.), 'and we forsake the Everlasting and worship the dead?' Here R. Abba b. Kahana teaches that 'everything perishes; only God remains alive'.[15] 'Man's work lives longer than its maker, God lives longer than His work'.[16] An illustration of the former is given in the names of cities built by or named after Constantine, Antiochus, Romulus, Alexander or Tiberius and Seleucus. 'They perished, their cities are destroyed, but God remains alive and exists.'[17]

(5) *Truth.*

The next attribute of God we have to describe, based on our sources, is that of Truth. God is called אלהים אמת (Jer. 10. 10, Ps. 15. 2, 31. 6, 119. 160). We find also in an Egyptian hymn the designation, 'The Lord of Truth'.[1] In Rabbinic theology this attribute is connected with God's eternity. He, who is eternal can be true, trustworthy, faithful to His creatures. A mortal being is unable, often prevented from discharging his duties.[2] Owing to God's eternity such a state of affairs cannot arise. There was a man, says an Haggadist,[3] whose countrymen used to deposit with him their articles. In spite of his best intentions, he is apt to make mistakes, because he does not know

---

[15] Lev. r. 19. 2; v. 1. Sam. 2. 2; Tanh. iii. 33.

[16] R. Judah b. Menasja, b. Meg. 14 A.

[17] M. Ps. 9. 8, ed. Buber, 85.

[1] v. Breasted, pp. 347, 351; cf. Farnell, *Attributes*, p. 107.

[2] v. above, p. 178.

[3] M. Ps. 25. 2, ed. B. 210; v. also R. Alexander's exposition, who develops this idea of God's truth on the assumption of God's tenderness and love to his creatures: בשר ודם מפקידין בידו חדשים והוא מחזירן בלויין ישינים אבל הקב׳ה מפקידין בידו בלויין ושחוקין והוא מחזירן חדשים.

the articles. God is different; He is the God of Truth
(Ps. 31. 6), ' In Thy hand do I trust my spirit'. Did it ever
happen that God interchanged the souls entrusted to Him ?
No, he returned them to their rightful owners, for ' He is a
trustworthy God'. Since God is omniscient such a mistake
is with Him excluded. The doctrines of immortality and
the future redemption of Israel are based, to a great extent,
on the belief that human souls are nightly deposited with
God, who faithfully returns them every morning. This act
of truthfulness is a symbol of their eschatological expecta-
tions.[4] ' God's seal is Truth ' is a teaching of R. Hanina b.
Hama.[5] The word אמת is explained after the Notarikon
fashion to imply a protest against Gnostic dualism and
Christological ideas. The א means God is the first, and not the
Demiurgos ; 'ת the last (He has no successor), and 'מ, besides
Him there is none.[6] An allegorist sees in all the characteristics of Ps. 15 an allusion to God. Similarly ודובר אמת ' He
who speaketh the truth, is God' (cf. Jer. 10. 10).[7] R. Isaac [8]
uses Ps. 119. 160 for the explanation of Gen. 1. 1 and as a
refutation of dualistic theories. God's word is Truth, i.e.
' God created in the beginning heaven and earth '. R. Isaac
b. Merjon connects also truth with Eternity when he expounds Hab. 2. 4 : אפילו צדיק חי העולמים מאמונתו הוא חי ' Even
the Righteous Eternal lives from His Truth, Faithfulness '.[9]
The attribute of God's truth is also the basis of the belief in
reward and punishment. God is truthful, and He will
reward the just and punish the wicked. The Tannaitic
Midrash sees in אני ה' of the text this doctrine expressed.
The inner bearing of these two doctrines is brought home
to students of Rabbinic lore in a story of Simon b. Shetach.
This teacher bought once an ass from an Ishmaelite.

---

[4] v. Gen. r. 48, 1 ; Lam. r. 3. 22 ; M. Ps. 25. 2 ; R. Alexander and Simon R.
b. Abba in the name of R. Simon.

[5] b. Shabbath 55 A ; Yoma 69 B ; Sanh. 64 A : חותמו של הקב׳ה אמת.

[6] v. pal. Ber 1. 5.   [7] M. Ps. 15. 4, ed. B. 116.

[8] Gen. r. 1. 7.

[9] Eccles. r. 3. 9 ; v. however Bacher, A. P. A. iii. 590 ; the passage
remains obscure.

The pupils of the master found a jewel on the neck of the animal. The pupils saw in this event a blessing of the Lord, and suggested to him to keep the ass with the jewel. The scribe thought otherwise; he said: ' I bought an ass, and not a jewel.' Simon b. Shetach duly returned it, and the Ishmaelite said: 'Blessed be the God of Simon b. Shetach.' Behold from the reliability, trustworthiness of man, thou canst learn that of God, who is faithful to reward Israel for the observance of the commandments.[10] Similar events are recorded in the stories told about great men of antiquity like R. Hanina b. Dosa, R. Phinehas b. Jair. The moral of the narratives was מאמונתו של בשר ודם את יודע אמונתו של הקב'ה.[11] If the words of a human being can be relied upon, though its fulfilment seems impossible or supernatural, how much more, argued the Rabbis, can we accept God's promises and threats as being trustworthy.

(6) Justice.

The attribute of Justice is even more closely attached to God's Eternity than Truth by the Haggadic theologians. This is manifested in the name צדיק חי עולמים, and is, as we saw, based on the conception of God's truthfulness. The justice of God appears in His character and name of Judge, ' Lord of Judgement', as a source of law and order, as the revealer of the moral, social, and political duties, and master of rewards and punishment. Many first-rate theological problems and teachings depend on this attribute.

Heretics and heathens, readers of the Bible and philosophers, seem to have had a special pleasure in finding fault with God's justice and impartiality. They referred to and cited Abraham's question: 'Should not the judge of the whole earth do justice?' (Gen. 18. 25). God could give no answer. Abraham asked also: ' Wilt thou also destroy the righteous with the wicked?' (ib. 23). God kept silent.

[10] Deut. r. 3. 5 and following note.
[11] b. Jeb. 121 A ; v. pal. Demai, ch. 1 ; B. M., ch. 2 ; Deut. 3. 5.

A Haggadist dealt with these questions, which were left without answers, in a homily based on Job 40. 4, ' I will not keep silent, so that people should not say: " We can also speak with God ", i.e. and criticize Him, as Abraham did, and He could not defend Himself '.   God replies : ' No, I will not keep quiet ; I did not answer Abraham, yet I will answer thee.   Why ?   Because Abraham did not doubt my truthfulness and justice, when I enjoined him to sacrifice his son Isaac, although I told him previously that Isaac will be called his seed ' (Gen. 21. 12).[1]   Abraham, owing to his strong faith in God's justice, was entitled to raise such questions.   The same right cannot be conceded to those who deny or doubt God's justice, or the vain-glorious gossipers who judge the Highest by their limited or super-ficial wisdom.   The idea in this Haggada illustrates the thought that God knows why He has chosen Abraham, why He enriched and exalted him, whilst others were neglected, poor, and humble.   There is no arbitrariness with God but strict judgement.[2]   If some tell thee : ' God makes rich and poor; whom He likes He makes rich, others He makes poor.   One becomes a king, the other a beggar ; Abraham becomes a king and rich !'   Reply to him : ' Could you accomplish those deeds which Abraham accomplished ? '   The same problem is met with in a dialogue between the Matrona and R. Jose b. Halafta : ' Your God ', says the lady, ' chooses whomsoever He likes !' i.e. is not just.   The scribe, instead of replying directly, passed on to her a basket of figs.   The lady selected the nicest and ripest of them and enjoyed them.   The scribe, looking at what she was doing, observed : ' You are clever in selecting the good figs out of the bad ones, and you assume that God does not know whom He has chosen as the best of His creatures !'[3]

A more serious discussion of this great and puzzling question is to be found in another dialogue between the

---

[1] Tanh. B. i. 91 ; Agadath Ber. B. 44.   [2] Gen. r. 55. 1.
[3] Num. r. 3. 2 and parall ; v. Tobit 4. 19.

Emperor and R. Joshua b. Hananja.[4] 'Where is your God's sense of justice? Why are children born deaf and dumb, blind and lame? Why should they suffer? They are innocent.' R. Joshua replied: 'God knows the deeds of man long before he was born, whether he is going to be good or bad.' Emperor: 'Let him repent, and God shall open his eyes!' Thereupon R. Joshua tests the case of a blind man, who turns out to be a greedy, faithless man, and convinces the Emperor of God's justice. The attribute of justice was and is a stumbling-block to all who look upon great and small events merely from a narrow and selfish point of view. Daily life and common happenings appear in a light, which can hardly be reconciled with God's justice. The old question: 'Why is the wicked prosperous and the righteous man miserable?' is not yet answered. R. Joshua, a thinker of great eminence, has no other answer than this, that God in His omniscience knows what He does. This teaching could not satisfy. As a matter of fact some teachers of the third century held just the contrary view. God judges man not according to his future actions but on his present deeds, worth, and merits.[5] R. Isaac taught: 'If one tells you, "I have sought and could not find!" do not believe him. "I did not seek, but I have found!" do not believe him. "I sought and I found", then believe him.'[6] Rabbinic opinions are at variance whether blessings of life, like health, wealth, and children, or poverty, illness, and barrenness, are a result of piety or wickedness, merits or sins, or independent of such qualities or faults. The problem was discussed at all times

---

[4] S. E. Z. ch. 23, ed. Friedmann, 41.

[5] j. R. H. 1. 3, 57 A; R. Joshua b. Levi: אין הקב׳ה דן את האדם אלא בשעה שהוא עומד בה; v. also Gen. r. 53; Th. 572; Exod. r. 3. 2; Tanh. Ps. Jon.; Gen. 21. 16; b. R. H. 16 B. The same idea in the *Logia of Jesus*, v. 10; v. Harnack, *Erforschtes u. Erlebtes*, Giessen, 1923, 50, 'Wherein I find you, therein will I judge you'. God does not judge man after his past or future, but as he is in the present; v. also Marmorstein, in *ZfNW*, 28 (1926), 257 f.

[6] b. Meg. 6 B; Tanh. f. 280 B.

without reaching a final answer.[7] R. Isaac advises people to seek and they will find. Apparently by his saying he refers to students of the law. Can it be also the same with seekers after wealth and happiness? The Gospels quote a similar saying: 'Seek ye and ye shall find!'[8] or 'He who seeks findeth'.[9] Speculation, philosophical as well as theological, has failed to answer this simple question up to to-day. They were not happier in the solution of the bigger problems of suffering and death, success and health of individuals as well as of nations. Rome, i. e. Edom, is successful and rich, Israel is poor and down-trodden. Rome enjoys the blessing of Isaac, his father.[10] Israel's suffering, poverty, exile, are all signs of God's love, of God's guidance. The happiness of the wicked is merely a faint dream of the future joy of the righteous; the might of God's enemies merely a shadow of Israel's future greatness and glory. One or two teachings testify to God's justice. The first is that God rewards the just and punishes the wicked. The second, that neither human life, nor the history of the world, whether in their darkest moments or at the height of their glory, can be thought of without, or divided from, God's providence. Therefore, whatever happens, must be according to a wise plan, and is just. Hence the doctrine of the great Day of Judgment depicted by prophets and apocalyptics, and elaborated by the Haggadists. We are here especially interested in a saying of R. Johanan b. Nappaha: 'God will in future sit in judgement over pious and wicked alike. The former go to the Garden of Eden, the latter to Hell. The wicked protest by saying: "God has not judged us properly. Whomsoever He likes, He justifies, and whom He dislikes He declares guilty." God says: "I did not want to publish your crimes." What does

---

[7] v. the material in my *The Doctrine of Merits*, 34 ; cf. W. Fowler, *The Religious Experience of the Roman People*, 432 : 'Prosperity and fertility, whether of man, beast, or crop, depend on the Roman's attitude towards his deities.'   [8] Matt. 7. 7.

[9] Ib. v. 8 ; v. *MGWJ.* 41, 74, and Hoenicke, *Neutest. Apokryphen*, p. 21. 8, and *Handbuch*, 37.

[10] v. *The Doctrine of Merits*, Index, s.v. 'Rome'.

God do? He causes their *elogium* to be read, and they go
to Hell.'[11] An earlier Haggadist, R. Jonathan b. Eliezer,
taught[12] that God does not condemn a nation before he
caused their books to be read aloud in Heaven. This gave
rise to the conception of the heavenly books of virtues and
crimes, preserved in Heaven. This doctrine made a great
impression on the popular mind, and is one which contributed a great deal to misrepresent the general trend of
Rabbinic theology.[13] The same teacher, R. Jonathan, taught
further that no wicked departed from this world until he
saw or experienced his own downfall.[14] R. Hanina b. Hama
strongly opposed those who held that God never punishes;
'He forgives all sins, no; He is long-suffering, but He
pays for all sins.'[15] This sounds like the saying of Sextus
Empiricus, who resembles in many of his sayings the Rabbis:

> Though the mills of God grind slowly, yet they grind
> exceeding small;
> Though with patience He stands waiting, with exactness
> grinds He all.'

At this point we arrive at the conflict between the attributes
of justice and goodness, which will be discussed in the next
chapter.

The individual tragedies and communal misfortunes
which befell Jews gave rise frequently to discussions and
observations on the meaning and origin of suffering. When
the four Elders, e.g. R. Tarphon, R. Joshua b. Hananja,
R. Eleazar b. Azarja, and R. Akiba entered the sick room
of R. Eliezer b. Hyrkanos, R. Akiba said: 'Beloved are the
sufferings!' The master said to them: 'Support me; I
will hear the words of my pupil, Akiba, who says that

[11] M. Ps. ch. 1, B. 24

[12] Gen. r., ch. 28; Th. 259; Midr. Sam., ch. 18.

[13] v. also Tanh., B. i. 11 A; Steinschneider, *Kobak's Jeschurun.* iii. 65;
Ozar Nehmad. ii. 113; Sachs, *M. Beiträge*, i. 11; Zunz, *Jubelschrift*, p. 145,
Löwenthal, *Ps. Aristoteles*, p. 126. 1.

[14] Esther r., ch. 3, 13 B : אין הרשע יוצא מן העולם עד שהקב'ה מראה
קניגין דידיה היאך הוה מיתציד.

[15] Esther r., ch. 8, 24 B, ch. 7, 24 B: מאן דאמר רחמנא ותרן הוא יתותרון
מעוהי ; Tanh., f. 126 B ; M. Ps. 10 D, ed. B. 93.

sufferings are precious ! Akiba, whence do you derive this
teaching ? ' Akiba replied : ' I derive it from the plain text
of the Scriptures ! It says : " Manasseh was twelve years
old when he began to reign, and he reigned fifty-five years
in Jerusalem, &c., and he did evil in the sight of the Lord ! "
(2 Kings 21. 1–2) Further it says, " These also are proverbs
of Solomon, which the men of Hezekiah, king of Judah, copied
out " (Prov. 25. 1). Is it possible that Hezekiah, who taught
the whole world Torah, should have neglected the education
of his own son, Manasseh ? No, in spite of all the great
trouble and pain Hezekiah took with his son, only sufferings
brought him (Manasseh) back to the right path, as it is
said : " And the Lord spake to Manasseh and to his people ;
but they would not hearken. Wherefore the Lord brought
upon them the captains of the host of the King of Assyria,
which took Manasseh among the thorns, and bound him
with fetters, and carried him to Babylon. And when he
was in affliction he besought the Lord his God, and humbled
himself greatly before the God of his fathers " (2 Chron.
33. 10–12). Hence thou dost learn that sufferings are beloved.' [16] At the same time, or another like occasion, the
Scribes wept bitterly, but R. Akiba smiled. When the patient
said : 'There is a mighty anger in the world !' the Scribes cried,
for 'the Scroll of Torah' was in pain. R. Akiba, however, said :
' I smile, for all the time that I see my master without trouble,
that his wine, his flax, his oil, his honey is good and well, I am
afraid, lest my master " has already received his world " ;
now that I see his pain I smile, because I am sure that he
has not lost his share in the world to come.' [17] R. Akiba
was the first to emphasize the teaching that God makes the
righteous pay in this world for the few ' evil deeds ' which
they have committed, in order to bestow upon them happiness and give them a good reward in the world to come.
Just the opposite is the case with the reward and punishment of the wicked. [18] Sufferings are, according to R. Akiba,

[16] Mekh. 72 B ; Sifre Dt., § 32 ; b. Sanh. 101 B.   [17] Ib. 101 A.
[18] Gen. r. 33. 1 ; Pes. B. 73 A ; Lev. r. 27 ; Agad. Ber. 4.

signs of God's justice and love. It is remarkable how often this great teacher recurs to this subject. In the refutation of Pappus's sermons R. Akiba retorts: ' There is no arbitrariness in God's deeds. The words of Him " who spake, and the world was created ", cannot be refuted. He judges everything in truth and in justice!'[19] Justice and love are God's thrones.[20] The great, almost unbearable, sufferings which Jews endured in this teacher's age, supply us with the commentary on these sayings. We have to thank God for the good and evil alike. The latter are signs of the Divine love and grace. The teachers made an impression in this age upon the visitors to the schools and places of worship by saying: ' Man should welcome suffering more than happiness (טובה), for if man is happy he cannot acquire forgiveness of sin ; how does he acquire it ? By suffering!'[21]

Seven contemporaries of the Bar-Kokhba war expressed their opinions on this problem. R. Eliezer b. Jacob refers to Prov. 3. 12, ' For whom the Lord loveth He correcteth ; even as a father the son in whom he delighteth '. What causeth the father to delight in his son ? The sufferings. R. Meir refers to Deut. 8. 5, ' Thou shalt also know in thine heart, that, as a man chasteneth his son, so the Lord thy God chasteneth thee'. ' Thou and thine heart are aware of the deeds thou hast done, and the sufferings by which I have chastened thee. The chastisements were not in accordance with thy deeds.' R. Meir means to say that our sufferings are always less than what we really deserve. R. Jose b. Judah exclaims: ' Beloved are the sufferings before God ! (המקום), for, through them the glory of God falls upon him who is being chastened.' R. Jonathan b. Joseph says that, 'just as God made a covenant with the Holy Land, He did so likewise with the sufferings '. That means to say : ' God fulfilled His promise to bring our forefathers into the Land, so He will keep His promise to pay reward in the world to come for the good deeds and sufferings in this

---

[19] Mekh. 33 A. [20] b. Hag. 14 A ; cf. Dan. 7. 9.
[21] Mekh. 72 B ; Sifre Deut., § 32 ; M. Tan. 26.

world'.   R. Simon b. Johai calls the sufferings 'beloved' (חביבים), for God gave three things to Israel, which the nations of the world eagerly desire, e. g. the Law, the Land of Israel, and the world to come.   All the three were given with sufferings. The Torah (cf. Prov. 1. 2 and 5. 12), Palestine (Deut. 8. 5), and the future life (Prov. 6. 22).   R. Nehemiah looks on sufferings as on the sacrifices.   Both of them atone for sins.   Moreover, chastisements have a greater atoning power than sacrifices.   The latter affect men's money, the former men's body, life, health.[22]   R. Judah b. Ilai depicts the righteous giving praise and thanks, seeing the retribution of the wicked, for the sufferings brought on them (the righteous) in this world (Lev. r. 32. 1).   R. Eliezer b. Parta goes even a step further when saying that God stipulated with Israel at the revelation : 'If ye receive upon yourselves the chastisements (for transgressing the law) with joy, then ye will receive reward ; if not, if ye murmur against them, then they will change into punishments. They, therefore, received the punishments with joy'.[23]

The sufferings which were the sources of these teachings repeatedly occurred in the third century. The problem did not lose force and actuality. R. Jochanan b. Nappaha visited his pupils and friends, R. Hijja b. Abba and R. Eleazar b. Pedath. In both cases he asked: ' Do you love your pain and suffering? ' The same question was asked of R. Johanan by R. Hanina b. Hama. In all the three instances the answer given was: 'No, neither sufferings nor their reward!'[24] The answers are the more remarkable since the great teachers of the second century decided that sufferings have to be borne with love and patience.[25]   R. Jochanan very

---

[22] v. Sifre Deut., § 32 ; Mekh. 72 B; M. Ps. 417–18 ; M. Tann. 26 ; b. Ber. 5 A.

[23] Mekh. 63 B ; Aboth R. Nathan, 47 A.   [24] b. Ber. 5 B.

[25] B. Ber. 5 A ; Cant. r. on 2. 16, with variants. The latter text throws light on the Babylonian report. The Bab. text reads : ר׳ יוחנן חלש על לגביה ר׳ חנינא א״ל חביבין עליך יסורין א״ל לא הן ולא שכרן א״ל הב לי ידך, ויהב ליה ידיה ואוקמיה, אמאי לוקים ר׳ יוחנן לנפשיה, אמרו אין חבוש מתיר עצמו מבית האסורים. R. Jochanan became ill. R. Hanina, who

often dealt with the problem of suffering. 'God visits with
pain those who are soft-hearted.' In another saying he
speaks of the potter who examines his pots. He does not
knock at the bad ones, but on the good ones. He knocks
many times, and they do not break. God likewise does not
chastise the wicked (מנסה examine by illness, trouble, &c.).
On whom does He cause suffering? The righteous, as it is
said: 'The Lord tests the just' (Ps. 11. 5).[26] That sufferings

was by profession a medical man, went to visit him. R. Hanina asked
the patient: 'Do you like sufferings?' R. Jochanan said: 'No, I do not
like them nor their reward.' R. H.: 'Give me your hand.' R. J. did
so, and was healed. 'Why did not R. J. raise himself?' Because no
prisoner can free himself without other people's help from the prison.
The version preserved in Cant. r. shows that a good deal is missing in
this relation. R. Jochanan suffered, according to that version, for three
years and a half from צמר מורייה (fever). R. Hanina went to visit him,
and said to the patient: 'What is with thee?' (lit. מה אית עליך 'What is
upon thee?') R. J. replied: 'I have more on me than I can bear!'
R. H.: 'Thou must not speak thus, but say: 'The faithful God!' When
his (R. J.'s) pain became very great, he said so. Once it became greater
than usual. R. Hanina again visited the sick, and he said a word (אמר
עלוי מלה) and the sick was at ease (והוה נסב נפש). After many days
R. Hanina became ill, and R Jochanan went to visit him, and said:
'What is with thee?' R. H. replied: 'How hard are the pains!'
R. J.: 'But how great their reward!' R. H.: 'I do not like them nor
their reward.' R. J.: 'Why dost thou not say that word which thou
didst say to me and thou wilt be at ease?' R. H.: 'When I was outside
I stood as surety for others; now that I am inside others have to pledge
themselves for my sake.' R. J. said: 'It is written, "he feedeth among
the lilies", that means that the staff of God touches only such men (Cant.
2. 16), whose heart is tender like the lilies.' The three and a half years of
R. Jochanan's illness remind us of the general use of this number,
e. g. Dan. 7. 25; 8. 13, 14; 9. 27; 12. 7, 12, 11 f. ; vgl. Hilgenfeld, *Apokalyptik*,
27; *Apocalypse of Elijah*, 87; R. Jochanan; M. Ps. 10 D: ג' שנים ומחצה
היתה שכינה עומדת בהר הזתים ומברת. The sentence: כד הוינא מלבר
הוינא ערב לאחרונין וכדון דאנא מלגיו לית אנא בעי אחרנין דיערבוני
agrees with the saying אין חבוש מתיר עצמו מבית האסורים. It is clear
that this was said by R. Hanina, and not by R. Jochanan, as assumed by
the Babylonian text. An outsider can stand surety or bail for the prisoner
who is inside, and not *vice versa*.

[26] Cant. r. on 2. 16; v. however Gen. r. ch. 32. 3, ed. Th. 290, in the
name of R. Jonathan b. Eliezer; v. also ch. 34. 2 and 55. 2; Tanh. וירא
20, the same in the name of R. Judah b. Shalom. The potter is often
mentioned in Rabbinic parables; v. Gen. r. 14. 7; v. Sirach 33. 12; Test.
Naph., § 2; cf. Aphraates, 386.

are brought on the righteous when they have a chance to study the Torah and they neglect it, is another teaching of R. Jochanan. His colleague, R. Simon b. Lakish, put it this way: 'Suffering departs from him who studies the Torah'.[27] Sufferings are, according to both, means and agents by which our sins are removed and wiped out. They are signs of love or of God's covenant with men.[28] We may find a clue to these sayings in the dispute of R. Jacob b. Idi and R. Aha b. Hanina. Both older pupils of R. Jochanan and contemporaries of R. Simon b. Lakish. They speak of sufferings of love. This term depends upon whether neglect of study, or of prayer, is entailed or not. We know that the persecutions in R. Johanan's time were aimed, in the first instance against the study of the Law and performance of the commandments. Jews in Galilee were burdened with communal slavery, police work, and other tiresome services, so that they were unable to perform their religious obligations. Besides the strenuous physical work, they were worried by conscientious troubles. There is a great resemblance between the conditions prevailing before and after the Bar-Kokhba war on one side, and in the middle of the third century on the other side. Now, just as then, the problem of the suffering, especially of the just, was the order of the day. Therefore, many other teachers of this age also deal with the cause and meaning of suffering. Thus, R. Joshua b. Levi says: 'He who rejoices at the sufferings which befall him, will bring salvation to the whole world, as it is said, "Through them (sufferings) will the world be saved "' (Isa. 64. 4).[29] Entirely in the spirit of this age rings another saying of the same teacher: 'All sufferings which befall a man and disturb him from study are sufferings of rebuke, otherwise they are sufferings of love'. We have seen that

[27] b. Ber. 5 A.

[28] AZ. 55 A; Ib. 5 A; Deut. r. 2; v. also Menahoth, 53 B.

[29] B. Taan. 8 A: כל השמח ביסורין שבאין עליו מביא ישועה לעולם שנ׳ בהם עולם ונושע.

R. Jochanan did not agree with this view, 'All sufferings
are signs of love'.[30]   R. Alexander says: 'There is no one
without suffering'.   It is a fallacy to assume that the
wicked are absolutely happy.   Righteous and wicked, good
and bad people, suffer equally under the foreign rulers, who
enslave men and women for their statute-labour.   'Happy
is the man who suffers, or upon whom suffering comes on
account of the Torah'.   That, surely, means to say that
the prohibition or the neglect of study causes him pain
and suffering.[31]   Owing to slavery, in the day-time the
scholars were prevented from study by day, and had to use
the hours of the night for this purpose.   This is the reason
why the duty of study is so emphatically urged by the
teachers of this age, and the greatness of the study in the
night exaggerated.

A third teacher, R. Jose b. Hanina, explains the suffering
of the righteous similarly to R. Johanan or R. Jonathan.
His parable illustrates the case by the dealing of the flax-
grower with flax.[32]   R. Eleazar b. Pedath brings home to
his audience this doctrine by the parable of the farmer who
had two cows, one is lean, the other strong.   'On which
will he put the burden? Surely, on the stronger!'[33]
These sayings reflect the sufferings of the righteous, which
we detected in another group of sayings by the same

---

[30] Gen. r. 92. 1: כל יסורים שהם באים על האדם ומבטלין אותו מד׳ת
יסורים של תוכחות הם, אבל יסורים שהן באים על האדם ואין מבטלין
אותו מד׳ת של אהבה הן; cf. Prov. 3 12 ; v. also Tanh. B. i. 201 f.

[31] Gen. r. 92.1: אין לך בן אדם בלא יסורים אשריו לאדם שיסורים
באים עליו מן התורה. Tanh. B. i. 202 has a different saying of this teacher
on our subject, which reads: אשרי אדם שיסורין באין עליו, והקב׳ה אמר להם
די, שיש להם סוף; Gen. r. 92. 1 gives it in the name of R. Hoshaja.
R. Alexander's statement is in the Tanhuma, attributed to R. Bisna.   It
reads: אין אדם בעולם שאינו בא לידי יסורין, הוי אדם חושש בעינו ואינו
יכול לישון, בשינו אינו יכול לישון ואלא ער כל הלילה, ואדם ער כל הלילה
ויגע בתורה זה ער וזה ער, הוי הוי אשרי אנוש שיסוריו בתורה.

[32] v. Gen. r. 32. 3 and parall. given above.

[33] Gen. r. 32. 3.

Rabbis also. Both go back to moral and religious conditions, the details of which are still to be discovered.[34]   The
very teacher of whom we are speaking here may help us to
find the key to these events. In two sayings are preserved
the causes of suffering as advanced by Eleazar b. Pedath:
'Chastisement is caused by giving alms or bread to a man
who has no knowledge.'[35]   Further, he sees the root of this
evil in scoffing: 'Upon him, who mocks, suffering will
come'.[36]   R. Ammi held a similar opinion: 'There is no
death without sin and no suffering without guilt.'[37]   R. Assi
taught also that Job had deserved much more suffering
than he actually suffered, because God said to Satan:
'Thou hast provoked Me against him, in order to destroy
him without cause!'[38]   R. Isaac, to whom we owe a direct
historical reference to the general suffering of the people in
this period, which throws light on the fact that nearly all
the teachers deal with this problem,[39] developed a new
theory that the sufferings in this world will be recompensed
by the wonders and rewards in the world to come. An idea
which is somewhat akin with that of R. Akiba and
R. Samuel b. Nahmani.[40]   Some of the more or less serious
losses and visitations vicariously exempt or free men from
more serious suffering. A man, who committed sin is guilty
of death by Heaven. He loses his fowl, breaks his bottle,
wounds his little finger. All these are substitutes for
greater losses, illness or death.[41]   Considering the general
poverty of the Jews in this time, it is no surprise that the
loss of a chicken or a bottle should be regarded as a matter

---

[34] v. Marmorstein, *The Doctrine of Merits*, 98.

[35] b. Sanh. 92 A: ‏כל הנותן פתו למי שאין בו דעה יסורין באין עליו.‏

[36] b. AZ. 18 B: ‏כל המתלוצץ יסורין באין עליו.‏

[37] Lev. r. 27. 1 ; Eccles. r. 5. 4 ; pal. Sabbath 55 A: ‏אין מיתה בלא חטא‏ ‏ואין יסורין בלא עון‏; cf. Ez. 18. 4 and Ps. 89. 33.

[38] Source unknown, in ‏מעין גנים‏ of Samuel b. Nimin, ed. Buber 8.

[39] Cant. r. 2. 5 ; Pes. B. 101 B: ‏וביותר שאני חולים מן המלכות אדם‏ ‏מתאוה לשמוע.‏

[40] Pes. B. 157 A.

[41] Pes. B. 165 B : Eccles. r. 7. 23 ; pal. Sota 17 A.

of great grief. R. Helbo connects likewise the problem of
suffering with the doctrine of reward and punishment.
Differing from the teachings we heard above, and with more
originality than 'There is none who does not suffer', he
asserts that even the greatest sufferer occasionally experi-
ences God's benefits. These blessings are due to the sufferings
they endure, which do by no means diminish man's reward.
This teaching is illustrated by a parable in which an
orphan boy figures, who was brought up by a farmer, who
provided him with food, drink, and clothes, and apprenticed
him. The boy thought that he was being provided for on
account of the work that he did. The provisions made for
him are his wages. The farmer, however, says: ' You get
your food and drink and clothes for occasional works, by
filling a barrel of water, or hewing wood; your real wages
are kept with me.' Israel is the orphan. Whatever Israel
enjoys in this world is due to the sufferings; their real
reward is kept for the next world.[42] R. Helbo repeats also
the doctrine of R. Akiba that the sufferings are destined
to free Israel from their sins in this world, so that they
shall be worthy to inherit the world to come.[43] R. Aha
regarded sufferings, Torah, sacrifices, and prayers as the four
things which God offered to the generation of the Flood;
yet they were reluctant to receive them: 'They said to
God: " Depart from us (יסורין = סור), the knowledge of Thy
ways, we desire not (= תורה); what is the Almighty that
we shall serve Him (קרבנות = עבודה), and what profit shall
we have if we pray unto Him (תפלה = נפגע) ? " '[44] The real
meaning of this homily points rather to the conditions of the
teacher's own age than to that of the people of the Flood.
He tries to show that suffering, study of the Torah, worship of God and prayer, have atoning power before God.

[42] Deut. r. 3. 4.

[43] Pes. B. 151 B, r.: ר' ברכיה ר' חלבו בש"ר שמעון בן יוסינא בש"ר
בש"ר שמואל r. perhaps ;מאיר; Lev. r. 29: בשם ר' שמעון בן יוחאי r.
בר נחמן; v. also Pes. B. 152 B, in the name of R. Jeremiah. The teaching
reads: מיסרך אני ביסורין בעולם הזה, בשביל לנקותך מעונותיך לעולם הבא•

[44] Exod. r. 30. 10.

N

The sufferings were divided, this teacher taught, in three
different parts. One part was apportioned to the Fathers,
the second to the generation of the persecution, and the
third part is preserved for King Messiah.[45] By the דורו של
שמד here the contemporary persecutions and sufferings were
meant, not those of the Hadrianic time. As to the sufferings of the Fathers, we have a remarkable passage by
R. Judah b. Simon. Abraham asked for old age (in order
that father and son could be distinguished by the signs of
old age), Isaac prayed for suffering, Jacob for illness (that
man should not depart from this world suddenly). We are
here concerned about Isaac, who prays: 'Lord of the
Worlds, if a man should die without suffering the measure
of judgement is spanned against him (מדת הדין מתוחה כנגדו).
When, however, Thou bringest upon him suffering, the
measure of judgement is not spanned against him!' God
said: 'Thou didst ask for a good thing, I will start with
thee!'[46] The same teacher sees in Israel's suffering in this
world a preparation for the next world.[47] A similar
thought is reported by R. Judan[48] and by R. Hanina b.

[45] M. Sam. ch. 19, ed. B. 101, R. Huna in his name: לשלשה חלקים
נתחלקו הייסורין, אחד לדורות, ולאבות, ואחד לדורו של שמד ואחד
למלך המשיח. Precisely the same saying is quoted M. Ps. 2. 9, ed. B. 28,
by R. Huna, in the name of R. Idi; read perhaps אחא ר' instead of
ר' אידי. The reading אחת נטלו אבות העולם וכל הדורות is to be preferred
to the reading לדורות ולאבות; v. also R. Levi in the name of R. Idi;
M. Ps. 16. 4, ed. B. 121.

[46] Gen. r. 65. 4. The passage shows that the Rabbis discussed the
question: Why was Isaac suffering from blindness? This teacher,
R. Judah b. Simon, gave one answer. The same is given by R. Levi,
who says: יצחק חידש יסורין. R. Hanina b. Papa suggested, 'In order
that Jacob should be enabled to receive the blessings'. There seem
to have been earlier disputes on that point. R. Eleazar b. Azarja, e. g.,
advances the view that Isaac became blind in order that he should be
spared to mix with people, who spoke evil of him, the father of Esau.
Anonymous sayings connect Isaac's infirmity with the sacrifice on
Moriah.

[47] Lev. r. 33. 2: אמר הקב'ה איסרם אני ביסורין בעוה"ז אבל לע"ל
לא אוסיף עוד עבור לו.

[48] Gen. r. 92. 1: ומה הללו שן (עבדו) שאינן בכל גופו שלאדם אלא אחד

Isaac.[49]   R. Hanin of Sepphoris, combining Gen. 12. 10 with Ps. 94. 12, derives from the example shown by Abraham that the sufferer must not murmur against God, or complain of his trouble, but bear it patiently like Abraham.[50]   A similar admonition is contained in a sermon of R. Tahlifa of Caesarea. ' In case of trouble or suffering coming on thee, receive them with joy, and do not despair at seeing the wicked Esau being happy and prosperous!'[51]   The great power of atonement vested in suffering is vividly described in a sermon of R. Dosithai of בירי.   He depicts David as a Samaritan merchant.   David says before God: ' Lord of the whole world!   Who can understand (avoid) errors ?'[52] God says : ' I forgive them.'   ' Cleanse me from my secret sins!'   God: ' I forgive them.'   ' Keep thy servant back from presumptuous sins!'   God: ' I forgive them.'   ' Let them not have dominion over me', i.e. the teachers should not speak of my sins in their lectures and sermons.   God: ' I forgive them.'   ' I shall be innocent from my great transgression', i. e. either it shall not be written at all, or forgive me that sin I committed!   God says: ' It is impossible !'   David: ' Am I lost altogether ?' (כל הכי נטרד ההוא גברא ' Is there no remedy for me?').   God says: ' Take upon thyself sufferings!'[53]   Finally, we notice that some of the

---

מאיברין אמרה תורה לחפשי ישלחנו, מי שיסורים באים עליו שהן בכל גופו של אדם עא עא כו"ב; v. also the story of R. Hama with the blind man, who used the term שאת בן חורין לעוה"ב.

[49] M. Ps. 90. 16, ed. Buber 393 : כל מי שקדמוהו יסורין בעולם הזה ישלו חלק לעולם הבא; ' he is like Abraham, who is called ירא אלהים '.   The idea is expressed in Ps. 90. 11 : וכיראתך עברתך ' and according to the fear of Thee, so is Thy chastisement ', e. g. of those who fear thee.

[50] Gen. r. 40. 2; cf. 92. 2 : מה כתיב באברהם ואברכה ואגדלה שמך, כיון שיצא קפץ עליו רעבון ולא קרא תגר ולא הקפיד אלא וירד אברם וכו' ויהו רעב בארץ.

[51] Deut. r. 1. 17 : אם באו עליך יסורין קבל אותן בחיבה אל תתחר במצליח דרכו זה עשו.

[52] Cf. Ps. 19. 13.

[53] b. Sanh. 107 A.   David's sins and deeds were commented on very unfavourably by some of the teachers and the people.   Many teachers of the third century preserved valuable material on this point, like R. Joshua

teachers saw in Job and his suffering, in his loss of wealth
nd children, in his illness and condemnation of his right,
a true picture of Israel's fate and history. As Job ultimately was rewarded and justified, so will Israel at the
end of the days regain the right place in the world.[54]

(7) *Goodness.*

How is God's justice to be reconciled with a beneficent
God ? How can God's goodness prevail in face of all the
evils of this world ? If God is compassionate, long-suffering, forgiving, then all the doors stand open to sin and
licentiousness! Since the teachers of Judaism opposed dualistic theories just as much as they combated polytheistic influence, these queries and doubts, answers and sayings reflect
an earnest grappling with these questions. If there is one
teaching which can be regarded as unquestioned and unop-
posed, it is the doctrine of God's love, which extends to
Jews and Gentiles, good and bad, human beings and the
animal world alike. Writers on Christian theology are
wont to point out this as a result of Jesus's teaching. They
boast, we can see with what right, that the spread of the
Christian doctrine of love changed the face of the world
and the hearts of mankind. This is just as great a fallacy
as the generally held view that Rabbinic theology teaches
a particular, and not a universalistic, God. One preacher
concludes his sermon ; 'Just as God's love extends to
human beings (אדם), so His mercy is upon the cattle and
birds'.[1] Another preacher calls attention to the fact that
God has mercy even at the time of punishment with the
wicked and their cattle.[2] ' He who loves his fellow crea-

b. Levi ; v. M. Ps. 5 c, R. Isaac, Gen. r. 41, R. Samuel b. Ami, Pes. B. 10 B,
Pes. R. 147 B, R. Samuel b. Naḥman, pal. Ber. 2. 1, b. Sabb. 30 A. The
heretics of the Church liked to display their animosity and malice when
referring to David ; cf. Clem. *Hom.* iii. 21 and 25 ; *Diodor of Tarsus,* ed.
Harnack, 113 and 129 ; cf. Hilgenfeld, *Ketzeraeschichte,* 421.

[54] v. Lam. r. 3. 1 ; M. Ps. 102. 8 ; Pes. B. 26 B.

[1] Deut. r. 6. 1.   [2] Exod. r. 12. 3.

tures (על הבריות) will be loved by God.'[3] God is, according
to R. Judah b. Simon, תוכו רצוף אהבה (Cant. 3. 10), the
midst of it being paved with love.[4] 'The Lord is good to
all, and His tender mercies are over all His works'
(Ps. 145. 9), repeated daily by Jews, took deep roots in the
minds and souls of all believers in God and worshippers in
the synagogues. God's loving providence extends to all
creatures, to all comers of the world (באי העולם). He is the
saviour of mankind, more so of Israel.[5] Even in battle, in
fighting the Egyptians, He deals mercifully with His creatures.[6] 'He feeds and sustains all.'[7] This act of lovingkindness is shown not only to those who are just and
righteous, but even to the wicked. They are supplied
according to their needs and provided sufficiently.[8] God's
love and providence know no limits between just and
wicked; moreover, He provides even for the beasts of the
field, big and small, sustains the plants and herbs in His
goodness and grace.[9] R. Gamaliel II stated: 'God feeds
the world, from the mighty unicorn to the smallest
vermin.'[10] Rab repeats this by saying: 'God is occupied
for a third of the day in feeding the mightiest and smallest.'[11] In another connexion R. Gamaliel II, or R. Zadok,
according to a variant, expresses this view of God's providence, in which all creatures share equally, in these words:
'God, who created the world, causes wind to blow, sun to
shine, rain and dew to descend, plants to grow, and decks
a ready table to all!'[12] It is noteworthy that Tineius Rufus,
in his dialogue with R. Akiba, uses the very words: 'Why
does your God cause the wind to blow? the rain to descend?
the herbs to grow on Sabbath?'[13] A Min (unbeliever) taunted
the Elders in Rome with the same question, using the very

[3] b. Shabb. 151 B.   [4] Pes. B. 12 B ; Cant. 3. 10 ; Num. r. 12.
[5] Mekh. 37 A ; M. R. S. b. J. 62.   [6] Ib. 38 A ; M. R. S. b. J. 62.
[7] Ib. 38 A.
[8] Ib. 59 A ; R. Zadok; v. also b. Kid. 32 B ; Midr. Prov. 12 A ; R. Gamaliel II, Sifre Deut., § 38.
[9] Mekh. 59 A.   [10] v. further in the chapter on the existence of God
[11] b. A. Z. 3 B.   [12] v. note no. 8 above.
[13] Gen. r. 11. 6.

same words.[14] Both the Roman general and the nameless
Min must have belonged to the Stoics, who believed in the
providence of the gods. God is the sustainer of all; of the
whole world. Yet their philosophy objected to God's resting and working on Sabbath in the same breath. To the
same school must have belonged the interlocutor of
R. Johanan b. Zakkai, according to some texts, of R.
Joshua b. Hananja, according to a second version, and of
R. Joshua b. Korha, to a third reading. Rain is provided
by God for all, without distinction of creed and race.[15]
In the time of great distress, before and after the Bar-
Kokhba war, there were Jews who doubted whether God
can supply even His people with food.

R. Jannai repeats the words of R. Gamaliel: ' A man
buys a pound of meat. How much trouble and pain does
it cause him till he sees it cooked. I, God, cause wind to
blow, clouds to lift, rain and dew to descend, plants to grow
and ripen, a table is ready before everyone, all the creatures
get all they need, each person according to his requirements.' The same words are varied by R. Phinehas b.
Hama.[16] R. Simon b. Pazzi compared God in the manner
of the Stoics with the soul, and saw in the soul the
sustainer of the body, in God the provider of food and
sustenance.[17] Joseph, in saying grace at the table of his
Egyptian master, thanked God, who supplies food for all.[18]
An anonymous Haggadist says: ' God supplies with food
all His creatures without expecting or receiving any
reward; are we not bound to thank Him ? ' [19] Another
dwells on the contrast between God and men. The latter
gives alms to a poor beggar once, twice, a month, or
a year, but God gives food to man all the days he is alive.[20]

[14] Exod. r. 30. 6 ; Pes. r. ch. 23 ; Tanh. חשא, 33.
[15] Deut. r. 7 ; Gen. r. 13 ; M. Ps. B. 479.
[16] Eccles. r. 1. 4.
[17] v. above, p. 196, for the Stoics, v. Diogenes of Babylon, 82, ed. Gomperz,
and Seneca, cp. 65. 24 ; Philo, de opif. mundi, 23 ; Bergmann, Judaica, 136.
[18] v. further on.   [19] M. Ps. ed. Buber, p. 482.
[20] Jelamdenu, ed. Grünhut, Genesis, 23 A.

This belief in God's providence was so firm and unshakable in the creed of the scribes that a man who worried about his food for the next day, was regarded as lacking in faith. Their trust in God's goodness and mercy knew no limit.[21] The immovable trust in God, taught and shown by Prophets and Psalmists, was not weakened and did not fade away in the times of the Rabbis, in the so-called age of the 'Spät-Judentum'. 'Do you know whom you shall trust? Him, who created Heaven and earth. He, who trusts Him, his reward will never cease!'[22] R. Simon b. Pazzi says in the name of R. Joshua b. Levi: 'He, who trusts in God is worthy to become like Him, but he who puts his trust in the idols is bound to become like them.'[23] This scribe sees in man's unchangeable and immovable trust in God the highest form of the imitation of God.

A second aspect of God's goodness is to be found in a teaching expounded by R. Johanan b. Zakkai, which was later on very often developed and enlarged upon. We mean the saying: הקב'ה חס על כבודן של בריות 'God pays due regard to the honour of the creatures.'[24] R. Eliezer b. Hyrkanos, a very rigorous judge of human character, said, according to Abba Hanin: 'God pays due regard even to the honour of those who transgress His will, how much more that He does so to the honour of those who do His will!'[25] That we have to supply here the words על כבודן של עוברי רצונו is apparent from a third teaching of this type. 'God has pity on the wicked', says an anonymous teacher

---

[21] v. the passages, Marmorstein, *The Doctrine of Merits*, 175. 11; cf. Epictetus, *Diss.* i, 9. 19: 'If ye get satisfaction to-day, and are despairing of to-morrow, what shall we eat to-morrow? wretched people! if you got to-day, surely you will be provided for to-morrow. If you do not get it, well, then commit suicide!' What a world of difference between the Stoic philosopher and the Jewish teacher! v. Bergmann, *loc. cit.*

[22] M. Ps. 434 f.   [23] Deut. r. 5. 9.

[24] Mekh. 88 A; Tos. B. R. 7. 10: בא וראה כמה חס המקום על כבוד הבריות; b. B. K. 79 B: כמה גדול כבוד הבריות; v. also Sifre Deut., § 192; Tanh. f. 11 A.

[25] Sifre Num., § 11: חס המקום על עוברי רצונו; v. pal. Sotah 2. 2; b. Sotah 14 A: אם ככה חסה תורה על עוברי רצונו; Num. r. 9. 13.

of the Tannaitic period, 'how much more on the honour of the righteous'.[26]   R. Joshua b. Levi goes even a step further! 'God did not reveal the name of the tree Adam ate from, neither to Adam, nor will He ever reveal it! See what is written! "And if a woman approach unto any beast, &c." (Lev. 20. 16). If a human being sinned, what is the crime of the beast? Why should one kill the beast? In order that people should not point at the beast, saying, "Through it X got stoned!" If God is so particular about the honour of His creatures, how much more is He considering His own honour?'[27] On the other hand, R. Huna in the name of R. Idi taught that God pays more attention to the honour of the Zaddik (righteous) than he cares for his own honour.[28] 'He shows honour to those who fear Him. God, certainly, guards the honour of all His creatures, even of those who sinned against Him, and became honourless by their misdeeds.' Those who fear Him, are put a grade higher. For God Himself honours them. How? 'Solomon sits on God's throne (1. Chron. 29. 23), Elijah rides on God's horse (cf. Nahum 1. 3), Moses uses God's sceptre (Exod. 4. 2), the Messiah will wear God's crowns (Ps. 21. 4), Israel, God's garment (Ps. 29. 1), Moses, God's name!' All these things are unthinkable with human kings. They would never tolerate that others should be called by the titles Καῖσαρ, Augustus, or Βασιλεύς, others should wear their uniform, crowns, or use their sceptre, horse, or throne. God makes those who fear Him share these honours. They are so near Him that they become like God![29]

We notice thirdly that the scribes have been contending against the opinion whether God could satisfy His crea-

---

[26] T. K. 84 A.

[27] Gen. r. 15. 8, ed. Th. 141–2, based on the Mishna Sanh. 7. 4.

[28] Pes. B. 15 A; Tanh. f. 36 A: חס המקום על כבודו של צדיק יותר מכבודו.

[29] Tanh. f. 71B; Tanh., Buber ii. 22 f.; Exod. r. 8. 1; M. Ps. 21. 2, ed. Buber 177, by R. Simon, with additions and variants; Num. r. 14. 3, by R. Abin.

tures.   R. Benjamin b. Levi, whom we know as a zealous
opponent of heretic ideas, deals with the problem whether
God can do justice to all parties.   We read that Ahasuerus
did ‘ according to the wish of each man ’.   God said to
him : ‘ I cannot do according to the request of each of my
creatures ’ (אני איני יוצא מידי בריותי), and thou dost seek to
fulfil the wish of each individual.   Supposing two men
were to ask for the hand of one woman, can both of them
marry her ?   No, either one or the other !   Further, if two
ships wait in the harbour, one for the north wind and the
other for the south wind, can one fulfil both ?   No !   Either
it is a south or a north wind.   In future there will stand
before thee in judgement two men, a Jew and a wicked
person.   Canst thou do justice ; satisfy both of them ?   No,
one will be exalted and the other crucified !   R. Benjamin
adds to this the thought which may be turned against those
who believe that God is not almighty, ‘ that this happens
in this world; in the world to come these things, like the
service of two winds at the same time, will be possible ’.[30]
R. Abbahu held to the contrary that God can fulfil the
desires of each of His creatures.   It was revealed and
known to Him, ‘ who said and the world was created ’
(גלוי וידוע לפני מי שאמר והיה העולם) that the nations of the
world will not receive the Torah.   ‘ Why did he attempt
to offer it to them (lit. מפני מה יצא ידיהן Why did He
desire them to acknowledge it ?) ? ’   ‘ For this is the measure
with Him.   He does not punish His creatures lest He
gave them a chance to do the right thing, for He does not
force His creatures ’ (שאין הקב׳ה בא בטרוניא על בריותיו).[31]

God’s love to His creatures, whether good or bad,
Gentiles or Jews, is as we see, one of the most emphatic
and characteristic doctrines of Rabbinic theology.   We are
taught by Dr. W. Newton[32] that ‘ various true views of

---

[30] Esther r., ch. 2, end ; Lev. r. 9. 5 ; Num. r. 13. 3 ; Cant. r. 4. 31 ; v.
also Yalkut Makh. 145. 26.

[31] Pes. B. 200 A ; Tanh. f. 283 B.

[32] *The Christian Doctrine of God*, ed. 1909, 84.

God have been entertained by men, but that *God is love*
has never been proclaimed as truth and wrought out into
a message of grace and help. This is the Christian
speciality; and a religion that has such a truth to offer
could not set in anywhere but at the front. No wonder
that the new song is a song of the love of God.' We dare
to challenge this statement, not only on historical grounds.
Jews, and as a matter of fact, Christians themselves, have
seen very little of its beneficial influence, and deplored
on very many occasions the application of this love. If
Christianity had acknowledged God's love as the highest
principle of religion and believed in God as the God of
love, if that had been the real conception of religion up to
this day, the history of the world ought to appear quite
different from that picture which lives in the mind of all
those who know it! There are in the Gospels glowing
passages of God's love; but many more, spoken or written
with greater force and power, which show a very uncom-
promising attitude towards all those who do not agree,
either in thoughts or in deeds, with the teachings of
Christianity. Rabbinic teachings extend God's love and
grace, goodness and mercy, to sinners. ' God is the Father
of all beings, of the whole world. "A wise son makes a
glad father" (Prov. 10. 1). The father is God, who is the
Father of the whole world!' [33] God provides food even to
those who provoke Him (e.g. the daughters of Lot), how
much more to those who do His will.[34] The same sentence is repeated in the teaching derived from the story of
Israel's rebellion in the wilderness, when they doubted
God's power to give them bread and meat.[35] He does not
desire the downfall and destruction of the wicked.[36]
R. Samuel b. Ami teaches 'that God desired to lodge with
His creatures since the first day of the creation', [37] or,
according to another version, he desired to make partner-

[33] Midr. Prov. 13 A on Prov. 10.1.   [34] Mekh. 36 A.
[35] Ib., pp. 48 A, B.   [36] v. above, note 31.
[37] Gen. r. ch. 3; Num. r. 13; Pes. r. 7. 27 B.

ship with the creatures. The classical verse of the Psalmist
(104. 9) expressing God's love to all is explained by three
teachers of the third century. R. Joshua b. Levi says:
'God is good to all, to all who are His works.' R. Samuel
b. Nahmani expounds: 'God is good to all, and His mercy
extends over all, for His nature is to be merciful.' R. Levi
sees in it a higher idea. 'God is good to all, and the
greatest good is that His creatures learn of Him to be
merciful to each other.' [38] Again the *imitatio Dei!* R. Hijja
puts this teaching somewhat differently. 'A human being
who has a friend, as long as the latter is rich, cleaves to
him, loves him; when he gets poor, he ridicules him. God
is different. When a man becomes poor, God lifts him up
and helps him.' Yet this teacher limits God's support only
to the righteous, and does not extend it to the wicked. His
view opposed a perhaps older view, which agrees with that
of the Mekhilta, that 'God supports and erects even the
wicked!' [39] To each living creature is granted the desire
of its heart. R. Abba adds: 'Even if it was not uttered,
only thought of in the heart.' [40] Owing to this nature of
God, He was called הטוב '*the Good*'. For rain and good
tidings the blessing in the time of the Mishna was: ברוך
הטוב והמטיב 'Blessed be He, the Good One, and who does
good.' [41] 'The world was created out of goodness.' [42] The
morning prayer expresses this with ובטובו מחדש תמיד and
המחדש בטובו. Further we come across the name רחמנא
'the Merciful', which is closely associated with our teaching. R. Akiba taught: כל מה דעביד רחמנא לטב עביד 'What
God does is done for some good purpose, though it seems to
us sometimes harsh, cruel, or incomprehensible'. R. Huna,
Rab, R. Meir, who are connected with the saying, bear out
that we have in it an adage known to and uttered by many
people. [43] The same teacher, R. Akiba, emphasizes that

---

[38] Gen. r. 33. 3, ed. Th. 304.

[39] Tanh. B., i. 151–2; v. also Ag. Ber. ch. 48. [40] Exod. r. 24. 3.

[41] M. Ber. 9. 2; pal. Ber. 13 D; pal. Taan. 69 A; b. Taan. 31 A; Gen.
r. 13, ed. Th. 123–4, 613.

[42] M. Tadshe, 29. [43] b. Ber. 60 B.

'all creatures are loved by God, all of them created in the image of God.' [44] Israelites took a somewhat higher place, for they are called God's children. They received the Torah. The love of God, however, knows no distinction, all are created in the image of God. When R. Akiba preached in גנזק של מדי on the subject of the people of the Flood, his words did not make the slightest impression on the audience. As soon, however, as he turned to the history of Job, all of them cried. He applied to them the verse in Job 24. 20, 'They have shown no love and mercy to their fellow creatures, so has God turned his love away from them'.[45] The generation of the Flood found no sympathy even in their tragic fate, for they were merciless. 'He who shows no love to his fellow-men can expect no love from Heaven.' [46] R. Aha said : ' When drought comes, and the creatures are merciful to each other, God is also filled with mercy toward them.' [47] R. Tanhuma preached at such an occasion of general distress : 'My sons ! Fill yourselves with mercy toward each other, and God will be filled with mercy to you !' [48] The teachers of Judaism never wearied of describing or speaking of the great mercy shown by God to mankind. The attributes and ways of God are full of mercy and lovingkindness. The character and the deeds of man are crooked. Those of God are full of mercy, as it is said : ' The Lord is merciful and gracious ' (Ps. 103. 8).[49] Another teacher taught : ' We know that the mercy of God will last for ever. We have not consumed it. His mercy is still with us. The nations say : " Come and let us cut them off" (Ps. 83. 5). " His compassions do not fail us ". Moreover, " Thou dost renew us every morning, and raisest us ". By this we know that Thy faithfulness is great to all Thy creatures ' (לכל באי עולם).[50] 'A

---

[44] Aboth iii. 15 ; Mekh. 94 A.　　　　[45] Gen. r. 33. 7.

[46] B. K. 6 c ; Sifre Deut., § 97 and 117.　　　　[47] Gen. r. 33. 3.

[48] Ib. 33. 3.　　　　[49] Exod. r. 2. 1.

[50] M. Ps., ed. Prague, ch. 67, ed. Buber, p. 314, with variants ; M. Lam., ed. Buber, p. 132.

worldly king sends his legions against a city which rebelled
against him. They kill all the inhabitants of the city,
whether faithful or rebellious; God, however, saves the life
of the righteous,[51] for His mercy is upon Him. The
mercy of men extends more to the male than to the female.
God's compassions are alike to male and female; moreover,
they include all creatures, even the cattle.' [52] This aspect
of Rabbinic theology is most concisely put by a Tannaitic
teacher, who says: 'I am the Lord your God, I am the
Lord, "who spake and the world was", I am the judge,
I am full of mercy, I am the judge to punish, and faithful
to pay reward!' [53] These ideas were so widespread and
well-known that we find besides the name רחמנא,[54] the name
בעל הרחמים for God. R. Levi says: 'The Lord of Mercy
does not touch the souls first', i.e. does not punish in the
first instance with death.[55] God says to Moses: 'Thou art
a human being, therefore thou couldst not hear them; I,
however, am the Lord, compassionate, the Lord of mercy;
I have mercy on them!' [56]

The conceptions of God's providence and love have been
subjected to criticisms in many quarters, and from many
points of view. The slightest doubt as to God's mercy and
love was considered heretical. An old Mishna enumerates
three instances, for which the reader in the public service
is removed from the reading desk. One of these instances
is, if he read: 'Thy mercy reaches the bird's nest, but for
me there is no mercy'.[57] The proper text of this Mishna
was a matter of contention as far back as the third century.
There were obviously two distinct readings. The first

---

[51] M. Tanh. i. נח 10, Ag. Ber. 9–10.

[52] Sifre Num., § 133; Yalk. i. 773.   [53] T. K. 74 A.

[54] v. the saying: רחמנא לבא בעי God wants the heart; v. b. Sanh.
106 B, where we read הקב'ה; further רחמנא ליצלן, b. Yeb. 63 A, B. K.
65 B, Sabb. 84 B, Taan. 9, B. Kid. 81 A, Ket. 111 A, j. Sanh. 8. 1, Gittin 17 A,
M. Ps. 436.

[55] Lev. r. 17. 4; Pes. r. ch. 17, 88 B; Ruth r. 2.

[56] Eccles. r. 7. 7; Exod. r. 6. 2.

[57] M. Ber. v. 33 B; M. Meg. iii. 25 A.

read: 'צ קן עד 'Thy mercy reaches up to the bird's nest'.
The second had: על קן 'Upon the bird's nest. God's love,
which is infinite, is limited.' [58] It is still doubtful of what
the heresy consists in this saying. It may be that the
heretics thought of the bird's nest as the smallest of the
small things to which providence may extend, but for
smaller things, like worms, insects, &c., it does not care.
Rab, the Babylonian teacher, taught: ' God provides for all
creatures, from the mightiest beast to the smallest worm.' [59]
There is another comment on this Mishna. Such heretics
are meant, according to it, who hold that only those commandments are obligatory which are as clear as that of
Deut. 22. 6–7, because they are natural; other commandments, which do not appeal to common sense, their reason
or intention being obscure, need not be observed.[60] The
words of the text seem to favour the first interpretation.
There must have been Jews who, under Epicurean influence,
doubted or limited God's mercy.

Others tried to prove the idea that God is *cruel*. The
Haggadists repeat the words of the critics, who say of
God ' that is His custom, He destroys the generations in
a cruel way (כך היא אומנתו לחייב את הבריות במדת אכזריות). He
destroyed the generation of Enosh, that of the tower-
building. He cannot leave off His ways!' God replies:
' Abraham, come and see for yourself! All the generations I have destroyed shall pass before thee; and thou
shalt see that they were not punished by me according
to the measure of their wickedness. If, however, thou
shouldst think I meted out their punishment too severely,
very well, teach me, and I will do according to what
thou dost say, for it is written, "That which I see not,
teach thou me; if I have done iniquity, I will do so no

<hr/>

[58] R. Phinehas b. Hama in the name of R. Simon b. Pazzi, j. Ber. 5. 3 ;
Meg. 14. 10 and R. Jose in the name of the same teacher; v. also b. Ber.
38 B, b. Meg. 25 A, where R. Jose b. Abun and R. Jose b. Zabdi give a
different Palestinian tradition.

[59] v. above, p. 197, and b. Sabb. 107 B ; v. Ass. Mosis 12. 4.

[60] v Aptowitzer, *MGWJ.* 57. 16 f.

more!"' (Job 34. 32).[61] We must presume that only strin-
gent reasons moved the Haggadist to invent this strange
dialogue between God and Abraham. Indeed, an earlier
teacher faced the same objection to the doctrine of God's
mercy. He assumes that before Abraham appeared, God
punished the world rather cruelly.[62] The latter Haggadist
wanted to weaken that impression. 'The sins men commit
changed the merciful and gracious God into a cruel God.'[63]
This reproach resounds in another passage also: 'God says
to Moses, "Enough! By thy prayers thou bringest me and
thyself into ill-fame. They will say, 'Moses must have
been a great sinner, so that God did not grant his request',
and further: 'God is cruel! See how much Moses prayed,
and he did not listen to him!'"'[64] The teachers of the third
century dealt with the same question. They derived hence
a new aspect of the relation between God and man.
R. Johanan said: 'Hence we learn that no creature can
claim anything of his Creator. Even Moses, the teacher of
all the prophets, does not dare to approach Him, only in
the way of supplication.'[65]

Another difficulty of the same type was the commandment: 'Remember what Amalek did unto thee' (Deut.
25. 17), which implies cruelty, and contradicts the words:
'Thou shalt not abhor an Edomite' (ib. 23. 8). 'Come and
see', says an Haggadist, 'not like the nature of God is that
of man. A man never rids himself of some wrong done to
him by his fellow-man. God is different. Israel was
enslaved in Egypt (Exod. 1. 13), and when they acquired
their freedom, then came Amalek, who was of the seed of
Esau, and did so many wrongs to Israel, God, notwith-
standing all these, enjoins them, "Thou shalt not abhor
an Edomite!"'.[66]

Thirdly, we notice that the teaching of God's mercy gave

---

[61] Tanh. B. i. 91 ; Ag. Ber. ch. 22, ed. B. 45.
[62] Sifre Deut., § 311.   [63] Tanh., Yalk., Hos. 527.
[64] Mekh., Yalk., Deut. 820.   [65] Deut. r. 2. 1.
[66] Pes. B. 22 B.

rise to the notion that God forgives all sins. 'God is gracious and merciful, full of lovingkindness and forgiveness; then all the lines between righteousness and wickedness, sin and virtue, are wiped off.' One of the greatest mercies of God is the Jewish aspect of forgiveness of sin. Whilst some thought the Merciful cruel, others taught that He is too compassionate; He never punishes. No deed is so bad that it should find no pardon with Him. This doctrine must have led to great and regrettable abuses. R. Hanina taught therefore in a very frequently reported and seriously pronounced saying: 'He who says, "God is too pitying", his life should be cut off!' [67] It may be that R. Hanina turned against Bar Kappara, who taught that God forgives all sins except immorality. [68] Judah b. Nahmani, the famous Meturgeman, also raised his voice against people of this caste. He rebuked them by pointing to the words of Micah (7. 5), '"Trust ye not in a friend; put ye not confidence in a friend!" If the evil inclination tells thee: "Sin, God will forgive thee!" do not trust such a friend (cf. Gen. 8. 21), and put not your confidence in a leader, i. e. God, who is compassionate.' [69]

(8) *Purity and Holiness.*

The real meaning of purity in the Haggada is applied to a life free from sexual errors and moral stains. Whatever the words טהור 'pure', and טהרה 'purity', might have conveyed to the primitive mind, in the ages of the Tannaim and Amoraim it was conceived in this sense. R. Jonathan says of the daughters of Israel, that they are קדושות וטהורות 'holy and pure'.[1] A Midrash fragment[2] contains an exposi-

[67] pal. Taan. 48 D; pal. Shek. 48 D; pal. Beza 62 B, Gen. r. 6. 4; b. B. K. 50 A; Esther r. chaps. 7 and 8; Tanh. f. 126 B; M. Ps., ed. Buber, 93; R. Judah.

[68] Tanh. 26; v. also M. Ps. 24 D, R. Abba b. Kahana's saying, Lam. r. 1. 2, and others.

[69] Cf. Jer. 3. 4; b. Hag. 16 A.

[1] Sifre Deut., § 214; v. also Büchler, *Types of Jewish Palest. Piety*, 53 f.

[2] v. Wertheimer, בתי מדרשות, i. 41.

tion of Lev. 18. 3, saying: בניי אם מבקשין אתם לירש את הארץ
הזאת שמרו עצמכם מן העריות ומכל דבר של קלקלה והיו טהורין
ו קדושים ואתם יושבין לבטח. R. Hijja bar Abba says: כל אשה
שמייתחמת מן בעלה בקדושה ובטהרה לא קפח הקב'ה שכרה אלא נותן
לה בן צדיק כמשה ואהרן, מנא לן משמואל הנביא דכת' בו וכו' אשר
שאלתי מעמו למה שנזרע בקדושה ובטהרה.[3] This conception contradicts a very wide-spread feeling among primitive and
advanced peoples, that all birth is intrinsically impure.[4]
Jewish religion in our period was free from this view.
R. Meir said that the sons of Aaron, Nadab and Abihu
died because they remained unmarried.[5] King Hezekiah
was visited with a severe illness because he did not want
to marry.[6] One Haggadist compares the fruit of the womb
(children) to the fruits of the ground. God says: 'Just as
the latter are produced without sin or iniquity, so bringing
forth offspring is without sin or iniquity.'[7] How is this
difference between Jewish religious feeling and the
generally conceived opinion of the Greek-Roman world[8]
to be explained? Surely by the doctrine of God's purity.
In Jewish thought there is no room for any sexual idea in
connexion with God. It is, as a matter of fact, *the* only
religious system where no goddess appears or figures in any
way. The influence of this omission cannot be highly
enough calculated in the development of Jewish religion.
The aberrations of antique religions as well as of Christianity are to a great extent due to this fact. God, however, is purity itself. This is admirably expressed by
R. Abdimi of Haifa, who teaches that God says to man:
'Behold, I am pure, my abode is pure, my ministers are
pure, the soul I give thee is pure: if thou shouldst return
her as I gave her to thee, unstained and undefiled, well; if

[3] Quoted in *Halakoth Gedoloth*, ed. Hildesheimer, p. 38.
[4] v. Farnell, *The Attributes of God*, 189 f.
[5] Num. r. ; v. Yalkut Sikili, MS. Bodl., 3 A, B.   [6] v. Ber. 11 A.
[7] Eleh Debarim rabba ; Yalkut Deut. 848.
[8] v. Abt, *Die Apologie des Apulejus*, 111 f. ; Fehrle, *Kultische Keuschheit in
Altertum*, 31 ; Harnack, *Origenes*, i. 60. Many traces of these doctrines
can be found in our sources as well. They imply, however, only physical,
and not moral impurity, as will be shown later.

not, I burn her before thee!'[9]   The purity of God and the
human soul are often compared, just as the providence of
God for the world and the care of the soul for the human
body.[10]   God shuns even the mention of an impure word,
therefore it is said אשר איננה טהורה in Gen. 7. 8, instead of
טמאה, according to R. Joshua b. Levi,[11] 'God is called pure
and He will purify Israel'.[12]   R. Akiba says that 'Israel
has no one else to purify him but his Father in Heaven'.[13]
R. Akiba meant purification from all kinds of sin and transgression.   Sin defiles man.   We find this idea expressed in
an ancient Boraita:

ת"ר ולא תטמאו בהם וכו'

אדם מטמא עצמו מעט, מטמאין אותו הרבה,

מלמטה מטמאין אותו מלמעלה,

בעולם הזה מטמאין אותו לעולם הבא,

ת"ר והתקדשתם והייתם קדושים,

אדם מקדש עצמו מעט, מקדשין אותו הרבה,

מלמטה מקדשין אותו מלמעלה,

בעולם הזה מקדשין אותו לעולם הבא.

'He, who defiles himself a little, will be defiled a good
deal.   Here, beneath, will be defiled from above.   In this
world, will become defiled in the future world.'   The same
happens to those, who sanctify themselves a little, beneath
and in this world, they will be hallowed in the world
to come, from above, and a great deal (b. Joma 39 A).
The threefold defilements and sanctifications respectively
describe the sins against ourselves, our fellow-men, and
God, and the virtues of pious deeds performed in this
world, towards our fellow-men and ourselves.   The sins
increase self-defilement from above, and in the future
world.   Virtues and merits have the opposite result.

[9] Eccles. r. 12. 7; Lev. r. 18.   [10] b. Ber. ; Midr. Ps. ; Lev. r. 18.
[11] Pes. B. 31 A; Gen. r. 32; M. Ps. chaps. 1 and 12; b. Pes. 3 A.
[12] Pes. B. 71 B. ; Exod. r. 15. 5.   [13] M. Yoma end.

Impurity stands for sin generally, and sanctification for a life according to the Law.

In spite of these conceptions we find that some of the Rabbis held the view of man's physical impurity. R. Jose the Galilean teaches that those who intend to enter the camp of the Shekhina have to separate (פרישה) from their ordinary habitation. Moses did so. The High Priest followed this example by removing seven days before the Day of Atonement to the precincts of the Temple. R. Nathan thought that Moses waited for forty days before he ascended the Mount, in order to rid himself of all chances of physical impurity. The washings before meals, prayers, entering the sanctuary, after certain natural functions are closely connected with this idea of purity. This is not the place to describe what role they played in ritual life among Jews. However great may have been the fear of and belief in evil spirits in certain circles and different periods, this cannot be denied, that the primary motive of these purifications of the body was the endeavour to attain physical purity, which is most befitting the vehicle of the soul, whose purity is akin to the purity of God. Body and soul together aspire to become like God's purity.

The teaching of God's purity gave rise to many questions. There seem to have been two different views. God's omnipresence presupposes that even in the defilement, impurity, and sin of idolatry and immorality, God's purity does not suffer. God is with His people in Egypt. Babylon, Media, and Persia. Yet, Moses left the city in order to deliver his prayer, or in order to hold communion with God. 'Why? Because the city was full of idols and abominations.'[14] Owing to this idea, the synagogues in the diaspora were built near the river, or on the fields, apart from human habitation. A similar conception is to be found with the Greeks. The Shekhina is not revealed outside the Holy Land, probably for this very reason (Mekh. 2 b). A sage of the third century, R. Abbahu, was

[14] Mekh. 2 b.

questioned by a Min: 'Your God is a priest; when He buried Moses, He became defiled; how did He purify Himself? surely not by water!'[15] The teacher proved God's purification by fire, which is greater than that of water. Whether the questioner was a Christian, which is quite probable, for R. Abbahu lived in the place of the Church-father Origen, or a Gnostic, is not certain. If he were a Christian, the answer might mean an attack against the doctrine of baptism with water. In reality the accepted thought may have been that of R. Johanan b. Zakkai, who taught: 'Neither is the dead defiling, nor the water purifying.'[16] Here Jewish religion reached a height which was rarely surpassed by theological speculation. Yet this lofty idea could not achieve great popularity. A teacher derives from Ps. 51. 5 that sin and transgression defile man like the dead body.[17] Sin and impurity are identical. The influence of sin on the Shekhina is expressed in the words of R. Isaac: 'He who commits sins in secret is as if he had pushed the feet of the Shekhina.'[18] Many sins are in such a degree impure that God's presence, the Shekhina, is being removed from earth. God and the sinner cannot live in the same world. God has removed His Shekhina from the place. The teachers must have felt the contradiction between God's omnipresence and the temporary disappearance of the Shekhina from a place.

R. Phinehas b. Jair also connected these two attributes. Purity and holiness are correlatives. This correlation is seen in the Biblical writings, and is frequent in our sources. The former apply this attribute to men and angels—to the whole community and nation. God's holiness must be man's highest guiding ideal. What it means was conveyed to the reader of the Scriptures, when he read such passages as: 'Ye shall therefore sanctify yourselves, and ye shall be holy: for I am holy' (Lev. 11. 45),

---

[15] B. Sanh. 39 A.
[16] Pes. B. 40 B, and Parall.   [17] M. Ps. ch. 51, ed. B. 281.
[18] b. Kid. 31 A; Hag. 16 A.

or, ' Ye shall be holy, for I the Lord your God am holy ! '
(ib. 19. 2), or, ' I will be hallowed among the children of
Israel ; I am the Lord which hallow you ' (ib. 22. 32), or,
' Be holy unto your God ' (Num. 15. 40), or, ' And ye shall
be holy men unto me ' (Exod. 22. 30), or, ' And ye shall be
unto me a kingdom of priests and an holy nation '
(ib. 19. 6) ? Surely the deep thought that by abstinence
from evil, by following God's commandments, by imita-
ting His ways, by attaining virtue and morality man can
acquire holiness was familiar with the readers of the Bible,
and the audience of the Rabbinic preachers. Even in the
Tannaitic period certain men were still called ' holy ones ' ;
R. Meir is introduced to the people of Sepphoris by R. Jose
b. Halafta with the words: a great man, a holy man,
a chaste man ! (אדם גדול אדם קדוש אדם צנוע, v. pal. Ber. 5 B,
ii. 7 ; Gen. r. 100. 7 ; Weiss, *Dor Dor we Dorshaw*, ii. 148 ;
Bacher, AT. ii. 5).[19] R. Simon ben Lakish is surprised at R.
Meir's teaching, and exclaims : פה קדוש יאמר זה, a holy mouth
should say such a thing ? (b. Sanh. 23 A). R. Phinehas
ben Jair states: ישראל קדושים הן (b. Hullin 7 B).[20] R.
Ishmael says : כשאתם קדושים הרי אתם שלי, Mekh. 98 A.
similarly, the great editor of the Mishna, who was styled
רבינו הקדוש. Great men were addressed in this way.
With the adoption of the name ' the Holy one ' for God,
a great change is to be observed. For this very reason
we are taught that with the death of Rabbi ' Holiness
ceased among men '. Men, even the greatest and most
pious, we hear from Haggadic teachers in this age, cannot
and must not be called ' holy ' any more. God alone is

[19] קדוש and גדול together also in Num. r. 4, 22. אמרו רבותינו שני דברים
היו קדושים וגדולים וכסבורין בני אדם שהן קשים, also with צנוע ; ibid.
כל בית אבי היו צנועים וקדושים.
[20] v. to this Num. r. 9. 5 : ומנין שישראל נקראו קדושים בעת ששומרים
עצמן מן הניאוף ומן הזמה לכן כתיב והתקדשתם וכו' מכאן בומן שהם
קדושים הוא להם לאלוה: . Special attention may be drawn to the saying
of R Judah b. Simon, Tanh. ii. 33, א'ל קדושים אתם ? מהו נרפים.

holy, *errare est humanum*; men whilst alive, are liable
to err and stumble.　No wonder that the teachers turn
away from the idea of man's holiness, and preach on the
subject of God's holiness.

'God's holiness is perfect.'[21]　The teaching preserved in
the name of R. Abba, שהוא קדוש בכל מיני קדושות, and explained
by R. Aha b. Hanina, deal with this subject.　'God is holy in
His speech (cf. Ps. 60. 8), in His walk (ib. 77. 14), in His
appearance (ib. 63. 3), in His praise (Exod. 15. 11), and the
revelation of His strength (Isa. 52. 10),[22]　Very instructive
is an anonymous homily, which throws welcome light on
our doctrine.[23]　God says to Israel: '*Before I created my
world* the angels praised me, and sanctified me with your
name by saying, "Blessed be the Lord, the God of Israel,
from eternity to eternity".'[24]　When Adam was created,
they said: 'Lord of the World, is this he in whose name we
praise Thee?'　God says: 'No, he is a thief!' (cf. Gen.
3. 17).　Then came Noah, and they said: 'Is this he?'
God: 'No, he is a drunkard!' (cf. ib. 9. 21).　Afterwards
appeared Abraham, and God said again: 'No, he is a
stranger (proselyte)'; 'Isaac?' and God said, 'He loves
mine enemies' (cf. ib. 25. 28); 'Jacob?'　Then God said,
'Yes, he is the man, who is called Israel' (cf. ib. 35. 10):
and after him his offspring.　Then God sanctified them
after His name (cf. Isa. 49. 3).　God said: 'Since ye were
sanctified after My name before the world was created, be
hallowed as I am holy'.　The homily concludes, after
quoting a parable of a king, who married a queen, with the
words: 'If ye are worthy, ye are called the "congregation
of the holy ones", if not, "the wicked community"' (cf.
Num. 14. 26).　This homily deserves a more detailed treatment from various points of view.　First of all, the idea
that there were ministering angels *before* the creation of
the world.　Teachers of the third century, under the heavy

[21] v. Josh. 24. 19: כי אלהים קדושים הוא.

[22] v. pal. Ber. 12 D; Tanh. iii. B. 73 f. ; M. Ps. 27 ; R. Isaac b. Hama.

[23] Tanh. iii. 72 f.　　　　[24] 1 Chron. 16. 36.

pressure of Gnostic propaganda, allied with Christian attacks against our doctrine, taught that God created the angels on the second or the fifth day.[25] These days were, as we know, kept as days of special importance.[26] Yet in the Tannaitic Haggada this teaching of the creation of the angels was not known at all. R. Jose the Galilean taught that 974 years before the creation the angels existed already.[27] An old Jewish exorcism has the same doctrine, that the angels were created about a thousand years before the Universe. That enables us to date the homily before the change introduced by R. Johanan and R. Hanina was effected. Secondly, attention may be paid to the rather harsh treatment of the Fathers from Adam up to Isaac. All the Haggadas which contain a more or less condemning word about the Fathers of old, could not have sought simply to exhibit human weakness and to belittle the greatness of the heroes of yore. Thirdly, the holiness of Israel is especially pointed out. The latter idea occurs in other homilies and sayings. 'Who are His holy ones? Israel,' cf. Deut. 7. 6, Jer. 2. 3.[28] Jews, the children of Jacob, are the *true Israel*, but not the *new nation*, the offspring of Adam, Noah, Abraham, Isaac, and Jacob, as the Church-Fathers taught.[29] Owing to this fact Jews are never called in our sources יהודים, as Greeks, or Romans, Syriacs or Arabs called them, but Israel. R. Menahem b.

[25] v. now Marmorstein, ' Beiträge zur Religionsgesch. und Volkskunde' in *Jahrbuch für jüd. Volkskunde*, ii. 377, note 5; Gen. r. ch. 1, ed. Th. 5, ch. 3, p. 24; Tanh. i. B. 1 and 12; Ex., pp. 15 and 22; M. Ps. chaps. 24, 86, 104; Pirke R. E. ch. 4.

[26] v. Graetz, *MGWJ*. 4, 1855, 191; Fabricius, *Hypomnesticum Josephi*, ch. 145; Codex Pseudep., v. 5; Halakhoth Gedoloth j. Taan. 64c; Luke 18. 12; Soferim 21. 3; v. Geiger's *Wiss. Zeitsch*. iv. 221; Hamanhig, 19 B; Gen. r. 76. 3; Tanh. B. וישלח 16; Geiger, *Nachgelassene Schriften*, iii. 318; Achelis, *Das Christentum*, 117.

[27] Aboth R. N. ch. 31, ed. Schechter, 47 A; Midr. Ps. 4 3; Tanh. לך לך 11; Seder El. r., ed. Friedmann, 9. 61, 130; Hag. 14 A; M. Ps. 90. 13; 105. 3.

[28] M. Ps. B. 540.

[29] v. on this question, my *Religionsgeschichtliche Studien*, i. 9–18.

Simai was called the son of the 'holy ones'.[30] This teacher belonged to the circle of Rabbi, who was also called 'holy,'[31] and who addressed the Exilarch Hananja לקדושת חנניה 'His Holiness'.[32] To this age belong the sayings: כל הנודר עצמו, כל המקבל עליו דברי חכמים נקרא קדוש and [33] מן הערוה נקרא קדוש קדוש,[34] in spite of the fact that the latter is taught in the name of Abajji, and the former by R. Judah b. Pazzi. Both, as the language and context prove, are older sayings. R. Joshua b. Levi, who was much older than R. Judah b. Pazzi, comments on the former saying. Abajji, as can be seen from the parallels in the Palestinian Talmud,[35] used here older material. But apart from this internal evidence we have other proofs that the ideas and conceptions about the holiness of man, must have experienced great changes. This alteration of attitude is discerned in a saying of R. Simon b. Lakish,[36] who says: 'Ye shall be holy; you might think like God Himself? No, it is written, "for I am holy"; my Holiness is of a higher degree than yours'. This change of outlook is even more apparent in the saying: 'No pious man is called holy whilst he is alive', cf. Eccles. 7. 20. 'Even the Fathers of the world are not called "holy" before their death.' This teaching must be of the third century because teachers of the fourth century dwell and comment upon it [37]

What was the reason for this change? We know the reaction in Christianity which took place in the Church after the middle of the third century.[38] The crudest superstition arose from the lowest parts of the population

---

[30] b. A. Z. 50 A; b. Pes. 104 A; v. Pal. A. Z., ch. 3.

[31] b. Shabb. 118 B; Pal. A. Z. 42 c.

[32] pal. Sanh. 19 A.　　　　　[33] Lev. r. 24. 6.

[34] b. Jeb. 20 A.　　　　　[35] ii. 4.

[36] Lev. r. 24. 9 : והדין קדושים תהיו יכול כמוני ת"ל כי קדוש אני קדושתי למעלה מקדושתכם.

[37] M. Ps. B. 120; R. Phinehas; Gen. r. 1. 9; b. Hama, and R. Aha b. Pappa. The latter name is not quite settled; some read R. Hama b. Pappa, others R. Hijja b. Pappa; one text reads erroneously R. Hama b. Hanina.

[38] v. Harnack, *Dogmengeschichte*³, 1894, ii. 6 F.

and covered with its darkness all the purity and morality of ancient Christianity, which it brought from the Father's mansion. The earliest Christians and Apologists would have hidden their faces in shame at beholding the union of paganism and Christianity. One of these dangers, which changed Christian religion, was the worship of saints, under which lurked the demons of idolatry. Jewish teachers saw the same peril hovering over their religion. The false beliefs, superstitions, saint-worship, crudeness, and perversity which arose from their surroundings and threatened the whole edifice of holiness. What Harnack sees in the Church of the third century can be observed by the study of Rabbinic writings of the third and fourth centuries. A change was therefore necessary. Man is not holy, even the Fathers are not holy. 'Only One is Holy: God'. This induced the leading Scribes to discard the old names and put in their place the name of הקדוש ברוך הוא.

The holiness of God is in Judaism the essence of religion. Holiness is not the *tabu* of primitive and more advanced religions. It is the expression of what the religious Jew feels when discharging his religious duties, observing his Sabbath and Festivals. All his deeds and words are emanating from the Divine Holiness. How far this and other attributes influenced the religion of the Rabbis, their changes and development, will be shown in the next chapters dealing with the anthropomorphism and imitation of God. If religion has a purpose in life and the world, it must bring God near to man, and man must become like unto God.

THE OLD RABBINIC
DOCTRINE OF GOD

II. ESSAYS IN ANTHROPOMORPHISM

BY

A. MARMORSTEIN, Ph.D., RABBI

KTAV PUBLISHING HOUSE, INC.

NEW YORK

First Published in 1937

INTRODUCTION

THE five essays presented here as a second part of the *Old Rabbinic Doctrine of God* cover merely some of the aspects of Rabbinic teachings and speculations on the subject of anthropomorphism and anthropopathism. In selecting certain problems connected with the doctrine of God in Judaism of the first centuries of the C. E. I was guided mainly by three principles: At what stage of Jewish history was objection raised to crude anthropomorphism and anthropopathism among the Jews, under what influences did such a movement arise, and where did it originate? Long before such a movement can be traced in post-Biblical literature Prophets and Psalmists arose in Israel who strongly and eloquently raised their voice against popular beliefs in God's corporeality, human forms of the deity, His needs and passions, His partial knowledge and imperfect justice. Yet their words did not dispel the clouds of criticism of exaggerations and narratives which attribute to God human limbs and human feelings. Neither critics, nor defenders of the Bible were fully aware of the great difficulty faced by all anthropomorphic religions, namely, that of harmonizing the highest conception of God's spirituality with man's shortcomings, of beholding and grasping the existence and rule of an entirely spiritual being. This problem formed a stumbling block which caused and will cause great danger to religious truth and enlightenment. It is, therefore, necessary to trace this fight between anthropomorphic and anti-anthropomorphic conceptions of the deity in early Judaism of the first centuries.

The general view that the movement originated on Hellenistic soil cannot be maintained, since the earlier Hebrew sources betray the prevalence of such tendencies as found in later Hellenic writings. Besides, similar questionings of anthropomorphic and anthropopathic passages of the Bible can be discovered also on Palestinian soil. Furthermore both movements, one in favour of the literal, and the other in favour of the spiritual understanding of the Bible, are equally represented in both camps and countries. It is true that historical evidence is more favourable for the earlier date of this treatment of the subject in Egypt rather than in Palestine. Yet, this may be due to the lack of documents on Palestinian soil in the pre-Mishnaic period, or to the uncertainty still prevailing whether Palestinian Jews exercised their influence on the Jewry of Alexandria and the rest of the Diaspora, or whether, vice versa, the latter shaped the ideas and teachings of the former. However that may be, the contact between them can be established and their common interest in the Bible plainly recognized. Religion and origin overbridged the considerable gulf of language and culture that cut asunder the two sections, and the bond uniting them, their monotheism and their Scriptures, was stronger and more intimate than accidental and external incongruities. This can be shown by Philo's reflections on assimilation—probably with special reference to his own nephew who deserted his God and his people, joined the Romans, and later led Rome's Imperial legions against Jerusalem—which would put some of our present-day champions of Jewish nationalism to shame. He says in his *Life of Moses* (Bk. I, ch. vi, par. 31, Loeb edition, vi, p. 294): 'They nevertheless look down on their relatives, relations, and friends and set at naught the laws under which they have been born and bred, and subvert our ancestral customs to which no blame can justly be attached, by adopting different modes of life, and, in their contentment with the present, loose all memory of the past.' These are words of an enlightened and experienced sage condemning unhealthy assimilation.

Secondly, I have tried to prove that the division between the pro- and anti-anthropomorphic theologians depends on the attitude taken towards the Biblical text. The strict literalist does not object to any kind of anthropomorphism, whilst the anti-anthropomorphist strives to divest the letter of its possible crudeness and corporeality. Here again it is almost impossible to decide with certainty whether the exegetical method produced the theological divergence, or whether, vice versa, theology influenced exegesis. Those who believe that allegorical methods of exegesis owe their very existence to apologetic and anti-anthropomorphic motives, will answer this query in the affirmative, others, like I. Heinemann in his essay, *Altjüdische Allegoristik*, Breslau, 1935, may reverse this process. But neither the question, nor the solution, is so simple as all that, since many cross currents and many serious obstacles held up the straight and unchecked development of the doctrines and conceptions of the deity in Israel. The numerous sects, which arose among the Jews, preached and taught many queer and quaint things, which had to be challenged by the official leaders of religious thought, and led either to a fierce combat of ideas, or to a modification of the then established theological views. Traces of this spiritual fight can be found in some chapters of these essays. The difference of exegetical method reveals itself not only in the substance, but also in the form, of Biblical interpretation. The terminology used by the school of pro-anthropomorphic teachers, who, as was stated, were literalists, was necessarily different from, if not entirely opposed to, that of the allegorists. This can be shown to be a fact from our literary documents. Another outcome of this religious split within the schools of Judea and Galilee was the controversial struggle about the value of the Haggadah, strictures against writing and studying Haggadic lore, its supremacy or inferiority in relation with the Halakah. No wonder that anti-anthropomorphic Haggadists who looked askance at Biblical anthropomorphism would raise a rather emphatic protest and utter their full disapproval of anthropomorphic Haggadoth with slight or no Scriptural support at all. This fundamental difference of view, described and discussed in these essays, had important, far-reaching repercussions on other problems and branches of Rabbinic theology as well. Thus, cosmology and anthropology, the relation between God and the world, the relation of God to man, the conception of the imitation of God, and other problems, took a characteristic shape in one school and an opposite form in another. One took an affirmative, the other a negative stand, to these questions, according to the light in which they taught of God and His word as embodied in the Bible. The consecutive parts of this work will prove the truth of this assertion. Here, a general remark may suffice.

This diversity of opinion and teaching, however, did not affect the unity of Judaism, or endanger the purity of doctrine, for the foundation of Israel's religion was safeguarded by the unshakable belief in the existence and unity of God which permeated all sections of the Jewish community. Only when and where dualistic and trinitarian theories crept into the synagogue and schools, there and then the very existence of Judaism was shaken and imperilled, and sectarianism wrought havoc in the rank and file of our people. That the victims of such heretic and sectarian movements were not even more numerous, although no doubt there may have been many of them, is entirely due to the preaching and teachings of the saintly and wise Haggadists whose sayings are described and analysed in the following pages. However great the distance in time and space between them and our contemporaries, however different the outlook of the Jew in the twentieth century may be compared with that of the Jew in the first three or four centuries, there are many puzzles which are still unsolved, as there are many ideas and views of those teachers recorded here which are still, and will for ever remain, vital forces for all generations to come. The Bible, without the monumental contributions of the Haggadah and Halakah, remains a book sealed with seven seals.

A. MARMORSTEIN.

LONDON
July 30, 1936.

CONTENTS

I

1. THE Jewish religion is classed with anthropomorphic religions. Such a designation is by no means of a degrading character and quality. The name 'anthropomorphic religion' is free from any mark of inferiority. No system of religious thought, or form of religious life, can be separated from anthropomorphic or anthropopathic conceptions. Only by such an equipment can religion proclaim the existence of an active and living God, and only thus can it adhere to a real, personal divinity. Deprived of it nothing remains but shallow theism. As long as people will crave after a personal deity they cannot do otherwise than, some with more, some with less skill, ascribe to God certain human attributes and speak of His qualities and functions in human ways and manners. Man cannot worship or show reverence to an impersonal power, nameless and impotent, without attributes of goodness or justice, not visible by deeds and unrecognizable by passions. Higher religions cannot exercise any influence, and rule the hearts of multitudes, if they are divested or robbed of their anthropomorphic and anthropopathic wealth inherent in their sacred narratives and teachings. Anthropomorphic and anthropopathic elements in a religion are thus not to be looked upon as disadvantages. On the contrary, they endowed men with spiritual strength and opened higher ways of thought leading to religious enlightenment. At many stages of cultural development religious values and doctrines cannot be brought home to mankind unless the meaning of God's existence and creative work is presented in forms of these two terms.

However useful and necessary these modes and expressions of religious instruction have been and still are, they were bound to produce drawbacks. Disadvantages grew up, which made themselves felt very early and very strongly in the synagogues and schools of the Jews. Historical causes are responsible for such an early opposition to, and such a strong criticism of, an anthropomorphic and anthropopathic presentation of the divine

character of God. As Jewish religion was embodied in the Holy
Scriptures which invested God with human forms and endowed Him with similar feelings, naturally misgivings were
aroused in the minds of Jews living among foreign cultures
and civilizations, with the result that early prophets raised their
voices against excessive humanization of the divine. The Greek
historian Herodotus speaks in terms of high praise of the Persians who banished all images from their divine worship and
abstained from depicting their divinity in human form.[1] He
apparently was not aware of the prohibition which forbids the
making of images or likenesses of God enforced among the
Hebrews. It is probable that the often expressed charge of
the Jewish Ass-worship and other similar groundless accusations current in those and later times among the Greeks reached
his ears.[2] Anthropomorphism was a very sore problem among
the Greeks. To Greek philosophers it meant much more than
to Jewish Bible-readers. The Greeks could see their Gods in
statues and images, which conveyed to the onlookers the idea
not only of a personal, but of a physical god appearing in a
form made by man from earthly material. However great the
art employed and the beauty conveyed may have been the limbs
and the features of the gods presented by art and genius manifested an obstacle to the spiritual conception and identity of
the divine being. *Such* an anthropomorphic menace was held
far away from Jewish religion; yet it was a danger in Greek
religion, which ultimately aroused the unbounded antagonism
of philosophy against the religion of the Greeks, and finally
brought about the downfall of the whole shaken fabric of Greek
and Roman civilization, resting as it did on such an unstable
basis. Religion was, and is still to-day, the soul of human
civilization; the strength or the weakness of the latter depends
on the force or feebleness of the former. The Hellenists felt

---

[1] Bk. II. 172; cf. J. Geffcken, 'Der Bilderstreit im Heidnischen Altertum', *A.R.W.*, xix (1919), p. 288.

[2] About the diverse accusations against the Jews v. *Monatsschrift*, iv.
126; Rahmer's *Jüdisches Literaturblatt*, viii (1879), 52; Kobak's *Jeschurun*,
viii, p. 16; Hennecke, *Handbuch der Neutestamentlichen Apocryphen*, p. 116;
Staehelin, *Anti-Semitismus*, pp. 15–24; and Reich in *Neue Jahrbücher für
das Classische Altertum* (1904), 707 ff.

very early in the course of their historic development what the Babylonian-Assyrians learnt before them, and the Egyptians experienced at an even earlier stage, that all treasures and might, power and force, cannot preserve even the greatest empire in the absence of spiritual values. Writers and thinkers coming from various camps and schools, poured out their biting ridicule over the makers of idols and laughed heartily at the poets of Greece who invented gods with human passions, human faults, and human forms.[3] Such a condemnation of anthropomorphic doctrines and conceptions, as being most dangerous superstitions, was bound to react on the religion of the Greek-speaking Jewish community of the Diaspora. The history of the last two hundred years offers a close parallel to the events which occurred among the Greeks during the last centuries before the Current Era. The Jews of the Diaspora, in the same manner as the German-speaking Jews, were most anxious to gain the good opinion of their neighbours and most zealous to adjust their religion to the standard of the general culture of their surroundings. The Jews of Alexandria dreamt of full emancipation and strove for full equality. In order to gain these they were prepared to go very far in sacrificing much of the religion of their ancestors, and losing some precious legacies of their religious and national inheritance. The general idea took root among them that by so doing they might find favour in the eyes of the Greeks, especially with the more advanced, cultured, and intellectual classes. The Jewish Hellenist Aristoboulos was interrogated by his king about certain passages in the Bible, in which the hands and arms, face and legs, walking and resting of God are mentioned.[4] This Hellenist did his best to bring home to his pagan inquirer, and indirectly as well to his Jewish readers, who were somewhat troubled by these anthropomorphisms, an allegoric version by which these passages would lose their crudeness. The educated circles of the Alexandrian community consisted of different classes with different tendencies. One class was evidently inclined to take the above

---

[3] v. Cicero, *de Natura Deorum.* II. xvii. 45.

[4] v. M. Friedländer, *Geschichte der Jüdischen Apologetik*, Zürich (1904), p. 29; cf. A. Schlatter, *Geschichte Israels*, Stuttgart (1925), pp. 82–7.

mentioned passages and expressions literally. This caused
many of them real spiritual misgivings and disturbed their
religious tranquillity. Others saw in this difficulty a most welcome opportunity to discard Jewish religion also, since it was,
in their view, antiquated and not worthy of perpetuation for
future generations. Aristoboulos is a very reliable witness for
the remarkable fact that among the intellectual Jews in the
Greek-speaking Diaspora there arose at least one man,—but
most probably he was one of many, whose names, however, are
forgotten—for the defence of his religion, and for the sanctity
of the ancient documents on which that religion was based,
destined as they were to survive many ages and cultures. If we
turn now from Aristoboulos to Philo we perceive that these
parties remained alive for many generations. The situation did
not change—at least not considerably—in spite of the great progress made by Hellenism in the Greek world. There are plenty
of traces of lively discussions regarding this problem in the
Greek Bible Translation, known under the title of the Septuagint.[5] If we add to this the repetition of the questions, and the
vehemence with which the opponents of the allegorical method
of interpretation are handled by Philo, the great importance
that this question assumed nineteen centuries ago among the
Jews of Alexandria can be easily realized. The influence of
these protracted discussions and lively disputes was, however,
by no means confined to Hellenistic Jews, but as will be shown
in the next paragraph, penetrated deeply the schools and places
of worship of Palestinian Jewry as well.

2. Anthropomorphism occupies a most prominent place in
the works of Philo. He asserts that God cannot have a human
form, for if He had, then it would unmistakably follow that He
has human needs and human desires. Such an assumption,
naturally, cannot be entertained or tolerated.[6] No reader of
Philo's treatise on the unchangeableness of God[7] can fail to
notice that the writer is deeply agitated by Biblical passages

---

[5] v. A. F. Dähne, *Geschichtliche Darstellung der Jüdisch-Alexandrinischen
Religionsphilosophie*, Halle (1834), ii, pp. 32 ff.

[6] *De Posteritate Caini*, ed. Mangey, i, p. 227; cf. Dähne, loc. cit., i, p. 122.

[7] *Philonis Opera*, vol. iii, pp. 20-1.

which convey anthropomorphic ideas and lend themselves to mischievous teachings about the Jewish doctrine of God. Not being the first either among the Greeks or among Jews, who faced this problem, he, in his elaborate interpretation, followed a well trodden path. This must be especially emphasized for the simple reason that it is very difficult, when speaking of Philo, to establish what is borrowed material and what is his own original view. Following an old tradition and stepping in the footsteps of a long line of religious and secular thinkers, one may assert that his words represent a good deal of the fruits of earlier theological speculations. Yet one thing is certain, that just as he was not the first, likewise he was not the last among Jewish theologians and Bible readers who devoted their attention to these great difficulties of Jewish religious thought. Philo will forever remain in the front line among the defenders of these sacred but incriminated texts, and his voice on this subject will find a hearing in all ages, whenever these passages cause anxiety and mistrust.

Philo speaks of these matters in a way as if he would defend something of personal concern, and therefore loses the philosophic calm which is proper in the treatment of philosophical subjects. He calls his opponents *some of those careless inquirers* and refers to them in quite uncomplimentary terms. No one would go so far in a quiet academic discussion as to say of his opponents the following words : ' Suppose that the lawgiver is hinting that the creator repented of the creation of man, when he beheld their impiety, and this was the reason why he wished to destroy the whole race. Those, who think thus, may be sure that they make the sins of these men of old times seem light and trivial through the vastness of their own godlessness.' Philo must have been provoked by grievous offence on the part of his opponents which caused him to lose his temper and utter such words of condemnation and abuse against them. Who were these opponents ? Surely they were thinkers who differed from Philo in his method of exegesis or interpretation of anthropomorphic and anthropopathic passages occurring in the Bible. Their offence was, in the eyes of Philo, that they took such a saying as is referred to in the previous quotation absolutely literally, and at its face value. That fact alone does not enable us to group these men; whether they belong to the more conservative section of the community who accepted the letter, or whether they were members of the more advanced party of Alexandrian Jews who cast overboard, with these misapprehended narratives, also the heavier and weightier parts of Jewish religion.

We know from other utterances and remarks, preserved in the works of Philo, that there existed some very extreme radicals in his neighbourhood, against whom he used very sharp language. Yet their fault was not adherence to the literal meaning of the Scriptures, but the reverse; they went so far in their extreme allegorization that nothing was left of real religion and of religious law which would mean anything to a Jew.[8] Therefore here must be sought another party of opposite extremists that could not sever itself from the belief in the literal meaning of this or similar narratives. Such antagonistic and contending parties were always unavoidable companions in the course of Jewish history, when decaying cultures and doomed civilizations were fighting their last battle and struggling for life. The advanced radicals, whatever their practical attitude towards their religion may have been, could not have failed to allegorize these narratives about the repentance of God, without being driven to that final path which led out of Judaism. If they were acquainted with, or influenced by, contemporary philosophy, they surely must have known the allegorical method of interpretation. Philo himself was not altogether free in his very defence of this passage from Stoic teachings which saw the chief requisites of the human sage in constancy, both in action and thought. The human sage, runs their teaching, takes in hand with unbending steadfastness and firm constancy all that it behoves him to do. How can one therefore ascribe repentance to God the giver of wisdom? This problem crops up in Philo's exposition of Gen. vi. 7. Here Philo takes some people strongly to task for falling victims to misinterpretation of an anthropo-

[8] v. M. Friedländer, *Der Vorchristliche Jüdische Gnosticismus*, Göttingen (1898), p. 96; and cf. A. Marmorstein, 'Les Épicuriens dans la littérature talmudique', in *R.E.J.*, vol. 54 (1907), pp. 181-93.

pathic expression in that verse. His words are: 'Again, some
on hearing these words suppose that the Existent (God) feels
wrath and anger, whereas He is not susceptible of any passion
at all'.[9] These people are most probably the same men who
in the previous quotation were stigmatized as worse sinners
than the wicked generation. How does Philo himself explain
these passages? Rebuke is surely no argument or justification.
Indeed Philo was not satisfied with mere reproach but laid
down general rules by which these and similar passages should
be handled and mastered. These directions are the connecting
links between the Hellenistic manner of religious thinking and
Rabbinic theology, and consequently must be considered here.
Philo's words seem to me of such importance for my subject
that they have to be quoted in their entirety. He says:

'All the same the lawgiver uses such expressions just so far as
they serve for a kind of elementary lesson to admonish those who
could not otherwise be brought to their senses. Thus in the laws
which deal with commands and prohibitions—laws in the proper
sense of the word—there stand forth above others two leading statements about the cause. One that God is not a man (Num. xxiii. 19),
the other that He is as a man, but whilst the former is warranted by
grounds of certain truth, the latter is introduced for the instruction
of the many, and therefore it is also said of Him 'like a man He shall
train His son' (Deut. viii. 5).[9]

Philo teaches how to deal with two contradictory Bible passages, and further how to remove the belief in God being a man.
The first method was highly developed and largely elaborated
by the Palestinian scribes, the latter problem requires a fuller
treatment in these essays. It is noteworthy that here again
Philo uses rather strong words for Bible readers who adhere to
the literal meaning of the text, and does not mind condemning
such a method as 'the mythical fiction of the impious'.

3. Early Rabbinic texts show clearly that such Biblical passages as those mentioned by Philo in which God is spoken of
as Ish (אִישׁ), required explanation and defence. In an earlier
part of this work the observation was made that אִישׁ was used
for the designation of God in early Rabbinic literature.[10] This

---

[9] Philo, loc. cit., pp. 36, 37.   [10] v. *Doctrine of God*, pp. 66–7.

divine name was primarily based on Ex. xv. 3 : 'The Lord is
a man of War, the Lord is his name'. Such a Scriptural reference could not be passed over in silence. Indeed in an early
text the question was raised : 'How can such a thing be said
of God?' To many readers, who were not used to poetic style,
it appeared strange that God could be called a *Man of War*.
That such a teaching is quite out of accord with old Hebrew
conceptions of the divine is further demonstrated with the help
of several prophetic utterances to be found in the writings of
Jeremiah, Isaiah, and Ezekiel; some texts adding 2 Chron. vi.
16. Jer. xxiii. 24 says : 'Indeed, I fill heaven and earth';
Is. vi. 3 says : 'And one calls to the other saying, Holy, Holy,
Holy, full is the earth of His glory'; and finally Ez. xliii. 2
says : 'And behold the glory of the God of Israel came from
the way of the East and His voice was like the noise of many
waters, and the earth was lit up with His glory'.[11] How can God
therefore be called 'a Man of War'? The quotation appended
from Chronicles adds to the amazement of the questioners,
for it says : 'Now, therefore, Lord, God of Israel, &c., behold
the heavens and the heaven of heavens contain thee.'[12] The
answer is such that it may have been given by Philo himself.
God is no man, yet owing to GOD's love and holiness, God
sanctifies his name among His children. The scribe confirmed
this doctrine by a word of the prophet, Hos. xi. 9 : 'For I am
God and not man yet in your midst holy', which means to say
that God reveals Himself as man for the sanctification of Israel.
This verse is put together in another place with that in
Num. xxiii. 19, mentioned above in the quotation from
Philo, to dispel the notion that God could be called or considered *a man*. A remarkable dialogue, which is supposed to
take place in the last days of eschatological bliss, between the

[11] Mekilta, p. 38 a. It is noteworthy that the whole passage is omitted
in the Mekilta of R. Simeon.

[12] Attention may be called to the order in which the verses from the
prophets are cited : Jeremiah, Isaiah, Ezekiel, 2 Chronicles; the first two are
in proper order, not so the last two. Apparently the text of the Mekilta is
composed of two different readings. The first version reads Jeremiah,
Isaiah, and Chronicles; the second reading had the quotation from the
three major prophets. Some later scribe combined the two readings.

community of Israel and God, discusses several problems bearing on and betraying more the polemical tendencies of the age
in which it was composed than those of Messianic times.[13]
Among the questions raised in that dialogue there is one which
has a close bearing on the subject here discussed. The community of Israel asks the following questions: 'It is written
in the book of the prophet Jeremiah (iii. 1), "Behold, if a man
sent away his wife and she went and married someone else, can
the former husband take her back again?"' In this question
God is paralleled to the איש of the Hebrew text, and the
divorced woman stands for the dispersed Jewish nation. God
replies: 'The law of the Pentateuch, forbidding the remarriage
of a divorced wife by her previous husband is in force only
when she marries someone else, meaning an איש (cf. Deut.
xxiv. 1–4), but not God, who is not an איש.' In the text of
the Sifre[14] there is a further Scriptural reference to Isaiah l. 1,
which bears out that Israel was never divorced and never driven
away by God. 'Where is the bill of your mother's divorce which
could prove that I sent her away, or to which of my creditors
have I sold you?'—asks the prophet in the name of God.
These words are repeated in several pamphlets and fill volumes
from the days of Isaiah up to the present day. Israel is forsaken by God, rejected, and despised. Such views are proclaimed
by pious and impious readers of the Holy Scriptures, and defenders of religious thought against Judaism. Early Christian
and late pagan readers of the Bible were delighted to discover
in these anthropomorphisms some support for their ideologies.
The rejection of the literal usage of this name for God, as these
two instances show, is traced to the school of R. Ishmael. This
school, as will be seen later, was opposed to exegetical methods
followed by R. Akiba and his school who took such anthropomorphisms literally as the identification of the Hebrew איש
with God.

4. Philo does not curtail or restrain remarks about people

---

[13] v. on the subject Marmorstein, 'L'épître de Barnabe et la polémique
juive', in R.E.J., vol. 60, 1910, pp. 213–20, and Religionsgeschichtliche
Studien, Skotschau, 1910, pp. 24–6.

[14] v. Sifre Deut., par. 306; Midrash Tannaim, p. 181.

who took anthropomorphic teachings literally, but he asks them in sermons or public discussions the following pertinent questions :

'Does Moses speak of feet and hands, goings in and goings out, in connexion with the Uncreated? or, of His armings to defend Himself against His enemies? For he describes Him as bearing a sword, and using as His weapon wind and death-dealing fire. His wrath, His moods of anger, His jealousy, and other emotions similar to them are spoken of by Moses, which he describes in the terms of human nature.'

The serious objections to the anthropomorphic and anthropopathic utterances of Moses which Philo compressed in a few lines may have originated either from the radical party of the community, or have been directed against the defenders of the strict letter of the Biblical narrative. It will soon be shown that the earliest Rabbinic Midrash retained many traces of similar discussions among Palestinian Jews. In this paragraph, however, attention may be concentrated on the reply which Philo had in store for his questioners in Alexandria. This reply is very interesting for more than one reason, and deserves fuller treatment. These are his actual words :

'Those admitted into the infallible mysteries of the Existent do not overlay the conception of God with any of the attributes of created beings. These find a moral most pertinent in the oracles of revelation. That "God is not a man", nor yet is He as the heaven or the universe. These forms are of a particular kind which present themselves to our senses, but He is not apprehensible even by the mind, save that He is.'

Philo employed this illustration from the world of Mysteries and reminded his readers of the oracles, in order that he might impress those of his audience who may have been attracted by the then fashionable cult of religions. Next to the refutation, in which he fully agrees with the Midrash that God is not a man, Philo lays great stress on the denial of the false idea that God can be spoken of either as *heaven* or as *universe*. This is again an unmistakable thrust against some of his radical contemporaries who regarded heaven or universe as deities. This doctrine refuted by Philo opens a new opportunity for observing

another similarity, and at the same time a contrast, between
Palestinian and Alexandrian Jewish theology. The former records a remarkable scholarly dialogue between the two leading
scholars of the Judaean schools in the first decades of the second
century in Palestine, R. Ishmael and R. Akiba. Unfortunately
the text is in a very bad condition and calls for some elaborate
treatment which must be relegated to the footnotes.[15] Here
follows the translation according to the revised texts. R. Ishmael

[15] v. Gen. R., ed. Theodor, chap. i, p. 12. Similar discussions are reported
as having taken place between these two scholars on Gen. iv. 1 in Gen. R.,
ed. Theodor, chap. xxii, p. 206, and on Gen. xxi. 20, ibid., chap. liii, p. 574.
All the three dialogues are modelled after one and the same scheme. Rabbi
Ishmael opens with a short reference to the teacher of Rabbi Akiba,
pointing out at the same time the number of years during which Rabbi
Akiba sat at the feet of his master and adopted his exegetical methods.
Then he inquires how that method can be applied to certain difficult
exegetical and theological passages. If the exegetical rules were accepted and
applied to Gen. i. 1 some heretical ideas would result as a consequence of
such teachings, namely, that heaven and earth are deities. Gen. iv. 1
would suggest the idea that Cain is a God, and in the case of Ishmael
another wrong conception might arise that Elohim is a lad. After these,
Rabbi Ishmael cites Deut. xxxii. 47 with an unfriendly remark about
his opponent's inability to expound these verses correctly. In the first
instance he says that the particle (את) means 'to include the creation of
sun and moon, &c., with the creation of heaven and earth'; in the second
case the teaching is underlined that Cain was the first of all creatures, who
was born in a natural way; and thirdly, that the superfluous particle in
the case of Ishmael purports to indicate that Ishmael was not alone but
accompanied by a number of beasts and animals and a large household.
The interpretations ascribed here to Rabbi Ishmael are strictly opposed to
the spirit and letter of his exegetical teachings. The original text can be
reconstructed by consulting all the available parallels and manuscripts.
Tanchuma, ed. Buber, Gen., p. 5 f., has the following reading, in which
R. Ishmael says: 'The expression (את) in Gen. i. 1 surely cannot be
explained according to your method; it is, however, the usual expression
of the text.' Rabbi Akiba says: 'Thou canst not explain it according to
your method, cf. (v. Deut. xxxii. 47) but I can, for if the particle would be
omitted one would think that heaven and earth are Godheads; now, since
the text puts את, the teaching can be derived that heaven and earth were
brought into existence fully furnished with their complete equipment.' It
is noteworthy that the rendering of the verse from Deuteronomy, which
is quoted here in the dialogue in the name of R. Ishmael or R. Akiba
respectively, is cited in the Palestinian Talmud four times in the name of
one of the younger Palestinian Amoraim, R. Mana, v. Peah i. 1, Shebiit
i. 6, Shabbath i. 1, Sukka iv. 1, and Ketuboth viii, end. This looks strange,
unless we take it as a later gloss. The Midrash Abḳir published
by me in *Dwir*, pt. i, pp. 127–8, enables us to render the question and

says to R. Akiba: ' Thou hast served Nahum the man of Gimzo for twenty-two years, who expounded all the particles as את, גם, אך, and רק. How did he explain Gen. i. 1 את השמים? Could we have said without these particles that heaven and earth are deities?' R. Akiba replies: 'את השמים includes the creation of sun, moon, stars, and planets, and את הארץ includes the creation of trees, herbs, and the planting of the Garden of Eden.' It is obvious that R. Akiba did not become angry on being challenged by his colleague, who advanced a theory which surely would lead to the suggestion that heaven and universe are deities. Philo's words make it certain that there were circles outside the schools about a century before, in Egypt, which propagated such views. M. Joel[16] has called attention to Irenaeus, who mentions Gnostics holding some tenets according to which Moses hinted in the very first sentence of the Genesis at a fourfold divinity, i.e. God, beginning, heaven, and earth.[17] Considering further that for many centuries Heaven (שמים) was one of the names used in Judaism for the designation of the diety [18], it is no wonder that such a conception should have become deeply rooted among the people, especially those who could compare the Greek with the Hebrew term. The designation of the divine power or powers was a common feature in the religious conceptions of the Persians [19] as well as of the Greeks,[20] and modern research has tried to trace the usage among these two peoples as far back as the Assyrian-Babylonian religious system.[21] It is remarkable that in spite of these resemblances between Jewish and pagan designations of the deity, neither scribes nor people refrained from calling God by this name in devotion or in solemn speech.

answer in this way: R. Ishmael asks what is the meaning of את in this verse? Surely no one of us will go so far as to suggest that heaven and universe are deities or that man is God, or that God is a lad? Thereon R. Akiba gives his interpretation.

[16] *Blicke in die Religionsgeschichte* (Breslau, 1880), pt. i, p. 169.

[17] adv. Heres, i. 18.   [18] v. above, pt. i, p. 105.

[19] v. Spiegel, *Eranische Altertumskunde*, ii, p. 15 ; cf. Moulton, *Early Zoroastrianism*, p. 66.

[20] v. Johannes Geffcken, *Zwei Griechische Apologeten*, p. xi.

[21] Farnell, *Greece and Babylonia*, p. 270 ; v. also D. Chwolson, *Ssabier*, ii, p. 124.

Most characteristically R. Ishmael used his argument as a *deductio ad absurdum* meaning by this to say that surely no Palestinian Jew would dare to advance such a view ; yet Philo's words unmistakably testify that among Alexandrian Jews there were elements that called for rebuke because of their belief that God is ' heaven or universe '.

5. Finally Philo solved these difficulties more in a homiletical than in a philosophical sense. He speaks of a physician who devises the treatment of his patient according to the condition of his sickness. Or, he illustrates with the example of the conduct towards the foolish and ill-behaved slave on the part of his master, in order to depict the relation of God to man. 'All such may well learn ', he concludes his peroration, ' the untruth, which will benefit them if they cannot be brought to wisdom by truth.' After this he sums up with the story of the husbandman who whilst digging his orchard to plant some fruit trees lighted on a great treasure and thus met prosperity beyond all his original hopes. Philo indicates that he copied this story from a much earlier source and claims for it no originality. It is not certain whether the application of the parable is his own or not; it reads: ' So does God deliver the lovers of his eternal wisdom without toil and labour'.[22]

The story of the husbandman who found the treasure deserves special treatment. It is one of the many intimate links connecting Rabbinic teaching with the Gospels and Hellenistic literature. In Philo's rendering there are some details missing which are very necessary for the understanding of the story, namely the manner of lighting on the treasure. Matthew [23] has this account of the discovery of the treasure in the field in an enlarged form. 'The kingdom of heaven is like unto a treasure hid in a field; the which when a man hath found he hideth, and for the joy thereof goeth and selleth all that he hath and buyeth that field.' It seems that in the Gospel the treasure is found in a field belonging to some one else, and it is difficult

[22] Philo, loc. cit., par. 91 ff., pp. 56–7.
[23] Chap. xiii. 44 ; cf. Maurenbrecher, *Von Nazareth nach Golgotha* (1900), p. 169, R. v. Pöhlmann, Geschichte der socialen Frage und des Socialismus in der alten Welt. München, 1912, ii. 396.

to understand what led the discoverer to light on the treasure.
The Rabbinic variants do throw some light on the fuller and
original form of both of these rather obscured versions. There
is no doubt that all the three Jewish writers, however different
they may have been in their mental outlook and their religious
beliefs, elaborated an old Jewish proverb or parable, which
is based on an ancient story. The Midrash preserved no less
than four different applications of this proverb to various anecdotes. The Midrash named after the school of Rabbi Ishmael
preserved the original proverb and applied it to Korah. The
proverb was rendered in this manner: 'For my benefit has
my cow broken its leg.'[24] This source is a guarantee of the
antiquity of the proverb as well as of that of the anecdotes on
which it is based. The teaching is that through the contention of Korah and his assembly, and their ultimate downfall,
Aaron and his descendants benefited and were granted the
twenty-four gifts of priesthood. In other words, the proverb
teaches that those whom God loves He protects and grants them
His Grace even at the expense of others. The second version,
in which a very characteristic anecdote is connected with this
proverb, relates it to an episode in the life of the first-
century scholars R. Elieser ben Hyrkanos and R. Joshua b.
Hananyah.[25] These two scholars visit the large and wealthy
Jewish community of Antiochia to collect funds in support
of their colleagues and students.[26] One version has it that they
were accompanied by their pupil R. Akiba.[27] Here in Antiochia lived a man called Abba Judan, who was a very liberal
supporter of the Palestinian academies. At the time of this
visit, paid by the scholars to the city, his financial affairs were
not very prosperous. He was aware of the fact that he would
be unable to contribute to the collection of the distinguished
guests in his usual manner. This fact filled him with grief and
shame, so that he was hiding before them. His wife who was
even more charitable than her husband—by the way quite a

---

[24] Sifre Num., § 119.

[25] v. pal. Horayoth 48 a, Lev. r., v. 4, Deut. r., iv. 8.

[26] The term used is: על עסק מגבת חכמים, in Deut. r. לגבות לעסק
מצות עמילי תורה.

[27] Omitted in Deut. r.

typical characteristic in Jewish folklore [28]—noticing her husband's anxiety and distress, advised him to sell the half of his
remaining field and give the price thus obtained to the col-
lectors. And he did so. Next time, when he was ploughing his
field, his cow fell into a pit and broke its leg; yet the very spot
contained a treasure of greater value than his previous fortune. People applied to Abba Judan the proverb: 'For my good
has my cow broken its leg'. A third story links this adage
with another event in the biography of R. Elieser b. Hyrkanos
and gives the words a more spiritual meaning, more like the
application made of the story by Philo. In the case of Abba
Judan the charitable person is rewarded by material treasure,
in the story of R. Elieser, however, with spiritual gifts, with
learning. This scribe spent his early youth as a labourer in his
father's fields near his native Galilean village. Thirsting for
knowledge, he was kept back by his father and brothers from
satisfying his scholarly ambitions. Once, while working in the
field, the cow broke its leg, and the labourer out of fear of his
father and brothers fled to Jerusalem, where he joined the
school of Rabban Yochanan ben Zakkai, and achieved fame
and leadership among the scholars. Through this accident in
the field he also was enabled to gain the greatest treasure in
life, the Torah.[29] Lighting on unexpected treasures is a well-
known motif in Jewish legends[30] as in general folklore. These
stories belong to the same type and group. There is a fourth
version by R. Simon ben Yohai, who compares the Egyptians
after the exodus of the Hebrews from Egypt to a man who
sold a field, which was situated, according to one version, in a
distant province, and according to another in an unseemly place.
The happy buyer found there a great treasure. When the previous owner heard of this, he took his own life in his grief.[31]

[28] v. Marmorstein, 'Beiträge zur Religionsgeschichte und Volkskunde',
ii, in Grünwald's *Jahrbuch*, ii, pp. 375 ff.

[29] v. Gen. r., ch. xli, ed. Theodor, p. 139 f., Pirke R. Elieser, ch. i, and
other parallels given by Theodor.

[30] v. Marmorstein, 'Beiträge zur Religionsgeschichte und Volkskunde',
in Grünwald's *Jahrbuch*, ii, pp. 345–51.

[31] Mekilta 27 a, Mekilta of R. Simon, p. 44, Cant. r., iv. 13, quoted as
תני ר' שבי. Here the place is not פלטיא בירושה במדינת הים but
במקום אשפה.

If we compare these four versions of the Rabbinic application of the proverb with the Gospel and Philo, we see, in spite
of the discrepancies between them, some common features.
The man in the Gospel sells everything, like Abba Judan, to
find a treasure. Philo's husbandman like the young Elieser
finds a treasure, namely the proper understanding of the Torah.
The treasure comes to the discoverer unexpectedly. Such dis-
coverers are the favourites, who, as Philo puts it, understand
the proper meaning of the words of the Law-giver, and are
not like the slow-souled dullards, taking anthropomorphisms
literally. We shall see whether that was the case with R. Elieser.
Yet, before doing so, another close parallel between the
Haggadah and an old report in Philo's writing shall be discussed here, for it has some bearing on the subject of anthropomorphism.

6. The Haggadic material preserved in Philo deserves fuller
and more detailed investigation than it has received till now.
The essays and studies, which have appeared since Gfroerer
and Dähne among Christians, and Fraenkel, who heads the
list of modern Jewish scholars, who devoted their studies to
Hellenistic writers, do not afford any precise answer to the
question as to the inner relation between Hellenistic and
Rabbinic Haggadah. I will show this connexion, apart from
the previous instances, in another case as well. Long before
Philo the question was raised and discussed among Greek
Jews, why man's creation was left till the end, and did not
anticipate that of all the others? The question is based on
the assumption that the more important things anticipate the
less important ones in rank and order. Philo records four
answers to this query, which he culled or copied from earlier
teachers. The first answer amounts to this. God furnished man
not only with the highest spiritual gifts, namely with a rational
inner relation to the deity, but also with material gifts which
prepared for him everything fit to advance a prosperous life and
physical well-being. Secondly, this order of things is a safeguard and promise that if his life and conduct are regulated and
carried on virtuously, in complete accord with the divine will,
then the earth will furnish him with all necessities without

trouble and toil. Thirdly, this order indicates that there is a close contact and intimate relation between the beginning and end of the work of creation. There is a unity between Man and Heaven, closely joined together by eternal ties. Heaven is the best among the celestial bodies, man represents the crown of creation among the lower creatures on earth. Finally, the sudden appearance of man on the stage of the universe was most dramatically arranged, so that he should inspire with fear and awe all the already existing beasts and creatures.[32]

The question was raised in Palestine as well as in Alexandria. One cannot ascribe priority to the Greek source on the ground that the theory that the greater and more excellent were older or more ancient than things that came later into existence was not known in the schools of the Palestinians. Considering the very strong sense of and feeling for honour and order developed in ancient Judaism, it is somewhat daring to see foreign influence in such a thought. The great consideration shown in life and action, in public and in private, to rank and precedence in religion and in wisdom seems to be some genuine innate growth of the Jewish character, and not to be due to extraneous thought. The amazement that the most important creature should be at the same time the last in the order of created beings, could well have been voiced first by a Palestinian Jew, who might have been quite immune from the influence of Greek intellectual activities.

The 'last but not least' principle translated into Hebrew as אחרון אחרון חביב is surely of a more recent date and a later development than the teaching of first things coming first.[33] The question, therefore, is quite natural in the mouth of a Palestinian Jew: 'Why was man created last?'[34] If man is—and there is nothing to gainsay it—the crown of the creation, then why was he not created before all the other creatures of

[32] Philo, *De Officio Mundi*, par. 77; v. the references in the German translation and in Theodor, *Bereshit rabba*, p. 137, and E. Stein, *Philo und Midrash* (1931), pp. 6–7.

[33] v. Gen. r. ch. lxxviii, ed. Theodor, p. 925.

[34] Tosefta Sanhedrin, ed. Zuckermandel, viii. 7–9, p. 428, ll. 2–12, pal. Sanhedrin iv. 9, b. Sanh. 38 a, Gen. r., ch. xv.

the world? If the anthropocentric conception is correct, then man should head all creation. The coincidence of the question in Philo and in an ancient Barayta is not the most significant part of the resemblance between the two different sources. The agreement in the answers and explanations offered is perhaps of even greater importance for students of theology. The style and the present place of the fragment show traces of high antiquity. The latter is an unmistakable piece of evidence for its use in the procedure of the ancient courts, when criminal law was still practised in Palestine. The homily was already in those early days made use of in addressing the witnesses and appealing to their sense of responsibility and honesty. The Barayta, just as Philo, offers four different interpretations and replies. This variety in both sources, in Greek and Hebrew, is a clear testimony to the general interest taken by all sections of Jews in this perplexing question. In the Palestinian source the first view recorded leads the reader to the arena of disputes between scribes and Jewish believers in a dualistic religious system. Man was purposely created after all other creatures, in order that the Minim should not be able to assert that man was the assistant or partner of God in the creation of the world.

In speaking of Minim most probably Gnostics are referred to, who propagated the theory of the two Gods, viz. the Highest God, and the Lower God, the Demiurgos. Yet, it is not impossible that Alexandrian Jews, who saw in the Logos the real Creator, were indicated by this designation. In any case such a solution would not appeal to Philo and we do not expect him to elaborate such a point of view, for it would be quite contrary to his philosophy and theology alike. The later dogma of the participation of Jesus in the work of creation is too young for our source. The second answer ascribes an ethical and moralistic reason for the present order of things. Man was created last in order that his pride shoud be defeated. Man should not become proud, for even the smallest insect preceded him in creation. This has no exact parallel in Philo's list of answers. Yet, it is worth while to compare the second theory in the Tosefta with the fourth in Philo. Here, the idea of man's creation is at least intended to imbue him with humility; there, however, it was staged in this way in order to overawe the stronger animal world. This contrast between Philonic and Rabbinic Haggadah is most remarkable. The last two theories reported in the Barayta bring home the idea, first that man was created last so that he shall immediately embark on his duty, the discharge and fulfilment of the Mizwah, the divine law. For this view there is apparently again no room in Hellenistic theology. The last, however, in the Barayta, agrees literally with the first taught by Philo. Since Philo honestly admits here that he owes these teachings to earlier systems, there can be no question regarding priority as far as Philo is concerned, but only regarding his source which is unknown at present. Adam was created last so that he should be enabled to partake of a banquet already prepared, without delay and waiting. This is illustrated in both of our sources by the story of the king's banquet. A king built and inaugurated a new palace. He invited guests for this purpose. The parable is further elaborated by an old Midrash on Prov. ix. 1 :

'"Wisdom built her house", that is the King of Kings, the Holy one blessed be He, who built His world in seven days by wisdom. " She hath hewn her pillars seven", these are the seven days of creation. " She hath killed her beasts and mingled her vine", these are the seas, the streams, deserts, and the other necessities of the world. " Afterwards she hath sent forth her maidens and crieth upon the highest places of the city, 'whosoever is simple may return hither'"', namely, Adam and Eve.'

The parable of the banquet arranged by the king in the Midrash has a close parallel in the words of Philo. He says: ' Just as a host does not call to a meal before he has prepared it, and made ready everything wanted for the meal, so God prepared everything before inviting man to partake of it.' Philo, or his source, added another parable taken from the life of the theatre and circus, which was dear to his Greek readers. Palestinian Bible students of his generation would have found less pleasure and amusement in a picture of that sort. A banquet prepared for guests is a very favoured, and therefore frequent, topic in the Haggadah to illustrate and illuminate various theological doctrines, e.g. the perfection of creation,[35] future reward and punishment,[36] and many others.[37]

The authorship of this parable is ascribed in the Genesis rabba [38] to R. Nehemiah. This is perfectly in accord with the ancient tradition surviving in the schools that the anonymous passages in the Tosefta go back to the teachings of this scribe.[39] The parable was further developed and elaborated in the Amoraic Haggadah in several variations. R. Samuel b. Isaac compares the creation of man by God to a king, who prepared a banquet and invited many guests to partake of it. He prepared for them many dishes full of great delicacies, and said: ' Whosoever eats and blesses the king, he will enjoy it, but he who eats and does not bless him, he will be beheaded by the sword.' [40] Closer connexion between the Tannaitic and the Amoraic Haggadah can be established in a long sermon of R. Aibo, a teacher of the fourth century, recorded by R .Huna.[41] God created man with full knowledge at the end of the creation, and not by any oversight. He was created after all creatures so that all necessities should await him when he came into this world. The angels objected to man's creation with the words of the Psalmist, Ps. viii. 8. God said to them : ' If so, all sheep and oxen wherefore were they created? Imagine a tower full of the choicest things, and there are human beings going by, what is the good of filling it with all the precious dainties ? ' The angels submitted to the will of God by saying: ' O Lord

[35] v. the answer given in the dialogue of R. Yose b. Halafta to the matrona, who inquires about the proper order of creation, similar to our Barayta; v. Tanhuma, ed. Buber, i, p. 2.

[36] v. R. Yohanan ben Zakkai; v. b. Shabbath 153a, Eccles. r., ix. 3, 8, Eccles.ᶻ., p. 121, Midr. Proverbs, ch. 16, Semahoth zutarti, p. 33.

[37] R. Joshua ben Levi, Midr. Psalms, ch. iv, ed. Buber, p. 48; R. Eleasar b. Pedath, Gen. r., ch. lxii, ed. Theodor, p. 671 ; R. Levi, Pes., ed. Buber, p. 22b, R. Samuel b. Isaac, Gen. r., ch ix, p. 73; Deut. r., ch. xi, 6, Midr. Eleh Deb. r., ed. Buber, p. 3, no. 7; b. Ber. 31a, cf. Luke xiv. 16, cf. E. Norden, *Die antike Kunstprosa*, p. 467.

[38] v. Gen. r., ch. xv, ed. Theodor, p. 137.

[39] v. Marmorstein, *Midrash Haseroth we Yeteroth* (London, 1917), p. 4, note 15.

[40] v. Gen. r., ch. ix, p. 73. The application is that the angel of life accompanies him, who performs the commandments and good deeds; the transgressors, however, are handed over to the angel of death.

[41] Gen. r., ch. viii, p. 61.

of the whole Universe, how glorious is Thy name over the whole world.'

There is a further resemblance between the third of Philo's arguments and some Haggadic interpretations on our problem, which requires a few observations. Whether Philo and Rabbis have drawn from a common source, or, whether Philonic theories penetrated into the Palestinian schools in the third century are questions which cannot be answered at present. The fact has to be established that the question of man's place in creation was just as vigorously discussed from the pulpit in this age as three centuries before. The views and theories advanced in this context centre around Ps. cxxxix. 5. ' Thou hast formed me behind and before, and thou hast put thine hand upon me.' The gross anthropomorphism called for explanation and mitigation. Teachers like R. Yochanan b. Nappacha and R. Simon b. Lakish, who were by no means troubled by such utterances of the Bible, found it necessary to soften the meaning of this verse. The former rendered the text thus : ' God has endowed man with two impulses, good and evil, therefore, says man, hast thou formed me with two formations, one leading forward, and the other backward. One enables man to inherit the world to come, the other, however, leads to punishment.' His colleague said: 'Man was created before all creatures.' The spirit of God in Gen. i. 2, meaning the spirit of the first man, Adam, who was the first and at the same time the last of the created beings.[42] Here, exactly as in Philo, we have before us the teaching which attempts to connect the beginning and the conclusion of creation, the physical with the spiritual, the creation of the body and the spirit of Adam.

Even if the main purpose of the homily was to explain the anthropomorphism of the passage, yet, the preacher contributes at the same time some solution to the question; ' Why was man created last ? ' His reply was in short that man may have been the last as far as his physical character goes—which is in reality of minor importance—spiritually he anticipated the

[42] v. Tanh., ed. Buber, iii, p. 32, Gen. r., ch. viii, ed. Theodor, p. 56, Lev. r., ch. xiv, 1.

whole creation. There are still some indications preserved, which clearly show that this solution did not enjoy great popularity, but called for opposition. Thus R. Eleasar b. Pedath, a contemporary of these teachers, adheres to the literality of our text. Adam was spiritually and physically created on the last day. The only concession which he is inclined and prepared to make is that on the last day of creation the spiritual Adam was created before the physical Adam. The spiritual part of man, his immortal soul, his spirit, anticipated the creation of the body as well as that of the animal world. Another teacher, R. Samuel b. R. Tanhum, (read perhaps: Nahmani) proves from Ps. cxlviii that the order of creation in Gen. ch. i has a complete parallel in this Psalm. Or, in other words, the things were created in the same order as that in which they are enumerated in this Psalm, where the praise of God is spoken of.[43] R. Simlai is even more outspoken in his opposition to R. Simon b. Lakish who maintained that man was created first. Just as man's praise and song is the last, so his creation came after that of all the other creatures.[44] It would be most tempting to investigate here the problem whether the preachers of the opposition did not reject the very basis of the question and teach that the most important things need not be first in order and rank. Many changes have taken place in contemporary Judaism which may have altered the standard conceptions of what is important and what is of no consequence in social as well as in religious life. Such an investigation, for which there is a great abundance of material, must be left for another place where the anthropological conceptions of the Rabbis will be described and analyzed.

[43] Gen. r., ch. viii, ed. Theodor, p. 56.
[44] v. previous note, ibid., p. 59.

II

1. THE comparisons between Philo and Haggadah teach one lesson, which leaves no room for any doubt. I mean that Alexandrian Jewry was divided into many religious groups and sections in the days of Philo. The conditions in Palestine differed not very much from those among the Greek-speaking Jews. Otherwise, one could not account for the many similarities of the questions raised in the one place as in the other. The different groups mentioned by Philo were of various colours and bore different crests. Next to the radicals at both ends, who defended the literality of the Scriptures out of piety and reverence, there were the Jewish Marcionites who adhered to the same principle out of hatred against the Bible and the Jewish teaching of God. The Jewish scoffers in Alexandria, who are characterized by Philo as 'persons, who cherish a dislike of the institutions of our fathers and make it their constant study to denounce and decry the Laws',[1] were not without sympathizers and coreligionists in Palestine. Between these two groups stood the allegorists, who tried to avert the criticism and misinterpretation of the Bible, and through the Bible of the Jewish doctrine of God.

If one turns to the anonymous Haggadah, there a door is opened to a mine of information on this subject from which material can be gathered, which may be of the same date as Philo, if not older. We saw above[2] that the literality of Exod. xv. 3 was rejected by Philo as well as by the allegoristic school of the Haggadah; so, too, other anthropomorphistic utterances were scrutinized in the same way. Thus Exod. xiii. 21, where God is spoken of as walking. Here as in the previous case the literality of the text is confronted by teachings of the prophets, which reduce such words to absurdity. Here again, the same verses from the prophets Jeremiah, Isaiah, and Ezekiel are cited to make such a notion of walking in the case of deity quite

---

[1] *De confusione linguarum*, § ii.   [2] v. above, p. 7 ff.

preposterous. A Haggadist, who bears a Greek, or according to other readings, a Latin name, Antigonos or Antoninus, offers an explanation, which also would do credit to Philo, when he says that such an expression means nothing else but the manifestation of God's love for Israel in delivering them from Egypt.[3] Another homily is devoted to the problem of God's jealousy mentioned in Exod. xx. 5. Is there such a thing as jealousy before God?[4]. Is God jealous on account of people who transgress His word and act against His will? Does He inflict punishment on sinners by throwing stones, arrows, or slings? Such Biblical passages, we see now, were criticized in Jerusalem as in Alexandria, as we read in Philo's words, quoted above. The answer given by Palestinian sages is on the same model and breathes the same intellectual atmosphere as that of the Greek-speaking teachers. There is no such feeling with or in the deity, and consequently the expression must not be understood literally. What does it mean? That those who are addicted to idol worship are changing the character of the real God into that of the non-existent idols. That is to say that these idolators proclaim ideas about God which cannot be justified. They think that just as idols are jealous when their worshippers turn to other deities, so likewise God may be jealous when Hebrews turn away from Him and embrace other religions. The school of R. Ishmael preserved another view to combat the literal meaning of such a passage. God is the Lord of jealousy, but divine jealousy has no room or place in the Jewish conception of God.[5] The same doctrine was taught with reference to Ps. cxxi. 4. Can one say about God that he is sleeping? No. God has dominion and rule over sleep, but sleep is far from Him. God's jealousy was frequently dis-

---

[3] Mekilta 25 a; v., however, Mekilta of R. Simon b. Yohai, p. 40, where a different interpretation is attributed to R. Yose, the Galilean, about which further on p. 110. Further Tanh., p. 80 a. In legends and popular tales the idea often occurs that God is walking about, M. Ps., ed. Buber, p. 464, Pes. ed. Buber, p. 212 b., v. Yalkut Makiri Hosea, ed. Greenup, *JQR*., N.S. xv. 1924, p. 209, אני ואתם נלך לנחמה. God goes for Israel's sake to a place of uncleanness, i.e. Egypt, Exod. r., ch. xv. His way and walk is in holiness, R. Aha b. Ḥanina, Tanh. B., iii, p. 73.

[4] Mekilta of R. Simon b. Yohai, p. 105.

[5] Mekilta, p. 67 b.

cussed in the dialogues held between rabbis and various inquirers. An interlocutor of R. Gamaliel II, who is given the
title of philosopher, asked: 'Why is God jealous of the idols?
There is nothing in them worth being jealous of.' He does
not object to the idea of divine jealousy, but he cannot see
the reason for such a feeling in the given instance. A wise
man, a rich person, a hero, might be jealous of his rival's
wisdom, wealth, or strength, but the idols are—especially
according to Jewish teaching—of no reality at all, then why
should God be jealous? R. Gamaliel in his reply admits the
jealousy of God, yet with the modification that the jealousy is
not directed against the idols, but against those who adore
them and ascribe divine rank to them.[6] Interesting in the reply
of the Patriarch is the story of a man's calling his dog by his
father's name and swearing by the dog, which is a plain reminiscence of Socrates' swearing by his dog.[7] Christian Apologists
frequently mention this episode in the life of the Greek philosopher. Somehow it had also become known to the Rabbis.
Stricter than this alleged philosopher, who discussed with R.
Gamaliel the question of God's jealousy, were the Gnostics, who
poured out all their contempt on the God of the Jews for His
jealousy. It seems to have been a special dogma of the Ophites.
The serpent said to Eve: 'By the life of God, I am sorely grieved
on your account, because you are as stupid as the beasts. . . .
Do not be afraid . . . for out of jealousy did God forbid you to
eat from the fruits of the tree. . . .'[8] The same accusation of
jealousy is repeated in the Palestinian Targum[9] and by one of
the foremost Haggadists of the third century,[10] R. Levi, as
illustrating Ophite polemics against Jewish religion. The same
teacher dwells also on the contradiction between Lev. xix. 18,
forbidding jealousy and vengeance, and Nahum i. 2, where
God is called an avenging God. His solution retains the literal
meaning of the text, which implies that God will avenge the

---

[6] Ibid., p. 67 b.

[7] For a fuller treatment of this point v. my remarks in the *Tarbiz*, vol. v,
p. 145, where all the particulars can be found.

[8] v. 'Life of Adam and Eve', ch. xviii, in Kautzsch, *Pseudepigraphen
des A. T.*, p. 521.

[9] Gen. iii. 4.   [10] Gen. r., ch. xix, ed. Theodor, 172.

misdeeds of his enemies, wicked people, and the nations of the world.[11]

A third problem which occupied the mind of the early Haggadists was the question of God's resting on the Sabbath. Here, as in the first instance, the idea is contradicted by a quotation from Isaiah, xl. 28, where we read: 'that there is no travail, nor weariness before Him. He fainteth not, nor is He weary.' This is opposed to Exod. xx. 11, where it says: 'And God rested on the seventh day'.[12] In the Mekilta there are further quotations from Isa. xl. 29, and Ps. xxxiii. 6, showing that the term 'resting' gives no sense if spoken of the deity.[13] The treatment of the subject is different in these two sources, which leads to the assumption that is fully borne out by the vast material at our disposal, that in Judea, and later in Galilee, there were two different theological systems, the one understanding the early religious documents more literally, the other more spiritually. The first source explains the contradiction by introducing the doctrine of divine retribution for the wicked, who by their evil deeds contribute to the destruction of the Universe, which was created with toil and trouble. The theological maxim further voices the opinion that sins and transgression cause all the evils and ultimately the destruction of the world. The second source represents the more spiritual, allegorical interpretation of the text. Surely, they would say, these expressions, rest and work, are not fit to be applied to God. When we speak of resting or working with reference to the Godhead we are employing mere figures of speech used for bringing home to human understanding the existence and greatness of God.

It can be explained in this, as well as in many other instances, why both schools of thought and exegesis paid such attention to these problems, which to many thinkers may appear trivial and not worth while. However, external as well as internal reasons compelled them to enlarge on this subject. It has not yet been recognized how much Jewish theology, in the centuries under review, was stimulated by the polemic onslaughts

---

[11] Eccles. r. on viii. 4, Gen. r., ch. 55, ed. Theodor, p. 586.
[12] Mekilta of R. Simon, p. 109.   [13] Mekilta 59 b.

directed against Judaism by the united forces of pagan religion
and philosophy, Gnosticism and Early Christianity. It is the
Sabbath which is attacked by all three of them. The Jews of
the Diaspora were especially distinguished by their faithful and
loyal observance of the Sabbath.[14] No wonder that that precious gift given to Israel by God became the subject of ridicule
by clowns and priests alike in ancient Rome and Alexandria,
wherever the poisonous hydra of Anti-Semitism lifted up its
ugly head. Philo, the Church Fathers, and the Haggadah preserved some material on this subject. One of the arrows aimed
against the Jewish Sabbath touched also at the same time the
Jewish doctrine of God. On the one side it was asked: 'If the
law of the Sabbath is of such importance and cannot be
abrogated, as taught by the teachers of Judaism, why does your
God not keep it?' On the other hand it was objected: 'How
can the Scriptures write about God resting on the seventh
day?' Philo addresses his words to such objectors, when he
says in good Haggadic manner: 'Excellently, moreover, does
Moses say "caused to rest", and not "rested"; for He causes
to rest that which, though actually not in operation, is apparently making, but He Himself never ceases making.'[15] One
can point to Celsus as a representative of ancient philosophy
as indicating the impression made on educated and intelligent
heathen readers of the Bible. 'After this work', says Celsus,
'He became tired like a clumsy artisan and bad worker, who
needs rest in order to recuperate from his labour.'[16] The whole
chorus of Church Fathers joins Origen in repelling such calumnies and misinterpretations.[17] The writer of the Book of Jubilees does not hesitate to say that God kept the first Sabbath,
just as Adam was the first among the earthly ones who
observed this day.[18] The same teaching is spread by the author
of the Pirke of R. Elieser,[19] who in so many of his teachings

[14] v. Gen. r., xi. 4, Pesikta r., 119 b, cf. further my remarks in my article
on 'Sabbath Observance in the Diaspora' in the *Hator*, vol. viii (Jerusalem,
1928), no. xi, pp. 7 ff.

[15] *Allegorical Interpretation*, i, 5, ed. Loeb, p. 151.

[16] *Origenes contra Celsum*, vi. 61.

[17] v. for a fuller treatment of this subject *Rheinisches Museum*, lxvi, 400 ff.

[18] Jub. ii. 18.   [19] Ch. xviii.

agrees with the Jubilees. As a reply to Christian and earlier
Gnostic anti-Jewish attacks, Rabbinic apologists introduced
the theory that God observes the Sabbath, just as the teaching
gained ground that God observes other particular laws, as will
be shown in the course of these studies.[20] A fourth ancient
objection was caused by the verse in Exod. xxii. 23. It says: 'I
will slay you with the sword.' Does God use a sword in order
to slay them? Surely not. Then what is the meaning of the
passage? God will bring upon them those who will slay them
with the sword.[21] Finally, there is Exod. xv. 7, to be mentioned
in this connexion. 'Thou hast overthrown them that rise up
against Thee.' Who can rise up against God? The answer is,
those who rise against God's children,[22] or according to another
version, against His beloved ones, they are regarded as if they
rose against God Himself.[23] The homilist gives instances.
Amraphel against Abraham, Pharaoh against Israel, Sisera,
Senacherib, Nebuchadnezzar, and Hiram, the king of Tyre, are
meant by this designation. The Mekilta does not supply this
list of individuals, whose hostility to Israel is known from the
Scriptures, but instead supplies a number of Biblical verses
which speak of God's enemies in a similar manner, as Ps.
lxxiv. 23, lxxxiii. 2, and cxxxix. 21. The words 'those that rise
up against Thee', 'those that hate Thee', and 'Thine enemies',
appear meaningless if taken literally. Their meaning, therefore,
had to be changed and applied to God's beloved or His people.
Mekilta as well as Sifre on Numbers [23] add here a long list of
Soferic alterations which aim at elimination of gross anthropomorphisms. The vicinity of these two lists may offer a clue
for the date of these early endeavours to remove or explain
allegorically passages in which God is invested with human
passions. Anyhow, one is justified in asserting that the allegorical exegesis in Palestine is not much younger than that of
the Greek Diaspora. The emendations of the Scribes as well
as these questions and answers belong to the oldest form and
material of the ancient Haggadah. It may be noted that in

---

[20] v. Tanh. i, ed. Buber, p. 12, Pes. r., 187 a, Gen. r., ch. xi, p. 94, Exod.
r., xxx. 9, Yalkut Makiri, Ps. cxlvii. 29.
[21] Mekilta 39 a.   [22] Mekilta of R. Simon, p. 63.   [23] Sifre Num., par. 84.

that age the difficulties raised were two-fold. First of all, how
can one speak of God as walking, as being jealous, as sleeping
or resting, as having a sword in His hand, or as having
enemies? The assertion appears even more absurd in cases
where statements to the contrary can be adduced, which show
that these assertions are impossible if applied to God. Here
again it can be shown that we are moving on the oldest ground
of the Haggadah, for, in its earliest form, the raising of contradictions plays a prominent part.

2. Besides these anonymous Haggadic utterances there are
some, which following the same tendency and imbued with the
same spirit are ascribed to R. Ishmael, a teacher of the early
second century. The resemblance in method and coincidence in
thought is so striking that one would be inclined to place the
anonymous ones under the name of this teacher. R. Ishmael followed the teachers of the allegorical school, in opposition to his
chief colleague R. Akiba, who, as we saw in an earlier chapter,
preferred the literal exposition, even where anthropomorphic
difficulties predominate. Here, mainly R. Ishmael's views
shall be recorded and analysed. In a sermon on Exod. xii. 13
'and I will see the blood', the question is raised in the style
which was noticed in the previous chapter: Is not everything
revealed before Him? Thereupon evidence is brought to
support this assertion from Dan. ii. 22 and Ps. cxxxix. 12.
The doctrine of God's omniscience is based on these verses.
God knoweth what is in the darkness, and light dwelleth with
Him. Further 'the darkness hideth not from Thee'. R.
Ishmael's answer would have caused joy to Philo, if he had
heard it. God naturally can see everything in the Universe, but
'I will see the blood', means something quite different, namely
'as a reward for your faithful observance of the commandment
in connexion with the Paschal Lamb I will reveal Myself to
you, and will have pity on you, and redeem you'.[24] A second interpretation removes the anthropomorphism by asserting that
the expression 'and I saw', does not mean seeing the blood, as
the literal sense conveys, but 'and I will remember the sacrifice
of Isaac, for whose sake or merit Israel shall be redeemed

[24] Mekilta 8 a.

from Egypt'.[25] There is a third exposition, which also
originated in the allegorical school, teaching that the verb does
not indicate God's seeing, but implies that the sacrifice should
be offered up in a place visible to all passers by, viz. in public.[26]
Secondly, there is R. Ishmael's question and exposition on
Exod. xv. 2 'this is my God ואנוהו '. R. Ishmael understood the
meaning of the verb as 'and I will adorn Him'. How can man
adorn God? No, that is impossible. The meaning is: 'I will
adorn myself before Him by performing the divine precepts
in the best way.'[27] There are other interpretations, like that
of R. Yose the Galilean, who renders it as: 'I will declare
His praise before all the nations of the world': R. Yose son
of the Damascene, as 'I will make Him a habitation': Abba
Shaul as 'I will imitate Him', and finally R. Akiba, who says:
'I will speak of God's beauty and praise before all the nations
of the world'.[28] R. Ishmael further expounded Num. xviii. 8,
the words 'and I behold': 'and I' stands for 'willingly', and
'behold' stands for 'joyfully or gladly'. His pupils asked
him: 'How is the same term in Gen. vi. 17 to be explained?
Does this convey the idea that there is such a thing as joy
before God or in heaven?' R. Ishmael says: 'Yes, indeed
there is joy in heaven, when those who provoke Him perish.'
The teacher supported this doctrine by quotations from
Prov. xi. 10, and Ps. ii. 4, and x. 16.[29] It is remarkable that
this teacher found nothing to object to in the conception

[25] This exposition is based on the similarity of the verb (ראה) used in Gen.
xxii. 14 and 1 Chron. xxi. 15. The latter verse is rendered: 'and as He was
destroying (scil. Egypt), the Lord saw (namely, the sacrifice of Isaac).'
In the Mekilta of R. Simon this Haggadah is omitted.

[26] Mekilta of R. Simon, p. 14, where the question is put in this way:
'What do I need? Is not everything revealed before Him'? But the text
means to say that he should not place the blood except on a spot revealed
to or seen by every passer-by.

[27] Mekilta, p. 37 a; Mekilta of R. Simon, p. 60, where the order is somewhat different, namely, R. Ishmael, Abba Shaul, R. Yose son of the
Damascene, R. Yose the Galilean, and R. Akiba.

[28] The difference between R. Ishmael and R. Akiba is quite apparent
in this instance. The former avails himself of the allegorical method in
removing the difficulty raised by him, the latter seemingly found no
stumbling-block at all in this text.

[29] Sifre Numbers, par. 117.

of the rejoicing of God, or in the idea of joy in Heaven.[30]
Moreover, he introduces a controversial point by saying that
God rejoices at the downfall of the wicked.[31] This teaching
was by no means general. On the contrary many teachers
emphasize God's goodness by preaching that God is grieved
by the misfortune of His creatures even if they are wicked and
guilty.[32] Yet, such utterances as 'when the wicked perish, the
city rejoices' or 'Thou hast smitten all my enemies upon
their cheeks and thou hast broken the teeth of the wicked',
and other verses were too strong for the Tannaite. R. Jonathan
supports this theory with Exod. iv. 14, where הנה implies joy.
The compiler of the Genesis rabba seems to have preserved
a teaching on this passage in Genesis which contradicts the
view of R. Ishmael and therefore may be regarded as the theory
of R. Akiba and his followers. God agreed with the exclamation of the angels: 'What is man that thou rememberest him',
&c., Ps. viii. 5, which is expressed by the word ואני הנני.[33]

Later teachers also speak freely of God's joy. A Barayta
says: 'On that day there was joy before God as on the day
when heaven and earth were created.'[34] R. Zeira, who by the
way opposed anthropomorphic ideas as R. Ishmael did, speaks
of God as being joyful when His children throng the court-
yard of the synagogues and come to pray before Him,[35] and
of rejoicing when giving His Torah to Israel.[36]

Yet the point of view represented by this teacher was by
no means the generally accepted teaching in contemporary
Judaism, nor did it succeed in securing the confidence and
assent of the schools and their leaders. As in the Halakah so
in the Haggadah victory fell to R. Akiba and his disciples.
One may rightly see a connexion between the controversies
in both branches of ancient learning. A teacher who understood Bible and Prophets allegorically differed in his view
of God from the rival who took all the Biblical narratives

---

[30] v. also Matt. xviii. 13, the rejoicing in heaven.
[31] v. further on the dialogue between Pappus and R. Akiba, pp. 42 ff.
[32] v. *The Old Rabbinic Doctrine of God*, pt. i, pp. 196–208.
[33] Gen. r., ch. xxxi, ed. Theodor, p. 285.
[34] B. Megillah 10 b.   [35] v. Midrash Psalms, ed. Buber, p. 42.
[36] B. Berakoth, p. 5 a.

in a literal sense. This dissension must have divided them
in their interpretation of the legal and ritual exposition of the
Bible as well. A rationalist takes an attitude towards the law
different from that of a mystic, who sees and perceives God
everywhere, walking and standing, praying and working. Historical conditions favoured the victory of R. Akiba. R. Akiba's
theology as opposed to that of R. Ishmael is expressed in many
controversies which they had on many important subjects,
as e.g. Exod. xii. 2, which is interpreted by R. Akiba in a literal
sense. God has shown unto Moses the New Moon. According to
R. Ishmael such a thing is out of the range of possibility. Moses
has shown the New Moon to the Israelites.[37] This was one of
the three things which God showed to Moses with His finger.
These things are the New Moon, the making of the lamp, and
the prohibition of unclean animals. Secondly, on Exod. xx. 18,
R. Ishmael taught that they saw the visible, and that they heard
what could be heard. R. Akiba favours the more literal exposition
that they could hear the visible, and could see that which was
conveyed to them by the ear. Everything which came out of
the mouth of the Geburah was immediately engraved on the
tablets.[38] Thirdly, the name Elohim in Exod. xxii. 27 is taken
by R. Ishmael as meaning 'judges', R. Akiba again renders it
literally, 'God'.[39] A further dispute between these two teachers
is connected with their attitude to esoteric studies, the Maaseh
Bereshith and Maaseh Merkabah. The same applies to
the public discussion of the Laws concerning prohibited
marriages עריות. R. Akiba, who took all these texts in their
literal meaning feared that they might have grave consequences
if treated in public; not so R. Ishmael, whose allegorical method
was a safe-guard against such possible misinterpretation.[40]

There is a further controversy between these two teachers,
which throws light on the one side on the principal antagonism

---

[37] Mekilta 2 b. Sifre Numbers, par. 61, where ed. Horowitz adds 'as if'
כאילו, which is, however, a gloss contradicting the real meaning of the
sentence. Menahoth 29 a quotes this Barayta as a תנא דבי רבי ישמעאל
Pesikta, ed. Buber, p. 54 b and Pesikta r., p. 78 a, as תני רבי שמעון בן יוחא
Exod. r., xv. 1, Num. r., xv. 4, Tanhuma Bo, and Shemini, ed. Buber,
p. 28. v. further b. Hullin 42 a.

[38] v. Mekilta 71 a.   [39] Ibid., 97 a.   [40] v. pal. Hagiga ii. 1.

of these two masters, and on the other side illuminates their
relation to earlier Jewish Hellenistic thought and religion.
R. Akiba expounded the word אבירים in Ps. lxxviii. 25 as
food of angels. He may have known the Greek version as used
by the author of the *Sapientia Salomonis*. When R. Ishmael
heard this interpretation, he became indignant and objected
on the ground that angels have no food and, consequently,
there is no eating in heaven. The meaning of the word is to
be derived by the change of אבירים [41] into אברים. It is a
food, which is absorbed by the limbs. R. Ishmael as an
allegorist concurs with the teaching of Philo, who likewise
explains all actions or feelings ascribed to God, but which are
too human, as carried out by angels. His words may be translated
here, for they throw welcome light on the development of the
Rabbinic allegorists as well. 'The unique or sole God is
surrounded by numberless forces destined for the salvation
of the world. . . . There is in the air a chorus of invisible
holy, bodyless souls, the partners of the divine beings. The
Scriptures call them angels. This whole host of angels is
arranged in perfect order, is devoted to the service of the
Most High, and ever ready to obey His command. For in
heaven there is no negligence of duties. Just as in the case of
a human king it is meet that ministers or officers should carry
out functions and duties which cannot be performed by the
king himself without loss of prestige ; truly the Father of the
Universe needs no creatures for His service, yet he deputes
and commissions, for the sake of decency or dignity, some of
the inferior power to discharge certain functions or duties,
without investing them with independent will or initiative.' [42]
These words of Philo guided all allegorists before and after
his time. They corroborate the experience of the student of
Rabbinic texts that R. Ishmael, or Pappus, and others made
room in their theological teaching for angels and spirits, when
they found themselves faced with anthropomorphic passages
in the Bible, so that they substituted for the name of God that
of an angel or spirit. Yet the angels of the allegorists were
different from those who lived in the speculations of the

---

[41] b. Yoma 75 b.   [42] v. *De confusione linguarum*, iii. 394.

literalists. R. Akiba taught that these angels require food,
not so R. Ishmael. This difference of opinion brought about
the controversy concerning the meaning of the word אבירים
in the Haggadah of the two teachers.

The contention of the two teachers and their schools can
further be shown in the following Midrash. We noticed above
that the two masters were at variance on the exegetical value
of the particles used in the Hebrew language. R. Ishmael
attached no importance to them. Yet, in three instances, he
admitted their usefulness. One of these is Deut. xxxiv. 6 'and
he buried him in the valley'. The subject is missing in this
sentence. Who buried Moses? R. Ishmael asked: 'Did others
bury him? No, he buried himself.'[43] R. Ishmael used his
opponent's method here, in order to reject a rather strong
anthropomorphic teaching. The rival school taught that the
subject in this sentence is no one else but God. A preacher
of the third century, R. Simlai, is credited with the following
remarkable teaching: The Pentateuch begins and ends with
the commandment to exercise charity. The Alpha and Omega
of the Law is lovingkindness and benevolence. How does
or did this Jewish teacher, who is often grouped together
with Scribes and Pharisees of the crude and gross legalistic
type, prove this? He saw in Gen. i. 28 that God was pronouncing the blessing over the bridal couple, like a minister
of religion in performing a wedding ceremony; further in
Gen. ii. 22, he saw an instance of God acting as best-man by
adorning the bride before the wedding; then in Gen. xviii. 1
an instance of God visiting the sick and ailing; finally in our
passage of Deuteronomy a case of God burying the dead and
comforting the mourners.[44] All these acts of charity are
frequently pointed out as the greatest virtues by which man
imitates the work of his Maker.[45] Some of these virtues and
qualities are especially elaborated by teachers of the anthropo-

[43] v. Sifre Numbers, par. 32.

[44] v. b. Sotah 14 a, Gen. r., ch. viii, ed. Theodor, p. 67, Eccles. r., vii. 2,
Tanhuma, i, ed. Buber, p. 83, Midrash Psalms, xxv. 11, Pirke R. Elieser,
ch. xvii.

[45] v. Marmorstein, 'Die Nachahmung Gottes (Imitatio dei)' in *Jüdische
Studien, Dr. J. Wohlgemuth gewidmet* (Berlin, 1928), pp. 144–59.

morphic school. R. Abbahu, whose Haggadah is exceedingly
rich in anthropomorphic material as will be demonstrated in
a following chapter of these essays, depicts God as blessing
the bridal-couple with a cup of wine in His hands and uttering the prescribed blessings which were customary in the days
of this Amora.[46] The interpretation of the text in the narrative
of Moses as meaning that God Himself busied Himself with
the funeral of Moses must be older than the third century, and
was propagated either by R. Akiba, the head of this school,
or by his followers.

This divergence of views existed also between R. Akiba
and R. Yose the Galilean, another contemporary scholar.
There is recorded an ancient Tannaitic dispute between these
two teachers on Gen. xxii. 1, concerning the meaning of the
verb נסה. R. Yose the Galilean taught that the verb means
'and God exalted Abraham', R. Akiba, however, is satisfied with
the literal meaning, and translates 'and God tested'.[47] This
interpretation of R. Akiba fully agrees with his method which
adheres to the literal meaning in spite of the anthropomorphic
idea conveyed by the text. He does not fear or care that a
literal exegesis may raise doubts about the omniscience of God.
His religious system is so firm that such trifles cannot disturb
it. This may perhaps be the result of his deep religious experience and his earlier intellectual endeavours. This scholar,
who once tasted the spiritual fruits of the Pardes which he
diligently frequented and left in perfect religious equilibrium,
must have become more confirmed in the more rigid conservative or literal perception of the Bible, allowing no compromise
or concession of any type or to any extent. Jewish history in
various periods shows similar appearances under similar conditions of intellectual growth and decline. Yet this school was
opposed by another train of thought, like that represented by
R. Ishmael and R. Yose ha-Gelili, expressing the rationalistic
point of view. The very characteristic terminology used by
these two teachers in their Haggadah, which, however, is
surely older than their time, is an eloquent witness to their

[46] v. Gen. r., ch. viii, ed. Theodor, p. 66.
[47] v. Gen. r., ch. lv, ed. Theodor, pp. 588–9.

theological trend of mind. R. Ishmael and his forerunners in introducing a question on a difficult passage of the Bible use the term וכי אפשר לומר כן, meaning: 'How is it possible to say thus?', whilst R. Yose ha-Gelili when facing anthropomorphic passages, asks: וכי תעלה על דעתך לומר כן? meaning, 'how can one entertain even the thought of saying such a thing?' Surely, R. Akiba would never dream of using such language even when reading the most irrational verse in the Scriptures.

The difference between the earlier anthropomorphic and the allegorical schools can be detected in the anonymous Haggadah in many instances. The anthropomorphic school explains the difficulty about God being a man of war, in which a close parallel between Philo and the earlier Palestinian allegorical school has been established above,[48] in different ways. To the literal interpretation, the difficulty is not 'is it at all possible to speak of God as a man of war?', but, will the fact that here God is called a young warrior, whereas at the revelation He is depicted as an old sage or scribe, not confound dualistic religious thinkers and they will proclaim that the Bible confirms a dualistic conception of deity?[49] That is all that they are concerned about. A literal exposition must face such threats and dangers. Here it was taught that God appeared with weapons. An exposition on Exod. xii. 12 will clearly show that both schools are represented in our sources one close to the other. 'And I shall pass through the land of Egypt.' An anonymous teaching endeavouring to avoid the gross anthropomorphism of the verb, namely God's walking, which, as we saw, was disliked by Hellenistic as well as by Palestinian allegorists,[50] offers the translation 'and I will pour out my anger', &c. The verb עברתי resembles the noun עברה. Just as R. Ishmael, the allegorist and opponent of anthropomorphic literality, acquiesces in speaking and reading of 'God's joy', so, for some reason to be investigated later, the idea of God's wrath and anger did not seem incompatible with the

[48] v. above, pp. 7 ff.
[49] Mekilta, p. 37 b and Mekilta of R. Simon, p. 60.
[50] v. above, p. 3 and p. 10.

theology of this school. The opposing or rival theology, as
taught by R. Judah b. Ilai, a pupil of R. Akiba, does not
hesitate to interpret: ' God passed from one place to another ',
merely adding ' like a king who does the same.' [51] The view
of R. Yose the Galilean about God testing man, recurs in
the following anonymous teaching on Exod. xx. 20. The text
has: ' in order to test you ', which is also interpreted ' that
God came in order to magnify (exalt) you before all the nations
of the world '. Here again, the opposition adds the significant
technical term used by the advocates of the literacy of the
text, בודאי, viz. the verb testing is to be understood in the
literal sense, and not allegorically.[52]

It will be necessary, before advancing further in our investigation of the ancient disagreement on this subject, to
consider the position occupied by R. Yose the Galilean in
this controversy. One is entitled, after the evidence produced
up till now, to group this scribe among the allegorical interpreters of the Tannaitic age. Allegorists were in many respects
in a queer position on several occasions, when they faced
difficulties which the literalists safely ignored or passed by.

A very instructive example of this observation is offered in
the controversy between R. Ishmael and R. Akiba on Exod. xx.
23, לא תעשון אתי. The former refers אתי to the image and
likeness of the ministering angels, Serafim, and Ofanim that
are in heaven. R. Akiba, however, translates ' do not make
Me, or of Me, a likeness, as the heathen make images of their
gods '.[53] Something similar can be observed in the Haggadah
of R. Yose ha-Gelili on Exod. xxxiii. 22, where the strong
anthropomorphism could not pass without mitigation by such
an allegorist as R. Yose. The verse has: 'And I will lay my hand
on thee till I pass over.' A scribe who adhered to the literal
interpretation of the text might have overlooked the anthropomorphism altogether. An allegorist could not abide by
the literal meaning of such expressions. R. Yose, therefore,
teaches that the expression indicates to Moses that he will be

[51] Mekilta of R. Simon, p. 13.
[52] Mekilta, pp. 7 b and 12 a, Mekilta of R. Simon, p. 13.
[53] Mekilta, 72 a, and Mekilta of R. Simon, pp. 114–15.

protected by special grace in dangers which he will encounter.
These perils arise from the action of demons and spirits
who at certain hours or on certain occasions, have power to
do mischief independently of God. Here, as in the case of
R. Ishmael, an angelological doctrine, a demonological conception, helps to overcome an anthropomorphic difficulty.[54] The
very same quaint teaching is used for removing the anthropomorphism in 1 Kings viii. 11, 'and the priest could not stand
in service owing to the cloud, for the glory of God filled the
house of God. Why could the priest not discharge his duties
and minister in the presence of God's glory ? ' R. Yose replies
that the priests could not minister because there are moments
when the demons and spirits are at liberty to do harm to
mankind independently of their divine master, or at their
own discretion. There is a third allegorical interpretation,
which some texts ascribe to the same teacher. Ps. xcv. 2
'which I swore in my anger, if they will come to my rest'. 'Till
God's anger lasts'—there was no objection to speaking of His
anger, as pointed out before on p. 36, and see also further
Pt. I, on pp. 196 ff.—yet ' to my rest' seemed hard, and had to
be rendered allegorically, namely, 'to my promised land'.[55]
Finally, it is to be observed that the demonological theory of
this teacher was also applied in solving the contradiction
between Num. and Exod. The Glory of God was visible, or
appeared in the cloud. What does that mean ? God is everywhere present. It means, says the allegorist, that whenever
Moses and Aaron were threatened by their enemies God
protected them. That is the meaning of this phrase. His
angels were sent to their guard, or the demons were given
free hand to bring havoc on the wicked.[56]

This difference between the leading teachers of the pre-
Bar Kochba period can be traced back to earlier times. The
teachers and predecessors of R. Ishmael and R. Akiba manifest

[54] Mekilta, 72 b, v. also Barayta b. R. H. 24 b, b. Ab. Zara 43 b.

[55] v. Introduction to Sifra, p. 2 b, further Jalkut Makiri Psalms, ed.
Buber, ch. 93, 20, where the sayings of R. Yose are quoted anonymously,
similarly in Num r., ch. xiv. 19.

[56] v. Mekilta 48 a.

the very same tendencies in their exegetical method, and consequently in their theological outlook, as their pupils and
successors in the schools of Judea, and later on in Galilee.
R. Joshua ben Hananyah, who propagated the idea that God
shares the trouble of his people, or that the Shekinah is journey-
ing with Israel from exile [57] to exile must be ranked together
with R. Akiba and his followers. There could be established
no link between R. Ishmael and this teacher, in spite of the
close personal relation that according to Rabbinic biographers
existed between them, namely that R. Joshua redeemed
R. Ishmael from Roman captivity after the destruction of
the Temple in Jerusalem. The young priest leaned more
towards the opinions, and favoured the wisdom, of his bene-
factor's opponents. The prophecy of the aged Levite that the
captive priest would become a great teacher among his people,
was verified to the letter, but the teacher developed in a different direction. Let us turn to the exegesis and theology of
R. Joshua and his opponents. R. Joshua is in favour of the
literal interpretation, whilst his colleagues R. Elieser b. Hyrkanos and R. Eleasar of Modiim, the native of the ancient
Hashmonean place, adopted the allegorical method. A few
instances may suffice to demonstrate this contention.

Exod. xiii. 18, 'the way of the wilderness, the Red Sea', is
explained by R. Elieser thus: 'the way, in order to fatigue
them', cf. Ps. cii. 27, 'in the wilderness in order to purify
them', cf. Deut. vii. 15, 'The Red Sea', in order to test them,
cf. Ps. cvi. 7. R. Joshua, however, expounds these words differently: 'The way', that is the Torah, cf. Deut. v. 30, and
Prov. vi. 23. 'The wilderness', in order to give them the
Manna, Deut. viii. 16; 'The Red Sea', in order to show them
miracles and wonderful deeds, cf. Ps. cvi. 22.[58] Both teachers
tried to answer the question raised: 'Why did God not lead
them straight into the promised land?'

Regarding Exod. xiv. 2 there is a dispute about the meaning of the geographical term פי החירות. R. Elieser takes
it as an idol of supernatural origin, which was destined to

[57] v. Mekilta of R. Simon, p. 1.
[58] Mekilta, p. 24 a, Mekilta of R. Simon, p. 38.

mislead the Egyptians, whilst R. Joshua saw in it a geographical name.[59]

R. Joshua understood Exod. xiv. 15 in the sense that there was nothing left to Israel except to continue the journey, according to R. Elieser, however, Moses was reproved for wasting time in long prayer in an hour of danger.[60]

Exod. xv. 22 offers a very eloquent proof of the difference in the exegesis of the two masters. The text ויסע משה requires some comment. R. Joshua taught that all the journeys made by the children of Israel were by God's command with the exception of this one, which was by the direction of Moses himself, as indicated in the letter of the Scriptures. Not so R. Elieser; according to him, this journey was also at the command of God, then why does the text say that Moses made Israel to journey? It seems to say that Moses forced them to move against their wish with a stick in his hands. For they beheld the corpses of their task-masters rotting on the field, and they thought that no one of the old people was left in Egypt, so they wanted to return to Egypt till Moses forced them to go on.[61]

Exod. xv. 24 was expounded by R. Joshua literally, the people murmured against Moses. R. Eleasar of Modiim teaches that they rebelled against God as well.[62] Similarly v. 22 is taken literally (כשמועו), namely, they could find no water. R. Elieser, however, renders the verse allegorically, namely, ' they were fatigued in order to try them.'[63] According to the allegorists ' water ' stands here for ' Torah '. The *Dorshe Reshumoth* explain also the word עץ in v. 25 as 'Torah' in opposition to R. Joshua, who understood the text literally. Moses taught them Torah, by doing so he healed the waters. Exod. xvi. 3 is taken by R. Joshua as an unjustified exaggeration on the part of the hungry Hebrews, who were starving in Egypt and wanting the necessities of life, whilst according to R. Elieser

---

[59] Mekilta 25 b, Mekilta of R. Simon, p. 41.
[60] Mekilta 29 a, Mekilta of R. Simon, p. 47.
[61] Mekilta 47 b, Mekilta of R. Simon, p. 71.
[62] Mekilta 45 b, Mekilta of R. Simon, p. 72.
[63] So Mekilta 45 b., v. a longer recension in Mekilta of R. Simon, p. 72, where the roles are changed.

they were telling the truth. For as slaves they had access to food and drink—but lacked freedom; in the wilderness they enjoyed freedom but lacked physical comfort.[64]

Exod. xvi. 4 הנני ממטיר לכם, R. Joshua stresses the literal meaning of לכם, by implying that the rain of food from heaven was only for Israel. R. Eleasar of Modiim sees in it an allusion to the merits of the fathers, which play a great part in his Haggadah.[65] Similarly the anthropomorphic expression הנני is understood by R. Eleasar as 'for the merit of the fathers I will, &c.', whilst R. Joshua favours the literal rendering by paraphrasing the sentence: 'I will reveal myself at once without delay'.

Exod. xvi. 9, לפני ד', R. Joshua explains that the expression קרבו לפני ד' means, come before judgment, cf. Is. xli. 21, whilst R. Eleasar of Modiim says that קרבו indicates the revelation of the Shekinah.[66] Apart from the obscurity in the interpretation of the statement of R. Eleasar, who probably tries to explain the term 'before God' as the revelation of the Shekinah—for any creature is everywhere in the presence of God—the saying of R. Joshua does not coincide with the observation that he champions the literal meaning of the text. As a fact, in the Mekilta, p. 48 a, the expositions are reversed in agreement with the general tendencies of these scribes.

In verse 10 R. Joshua takes the verb ויפנו literally, explaining that they did not turn to the wilderness till the revelation of the Geburah. R. Elieser takes the meaning allegorically, that they turned to the merits of the fathers.[67] The reading of the Mekilta of R. Simon, p. 76, is wrong.

The anthropomorphism in verse 12 is weakened by teaching God's omniscience. He knows what Israel said and what the people will say in future.[68] In the Mekilta of R. Simon, p. 76, this teaching is ascribed, surely wrongly, to R. Joshua. Doubtless the copyists omitted his teaching, and credited him with that of R. Elieser.

[64] Mekilta 47 a, Mekilta of R. Simon, p. 74.

[65] Mekilta, p. 47 a, Mekilta of R. Simon, p. 75, v. also ed. Horovitz-Rabin, p. 160, R. Joshua uses the term בודאי.

[66] v. Mekilta of R. Simon, p. 75.

[67] v. Mekilta, p. 47 a.   [68] Mekilta 47 a.

An instructive instance can be brought forward from the contradictory explanations by these two teachers of verse 14. R. Joshua interpreted the phrase as the hoar frost on the earth, דק ככפר על הארץ, literally, that the Manna fell down like the frost on the earth. R. Eleasar the Modite explained that the Manna came down as a consequence of the prayers of the fathers, who sleep in the dust.[69] This Haggadah is supplemented by an anthropomorphic legend, that God stretched out both His hands in order to receive the prayers offered by the patriarchs, which is entirely opposed to the spirit of R. Eleasar's teaching. It is evidently a later gloss.

Another example: on Exod. xvii. 12: 'And the hands of Moses were heavy.' R. Joshua says that the hands of Moses were as heavy at that moment as that of a man on whose hands are hanging two pitchers of water. R. Eleasar of Modiim takes this sentence figuratively. Moses was disappointed or did not succeed immediately because he delayed the performance of his duty from that day to the next.[70] Consequently the phrase does not convey the meaning that the hands of Moses became heavy, but that Moses came to grief, or pain. In a duplicate passage the view of R. Joshua is rendered thus: 'The sin of Moses became so heavy on his hands that he had to return or rely on the merits of the fathers.'[71] This teaching is, as we saw, a typical feature of R. Eleasar's Haggadah. One may mention some more instances to make still clearer the statement as to the difference between the two teachers. Exod. xviii. 24: 'Moses hearkened to the words of his father-in-law and did all that Jethro said.' Thus the literal meaning is accepted by R. Joshua. R. Eleasar of Modiim modifies this by saying that Moses did all God commanded him.[72]

3. Besides the controversies between R. Akiba and his two contemporaries, R. Ishmael and R. Yose the Galilean, there are four disputes recorded which took place between him and another scholar of his age, whose name is not so well known as

---

[69] Mekilta, p. 39 a, Mekilta of R. Simon, p. 77.
[70] v. Mekilta of R. Simon, p. 83, anonymously, Mekilta, p. 54 a.
[71] Mekilta, p. 54 b and Mekilta of R. Simon, p. 83.
[72] v. Mekilta 60 a, Mekilta of R. Simon, p. 91 ; v. further on vers. 23, 27, 21, v. 18.

that of the two scribes mentioned previously. I mean the four remarkable sermons of Pappus, or Pappayos, which met with serious criticism on R. Akiba's part. They belong to the subject under discussion in this chapter and require fuller treatment. The texts on which the sermons of Pappus are based give rise to speculation on the doctrine of God generally, and on the problem of anthropomorphism particularly. The name of the preacher is little known and was at one time identified with that of an early bishop of the Church.[73] This, however, is not to be taken seriously. In the infancy of the modern science of Judaism such ingenious suggestions were frequent and permissible; now-a-days greater care and reserve is to be exercised. Whosoever this preacher may have been, his sermons deserve fuller investigation. He preached in public, in a Jewish synagogue, and R. Akiba, who was present on these occasions, stopped him, by telling him: 'Enough'. This happened to other preachers as well[74] and makes the sermons even more interesting and instructive. The very fact that the orator is silenced in public for some reason or other points to some intellectual or spiritual crisis in the midst of that community, when the divergence of views or doctrinal contention reaches such a height that the ideas or utterances of a preacher sound or are looked upon as dangerous. The order of the sermons which have to be mentioned here cannot be established, for it varies according to the sources at our disposal. The compilers of the different Midrashic collections put that sermon which has a bearing on their special text either in front or at the end of their list. I shall treat them according to the order given in the Mekilta,[75] which is as follows: (a) Cant. i. 9; (b) Job xxiii. 13; (c) Gen. iii. 22, and (d) Ps. cvi. 20.

I. 'To the horses of Pharaoh's chariot have I compared thee my love.' The preacher takes for granted that each member of his audience present is fully aware of the fact that Canticles

---

[73] v. L. Löw, Ben Chananja, vi. 827..

[74] v. f.i. Gen. r. ch. xxxvi, ed. Theodor, p. 339, and parallels, where R. Judah b. Ilai tells R. Meir : דיִּיק.

[75] Mekilta 33 a, Mekilta of R. Simon, p. 54. Gen. r. ch. xxi. 5. Cant. r., i. 45, Tanhuma, ed. Frankfurt a. O. 65 b., Midr. fragment *MGWJ.*, 1894, p. 172.

is composed of dialogues between God and the Kenesseth
Israel. What does such a comparison, as spoken of in this verse,
mean? asked Pappus. Can such a comparison be made at all?
His explanation would not satisfy Philo or any of his colleagues
of the allegorical school. He interprets the poet's words thus:
If Pharaoh appeared on a male horse, God did the same,[76]
on a female horse, then God did the same.[77] R. Akiba indignantly tells him to keep silent. R. Akiba, on his own part,
advances this exposition of the verse, that God rejoiced at the
downfall of the Egyptians, but He would have rejoiced more to
destroy Israel, if it were not for the Torah. This quaint idea
is based on the similarity between the word for ' horse ' סוס,
and the verb for ' rejoice '. I have serious doubts whether the
explanations in the text are properly recorded at all. The
preacher in raising his difficulties must have belonged to the
school of allegorists, that is, to the circle of R. Ishmael, or that
of R. Yose the Galilean. The method of R. Akiba, however,
as we learnt on the previous pages, was to take such passages
literally. Furthermore, it was shown above[78] that R. Ishmael
propagated the view that God rejoices at the defeat of the
wicked. The views expressed here, have to be, therefore, simply
transposed. The allegorical view was that of Pappus, the literal
interpretation is that of R. Akiba.

There is some external evidence that such literal explanations
were given in the schools and synagogues of Judea in the first
decades of the second century. Justin Martyr in his attack
against the Jew Tryphon mentions something of this type. The
Church Father may have listened to such, or to a similar,
exposition by R. Akiba or by some of this teacher's numerous
pupils, who adopted his exegetical norms. Justin reproaches
the sages of Israel for pondering on such futile questions, as,
why are only male and not female camels mentioned or spoken
of ?[79] There is another anti-Jewish dialogue of the second
century preserved, in which the attack is expressed more distinctly. We read there:[80] ' Do not, like a Jew, suppose concerning an incorporeal being that distinctions of male or female

---

[76] Mekilta 33 a.   [77] v. Habakkuk iii. 15, and Ps. xviii. 11.
[78] v. above, pp. 29 f.   [79] *Dialogue* ch. cxii; cf. Harnack, p. 69.
[80] Published in the *Expositor*, April (1897), p. 304.

hold good. You may hold such language about them, just as you would even about your own body; for your soul is nominally called feminine, yet in reality it is neither male nor female.' The Haggadah actually speaks of male and female in the creation, for instance, about the upper and lower waters being male and female respectively,[81] yet it is a general tendency in folk-lore to call the stronger elements male, and the weaker female.[82]

That the transposition of the names of the teachers, suggested a few lines earlier, is justified, seems the more probable because the pupils of R. Akiba would otherwise be adopting and broadcasting teachings silenced by their master, which is surely unlikely. Thus R. Meir says that just as Pharaoh appeared on a female horse, so God rode on a female horse on His throne of Glory. The later Haggadists joined a legend as commentary to these words. Pharaoh asked his servants about his swiftest animal with which he could pursue the escaping Hebrews. They advised him to take a certain coloured mare, after which all the males will run with the greatest possible speed. God asked His ministering angels a similar question. 'Which is the quickest among all my creatures?' They replied : 'Thou art omniscient and Thou knowest best that the wind coming out of the wings of the Cherubim is the swiftest of all Thy creatures.' Consequently God appeared on it.[83] If the legend is eliminated from the Haggadah it would appear that R. Meir agreed with Pappus. In another legend a somewhat similar teaching is connected with the name of R. Joshua b. Korha. He says: 'Pharaoh was riding a mare when he appeared at the sea. God rode a mare. Yet, how can one say such a thing, was He not riding a Cherub ? This is true, but the Cherub had the likeness of one of Pharaoh's mares, so that all the horses of Pharaoh were swiftly running after it into the sea.' [84] Here

[81] R. Levi, Gen. r., ch. xiii, Eccles. r., p. 67. pal. Berakoth 14 a; ibid. Taanith 64 b, Bathe Midrashoth, ed. Wertheimer, i, p. 6; cf. further *Ethiopic Enoch*, ed. Charles, p. 107.

[82] v. *Zeitschrift des Vereines für Volkskunde*, xx, 143.

[83] Midrash Agadath Shir Hashirim, ed. Schechter, p. 17, ed. Buber, p. 15.

[84] Aboth of R. Nathan, ed. Schechter 83 a, where the text has to be adjusted according to the Mekilta.

again it is a most unlikely assertion that R. Joshua b. Korha
should have propagated an idea publicly rejected by R. Akiba.
There is finally textual confirmation for reversing the names
of these two scribes in the version of the later Midrash on
Canticles, which may here be relied on.[85]

II. The second homily teaches that God judges mankind all
by Himself, without the assistance and counsel of His heavenly
host of ministering angels, and that there is no gainsaying His
words. R. Akiba, however, explained the words as meaning
that God's judgments are perfectly just and well-balanced
and true.[86] Pappus followed here the exegesis of the allegorical
school, which favoured angelological theories, as demonstrated
above.[87] Consequently some emphasis had to be laid on the
strict unity or independence of God's justice from external
powers. R. Akiba, probably thinking of Gnostic speculations
about the justice of God, teaches the perfect truth of God's
justice, which cannot be assailed or doubted. The later teaching
that God consults His *familia* was not yet known in this age.[88]
It is, however, most remarkable that in one passage belonging
to R. Akiba the term בית דין של מעלה, i.e. 'the Heavenly
Court' is used [89] which would perfectly fit in with his opposition to Pappus in this instance. The allegorist opposed the
conception of the participation attributed by the literalist to
the Heavenly Court or *familia*, and was consequently rebuked
by R. Akiba.

III. The third sermon of Pappus is built on the same principle as the previous one. An allegorist could not accept the
interpretation 'behold, man is like God', he naturally would
see in ממנו the ministering angels. R. Akiba retorts that
one can explain the text literally without bringing in the name
of God at all. God put before man two ways. One of life
and the other of death. Man chose that of death. This text
requires some elucidation. It is quite clear why Pappus

---

[85] v. Cant. r., ad loc.

[86] v. the version in Masmuth's מעין גנים, ed. Buber, Berlin, 1889, p. 74.

[87] v. above, p. 33.

[88] v. Marmorstein, 'Anges et hommes dans l'Agada', *RÉJ*. 84 (1927),
pp. 37–51, and pp. 138–141.

[89] v. Makkoth 13, a b.

offered his exposition, which is in agreement with that of the
allegorical school. Yet, surely, R. Akiba could have raised no
objection to such an interpretation on dogmatic grounds.
Secondly, how did R. Akiba force his doctrine of the two
ways into the text, which contains not the slightest allusion
to it? All one can say is that R. Akiba expounded: Behold,
man (has chosen) one of them (the two ways). Here again
Canticles rabba helps to re-establish the original text. Accordingly, Pappus referred to God, the Unique of the World,
R. Akiba, however, to the ministering angels. This variant is
helpful, but by no means decisive. For the critic of the text
may ask the question, how did the reference to the ministering
angels creep into the sermon of Pappus in all the parallel
texts? Furthermore, it cannot be denied that R. Akiba prefers
the literal and his opponent the allegorical method of exposition. One has again to reverse these two views, as was
necessary in the first sermon. The allegorist says that אחד
ממנו cannot mean 'like God', but 'as one of the ministering
angels'. R. Akiba replies that there is no obstacle in the way
of rendering the phrase literally: 'Like God Himself'. How
is now the omission of this view in the Mekilta and the insertion of the teaching of the two ways to be accounted for?
The text in Ecclesiastes rabba records three comments on
this verse. There the third view, that of the Hakamim, is
identical with the teaching ascribed to R. Akiba in the Mekilta.
This introduces a second allegorical interpretation, which
avoids anthropomorphism and angelology at the same time.

IV. The fourth sermon is based on the original text of
Ps. cvi. 20, which reads כבודי instead of כבודם: 'They
changed my glory into the image of a grass-eating ox'. Pappus
said, 'One might think that the Hebrews made a golden calf
after the image of the ox above; therefore, the text says, "a
grass-eating ox".' Akiba says that they made the calf after the
image of an ordinary grass-eating beast, taking the words of
the Psalmist quite literally.[90]

---

[90] v. Tanhuma כי תשא, par. 21-2; Yalkut Makiri Ps. 106. 48, R. Simon
b. Lakish, b. Hag. 13 a b.

4. Justin Martyr in his dialogue with the Jew Tryphon [91] asserts that the Jewish teachers of his age ascribe to God human forms, picture Him with physical qualities, invest Him with a human figure and think of Him as in possession of human limbs. The references in the Bible to God's limbs are interpreted literally and they speak of God as taking on the image of angels or of man. This charge was often repeated by scholars of the last and of this century, whenever the old-Rabbinic doctrine of God was discussed or criticized. A German scholar of our time writes: 'Die ganze Entwickelung der alttestamentlichen, und nachher der nachalttestamentlichen-talmudischen Theologie ist von der Idee der Geistigkeit Gottes niemals so bestimmt erfüllt, dass der Gedanke an irgend eine irgendwelche Körperlichkeit Gottes im Judentum vollständig abgestreift worden wäre.' [92] Finally, there is an historian who spent some time in writing about Judaism, who characterizes the Jewish teaching of God as being first of all exclusive, secondly jealous, thirdly as anthropomorphic. [93] I think it is high time to examine these charges against the Rabbinic conception of God with the aid of the Rabbinic material at our disposal. From the foregoing paragraphs it seems pretty evident that there were two trains of thought in Judaism, one favouring the allegorical method, which was never open to Justin's challenge. What about the opposing school of R. Akiba? Is the description of Justin not true about them? The following paragraph will be devoted to the investigation of this problem.

Contemporaries of Justin, R. Dosa and R. Akiba, followed by the pupils of the latter, left some remarks on the verse ' for no man can see Me and live '. R. Dosa taught that man cannot see God and live, but he will behold Him after death. He based his pronouncement on Ps. xxii. 30, ' before His countenance bow down all those, who descend to dust, whilst his soul is no more alive '. R. Akiba, who is in favour of literal exegesis, as we have noticed, says that even the holy creatures

[91] Ch. 114, cf. Harnack, *Texte und Untersuchungen*, xxxix, p. 57.

[92] Baudissin, *Archiv für Religionswissenschaft*, xviii, 1915, p. 200.

[93] Ed. Meyer, *Entstehung des Christentums*, ii, p. 23.

who carry the Throne of Glory cannot see the Glory, namely
God, as it is said 'no one can see Me, and live' (Num. xxxiii.
20).[94] R. Simon ben Yohai adds to this: 'I am not refuting
or contradicting the words of my master, I merely supplement
his teaching by saying that even the ministering angels, who
are endowed with the blessing of eternal life, cannot see the
Glory. The text applies to them as well as to all creatures.'
These three views which have to be considered here are taught
with some variants in another source.[95] R. Akiba teaches
there that even the ministering angels are unable to see God.
The view of R. Dosa in the Sifra is here ascribed to Simon
the Yemenite and that of R. Dosa is given in the name of
R. Eleazar, the son of R. Yose the Galilean, with the further
remark that neither the figure nor the place of God can be
seen or ascertained by man in this life. Did these scribes hold
that God has a figure, which can be seen? Was there in their
theology room for a visible God? To answer these questions
one must gather more material garnered in the store-houses of
Jewish theology, religious thought and teaching.

A legend has it that when the High-Priest Simon the Just
on his last Day of Atonement was ministering in the Temple,
his usual companion, a venerable old man, clad and wrapt in
white, entered the Holy of Holies with him, but did not leave
with him. Hence he inferred, and correctly so, that it was his
last year of office.[96] In the circle of R. Abbahu this report
roused some surprise, for it is written that no one shall be in
the Tent of Appointment during the time when the High-
Priest is atoning in the Sanctuary (Lev. xvi. 17). Not even
one of the angels was permitted to stay there at that moment.
R. Abbahu says that surely the venerable old man was not
a human being, but God Himself. R. Abbahu was favourably
inclined to anthropomorphic ideas, as will be proved further
on, yet this answer may have been familiar to the contemporaries of the High-Priest who circulated that legend as well.
There is another High-Priest about whom it is told that he
encountered in that sacred place Akathriel, who is God, if

94 Sifra 3 b. Yalkut Makiri Psalms, p. 154.
95 Sifre Numbers, par. 103.   96 pal. Yoma v. 2.

the text is to be taken literally. R. Ishmael ben Elisha saw
Akathriel sitting on His throne appealing to the High-Priest
that he should bless Him, which he did.[97] The passage gave
rise to vehement attacks on the part of various heretical
writers, which were repelled by scholars of the Geonic age, and
after.[98] The difficulty is not removed by seeing in Akathriel
an angel or the Light of Glory, for the ancient readers saw
in this name God Himself. Besides, the older as well as the
younger Haggadah preserved numerous traces of a religious
conception in which God is spoken of or imagined as a visible
figure. Rabbis in the Middle Ages still adhered to such a presentation of religious teaching.[99] The Midrash depicts the
Hebrews as seeing God as warrior or as a learned scribe [100]
The Hebrews on the Red Sea were able to point at God with
their fingers, 'They beheld His image as a man is able to
look his friend in the face.'[101] Hillel may have taken the
words of Gen. i. 27 literally, when he compared himself, the
man created in God's image, with the eikon or statue made
for the honour of the ruler that is well looked after and carefully preserved.[102] R. Meir follows in the footsteps of this
great teacher in expounding the prohibition not to leave the
hanged man over-night on the tree; for he is bearing the very
image of God, which, as developed at some greater length in
a parable, would lead to blasphemy.[103] These observations
lead to a Barayta that has a close bearing on the subject
under discussion. Five persons, we are taught, were created
מעין דוגמא של מעלה [104], which means 'in the likeness or
image of the Above'. 'Above' signifies the name of God.[105]
What did this saying convey to the reader? It could mean
that Samson in strength and force was almost like God, the
all-powerful and almighty. Saul, Absalom, Zedekiah, and

[97] b. Berakoth 7 a. Barayta Aziluth 76 b. Zunz, *Syn. Poesie*, 474;
Perles, J., *Miscellen*, p. 10, derives the name from the Persian.

[98] v. Geonic Responsa, ed. Lyck, no. 115. Commentary on the Sepher
Yezira by R. Judah Barzeloni, pp. 20-1.

[99] v. the Ketab Tamim of Moses Tachau in Ozar Nehmad iii. pp. 54 ff.

[100] v. above, p. 36.   [101] Mekilta 37 a. Mekilta of R. Simon, p. 60.

[102] v. Lev. r., ch. xxxiv.

[103] b. Sanhedrin 46 b.   [104] b. Sotah 10 a.   [105] v. pt. i, p. 91.

Asa excelled in the beauty of their limbs or figures all their fellow creatures, and were almost similar to God. This teaching sounded so anthropomorphic that it had to go through some important modification. Younger texts read instead of נדמו מעין דוגמא של מעלה the less dangerous phrase נדמו לאדם הראשון. They were like Adam in beauty and physical perfection.[106] It seems that the older expression was altered in order to avoid criticism and objection. According to an old commentary the original expression refers to the heavenly beings who serve before Him, but not to God Himself, who has no figure.[107] Accordingly, the Barayta attempts to show that Samson and the other personages enumerated there reached in beauty and strength respectively a very high degree, surpassing the usual measure of these qualities and bordering on those of the celestials. About God such phantasies are not only impossible but blasphemous. Nevertheless, the original text favours a more literal exposition, in agreement with the conceptions advanced from the available sources.

A literary remnant of this anthropomorphic movement in Palestinian Jewry of the first century is the little booklet circulating under the name of Shiur Komma. Here, anthropomorphism reaches its climax. God is not only spoken of as a man with a figure and limbs, but fantastic measures and numbers are supplied to the reader in order to convey an idea of God's physical greatness. It was rightly pointed out by Dr. Gaster that the Church Father Irenaeus in his book against the Heresies speaks against similar tendencies among contemporary sects,[108] and refutes these mystical tendencies and Gnostic speculations. Yet it was perhaps not only Gnostic Jews or Christians who indulged in such theological teachings.

---

[106] v. Pirke de Rabbenu ha-Kadosh, ed. Grünhut, ch. v. 14, ed. Schönblum, vi. 28, where six names are mentioned. Uzziah is added to the previous list, v. further Pirke of R. Elieser, ch. liii, Tanhuma Deut., ed. Buber, p. 8, Lev. r., ch. xx, and Tanhuma, ibid., where the total is increased by another name.

[107] v. the Yezira-commentary of R. Judah of Barzelona, p. 39.

[108] v. *M.G.W.J.*, xxxvii, vol. 1892, pp. 179 ff., now in his *Texts and Studies*, vol. ii, pp. 1330-34.

The material quoted in this chapter, which could be enlarged, leaves no doubt that there was a school in Judaism, and an important one too, that believed in a God who accompanies man in human form and shape. These mystics, who were far removed in their religious life and thought from any rationalism, were so near to and one with their Maker that they could think of Him as invested with human figure and limbs. The very fact that such a piece of literature survived for centuries in Hebrew is strong evidence for the immense influence that this non-rational theology exercised in the course of Jewish history. Even the opponents of this work, like the Gaon Saadyah,[109] do not deny the antiquity of the book; they merely harp on its pseudo-epigraphic character. Yet the very fact that the story of Akathriel found a place in the Talmud is undisputable evidence that such beliefs must have been widely held during the first centuries of the Current Era. The Shiur Komma was originally a part of the Midrash on the Alpha-betha ascribed to R. Akiba, and not of the Hekaloth, as suggested by Dr. Gaster.[110] The Bohemian writer and scholar Moses of Tachau, at all events, saw in the Shiur Komma a part of R. Akiba's Midrash.[111] Anyhow, the mystics of the Middle Ages must have known something about the origin of this literature, and their tradition coincides remarkably with the observation of the tendency which ruled in the school of R. Akiba. The fiercest opposition against and unmerciful strictures passed on the little book by Karaite, Christian, and Jewish scholars and writers did not prevail to rob it of its popularity in the circles of mystics and saints.[112] It satisfied the craving of man after nearness to and oneness with God, which rationalism and pure wisdom cannot supply and offer.

Aboth of R. Nathan preserved [113] a remarkable piece of

[109] v. Yezira Commentary, loc. cit.

[110] v. loc. cit., p. 1338.

[111] v. Kethab Tamim loc. cit., p. 61.

[112] v. *Cat. Ohel Dawid*, p. 444 and p. 896; further *Orient. Literaturblatt* (1842), 812; *Hatehiyah*, pp. 41–3; *Hammagid*, iv. 46; Responsa Shaare Teshubah, no. 122; Epstein, *Mikadmaniyoth*, p. 120.

[113] Chap. 43, 2nd version, ed. Schechter, p. 120.

disquisition on the subject of the visibility of God. There
are three groups enumerated. The first sees the king and his
countenance, the second can see the king but not his countenance, and the third can see neither. The three different
groups are alluded to in Ps. cxl. 14, Isa. xxx. 20, and Isa. xxx.
21. The first verse is rendered thus: 'Surely the righteous
give thanks to Thy name, they sit beholding Thy countenance', cf. Ps. xi. 7. The Haggadist understood, therefore,
ישרים as 'beholding', and not as 'the upright' shall sit or
dwell before Thy countenance. Further, the second verse,
which means 'and thy teacher shall not be hidden any more',
was expounded as 'and thou wilt not behold, or the countenance of God will not be seen, yet thine eyes shall see thy
teacher, God.' Finally, there is the third set, about which
the continuation says: 'and thy ears shall hear behind thee
saying.' The teachers classify the prophets here in three
groups, according to their standard and degree, and air their
views about the visibility of God. For, it is added, some see
Him in a dream, others in prophetic vision, and the third in
an ordinary vision. Yet there will come a time when God
will 'pour out His spirit on mankind and every one will
prophesy in the name of God', cf. Joel iii. i f. In an Haggadic exaggeration, this Haggadah makes even the animal world
participate in sharing the blessing of the Holy Spirit. For
my purpose it is of importance to establish that the author of
this saying believed in a corporeal visibility of God, in distinction from other Haggadists, who rejected such an idea
entirely, and meant by this term merely a more or less intimate
nearness of the created being to his Creator.

A parallel to this passage can be read in the Midrash on
Psalms [114] where seven groups of pious men are enumerated.
The first of these dwells with the king, and sees the king face
to face. These seven groups enjoy the presence of God after
this life, in Paradise; the groups spoken of in the Aboth of
R. Nathan, however, in their lifetime. Nevertheless, a connexion between the two sources certainly existed.

Such a view, of God's visibility and corporeality, was not

[114] Chap. xi, 6, v. also Yalkut Makiri, ed. Buber, p. 70.

general. It could not prevail. Even if all the traces of
opposition to such a teaching had been obliterated by the more
successful school of the defenders of the letter of the Scriptures, it would be pretty obvious that it was not the only one.
Fortunately enough there is good evidence for the existence
of allegorical teachers who challenged these doctrines. On
Num. xii. 8, there is a remarkable controversy between the
school of R. Ishmael and R. Joshua b. Korha, whom we have
recognized as a representative of the literal way of exegesis.[115]
The former expound the text, 'He spoke to him from mouth
to mouth, and not in riddles, and even the likeness of God was
shown to him', similarly to the exposition of Exod. xxxiii. 23,
that God allowed Moses to see the happiness of the wicked and
the trouble of the righteous in this world, and the reward of the
pious as well as the punishment of the sinners in the world to
come. Such an exegesis is strictly allegorical and has no room
in its theological system for a likeness or figure of God.[116] Not
so the other school. R. Joshua b. Korha interprets the text literally. Moses, he says, did not do the right thing by hiding his
face, he might have seen all that is below and above, the past
and the future. When he finally said, 'Show me Thy glory',
God said to him, 'When I wanted to show thee My countenance
thou didst hide thy face from before Me, now no one shall
see My countenance and live'.[117] Later Amoraic Haggadists
defended the respectful conduct of Moses, and teach that he
was not punished but awarded the privilege of enjoying for
forty days the splendour of the Shekinah.[118]

Another very interesting piece of Haggadah gives us a glimpse
of the theological contests of the schools carried on in the
early years of the second century in Palestine. Simon b. Azzai,
a contemporary of R. Akiba, tells of a great discovery made
by him in Jerusalem. He found there a book entitled Megil-
lath Yuhasin, in which was written: (a) that a certain person,

---

[115] v. above p. 45.   [116] Sifre Numbers, par. 103.

[117] v. Exod. rabba chap. iii, quoted in B. Berakoth 7 b as תנא משום רבי
יהושע בן קרחא

[118] So R. Hoshaya, R. Samuel bar Nahmani in the name of R. Jonathan
ben Elieser, and R. Joshua of Siknin in the name of R. Levi. For the
sources, v. previous note.

whose name is not revealed in our sources, was a bastard, born from a married woman; (b) that the Mishnah of R. Elieser b. Jacob was measured and pure; and (c) that the prophet Isaiah was put to death by King Manasseh.[119] This tradition recurs also in the apocryphal writing called 'The Ascension of Isaiah'.[120] The report that the prophet was cut asunder by a saw whilst hiding in a cedar tree, is given, in Aramaic, in the Talmud as well as in the Apocalypse of Paul, an early Christian literary document.[121] For my purpose the passage is of importance, for the Hebrew part of the story recounts in detail the theological controversy which, it is alleged, took place between king and prophet, and which led to the death of the latter. The king discovered three contradictions between Isaiah and the Pentateuch. Moses said: 'For no man can see Me and live', whilst the prophet proclaims: 'And I saw God sitting on a high and exalted throne'. Secondly, Moses said: 'Who is like the Lord our God everywhere, near where we cry unto Him?' whilst Isaiah says: 'Seek the Lord when He is to be found'. Thirdly, Moses said: 'I will fill the number of thy days'. Isaiah, however, prophesies in the name of God: 'I will add unto thy days fifteen years'. We notice here that the idolatrous king plays the role of the defender of the Mosaic law and religion, whilst the prophet is accused of introducing a reformed or modernistic theology. Furthermore, the king represents the conservative but more spiritual religion against Isaiah, whose conception of God is more material and reactionary. Manasseh adheres to the teaching of Moses that God is permanently near to him who cries unto Him, whenever and wherever the prayer may be delivered, the prophet makes it dependent on time and season. Then there is a second point as to whether God's decrees are changeable or immutable. Finally the question is put: 'Can God be seen or not?' Here a fragment of some disputes which agitated the minds of theologians in the first or the

---

[119] b. Yebamoth 49 b.   [120] v. ed. Charles, chap. iii. 10.

[121] v. Heidenheim, *Vierteljahresschrift*, iv, 171; Hennicke, *Handbuch der Neutestamentlichen Apokryphen*, p. xv; Kautzsch, *Pseudoepigraphen*, p. 172, note c.

second century is recorded in a shortened form. Possibly the members of the Pardes indulged in such discussions. Their views are clad in the words of the Scriptures. The members of the allegorical school merely quoted the words which declare that God cannot be seen, He has no form or image; the opposing school pointed to the literal meaning of the words of Isaiah. Is it possible that the narrator allegorized, in the death of Isaiah, the predicted downfall of his rivals? If he did so, he was right, for ultimately the allegorical method conquered the literal interpretation of the Bible; yet this victory was long delayed, and is by no means won yet. As the next paragraph will show, the literal method of interpretation enjoyed great popularity among the Amoraic Haggadists, and regulated and directed their theological outlook and ideas.

5. I turn now to the Haggadic material in the teachings of the Amoraim on the subject of anthropomorphism, by which their contributions to the development of this doctrine can be illuminated. Although the whole Tannaitic material could not be brought forward in the previous paragraphs under discussion, yet these sufficed to establish the fact that there were two schools, one opposing, and the other defending, the literality of the Biblical text on which their theological outlook depended and their conception of God was based. This division was carried on by the great teachers of the Amoraic period. On the whole, one can say so at the outset, the anthropomorphic trend of mind so warmly defended and propagated by R. Akiba and his followers, gained the upper hand first, and the greater number of teachers adopted his view; whilst only a small minority cherished and dared to propagate allegorical doctrines.

It will be advisable to illustrate this observation first by the teachings of the Amoraim on the creation of the world. R. Simon b. Yehozadak, a teacher of the third century, asked R. Samuel bar Nahmani to explain to him how God created light. He, the questioner, does so, since he had heard that R. Samuel was a Baal Haggadah, i.e. a Haggadist, and such a man is supposed to know about similar subjects. The answer was that God wrapt Himself in a garment of light, and light spread from one end of the world to the other. The information was given in a whisper, as customary with mystic teachers, which surprised the questioner, for the idea is clearly conveyed by the words of the Psalmist (civ. 2). Both teachers must have understood this verse literally.[122] The Psalmist kept alive some ancient myth and the mystic Haggadist took it in its literal meaning. One can easily verify the fact by observing that whilst the writings of the wisdom literature are very poor in anthropomorphic passages, Psalmists and Prophets furnish a great abundance of such material, derived from old mythical reminiscences. The influence of these poetical or mythical figures of speech penetrated into synagogues and schools through these Haggadic teachers.

The cosmological doctrines of the contemporary Haggadah are full of anthropomorphic colour. R. Simon b. Lakish makes God say that the sin-offering brought on the New Moon's day should be an atonement for Him, for He diminished the moon, which was first equal in size and strength with the sun.[123] God said: 'This offering shall be an atonement for Me, because I made the moon smaller'. The same teacher has further another very strange teaching of a similar type. God, he says, required levitical purification through Aaron for His stay in Egypt, in a place of impurity, during the delivery of the Israelites from that land.[124] For, this is the underlying idea of this legend, Israel was delivered neither by the Logos, nor angels, but by God Himself.[125] This teacher

[122] Gen. r. chap. iii, ed. Theodor, p. 19 f., b., Pes. 145 Lev. r. xxxi. 7, and v. also xv. 21 Tanh. בראשית, 10, ויקהל, 7, Midr. Psalms xxvii. 1, civ. 4, Seder El. r., ch. iii. Pes. reads 'in a white stola', איצטלא בנה ?, Tanh. i, p. 6, has R. Nathan, i.e. Jonathan; v., however, Tanh. ii, p. 122, where the right name of the questioner is given. Here, however, the question is not about the creation of light, but as to the creation of the world. In Midr. Psalms xxvi, ed. Buber the saying is by R. Abun ha-Levi; v., however, p. 330, like the other sources.

[123] v. Gen. r. chap. vi, ed. Theodor 42, further b. Hullin 60 b, Shebuoth 9 a, Pirke R. Eliezer chap. li, v. also ch. vi, in the name of R. Zachariah, further Midrash Konen, p. 2.

[124] Exod. r. chap. xv. 6, v. also ibid. xviii. 1, where God appears in the palace of Pharaoh in order to communicate with Moses, v., however, Mekilta, p. 1 a f., God does not reveal Himself outside Palestine.

[125] v. the Geniza fragment of the Passover Haggadah published by I. Abrahams, *J.Q.R.* vol. x, pp. 41 ff.

held the view that the creation was actual work, and not a creation by word. R. Simon b. Judah, in whom one may see an allegorist, teaches that one cannot speak in regard to God in the terms of labour. All the terms of making and creating and so forth have to be taken allegorically. God spoke, and through His Logos everything came into being. Toil and fatigue have no meaning in speaking of God.[126] Not so R. Simon b. Lakish, who emphatically asserts that the world was created by toil and work.[127] Another anthropomorphist connects with this lore an ethical doctrine. The righteous, who contribute by their piety and good deeds to the preservation of the world, will be rewarded for supporting and keeping alive God's work; the wicked, however, will be chastised for destroying God's creation by their misdeeds.[128]

The position taken by R. Simon b. Lakish in the matter of anthropomorphism was fully shared by the leading teacher of this age, the head of the school of Tiberias, R. Yochanan b. Nappacha. This is the more significant, since these two teachers could not see eye to eye with one another in most of the Halachic and Haggadic questions that agitated their minds. By this time, one can assume, the anthropomorphic view held the upper hand in the school of Tiberias. R. Yochanan, whom one copyist credited with the doctrine of the Logos,[129] is reported in another source as having depicted the creation of the world in a real anthropomorphic way. He makes God take two balls (פקועות), one of which was of fire, and the other of snow, then He mixed them up together, and out of them the world was created. R. Hama b. Hanina teaches that God took four such balls with which He created the world.[130] Such cosmological

---

[126] v. Gen. r. chap. iii, chap. x, ed. Theodor, pp. 19 and 85 f. based on Ps. xxxiii. 6, further on Isa. lxvi. 2, chap. xii, ed. Theodor, p. 99, further ch. xii, ed. Theodor, p. 108, the teaching is ascribed to R. Yochanan, taught by R. Abbahu, most probably, wrongly.

[127] v. Tanhuma i, ed. Buber, p. 7.

[128] R. Yose bar Nahorai, R. Levi in his name, chap. x, ed. Theodor, p. 86, speaking of ידי קוניהם ממשמשות, v. however, R. Aha ibid., chap. viii, p. 37.

[129] v. above, note 126.

[130] Gen. r. chap. x, ed. Theodor, p. 75, b. Hagiga 12 a, has a similar teaching in the name of Rab, R. Abba bar Kahana records this teaching of Rab in Gen. r. chap. iv., p. 31.

theories cannot be reconciled with the teachings of the earlier or later allegorical views. It would be useful to discover how and why the ancient, by then long discarded, pre-Socratic cosmological philosophies crept into Jewish theology in the third century. That such was the case can be gathered from several instances. R. Abbahu, a pupil of R. Yohanan, who lived in Caesarea, a Greek city, taught that God experimented and created several worlds till this world seemed the best and most fitting in His eyes.[131] Such a view could not be harmonized with the teaching of a world created by the Logos. Ancient Jewish apologetic dialogues show that the doctrine of the Logos was disputed by pagan inquirers.[132]

The creation of the world was a favourite topic in the early dialogues between the scribes and their heathen interlocutors. Thus R. Gamaliel and a philosopher,[133] Hadrian and R. Joshua b. Hananyah,[134] a Roman matron and R. Yose b. R. Halafta,[135] exchanged words on this subject. Now our sources report that R. Joshua b. Hananyah replied to Hadrian with the theory expounded in the third century by R. Hama b. Hanina, which proves the earlier date of this teaching. R. Joshua b. Hananyah, as we know from several indications,[136] was well versed in Greek philosophy and literature, may have adopted and adapted the theories of the early Greek natural philosophy and planted it in Jewish soil. This accounts also for the attention given in the Haggadic controversies between this teacher and

[131] v. Gen. r. chap. iii. 9. Exod. r. 30. 2 Eccles. z. 37. Eccles. r. iii. 13.
[132] v. f. i, R. Meir and the Samaritan, Gen. r. ch. iv, 3, ed. Theodor, p. 27. As to the doctrine of the Logos in Rabbinic theology, v. Mekilta 31 b, 32 b. 43 b. Sifre Deut. par. 330, Aboth v, 1, R. Yohanan b. Zakkai, Pirke R. Elieser, ch. xlviii, Simon b. Zoma, Gen. r. ch. iv, 7, ed. Theodor, p. 30, pal. Hagiga 71 c, further ii Baruch, xiv, 18, God can do everything by His word, cf. Gen. r., ch. 28, 2, ed. Theodor, p. 261, Tanhuma Gen. ed. Buber, p. 25. Agadath Bereshith, ed. Buber, p. 2, Yelamdenu Genesis, ed. Grünhut, p. 18 b, Deut. r. v. 13. Finally it penetrated into the Jewish-Aramaic magic incantations, v. ed. Montgomery, p. 121.
[133] v. Gen. r. ch. i, ed. Theodor, p. 8, v. Graetz, Gnosticismus u. Judenthum, p. 33.
[134] v. Gen. r. ch. x, ed. Theodor, p. 75.
[135] v. Tanhuma 1, ed. Buber, p. 2.
[136] v. Marmorstein, R. Josue b. Hananiah et la sagesse grecque, in R.É.J. 87, 1929, pp. 200 ff.

his opponent, R. Elieser b. Hyrkanos, to cosmological and cos-
mogonic questions. Thus the dispute about the origin of the
material with which the celestial and earthly things were
created by God[137] betrays foreign influence. There is some
evidence also in Philo for this assertion.

The divergence of these two schools found expression in the
different divine names used by them. The teachers who taught
that the world was created by the use of the *word* or *logos*
coined the name 'He who spake and the world was created'
(מי שאמר והיה העולם) for God, whilst the literalists speak of
בורא or יוצר, i.e. Creator or Former of the world.[138] To this
school belonged the anonymous preacher who developed his
theory on the text of Eccles. iv. 8. *There is One*, that is the Holy
One blessed be He. *There is no other*, for He has no mate, nor
partner. *He has neither son, nor brother.* Since there is no companion to Him, how could He have a son ? It means that the
Israelites are called His children and brothers out of love. *His
trouble is endless.* This signifies the great trouble taken by Him
in the creation of the world during the six days of creation.
For whom do I toil and deprive Myself?—asks God. Is it not
that Israel shall cleave unto my ways ? This means that if the
pious are not zealous in the diligent performance of the commandments and good deeds, is the trouble and toil of the
creation not in vain ? [139] Another example of the theological
teaching of this school is to be found in an exposition on
Ps. civ. 16. 'The cedars of the Lebanon which He planted.'
These cedars were like grasshoppers. God took them, tore them
up, and planted them in the Garden of Eden ; that is why they
are called the Trees of God.[140]

These strange theological teachings are in great contrast to
the teaching that God created both worlds by pronouncing two
letters. God says to His creatures: 'Know in whom ye put your
trust; in Him who created both worlds with two letters.' The
teaching is derived from Isa. xxvi. 4 כי ביה צור עולמים, which

---

[137] v. Gen. r. ch. xii, ed. Theodor, p. 109, b. Yoma 54 b, Eccles. r. iii, 20,
Eccl. zutta, p. 99.

[138] v. pt. i, pp. 74–76, 86–87, and p. 89.   [139] Eccles. r. iv. 8.

[140] Gen. r. ch. xv, ed. Theodor, p. 135.

means through the letters י and ה did He create the worlds. With the letter ה this world, and with the letter י the world to come. The ה indicated that there was neither toil nor labour in the divine creation, but simply the application of the Logos, cf. Ps. xxxiii. 6.[141] This teaching is taught by R. Abbahu in the name of R. Yochanan. Such a tradition is most surprising and contradicts all that we know about these two teachers, master as well as pupil. In one Haggadah R. Yochanan, as we have shown before, depicts God as creating the world by stretching out two balls, and here he speaks of God as creating the world by the Logos. Apart from this saying, there are others to be found in Rabbinic literature which credit him with anthropomorphic utterances. Similarly R. Abbahu can safely be placed among the sages who favour similar physical teachings regarding corporeal actions of God? Two examples will suffice to demonstrate their attitude towards our problem. R. Yochanan as well as R. Abbahu uses the term אילמלי מקרא שכתוב אי אפשר לאמרו (if it had not been written in the text, one could not say such a word). This, as will be shown in these essays, is a typical expression of those who not only take anthropomorphic expressions literally, but, moreover, strengthen the anthropomorphic meaning of them. Thus, when R. Abbahu declares on the strength of Exod. xxxii, ' Moses took hold of God just as a man of his fellowman by his coat, and said to Him : " Lord of the Whole Universe, I will not leave Thee alone till Thou wilt pardon the sin of Israel ".' [142] Similarly R. Yochanan depicts God standing before Moses wrapt in a praying-shawl and teaching him the order of prayers and supplication.[143] These anthropomorphic sayings shared, after centuries, the fate of the Bible. Just as the allegorists turned the accounts of the Scriptures into allegories, so the teachings of the literalists, by a strange irony, were understood and expounded allegorically. Yet there arose some mystics and sages who opposed such treatment of the Haggadah, and insisted on strict literality. It is, at any rate,

[141] v. Midrash Psalms ch. lxii, 1, ed. Buber, p. 307, without these names of teacher and pupil, pal. Hagiga 16 c. Gen r. ch. xii. 10, Pes. r. ch. xxi, p. 109 b. Menahoth 29 b. Tanhuma gen. ed. Buber, p. 11.
[142] b. Berakoth 32 a.   [143] b. Rosh Hashanah 17 b.

very quaint that these teachers should be enumerated among the allegorists, or opponents of the literal way of interpretation.

6. It seems that the friends of the anthropomorphic interpretation of the doctrine of God prevailed and held the upper hand over the allegoristic preachers. Yet there can be detected survivals of the once strong and influential school of R. Ishmael and his followers. Historical changes and fluctuations in thought may have weakened or counteracted these teachings, but there remained influential preachers who propagated and perpetuated this aspect of religious thought. The teacher who unearthed the older idea of Logos, creation by the Word, is one instance. Another preacher to be mentioned here is R. Isaac Nappacha, who flourished in the second half of the third century, contemporaneously with the majority of the Haggadists referred to in the previous paragraph. Several of his Haggadic sayings leave no doubt that he was strongly opposed to the literal understanding of the Bible and disliked any sign of religious instruction which might lead to a material or physical conception of the Godhead. To begin with, there is his explanation of the figure of speech פנים אל פנים, which represents God as speaking to Moses 'face to face'. It was meant in an allegorical sense. R. Isaac's rendering is preserved in two versions. According to the first it means to say, 'I and thou', says God to Moses, 'we, both can clarify the Halakah'. According to the other way of exegesis God said to Moses: 'Treat Israel in the same friendly manner as I treated thee.' Face to face, therefore, means: 'show them the same friendliness or encouragement', this is the allegorical sense of the word פנים, 'which I have shown thee'.[144] There have been Haggadists who took this term quite literally, against whom this exposition is directed. A further proof for the allegorical tendency of this Haggadist can be brought forward from his teaching based on 1 Chron. xxix. 23: 'And Solomon sat on the throne of God'. The very question raised in this connexion betrays the terminology of the allegoristic teachers. How can a mortal sit on God's throne? God is a consuming fire, cf. Deut. iv. 24. Surely, this must not be taken literally. It means that just as God's kingdom extends from

[144] Berakhoth 63 b.

one end of the world to the other, or is limitless, so will the rule of Solomon be on earth.[145] Furthermore, there is another similarity between Solomon's judgment and that of God. Before God's seat of judgment, man is tried without witnesses and previous warning; the same will occur before Solomon. In some parallels of this Haggadah, many more resemblances are elaborated, which need not be given here, since these two suffice to show the allegorical method of this teacher. A third allegorical Haggadah by our teacher combines a long list of anthropomorphic passages with an allegorical interpretation. These verses speak of God as speaking, sitting, walking, dwelling, laying bare His arm, and being fearful and awful. R. Isaac collects several passages bearing on these topics, and adds that all these actions are not to be taken in their literal sense, but allegorically. God's actions are meant in 'holiness'. With great ingenuity he discovers that wherever these anthropomorphic deeds are spoken of, the text always adds some qualification of 'holiness'. This served to indicate that God's actions are not like those of an ordinary human being.[146] R. Isaac pursued some homiletical aim in compiling this long catalogue of anthropomorphic passages that are always combined with some adjective or appellative of holiness. This indicates their allegorical value or bearing.

Here attention must be paid to some teachings recorded in the Talmud [147] under the name of this teacher by R. Abun b. R. Ada which apparently contradict the result arrived at through the material brought forward in the previous lines. The first sentence does not cause much trouble, since there appears no reason why an allegorist should not indulge in such teaching. The question raised is put in this way: Whence do we derive the idea that God is present, or to be found, in the synagogues?

[145] Cant. r. i, i, 10, v. also Midrash Psalms, ed. Buber, p. 324, Exod. r. xv, 26, anonymous, with further parallels.

[146] The Scriptural references are: (I) God speaking in Ps. ch. v. 5; (II) God walks, cf. ibid., lxviii. 25; (III) God lays bare His arm, Isa. iii. 10; (IV) God sits on His holy throne, cf. Ps. xlvii. 9; and (V) His might, Exod. xv. 11. The sermon is quoted in pal. Berakoth ix. 1, Midrash Psalms, ed. Buber, p. 27, Tanhuma iii, ed. Buber, p. 73; the names of the Haggadists vary in the various sources.

[147] b. Berakoth 6 a.

He saw the Scriptural basis for this belief in Ps. lxxxii. 2,
where it is said that God stands in the assembly of the godly.
It may be that here an earlier Tannaitic view found its elabora-
tion. R. Halafta b. Dosa of Kefr Hananyah taught that where-
ever ten persons are gathered and are occupied with the study
of the Torah, there the Shekinah is present.[148] The presence of
the Shekinah need not be understood or expounded in an
anthropomorphic sense. The Shekinah is present with five, or
three, or two men, or even with one when devoting time and
energy to the Torah. The idea was known in the first century
outside the Rabbinic schools as well. A witty pagan sought to
catch Rabban Gamaliel by asking him: 'How many Godheads
does Judaism recognize, since, according to this teaching, there
must be quite a number of them?'[149] The writers of the Gospel
were familiar with this Haggadah.[150] The question, therefore,
was not a challenge or doubt of God's omnipresence, as in the
case of the pagan interlocutor of R. Gamaliel, but to encourage
the visitors of the synagogues by showing that God is always
ready to accept the entreaties of the worshippers.

It seems more difficult to reconcile or adjust the second sentence recorded in this connexion with R. Isaac's recognized
religious point of view. In this passage, the question about the
phylacteries worn by God and their contents is discussed at
some length. The gross anthropomorphism was averted by some
of the earliest commentators of the Talmud by an allegorical
revaluation of the question and answer, which by no means
deterred later scholars, heirs to the literalistic conception,
from defending the letter of this Haggadah. However that may
be, the text, as it stands, does not condemn those who are inclined to support a literalist exegesis of the teaching. Of course
a rationalist will never be able to descend to the depth of such
a feeling, or ascend to the height of such a vision, of which
only a mystic thinker is capable. At this point the contradiction
in the Haggadah of R. Isaac is to be explained. The fact is that
R. Rabbinowitz, the compiler of the Dikduke Soferim, noticed
that the tradition of the names of the teachers is troublesome.

---

[148] Aboth, ch. iii. 7, Mekilta 73 b.   v. also Aboth iii. 4.
[149] b. Sanhedrin 39 b.   [150] v. Matt. xviii, 20.

The editions point to Rabbi Isaac, whilst the manuscript has Rab
Isaac. The first reading is, however, erroneous, as proved there.[151]
The teaching cannot belong to the Palestinian R. Isaac, but the
Babylonian teacher has to be credited with this Haggadah. This
conclusion is now confirmed by the observations made in the
course of the investigation of R. Isaac Nappacha's Haggadah.

This Haggadah was often misinterpreted by Christian as
well as by Jewish scholars. This is not astonishing, since it
was never examined in its proper context and light. It belongs to a whole complex of ideas and teachings without which
the sentences cannot mean anything. The homilies which
the preachers intended to convey to their hearers and pupils
were delivered in order to answer such questions as: 'Does
your God observe the commandments.' This was an often repeated slogan in the spiritual fight of the Church against the
Law? Secondly, the more philosophic heathen, especially the
Stoic sage, asked the rabbis, what is God doing? A God who
finished the work of the creation and removed into idleness has,
according to the ruling philosophy of the age, no reason for
existence at all. Thirdly, God was thought to be an ideal to be
followed by man. Hence developed the teaching that what God
commands us to do He observes and fulfils, unlike a human king
who does the reverse, in making laws for others that are not
binding on himself. These principles guide the investigator to
understand some quaint sayings and their background.

I turn first of all to the teaching that God is a student of
the law. It is an extraordinary notion to depict or imagine,
that God is studying or teaching the Torah, like a teacher or
a student. One is justified in inquiring how such a teaching
crept into Jewish theology, and how it could find favour in the
synagogues and schools. It is, of course, quite natural that
scholars and students should exalt their occupation as divine
and worthy of God Himself. This presupposes that such conceptions were taken literally, and not allegorically. Allegorically they mean nothing. Rab,[152] the leading teacher of the
Babylonian schools in the first half of the third century, makes

[151] Variae Lectiones, Berakoth, p. 18.
[152] b. Aboda Zara 3 b.

F

for us a time-table of God's daily occupation. God's day is
divided into study of the Torah, judgment of the world, the
feeding of all the creatures from the biggest to the smallest,
and finally the last part is devoted to play with the Leviathan.
A somewhat later teacher expresses the opinion that since the
destruction of the Temple there are only the 'four cubits of
the Halakah left to God'. This is the teaching of R. Hiyya bar
Abba.[153] R. Berekyah preserved the teaching of R. Judah b.
Ezekiel that there is no day without a new teaching produced
by God in His heavenly Beth Hamidrash.[154] There is no end
to the remarks and views about God's role as teacher in the
eschatology of the Amoraic period.[155] All these endeavours of
the Amoraim to portray God as learning and teaching can be
understood as replies to the questions raised about the value
of the Torah on the one side, and the inquiry about God's occupation on the other side.

For the question whether God observes the Law was often
repeated and seriously meant. Justin Martyr quite bewilders
his poor Jewish interlocutor, Tryphon, with this ingenious
question. It cannot be accidental that, somewhat earlier, a
Min asked a similar question in a Roman synagogue of scribes
who visited Rome and preached in one of the numerous synagogues in that city. The scribes were R. Gamaliel, R. Eleasar
b. Azaryah, R. Joshua b. Hananyah. The subject of their speeches
was characteristically enough the theme of the nature of God and
the nature of man. Man decrees laws and demands of others that
they should carry them out, he himself, however, does not keep
them. God decrees and He is the first to discharge the duties
imposed upon others.[156] That this was a live subject can easily
be imagined if we recall the spiritual and religious cross-currents
among the Jews of Rome about the end of the first and beginning of the second century, which necessitated a visit from the
leading scribes of Judea. The subject must have touched one
of the sore points of Jewish contemporary life, namely, the
attitude to the Law. It is certain that the sermon preached in

---

[153] b. Berakoth 8 a.   [154] Gen. r. lxiv. 4, ed. Theodor, p. 104.
[155] Seder El. r. ed. Friedmann, p. 4; Finn, *Heassif* (1884), 99.
[156] Exod. r. xxx. 1.

the metropolis of Rome was by no means purely academic, but of practical guidance to the assembled Jews. M. Joel[157] thinks that this—and this applies to many other passages of a similar nature and form—was designed to impress the hearer with the absolute value and the permanent duration of the observances. The observances are not only prescribed by God to man, but kept in the first instance by Himself. The due distance between God and man, says Joel, should not be overlooked. His words are: 'Sie sind nicht nur ein Weg, den Gott dem Menschen zugeschrieben, sondern den er unter schicklicher Berücksichtigung des Abstandes zwischen Gott und Menschen auch von Gott selbst eingehalten glaubt'. The topic was even of greater relevance than is assumed by Joel. The question was again and again asked of Christian apologists and Jewish sages, What is God doing after having finished the work of creation?[158] The reply was that God observes the law, just as the teachers, for the very same reason, were eager to propagate the teaching that the patriarchs kept the minutest particulars of the Law.[159]

The problem, which agitated the minds of the Roman Jews in the first century, was alive among the Galilean Jews of the third century, and called for solution. R. Eleasar b. Pedath shaped the teaching in this form: 'Usually, an earthly king after issuing a decree, either keeps it himself, or insists that it shall be obeyed by others. God is quite different. Whenever He issues a statute, He is always the first to observe it.' The Scriptural evidence is somewhat complicated. It is based on Lev. xix. 32, 'thou shalt rise up from before the hoary head, and honour the face of the old man, and fear the Lord'. God was the first to discharge this duty when He rose before Abraham.[160] This Haggadist must have been aware of the older

---

[157] *Blicke in die Religionsgeschichte*. Breslau, 1880, ii, p. 172.

[158] v. the question of King Ptolemy in Rome, Gen. r. ch. vi, v. also Mekilta, p. 104 b, 'God is heating the hell for the wicked'. An unbeliever, Min, mockingly says to R. Gamaliel II: 'I do know what your God is doing at present', v. b. Sanhedrin 39 a, a Roman Matron asks R. Jose b. Halafta the same question, and receives a jocular reply, v. Tanhuma, Num. ed. Buber. Gen. r. ch. lxviii. 4, Num. r. iii. 6, xxii. 8, Midr. Samuel, ed. Buber, ch. v, Pesikta 11 b, Lev. r. viii.

[159] v. Marmorstein, 'Quelques problèmes de l'apologétique juive', *R.É.J.* 68, 1914, 161 ff. [160] Lev. r. xxxv. 3.

tradition, although this is, in our sources, reported by a contemporary teacher, R. Levi,[161] that God stood as a sign of honour before the patriarch.[162] In another source the same teaching is ascribed to R. Simon. Significantly, it is introduced by three Greek words βασιλεύς, νόμος, ἄγραφος, and based on the verse ושמרו את משמרתי, reading, 'I the Lord observe my ordinances first'.[163] A third Haggadist bases this doctrine on Ps. xii. 7, ' God's words are pure, not so those of a mortal which are not pure ', i.e. are unreliable, because he is often unable to keep his promise, or carry out his plan. God, however, who is everlasting and almighty, is always true to his word.[164] An anonymous preacher uses this argument, 'a king orders and does not do what he decrees', in a diatribic speech of God to Moses, when He commanded him to erect the Tabernacle,[165] implying the idea that God's deeds are different altogether. In later Rabbinic homiletics, when the custom spread of introducing a sermon by more or less elaborate eulogies of God, the term ' He decrees and He fulfils' became a standing feature of the Haggadah.[166] In brief, one may deduce from these sayings and the emphasis laid on the doctrine that God not only decrees but also observes His laws, that they are due to apologetic motives, which in Jewish theology as well as in that of the Church influenced the history and the development of doctrine. That this is not the only anthropomorphic doctrine developed by the Rabbis under the influence of apologetic tendencies will be demonstrated in the next paragraph.

7. Students of the Haggadah are often faced by a peculiar type of utterances, that ascribe human actions to God and invest Him with human feelings, in which expressions of anthropopathism are attributed to Him. This can be observed already in the Tannaitic Haggadah. R. Elieser b. Hyrkanos depicts God sitting, roaring like a lion in His pain over the destruc-

---

[161] Gen. r. xlviii. 7, and parallels, ed. Theodor, p. 482.

[162] v. Gen. xviii. 1.

[163] pal. Rosh-Hashana 57 a b, cf. S. Brann, *Orient. Literaturblatt*, 1847, col. 330.

[164] v. Pesikta, ed. Buber, p. 30 a b and parallels.

[165] Exod. r. xl. 2.

[166] v. Pesikta rabbati, ed. Friedmann, p. 57 a, Tanhuma, f. 74.

tion of the Temple. It is certain that without the Scriptural support of Jer. xxv. 30 this teacher would not have made such a daring, anthropomorphic statement. 'The Lord roars from High, from His holy habitation does He give His voice.' He is roaring on account of the loss of His habitation.[167] In comparing God to a lion, the teacher of Lydda was guided by the often praised simile of the prophet Amos.[168] Yet a Barayta speaks without restraint of God weeping on account of the fate of three men, and He is supposed to do so daily. These three unhappy beings are: (a) a scholar, who has an opportunity of studying the Torah and neglects it; (b) a scholar, who has no leisure for study, and in spite of it devotes his time to learning; and (c) a *parnas*, a communal leader, who is overbearing or proud towards the members of the community.[169] Such an expression found its critics among the Amoraim, who asked: 'Is there weeping before God? Can one use such a word about God?' Yes, they taught, there is such a thing before the Godhead. God mourns and weeps over the loss of His Sanctuary. Here again the later Rabbis followed the lead of earlier teachers. Thus Rab elaborates the earlier Haggadah of R. Elieser b. Hyrkanos.[170] Further, commenting on Jer. xiii. 17, 'I shall weep in secret owing to your pride', R. Samuel b. Inia reports in the name of Rab that there is a place called מסתרים, where God weeps, but it is not in secret. R. Samuel b. Isaac explains the phrase מפני גאוה as meaning 'because the pride of the Jewish people is taken away from them, and given to the nations of the world'. A third Samuel, namely b. Nahmani, renders the teaching somewhat differently. God is weeping because the pride or glory of the Kingdom of Heaven is crushed.[171] The destruction of the Temple, an event never to be forgotten, appeared to earlier and later witnesses as causing weeping in heaven. In other words: as we saw that there is rejoicing in heaven, so there is weeping and mourning before God.[172] Both are connected with the rise and the decline in the fortunes of the Jewish people. None of these teachers, therefore, could take

---

[167] b. Berakoth 3 a.   [168] Am. iii. 8.
[169] b. Hagiga 5 b, cf. Pirke Rabbenu ha-Kadosh, ed. Schönblum iii, 6.
[170] b. Ber. 3 a.   [171] b. Hagiga 5 b.   [172] v. above pp. 43–4.

exception to the idea of God weeping, although Rab disliked
to hear of God weeping in secret, because it contradicted the
doctrine of God's omnipresence.

Further, one can make the observation that the Rabbis do
not mind speaking of God as being in trouble or pain, thinking
of Him as sharing His people's distress and exile. R. Meir, in
the second century, translates Deut. xxxii. 18, 'and thou hast forgotten God מחללך', not 'who hath formed thee', but, based
on Ps. xlviii. 7, 'who shares thy suffering and thy distress'.[173]
There is further a very old exposition on Esther vi. 1 referring
the text to God, presupposing the identification of the word
המלך in the Scroll of Esther with God. The king's sleep was
disturbed. The throne of heaven was terribly shaken, for He
saw the awful distress of Israel. How can there be sleep before
the Omnipresent? asked the orator. Does it not say, Ps. cxxi. 4,
'behold the guardian of Israel slumbereth not and sleepeth
not'? The text means that when God beholds Israel's trouble,
and the nations of the world all in comfort, then it appears as
if God must be fast asleep. This is what the Psalmist exclaims,
Ps. xliv. 24, 'awake, O God, why sleepest Thou?'[174] Besides
the verses just quoted from the Book of Psalms, there was a
third one, Ps. lxxviii. 65 'and God awoke as from sleep', which
gave rise to serious consideration. The answer is given anonymously, but may be traced back to R. Elieser b. Hyrkanos, who
favours such distinctions. God sleeps when Israel is neglecting
the divine ordinances, and is awake when the Law is faithfully
carried out.[175] Another attempt to avert the strong anthropomorphic feeling of this passage advanced the theory that
God masters sleep, but sleep has no mastery over Him.[176]
When Israel is in trouble, God seems to be asleep. The intimate connexion that is supposed to have existed between God
and Israel and which lived in the minds of the Jewish teachers,
induced them to preach the strange anthropopathic doctrine

[173] Midrash Tannaim, ed. Hoffmann, p. 195.
[174] Midrash Esther r. x, 1., v. also b. Sotah 48 b, in the name of Rabbahu,
yet the use of the divine name Makom suggests Tannaitic origin.
[175] Mekilta, p. 39 a.
[176] Ibid., p. 68 a, cf. p. 95 a, and above p. 24.

that God weeps or mourns. This view alone, however, would not have sufficiently emphasized the grief and distress felt by God at the tragic fate of the Jewish people. Another, weightier, cause must be sought to explain this strange doctrine.

R. Akiba, the great religious teacher and the immortal national martyr of the Jewish people, is credited with the teaching that the Exodus of the Hebrew slaves from Egypt meant much more than the freeing of serfs from bondage. It signified the release of God Himself, if one may say such a thing of God. The teaching goes back to Ps. xci. 15. God was in servitude and bondage during the whole time that His children were subjugated by the taskmasters of Pharaoh.[177] This teaching was further extended by adding that not only in Egypt, but wherever His people were exiled and persecuted the Shekinah, the Divine Presence, or God Himself, is with them. This was the case with the exiles of Egypt, of Babylonia, of Elam, and of Edom. This teaching of R. Akiba was not original, and is merely a reiteration of the words of his teacher R. Joshua b. Hananyah, who taught: 'Come and see God's boundless love and gracious protection that He granted to His people, Israel. His Shekinah went down with them to Egypt, was with them at the crossing of the Red Sea, He accompanied them during their journey through the desert, and brought them to His Sanctuary. God is with Israel everywhere and under all circumstances, in their good fortune as well as in their misfortune.'[178] These eye-witnesses of the Destruction of the Second Temple felt what the dreamers of a speedy Restoration of the Temple did, who comforted their contemporaries and fellow sufferers with the belief in the immutable presence of their God.

Successive generations of teachers often repeated these words, and with them dispelled the people's despair and raised their hope and trust in God. Such an action was especially called for since Christian teachers renewed and reiterated the old defamation of the Jewish nation, first broadcast by pagan

---

[177] v. Mekilta, p. 17 a, the Scriptural proofs are: Isa. ii. 27, Isa. xliii. 14, Jer. xlix. 39, and Isa. lxiii. 1,

[178] Mekilta of R. Simon b. Yohai, p. 1 f., cf. Gen. xlvi. 4, Exod. xiv. 19.

writers and orators. *God has forsaken the people of Israel!
He is no more dwelling in their midst.* This was manifested by
the Exile of Israel, the defeat of the Jews on the battlefields
of Galilee and Judea, the downfall of the City of Jerusalem,
and last but not least the Destruction of the Temple in
Zion. Such a proof appeared conclusive to the mind of
Greeks and Romans, whose religious ideas and conceptions
accepted these reasonings. A defeated and destroyed people
or land is forsaken by the gods. The gods become either too
weak to protect their worshippers any longer, or they themselves are perishing and broken. One or the other of these
two causes must be operating in the case of the Jews. The
new Christian community coming from the heathen varied, or
had to change, this teaching into a defamation of the Jews, proclaiming that God had abandoned and forsaken the Jews, whose
share and position was taken by the new nation, the true Israel,
the real people of God, the Church of Christ. The Christian
anti-Jewish campaign against God's people was even more
intensive and not less poisonous than that of the gutter-press
of Alexandria or Caesarea, and the results even more harmful
than the attacks of the philosophic adherents of the decaying
Greco- Roman religion and civilization. The tragedy of Jewish
history is up to this very day a cry for defamation—and an
appeal for persecution. R. Joshua b. Hananyah frequently
defended Israel and the Torah against calumnies and misrepresentations on the part of many critics and hostile interlocutors,
among whom is to be counted one who tried to demonstrate
forcibly by mimicry the doctrine of Israel's rejection by God.
It may therefore reasonably be assumed that such a statement
as that of R. Joshua was intended to emphasize the truth that
God is and will remain for ever in the community of Israel.
The scattered and down-trodden nation is still God's people.
That this polemical attitude against the unfortunate victims
of Imperial Rome did not weaken when the Church became
consolidated and assumed the legacy of the Greco-Roman
world, thereby christening the anti-Jewish weapons, can be
attested from numberless utterances of Church Fathers and
preachers of the first four centuries. They initiated through-

out the whole world a pernicious campaign against the race that had produced their Saviour and their literature. No wonder that the teachers of Judaism could not remain silent, but used every available means of defence and justification. Many generations sighed under the unbearable burden of these cruel accusations, losing courage and self-respect in face of these irreligious allegations, which, mingled with fanatic hatred, tried to rob the Jew of his religion, his future and his past, blot out all he held divine and precious in life and death. The enemies could not overcome and destroy Israel's love of God and God's love for Israel. Israel was not forsaken by God. The gigantic task of these Jewish teachers was to keep alive Israel's attachment to God. The history of this attack and defence is not yet written, and requires a monograph of its own. Yet the very attacks enable us to understand and grasp the deeper value and real meaning of sayings that attribute to God such feelings and ascribe to Him such actions, as grief and exile, as shown above.

The passages cited are not the only ones which emphasize this teaching. The Sifre, like the Mekilta, repeats the same idea. The Shekinah suffers, when Israel is in trouble.[179]

R. Abbahu, a native of Caesarea, where not long before him the Church Father Origen lived and taught, preached a most remarkable sermon: 'Whenever salvation is granted to the Jews, this means simultaneously the salvation of the Holy One, blessed be He'. The idea is based on Ps. xci. 15–16: 'With him am I in distress', says God; 'And I will share with Him my salvation', says Israel. R. Abbahu expresses the fervent prayer of his contemporaries and fellow sufferers in these beautiful, although quaint words: 'Lord of the Universe, Thou hast said with him am I in distress. Be saved, by hearkening to my supplication for redemption, come to Thine own salvation.'[180] One cannot miss the strong anxiety felt by this teacher for the existence and continuity of his people as a religious community, in the presence of the wild and dangerous tempest raging around him. There is a second Haggadah, which justifies the inference that this topic played a not

[179] Sifre Num 84.   [180] Midrash Tanhuma, iii, ed. Buber, p. 71.

unimportant part in the theology of this teacher in Caesarea.
He proclaimed that this idea of Israel's salvation being simultaneously the salvation of God, is taught in many passages of
the Scriptures.[181] Ps. ix. 15 'I will rejoice in Thy salvation',
is one of them, Isa. ii. 1 'I rejoiced in Thy salvation', is
another. Altogether, there are five of these verses. A third
verse is Ps. xiii. 6, 'My heart shall rejoice in Thy salvation'.
The remaining two are Ps. lxxx. 3, and Ps. xci. 16. The two
last verses combine the conception of God sharing Israel's
distress and future salvation. One depends on the other. The
present is a sign for the future, as well as a witness for the
past relation between God and Israel. The ages refute that
cruel doctrine of God having forsaken His people.

The combining of God's exile with the fate of Israel on
the one side, and the salvation of both on the other side, based
on Ps. xci. 15, was also a strong point in the Haggadah of
R. Simon b. Lakish, who was likewise not averse from anthropomorphic ideas. According to a legend used by this teacher,
God said when the enemies forced their way into the Sanctuary,
that He must share the servitude of Israel. This secret was
revealed to Daniel. 'And thou wilt arise at the end of the
days.'[182] Daniel asked: 'At which end?' God: 'At the period
of judgment and trial.' Daniel: 'And wilt Thou rest?' God:
'Rest for the world.' Daniel: 'Thou wilt rise: with whom?
With the righteous or with the wicked?' God: 'With the
righteous.' Daniel: 'When?' God: 'At the end of the right.'
It does not say לקץ הימים meaning 'the end of the days', but,
לקץ הימין 'at the end of the right'. 'My right hand', says God,
'is in servitude, as long as my children are subjugated by the
nations of the world, I share their trouble and suffering.
When they are redeemed, my right hand will be freed.' This
idea was also found expressed in the words of the Psalmist
(lx. 7): 'In order to save thy friends strengthen or help Thy

---

[181] Midrash Psalms, ed. Buber, p. 89, and p. 111, Tanh. iii, ed. Buber,
p. 71, v. Yalkut Makiri Psalms, p. 304, Exod. r. ch. xxx, Lev. r. ch. xxxix,
cf. *Monatsschrift* (1887), 179, the interpretation given there is an historical
document for the mentality of German Jews at the end of the last century,
but not of those of the third century in Palestine.

[182] Dan. xii. 13.

right hand.'[183] It is quite likely that R. Abbahu and R. Simon b. Lakish only developed teaching which was widespread much earlier.

The danger was felt most poignantly in Caesarea and other Greek-speaking cities with large Jewish populations. The struggle was a permanent and intensive one. No wonder that the teachers of Judaism saw in the fate of their religious community the distress or the salvation of their God. A teacher who lived somewhat later and may have survived the Christianization of the Imperium Romanum by Constantine the Great and his bishops, and shared the great dream of a restoration of the Jewish people under Julian the Apostate, R. Berekyah, addresses his audience with the words of the Prophet Zacharia (ix. 9): 'Rejoice, O daughter of Zion, for the Righteous is approaching, and He will be saved.' The text does not say 'and He will save thee', but 'and He will be saved'.[184] Likewise in Isa. lxii. 11 it is indicated that through His people God Himself also will be saved. These scribes were convinced that, with the fall of Israel, the divine idea as taught by Moses and by prophets, developed by sages and by scribes, is condemned. Their divine message can be saved only by the salvation of the Jewish people. This is their teaching and it contains the key to the understanding of the history of Judaism.

The teaching of God's participation in Israel's redemption and persecution anticipated the age of the teachers in the third and fourth centuries. The nephew of R. Joshua b. Hananyah, likewise called Hananyah, found in the opening words of the Decalogue the teaching that God was redeemed with Israel from Egypt. He read: 'I am the Lord thy God, who was redeemed with thee from the land of Egypt.'[185] The teaching of R. Akiba, quoted above, is cited as belonging to the School of R. Ishmael.[186] R. Yannai, who lived in the early decades of the third century, sees in the relation of God and Israel the

---

[183] v. Midrash Ps., ed. Buber, p. 110–11. Pesikta, ed. Buber, p. 131 b, Midrash Psalms, ch. 137, end, R. Azarya and R. Abbahu in the name of R. Simon b. Lakish.

[184] v. Midrash Tanhuma, iii, ed. Buber, p. 71, v. also Pes. rabbati, p. 30 b. Yelamdenu, *R.É.J.* xvi, p. 221.

[185] pal. Suka 45 c.   [186] pal. Taanith i. 1, b. Meg. 29 b.

mutual relation of twins to each other. The pain felt by one
reacts on the other.[187] Anonymous teachers derive from the
name of Levi[188] and from the thorn-bush the symbolical teachings of God's immutable adherence to Israel and His share in
His people's misfortune.[189] Instead of long comments on these
extracts a parable of R. Judan may bring home quite clearly the
assumed apologetic tendency of this anthropomorphism of the
Haggadists.[190] There lived once side by side a mother and her
daughter who, as was well known to all their neighbours, were
not on the friendliest terms. When the daughter was in travail
and great pain, the mother joined her daughter in her lamentations and cries of anguish. The neighbours were surprised and
asked her: 'Wherefore dost thou cry? Thou art not giving
birth to a child; besides, thou art not on such friendly terms
with her.' The mother replied: 'Is she not my daughter?
How can I bear the pain of my child, without sharing it?'
Similarly, after the Destruction of the Temple loud weeping
and lamentation was heard in the whole Universe coming
from God.[191] The ministering angels said to God: 'Is there
such a thing as weeping before Thee? Is there weeping,
mourning, and lament in heaven? Does it not say: "Glory
and Majesty is before Him"?'[192] God replied to them: 'Is My
house not destroyed, are My children not driven into exile,
should I not be grieved?' Indeed, the prophet Elijah informs
R. Jose, who visited the ruins of Jerusalem, that God mourns
daily the fate of His Sanctuary and of His children. 'Woe
unto the father, whose children are driven from the mansion
and table of their father.'[193] Of a truth, God has not forsaken
Israel.

8. There is a third problem of Jewish Apologetics, the
discussion of which tended to strengthen anthropomorphic
thought in Jewish theology. It is the question of God's needs
in general, and of the command to erect a sanctuary and to
offer sacrifices in particular. One of the strongest attacks

---

[187] Exod. r. ii. 5.   [188] Exod. r. i. 5.
[189] b. Taanith 16a, Tanh. ii. 14. Pirke of R. Elieser, ch. xl.
[190] Midrash Psalms, ed. Buber, 173.   [191] Cf. Isa. xxii. 12.
[192] Cf. 1 Chron. xvi. 27.   [193] b. Berakoth 3a.

framed, and one of the most effective weapons forged in the schools of ancient philosophy, in the combat against polytheism, lay in the argument regarding the absurdity of belief in the needs of the gods.[194] It was re-echoed many a time from Jewish as well as from Early Christian lips and pulpits, before Christianity was severed from Judaism. Yet in turn, with the spread of the Hebrew Bible, similar objections were raised to the Jewish teachings of God as propagated by the Biblical writings. A homily of R. Yochanan bar Nappacha may serve as an indication to show the effect of this argument on Jewish teachers and their pupils in the third century. Moses, it is taught, experienced a setback when three commandments were given to him. First of all, when he was enjoined to erect a Sanctuary (Exod. xxv. 8), secondly, when he was ordered to prescribe the daily offerings (Num. xxviii. 2), and finally, when the law of taxation, the Half Shekel, was about to be promulgated, and he was told that this contribution means a 'ransom of the soul' for him who pays it (Exod. xxx. 12).

As to the tabernacle, Moses was amazed. How can a mortal being erect a Sanctuary unto God? Whereas it says about Him 'behold neither the heavens nor the heaven of heavens can contain Him' (1 Kings viii. 27). As to the sacrifices, the prophet Isaiah says: 'the Lebanon cannot supply enough fuel, nor all the cattle thereof enough burnt offerings' (xl. 16). Finally, how can one give the ransom of one's soul?[195] The last point belongs to our group only so far as the passage might have conveyed the wrong impression that God needed the Half Shekel for such a purpose. The questions involved in this sermon, and the difficulties underlying them, are of a much earlier date, and call for fuller treatment than the abridged homiletic sketch, preserved in the literature of the Midrash, presupposes. It is first of all necessary to consult again the theology of the Hellenistic writers and connect the two divergent schools.

[194] v. the literature in Geffcken's *Zwei Griechische Apologeten*, pp. 202 ff.

[195] The sources of the sermon are: Pesikta, ed. Buber, p. 20 a, R. Judah b. Simon in his name. Pesikta rabbati, ed. Friedmann, p. 84 b, shortened. Further Tanhuma, ed. Buber, Num., p. 34, where, however, the order of the subjects is: (a) the half shekel, (b) sacrifices, and (c) the Tabernacle. Num. r., xii. 13, Midrash Psalms, ch. 91. v. also Pes. B., p. 68 b.

A people living in a strange environment is more sensitive to external influence and more likely to listen to outside criticism than a nation enjoying full political and intellectual independence in a more or less secure home. Alexandrian writers and preachers faced earlier polemics and questions on the subject of God's dwelling place. The Jews in Palestine did not mind what Zeno or other Stoics thought of temples, erected by human hands.[196] To them the Sanctuary on the Temple Mount represented the most sacred and beautiful spot in the whole universe. Not so to the Jew in Rome or Alexandria. It may be that when Philo was coming back from his pilgrimage to Jerusalem some sceptic or stoic whispered in his ears: 'Is there anything sacred in the most magnificent edifice? Or, in other words, does your God need a Sanctuary? Can a building contain God?' It cannot be accidental that the LXX, Philo, the author of the Psalms of Solomon, and later Josephus, use the text of Solomon's prayer as the basis for their discussion of this question, in the same way as is done later by the Galilean teacher of the third century. It will be useful to give to these sources special attention and consideration. The Glosses added in the text of the LXX to 1 Kings viii. 53 and 2 Chron. vi. 1 must have been written by a theologian who felt the difficulty and the incongruity of the passages as keenly as did later on the contemporaries of the teacher of Tiberias, or, according to the legend, Moses himself. In the first gloss so much is clear, that the glossator was deeply troubled by the prayer of Solomon on one side, and the erection of the Sanctuary on the other side. The answer to this query is borrowed from some earlier source, unknown to us, and means that it is absurd to assume that God lives in a house. His dwelling is in the dense darkness, wherever that may be. The second gloss translates the prayer more definitely than the first. Solomon prayed: 'A house

---

[196] Pythagoras taught that God has no fairer temple than the pure soul, v. Farnell, *Higher Aspects of Greek Religion*, p. 147, v. also Seneca, *Ep.* 95, Lactantius, *Inst. div.* vi, God dwells not in temples of wood and stone, and needs no ministration of human hands. Zeno spoke with contempt of the erection of sacred edifices; for how can an edifice be sacred when built by labourers and builders?

fitting for a king like Thee, where Thou mayest dwell for my adoration of Thee, in this present period.' The Temple of Solomon is, therefore, built for man's sake, and not for God's need or comfort. Further, this institution is ordained for the present age, when man is weak and frail; the real perfect age will see more glorious and more appropriate buildings, built by God himself. We learn here the idea that the erection of the Temple is for man's sake, but, as will be shown further on, even observances and other institutions are made for the same purpose. Philo [197] seemed to have solved the difficulty by a similar theory. The Temple made by Moses was a necessity for the present world; the more perfect world will not need such an outward symbol of God's dwelling among man. Whilst, however, Philo sees the ideal Temple in the future, the author of the Wisdom of Solomon saw it in the past, when he says: [198] 'Thou hast commanded to erect a Sanctuary unto Thee on the Holy Mount and a place for sacrifices in the city of Thy residence, an imitation of the holy Tabernacle which Thou hast prepared from the beginning of creation.' The earthly temple shall serve as a reminder to man of the divine habitation in heaven. Here again, there is a teaching, which either was borrowed from, or has made a lasting impression on, Palestinian Haggadists. Finally, there is Josephus, who paraphrases the words of Solomon in a similar way to that of the LXX. God has an eternal abode. Perhaps it is that abode spoken of by the author of Solomon's Wisdom, and surely that which is contrasted by the Glossator of the LXX and Philo with the Temple built by human hands and human labour. This habitation is made of all the elements created by God: Heaven, earth, air, water, which are all of them imbued throughout by Him, but they do not suffice to contain His divinity.[199] Let this suffice for the Hellenistic literature, in order to convey some idea of the agitation caused by this problem among Greek-speaking thinkers.

Turning to the Palestinian sources, we see that as far

[197] v. on LXX and Philo, Dähne, *Geschichtliche Darstellung*, ii, pp. 44–5.
[198] Ch. ix. 8, v. Weinstein, *Genesis der Agada*, p. 17.
[199] *Ant.* viii. 9.

as the material available can teach the question does not arise before the middle of the second century. R. Judah bar Ilai is the first who dispels the scruples aroused on this account. God is like a king who used to talk to his little daughter where he chanced to meet her. Yet, when she grew up, he built a pavilion for her, for he considered it not polite to continue to behave in such a manner towards his daughter. Similarly God wanted to show honour to His people, when Israel became a nation and received the Law on Sinai.[200] The Tabernacle was not built because of God's need of a worthy habitation, but as an eloquent sign of the great honour shown to Israel. The same teacher uses a similar argument in explaining the commandment about the kindling of the lamps in the Sanctuary.[201] God does not require light, but the commandment was given in order that Israel should be able to acquire merit so as to inherit a share in a future life.[202] On similar lines is the expression in the Mekilta [203] where the command for making the Tabernacle is contrasted with the saying of the prophet Jeremiah, ch. xxiii. 24, 'God fills heaven and earth, how can He dwell in a house built by a human being?' The answer given is that the command was issued in order to enable man to receive reward. It is noteworthy that out of the three points raised in the Haggadah of R. Yochanan b. Nappacha two are raised as contradictions in the older Mekilta.

A contemporary of R. Yochanan, a teacher of Lydda, R. Joshua b. Levi, advances the teaching that the Exodus of Israel from Egypt was conditional on the erection of the Tabernacle; otherwise the liberation would not have taken place, or might have later on been annulled.[204] The exegetical force of this Haggadic teaching appears so weak that one cannot help assuming that the idea of the Tabernacle was at this time sorely in need of apologetic support. The Law of the erection of the Tabernacle, as this teacher is endeavouring to imply, is of greater importance and significance than is commonly assumed. He may have developed an earlier idea of R. Simon b. Yohai, according to

[200] Pes., ed. Buber, p. 2 a.
[201] v. Num. viii. 1 ff.   [202] Tanhuma iv, ed. Buber, p. 36.
[203] Mekilta 18 b.   [204] Pes., ed. Buber, p. 18 a.

whom the world exists for the sake of the Tabernacle.[205] Here also one would like to know whether the idea owes its origin to some tangible cause in the background, or was it the result of learned, but unauthoritative, exegesis? There are other Haggadists who emphasize the merit of the Tabernacle, i.e. that of erecting the Sanctuary, e.g. R. Samuel bar Nahmani.[206] Yet, in the case of R. Joshua b. Levi an indication is still at our disposal which makes it more than probable that in uttering these words he intended to defend this institution and its religious meaning against evil-minded critics. He emphasizes in another homily the great blessing and source of welfare which the Temple has been to the Gentile world.[207] He, surely, meant to say in the face of sharp opposition that ridiculed the whole conception of building Sanctuaries generally, and the rebuilding of the Temple in Jerusalem in particular, that Jews as well as Gentiles have to look to the Temple as to a source of blessing in the present and as to a safeguard of their existence in the future. Are there, one might ask, any traces of such opposition discernible in the literature at our disposal? If we may trust the author of the Clementine Homilies (II, XLIV) there were people who raised such questions as: If He dwells in a Tabernacle, who is without bounds?

Another theory about the influence exercised by the erection of the Tabernacle deserves mention in this connexion. R. Eleasar b. Pedath and R. Yochanan b. Nappacha taught that on the very day when the Tabernacle was erected the evil spirits, the rule of demons, and the fear of ghosts disappeared from the world.[208] Did these preachers understand the function of the Tabernacle as that of dispelling for ever the dominion of dark superstition as represented by idolatry and the end of an antiquated and misplaced form of religion? Or did they mean to convey the thought that contemporaries of Moses saw in the sacred building a place of refuge for superstitious men and women? The exegetical proofs, without which such teaching

[205] Ibid., p. 136 a.   [206] v. Marmorstein, *Doctrine of Merits*, p. 82.
[207] Lev. r. i. 2, Cant. r. on ii, 3, Num. r. i. 3.
[208] Pes., ed. Buber, p. 6 b. Pes. r., ch. xxi, Tanhuma iv, ed. Buber, p. 39, Midrash Psalms, p. 47 d.

could not be accepted, do not help us to see any more clearly behind the scenes. Most likely they saw in the fulfilment of this commandment a reward, granted as a weapon against dangerous forces of demons and ghosts, in which people still believed.

A most remarkable sermon on this subject is preserved in the Yelamdenu, one of the latest Midrashic compositions, which is, however, rich in thoughts and teachings proclaimed in earlier ages. The subject of the homily is the question: ' How many things preceded the creation of the world ? ' Answer: Seven. The reply, borrowed from a Barayta, is several times quoted in Talmud and Midrash.[209] Among these seven pre-existent things there is also the Sanctuary. This leads to the very theme of the sermon introduced by the rhetorical catch-word: בא וראה, ' Come and see '. The preacher introduces or invents a legend for the benefit of his audience. In this God says to Moses, when transmitting the command to erect the Tabernacle, that he shall impress the people by saying to them the following words: ' It is not because I have nowhere to dwell that I enjoin you to build a Sanctuary unto Me, truly not so, for I erected My Sanctuary on High before the creation of the world.' Then the preacher supports this assertion by citing passages from Jer. xvii. 12, Hab. iii. 20, and Isa. vi. 1. Yet why does God want such a building on earth below ? In order to give expression to His love for Israel. God leaves His pre-mundane palace and descends to Israel's Tabernacle. We see here, first of all, the idea of the Heavenly Sanctuary, which occurs also in the Wisdom of Solomon, secondly the teaching that the building of the Tabernacle is for the sake of Israel, as taught in the synagogues of the Hellenists, and moreover to show the appreciation and love vouchsafed to His people, as proclaimed by R. Judah b. Ilai.[210]

That the command to build an abode for the Divinity is a manifestation of God's love for Israel led to two very remarkable trains of thought in the theology of the Palestinian scribes. The presence of God in Israel is a sign of grace, but also of Israel's purity and holiness. There is to be mentioned first a

---

[209] Tanhuma Num. ed. Buber, p. 34; for parallels v. Buber's note loc. cit. no. 5, and Theodor, Genesis rabba, p. 6.

[210] v. above, p. 79.

homily of R. Isaac.[211] The righteous cause the Shekinah, the Divine Presence, God, to dwell on earth, whilst the wicked people drive away the Shekinah, removing Him to the heights of heaven. This meaning is put with Haggadic skill into the words of Ps. xxxvii. 29. Originally the Shekinah dwelt on earth, the transgression of Adam, the misdeeds of the generations of Enosh, the sins of the people of the Flood and of the Tower, of Egypt in the days of Abraham, of Sodom, and of Egypt in the days of Moses, removed the Divine Presence into the seventh heaven.[212] This happened gradually. Similarly seven pious men, viz. Abraham, Isaac, Jacob, Levi, Kohath, Amram, and Moses brought the Shekinah down from the seventh heaven to earth, till the Tabernacle was erected. Some of the Rabbis believed and taught that originally there was a divine immanence which became, to a certain degree, transcendent, owing to the sin of the creatures. R. Levi illustrates the presence of God in the Tabernacle by the simile of a cave situated near the shore of the sea. At high tide the water fills the cave, yet the sea is not lacking any water. Likewise here, the Tabernacle is full of the glory of God without diminishing in the least the extent or strength of the Shekinah.[213] The same teacher expressed his view on the present subject in another homily which was reported in the synagogues in two different versions. According to the first, taught by R. Joshua of Sikenin, the usual narrator or reporter of R. Levi's homilies, Moses was shown in heaven four patterns of fire in four different colours, viz. black, white, green, red, which Moses was to follow in building the Tabernacle. R. Berekyah handed down this teaching in the form of a parable. Once a king appeared to his Ben Bayyith in a cloak covered with jewels, and told him to procure a similar precious garment. The poor man apologized, and said: 'How can I satisfy such a wish of yours?' The king answered: 'Thou in

[211] The names of the scholars are given in the sources with variants. Pes. has R. Tanhum, the son-in-law of R. Eleazar b. Abina in the name of R. Simon b. Joseph, Cant. has R. Menahem b. R. Eleazar b. Abina in the name of R. Simon b. Yasina.

[212] Pes., ed. Buber, i b, v. note 22, Cant. r., v. 1. Gen. r., ch. xix, p. 176 where Cain is mentioned instead of Adam.

[213] Pes., ed. Buber. 2 b, and parallels.

thy capacity and I in my glory.' Thus said God to Moses: 'If thou dost below that which is above, I will leave my household of above and draw my Shekinah below among you.'[214] Here again God leaves the high heavens, his familia above,[215] and finds His place below, (Zimzum.)[216] In spite of such anthropo-morphic expressions as ascending and descending, R. Levi, in common with other Haggadists, found nothing objectionable in them. Thus an anonymous preacher on Prov. xxx. 4 thinks it quite proper to apply all parts of that sentence to God, 'Who ascended high and descended below? God', cf. Ps. xxiv. 3, and Exod. xix. 20. The rest of the sentence refers to God as the Lord of life, the giver of rain, who revives after death, &c.[217]

Nevertheless, there was also a different voice heard in the synagogues, according to which the Shekinah never found an abode on earth before the erection of the Sanctuary.[218] This teaching is recorded in the name of Rab, apparently disputing the opinion represented by R. Isaac who was an Amora of a later date. Yet the younger scholar may have continued a Tannaitic view ascribed to R. Simon b. Yohai, who also speaks of the Shekinah abiding first below. This presence of the Divine Glory on earth was temporarily interrupted, but later on, with the building of the Temple, again restored.[219] These op-posing views appear further in the following Haggadah. The angels moaned and said: 'Woe!'—because God was about to

[214] Pesikta ed. Buber, 4 b. Cant. r. iii. 2, Num. r. xii. 18. The Haggadist tries to answer the question, how could a human being, a mortal being, undertake such a task?

[215] About the conception of the Heavenly Familia, v. Marmorstein 'Anges et hommes dans l'Agada', in RÉJ. 84 (1927), pp. 37 ff., 138 ff

[216] The term Zimzum, viz. that the Omnipresent God contracts and confines His Shekinah on, or to, a certain spot, is a creation of the Amoraic Haggadah of the third century. The term occurs, besides, in the sayings of R. Levi, also in those of R. Yochanan, v. Pes. ed. Buber, p. 20 a, v. also Midrash Cant., ed. Grünhut, p. 15 b.

[217] Pesikta, ed. Buber, p. 8 a.f., v. Yalkut Shimeoni, Proverbs no. 962. Pes. r. quotes the saying in a Petiha of R. Tanhuma b. Abba.

[218] Pesikta rabbati, ch. viii, ed. Friedmann, p. 18 b.

[219] It is most extraordinary that the compiler should record a controversy between an Amora and a Tanna in this order and in such a manner. The parallels in Tan. and Num. r. agree with the text of the Pes. r. as far as the names of the teachers are concerned.

depart from the upper ones, and descend to the lower beings.[220]
God comforted them by saying: 'Indeed, my original principal
dwelling is amongst you', cf. Hab. iii. 3. Another teacher,
whose name [221] cannot be established precisely, remarks that
God mocked at them by asserting that the principal place of the
Shekinah was with the angels; no, the Divine Presence abode
first on earth, and then departed to the high, whence it was
restored after the building of the Sanctuary.[222] An Amoraic
Haggadist of the third century elaborated some compromise of
these two divergent views. When God created the world, says
R. Samuel b. Nahmani, He desired to have a habitation in the
lower world, just as He possessed one in the upper regions;
therefore He commanded Adam not to eat from the fruits of the
tree of knowledge. Adam transgressed this command and therefore God removed His Divine Presence from the earth to the
first heaven.[223] Apparently this teacher tried to find a deeper
justification for the erection of the Tabernacle.

This discussion, and the same applies to similar discussions
in the ancient Rabbinic writings, which seem to the uninitiated
artificial and futile at the same time, must have meant a great
deal to the teachers who shared in it. We are led to the second
teaching derived from this complex of ideas; namely, that the

[220] Yelamdenu, v.Yalkut Machiri, ed. Greenup, Habakuk, p. 31, Tanhuma
Terumah, 9, the author of the Haggadah is R. Samuel b. Nahmani, yet v.
the following note, which discusses this point at greater length.

[221] There seems to be confusion in the sources about the author of this
view and legend. In Num. r. R. Joshua b. Levi, R. Simon b. Judah being,
as usual, his reporter, is credited with this saying. In the Yelamdenu, at the
end of the Haggadah of R. Samuel b. Nahmani, the words are put into
the mouth of David.

[222] v. Yelamdenu, *supra* note 220, further Num. r. xii. 6–7. The subject
recurs also in the Haggadah of R. Alexandri, Cant. r. viii. 2, but not in
connexion with the erection of the Tabernacle; he refers to the objection
of the angels to the revelation of the Torah to Israel and to their fear that
the Divine Presence will move from heaven and dwell among mankind on
earth.

[223] Tanhuma Num. Naso, 16, v. also Tanh. Lev. ed. Buber, p. 110, where
R. Samuel b. Abba figures as the author. Buber prefers to read R. Samuel
b. Ammi, on account of Gen. r. iii. 9. The Haggadah is remarkable for
more than one reason. There was surely some external motive which led
him to connect the rather wide-spread conception of the Heavenly Sanctuary
with the transgression of Adam?

erection of the Tabernacle served as a witness of God's pardon
and forgiveness to Israel. There is a lengthy sermon on this subject, which preserves the apologetic tendencies without any
attempt to disguise the emphatic apologetic aim in it. The
homily is ascribed to a teacher R. Ishmael, hardly the Tannaite
of this name.[224] The tent of testimony is a sign for all the
creatures of the world that God has pardoned the sin of the
golden calf. He illustrates this teaching by a parable. Once a
king married a wife, whom he loved very dearly. Yet once he
became angry and left her. The neighbours said to her: ' He
will never return to you.' After a time the king made peace
with her and took her back in his palace and she dined and
drank with him as before. The neighbours were reluctant to
believe that such a change had come over the king, till they
recognized the fact by the odour of perfume on her. The application of this rather extraordinary parable is this. God is the
king who loves Israel dearly, yet for a short while He is angry
with the community of Israel, on account of their sin in making
the calf. The nations of the world are the neighbours who assert
that God has forsaken Israel, or that His covenant with the
people is invalidated. Now the erection of the Tabernacle at
the command of God was a visible testimony that He pardoned
the sin of His people, restored the old relationship, and, moreover, caused His Shekinah to rest among them. It is highly
noteworthy that most of the teachers, if not all mentioned in
the previous paragraph, in their discussions or in their sermons
on the conclusions drawn by Christian writers and clerics
from the story of the golden calf, i.e. the rejection of Israel
by God, the broken and lost covenant, and the transfer of His
love to the new nation, the Church, used this apologetic weapon.
The force of their rejoinder rested on the argument that the
Shekinah does not dwell among evil-doers. To the Jewish
scribes the erection of the Tabernacle was a mere restoration
of the earlier dwelling of God amongst the pious and righteous.

Another Haggadist likewise used the Tabernacle as convincing proof for the appeasement between God and Israel.
R. Judah b. Simon depicts rather dramatically the doubts of

[224] Tanhuma, Exodus, ed. Buber, p. 127 f. and the editor's note no. 13.

Moses as to the efficacy of his prayers on behalf of his people. When God told him to erect a sanctuary, he was assured that the sin of the calf was forgiven and he became satisfied.[225]

The second subject of R. Yochanan's sermon is also of great interest and occupies a prominent place in Jewish apologetics. It is quite natural that the question of sacrifices, their nature and meaning, their purpose and interpretation, their Biblical foundation, and their relation to other religious systems, should have aroused curiosity and opposition within and without the Jewish community. Jews could not remain indifferent to the general cry raised by philosophers and students of religion with unmistakable vehemence against this form of divine worship among the Greeks and Romans.[226] Consequently very early apologists among Jewish Hellenistic writers generally, and Philo and Josephus particularly,[227] endeavoured to defend the Mosaic system of sacrifices. With the rise of Christianity this dispute was intensified, in spite of the fact that the first Christians made the pilgrimage to the Temple Mount in order to discharge their duties like all other pious God-fearing Jews.[228] Moreover, although some fundamental christological conceptions are actually based on the Biblical sacrificial system,[229] nevertheless

[225] Midrash Eleh Debarim, ed. Buber, p. 2.

[226] v. especially Johannes Geffcken in *Jahrbücher für kl. Philologie*, vol. xv (1905), 631.

[227] The material is conveniently collected in P. Krüger's *Philo und Josephus als Apologeten des Judentums* (Leipzig, 1906); v. also P. Wendland, *Hellenistisch-Römische Literatur*, p. 153.

[228] v. Matt. v. 23, also Acts ii. 46, cf. H. Achelis, *Das Christentum in den ersten drei Jahrhunderten* (Leipzig, 1912), p. 4. There is no foundation for Harnack's assertion in his *Dogmengeschichte*, vol. i, 3rd ed. (1894), p. 67 note: 'Damit war vor Allem das ganze Opferwesen, das schon auch Jesus Christus wesentlich ignorirt hat, zurückgewiesen'. Harnack's assumption lies here in the German 'wesentlich', for which no foundation can be found.

[229] v. Heb. ix. 13. 'For if the blood of rams and bullocks and the ashes of the heifer, which sprinkled upon the defiled ones, sanctified for the purification of the flesh, how much more shall the blood of Christ, who offered himself without stain by the eternal spirit, purify your conscience from dead works to prepare you for the service of the living God?' A noteworthy parallel, and perhaps simultaneously a strong rejoinder against these words may be read in the Haggadah of R. Isaac, whose theological teachings, as shown by me in several places, are of the greatest

the Mosaic laws about sacrifices became a strong weapon
in the fight against Judaism. It is not without great significance that the Tannaitic Haggadah has very little to say
on this subject. No doubt the words of the writer of the
Barnabas-letter, referring to all the prophets as having described the offerings of sacrifices as unnecessary to God, were
known and shared by the earlier and later scribes of Israel.[230]
Yet sacrifices remained an integral part of Jewish religious life
up to the destruction of the Second Temple, and even after that
period pious Jews and learned scholars could become used only
with the greatest difficulty to a religious practice deprived of
this approach to God.[231] For several reasons, which can here
be merely indicated, the Early Church took a different attitude
in this matter. The discontinuation of sacrifices, owing to historical conditions, was a convenient argument in favour of the
abrogation of other Mosaic laws, as Sabbath, circumcision,
dietary prescriptions, and so on. Just as the sacrifices had a
temporary character, why not the rest of the laws ?—was a frequently heard argument, which, when propagated with necessary backing, found willing ears among Jews and Gentiles
alike. Secondly, it helped the consolidation of the christological conception of Jesus's death as the real sacrifice and
substitute for animal sacrifices for the whole of mankind.
Thirdly, it helped a good deal to silence Gnostic and philosophic criticism directed against the Church. These arguments
and theories did not help to soothe the conscience of the
more serious and devout adherents of the new religion among
the Gentiles as well as among those of Jewish origin. They

importance for the understanding of the relation between Christianity and
Judaism in the third century, based on Gen. xviii. 1, where he makes God
say in a legend: 'Whosoever slaughters a bullock or a lamb, and pours
out a drop of blood, I do come and bless him'; cf. Exod. xx. 24, 'Abraham
is sure of my blessing, out of his mansion a whole stream of blood flowed,
when he obeyed my command and circumcized the male members of his
household'; v. Tanhuma Gen., ed. Buber, i, p. 84. This is not the only
passage in the Haggadah where the death of Jesus and the duty of circumcision are contrasted; v. also Gen. r. 48. 4, Ag. Ber., ch. xix.

[230] Ch. ii. 4; v. Windisch, *Der Barnabasbrief* (Tübingen, 1920), p. 311,
and the notes given there.

[231] Aboth of R. Nathan, ch. iv. 5, cf. Marmorstein, Midrash Haseroth we
Yeteroth. London, 1917, p. ix.

could not help wondering how a considerable portion and a most
integral part of a legislation could be bluntly discarded and
cast overboard for no sufficient reason, if the Pentateuch
as a whole was to be considered the basis of the new religion.
Long before Julian the Apostate asked his Christian citizens
about the neglect of this law, honest Christians recognized
the incompatibility and the contradiction in their religious
system.[232]   The earlier reply that these laws were the result of
Israel's stiff-neckedness and sinful behaviour, in a word a
punishment and burden, but were no longer binding or appli-
cable to the new nation, was often repeated and found apparently
many believers and apostles. The more Jewish-minded Christians were taught that these commandments were really no
integral part of the Mosaic laws, but later forgeries, which
were added by misguided teachers or false law-givers.[233] Such
a solution could not find general acceptance and actually did
not satisfy deeper seekers after religious truth. Why did Moses
order such laws? Surely, God needs no food? There is no
eating in Heaven? Marvellous, indeed, that a Jewish teacher
of the third century and one of the sources used by the Clementine writers should have supplied one and the same answer.
The coincidence gives food for thought, but it cannot here be
dwelt upon. When meantime—says the author of the Recognitions of Clement [234]—Moses, that faithful and wise steward,
perceived that the vice of sacrificing to idols had been deeply
ingrained in the people from their associations with the Egyptians, and that the root of this evil could not be extracted, he
allowed them indeed to sacrifice, but permitted it to be done
only to God, that by any means he might cut off one half of
the deeply ingrained evil, leaving the other half to be corrected
by another, and at a future time; by Him, namely, concerning
whom it is said: 'A prophet shall the Lord your God raise
unto you, whom you shall hear even as Myself, according to

[232] The question is discussed more fully in my essay: 'Juden und
Judentum in der Altercatio Simonis Judaei et Theophili Christiani', in
Theologische Tydschrifs, vol. xlix, pp. 360–82.

[233] cf. Marmorstein, 'Judaism and Christianity in the middle of the
Third Century', in *H.U.C.A.* vol. x, 1935, pp. 247 ff.

[234] *Recognitions of Clement*, i. 36.

all things, which he shall say unto you. Whosoever shall no
hear that prophet, his soul shall be cut off from his people.'
R. Levi, a teacher belonging to the circle of R. Yochanan in
Tiberias, teaches the Jewish version of this doctrine.[235] R.
Phinehas relates a parable and its homiletic application of this
Haggadist in this way: 'There was once a king, who had a
son whose favourite food was flesh of fallen and torn animals.
The king said: "This kind of food shall never fail on my
table, till he will get sick of it".' Similarly God treated his
people. They were prone to worship idols in Egypt, consequently, they offered sacrifices to the idols and demons. They
offered them on high places, and many plagues broke out in
their midst. God said: 'Let them offer sacrifices before Me
in the Tabernacle at all times, so that they may abstain from
idolatry and be saved from punishment.' According to both
versions, the admission of sacrifices was a concession to the
people, who cleaved to the old form of divine service, learnt
in Egypt. It is not without interest and usefulness to inquire
here after the possible common source of which the Galilean
Amora and the Clementine theologian availed themselves in
expressing their views. In order to do so one has to turn to
Philo. Did Philo know or share such a conception of the
origin of sacrifices among the Hebrews, as taught by those
two representatives of the Church and Synagogue, or not?
From some of his utterances in his work on the life of Moses
(Book I, xv. 87, Loeb edition, vi, p. 320 f.) one would gather
that such an idea was unknown and strange to Philo. He makes
Moses say this to Pharaoh, in laying before him his request
and that of his companions that he would send the Hebrews
out of his boundaries in order to sacrifice. Moses told him that
their ancestral sacrifices must be performed in the desert, as
they did not conform with those of the rest of mankind, and
so exceptional were the customs peculiar to the Hebrews that
their rule and method ran counter to the common course.
Philo plainly denies in these words the possibility of the
Hebrews having been influenced in their sacrificial system by
Egyptians. He would, no doubt, have indignantly rejected such

[235] Lev. r. xxii. 5.

a theory of Egyptian influence. Philo, in good Haggadic style, offers an answer to the obvious question why Moses and his Hebrews could not perform their sacrifices within the frontiers of Egypt. Yet the strong emphasis laid on the antiquity and peculiarity of the Hebrew sacrificial system suggests to those who are accustomed to read between the lines of Philo's long sentences, that he aimed at combating the very doctrine taught later on by teachers of Judaism and Christianity.

Yet in spite of the considerable resemblances between the Christian and the Jewish variations of a probably older Rabbinic Haggadah,[236] the contrast is rather pointed according to their religious position. There, in the Christian recension, the law of sacrifices was a temporary; here, in the Jewish relation, a divine institution. There, a mere concession, unavoidable and dictated by the force of circumstances; here, a measure of love and benevolence. This latter point of view can be made even clearer by examining other sayings and teachings of R. Levi on the subject of sacrifices. Some of them will be adduced here. First of all, the saying that God warned Israel about the great importance of the sacrifices commanded in the Pentateuch, for there is no better pleader for them, at the time of drought, than the performance of the sacrifices;[237] meaning to say, that for the merit of this observance God grants them their request. Further, there is a teaching of this sage reported in which he emphasizes the fact that God likes, or better, finds pleasure in, Israel's sacrifices.[238] This statement seems to be directed against some opponents, either Jews or Gentiles, who were teaching or asserting that God does not find pleasure, or never did find pleasure, in performances of this kind. In spite of the fact that the whole discussion had no bearing on practical religion, since sacrifices belonged to the dead past, nevertheless, the academic discussion and the confessional strife as to their value was not silenced in the third century.[239] The root

---

[236] Tanhuma, Lev. iii, ed. Buber, p. 94. Sacrifices are regarded as atonement for the golden calf.

[237] Pes. ed. Buber, p. 191 a, Pesikta rabbati 201 a, Eccles. r. on vii. 14.

[238] v. Pes. ed. Buber, p. 192 a, 192 b.

[239] v. Marmorstein, *Deux renseignements d'Origène concernant les Juifs* *RÉJ*. vol. 71, 1920, pp. 190 ff

of the problem touched a fundamental question of the doctrine of God. Does God require sacrifices?, was asked. God has no needs; if so, then there is no meaning in these ordinances enumerated in the Bible. The age of R. Yochanan very often repeated this question, as can be gathered from the number of Haggadists, who tried to answer this difficulty. R. Yochanan returns to this problem in another Haggadah. He says, with reference to Ps. l. 12, 'There are some creatures of God, who can exist without any assistance from other creatures; how can one say that God, the Creator of all creatures, is in need of His creatures' "help"'? As an example, the growth of the olive is quoted. The olive-tree produces abundance of olives without being watered or tended by human cultivators.[240] His colleague, R. Simon b. Lakish, asked in his sermon on Num. xxviii. 6, 'Is there eating and drinking before God?'. He goes even so far as to disprove such an assertion by citing the case of Moses, who spent forty days and nights in heaven without food and drink; how can one ascribe such needs to God?[241] These teachers were surely confronted by persons who argued, even if they did not believe, that the Mosaic conception of religion has room for such religious ideas as that God requires food or drink. A third teacher who taught and preached in the neighbourhood of these two scholars, R. Isaac Nappacha, repeats the very same question: 'Is there food and drink before Him? If you say that there is, learn from the angels and servants, who are with Him, who need no food and drink; how much less He who sustains all?'[242] This Haggadist often dwelt on the problem of sacrifices, as has been shown by me on several occasions; he proclaims that prayers are a suitable substitute for sacrifices.[243] Most interesting is a saying of his on Lam. ii. 7 that the Jews are like certain citizens who first arranged tables, i.e. supplied food, for their king, then provoked him, and he tolerated their

---

[240] Pes. r. 80a, R. Hiyya b. Abba in R. Yochanan's name.

[241] v. Pes. r. 10a, and with some variants, ibid., p. 194a; v. also Tanhuma Num., pp. 244b–245a, Num. r., ch. xxi.

[242] v. the sources in the previous note.

[243] v. my Midrash Haseroth we Yeteroth, p. 10, where the sources are given in notes 40 ff.

conduct. The king said to them: 'Why do you take this liberty to provoke and annoy me, because you prepared this banquet for me? Well, I reject your gift.' The same happened to God. Similarly God says to Israel: 'You assume that you may provoke Me indefinitely because you offer Me sacrifices. Well, I will reject your altar.' [244] This sermon, with a good deal of irony, ridicules the childish notion, which was widespread among his contemporaries, that the sacrifices, if acceptable before God, should at least have saved the Temple from destruction, and that animal sacrifices are a cover or a permit for transgressions. Against these views the extraordinary sermon of R. Isaac is directed. There is a fourth refutation of this erroneous teaching, that God requires food, which is, however, anonymous, demonstrating by the example of Solomon whose requirements could not be satisfied (cf. 1 Kings v. 2 f.). How could human beings furnish sufficient food for the deity? [245] A parallel sermon, which may have been a variant of the last, proves the inability of man to sustain the deity from the example of the Behemoth Ps. l. 10.[246] Finally, we find the view, expressed by, and ascribed to, R. Samuel b. Nahman that sacrifices do not mean that God needs food, but are a revelation of God's grace in providing for a man a means of repentance and atonement, by which he can acquire reward and merits.[247]

[244] v. Midrash Lamentations, ed. Buber, p. 113; a similar Haggada is given in the name of R. Samuel b. Nahmani.
[245] v. Pesikta rabbati 194 b.
[246] v. ibid. and Tanhuma III, ii. iv. 46.
[247] Pes. r. 194 b, v. also about this teacher's views on sacrifices pal. Ber. ii. 1. Rosh Hashanah i. 1.

III

A HAGGADAH, of uncertain age and origin, voices a very strange
teaching, which may serve as text for this chapter devoted to
the Rabbinic conception of the visibility or invisibility of God.
Seven groups of righteous will be granted, in the eschatological
age, the great privilege of seeing God. Their countenance will
be like that of the sun, or moon, of the firmament or the stars,
of the lightening or the lilies or the pure lamp in the Sanctuary.[1] As to the origin of this important and interesting doctrine
there is only one clue. In the Tannaitic Midrash on Deuteronomy[2] the latter part of this Haggadah is quoted in the name
of R. Simon b. Yohai, whilst the first part is given anonymously.
It is quite likely that the compiler of the Leviticus rabba may
have used a fuller version of the Sifre, or combined the teaching
of R. Simon b. Yohai with the earlier anonymous one.

The term used for seeing God is here, as in many other
places, מקבל פני שכינה. The doctrine of the relation of the
righteous to God, and God's relation to them, occupies a most
important chapter in Rabbinic teaching about God. Its full
meaning and extent has not yet been investigated, but deserves
fuller treatment than can be accorded here. Its proper place
is really in Rabbinic anthropology. The pious stand higher
than the ministering angels, or at least are equal with them.
Some climb to this height of perfection in their life-time, others
after their death. Some reach this excellency in this world,
others in the world to come. There are righteous men spoken
of as God-like in their earthly pilgrimage, others see God at
their departure from this valley of death. It is nevertheless
worth while investigating this term. What was meant by this

---

[1] Lev. r. xxx. 2, cf. Pirke of Rabbenu ha-Kadosh, ed. Schönblum, vii. 11,
reading מאורות פני צדיקים לעתיד לבא, instead of שעתידים להקביל
פני שכינה, v. Marmorstein, *Jüdische Archaeologie und Theologie*, ZfNW.
xxxii, 1933, 32–41.

[2] Sifre Deut. 67 a, cf. Pirke loc. cit. where the sentence is ascribed to
R. Simon b. Menasyah.

teaching that 'seven sets of righteous will be enabled to receive, or see the countenance of the Shekinah'? There are numerous passages in the Scriptures suggesting or conveying the idea, either explicitly or otherwise, that the mortal will or can see God at one time or another.[3] This chance or possibility is opened to man, in spite of the understood and presupposed invisibility and incorporeality of God. In spite of this fact generally acknowledged in Rabbinic theology, the Rabbis use this term, which implies that man will behold God, or see the Shekinah, which is virtually the same, since Shekinah is used as one of the divine names.[4] To make this fact clearer, and in order to dispel any possible doubt on this matter, some more material may be elaborated here. One homilist concludes his oration with the following words: 'In this world they (the Levites) perished[4] because their eyes saw My glory (cf. Exod. xxxiii. 20); not so in the world to come, when, returning to Zion, I will reveal Myself in My glory before all My people, and they will see Me, and live for ever (cf. Isa. lii. 8). Moreover, they will point with their fingers and will exclaim: "For this is the God, our God" (cf. Ps. xlviii. 15). Further it says (cf. Isa. xxv. 9): "And he will say on this day, behold our God, &c."'[5] In another version the same peroration is put with some variants.[6] Isa. lxvi. 14 says: 'And ye will see and your hearts will rejoice.' What shall we see, and what shall we rejoice at? In this world, owing to our sins, we have no prophetic vision, no Holy Spirit (cf. Ps. lxxiv. 9), even the Shekinah is departed from our midst (cf. Isa. lix. 20). In the world to come, however, God will reveal Himself again (cf. Isa. lx. 5) and man will see Him (cf. Ps. lii. 8). According to a third source at our disposal[7] this grace is granted to the living as well. The pilgrims at the

---

[3] v. the essay of Graf Wolf Wilhelm Baudissin, 'Gottschauen in der alttestamentlichen Religion', *A.R.W.* xviii, 1915, pp. 173–239.

[4] There is an ancient belief among Hebrews as well as among other nations that the beholding of divine things causes death, or at least blindness, how much more the sight of God. v. Lev. r. xxxi. 7. Pirke of R. E., ch. xiii, cf. Keim, *Rom u. Christentum*, p. 30, P. Wendland, *Hell.-Röm. Kultur*, p. 125, Folklore i, 108–14 and Philologus, lxiv, 1905, p. 164.

[5] Tanhuma, ed. Buber, iv, p. 18.

[6] Agadath Bereshith, ed. Buber, ch. lxxiii, p. 48.

[7] Sifre Deut., par. 143, cf. the reading of R. Hillel b. Elyakim.

festivals who appeared before the Lord, experienced such a revelation, seeing God.

In order to establish an approximate date for these teachings and ideas, one has to search for the spread of such conceptions in the Haggadah of teachers whose date is known from the usual sources. A well-known teacher of the second century, R. Yose b. Halafta of Sepphoris, told his son, R. Ishmael, who moved by mystic longings wanted to see the Shekinah: 'You are longing to see God during your life-time in this world, your wish may become true if you devote all your time to the study of the Torah in Palestine.'[8] The advice given by R. Yose b. Halafta to his son, very significant as his words are, becomes even more noteworthy, when two important facts are not lost sight of; first of all, this teacher's attitude to Christianity and Gnosticism on one side, and secondly, the striking parallel to his words which is found in an early Christian document.[9] The writer of the Epistle to the Hebrews says likewise that without *holiness* one cannot see God. Is there a connexion between these two sources? It is a well attested fact that the author of this Epistle availed himself of Jewish Haggadic material, Rabbinic as well as Hellenistic, consequently there is nothing surprising in the resemblance between his words and those of R. Yose b. Halafta. Naturally one would not expect the ideal of *Talmud Torah* in an early Christian document. Yet the ideal of Study of the Torah was to the ancient Jew the beginning and end of *holiness*, which enables man to see God. Similarly, Paul preaches in the spirit of the ancient sages of the Haggadah, merely christianizing their words slightly, when he says: 'Now, we see through a mirror, in a riddle, then, in the future, we shall see eye to eye.'[10] The Rabbis, therefore, must have been divided on the question of θεὸς ὀφθείς, on the experience of seeing God. The teachers who belonged to R. Yose's group or followed him taught that God can be seen in this world, the other school relegated this experience to the future world, as Paul did.

[8] Midrash Psalms. ch. cv, ed. Buber, p. 448, based on Ps. cv. 4, 'Seek the Lord, and His strength, i.e. the Torah, Seek His countenance evermore'.

[9] Heb., ch. xii. 14.

[10] 1 Cor. xiii. 12, v. also 2 Cor. v. 7.

Surely, among the mystics of Palestine there was the same yearning to see God, which burnt in the hearts of so many contemporary Greeks and Romans.[11]

A dialogue held between two scholars of the middle of the third century, both of whom are called by the name R. Hananyah, the Elder and the Younger, contributes some new information to our knowledge on this subject. The younger scholar ventured, in an apocalyptic utterance, so far as to announce that in future God will show His glory to all the creatures of the world, by lowering His Throne of glory from the midst of the sky, placing it on the very spot where sun and moon shine in the solstice of the month of Tebeth.[12] The older teacher of this name denies such a possibility by quoting the verse Exod. xxx. 20. The difference between this later Amoraic statement or picture of the future revelation and the earlier Tannaitic assertion is most remarkable. Here not merely Jews, but the creatures of the whole world, without distinction of race and creed, nationality and culture, share this unique religious experience, which is in store for mankind. Furthermore, the older scribe cites in his reply Ps. lxxxiv. 12 as a proof that God will endow frail humanity with the faculty to see God. One cannot read these lines without having the impression that speculation about the form of the eschatological revelation of God played a considerable part in the theological teaching of these Galilean rabbis. God will be visible to mankind as He was seen by earlier generations of Hebrews. About the final form of this world-shaking historical act the views clashed, then as before. Some thought that God Himself would be seen, others dreamt of a great theophany, which would inspire humanity and open the blind eyes of men and women to behold God's appearance. Mystics and rationalists cannot, naturally, see eye to eye on such points. This Rabbinic Haggadah leads the way to establish a closer contact between the teachings of the Rabbis and those of the unknown authors of the Pseudepigrapha of the Old Testament. The writer of the Book of Jubilees and that

[11] v. R. Reitzenstein, *Die hellenistischen Mysterienreligionen*, Leipzig, 1910, 118 ff., 124 ff.

[12] Tanhuma v, ed. Buber, p. 31, a fuller version in Tanhuma, f. 267 a.

of the individual Testaments of the Twelve Patriarchs were fascinated by the thought that God will become or is visible to His creatures. These authors and their circles, out of which they grew, or to whom they addressed their words, attached some special meaning or particular importance to this thought. A few instances may suffice to bring this home to the reader. The Book of Jubilees preaches in the same strain as our Haggadist that at the end of the days God will descend from His heavenly heights and dwell with a purified Israel for all eternity. Then the Lord will appear to the eyes of all, or will be seen by all.[13] This close agreement between the two streams of the Haggadah presupposes between the two branches of Jewish literature a more intimate relation than our historical knowledge can explain or warrant. The author, or authors, of the Testaments repeatedly point to a new revelation, in which God will appear and will be seen in Jerusalem.[14]

It is most remarkable that whilst Rabbinic eschatology and Pseudepigraphic visionaries freely speak of God's visibility, this possibility is never mentioned in the dialogues between pagans and scribes, when the latter are challenged by the unmistakable direct appeal: *Show me your God.* Jewish as well as Christian apologists have only one answer to this provocation, namely, that God is invisible.[15] The problem of God's visibility so often raised in Jewish Apologetics, is most significantly touched on by Philo in his writings on the Life of Moses (Bk. I. xv, 8, Loeb edition, p. 320), faithfully reflecting the mentality of his pagan contemporaries, when he introduced Pharaoh's reply to Moses with the following remark: 'The king whose soul from his earliest youth was weighed down with the pride of many generations did not accept a God discernible only by the mind, or any at all beyond those

---

[13] Ch. i. 25.

[14] Test. Zebulun ix. 8, cf. Henry T. Wicks, *The Doctrine of God in the Jewish Apocryphal and Apocalyptic Literature*, London, 1915, p. 121.

[15] Cf. the material given in Marmorstein, 'Die Gotteslehre in der Jüdischen Apologetik', in Dr. Wohlgemuth's *Jeschurun*, vol. vii, 1920, p. 175, further my essay, 'Jews and Judaism in the Earliest Christian Apologies', *Expositor*, vol. xlv. 1919, pp. 104 ff., and Midrash Abkir, ed. Marmorstein, *Dwir*, i, 1923, p. 125.

whom his eyes beheld.' Within the Jewish community there were not lacking groups and circles divided on the doctrine of invisibility or visibility of the divine being. R. Akiba, as was shown before in these essays,[16] generally cleaving to the literal meaning of the text, thought it necessary to proclaim that even the ministering angels *cannot see* God. Another early teacher, R. Dosa b. Hyrkanos, however, approaches some of the views treated earlier in this chapter by saying that no human eye can behold the deity whilst alive, but after death the human soul is granted such a privilege.[17] According to another teacher, whose date and name are not indicated in the sources, all departing souls, when taking leave of the body, are granted the sight of God.[18] For God says to Moses: 'In this world you are not able to see My glory, yet you shall see Me in the world to come. When did Moses behold Him? When He died. That teaches you that all departing souls see God.' This teaching must have filled many generations of believing Jews with comfort and strength at the moment of departing from their earthly abode, and before starting their journey to the great beyond. Modern students of the history of religions [19] are inclined to discover in all these passages of the Old and New Testament, Apocrypha, and Pseudepigrapha sharp, undeniable traces of the immense influence exercised by the Greek mystery religions on Jewish religion. Is it possible to apply these theories to the origin and development of this conception in Rabbinic theology? Before reflecting on this question, another more relevant query has to be raised. What is the difference between the meaning of מקבל פני שכינה, and that of 'seeing God'? The first expression occurs in the sentence which served as the starting-point of this discussion.[20] There are many more which deserve consideration.

To begin with there is R. Jeremiah (b. Elieser) who speaks of

---

[16] v. above p. 48.

[17] v. above, pp. 48–9.

[18] Sifra 3 b, Num. r. ch. xiv, Lekah Tob Exod. p. 205, Midrash Agada, ed. Buber, p. 185.

[19] Reitzenstein. *Poimandres*, p. 240, Hennicke, *Neutestamentliche Apokryphen*, p. 183, *Handbuch*, p. xiv.

[20] v. above, p. 92 ff.

four groups of people who are barred from *seeing the Shekinah*.
They are: the scoffers, the hypocrites, liars, and those who
spread evil reports.[21] The meaning of this term, used here in the
negative, will become clearer when the preacher's Scriptural
references are investigated. Hos. vii. 5 says that He withdrew
His hands from scorners.[22] Job xiii. 16 indicates that 'a hypo-
crite shall not come before Him'. Ps. ci. 7 declares that 'he that
telleth lies shall not tarry in My sight'.[23] Ps. v. 5 teaches that
speakers of evil shall not dwell with God. The term קבלת פני
שכינה, consequently, covered a wide range of nearness to and
intimacy with God. Yet those who were estranged from Him
by moral defaults and shortcomings, could not come near Him.
To see God, to receive the countenance of the Shekinah meant,
therefore, to the ancient teachers nothing less than to be near
to God, to dwell in His vicinity, to be protected by His hand,
and to tarry in His sight.

From the negative use of this expression one may turn now
to its affirmative application. Haggadists of all ages are familiar
with this phrase and use it for various purposes. R. Meir en-
courages those who minutely observe the law of wearing fringes
at the corner of their garments by saying: 'Whosoever is particular in observing this commandment is to be regarded as if
he had seen the countenance of the Shekinah.'[24] A younger
scribe renders this thought somewhat differently, teaching that
when the Jews look at their fringes, then they cause the Shekinah to dwell in their midst.[25] R. Simon b. Yohai fully agrees

[21] v. b. Sotah 42 a, cf. Pirke of Rabbenu ha-Kadosh, ed. Schönblum, iv,
25, where, however, instead of אין מקבלות פני שכינה the term נידונות
חוץ לפרגוד is used, v. also Yalkut Makiri Hosea, ed. Greenup, p. 186, and
b. Sanhedrin 106 a, where the sentence is given in the name of R. Hisda
by R. Jeremiah b. Abba, cf. further Mayyan Ganim on Job, ed. Buber,
p. 44, and Yalkut Makiri on Ps. v. 11.

[22] Rab taught that scoffers are destined to go to hell, v. b. Aboda Zara
18 b. R. Eleasar b. Pedath adds that severe chastisement is awaiting them,
ibid. R. Ketina deduces from the passage quoted in the text, that scorners
will encounter poverty, v. ibid.

[23] R. Judah in the name of Rab says regarding this verse: 'Leave My
boundary on account of telling lies, they cannot stand before My eyes.'

[24] v. pal. Berakoth i. 4.

[25] Midrash Psalms xc. 18, ed. Buber, p. 394.

with R. Meir in preaching that whosoever is zealous in the performance of this commandment is worthy to perceive the countenance of the Shekinah.[26] Great importance was, as we see, attached to this observance, the more so since, as we read in our sources, it was, at an earlier period, much neglected, and gave cause for complaint. This gave rise to threats and admonitions which predict the death of little children as a result of neglect of this commandment.[27] Whilst the neglect of the law of fringes is condemned so strongly, the fulfilment of the precept is magnified as if one had, in obeying this regulation, minutely discharged all the precepts of the Torah.[28] It is not unlikely that these valuations of the law of Zizith owe their origin to the great importance attached to it as a deterrent from sexual aberrations, examples of which were current in legend and folk-tale, known to students and laymen alike.[28] Consequently, the teachings can be translated thus: 'He who abstains from impurity and lewdness, he who leads a chaste life of abstinence, deserves to experience the nearness of God.'

The very same motive induced a scholar, R. Menasyah, the grandson of R. Joshua b. Levi, to say that a man who happens to be in view of an immoral act or object, and does not look at it, will be rewarded by *seeing God*.[29] The teaching is based on Isa. xxxiii. 15, 'he shutteth his eyes from seeing evil',[30] and on the continuation in verse 17, 'the king (i.e. God) in His beauty shall thine eyes see, they shall see the land which is far off'. This teacher was indebted for his saying to his grandfather, the famous scholar of Lydda, who referred the passage in the Book of Isaiah just cited to those people who refrained from looking at women doing some laundry-work who probably stood half-naked.[31] Not to glance or look at women is a well-known prohibition and a warning frequently repeated in Jewish

[26] b. Menahoth 43 b.

[27] b. Shabbath 32 b and 22 b.

[28] v. my ed. of Midrash Haseroth we-Yeteroth, p. 8 note 26.

[29] v. the story of Nathan dezuzitha, Gaster, *Exempla* no. xxxv, and for parallels ibid., p. 192.

[30] 'Evil' means lewdness and immorality. The saying is quoted in Lev. r., ch. xxiii. 13 c, Pes. r. 125 a, Derek Erez, ch. i.

[31] v. b. Baba Bathra 57 b, cf. also R. Phineas in Pes. r. 2 a.

moralist writings of all ages and climates, which is based on Old-Rabbinic teachings.

A pupil of R. Meir, R. Dositheus b. R. Yannai by name, attaches to charity and lovingkindness the same meaning and weight that the master ascribed to the observance of the Zizith-commandment. This teacher formulates his doctrine in this way: A man offers some gift to a king. It is altogether doubt-ful whether it will be accepted. Moreover, assuming that the ruler will accept the gift, it is still uncertain whether the donor will have an opportunity to see the king or not. It is quite different with the King of Heaven. A man gives a penny to the poor, he at once becomes worthy of seeing God. For this is the teaching of the text: 'I will "through charity" see Thy counte-nance, I shall be satisfied, when I awake with Thy likeness.'[32] The compiler of the Midrash on Psalms [33] used an interesting variant from some unknown source. Here the following reading is supplied: a 'matrona' is desirous of seeing the king; she tries by all available means to be received by him in audience. She adorns herself with a crown, which she uses when appear-ing before him. Owing to her adornment she is able to stand before him. The same with man; the gift given to the poor is his adornment which enables him to see God. This text shows that to see the countenance is equal to the expression להקביל פני שכינה in the parallel. A third parallel further adapts this teaching by extending this privilege to all givers of charity, whether righteous or wicked. All, without distinction, are worthy of seeing God, or perceiving the countenance of the Shekinah, because of the great merit of charitable deeds and actions.[34] This idea is derived from Isa. xl. 5, 'All flesh, with-out discrimination, even Gentiles, are promised that they shall partake in the great future revelation of God and His glory'.

There is further to be recorded the teaching of R. Yochanan b. Nappacha who extends and promises this sign of grace to those who pronounce the blessing at the sight of the New Moon.[35] To bless the Moon in the due season or time seems

---

[32] b. Baba Bathra 10 a, cf. Ps. xvii. 15.

[33] Midrash Psalms, ch. xvii. 18, ed. Buber, p. 134 f.

[34] Pes. r. 2 a.   [35] b. Sanhedrin 42 b.

to this teacher of such great religious importance that its performance is looked upon as if the performer of this duty had
seen the Shekinah. The view found support in the זה mentioned in Exod. xii. 2, in connexion with the law concerning the
New Moon, and the זה in Exod. xv. 2 in the Song of Moses.
The teaching of the Amoraic Haggadist is based on the older
teaching of R. Akiba against R. Ishmael, seeing in the first זה an
indication that God has shown Moses the moon with His finger,
whilst R. Ishmael interprets the passage as meaning that Moses
had shown the Hebrews the moon, pointing out to them the
particulars of this ordinance.[36] It is true that in the Babylonian
Talmud there is a Baraytah quoted in the name of the school
of R. Ishmael saying: 'If the Jews had no other merit except
that of seeing the countenance of their Father in Heaven only
once every month, it would be sufficient unto them.'[37] Yet
it was demonstrated on a previous occasion in these essays
that this Barayta collection handed down under the name of
R. Ishmael or his school does not always represent the point
of view of R. Ishmael or of his school.[38] There is further a
difference between the Amoraic מקבל פני שכינה and the
Tannaitic להקביל פני אביהם שבשמים. The real meaning
of R. Yochanan's teaching can be guessed by combining the
teaching of R. Akiba with that of another earlier teacher, who
saw in the verse זה אלי ואנוהו the doctrine of the *imitatio dei*.[39]
The visibility of God when commanding the rules of the New
Moon and His appearance on the Red Sea are guarantees for all
who observe the commandment of the blessing to be said in
due time at the sight of the moon that they will see God.

It is by no means improbable that both sayings arose out
of prevailing historical conditions in the days of these teachers.
A religious persecution, which caused great mental suffering
and anxiety to Palestinian Jewry in the second half of the
third century C.E., affected to a considerable extent the carrying

---

[36] v. Mekilta, p. 2 b and supra, p. 32. [37] b. Sanhedrin, p. 42 a.
[38] v. *MGWJ.*, ii. 390, iii. 149, Frankel, מבוא הירושלמי, p. 108. Friedmann, Mekilta, Introduction, Berliner, *Hebräische Bibliographie*, x. 138,
Königsberger, *Quellen der Halachah*, p. 43 f.
[39] Mekilta, p. 37 a.

out of this observance. The rulers looked askance at this
religious performance. R. Yochanan, therefore, praised and
encouraged those who, in spite of physical discomfort and
perhaps danger of life, sanctified the New Moon. The neglect
of this performance would entail serious disturbance in religious life, for on the regulation of the Calendar depended the
celebration of the festivals.[40]

The Amora promises further this high degree of nearness to
God to a student who goes from the synagogue directly to the
house of study in order to spend his time in study of the Torah.[41]
He bases his doctrine on Ps. lxxxiv. 8 interpreting it thus:
'He who goes from strength to strength will see God in Zion.'
The reading justifying such a homily must have differed from
the Massoretic text, which has got יראה אל אלהים, i.e. ap-
peareth before God, whilst the Haggadist makes of it יראה
אל אלהים בציון, viz. seeth the God of gods in Zion. Most
likely the Massoretes would reject such an interpretation as too
anthropomorphic. The LXX, however, renders the sentence
in agreement with the Haggadist: ' The God of gods shall be
seen in Zion.'

The expression to be found in Exod. xxxiii. 7 כל מבקש
יהוה is explained by some Haggadists as seeking the nearness
of, or visiting, Moses, surely because the literal meaning of the
text, seeking God, did not appeal to them. This gave rise to a
general teaching that he who visits or appears before a scholar
full of Torah, is as if he has approached God.[42] Another version puts this teaching somewhat differently, in applying it to
the visit paid or to be paid, at regular intervals, by a disciple
to his master.[43] The text כל מבקש ה' was understood by
these teachers as מבקש פני ה', seeking the countenance of
God. Similarly, in an allegorical sermon on Cant. viii. 8 ' what

[40] v. Marmorstein, ' Les persécutions religieuses de l'époque de R.
Jochanan b. Nappacha ', RÉJ., 77, 1923, pp. 166 ff., and Graetz, MGWJ.,
1884, 548; further Hamagid, 1863, 93, Heasif, ii. 447.

[41] b. Berakoth 64 a, b. Moed Katan 29 a, R. Levi, v. Yalkut Makiri,
Psalms lxxxiv. 15, R. Levi b. Hanina, instead of Hiyya.

[42] Tanhuma, ed. Buber, ii. 115.

[43] pal. Erubin v. 1. v. also Gen. r., ch. lxiii. 8, where the reading agrees
with Tanhuma.

shall we do to our sister on the day when she will be spoken for', a preacher makes the community of Israel address the question to God: How can we see the countenance of the Shekinah ? Through the observances of the Torah.[44] Faithful observance of religious duties as laid down in the Law, enables man to reach complete nearness to God. Moses in his last prayer for the prolongation of his life, used the words פנים שהקבילו פני שכינה, 'the countenance which was received before God, or, the countenance of mine which saw God's countenance, should it experience death ?' Finally, there is an eschatological saying, as usual in Haggadic perorations, which makes the visibility of God dependent on the unity of Israel which is also the first requirement for the redemption of man (cf. Jer. iii. 4, and iii. 18).[45] This however, as has been shown, was the teaching of R. Haninah,[46] which was not generally accepted.

Before concluding this chapter two more similar phrases used by the Rabbis have to be considered. The first is נידונין ליזון מזיו השכינה or מזיו השכינה, the second reads: נהנין מזיו השכינה. R. Abbahu, in one of his diatribes, makes the earth say to God, 'The upper ones are sustained by the splendour of the Shekinah, whilst the lower ones, if they do not toil, will starve'.[47] To be fed by the splendour of the Shekinah is opposed here by to be fed or find sustenance by work and labour. Yet, Moses, we are told, when spending forty days on the mount, was sustained by the splendour of the Shekinah.[48] The splendour of the Shekinah was granted, according to R. Samuel b. Nahmani, reported by R. Haggai in his name, to every Hebrew who witnessed the revelation of God on Mount Sinai.[49] The Biblical support for such a doctrine is found in Ezek. xv. 14, where the beauty of Israel which made the nation

[44] v. Midrash Canticles, ed. Grünhut, p. 48 a, where the text has to be read as above.

[45] Tanhuma, ed. Buber, v, p. 12.   [46] ibid., p. 49.

[47] Gen. r. ii. 2.

[48] Tanhuma, ed. Buber, ii. 119, Exod. r. xlvii. 5, where it is added that the living creatures carrying the Throne of Glory are sustained by the splendour of the Shekinah.

[49] Pes. r. ed. Friedmann, p. 101 a.

famous among the Gentiles, is spoken of. This beauty is nothing else but the giving of the law on Sinai. A Mishnah teacher, R. Tahlifa (identical with R. Halafta b. Saul) expounds the word שמחים in 1 Kings viii. 66 as meaning that all who partook of the festivities enjoyed the splendour of the She-kinah.[50] Similarly to the conception of הקבלת פני שכינה, Rabbinic apocalyptists developed the eschatological vision of the righteous sitting with crowns on their heads and being sustained or fed by the splendour of the Shekinah.[51] They found this vision indicated in their exposition of the words in Exod. xxiv. 11, where it is said ' and they saw the God of Israel, meaning the glory of God, which supplied them with food and drink ', i.e. the joy of seeing the Shekinah supplied them with food and drink. Properly understood, all these terms conveyed the idea that the righteous—but also wicked people who have charitable works to their credit, or Gentiles of a similar dis-position—will see God, or be received by Him. In other words, this seeing of God means that certain merits enable man to attain a nearness to God, which to most of these theologians was equivalent to seeing God. Yet there were some, as was shown in the course of this chapter, who were so steeped in their mysticism that they spoke of and believed in a real visi-bility of God. This sight of God, in one form or another, meant to some teachers of Judaism a manifestation of God's immense love to His creatures generally, and to His near ones particularly. This subject, which can here be merely touched upon, belongs to another chapter of the Rabbinic doctrine of God, namely the relation of God the Creator of man to His creatures, which will find its place in the treatise on Rabbinic anthropology.

[50] Pesikta, ed. Buber, p. 37 a, b. Moed Katan 9 a.
[51] Aboth R. Nathan, i, ch. i, ed. Schechter, p. 3 a.   v. also b. Rosh Hashanah 8 a, b. Berakoth 16 a.

IV

1. THE difference between the two contending schools of thought manifested itself not only in doctrine, but most significantly also in style and in expression. Such a division in thought, naturally, must have penetrated likewise the terminology of the schools. An adherent of allegorical methods will use different words and terms in introducing his teachings from those familiar to teachers who would not deviate from the letter of the Scriptures. If such a suggestion can be maintained, then the apparent grouping of the two schools is established; and secondly, the individual members belonging to this or that school or group can be named and classified. Chronologically as well as materially the first place has here to be given to the school and scholars, which and who believed that the words of the Torah have to be understood literally, strictly according to their writing, דברים ככתבם as their phrase runs. R. Elieser b. Jacob applied this rule to Deut. xxii. 17. 'They shall spread out the cloth before the Elders of the city'. It cannot be questioned that, in early times, the literal carrying-out of the rite was the usage, and it persisted up to a very late date in Jewish history, when the change of manners brought about the discarding of primitive customs. It is impossible now to fix the date when this alteration took place. Undoubtedly in some places the custom survived till very late. This does not contradict the fact that already at the beginning of the second century, if not earlier, some objections to the crudeness and coarseness of early conduct were actually raised. R. Ishmael, the well-known allegorist, actually disregards the literal application of the procedure, and declares himself satisfied with the figurative performance of the action resulting out of the bridegroom's accusation.[1]

[1] Sifre Deut. par. 237, Midrash Tannaim, p. 140, b. Ket. 46 a; v. however pal. Ket. iv. 3, where R. Jose b. Abun corrects the Barayta. A similar controversy between the literalists and R. Ishmael is recorded regarding Deut. xxv. 9, v. Sifre, Deut. par. 291, Midrash Tannaim, p. 167.

A second teacher, to whom the method of taking the letter at
its face-value is attributed, was R. Judah b. Ilai.[2] Yet he
applies it only in certain cases and with certain reservations,
namely, when the text contains a redundant word or a superfluous expression, only then can the rule be applied. Otherwise it would be impossible to harmonize such an attitude
with the fact that R. Judah b. Ilai employs allegorical interpretations in his numerous Haggadoth, and strongly objects to
literal translations.[3] The two instances in which R. Judah
finds exceptions to the general rule by applying the term of
דברים ככתבן, are of Haggadic and Halachic nature. A conflict between letter and life is inevitable in the long course of a
nation's history, and can be harmonized by admitting progress
in thought without taking refuge in legal fictions, as was done by
Roman lawyers.[4] Such difficulties arise also in the courts and
academies of the Scribes.[5] In some sources the term דברים
ככתבן was interchanged with בעינן קרא כדכתיב 'we read
the text according to its literal meaning'. Another term frequently used by the literalists is כמשמעו i.e. the text has to be
taken literally, of which several instances are preserved in the
Halachah as well as in the Haggadah.[6] Finally, the terms ממש
and ודאי may be added as typical of the literalist school,
before embarking on a fuller investigation of the terms used
by the literalist and allegorical interpreters of the Bible.[7]

[2] v. b. Pes. 21 b and Sotah 48 b.

[3] v. further on pp. 142–6.

[4] v. Otto v. Seeck, *Geschichte des Untergangs der antiken Welt*, vol. vi,
Stuttgart, 1920, p. 133.

[5] v. Sanhedrin 45 b. According to R. Ishmael, if a condemned city has
no road the prescribed punishment cannot be carried out, because the text
stresses the point of having a road, though R. Akiba prescribes that a road has
to be built, yet afterwards destroyed. R. Ishmael favours the abolishing
of the whole ceremony or punishment in such cases. R. Akiba is inclined
to do justice to the letter of the law, although it appears absurd to pave
a street which will have to be destroyed afterwards in order to execute
judgment on the condemned city. This point of comparison between
Jewish and Roman law requires and deserves fuller investigation. It must
be considered under the aspect of the validity of the law under changed
conditions where it has become out-moded.

[6] v. Bacher, *Terminologie*, vol. i, s.v. משמע.

[7] v. for instance R. Akiba, Mekilta, p. 14 b, סוכות ממש; cf. Mekilta
of R. Simon, p. 26, where the term ודאי occurs. As to the term ודאי

The first term to be dealt with here, at greater length, is : אלמלא מקרא כתוב אי אפשר לאומרו, i.e. were this or that not explicitly written in the text, one could not say or utter such a statement. Such a phrase, naturally, assumes that the teacher is inclined to take the words of the Scriptures literally, and moreover, he adds to it some anthropomorphism expanded by himself. In some cases, here as well as in the previous instances, the tradition clashes with the very character of the respective teacher's attitude to the problem of anthropomorphism. The teachers who are credited with the use of this term are here enumerated in their chronological order :

(1) R. Elieser b. Hyrkanos.[8] He explains the verb נשא God carried Israel like a father carrying his child. The term does not fit in this connexion, and ought to be joined with the view of the rival Haggadist, who connects the verb with דלג *steps*, which is less spiritual than the former explanation. R. Elieser

v. *Hamagid*, 1866, col. 368, further *Hakarmel*, 1872, pp. 72 and 448, L. Blau, *Massoretische Untersuchungen*, Strassburg, 1891, pp. 56 f. The term is to be found in the teachings of R. Joshua b. Hananyah, v. Mekilta of R. Simon, p. 75, on Exod. xvi. 4. לכם, unto you, is expounded as בודאי לכם, 'as fit unto you and to none else', which is opposed by R. Eleasar of Modiim, who sees in the word an allegorical reference to the merit of the fathers. Similarly a dispute is recorded between the same teachers on Exod. xviii. 3 on the word נכריה, where R. Joshua again uses the term ודאי to indicate that the word is to be understood literally, whilst R. Eleasar saw in it a reference to idolatry practised in that land, Mekilta, ibid., p. 86, v. also Mekilta, ad. loc. R. Akiba, in opposition to R. Elieser, sees in Exod. xiii. 5 in the expression 'a land overflowing with milk and honey, חלב ודאי, actually mountains flowing with milk, cf. Joel iv. 18, whilst his opponent, an allegorist, sees in it the produce of fruit trees (v. Mekilta of R. Simon, p. 32). There is an instance in which the term ודאי is cited in the Haggadah of R. Ishmael; it seems, however, that it was meant as a question to the literalist R. Akiba, v. Exod. r. v. 23, v. also J. Bassfreund, 'Über ein Midrasch-Fragment in der Stadt-Bibliothek zu Trier', *MGWJ.*, vol. xxxviii, 1894, p. 175, and Marmorstein, 'Zur Erforschung des Jelamdenu-Problems', ibid., lxxiv, 1930, p. 280. R. Judah interprets Lev. xix. 4 as 'do not look at the idols', using the term ודאי, whilst the anonymous interpreter renders the sentence as 'do not turn to the idols in order to worship them' (v. Sifra, p. 76 a). The term is somewhat strange in this connexion, since the literal meaning of the verse can apply to both, looking at or worshipping before idols. For other instances cf. Mekilta of R. Simon, pp. 101, 114, 115, pal. Yebamoth 8 d, Kiddushin i. 7, Gen. r., p. 142, Tanh. iv, ed. Buber, p. 114.

[8] Mekilta of R. Simon, p. 14.

agrees with the view of R. Jonathan. The Sages who speak of God's jumping or skipping, concur with the anthropomorphic exposition of R. Josiah in the Mekilta.[9] R. Elieser, we know, belongs to the allegorical interpreters of the Bible,[10] and the Rabbinic text has to be amended accordingly.

(2) R. Akiba[11] propagates the theory, discussed earlier in these essays, that the redemption of Israel is the salvation of God. His remark refers to 2 Sam. vii. 23.[12]

(3) R. Yose the Galilean is credited in one place in the Mekilta of R. Simon with this term, which, however, cannot be correct.[13]

(4) R. Judah b. Ilai[14] delivers a very anthropomorphic Haggadah under the cover of this term; it is also very doubtful whether the sentence really belongs to him.

(5) R. Simon b. Yohai on Gen. iv. 10, ' thy brother's blood cries to me ' &c.[15]

(6) Bar Kappara.[16]

(7) R. Joshua b. Levi on Deut. vii. 10, explaining the words אל פניו.[17]

(8) R. Yochanan b. Nappacha uses this term three times in order to convey anthropomorphic teachings, which are not at all warranted in the Scriptures.[18]

(9) R. Simon b. Lakish shares fully the anthropomorphic views advanced by his colleague, and adds many more of his own to them.[19]

---

[9] p. 8 b.   [10] v. above, p. 39.   [11] v. above, pp. 40 ff.

[12] Sifre Num., § 84, Mekilta 16 a, Agadath Shir ha-Shirim, ed. Schechter, p. 20, l. 519.

[13] Ed. Hoffmann, p. 40; v. however Mekilta, p. 25 a, where this teaching is recorded in the name of another teacher, v. above, p. 37.

[14] Sifre Num., § 106, cf. also pal. Sotah i. 1, b. Sotah, p. 13 b.

[15] Gen. r., ch. xxii, ed. Theodor, p. 216; v. also A. Kaminka, *HUCA.*, x, 1935, p. 161.

[16] Gen. r., ch. i. 1.   [17] b. Erubin 22 a.

[18] v. Rosh Hashanah 17 b, God is wrapt in a praying-shawl like a precentor in the congregation; b. Baba Bathra 10 a, God is indebted to a charitable person as is a debtor to his creditor; v. also Lev. r. xxxiv. 2, where the same teaching is ascribed to R. Simon b. Lakish, cf. further Lev. r. xxxvii. 2; b. Baba Bathra 26 a on Job ii. 3.

[19] Tanh., ed. Buber, v. 54, Tanh. f. 283 a, Pesikta, ed. Buber 93 a; the correct reading is preserved in Yalkut, i. § 931, Moses decrees, and God

(10) R. Hama b. Hanina.[20]

(11) R. Abbahu.[21]

(12) R. Reuben.[22]

With the exception of two teachers in this list, R. Judah b.
Ilai and R. Joshua b. Levi, all of them belong to the class of
Bible commentators who took the text in its strict literal sense,
and felt no objection to the grossest anthropomorphic expressions. Moreover, they overdid the Biblical anthropomorphism
by creating situations for which there is no warrant in the
Scriptural text. Extreme literalism alone could dare to proclaim
that God is suffering in Israel's exile, that God is judged by
human judges, and in fine, that God acts as a congregational
leader, that God obeys the decrees of mortal beings, and so on
and so forth. The formula used by them is a far-reaching
tribute to the letter of the Bible. Although being fully aware
of the fact that such terms, in an ordinary way at least, cannot
be applied to God in any sense, yet the Biblical expression
entitles the reader to say so, and if so inclined, to exaggerate it.

The same experience, namely of the interdependence between
literalism and anthropomorphism, can be gained from the
anonymous Haggadah, i.e. teachings and homilies which are
preserved by the compilers and editors of the Midrashim without mentioning the name of their authors. Some of them deserve full and careful attention, and will be discussed here.

There are numerous such Haggadoth which are rendered in
the same phraseology, speaking of God as mourning, or as suffering exile. Thus Midr. Lam. r., p. 138: אמר הקב״ה פלגי
מים תרד עיני על שבר בת עמי, אילולא שהכתוב מדבר
היה הלשון שאומרו חייב לחתכו אבר אבר, אלא קדמו
הראשונים שנ׳ וקדמונים אחזו שער (Job xviii. 20); ibid., p. 148,
כיון שראה אותם הקב״ה חגר שק ותלש בשערו, ואלמלא וכו׳.
הה״ד ולקרחה ולחגור שק (Isa. xxii. 12); ibid., p. 161 = p. 138·

---

complies with it. Midr. Psalms, xl. 5, ed. Buber, p. 388 f., further b.
Hullin 99 b.

[20] Tanh., ed. Buber, v, p. 30.

[21] b. Ber. 32 a and b. Sanh. 95 a.

[22] Cant. r. ii. 4, Ginze Schechter, i, p. 87, omitting the name of this
Haggadist.

האמורה הזו שהלבישו אותך מה היא עושה Pes. r. p. 134a,
עליך ? אילולי שהדדבר כתוב אי אפשר לאומרו עשה ה'' אשר
לא מלאכי (Lam. ii. 17); ibid., p. 135, זמם בצע אמרתו
השרת בלבד אלא הקב''ה נשא עמהם, אלמלא וכו' למענכם
קרובה שלחתי בבלה (Isa. xliii. 14); Exod. r., ch. xxx. 21,
ישועתי לבא, כי קרובה ישועתכם אינו אומר אלא ישועתי, יהי
שמו מבורך אילולא שהדדבר כתוב וכו' אל הקב''ה לישראל
אם אין לכם זכות בשבילי אני עושה כביכול, כל ימים שאתם
בצרה אני עמכם שנ' עמו אנכי בצרה, ואני גואל לעצמי שנ'
וירא כי אין איש, וכה''א גילי מאד בת ציון וכו'. ומושיע אין
כתיב כאן אלא ונושע, הוי אפי' אין בידכם מעשים עושה
הקב''ה בשבילו. Here again ideas are conveyed and supported
by Biblical references which were mentioned in an earlier chapter as the teachings of Haggadists who belong to the school of
literal interpreters of the Bible. Considering that most of the
teachers who use this term cannot be grouped with the allegorists, and furthermore that the anthropomorphisms in the
Haggadic sayings introduced by this formula were taught by
teachers of the opposite camp, the proof seems to be decisive
that the formula אלמלא מקרא כתוב אי אפשר לאומרו belongs to the terminology of the school of R. Akiba and his
followers. It is surely more than a blind coincidence, and
confirms the result of this investigation, that R. Akiba is
credited in Midrash Canticles zutta, ed. Buber, p. 17, with
the phrase: 'A man would surely be guilty of death if he
should utter such a word, now, however, as it is written in the
text, it is permitted to say so.' Thus he defends the conception
that God is really indebted to the person who acts charitably
towards His creditors. A man who lends money to a centurion
will boast of it, more so if he put the hegemon under obligation
to him, how much more if the king himself is his debtor.
This applies also to God.

This phrase offers another opportunity to establish a link
between the Palestinian and the Alexandrian Haggadah. Philo
in the third book of his *Allegorical Interpretations*[23] makes

[23] Ch. ii, ed. Loeb, v. 1, p. 303.

the following remark: 'Were one not to take the language as figurative, it would be impossible to accept the utterance (the statement that man is said actually to hide himself from God), for God fills and penetrates all things and has left no spot void or empty of His presence.' This sentence might have come from R. Ishmael, or R. Yose the Galilean who would have adorned it with many Biblical references. Philo, and perhaps before him some Palestinian allegorists likewise, may have emphasized the figurative meaning of the text. The opposition, however, laid stress on the written words which must be understood literally. They retorted that if it had not been *written*, then, surely, it would be *impossible* to say so; now that it is written there is no obstacle in the way of uttering, or believing, such things. A trace of the Philonic terminology is still preserved in the Haggadah of the Rabbinic allegorists. Such Haggadoth will be the subject of the next paragraphs.

2. In the first place attention will be called to some passages in which the Haggadists raise the question: וכי אפשר לומר כן ? is it possible to say so? The question fully coincides with the words of Philo. Furthermore the teacher or preacher who believed and adhered to the letter of the text would be reluctant to ask such a question. To him the letter, whatever there may be behind it, is sufficient to guarantee the sacredness of the narrative. Mekilta, p. 28a, וה' הולך לפניהם; ibid., p. 37a, *R. Ishmael*, יומם, אפשר לומר כן והלא כבר נאמר ?; ibid., p. 38a, זה אלי ואנוהו, וכי אפשר להנוות קונו?; ibid., p. 54a, יי איש מלחמה אפשר לומר כן? והלא כבר נאמר והיה כאשר ירים משה ידו וכו' וכי ידיו של משה מגברות ויגד משה, p. 63b, ישראל או ידיו שוברות עמלק? אלא וכו' וכי מה אמר המקום למשה לאמר לישראל או מה אמרו לו יכול ממש שירד הכבוד p. 65b, ישראל לאמר למקום? וירד יי על הר סיני וכו' שומע אני p. 72b, והציעו על הר סיני? כמשמעו אמרת ומה אחד משמש וכו'. It can be observed that these questions were asked in the school of R. Ishmael, which represented the allegorical method of exegesis. In some places the introductory formula was omitted, like Mekilta, p. 8a, in the saying of R. Ishmael on וראיתי את הדם, where the question is

raised: ‏והלא הכל גלוי לפניו?‏ (repeated on p. 12 a). There
are many indications that the seemingly daring and irreverent
question ‏וכי אפשר לומר כן‏ was omitted. Tanhuma, f. 80 a
renders the quotation given above from Mek. 28 a thus: ‏וה, הולך‏
‏לפניהם יומם הלא כבר נאמר הלא את השמים וכו'‏. The
formula is also used in the Haggadah of the Amoraim. R. Jonathan b. Eliezer, who asks: ‏קול ה' בכח אפשר לומר כן?‏ [24] and
R. Isaac Nappacha [25], who asks: ‏וכי אפשר לו / אדם לישב‏ [26]
‏על כסא יי?‏ are two witnesses that the school of the allegorists survived the epoch of the Tannaim and found loyal
successors in the third century.

It will be useful to revert again to Philo. The very question
of Philo, or of his predecessors, how can a mortal hide before
God?, was discussed by the teachers of Palestine. The report
about Jonah's flying from before God is questioned: ‏וכי מפני‏
‏יי הוא בורח והלא כבר נאמר וכו'?‏ (Mek. 1 b). Thereon the
usual Biblical verses are cited proving the omnipresence of
God. Similarly, the passage Gen. iv. 16 about Cain ‏ויצא קין‏
‏מלפני יי‏, was explained allegorically by several Haggadists of
the Amoraic age who hesitated a great deal before taking the
meaning of the word literally.[27] Such questions may safely be
ascribed to the school of R. Ishmael, or to other allegorical
interpreters of the Scriptures. Looking for further material of
this kind, the Mekilta of R. Simon b. Yohai offers some help.
On p. 109 the question is raised: ‏וכי יש לפניו עמל ויגע הלא‏
‏וכי יש לפניו קנאה?‏ (Isa. lx. 28), or, p. 105, ‏כבר נאמר וכו'?‏.

3. Another term used by this school is the question: ‏וכי‏
‏תעלה על דעתך לומר‏ by which the Haggadist raises doubts
about the literal meaning of the text, anticipating an allegorical
interpretation. It is not at all surprising that R. Yose the
Galilean, whom one has to recognize as a prominent representative of the allegorical method, is very frequently named
as author of these sentences in which this formula occurs.

[24] v. Exod. r. xxviii. 5, cf. Yalkut Makiri Ps. lxviii. 27.
[25] v. above, p. 62.
[26] v. Cant. r. i. 10, Pesikta, ed. Buber 28 b.
[27] v. Gen. r. ch. xxiii, ed. Theodor, p. 220, and parallels.

A few instances may suffice to show this. Sifre Deut. § 277,

ולא תשכב בעבוטו, וכי תעלה על דעתך שישכב בעבוטו
ובאת אל הכהן ;ibid. § 298, אלא שלא ישכב ועבוטו עמו
אשר יהיה בימים ההם זו היא שאמר <u>רבי יוסי הגלילי</u> וכי
תעלה על דעתך שתלך אצל כהן שלא יהיה בימיך אלא כהן
לפני מותו, וכי תעלה על דעתך ;ibid. § 342, שהוא כשר
שלאחר מותו היה משה מברך את ישראל וכו' וכיוצא בו
הנה אני שולח לכם את אליהו וכו' וכי עלתה בדעתך שלאחר
וסוף דבר ;Exod. r. chap. xix. 4, ביאת היום אליהו מתנבא וכו'
לא תעלה על דעתך שיעקב לחם ושמלה שאל, אלא אמר
יעקב הבטחני הקב"ה שהוא עמדי ויעמיד ממני את העולם,
והיה אלהים ;Exod. r. xiii. 8, אימתי יודע אני שהוא עמדו וכו'
עמכם, וכי תעלה על דעתך כשהיה יעקב חי לא היה הקב"ה
אשר שם צפרים יקננו וכי תעלה על ;Exod. r. xxxv. 1, עם בניו?
דעתך ששם (כלומר בבהמ"ק) צפרים היו מקננות? אלא
הצפרים שהיה כהן שוחט ומקריב בבהמ"ק. These instances
could easily be multiplied. Yet further instances would merely
confirm the theory which can be proved by the examples cited
here. Only an exegetical method which rejects the literal meaning of the text could raise such a question, and, finally, supply
an allegorical interpretation as is done in all the cases at our
disposal. A fuller and elaborate discussion of one of R. Yose's
teachings, who like R. Ishmael opposed R. Akiba's literal expositions, will throw light on the attitude of both schools. Sifre
Deut. § 153 brings the following Barayta in the name of R. Yose
the Galilean : <u>אשר יהיה בימים ההם</u>, וכי תעלה על דעתך
שאדם הולך אצל שופט שלא נמצא בימיו? אלא מה ת"ל אל
השופט אשר יהיה בימים ההם? אלא שופט שהוא כשר ומוחזק
באותן הימים, היה קרוב ונתרחק כשר, וכן הוא אומר, אל
תאמר מה היו שהימים הראשונים היו טובים מאלה כי לא
מחכמה שאלת על זה (Eccles. vii. 10). Any careful reader
must observe that the verse taken from Ecclesiastes contradicts
the first part, the teaching of R. Yose the Galilean. There is
a *lacuna* between the first and the second part of this Barayta.
This Barayta is quoted in a shortened form in the same

Midrash, § 298 (v. above, p. 115) with reference to the priest. Further, see b. Sanhedrin 28 a, and b. Kiddushin 15 b. These two extracts from the original Barayta throw light on the difficult expression באותן הימים in the text of the Sifre. Accordingly R. Yose says that a man may call on a judge who is a קרוב ונתרחק, i.e. whose earlier relationship which would disqualify him to act as judge had ceased, and on the other hand may not bring his offerings to a priest, who is כשר ונתחלל, i.e. was at one time a fully qualified priest, but for some reason had forfeited his qualification. Therefore the text, in the words בימים ההם, conveys the meaning that the judge or the priest has to be fully qualified to function on that occasion. Rabbinic sources preserve this Barayta further in the Tosefta Rosh Hashanah, chap. 1, and b. R. H. 25 a f., where, however, first of all the name of the teacher is omitted, and which secondly contains an additional sentence which enables the student to complete, or supplement, the part missing from the Sifre. There the teaching is deduced that הא אין לך לילך אלא אל שופט שבימיך, i.e. the judge, whether good or bad, qualified or not, has the authority in his days. This is proved by the passage from Ecclesiastes. This means to say that the text is to be interpreted quite literally, and not allegorically as suggested by R. Yose the Galilean. This second interpretation helped the defenders of the Patriarch R. Judah II, who appointed unqualified, ignorant judges to offices, to justify the action and confirm the authority of these judges in spite of vehement opposition to them.[28] R. Yochanan b. Nappacha, one of the foremost advocates of these appointments, derived from this incident his view that men like Gideon, Samson, or Jephtah, the קלי העולם, are to be respected and obeyed, if they attain high positions in life, like Moses, Aaron, and Samuel (Eccles. r. on ch. i. 5). The original text of the Sifre may be, therefore, emended as follows:

1. אשר יהיה בימים ההם

---

[28] v. Marmorstein, ' L'opposition contre le patriarch R. Juda II ' in *RÉJ.*, vol. lv, 1912, pp. 59 ff., and ארבעה מחקרים בתלמוד ובמדרש ס׳ היובל לכבוד הרב הכולל דר׳ צדוק העוועשי, Budapest, 5694, pp. 66–67.

2. וכי תעלה על דעתך שאדם הולך אצל שופט <u>או אצל</u>
<u>כהן</u> שלא נמצא בימיו?

3. ומה ת״ל אשר יהיה בימים ההם?

4. אלא זה שופט <u>או כהן</u> שהוא כשר ומוחזק באותן הימים,
היה קרוב ונתרחק כשר, כשר ונתחלל פסול.

5. [ד״א הא אין לך לילך אלא לשופט שבימיך] וכה״א
אל תאמר וכו'.

It can be shown that R. Ishmael also used this term: וכי
תני ר', תעלה על דעתך, for instance, pal. Ketuboth iv. 5,
ישמעאל זה אחד משלשה מקריות שנאמרו בתורה במשל, אם
יקום והתהלך בחוץ וכו'. וכי עלה על דעתך שיהא זה מהלך
בשוק והלה נהרג על ידיו? For further instances cf. b. Sabb.
10a; M. Sota ix. 4; Sifre, ad. loc., Sifre Deut. § 222. It must
not be considered as accidental that R. Akiba prefers the term
עלת על לב, v. Sifra, p. 10b, v. also R. Simon b. Yohai, ibid.,
p. 8a; R. Yochanan b. Nappacha pal. Ber. ii. 1. Other instances
for תעלה על דעת, v. Exod. r. xix. 4.

That R. Yose the Galilean was fond of the allegorical method,
and rejected the literal interpretation of the text, can be demonstrated by numerous instances. Here a small number of them
will suffice:

(1) Deut. xxxii. 2 where the verb ערף is explained as *atonement*, cf. Deut. xxi. 4, וערפו שם את העגלה, just as the calf
atones for bloodshed, so the words of the Torah for all the sins
committed. Sifre Deut. § 306, p. 131b where R. Eleasar, the
son of R. Yose the Galilean, is mentioned as the author of this
explanation, v. however Midrash Tannaim, p. 184, v. however
Sifre Deut. § 207, belonging to the school of R. Akiba, where
the verb is taken literally.

(2) Deut. xxi. 21. R. Yose the Galilean questions the justice
of the stoning of the בן סורר ומורה by the question raised:
וכי מפני שאכל זה טרטימר בשר ושתה לוג יין אמרה תורה
יצא לבית דין ויסקל? אלא הגיעה התורה לסוף דעתו של בן
סורר ומורה, Sifre Deut. § 220, Midr. Tann., p. 131, M.
Sanh. 72a.

(3) Deut. xx. 8, R. Akiba explains the term הירא ורך הלבב
literally, a man, who is afraid and cannot stand the hardships
of the battle, R. Yose the Galilean, however, זה שהוא מתירא
מן העבירות שבידו, Sifre Deut. § 197, where this teaching is
given anonymously, probably by R. Ishmael. R. Yose is represented by the explanation זה בן מ' שנה, v., however, Midr.
Tann., p. 120, M. Sota iv. 5, Tosefta, ch. vii, v. J. Brüll, מבוא
המשנה Frankfurt, 1876, p. 127.

(4) Gen. iii. 16, והוא ימשל בך, אומר ר' יוסי הגלילי יכול
ממשלה בכל צד? ת"ל לא יחבול ריחים ורכב (Deut. xxiv. 6),
v. Gen. r. ch. xx., ed. Theodor, p. 191. For the history of the
allegorical interpretation of the verse, v. Ps.-Jonathan Targum,
Jerushalmi, Deut. xxiv. 6, Grönemann, *Die Jonathan'sche
Pentateuch-Übersetzung in ihrem Verhältnisse zur Halacha*,
Leipzig, 1879, p. 96. Chajes, Z. Hirsch, אמרי בינה, p. 19,
Geiger, *Urschrift*, p. 471, Poznanski, *Kohler Festschrift*, p. 294.

(5) An exception to this experience seems to be the exposition of R. Yose the Galilean, on Ps. lxviii. 17, where he explains the verse literally, whilst R. Akiba is credited with the
allegorical method. No doubt the text has to be reversed.
R. Akiba expounds the verse literally as the race of the mountains, and R. Yose the Galilean as that of the tribes to receive
the Torah. The proper reading ought to be first R. Akiba,
then R. Yose ha-Gelili, v. Gen. r. ch. xcix, ed. Theodor, p. 127 f.;
v. Mek. p. 65b, Midr. Ps., ed. Buber, ch. lxviii, 9; Pes. r. ch. 7,
Num. r. xiii. 2.

4. There is a third phrase used by the adepts of the allegorical exegesis of the Scriptures, namely דברה תורה כלשון
בני אדם, the Torah speaks in the language of man. Such a
term could be used only by a teacher who does not accept the
literal meaning of the text as binding. A few instances may
prove this assertion. Sifre Deut. § 42, R. Ishmael, ד"א ואספת
דגנך, למה נאמר? לפי שהוא אומר לא ימיש ספר התורה
הזה מפיך, שומע אני כמשמעו, ת"ל ואספת דרך ארץ דברה
תורה [כלשון בני אדם]. R. Simon b. Yohai, surely following
his teacher's, R. Akiba's, view, takes the text literally. Ibid. § 34,
בשבתך בביתך בלכתך בדרך דרך ארץ דברה תורה כלשון

בני אדם. B. Ber. 31 b records a controversy between R. Ishmael and R. Akiba which at first sight would upset the theory that the term דברה תורה כלב״א belongs to the school of R. Ishmael, for there we read: דתניא ונקתה ונזרעה זרע מלמד שאם היתה עקרה נפקדת דברי ר׳ ישמעאל, ר׳ עקיבא אומר אם כן ילכו כל העקרות כולן ויסתתרו וכו׳ מאי ראה תראה דברה תורה כלשון בני אדם. The correct reading is, however, given in b. Sota, 26a, where the names are given in the right order, first R. Akiba, and in the second place R. Ishmael; v. also Sifre Num. § 19, b. Sanh. 56a. The discussion in the Talmud assumes that R. Isaac Nappacha, whom we recognized as belonging to the late adherents of the allegorical school, was guided by the same principle, דברה תורה ? איש איש למה לי הכרת תכרת הכרת בעוה״ז תכרת, b. Sanh. 64b, כלשון ב״א לעוה״ב. דברי רבי עקיבא, אמר לו רבי ישמעאל והלא כבר נאמר ונכרתה וכי שלשה עולמים יש? אלא ונכרתה בעולם הזה, הכרת לעולם הבא, תכרת דברה תורה כלשון בני אדם. This reading cannot be correct. First of all because it is not in the spirit of R. Ishmael's exegesis, and secondly, because there is no difference between R. Akiba and R. Ishmael. The correct reading is preserved in Sifre Num. § 112, הכרת תכרת הכרת בעוה״ז תכרת לעולם הבא, דברי ר׳ עקיבא, א״ל רבי ישמעאל לפי שהוא אומר ונכרתה הנפש ההיא שומע אני שלש כריתות בשלשה עולמות ת״ל הכרת תכרת הנפש ההיא דברה תורה כלשון בני אדם. There are further more instances, where the duplication of the noun (איש איש), or the verb (המול ימול) indicates, according to R. Akiba, some new teaching, whilst R. Ishmael's school understood them as דברה תורה כלשון בני אדם.[29] For my purpose it is sufficient to establish the division which existed and the guiding principles underlying these controversies. The same method was applied to the problems of anthropomorphism, which underwent entirely different treatments in the two opposing schools and in those of their successors.

[29] v. Sanh. 85b, 90b, Abodah Zarah 27a, Zebahim 108b, Niddah 32b, 44b, Arakin 3a, Maseroth 12a, b. Kid. 17b.

Geiger teaches that the application of this term to the re-
moval of anthropomorphic passages of the Bible is of a later
date, and of post-Talmudic origin.[30] Yet, apart from the
remarkable coincidence demonstrated in the previous lines
that the term is mainly used by teachers of the allegorical
school, there is some external proof for the earlier date of this
term and its meaning. Apart from Justin Martyr, a contemporary of R. Ishmael and R. Akiba,[31] there is Clement of
Alexandria who enjoyed the tuition of a Jewish teacher, whose
words are quite unmistakable : ' To interpret the will of the
passionless God as akin to our emotions is to interpret the
Scriptures carnally. The ascription of joy or pity to Him is
a concession to our weakness.' [32] What does that mean if not
דברה תורה כלשון בני אדם ?

5. In the same Tannaitic school a term was used to mitigate some more or less gross anthropomorphic expressions.
There is a legend that when God first revealed Himself to
Moses he imitated the voice of Amram, the father of Moses,
so that he should not be frightened.[33] Because, it is added,
one makes the ears hear, what they can grasp. The editor of
Exodus rabba [34] records this legend in the name of one of the
latest Palestinian Haggadists of the fourth century, namely,
R. Joshua b. R. Nehemayah. This fact, however, does not rule
out the Tannaitic origin of the legend, as confirmed by the
defence of the anthropomorphism in the language of the earlier
school. The same term is applied to several passages which
are arranged in the same Mekilta [35] namely, (a) on Exod. xix. 18,
' like the smoke of the furnace'. You might think actually like
the smoke of a furnace. The text says, Deut. iv. 11, ' and the
mount was burning in fire'. Wherefore, then, does the text say:
' like a furnace ' ? One makes the ears hear what they are
capable of grasping. (b) Ezek. xliii. 2, ' and the glory of the God
of Israel came from the eastern way and His voice was like
that of many waters'. Is that possible? But the ear hears what

---

[30] v. now his *Qebuzath Mamarim*, p. 308 f.
[31] v. Goldfahn, *Justin Martyr und die Agada*, p. 18, note 1.
[32] v. Patrick, *Clement of Alexandria*, p. 274.
[33] v. Mekilta R. Simon, ed. Hoffmann, p. 167.
[34] Ch. iii. 1.   [35] v. pp. 100–1.

it is capable of grasping. (c) Ps. xxiv. 8, 'The Lord is strong
and mighty, the Lord is strong'. (d) Amos iii. 8, 'the lion
roars, who is not frightened?' (e) Deut. xxxii. 2, 'let my
teaching come down like rain.' Is it possible that the rain is
greater than the words of the Torah, to which they are compared? We find further the same term in the Mekilta p. 94,
on the words 'and I carried you on eagle's wings', Exod. xix. 4.
In the Mekilta of R. Ishmael, p. 68 b, only the passages from
Ezekiel and Amos are enumerated; further the answer given
is not אלא משמיעין את האוזן מה שיכולה לשמוע, but
לשכך את האוזן מה שיכולה לשמוע. Rashi on Exod. xix. 18,
copies the instances brought forward in the Mekilta of R.
Ishmael, and reads לשבר את האוזן, perhaps read לסבר ?
Rashi applies this rule also in his commentary on Exod. xxxi.
17, probably taken from an ancient Midrash, where the often
discussed difficulty about God's resting on the day of Sabbath
is spoken of. Since God did not toil or work in accomplishing
His creation but did so by His mere word, the logos,[36] how can
one say God rested? Later in the Haggadah of the Amoraim
the more literal view was upheld and it was taught that God
finished the work of creation, but that his work still goes on,
scil. rewarding the righteous and punishing the wicked which
is regarded as work.[37]

Besides the two Mekiltas there are other ancient literary
documents in which this rule occurs. Thus in the fourteenth
paragraph of the Baraytah of R. Elieser b. R. Yose ha-Gelili
where the rule is styled: מדבר גדול שנתלה בדבר קטן
כדי להשמיע האוזן כדרך שישמע, i.e. 'from a great thing,
which is made dependent on a small one, in order to make the
ear hear what it may understand'. As instances the passages
from Deut. and Amos are adduced. In later sources the saying
is ascribed to R. Elieser, the son of R. Yose the Galilean.[38]
The teaching took a more elaborate form in Aboth de Rabbi

[36] v. the view of R. Judah b. Simon, Gen. r., ch. x, p. 85.
[37] Cf. Gen. r., ch. xi, p. 96, R. Phineas in the name of R. Hoshayah,
Pes. r., ch. xxiii, p. 120 b, and ch. xli, p. 174 a. Midrash haggadol, p. 64,
R. Huna in the name of R. Aha.
[38] v. Yalkut Deut., par. 942.

Nathan,[39] where first of all Isa. xlii. 13, then the verses from Amos and Ezekiel, are quoted. Finally the rule is somewhat enlarged in the saying: מראין את העין מה שיכולה לראות ומשמיעין את האוזן מה שיכולה לשמוע. The first version differs from the second where the verses from Amos, Ezekiel, and Deuteronomy are enumerated. Thirdly, the passage occurs in a Yelamdenu fragment, published by Neubauer, *RÉJ*. xiv. 97, from Makiri (Tanhuma), where, however, only Exodus and Amos are given. In conclusion attention may be drawn to a figure of speech, similar to this, used more than once in Gnostic documents: ' and he saw, what an eye cannot see, no ear hear, and the heart cannot grasp', where the Biblical wording seems obvious, and may have a closer bearing on the Haggadic phrase discussed here.

6. One may infer from the material brought forward in the previous paragraphs that neither the Tannaim, nor the Amoraim, their successors in the schools and synagogues, were unanimous in their views and teachings about the problems of anthropomorphism and anthropopathism. This subject still requires some further elucidation. On the one side high praise is bestowed upon the great prophets of Israel for ' being invested with the great gift of comparing the creature to the Creator', מדמין את הצורה ליוצרה; on the other side such an attempt is condemned as rather daring and beyond the power of human faculties. In order to make clear these divergent points of view, one has to examine the sayings of the two schools and their representatives, which course may enable the student to establish their proper place in the history of Jewish religious speculation.

To begin with, there is Hezekiyah b. R. Hiyya, who partly belongs to the age of the Tannaim, having sat at the feet of the last great masters of that period, and repeated their words by saying: ' Blessed are the Prophets, who are capable of comparing the creature to its Creator, the plant to its planter, as it says in Ps. lxxxiv. 12, " for sun and shield is the Lord God"; further Amos iii. 8 " a lion roareth, who will not fear?", and finally Ezek. x. 2 " and the Lord God of Israel cometh from,

[39] Cp. IX, ch. ii, ed. Schechter, p. 12.

&c., and his voice is like the voice of many waters and the earth was lit up by his glory". Yet one makes the ear hear what it can grasp, and the eye see what it can behold.'[40] The actual closing remarks themselves, as was shown in the previous paragraph, are borrowed from the terminology of the allegorical Haggadah[41] and are to be found in Tannaitic sources on these very same Biblical verses. This is quite natural since this teacher is considered as one of the compilers of Tannaitic works.[42]

Another source at our disposal attributes an almost identical saying to an Amoraic Haggadist who lived near the end of the third century. He illustrates his teaching by quoting Scriptural proofs quite different from those of Hezekiyah. The anthropomorphism of his passages centres around the term איש—אדם used for God. These passages are: Dan. viii. 16, 'and I heard the word of Man'; Man, as we saw above, stands in Rabbinic theology for God.[43] R. Judah b. Simon, belonging to the same period and circle, asserts that there are even more eloquent testimonies to confirm the veracity of the thesis. Ezek. i. 26, 'and on the throne there was the likeness of the appearance of Man';[44] Then Eccles. ii. 21 'The man whose travail is in wisdom, &c.', meaning God.[45] The tendency of these three teachers cannot be interpreted otherwise than as aiming at an attempt to weaken such anthropomorphic expressions as are enumerated in their Haggadah.

In strong contrast and unmistakable opposition to the aims of these teachers, magnifying the glorious seers of old for their great skill in anthropomorphism, are others, condemning and rebuking such an undertaking as that of comparing the creature to the Creator, the form to the former, the vessel to the potter, and the plant to the planter, as utterly futile. The

[40] v. Midrash Psalms, ed. Buber, p. 5.   [41] v. above, p. 7.

[42] v. D. Hoffmann, *Einleitung in die halachischen Midraschim*, Berlin, p. 21 and מכילתא דרבי שמעון, Frankfurt a. M., 1905, p. xii f.

[43] Gen. r., ch. xxvii, ed. Theodor, p. 255.

[44] v. above, pt. i, p. 64 and p. 65.

[45] Eccles. r. on ii. 26, Eccles. z., p. 116, Tanh., ed. Buber, i, p. 24, anonymous; v. also Pes., ed. Buber, p. 36 b, Pes. rabbati, p. 61 b and p. 197 b, Tanhuma Num., Num. r., ch. xix. 4.

literalist, naturally, would see much harm done by such exaggerated and far-reaching comparisons. One cannot say whether these teachers have been cognizant of the fact that the author of the Wisdom of Solomon[46] taught similarly, anticipating them, when he wrote: ' For no man is able to depict God that the picture should convey an idea of His likeness '. The rabbis say that the prophets could do so. Philo concurs with the writer of the 'Wisdom' that the Creator is infinitely superior to the created thing, consequently no attempt at a comparison has the slightest chance of success.[47] Among the Haggadists R. Hoshayah and R. Samuel b. Nahmani offer similar emphatic denials of ability on the part of a human being to emulate God. There is, however, an obvious and radical gulf between the Hellenistic and Palestinian Haggadists on this subject. The former speak and write against idol worshippers, the latter are addressing their words to Jewish Gnostics, by no means less dangerous than the fanatical pagan revivalists of the third century. R. Hoshayah in a most remarkable and significant sermon based on Isa. xxix. 46, illuminates the prophetic 'woe' by the following parable. Once an architect was entrusted with the office of tax-gatherer. As it happened, he had built a city with all her palaces and mansions, secret and hiding places. His new duties brought him to that very place. When he noticed that the inhabitants tried to evade payment of taxes and duties by availing themselves of the convenient trenches and caves and other secret places for hiding themselves, the former architect and present tax-collector exclaimed: ' How stupid of these people who are thinking that they can make use of some secret places by hiding themselves therein, as if I, the builder, had no knowledge of them ? ' Like them, says the prophet, are those men and women in his generation who believe that they have a chance to keep secret their plans and thoughts of evil from their Maker. Doing their deeds in darkness, they assert that God does not know and see their deeds. Such people turn things upside down. Can one attach the same value to the clay or the matter as to the potter who fashions them ? Can the creature be compared with the Creator ? Can the plant be

---

[46] Ch. iv. 16. [47] De decal., ii. 189 ff.

the same as the planter? These apparently wicked people invest
God with human deficiencies. God, they teach, is not omniscient, just as man cannot know or see everything.[48] The
homily is clearly directed against extreme Gnostics whose
theology vigorously deprived the God of the Bible of His
omniscience. The retort was, therefore, most appropriate.
The architect, the Demiourgos, the Creator cannot be told
by the creature: 'Thou hast not made me!'

Gnostics who defended, or rather made use of, the letter of
the Scriptures for the propagation of their pernicious doctrines
and anti-Jewish bias, could not be refuted otherwise than with
their own weapons, with the letter of the Bible. Allegorical
art and skill would not appeal to or satisfy them. R. Hoshayah,
living in the vicinity of the Church Father Origen in Caesarea, defended the Bible as representative of the Jews, just as
Origen did the same as the spiritual head of the Church.
Origen spoke as an allegorist, R. Hoshayah as a literalist. The
Haggadists who were brought into contact with Gnostics could
not shut their eyes, guided by their deep penetrating insight
in, and understanding of, the Hebrew Scriptures, to the movements of the day in their own surroundings which manifested
most striking resemblances to the problems and occurrences
faced by the Prophets and Psalmists of yore. R. Samuel b.
Nahmani who lived and preached in the late years of the
third century expounds Ps. l. 21, seeing in the verse a reflection of the events connected with the making of the golden
calf.[49] אלה (these)—namely the words of greeting, applied to
the golden calf—'thou hast made, and I kept silent'—meaning
God pardoned the nation's crime owing to the supplication of
Moses—'yet, if thou dost think that I am like thee'—namely
the creature like the Creator, the plant like its planter—'then
I will reprove thee, and set them in order before thine eyes'.
This Haggadist as well as R. Hoshayah demonstrates eloquently that none, not even the Prophets, can convey the idea
of God's likeness by parables or allegories. There are limits

---

[48] v. Gen. r., ch. xxiv. 1. Some readings have this teaching in the name
of R. Levi, v. Midrash Psalms, ed. Buber, p. 111.

[49] Deut. r., i. 3.

set to the human understanding and its endeavours to imitate
God.   Allegorical interpreters of the Bible can indulge in
teaching the doctrine of *imitatio dei*, not so theologians whose
teachings are too closely connected with the letter of the Sacred
Writings.

7. The philological meaning of the כביכול, to be registered
here, was discussed by N. Brüll in the *Jeschurun* (ed. Kobak),[50]
but he recognized the theological bearing of this term as well.
He found, first of all, that R. Akiba was the first to make use
of it together with the expression discussed earlier in this
chapter אלמלא מקרא כתוב אי אפשר לאומרו which is the
characteristic way of teaching in the schools of the anthropomorphic Haggadists.   According to Rashi the two terms are
actually synonymous and mean to say or convey the idea: 'if
one could say or assert such a thing of God, one would say'.[51]
R. Joshua b. Joseph of Tlemcen, the author of the methodological work הליכות עולם takes the first two letters כב to
mean 'the Torah which is written in twenty-two letters, can
say thus, but we human beings could not utter such a word.'[52]
Geiger[53] translates the phrase: 'als spräche man von einem,
bei dem so etwas möglich wäre'.   There are many others who
have tried to explain this term in various ways.   Brüll saw in it
the expression otherwise used בנוהג שבעולם, and translates:
*was gewöhnlich geschieht, in dem was in der Welt gebräuch-
lich ist.*   He substantiates his suggestion by the frequent use
of the 'ב in Mishnaic Hebrew in the sense of 'the amount, the
quantity', and יכול in the meaning of ' possibly ', as applied
in the terminology of the Tannaitic Midrash.   Accordingly the
rendering of the term will be: ' wie in der Möglichkeit, als
ob es möglich wäre ', corresponding to the term אתמהא,

[50] Bamberg, 1871, vii, pp. 1–6.

[51] v. Rashi, Yoma 3 a and other passages to be quoted later on in the
course of this paragraph.

[52] Eliyahu Bahur, the grammarian, objects to this interpretation for
several reasons.   They have been endorsed by the Talmudist Yom Tob
Lipman Heller.

[53] *Zeitschrift für wissenschaftliche Theologie*, v. 271, L. Löw, in *Ben
Chananja Forschungen*, p. 91, Pineles, דרכה של תורה, p. 203, Buber,
Pesikta, note 24 on p. 120, Dukes, *Sprache der Mishna*, p. 84.

which occurs in the group of later Midrashim collected in Rabboth.

Brüll's assertions require some modification. First of all it does not hold good that R. Akiba was the first teacher to avail himself of this term. R. Yochanan b. Zakkai, if we may rely on our present textual evidence, used it before R. Akiba in explaining the difference between the treatment of the chief and robber, as to their fines and punishment. R. Yochanan said: 'The robber made equal the honour of the slave with that of his master: the thief, however, put the honour of the slave higher than that of the master. כביכול, he made the Eye of Above (the All-seeing) as if he could not see (as if it were blind) and the Ear of Above as if it were deaf.' He connects this teaching with the following Scriptural references: Isa. xxix. 15, Ps. xciv. 7, and Ezek. ix. 9–10. All the texts have here כביכול.[54] Of the contemporaries of R. Akiba who mention this term in their teachings I refer to Hananyah, the nephew of R. Joshua b. Hananyah, and Simon b. Azzai. The former says: 'It is written כביכול הוצאתיך, I went out with you from Egypt.' By a textual alteration from הוצאתיך into הוצאתיך the meaning given by this Haggadist could be read into the text.[55] The latter uses the term in the sense of 'not even God would do so and so' in teaching 'כביכול God does not mention His name, scil. Elohim, before He said בראשית ברא'.[56] If it should be the case that the term is applied more frequently in the Haggadah of R. Akiba than in that of earlier and succeeding teachers, it can easily be accounted for by the very fact that R. Akiba's Haggadah is richer in anthropomorphic thoughts and his anthropomorphism exceeds that of others, so that either he himself, or later teachers, or even scribes and copyists saw the necessity of inserting or appending this

[54] v. Mekilta 91 b, Tosefta Baba Kamma vii. 2, b. B. K. 79 b.

[55] v. pal. Sukka iv. 3, Pesikta rabbati, ch. xxi, p. 110 a, as to the idea of God's redemption; v. above, pp. 68 ff.

[56] v. Midrash Tannaim, p. 186; cf. parallels to this saying in Gen. r., i. 12, Midrash Psalms xviii. 29, ed. Buber, p. 156, where Simon b. Azzai compares God's ways with those of a king. The latter mentions first his name and title, then his קטיזמא, scil. his works. God does the reverse, namely, 'in the beginning created', is followed by 'Elohim'.

somewhat mitigating and explanatory term. It will be necessary, therefore, in order to make clear the attitude of R. Akiba
on the subject of anthropomorphism, to examine some of his
homilies and sermons in which the term כביכול occurs. Some
have been treated in earlier parts of these essays, but it will
not be entirely unprofitable to read them in this context.

It should, however, first be remembered that in several instances the term כביכול follows that of אלמלא מקרא שכתוב,
as will be shown immediately. Preachers who coupled both of
them together must have been aware of the fact that they could
not be synonymous, unless they were regarded as duplicates, a
point which can be easily demonstrated. Thus, Mekilta p. 16 a,
we read: R. Akiba said אלמלא מקרא כתוב אי אפשר לאומרו
כביכול Israel says to God : ' Thou hast redeemed Thyself'.
It is the same idea which is to be found in the teaching of
Hananyah, the nephew of R. Joshua b. Hananyah [57] Now what
does the duplication of the expression mean ? None of the interpretations registered previously fit in this context. It is not
the only instance in our sources in which these two terms
occur together. R. Abbahu, who belongs to the anthropomorphic school of theology, uses them both together to indicate
that God is also reading the Torah, whilst standing.[58] The
teacher of R. Abbahu, R. Yochanan, uses both terms to indicate
the idea that God is under obligation to him who is charitable
to the poor.[59] The term כביכול by itself is used by a number
of Tannaites and Amoraim. A small collection of such passages
by these teachers may help to establish the exact meaning of this
difficult word for which no adequate explanation is yet forthcoming. R. Eleasar, the son of R. Yose the Galilean, teaches
the great value and the immense importance of peace. For,
כביכול the Satan has no power to touch the worst kind of
idolators who keep peace.[60] Even the best text will remain
obscure if the term be understood to convey some attempt to
remove anthropomorphic teachings or expressions unsuitable

---

[57] v. above, p. 71 f.   [58] b. Meg. 21 a.   [59] b. B. B. 10 a.
[60] v. Sifre Num. Editio Horowitz reads the sentence in the name of
R. Eleasar the son of R. Eleasar ha-Kappar, and adds כביכול אמר
המקום א   השטן וכו' (v. 46).

for use in speaking of or referring to God. Surely, the meaning must be somewhat different! Another interesting case is given in an anonymous Haggadah[61] where a number of difficult passages like Deut. xi. 12, Ps. cxxi. 4, further 1 Kings ix. 3, and Ps. xxix. 8 are contrasted with several passages that prove and assert that God is omnipresent, all powerful. The first passage implies that God's providence is limited to Palestine, whilst Job xxxviii. 26–7 extends it to all the countries of the earth. The second verse limits God's guardianship to Israel, Job xii. 10 teaches that all the living creatures without distinction of race and tongue are in His hand. The third implies that His eyes are THERE all the days, whilst Zech. iv. 10, Prov. xv. 3 convey the teaching that nothing is hidden from Him wherever it may be. The reference to Midbar Kadesh is surprising. In the first three instances the explanation and solution introduces the form of כביכול. God has a special care and providence for the land of Israel, for the people of Israel, for the Sanctuary, but He extends it to all countries, to all flesh, mankind, and to all places. The term, in all the passages, does not avoid anthropomorphism but makes room for both universalism and particularism, general and special providence, in the same breath. The meaning, therefore, attached to the term by ancient and modern scholars, cited above, does not fit here and does not cover fully the proper sense of the sentence.

It is true that there are instances in which anthropomorphic conceptions are introduced and conveyed by such a term. For instance Sifre Deut. 326, Midrash Tannaim p. 201, where we read: 'When God judges the nations there is joy before Him, whilst when He judges Israel כביכול there is regret before Him.' It was observed[62] that the anti-anthropomorphic school did not refrain from ascribing joy and rejoicing to God, nor did they hesitate to speak of His anger; therefore the term need not suggest that it was applied in order to remove anthropomorphic conceptions. There are besides several more indications that the term כביכול is used by both parties, by

[61] Sifre Deut. 40, p. 78 b, Midrash Tannaim, p. 32.
[62] v. p. 44.

anthropomorphic as well as anti-anthropomorphic Haggadists. Exception must be made in the case of passages where both terms, viz. אלמלא and כביכול, are coupled together.

In the dialogues between Pappus and R. Akiba about which v. above pp. 42–47, the term is used in the explanation given by R. Akiba. 'כביכול the Holy One blessed be He appeared on a mare, &c.', v. Mekilta, p. 33 a. An anonymous homilist, probably R. Akiba, depicts the influence of the state of God's relation to Israel when they do or do not do, respectively, His will. In the first case the left of God becomes right, otherwise כביכול the right becomes left. Similarly, when Israel does God's will, there is no sleep before Him, otherwise there כביכול is sleep before Him. Further in the first case, there is no wrath, contrariwise there is. Finally, God fights for His people in the first case, but changes His mercy to cruelty otherwise (Mekilta, 39 a). It is to be observed that only in the first and second antitheses is the term applied, and there also only in the negative parts, and not in the affirmative assertions, although all are of an anthropomorphic character. This fact is to be noted as contradicting all the suggestions offered for finding the possible meaning of the term which do not work in this, as in many other cases. If the term served the purpose, as generally assumed by the scholars mentioned earlier in this chapter, of avoiding anthropomorphic expressions, it is impossible to see how this was achieved by adding it to one anthropomorphism, and omitting it in another. R. Meir, a pupil of R. Akiba, uses this term M. Sanhedrin, vi. 5, where, however, the exact reading is doubtful, v. מתניתא דבני מערבא vi. 10. In some editions of the Exod. r. xv. 12, the teaching, familiar to the Tannaitic Haggadah, is ascribed to him that 'the redemption is to me and you, כביכול I was redeemed together with you'.

A few instances from the Haggadah of the Amoraim shall conclude our collection of the rich material at our disposal in the Rabbinic writings. R. Jonathan b. Elieser remarks anent the commandments קח לך and ויקחו אליך that כביכול 'I prefer yours to theirs' (b. Yoma, 3 b). R. Yochanan b. Nappacha uses

V

1. IT was unavoidable that a literature extending chronologically over a millennium, and geographically over many
lands with different religious and cultural influences, should
lose the traces of its origin and date. Theological discrepancies
and intellectual incongruities, progressive and retrogressive
thoughts, stand peacefully registered and recorded next to one
another. Late compilers and early editors did well to preserve
them both in their Midrashim, affording posterity more than
one clue to the long and arduous history of religious thought,
thus offering a key to open the storehouses of Jewish theology.
They demonstrate and establish with certainty that the most
sublime questions of Jewish religion reached their unanimity
only after passing through many spiritual tests and struggles.
The picture generally drawn of the scribes as dry and pedantic
lawyers and punctilious mincers of words has no chance of
existence when faced with the wealth of material reproducing
their teachings and views about God. Whether a legal or a ritual
question is the centre of their discussions, whether religious
praxis or ethical theory is involved, whether the glorious past
is reviewed or the dream of the future is visualized, they can
touch none of these without bringing dream or reality, law or
prayer, worship or preaching, into living contact with God
Himself. It was only right, therefore, that the דורשי רשומות,
the masters of allegorical studies of old, should have extolled
their branch of religious activity as leading to the recognition
of God.[1] It is consequently the more surprising and perplexing
that the very same literature should tell of unmistakable
antagonism and considerable opposition which arose in the
schools against the writing of the Haggadah, or its study or
propagation from (written) books. The minute details of
this antagonism between Haggadists and Halakists are hidden
from the searcher's eyes to-day, yet the few clear indications

[1] v. above, pt. i, p. 7.

require further illumination and investigation. The material at our disposal for such an investigation is of various dates, and offers no support for any theory of the continuity of such a movement. Nevertheless the fact remains that from time to time condemning or even hostile voices were raised against Haggadic studies and research. It really does not matter whether this opposition arose sporadically or was continuous; sufficient it is to say that it existed. If so, then the theologian or the historian must find out the deeper causes of such an intellectual appearance in Jewish life. First of all, the dates of these extraordinary manifestations have to be discussed.

It may not be accidental that the first period of anti-Haggadic feeling is somehow linked up with the name of R. Akiba. His colleague, R. Eleasar b. Azaryah, calls on him to leave the Haggadah alone, and turn his attention to Ahaloth and Negaim.[2] Surely R. Eleasar b. Azaryah himself taught Haggadah as well as Halakah; then why this rebuke? As from Judea in the first decades of the second, so from Galilee in the last decades of the third century, words of censure against Haggadah and Haggadists reach the student. We are told that R. Zeira, a contemporary of the great Haggadists of Tiberias and Caesarea, abused Haggadic lore by referring to it as to 'books of magicians'.[3] The only way to discover the real significance of these reports is by scrutinizing and analysing them.

The retort of R. Eleasar b. Azaryah was provoked by some of R. Akiba's most remarkable utterances. A dispute arose between R. Akiba and R. Yose the Galilean, whose antagonism to R. Akiba in exegesis and doctrine was duly established in previous chapters, in which the difficulty in Daniel vii. 9 was discussed, where the singular of the one throne and the plural of the many thrones was surely irritating to the advocates of Scriptural literacy. R. Akiba suggested that one throne is for God, the other for David. R. Yose the Galilean thought such

[2] v. b. Hagiga 14a, b, Sanh. 38b, ibid. 67b, Sabb. 96b, Midr. Psalms, ch. 104.

[3] pal. Maaseroth 51a.

an interpretation impossible, and said: Akiba, how long are
you going to profane divine things? As a good allegorist he
suggested that the two thrones represent two attributes of
God, namely, those of justice and mercy. In a later source
R. Akiba is credited with a change of his previous opinion
and as having adopted the point of view of the Galilean
scribe. In spite of this admission he was urged by R. Eleasar
b. Azaryah to refrain from Haggadah and concentrate on
Negaim and Ahaloth. The final result of the protracted controversy was that in reality there was only one throne, yet
that the plural indicates that there was a chair and a footstool
(based on Isa. lxvi. 1). The fact that a pupil of R. Akiba,
namely R. Meir, adopted the allegorical interpretation of
R. Yose the Galilean would tend to show that the master himself abandoned his earlier position.[4] The anthropomorphic
idea of God's using a throne seemed too strong even to the
School of R. Akiba, and became untenable. No wonder that
such anthropomorphic Haggadoth gave rise to and engendered
protests. The same is the case with the second report in which
R. Akiba is firmly requested to leave Haggadic studies and
turn his attention to other branches of learning. R. Akiba
indulged in the following exaggeration: 'One frog filled the
land of Egypt and brought about that terrible plague.'[5] The
singular in Exod. viii. 2 caused the literalist to produce such
extravagant homiletics. Now, apart from these instances,
there are several others which leave no doubt that the literal
adaptation of the Hebrew text of the Bible led to crude anthropomorphisms which the allegorists could not hear without
misgivings and fears for the purity of their religious teachings.
Hence the opposition to the Haggadah as taught and proclaimed by R. Akiba.

About the middle of the third century a movement which
disapproves of spreading Haggadic lore in writing appears in
contemporary literature. R. Joshua b. Levi is inclined to
deprive the writers of such books of their share in the world

---

[4] v. Exod. r. x. 5.
[5] Tanhuma ii, Seder El., ch. vii, Midr. Ps., ch. 78, 6, Sanh. 67 b, Midr.
Lekah Tob, ii, p. 37, v. R. Ilai, Midrash Agada, p. 136 f., anonymous.

to come. He is not less averse to those who look into, or read out of, such manuscripts.[6] R. Hiyya bar Abba who is a younger contemporary of the just named teacher makes no secret of what he thought of the writers of Haggadic documents. He wishes that their hands may be cut off.[7] Finally, there is a third teacher of this age who likewise condemned not only the written, but expressed his undisguised disapproval of the living word of the Haggadah, so that some of the famous Haggadists in his neighbourhood felt justifiably hurt.[8] These rather sharp reprobations of Haggadic lore could not have been directed against the Haggadah as such. On the contrary, the Haggadah was favoured by these preachers as much as by their opponents. The proof of this fact is the rich Haggadic activity of all the above three teachers as documented by their sayings and sermons preserved in the Midrashic literature. The reason for their strange utterances on Haggadic writing and teaching has to be sought for in the same direction as observed in the attitude of R. Eleasar b. Azaryah towards R. Akiba, which points to a dislike of anthropomorphic tendencies in the Haggadah. This significant split in Palestinian Jewish life is merely the continuation of earlier divergences between allegorists and literalists in the Diaspora as well as in Palestine. The under- and cross-currents of these streams can be observed in the Amoraic period, and did not stop during the many centuries of the Geonic and later Rabbinic epochs. That this is the real reason for Zeira's attitude against the Haggadah as taught by his colleagues R. Levi and R. Abba b. Kahana can be confirmed by two facts. First of all by a fuller examination of the report in the Palestinian Talmud, and secondly by investigating Zeira's Haggadah. It cannot be expected that the great masters of the Haggadah would allow to pass unchallenged such a depreciatory statement about the Haggadah and Haggadists made in their presence. As a matter of fact they asked Zeira to suggest some problem for solution which could or would confirm his judgment. He asked them for the meaning of Ps. lxxvi. 11, ' surely the wrath of man shall

[6] Soferim xvi. 10–11.   [7] pal. Shabbath xvi. 1.
[8] pal. Maaseroth 51 a.

praise (or, acknowledge thee), the remainder of wrath shalt thou restrain'. It cannot be accidental that Zeira chose this verse, which has baffled generations of perplexed scholars and commentators for more than two thousand years, to test their skill in their literal exegesis. They actually were not at a loss to understand the verse in its literal meaning as speaking of the divine wrath in this and in the future world. This test case should condemn the literalistic tendency of the Haggadah, for which a man like Zeira has nothing but contempt and condemnation.

If Zeira's Haggadah is carefully reviewed one cannot fail to notice that his was the allegorical method which, as shown, continued the method and view of earlier schools and teachers. It is clear that in spite of the paucity of Zeira's Haggadah, there are still a number of his teachings left which bear out the truth of this assertion. No doubt only an adept and a friend of allegorical exegesis could see in Exod. v. 4 the often neglected yet very true teaching that a man who aspires to a dignity or leading position that is above him, and so is unable to fill the place conscientiously, sins against the sense of the second commandment of the Decalogue.[9] This rebuke of unjustifiable communal, spiritual as well as political, leadership, at the end of the third century, was of more than a mere academic nature.[10] Secondly in Lev. xvi. 2 there is an anthropomorphism which no allegorist can leave unnoticed. ' I will appear in the cloud upon the mercy seat', means according to R. Zeira that God does not punish without a preceding warning.[11] His derivation is based on the use of the future, instead of the past. No doubt the endeavour to mitigate the anthropomorphism tempted Zeira to offer this explanation. Thirdly, his remark on Ps. vii. 12 could be quoted, where he adds to the text that although God is angry, yet He does not punish every day, but at the end.[12] Here again R. Zeira tried to weaken the obvious anthropopathism by seeing in God's anger the

---

9 Pesikta rabbati, p. 111 a.
10 v. the literature quoted on p. 148, note 30.
11 pal. Yoma, ch. i, end, p. 3 b.
12 pal. Sota 24 b, Midrash Psalms, ad loc.

due punishment for offences accumulated and committed against God. Finally, mention may be made of his argument given for the inclusion of the Scroll of Ruth in the Scriptures. This Scroll teaches nothing about pure and impure, about forbidden or permitted things; then why was it included in the Holy Bible? Because, says Zeira, it is a most eloquent testimony for the great value and virtue of charity.[13]

In these selected passages, which convey an idea of the allegorical and anti-anthropomorphic tendency of Zeira's exegetical trend of mind, and moreover the lack of anthropomorphic and anthropopathic Haggadah in his teachings in contrast to some of his contemporaries, R .Yochanan, R. Simon b. Lakish, R. Abbahu, and many others, referred to in earlier chapters of these essays, one may find some confirmation of the view that Zeira was opposed not to Haggadah generally, but to the anthropomorphic Haggadah, whether based on the Biblical text or added to it by legends and speculations. The next step will be to find out whether this view holds good also in the case of the other two earlier and older Amoraim, R. Hiyya bar Abba and R. Joshua b. Levi, or not. We saw that they opposed the writing of Haggadic books and their use for reading purposes or study. It is not without significance that it was on record that R. Yochanan and R. Simon b. Lakish used Haggadic compilations in manuscript.[14] Although R. Joshua b. Levi also confesses with great regret that he sometimes used a Haggadic compilation on Psalms[15]—but this may have happened before he made his condemning announcement. In comparing their respective attitudes about writing Haggadic matters, the contrast and antagonism between the teacher of Lydda, R. Joshua b. Levi, and the teacher of Tiberias, R. Yochanan b. Nappacha, are most striking. In contrast to the words of R. Joshua, we read in the name of R. Yochanan: 'It is a solemn covenant (lit. a covenant cut or sealed) that he who learns Haggadah from a book will not so easily forget his learning.'[16] This sounds pretty plain. It is definitely and deliberately directed against the view held and proclaimed

[13] Ruth r. i. 1.   [14] v. b. Gittin, 60 a; Temura 14 b.
[15] pal. Shabbath, x. 1, Gen. r. xxxiii. 2.   [16] pal. Berakoth 13. i.

by the teacher of Darom. It is surely not accidental that
some data and indications about written Haggadoth in the
circle of R. Yochanan are still preserved. R. Hanina b. Hama
made a remark with reference to what R. Simon b. Lakish
wrote ר׳ חנינא אמר על הדא דכתב ר׳ שמעון בן לקיש.[17]

I turn now to the Haggadah of R. Hiyya b. Abba for
material to establish his opinion on the question of anthropomorphism and, what goes hand in hand with it, his application
of the allegorical method of Bible-exegesis. The place occupied
by R. Hiyya b. Abba requires a more circumstantial description
than any that is possible here in this work. The very fact
that he is to be looked upon as the antithesis of R. Abbahu
speaks eloquently enough for the character of his Haggadah.
This alone may have induced him to give vent to his dislike
of certain Haggadic writings. The literal exposition of the
Bible and the consequences arising out of that method must
have filled him with uneasiness about the future development
of religious thought in Judaism. His Haggadah is far removed
from literality and consequent anthropomorphisms. He, like
his Tannaitic forerunners, dwells on Exod. xiii. 21, 'and God
went before them'. The anthropomorphism is mitigated on
the same lines as those of the earlier allegorist.[18] Further,
he found it necessary to expound the anthropomorphic expressions in 1 Sam. iii. 1 and 1 Kings xviii. 8, where it is said
'and the lad Samuel was serving God before Eli', and 'by
God before whom I stood'. What does the text mean by saying
'he stood before God'? Can one say such a thing? Is God
not omnipresent? The meaning is, that as long as he stood
before Eli, or Elisha before Ahiya ha-Shiloni, it was considered
of the same value as if he had done service before the Shekinah.[19]
In a third Haggadah the anthropomorphism in Num. xiv. 10,
'and the glory of God appeared in the tabernacle, &c.', with
the preceding words of the verse 'and the whole congregation
said that they will stone them with stones' is expounded as

[17] v. Yalkut Makiri Ps. ii. 34; v. also Midr Ps. ii. 13, where, however,
the word דכתב is omitted. The omission is surely due to scribal correction.

[18] Midrash Psalms, ch. xviii, ed. Buber, p. 156, and above, p. 23.

[19] Midrash Samuel, ch. viii, ed. Buber, p. 23.

meaning that they cast stones against Heaven.[20] Finally there is his exposition of Num. xxvii. 21, where the oracle through the Urim and Tumim is rendered in the following way: It does not say according to the order of the Urim and Tumim, but according to the judgment of the Urim and Tumim, which implies that it depends on the heavenly court's decision whether Israel, going to war, will conquer or suffer defeat.[21] This teaching confirms the truth of the observation made by me before[22] that allegorical Haggadists are prone to substitute angels when faced with anthropomorphic difficulties or irrational utterances. Urim and Tumim were, therefore, not oracles, but simple decisions by angels, or other celestial beings.

It remains to demonstrate that this Haggadist combined an anti-anthropomorphic attitude with allegorical exegesis. Thus the word צפונה in Deut. ii. 3 is not translated as 'to the north', according to its literal sense, but allegorically.[23] He says, surely with reference to contemporary political conditions as witnessed by historical evidence,[24] that Jews when threatened by Rome (Edom) with persecution do not offer any resistance to Imperial Rome, but seek a hiding-place till Edom's rule shall disappear. Another instance: R. Phinehas and R. Jeremiah in the name of R. Hiyya b. Abba raised a question regarding 1 Kings ii. 34, 'in his house, in the wilderness'. Surely the

---

[20] b. Sota 55 a.   [21] pal. Shabbath 5 a.
[22] v. above, p. 46.   [23] Deut. r. i. 19.

[24] v. Marmorstein, *Eine messianische Bewegung im dritten Jahrhundert*, *Jeschurun*, ed. Wohlgemuth, xiii, 1927, 16–28, 171–86, 369–85. Attention may here be drawn to another opponent of the messianic party eager to overthrow the heavy and hated yoke of Rome, whose homily is given Midr. Ps., ed. Buber, p. 73, cf. Yalkut Makiri, viii. 1. The preacher speaks first of the Four Kingdoms. The last one is Rome. Then he proves that the 'Redemption is caught in four different forms', quoting Jer. xlix. 9 (harvest), Joel iv. 13 (childbirth), Mic. ii. 2, and Cant. viii. 14 (spices). In all four verses the idea of salvation is expressed with reference to material or physical deliverance. What is the common teaching to be derived from all of them as far as spiritual or political redemption can be considered? A common feature in all four instances is that if they are plucked before their time they bring destruction and are useless to their owners. The application to Israel must be that premature efforts by forcible intervention or military attempts against the Empire are bound to fail and will be harmful to the national cause.

house of Joab was not in the wilderness. This cannot be understood in its literal sense. It means that with the death of Joab the whole of Israel became desolate like a wilderness.[25] Thirdly, Ps. cv. 19, 'till the time when his word comes' (*scil.* fulfilled or true). The context suggests that the word of God is meant, as actually interpreted by the Rabbanan, yet R. Hiyya b. Abba refers it to the word of Joseph.[26] These three instances may suffice for the present purpose.

R. Joshua b. Levi, the third opponent of written and the writing of Haggadoth, holds an altogether exceptional position in the history of the Haggadah. It would require a bulky volume to do justice to his Haggadic activity and production which cannot be discussed here. I confine, therefore, my observations to a few necessary remarks. Legends and traditions of various sorts occupy a great space in this teacher's Haggadah. Their source may have been the so-called Massoreth Haggadah, alluded to in some instances. They abound in anthropomorphist thoughts and ideas. The nature of these sources involves more or less pronounced anthropomorphism as is the case in all popular secular or religious tales and narratives. Significantly enough, these legends or tales about Biblical heroes are supported by Biblical references, or are skilfully interpolated into the Scriptures. This, of course, cannot be attempted, and cannot be achieved only by applying the method of literality, but one has to have recourse also to the allegorical method, of which several examples can be cited. The fact that Zeira figures among the teachers who perpetuated R. Joshua b. Levi's Haggadic teachings, is an additional proof for the agreement between these teachers as to their attitude towards anthropomorphism and literal interpretation of the Bible. The anthropomorphic trend in R. Joshua b. Levi's Haggadah may go back either to his earlier way of thinking and teaching, which he later on abandoned, or to his dependence on his sources, Haggadic traditions and compositions, the origin of which is in most cases unknown to us.

[25] Midrash Samuel, ch. xxv, ed. Buber, p. 124.
[26] v. Gen. r., ch. lxxxvii, end, Midr. Psalms, ch. cv, ed. Buber, p. 451, Yalkut Makiri, cv. 26.

2. An earlier attempt to counteract anthropomorphic conceptions by avoiding literal translations of the Biblical text is recorded in the name of R. Judah b. Ilai, who lived about a hundred years before the antagonists of Haggadic writings and studies in Galilee. He is credited with the teaching that 'whosoever translates the text of the verse literally, tells lies, and whosoever adds to the text is guilty of blasphemy'.[27] Significantly enough early commentators of the Geonic period referred the first part of the sentence to passages like Exod. xxiv. 17, where the visibility of God is spoken of, whilst the second part would condemn such substitutes as 'and they saw an angel of God', instead of 'the glory of God'. One may rightly doubt whether the Geonic commentators faithfully interpreted the words of the Tannaite. It is an established fact that allegorists and teachers of an anti-anthropomorphic tendency are not averse from such substitutes, as shown above.[28] The numerous exegetical and homiletical controversies which took place between R. Judah b. Ilai and R. Nehemayah, and which are recorded in the Talmudim and Midrashim, leave not the slightest shadow of a doubt in which camp R. Judah is to be sought and found. It is sure that he has to be counted among the allegorists, and at the same time among the anti-anthropomorphists. Thus R. Judah followed the line along which R. Ishmael and R. Yose the Galilean went in the footsteps of R. Eleasar of Modiim and R. Elieser the son of Hyrkanos, carrying on the learned tradition of the School of Hillel, and concluding in the Tannaitic period the legacy of the anonymous and to us only faintly known sages who adhered to the figurative interpretation of the Pentateuch and Prophets. The exegesis and theology of R. Judah requires a full monograph; here a few instances will be given to demonstrate on one side that he favoured the allegorical method, and on the other side that he was opposed to anthropomorphisms not only in popular Targumim, but also in the Haggadah. In some cases this rule does not seem to work, as was the case with the controversies

[27] v. Tosefta Megilla, b. Kiddushin 49 a, cf. A. Berliner, *Targum Onkelos*, p. 87, H. Chayes, *Orient. Literaturblatt*, 1840, col. 43.
[28] v. p. 46.

between R. Ishmael and R. Akiba, or R. Joshua and R. Elieser, yet here, as there, these irregularities are due to, or can be accounted for by, negligence or carelessness of scribes and copyists. The following instances are taken from the Genesis Rabba (ed. Theodor-Albeck).

(1) Gen. ii. 8, 'and put there', is explained figuratively as: 'God exalted man', in order to avoid the anthropomorphic implication of the literal meaning of וישם שם, cf. Deut. xvii. 15. R. Nehemayah explains the text as 'invited', or 'persuaded', like a king who has prepared a banquet and invites guests (Gen. r., ch. xv, p. 137).

(2) A similar controversy is recorded on Gen. ii. 15, 'and God took', which means 'exalted' according to R. Judah, cf. Isa. xiv. 2, and 'persuaded' according to R. Nehemayah, cf. Hos. xiv. 3 (Gen. r., ch. xvi, p. 148). Both teachers endeavour to mitigate the anthropomorphism of the text.

(3) Gen. iii. 23, 'and God drove him from the Garden of Eden'. R. Judah explains that he was deprived of his share in Eden in both worlds, whilst R. Nehemayah allows such a possibility only as to this world but not as to the future world (Gen. r., ch. xxi, p. 201).

(4) Gen. iv. 15, 'and God made (put) unto Cain a sign'. R. Judah understood under this anthropomorphism that God caused the sun to shine upon him, as a sign of forgiveness. R. Nehemayah, however, explains the sentence: Cain was afflicted with leprosy because of his crime (Gen. r., ch. xxii, p. 219).

(5) Gen. vi. 6, 'and God repented'. This often discussed anthropomorphism is weakened by R. Judah in his explanation that God regretted to have created man from the lower, and not from the upper world, for if he had done the latter, man would not have rebelled against God. R. Nehemayah does not mind taking the verb literally (Gen. r., ch. xxvii, 6, p. 258).

(6) Gen. vi. 19, 'and from all the beasts'. R. Judah says that the unicorn did not enter the ark, but its young ones did. R. Nehemayah denies this, but thinks that Noah tied the unicorn next to the ark, and thus it was preserved. The exactness of the word 'and of all the beasts' was probably

questioned by critics, which necessitated this discussion (Gen. r., ch. xxxi, p. 287).

(7) 1 Kings xvii. 6, ' and the ravens brought him bread and meat'. R. Judah says that there is a city in the vicinity of Scythopolis (Bethshan) called Arbu, consequently, the 'Orbim' were not ravens, but people of that place who supplied the prophet with food. R. Nehemayah takes the text literally, ravens brought him food from the table of king Jehoshaphat (Gen. r., ch. xxxii, pp. 309–10).

(8) Gen. xiv. 13, ' Abram the Hebrew'. R. Judah explains העברי allegorically, the whole world was on one side, Abraham on the other. R. Nehemayah renders it literally as ' who came from Eber'; the Rabbis take it geographically, from the other side of the river (Gen. r., ch. xli, p. 418).

(9) Gen. xiv. 22, הרימותי, ' I lifted up'. R. Judah finds in the verb an allusion to the ceremony of the heave-offering, cf. Num. xviii. 26. R. Nehemayah interpreted it as an expression of an oath, cf. Dan. xii. 7 (Gen. r., ch. xliii, p. 423).

(10) Gen. xvi. 1, ' and she did not bear him'. R. Judah explains the לו (him) in the sense that if she had married some one else she would have been blessed with children. R. Nehemayah renders the text thus: לא ילדה שרה לה ולאברם Sarah did not bear for herself or for Abram (Gen. r., ch. xlv, p. 447).

These ten instances may bear out my contention that R. Judah, and partly also R. Nehemayah, belong to the allegorical school. A fuller investigation of the Haggadah of these two Tannaites shows that the two contending schools still struggled for supremacy in the age after the death of R. Akiba and R. Ishmael, and could come to no agreement even in the schools of Galilee, whither the scholars repaired after the defeat of Bar Kochba in Judea.

This contest of the schools and scholars of the early centuries of the Current Era on the topic of figurative and literal exegesis and translation of the Sacred Writings of the Hebrews was not without serious repercussions on the weighty problem of elementary education. R. Elieser b. Hyrkanos, when visited by his pupils before his departure from this world, was requested

to teach them *the paths of life.* His sayings, which by the way
are among the most precious gem﹄ of old Rabbinic teaching,
cover more than one aspect of religious life and reflect many
sides of the master's religious experience. Apart from the
emphasis laid on the right attitude in prayer and proper
conduct in scholastic life, the teacher admonishes them :
'Keep back your children from הגיון and place them between
the knees of the disciples of the wise ' (v. Ber. 28 b). The noun
הגיון puzzled many generations of students and commentators
of the Talmud, and all their skill and efforts led to no satisfactory result. Rashi, our best teacher and guide, leaves us
here in the dark. For according to him the master enjoined
his pupils to refrain from too much Bible study when educating
children in private or in public. Is it likely that a man, a
scholar of R. Elieser's calibre, should wish to restrict the duty
of such studies, instead of stressing the necessity of diligent
study of and daily and nightly meditation on the words of the
Torah? Furthermore, how is the injunction contained in the
first sentence to be brought into accord with the warning to take
great care in the choice of proper, worthy, and qualified scholars
for the education of the growing youth? More helpful is R.
Nathan ben Yehiel, the author of the Aruk, who interprets the
words as follows: 'Avoid teaching your children by translating
or expounding the Biblical text in a strictly literal way, or by
any such method.' Such an education calls for teachers who
are skilled and able to teach the Scriptures in a proper way.
The lexicographer derived this explanation from older Geonic
sources which on their part may have drawn from authorities
no longer available to us. Yet one may see in this explanation
of the words of R. Elieser a remarkable confirmation of the anti-
literal and anti-anthropomorphic attitude in his Bible-studies
demonstrated in these pages from the material still available in
the old Tannaitic literature. R. Elieser, apparently, reviewing
on his death-bed his activity and the results of his life, could
not help expressing a personal note, an innermost feeling, a
serious self-defence. His words are, therefore, directed against
his colleagues of the opposition who propagate the method of
literality. His words must have made a very deep impression on

the witnesses of that memorable scene in the scribe's mansion
in Lydda. For somewhat later R. Akiba thought it opportune,
or was perhaps compelled, to warn his pupil R. Simon b. Yohai
from following the teaching of R. Elieser. He said, 'When thou
teachest thy son, instruct him from a properly corrected book',
meaning to say put the utmost stress on the letter and writing
of the text and avoid the figurative sense of the Scriptures (b.
Pes. 112 a). R. Simon b. Yohai, like R. Judah b. Ilai, although
both were pupils of R. Akiba, did not adhere to the teaching of
their master in this question of method and principle (v. further
about הגיון Hebr. Bibliographie, xiv. 47. Further instances of
the interchange of the names of teachers in our sources occur
in Siphre Deut. 212, cf. b. Yebamoth 48 b, b. Sanhedrin 28 b,
and Midr. Lam. r. Petihatha, no. 2).

3. The literal or anthropomorphic understanding of the
Bible was bound to engender new anthropomorphic and anthropopathic teachings which, on their part, met with the fate of
the earlier Biblical anthropomorphisms. Preachers and homilists, philosophers and mystics, commentators and grammarians
treated them according to their proclivities, either literally or
allegorically. A number of sages and scholars could be registered
with the former, and an equally strong set represents the other
group. My task cannot be to account for, or to describe at any
length, the history of anthropomorphism in the long course
of Jewish literature; in this paragraph the background of a
few such anthropomorphic Haggadoth shall be demonstrated.
Without the historical and archaeological, the religious and
cultural understanding of the Rabbinic texts the inner meaning
of them will remain either partly obscure or will be entirely
misunderstood, just as it happened to the Scriptures, in spite
of good translations and a wealth of commentaries. Two
examples of anthropomorphic teachings shall be analysed here
which, on the one hand, throw light on contemporary history,
and on the other, gain light from historical knowledge.

The first Haggadah is by the Babylonian teacher Rab, in the
first half of the third century, who preached the following
sermon. 'When sun and moon enter to ask permission (or to
take leave) of God in order to go forth and spread light on the

world, their eyes become dim from the splendour of the Shekinah,
so that their dim eye-sight prevents them from discharging
their duties. What does God do unto them? He shoots arrows
in front of them, so that they are enabled to walk forth guided
by their light, i.e. by the light of the divine arrows.' The
preacher found this quaint idea confirmed in Hab. iii. 2, where
the prophet says: 'Sun and moon stood in the Zebul (the
highest of the seven heavens), at the light of thy arrows they
walk, at the shining of thy glittering spear'. Further he combined with this verse Joel ii. 10, 'Sun and moon shall become
dark, and the stars lose their splendour'.[29] For a Haggadist,
who took the verses in Habakkuk and Joel literally, it was quite
natural to indulge in such mythological descriptions, but one
is inclined to ask, whence did Rab learn or deduce that sun and
moon *take permission* before starting their functions for which
they were ordered from the beginning of creation? How did
he get hold of the idea that this happens every day, which is not
indicated in the words of the prophets quoted? Yet this new
and original contribution of the preacher is the very key for
the understanding of the whole situation. The expression
נטילת רשות designates the sermon preached by the candidate
for scholarly authorization or ordination on leaving the academy
before starting his independent scholarly and judicial activities.
When leaving his *alma mater*, as an honour, he was obliged to
deliver an address, mostly of a Haggadic nature. Rab, therefore, when his turn came to leave Sepphoris for his native
Babylonia, compared the going forth of the qualified Rabbi
from the school to the exit of the sun and moon. Both, scholars,
the earthly torchbearers of the Torah, as well as the celestial
luminaries, go out into the world to become the bearers of the
light of the Torah to mankind, to carry the light of mind and
warmth of soul to humanity. Just as the celestial beings cannot
rely on their own natural powers but require the assistance of
Heaven in order to discharge their duties, so the scholar, like
Rab himself, must faithfully acknowledge the past instruction
of his teacher, and look forward to the future guidance of his

[29] Lev. r. xxxi. 9, Yalkut Makiri, Habakkuk, ed. Greenup, London,
1910, p. 51.

master after he has settled in the place of his new activity, far away from his spiritual home. Considering the history reported of the circumstances accompanying the ordination of this scholar, the sermon delivered offers a new support to the historical report known from other sources.[30] The anthropomorphic setting is merely the rhetorical corollary of the preacher's thoughts and feelings.

The second instance is also taken from the world of Rabbinic legends. Its author is R. Jonathan b. Elieser, reported to us by R. Samuel b. Nahmani. The teacher himself, as demonstrated by our references to several of his teachings above,[31] belongs to the school of the allegorists. He flourished in the third century in Galilee. The plural נעשה in Gen. i. 26 was a source of constant trouble to Bible readers from early ages up to the present. First pagans, then Gnostics, and later Christians availed themselves of this verse in their attacks on Hebrew and Jewish monotheistic conceptions, and in their propaganda for their peculiar teachings, viz. polytheism, dualism, and christology. R. Jonathan faced Gnostic arguments which induced him to invent a legend depicting Moses writing the Torah from the beginning till verse 26. When Moses arrived at that verse, he lifted up his eyes and said : ' Lord of

[30] v. b. Sanhedrin 5 a. R. Hiyya asked R. Judah I for his nephew's ordination. This permission was granted, withholding the candidate's right to settle cases of the ' firstborn animals ' ; it may be that the preacher alluded to this fact in dwelling on the restrictions put on the celestial luminaries. On the subject v. Grätz, *Geschichte*, vol. iv, 4th ed., p. 255 f. ; Weiss, *Dor Dor*, vol. iii, p. 132 ; Halevy, *Doroth ha-Rishonim*, vol. ii, p. 216 ; A. Epstein, 'Le retour de Rab en Babylonie', in *RÉJ.*, vol. xliv, 1902, reprint, p. 4. Pal. Hagiga i. 8 has the report that R. Gamaliel III did not concede after the death of his father the supplementing of the ordination of Rab. It may be that the נטילת רשות has a special point in referring to the restrictions imposed upon the candidate. It is, however, difficult to believe that, as Weiss thinks, the Patriarch may have been guided by dynastic or personal feelings. As a matter of fact Rab himself may have felt that he was not quite qualified and equipped in that branch for which ordination was not granted him. For a similar conception of God helping sun and moon by spreading light before them v. also the teaching of R. Joshua b. Levi based on Ps. lxxxix. 16 and Hab. iii. 11. The point of נטילת רשות does not occur here at all, Midr. Psalms, ch. xix, ed. Buber, p. 169.

[31] v. Index, s.v., and pp. 114, 130.

the Whole Universe, Thou givest an opportunity to heretics to criticize (or to object).' God said to him: 'Write, and do not care about them, he who will err let him do so.' Further, God said to Moses: 'Among men whom I created, there will always be different classes. They will produce men who are great and small, socially and intellectually. Now, when it shall come to pass that the greater one has *to take permission* from the smaller one, the former should not argue: "How shall I, who am a greater scholar, or of greater importance in social life, take authorization from a man who is smaller in learning or in piety?" If such a case aris eshe may be told: "Go, and take a lesson from thy Creator who created the upper and lower ones, nevertheless consulted the ministering angels before creating man." ' [32] It is pretty clear that the latter part of the sermon is directed against some of the preacher's contemporaries, who, proud of their learning or academic successes, were loath to submit for ordination or authorization to leaders who were smaller or less important in learning or even in character. Such episodes are recorded in the history of the third century. These show that after the death of R. Judah the Prince, the compiler of the Mishnah, and especially under his successors, really gifted scholars hesitated to submit to the spiritual leadership of men altogether inferior in learning and perhaps also in character. The innate antihierarchic feeling of the Jew during the ages manifested itself at all times. R. Jonathan, however, thought it to be for the good of the religious life of his age to support and strengthen the Patriarchs in their inherited rights. With what feelings these well-meant words were received by the scholars to whom they were addressed, is not known to us, but the changes recorded in the proceedings of the ordination occurring in these days may not have been to the liking of the leaders and authorities. [33]

[32] Gen. r., ch. viii, ed. Theodor, p. 61.
[33] It is quite likely that some of the junior members of the academy of Sepphoris during the presidency of Rabbi hesitated and manifested reluctance to submit later on to R. Gamaliel III whose prominence in learning was not recognized and original merit for leadership not sufficiently manifested. The Patriarch had foreseen trouble and warned his son to put fear into the hearts of the students by taking the reins of leadership

4. Porphyry, who lived in the third century C.E. and dreamt of a rejuvenation of paganism, criticized very strongly the figurative interpretation of the Hebrew writings as practised by Jews and Christians alike, and objected especially to the exegetical activity of Origen. The Church Father, Porphyry asserts, borrowed his method from the allegorical exegesis of the old Greek philosophers, and adapted it for his purposes.[34] This judgment is quite justified, and can be equally turned against Philo and some of his fore-runners. It is more difficult to accept such a view when extended to the Rabbinic adherents of the allegorical method, some of whom have been named in the foregoing pages. The connecting link between the Rabbis and earlier Hellenistic allegorists, Philo included, is, at present, impossible to discover. The communal and literary intercourse between the Greek diaspora and the Palestinian community is too little known to afford material for a working hypothesis. The hypothesis, however, that Philo and his sources may have used more of the earlier Palestinian wisdom and scholarship than they are credited with, is seen to have more basis when the Greek writings are examined and searched in the light of the Palestinian Midrash. A few instances may exemplify this in addition to the examples brought forward in the earlier course of these essays.

In his essay ' On Flight and Finding '[35] Philo says: ' And well may she say this (Thou art the Maker of my wishes and my offspring), for of free and really high-born souls He who is free and sets free is the Creator, while slaves are makers of slaves; and angels are God's household-servants, and are deemed gods by those whose existence is still one of toil and bondage.'

energetically into his hands (b. Ketuboth 103 b). A long fight ensued for many decades, till the leaders of the school succeeded in acquiring some influence in granting authorization, academic titles, and scholarly prefer-ment to students. The movement was already in full swing in the time of R. Jonathan; hence his admonition. About the history of ordination, v. Bacher, 'Zur Geschichte der Ordination', *MGWJ.*, xxxviii, 1894, 122-7; Marmorstein, 'L'Opposition contre le patriarche R. Judai.', in *RÉJ.*, vol. lxv, 1912, pp. 59-67, and 'La Réorganisation du doctorat en Palestine au IIIe siècle', ibid., vol. lxvi, 1913, pp. 44-54.

[34] Eusebius, *Ecclesiastical History*, vi, ch. xix.

[35] Philo, vol. v, London, 1934, § 212.

The context is obscure, as remarked by the translators.[36] Yet
Philo tries to overcome a difficulty, which was equally felt by
the teachers of the Rabbinic Midrash. There is a discrepancy
between Gen. xvi. 13, 'and she called the name of God, who
spake to her', and verses 9 ff. which teach that an angel spoke
to her. The Haggadists, in addition, disliked the idea that God
should converse with a woman.[37] It was, therefore, suggested
that in this place as well the word 'angel' should be inserted.
Philo, however, must have had before him an older Jewish interpretation on this question. Before man saw God, or was looked
upon by God, in toil and bondage, he conceived only of angels,
not so afterwards when he was endowed with knowledge of
God, free and 'really high-bred', then he could call on the
name of God who spake to him.

In the same essay [38] Philo, on Exod. xv. 27, elaborates the
deeper meaning of the text that the twelve springs correspond
to the twelve signs of the zodiac, the twelve months, the twelve
hours of the day and the night, the twelve tribes of the nation,
the twelve loaves of the sanctuary, and the twelve stones on the
oracle. The seventy palms, in their turn, correspond to the
seventy Elders and the seventy sacrifices offered on the Feast
of Tabernacles. R. Eleasar of Modiim, who was one of the
staunchest allegorists, as shown previously, teaches that God
created twelve wells from the beginning of the creation, corresponding to the twelve tribes of the children of Israel, and
seventy palm-trees corresponding to the seventy Elders.[39] Just as
in the first Philonic Haggadah the idea of angels as God's household-servants deserves fuller attention with reference to the
familiar Haggadic teaching of the heavenly familia [40] or Court
of Above, similarly the Rabbinic term כנגד (' corresponding

---

[36] Ibid., p. 124.
[37] Gen. r., ch. xlv, ed. Theodor, p. 457; v. also ch. xx, ibid., p. 188;
for a fuller text v. pal. Sota vii. 1; Midr. Ps. ix. 7, ed. Buber, p. 83. The
view that God did not speak directly to a woman is not general.
[38] §§ 184–6.
[39] v. Mekilta 49 b, Mekilta of R. Simon, p. 74; cf. Yelamdenu in Yalkut
Jos. 15, Midrash of R. Phinehas b. Yair, quoted in Midrash Hahefez,
Ms. Haftara for the first Day of Tabernacles.
[40] v. Marmorstein, 'Anges et hommes dans l'Agada' in RÉJ., vol. 84,
1927, pp. 37 ff. and ibid., pp. 138 ff.

to ') could be enlarged by comparison with the Hellenistic Haggadah. Here one remark must not be omitted that in the Rabbinic Haggadah the very same juxtaposition of subjects connected with the numbers twelve and seventy, respectively, is to be found, as also in Philo, which surely cannot be purely accidental.[41]

Philo makes a third remark in the treatise just mentioned [42] which throws light on a Haggadah of R. Judah b. Ilai, an adept at allegorical teaching, and gains fresh meaning from a knowledge of Rabbinic doctrines. In dwelling on Gen. ii. 6 the writer says: 'Those who are unversed in allegory and the nature-truth which loves to conceal its meaning, compare the spring mentioned with the river of Egypt which rises in flood yearly and turns the plain into a lake, seeming to exhibit a power wellnigh rivalling the sky.' R. Judah, who lived about fifteen decades after Philo, preserves this interpretation rejected by Philo. He answers a question which was raised and discussed among the scribes in his days: 'How does the earth get watered? Like the Nile, supplying water again and again.' This theory is based on the Scriptural evidence that a well or a cloud rises from the ground, to which is added the remark: 'First the fields were watered from below, then God changed the order by decreeing that rain should come from above.[43] This change of nature was

---

[41] v. Tanhuma Gen., ed. Buber, p. 221. The twelve tribes correspond to the order of the world. Day and night consist of twelve hours respectively, the year has twelve months, and finally there are the twelve houses or divisions of the zodiac. Another Haggadist connects the twelve stones in the contest of Elijah with the same line of thought, v. Pesikta rabbati, ch. iv, ed. Friedmann, p. 13 a; v. further Midrash Tadshe, ed. Epstein, p. xxvii, and Midrash Othioth of R. Akiba, ed. Jellinek, Beth ha-Midrash, iii, p. 24; cf. also *JQR.*, v. 47 as to Josephus *Antt.* iii. 7. 7, and Marmorstein, *Kiddush Yerahim derabbi Phinehas*, Budapest, 1921, pp. 5 ff. and Q. S. P. E. F., July 1920, pp. 139 ff. and July 1930, p. 156 f. The combination with the number 70 similar to that of Philo's is to be found in the late Midrash called Esfa, v. Coronel, *Geonic Responsa* no. 106, where the 70 Elders figure together with 70 Sabbaths and Festivals of the year, 70 children of Jacob who went down to Egypt, and 70 calves; cf. Midrash Tadshe, ed. Epstein, p. xxvi.

[42] par. 170 ff.

[43] Gen. r., ch. xiii. This question whether rain comes from above or from below is disputed by R. Elieser b. Hyrkanos and R. Joshua b. Hananyah, and later by R. Yochanan b. Nappacha and R. Simon b. Lakish, v. ed. Theodor, pp. 119–20.

due to the wickedness of man who took his prosperity and safety
for granted, and excluded any consideration for God from his
conduct and actions.' [44] The same idea was already current in
the days of Philo, or before his time, for he alludes to it,
naturally as a patriotic Alexandrian Jew disapprovingly, by saying: 'This afforded Moses ground for branding the Egyptian
character as atheistical in its preference for earth above heaven,
for the things that live on the ground are [in Egypt] made out
to be above those that dwell on high, and the body above the
soul.' These may have been the words of some Palestinian
moralist rebuking Epicureans for their materialistic views and
for the lack of fear of heaven caused by their material independence or spiritual blindness.

These comparisons between Hellenistic and Palestinian
Haggadah testify not only to an early contact between these
two branches of the same tree, but, as demonstrated in the
opening chapter of this work, to the parallel growth of literal
and figurative exegesis in both countries. They may be looked
upon either as a cause, or as a result of the ruling forces in
the realm of religious thought. One party objected to the
literal meaning of the text: the other could detect nothing
therein which would give rise to objection or argument. One
example will suffice to elucidate this. Many a Greek Jew read
with amazement Num. xxxv. 25 ff., and asked the queries
penned by Philo in the following words:

' The fourth and only remaining point of those proposed for consideration was the time prescribed for the return of the fugitives,
namely, that of the death of the High Priest. If taken literally, this
point presents, I feel, great difficulty. The penalty inflicted by law
on those whose offences are identical is unequal, if some are to be
fugitives for a longer, some for a shorter period; for of the High-
Priests, some are to be long-lived, some the reverse, some are
appointed in youth, some in old age; and of those guilty of un-
intentional homicide some went into exile at the outset of the High-
Priest's priesthood, others when the holder of the sacred office was
nearing his end.' [45]

The consequence of a literal interpretation will be that some

[44] v. Gen. r., ibid., p. 119.   [45] *De fuga*, § 106 f.

may be imprisoned for a very long time, and others may be lucky to escape after a very short internment. Philo's friends felt very uncomfortable in reading the Biblical ordinance about the fugitives. His explanation was that the High Priest here stands for the Divine Word, which anticipated a kind of Trinity consisting of Father (God), mother (Wisdom), and Son (the Logos), which, however, found no echo in early Rabbinic theology. Palestinian Haggadists found no fault with such a law, in spite of the difficulties possibly raised. An ancient Mishnah teaches that the mothers of the priests supplied the fugitives with plenty of food and raiment, so that they should not pray for the death of their sons.[46] The pious ladies believed in the efficacy of prayer, even if coming from the lips of murderers. Another rationalistic explanation given, is that the High Priest is responsible for life in the community, therefore his life is shortened as a punishment for neglected duties. The Sifre on Numbers records two statements on this subject, one by R. Meir, and the other by Rabbi if the reading is reliable. The former says that the connexion between the High Priest and the murderer expresses a contrast. The latter shortens human life, the former lengthens human life by worshipping in the Sanctuary. Rabbi formulates the contrast thus: 'Murder defiles the land and causes the Shekinah to depart from it, whilst the High Priest serves to cause the Shekinah to rest upon the people in the land.'[47] These homilies, however enthusiastically they may have been received or applauded by the listeners in Tiberias or Sepphoris, would not have satisfied a Greek-speaking assembly in Alexandria or Ephesus, for they touched merely the fringe of the difficulty. Advanced religious thinkers or rationalistic Bible readers, either in Palestine or in the Diaspora, could not accept the letter of some of the Biblical narratives or utterances, ordinances or observances, without formulating their scruples; teachers or students who were inclined towards mysticism or irrationalism, however, were quite willing to acquiesce in acknowledging the letter of the Bible.

[46] Maccoth, ch. ii, p. 11 a.

[47] v. § 160. Perhaps instead of רבי אמר, as often, דבר אחר is to be read. In this case R. Meir's teaching is preserved in two versions.

This fact leads to a very perplexing situation which repeated itself several times in the course of the history of Judaism. It can be observed that scribes like R. Joshua b. Hananyah, R. Akiba, R. Meir, R. Abbahu, and others, whose acquaintance with Greek philosophy, Greek literature, secular law, and general life is more or less well documented, are opposed, if not hostile, to allegorical interpretations, and consequently do not mind anthropomorphic conceptions about God. Yet others whose whole life and upbringing betray no sign of philosophic knowledge or external influences favour allegoristic expositions of the Sacred Writings on which their religion and theology are founded. The solution of this puzzling contrast may be seen in the very fact that the wider experience and knowledge acquired by the former served as a warning against the dangers and pitfalls of allegorizing the Bible. Living in an age when, among other enemies, Gnostics menaced the very existence of Judaism by undermining the stronghold of Judaism, the Bible—and Marcion was not the first and not the last of the long line of enemies of the Bible—they thought it appropriate to defend the Bible with the same weapons with which Gnostics tried to destroy it, namely, by insisting on a literal exegesis. These rabbis who imbibed foreign culture essayed to defend the literal meaning of the Scriptures, whatever the result as far as the Jewish teaching of God was concerned might be. What appeared to the Gnostic writers to be gross corporality, crude anthropomorphism, coarse sensuality, these freed and high-bred souls—to use a phrase of Philo—thought to be the true spiritual significance of Scripture, hidden from the blind eyes of the apostles of an abortive and imaginary learning. Further, they were fully aware that in divesting the heroes of the Bible of their real existence, whether faults or virtues, by transforming these into abstract virtues or academic faults, the most vital forces of historic consciousness become weakened and falsified. Then they were alert enough to notice that by pouring new philosophies and old primitive conceptions into the observances and ceremonies, hallowed by ages and tested by exiles, they not merely imperil the religious development but would knock out the bottom of the very safe-guards of the nation's hope. The words of these scribes, who guided the Jewish community in many lands from the Maccabean period up to the rise of the Byzantine Empire, breathe a continuous sigh of prayer to God for life, coupled with an indestructible trust in the Eternity of their task. Such a work cannot be undertaken, carried on, and accomplished by men and women whose religion is lifeless and whose God is an allegory. What did it matter if pagans spread rumours that Jews in Jerusalem were ass-worshippers, or philosophers reproached the Jews that their idea of God was not spiritual enough, and, finally, Christians joined the choir with their disharmonious song that Israel had falsified the message of the old law-givers and prophets and psalmists ? They sought the nearness of their God, craved for the presence of their Creator, whether in the Land of their Fathers, or in the countries of their Dispersion, sang new songs of hope, of trust, and belief in God, intensified the rule of the heavenly King in their homes, schools, and places of worship.

It would be a mistake to ascribe the lion's share of victory and triumph to one party or section of spiritual guides of Judaism without doing justice to the endeavours and work, achievements and contributions of their rivals as well. The unparalleled course of Jewish history, the unique tragedy and triumph of the Jew on the stage of the history of the world, engendered a more or less constant division in their midst. Other nations, living on their own soil, experienced in longer or shorter intervals spiritual upheavals, intellectual revolutions, moral and religious changes, which mark new epochs and tear asunder fathers and sons, families and classes. Social and political life cause such eruptions and results, for good or for evil, in progress or disaster. The Jew, among the nations, passes through a crisis even in peaceful days, in quiet times, and in well-organized communities. For under the inevitable process of assimilation, he has to listen with one ear to domineering fashions, current wisdom, widespread follies, the everchanging outlook on life and society, the sympathies and antipathies of his age and his neighbours, whilst with his other ear, he has to hearken, whether he likes or dislikes it, to the voice of his religion, of his sacred documents of old, to the messages of his teachers, to the cries of his history, and to his constant companion, his God. Now these contrasts between the legacy of old and the voice of the age have to be harmonized, if the community and the religion, from which it draws its strength, vitality, and force of rejuvenation, is to survive. This fight between the modernists and the antiquarians, the assimilationists and dissimilationists, liberals and conservatives —there may be found scores of names for these movements and shibboleths—ultimately goes back to the very fount of the disputes discussed in these essays. The question was, and still is, how we shall adjust the knowledge of the ages, advanced and progressive thought, with the word of the Bible. Shall we take the latter in a literal or in a figurative sense? The attitude of the Jew to his God, to his people, to his religion and community, depends on this very question and the answer given to it. The allegorists suggested that the teachers of Israel are entitled to put new wine into old bottles, to invigorate the old, weakened religious life with new methods and forces. And they also succeeded. A legend tells posterity that when the Schools of Shammai and Hillel reached the climax of their spiritual controversy, a heavenly voice was heard, saying that both schools proclaimed the words of the living God.[48] The ups and downs of the history of the Jewish people, the advances and retrogressions of Jewish life, the triumph and fall of Jewish thought, testify clearly that both views of God, the literal and allegorical, have their rights and places in Judaism. There are times when one preponderates over the other. Both are the words of true religion, of the living God.

[48] pal. Berakoth i. 4, b. Erubin 13 b.

INDEX

Compiled by the Rev. Dr. Joseph Rabbinowitz, b.a., ph.d. (Lond.)

I. INDEX OF BIBLICAL PASSAGES

Genesis.

i. 1	. . . .	12
2	. . .	21
26	. . .	148
27	. . .	50
28	. . .	34
ii. 6	. . .	152
8	. . .	143
15	. . .	143
22	. . .	34
iii. 16	. . .	118
22	. . .	43
23	. . .	143
iv. 15	. . .	143
16	. . .	114
vi. 6	. . .	143
7	. . .	6
17	. . .	30
19	. . .	143
xiv. 13	. . .	144
22	. . .	144
xvi. 1	. . .	144
13	. . .	151
xviii. 1	. . .	88
xxii. 1	. . .	35
14	. . .	30

Exodus.

iv. 14	. . . .	31
v. 4	. . .	137
viii. 2	. . .	135
xii. 2	. .	32, 103
12	. . .	36
13	. . .	29
xiii. 5	. . .	109
18	. . .	39
21	. .	23, 139
xiv. 2	. . .	39
15	. . .	40
xv. 2	. .	30, 103
3	. .	8, 23
7	. . .	28
22	. . .	40
24	. . .	40
27	. . .	151
xvi. 4	. .	41, 109
9	. . .	41
10	. . .	41
14	. . .	42

xvii. 12	. . . .	42
xviii. 3	. . .	109
24	. . .	42
xix. 4	. . .	121
18	. .	120, 121
20	. . .	84
xx. 5	. . .	24
11	. . .	26
18	. . .	32
23	. . .	37
24	. . .	88
xxii. 23	. . .	28
27	. . .	32
xxiv. 11	. . .	106
17	. . .	142
xxv. 8	. . .	77
xxx. 12	. . .	77
20	. . .	97
xxxi. 17	. . .	121
xxxii. 2	. . .	61
xxxiii. 7	. . .	104
20	. .	49, 95
22	. . .	37
23	. . .	54

Leviticus.

xvi. 2	. . . .	137
17	. . .	49
xix. 4	. . .	109
18	. . .	25
32	. . .	67

Numbers.

xii. 8	. . . .	54
xiv. 10	. . .	139
xviii. 8	. . .	30
26	. . .	144
xxiii. 19	. . .	7, 8
xxvii. 21	. . .	140
xxviii. 2	. . .	77
6	. . .	92
xxxv. 25 ff.	. . .	153

Deuteronomy.

ii. 3	. . . .	140
iv. 11	. . .	120
24	. . .	62
viii. 5	. . .	7
16	. . .	39

II. INDEX OF NAMES